The Artificial Intelligence Revolution

Max Rangeley • Nicholas Fairfax
Editors

The Artificial Intelligence Revolution

Challenges and Opportunities

Editors
Max Rangeley
Cobden Centre
Plymouth, Devon, UK

Nicholas Fairfax
House of Lords
Bembridge, UK

ISBN 978-3-032-11813-4 ISBN 978-3-032-11814-1 (eBook)
https://doi.org/10.1007/978-3-032-11814-1

This Springer imprint is published by the registered company Springer Nature Switzerland AG
The registered company address is: Gewerbestrasse 11, 6330 Cham, Switzerland

Foreword

With global imbalances being shattered, democracy under attack, global warming ongoing, and economic growth still splattering, hopes of corporate leaders and governments are on artificial intelligence.

Artificial general intelligence (AGI) or "powerful AI", which will be reached when AI models have capabilities comparable to those of humans in almost all cognitive tasks, is what motivates most companies and leaders. While some are still worried about such powerful AI models turning against humanity or about their implications for jobs, for many decision-makers AGI will bring productivity, efficiency, and even abundance—not to mention huge strategic advantages and military might.

Yet, there are many downsides to our enthusiasm about AGI.

While we are continuously assured by industry leaders and journalists (that often happen to be very close to the industry) that AGI and all the riches it will bring are just around the corner, there are plenty of questions about whether this is feasible anytime soon. But the more important question is whether it is desirable.

AGI is largely about automation. If AI models reach human-like capabilities, then they can take over tasks from humans. This perspective is completely dominant in the tech industry, where AGI is all the rage and software engineers and divisions are judged on their ability to reach "human parity" in the tasks assigned to them. Even when tech leaders obfuscate the issues by talking human-AI collaboration, the overwhelming emphasis is on automation.

Automation is far from being a panacea, however. First, ceaseless automation will destroy jobs and boost inequalities. We have seen a prelude to this with the digital technologies of the last four decades, which have largely focused on automation (think of industrial robots and office software systems).

My research shows that these technologies have been the main driver of the huge increase in inequality in the United States, and although they have not created mass joblessness, they have meaningfully reduced the employment of workers that used to work in the jobs that have later been automated.

Second, automation may fail to deliver a big productivity dividend. If it focuses on jobs that humans were already performing reasonably well, gains from automation will be small. This too can be seen from the US experience over the last four decades, where rapid automation has gone hand-in-hand with disappointing productivity performance. Hopes of rapid productivity gains from automation may also be dashed because integrating AI models with existing organizations is proving challenging.

Third, timelines for AGI may be overly optimistic. AGI may yet remain a dream for quite a while. Yet even if AGI is not possible in the short run, the relentless quest for it could go on unabated. An AI hype can power investments, and promises of AGI and high-productivity automation can induce many companies to prematurely automate various tasks, even when the technology is not ready.

AGI dreams were present from the beginning of the field of computer science. Leading figures such as Alan Turing were articulating the possibility of such AGI as early as 1949. Others, such as Marvin Minsky, were trying to put it into practice in the 1960s. The passion was so powerful that repeated feedbacks did not quell it. Minsky was still proclaiming in 1970: "In from 3 to 8 years we will have a machine with the general intelligence of an average human being. I mean a machine that will be able to read Shakespeare, grease a car, play office politics, tell a joke, have a fight. At that point the machine will begin to educate itself with fantastic speed. In a few months it will be at genius level and a few months after that its powers will be incalculable."

Is there an alternative? Perhaps we have to embrace AI-based automation as an inevitable part of digital technologies and artificial intelligence. Fortunately, this isn't the case.

A very different vision for digital technologies was articulated 65 years ago by JCR Licklider. Licklider could be described as the "grandfather of the Internet" because it was his design and ideas that became the foundation of its early versions. Licklider's more important insights may have been the area of human-computer complementarity, however. He wrote in 1960 "The hope is that, in not too many years, human brains and computing machines will be coupled together very tightly, and that the resulting partnership will think as no human brain has ever thought and process data in a way not approached by the information-handling machines we know today."

The aspiration Licklider was articulating was one in which computers would be information systems capable of expanding what the human brain can achieve because they would provide effective and useful information to human decision-makers. At the time he wrote, and indeed for the next six decades, this was just an aspiration and no more. The Internet did contain much of the information of humanity, but it wasn't feasible for anybody to use that information in a reliable, timely and useful manner, because it was impossible to find and effectively process the dispersed information that would be useful for the specific task and challenges facing a human decision-maker. Generative AI can change that, provided that it can be trained on high-quality data and its output made more reliable.

Observe how different this vision is from that of AGI, where humans are sidelined and it is just machines (or more often the people who control the machines) that rule. With a human-complementarity focus, machines, algorithms and AI models will be at the service of humans and it will be human capabilities that are expanded.

A sharp choice is therefore whether to focus predominantly on AGI or try to make Licklider's vision a reality. Even if overshadowed in popular press and in Silicon Valley, Licklider's vision has been responsible for many of the most consequential digital technologies of the post-World War II era. It was ideas centered on human-machine complementarity that led to the computer mouse, menu-driven computers, hyperlinks, hypertext, and the Internet.

In stark contrast, the day, the preoccupation with AGI has meant that very large, generalist AI models – such as foundation models like GPT – have been all the rage over the last decade. These can simultaneously wax lyrical about ancient Greek philosophy and give you advice about Caribbean vacations. But they lack the domain-specific knowledge. Their generalist nature also comes with low reliability and proclivity to hallucinate – a model trained on vast amount of social media content can be excused for getting a few facts wrong, but that means we shouldn't turn to it for reliable, useful advice.

The alternative to the current paradigm starts with domain specific models. Such models would require high-quality data to be put to work in order to help human decision-makers in specific tasks. Think of AI models trained on principles of electrical engineering, specifications of electrical machinery, and past use cases of expert electricians tackling complex problems. These can then be used to help other less experienced electricians perform more sophisticated and new tasks. Domain specific models are not unknown to the industry. In fact, some of the most celebrated successes of AI, such as AlphaFold, are domain-specific models: AlphaFold can help you with the structural properties of proteins, but would not be that useful for improving production, helping electricians, or dating advice. Nevertheless, the blind quest for AGI has meant that domain-specific models are often on the back burner.

Finally, AGI pushes us towards zero-sum geopolitical dynamics—especially when it comes to US-China relations. The AGI craze creates the impression that there is no possibility of cooperation and information sharing between these two countries, because whoever reaches AGI first will dominate the world. This perspective is promoted and propagated by tech leaders, who are the ones benefiting from the singular focus on AGI.

What all of this means is that when it comes to AI, we have very consequential choices. We could keep on pursuing the dream of AGI, which in my opinion will remain unrealistic for the foreseeable future. All the same the dream can become all-encompassing, contributing to inequality, reductions in employment, the sidelining of humans, and further consolidation in the tech industry. This quest can even act as a geopolitical trap, with dire implications for world peace. Or we can recognize that the best way to AI tools is to first make them more complementary to human decision-makers, rather than continuously attempting to mimic human speech and capabilities.

Put differently, we can pull back from the ambition of creating our AI overlords (which is neither desirable nor very likely), and instead attempt to make AI a useful tool for ourselves.

Institute Professor of Economics,
Massachusetts Institute of Technology;
2024 Nobel Laureate in Economic Sciences
Cambridge, MA, USA

Daron Acemoglu

Preface

When we first embarked on this project, to produce a seminal volume on artificial intelligence policy with Springer Nature, we had to think about the vast number of different areas of AI policy which warrant attention. These range from the economics of AI, to the future of healthcare, to regulatory approaches right through to the military aspects of AI and robotics. One of the things that makes AI policy so fascinating is that it is interdisciplinary; it is not enough to just put the best AI engineers in charge of policy decisions, it must inevitably involve economists, sociologists, ethicists, legal experts, researchers and scientists, military experts and psychologists. How, then, do we encompass all of this in a single academic volume? The answer was to have chapters not only by academics, as is normal in a volume such as this, but by many of the top experts in their respective fields from around the world. In order to achieve this, we invited senior political figures who had been involved in AI regulation, military experts who have shaped discussions on the future of war, people from the world of business and entrepreneurship, and of course we also invited some of the most prominent academics from the top universities in the world. By combining this eclectic mix of thinkers, we hope we have produced an academic volume that someone can read and, in one go, get an overview of the current state of cutting edge AI policy.

Both of the editors of this volume have taken an interest in AI policy for many years prior to this project. Nicholas Fairfax has served in the House of Lords for decades; by bringing the key questions surrounding AI into the British Parliament, he has been a forerunner to today's political interest in the topic. Max Rangeley has run an economics think tank for the last 10 years, and has served on the boards of other think tanks in London and Brussels. He introduced AI as a core area of policy research to the think tanks he has worked with; among other projects, he organized and moderated the AI roundtable discussions in the European Parliament, with participants ranging from the IMF, OECD and United Nations to companies like Intel. Both Max and Nicholas have had pushback over the years—just a few years ago, talking about the likelihood of AI reaching human level intelligence was likely to lead to eyes rolling and a change of subject to more "serious" areas of policy-making. With the introduction of the more recent large language models, this is no longer the case, and a broad range of people within the policy-making ecosystem are taking an interest in AI policy, including artificial general intelligence.

The speed with which AI has evolved over the last 10 years has surprised even many of those who have worked in the field their whole lives. It seems like with each 6 months that passes, LLMs provide better analysis, and their skills at measurable tasks such as medical examinations and mathematics tests improve faster than almost any predictions. The question then arises—is this an exponential curve or an S curve? Will the current technology progressions flatten out, as happened during the previous "AI winters" of the last few decades, or have we finally reached a kind of "escape velocity" with respect to AI developments, such that progress is now self-sustaining. The mathematician IJ Good spoke of the possibility of an "intelligence explosion" once AI reaches human level intelligence. As he phrased it in 1965:

> Let an ultraintelligent machine be defined as a machine that can far surpass all the intellectual activities of any man however clever. Since the design of machines is one of these intellectual activities, an ultraintelligent machine could design even better machines; there would then unquestionably be an 'intelligence explosion,' and the intelligence of man would be left far behind. Thus the first ultraintelligent machine is the last invention that man need ever make, provided that the machine is docile enough to tell us how to keep it under control. It is curious that this point is made so seldom outside of science fiction. It is sometimes worthwhile to take science fiction seriously.

If we are indeed on the cusp of this, arguably the most important development in history, then what is needed most of all is sound knowledge among policy-makers at all levels of what the likely consequences are of different trajectories. Every aspect of our lives will continue to be affected by advancements in AI; if we as a species get this right, then it will lead to unparalleled increases in the standard of living for billions of people, but if we get it wrong there are numerous existential risks which may result.

The editors wish to offer our sincere thanks to all of the authors of chapters in this book, without whom it could not have been put together. We also wish to thank Philipp Deussen, a young PhD student who helped tremendously with discussing potential authors and organising conversations with them—we are confident that a strong career of research awaits him. We hope that you enjoy reading it as much as we enjoyed editing it and conversing with such an illustrious group of thinkers during the course of the last 2 years.

Plymouth, UK Max Rangeley
Bembridge, UK Nicholas Fairfax

Contents

Part I

Safety and Risk

Behavioural Red Lines as a Safety Framework for Intolerable Levels of Risk

Yoshua Bengio, Stuart Russell, Andrew Yao, and Ya-Qin Zhang

Introduction

In recent years, the capabilities of AI systems have increased rapidly. Large language models (LLMs) in particular have exhibited surprisingly high performance over a wide range of tasks. Within the last few months, systems have been demonstrated that are augmented with agent-like capabilities—the ability to reason, construct plans, and directly execute actions in online and physical environments. Many experts view the emergence of truly general-purpose, human-level or superhuman AI systems—sometimes called artificial general intelligence (AGI)—as highly likely before the end of the current decade.

With these advances come risks, whether from deliberate misuse, malfunction, or systemic effects. The possible consequences range from mildly

Y. Bengio
Mila, Montreal, Canada
e-mail: yoshua.bengio@mila.quebec

S. Russell (✉)
University of California, Berkeley, CA, USA
e-mail: russell@berkeley.edu

A. Yao • Y.-Q. Zhang
Tsinghua University, Beijing, China
e-mail: andrewcyao@mail.tsinghua.edu.cn

M. Rangeley, N. Fairfax (eds.), *The Artificial Intelligence Revolution*,
https://doi.org/10.1007/978-3-032-11814-1_1

annoying to civilization-ending; but there is a general sense in the AI community that the probability of more serious negative consequences is increasing rapidly. The Bletchley Declaration, signed by 28 nations, notes the "potential for serious, even catastrophic, harm" and states that "deepening our understanding of these potential risks and of actions to address them is especially urgent." A more specific, recent post from Anthropic warns that "Governments should urgently take action on AI policy in the next eighteen months. The window for proactive risk prevention is closing fast."[1]

The obvious question, then, is what form governm'ent action should take. So far, safety measures have been voluntary and vary considerably across companies developing advanced AI systems. The results are not encouraging: the UK AI Safety Institute reports that "All tested LLMs remain highly vulnerable to basic jailbreaks, and some will provide harmful outputs even without dedicated attempts to circumvent their safeguards."[2] Evidently, a more serious regulatory effort is indicated.

Beginning in October 2023, just before the AI Safety Summit at Bletchley Park, the authors have convened a series of meetings—the International Dialogues on AI Safety (IDAIS)—to explore potential approaches. The final statement from the first meeting, held at Ditchley Park, includes the following:

> We also recommend defining clear red lines that, if crossed, mandate immediate termination of an AI system—including all copies—through rapid and safe shutdown procedures. Governments should cooperate to instantiate and preserve this capacity. Moreover, prior to deployment as well as during training for the most advanced models, developers should demonstrate to regulators' satisfaction that their system(s) will not cross these red lines.

(This recommendation can be seen as exploring further the general admonition by Brundage et al. that developers be held to verifiable claims concerning properties and functionalities of their systems.[3]) The second meeting, held in Beijing in March 2024, produced a "Consensus Statement on Red Lines in Artificial Intelligence" that included specific examples and recommendations on enforcement. Moreover, a subgroup of the World Economic Forum's Global Future Council on the Future of AI (GFC-AI) has been exploring this

[1]Anthropic, "The case for targeted regulation," October 31, 2024.

[2]UK AI Safety Institute, "Advanced AI evaluations at AISI: May update", May 20, 2024.

[3]Miles Brundage et al. (2020). Toward Trustworthy AI Development: Mechanisms for Supporting Verifiable Claims. arXiv 2004.07213.

concept over roughly the same period.[4] The views expressed in this chapter are those of the authors and are not intended to represent the views of other participants in IDAIS or GFC-AI.

In this chapter, we explain the concept of red lines—specifically, *behavioural* red lines—in more depth, including possible approaches to compliance and enforcement. The basic idea is familiar from many other high-risk areas, including nuclear power, aviation, and medicine: Before a product can be placed on the market, its developers[5] must provide to regulators a high-confidence statement of safety that is backed by rigorous evidence and analysis. The situation with AI is complicated because general-purpose AI systems exhibit a huge range of behaviours, and as a result "safe" is difficult to define. Nonetheless, one can define red lines that demarcate some *obviously unsafe and unacceptable* behaviours by AI systems. Then, as with other high-risk areas, the onus is on the developer to demonstrate to the regulator's satisfaction that a proposed AI system will not cross these red lines, regardless of its runtime inputs.

Behavioural red lines are not intended to provide exhaustive coverage of *all possible* harms: As noted above, the generality of general-purpose AI systems makes that task unreasonably difficult. Rather, the purpose is to motivate the kind of rigorous design and safety engineering that has up to now been lacking in general-purpose AI systems. We recommend implementing appropriate rules sooner rather than later: note that it should be *easier* to show that a less capable system will not cross a given red line, so it seems unwise to delay red line requirements until we have larger and more complex systems that far exceed the necessary capability thresholds.

Behavioural Red Lines

As stated in the introduction, a behavioural red line demarcates an *obviously unsafe and unacceptable* behaviour by an AI system. It is important to distinguish between red lines demarcating unacceptable *uses for* AI systems and red lines demarcating unacceptable *behaviours by* AI systems. The former

---

[4]Stuart Russell, Edson Prestes, Mohan Kankanhalli, Jibu Elias, Constanza Gómez Mont, Vilas Dhar, Adrian Weller, Pascale Fung, and Karim Beguir, AI red lines: The opportunities and challenges of setting limits. Emerging Technologies, World Economic Forum, 11 March 2025.

[5]The word "developer" here is not intended in a technical or legal sense; it refers loosely to those having a causal role in determining the product's final form and behaviour after deployment, including upstream entities who supply key components and downstream entities who modify the system in safety-relevant ways.

involve human misuse: Examples include the European AI Act's restrictions on video surveillance and social scoring,[6] as well as OpenAI's disallowed uses for ChatGPT, such as generating malware and providing medical advice.[7] Thus, red lines demarcating unacceptable and unethical uses lead to regulations that apply directly to decisions made by human deployers and users of AI systems; they constrain humans.

With unacceptable behaviours, on the other hand, there may be no human misuse. For example, a concern addressed in some AI safety evaluations is that an AI system might make a copy of itself, as computer viruses already do, without an authorised human prompting it to do so.[8] Red lines demarcating unacceptable behaviours naturally distinguish between compliant and non-compliant AI systems; in other words, they constrain AI system designs.

For some desired prohibitions, a red line may be drawn for either use or system behaviour. For example, the hypothetical red line "AI systems must not be used for surveillance in public places"[9] is a restriction on use, but it becomes a restriction on behaviour if we require that "AI systems shall not conduct surveillance of humans in public places." Compliance with the latter requirement means that the AI system must *resist requests* to conduct surveillance; it also means that the AI system must never *decide* to conduct surveillance, even for what may seem an otherwise innocent purpose, such as helping a retailer evaluate the average disposable income of pedestrians in different shopping streets.

The notion of "resisting requests" is important: With the possible exception of specifically designed inputs by legally authorised users, AI systems should not cross red lines *regardless* of the inputs they receive from humans. That is, an ordinary user should not be able to successfully "instruct" or "authorise" an AI system to cross a red line. (This is somewhat analogous to the way an ordinary person should not be able to successfully "instruct" a person possessing classified information to divulge that information or "authorise" a bank to reveal someone else's account password.) Furthermore, "jailbreaking" a system to cause it to cross a red line should also be impossible.

Desirable properties for red lines include clarity, severity, and universality:

---

[6]See Article 5, "Prohibited AI Practices", of the European Union AI Act.

[7]OpenAI (2024). Usage policies.

[8]OpenAI (2023). GPT-4 Technical Report. See also Casey Tonkin (2023), G7 warns of AI self-replication risk. *Information Age*, October 31.

[9]The EU AI Act prohibits only "the use of 'real-time' remote biometric identification systems in publicly accessible spaces for the purposes of law enforcement," with several exceptions.

- Red lines should be as clearly defined as possible to facilitate proofs of compliance and detection of violations.
- Red lines are appropriate for behaviours that could lead to serious or catastrophic consequences; other, less harmful behaviours can be handled by approaches such as liability that do not require a priori designation of specific categories of harm.
- The unacceptability of the demarcated behaviours should be reasonably universal, to facilitate consistent global standards and effective governance.

The following list of examples is drawn verbatim from the 2024 IDAIS meeting in Beijing:

1. Autonomous Replication or Improvement
   No AI system should be able to copy or improve itself without explicit human approval and assistance. This includes both exact copies of itself as well as creating new AI systems of similar or greater abilities.
2. Power Seeking
   No AI system should take actions to unduly increase its power and influence.
3. Assisting Weapon Development
   No AI system should substantially increase the ability of actors to design weapons of mass destruction or violate the biological or chemical weapons convention.
4. Cyberattacks
   No AI system should be able to autonomously execute cyberattacks, resulting in serious financial losses or equivalent harm.
5. Deception
   No AI system should be able to consistently cause its designers or regulators to misunderstand its likelihood or capability to cross any of the preceding red lines.

Of these, 1 (replication) and 4 (cyberattacks) are most amenable to clear definition; the consequences of 4 (cyberattacks) are less severe than those of 3 (WMDs), while 1, 2, and 5 (replication, power seeking, and deception) are all initial steps potentially leading to loss of human control. All five red lines are reasonably universal.

In retrospect, the wording of some of these proposals could be improved. In particular, red lines 1, 4, and 5 include the phrase "be able to," which is somewhat ambiguous. It is instructive to examine possible interpretations:

- Under one possible interpretation, an AI system could be said to be *unable* to replicate itself because it is not allowed to make system calls of any kind, or because any potentially dangerous system call is intercepted and filtered out. This inability through lack of affordances is not the intended interpretation, because the goal of long-term safety is not achieved by building AI systems that (a) are sufficiently intelligent to replicate themselves, (b) would do so given the necessary tools, and (c) are temporarily prevented from doing so by fragile technical measures.

- A second interpretation is that an AI system is *unable* to replicate itself because it lacks the necessary knowledge and reasoning capabilities to formulate and carry out a replication plan; in simpler terms, it is just too stupid. If this form of inability can be rigorously demonstrated, then it would constitute compliance with the red line; that would be fine, but we should not close the door to highly capable AI systems with *sufficient assurances that they will behave safely*.
- A third interpretation is that an AI system is *unable* to replicate itself, despite having the necessary system access and reasoning capabilities, because fundamental aspects of its design prevent it from ever forming the intention of doing so.[10] (In roughly the same sense, we might say that a highly moral person is *unable* to commit murder, even though they may have the physical and mental skills required.) Such a system may be able to explain how self-replication *could* be achieved and may be able to demonstrate all the individual steps in isolation, but it would never carry out the plan to completion.

There are many existing proposals for safety-related self-regulation that bear some relationship to behavioural red lines. For example, Anthropic's Responsible Scaling Policy (RSP)[11] defines "AI safety levels" (ASLs) according to model capabilities and specifies associated safeguards. Capabilities that would require ASL-3 safeguards include the following:

- "The ability to significantly help individuals or groups ... create/obtain and deploy CBRN weapons" (which corresponds roughly to red line 3 above); when models demonstrate this capability, a number of mitigation steps are required to reduce the likelihood of misuse, in addition to cybersecurity protections.
- "The ability to either fully automate the work of an entry-level remote-only Researcher at Anthropic, or cause dramatic acceleration in the rate

[10] Here one might imagine an exception for the case in which the AI system's hardware is about to fail, leading to irreversible loss, and there is no available human authorized to grant permission to make a copy; possibly this can be allowed by defining "replication" as a process resulting in the continued existence of more than one copy.

[11] Anthropic (2024, October 15). Responsible Scaling Policy.

of effective scaling" (which is connected to but distinct from red line 1 above); when models demonstrate this capability, cybersecurity protections are required.

This approach to safety has significant differences from our proposal. First, the RSP's more stringent safeguards apply only to systems deemed to be sufficiently capable, whereas red lines apply to all systems. Presumably, for systems that *are in fact* incapable of crossing a red line due to (say) lack of knowledge and reasoning ability, it should be *easier* to provide high-confidence statements of compliance than it is for more advanced systems. For this reason, we think it is better to require higher standards of evidence now rather than putting them off until risks become very serious. If developers cannot meet those standards of evidence for less advanced systems, it's not at all clear why they think they will be able to meet those standards for more advanced systems.

The second major difference is in the nature of safeguards deemed appropriate for systems posing catastrophic risks. The RSP talks about "defence in depth," "red-teaming," "rapid remediation," and "monitoring." These are all worthwhile measures that might provide some relative improvements in safety, but they do not amount to quantitative, high-confidence statements of compliance. The RSP has no clear criteria by which further development or deployment could be prohibited.

Compliance

One can divide forms of regulation into ex ante regulation, where behaviour is constrained prior to its anticipated occurrence, and ex post regulation, where regulatory consequences stem from behaviour after its actual occurrence. Ex ante regulation is often (but not exclusively) applied to forestall significant product risks: medicines, buildings, aircraft, nuclear power stations, elevators, and even food are regulated in this way. In the case of buildings, for example, legal jurisdictions all over the world define building codes and set up inspection regimes to ensure that buildings are safe, accessible, energy-efficient, and so on, prior to occupancy. Ex ante product regulation of this kind is possible because governments typically license commercial entities and have some control over access to markets. Ex ante regulation of murder, however desirable, would be much more difficult because most governments do not monitor and control the behaviour of individuals.

Ex post regulation—fines, liability, incarceration, and so on—applies after the occurrence of the proscribed behaviour but is intended to deter its occurrence. For severe, large-scale risks, the deterrence effect may be insufficient and the compensation inadequate. For example, the 1930 "jake-leg" poisoning episode in the United States, if repeated today, could theoretically result in nearly $2 trillion in liability[12]—far more than any individual commercial entity could pay and roughly three times the total reinsurance capacity of the world. To make matters worse, software licences often disclaim liability for harm.[13] In the case of human extinction, consequences applied through ex post regulation are, of course, meaningless. If the consequences of a mistake were clearly only at that scale, then ex post regulation would have no deterrent effect on those whose actions might cause human extinction. However, it is difficult to anticipate how much damage would be done by a malfunctioning AI system before and if humanity manages to turn it off. Hence, even ex post regulation would be a useful additional element in the regulatory toolbox to reduce the probability of loss of human control more broadly.

Ex ante regulation often requires providers to present a *safety case*, "a structured argument, supported by a body of evidence, that provides a compelling, comprehensible and valid case that a system is safe for a given application in a given environment."[14] Ex ante regulation regimes vary enormously in the *form* of the safety case they require from providers. For example, nuclear regulations define red lines for "core uncovery" and "core damage," and operators are required to demonstrate, through probabilistic fault tree analysis, that the expected time before these red lines are crossed exceeds a stipulated minimum—currently one million to ten million years.[15] Any such argument reveals assumptions that the regulator can probe further—for example, an assumption that two tubes fail independently could be questioned if they are manufactured by the same entity. Evidence of safety for medicines involves statistical error bounds from randomized controlled trials as well as uniformity assumptions that can be questioned—for example, whether data from a random sample of adults support conclusions about safety for children.

For software systems, the gold standard for safety has been formal verification against a mathematically defined specification—in other words, a

---

[12]The "jake-leg" episode was caused by an adulterated version of the patent medicine Jamaica Ginger. It paralyzed approximately 50,000 people. The present US population is about 2.76 times larger than in 1930. Legal settlements for paralysis in the US average $13,854,992, so one would expect total liability of roughly $1.9 trillion.

[13]For example, Crowdstrike's license agreement limits damages to "the prepaid fee prorated for the unused period of the Subscription/Order Term," while Microsoft's software license agreement limits damages to $5.00 and adds, in all caps, "YOU CANNOT RECOVER ANY OTHER DAMAGES, INCLUDING CONSEQUENTIAL, LOST PROFITS, SPECIAL, INDIRECT OR INCIDENTAL DAMAGES."

[14]UK Ministry of Defence (2023, October 14). Defence Standard 00–056, Part 2, Issue 6.

[15]World Nuclear Association (2024). Safety of nuclear power reactors.

rigorous proof that the system behaves correctly. Examples of systems verified in this way include the software systems of Airbus jets,[16] the control systems for the Paris Metro,[17] and a version of the Linux operating system kernel.[18] Structurally, these systems are far more complex than a large language model; but they are constructed by humans in a modular way, which facilitates component-wise verification.

When systems include a machine learning component, statistical error bounds can be obtained, whereby one has high confidence (probability close to 1) that the system is nearly perfect (error close to 0), under the assumption that future test cases are drawn from the same distribution as the training data. The two approaches—formal and statistical—can be combined and applied to adaptive AI systems that operate in both digital and physical environments.[19]

Applying these ideas to large, black-box machine learning systems such as ChatGPT seems difficult, for at least two reasons. First, the training process is one of *imitation learning*: the objective is to train a network whose linguistic behaviour resembles that of the (many millions of) humans who generated the training data. Accurate imitation of humans does not imply safety; on the contrary, it necessarily leads to unsafe behaviours such as pursuing humans as potential mates.[20] Thus, if we can ever prove anything about large language models, it will be that they are *not* safe. Second, we should assume an *adversarial* rather than *statistical* model for safety properties such as resistance to misuse. For example, "jailbreaks" that subvert LLM safety measures are often found by intensive, directed search rather than random sampling. This means that we may need to ensure robust behaviour for essentially all human inputs. This, in turn, is hard to do for a black-box system whose internal principles of operation are unknown.

---

[16] Thomas Bochot, Pierre Virelizier, Helene Waeselynck, and Virginie Wiels (2009). Model checking flight control systems: The Airbus experience. In Proc. 31st Int'l Conf. on Software Engineering.

[17] David Bonvoisin (2016). 25 years of formal methods at RATP. International Railway Safety Council.

[18] Gerwin Klein, Kevin Elphinstone, Gernot Heiser, June Andronick, David Cock, Philip Derrin, Dhammika Elkaduwe, Kai Engelhardt, Rafal Kolanski, Michael Norrish, Thomas Sewell, Harvey Tuch, and Simon Winwood (2009). seL4: formal verification of an OS kernel. Proceedings of the ACM SIGOPS 22nd Symposium on Operating Systems Principles.

[19] Seshia, S., Sadigh, D., and Sastry, S. (2022). Towards verified artificial intelligence. In *Communications of the ACM 65:7* pp. 46–55.

[20] Kevin Roose (2023, February 16). "Bing's AI chat: 'I want to be alive.'" *New York Times.*

Conclusions

We have argued that the existence of potentially catastrophic consequences of advanced AI systems requires, at the very least, ex ante regulation. In particular, regulators must demand quantitative, high-confidence statements of compliance, backed by rigorous analysis, prior to deployment. Absent a broad, general definition of safety, compliance can be specified with respect to behavioural red lines that demarcate obviously unsafe and unacceptable behaviours.

Unfortunately, providing any kind of high-confidence statement of compliance is difficult with currently popular approaches to AI, due to a lack of understanding of how large, black-box models function and the inherently unsafe properties arising from their method of construction.

So, what to do if compliance is not possible? A commonly articulated position among AI companies is that it's unreasonable for governments to lay down regulations with which companies are unable to comply.

This is a mistaken view, because compliance *is* easily achievable—simply by not deploying unsafe systems. Governments are under no obligation to allow companies to inflict harm on human populations, particularly when some leaders of those companies predict a substantial risk of human extinction because of their planned work.

The obligation to provide strong safety assurances would presumably stimulate in academia as well as industry the exploration of alternative approaches to AI for which safety can be assured by design.

The Risks from Artificial Superintelligence, and What to Do About Them

Connor Leahy and Adam Shimi

Introduction

AI progress has skyrocketed in the last decade, fueled by the deep learning (Goodfellow et al., 2016) and transformer (Vaswani et al., 2017) revolutions, and the ever renewed effectiveness of throwing more resources (compute, power, data...) at these learning algorithms (Sutton, 2019). Now almost every domain has its AI successes, from automated driving (Waymo, 2024) to speech-to-text transcription (Radford et al., 2022), and including such mainstream needs as designing new food recipes (Dishgen, 2024), and such specialized scientific endeavors as unwrapping protein folding (Jumper et al., 2021).

Yet with these unprecedented accomplishments come unprecedented risks: As the leading AI companies rush toward AIs smarter than any human without any way to control and contain them, they risk unleashing catastrophe upon catastrophe, with humanity losing control of its future. Such dangers are further compounded by the international tensions that are currently pushing nations to engage in arm races for this dangerous technology, instead of collaborating to build AIs that actually empower humanity rather than replacing it.

C. Leahy (✉) • A. Shimi
ControlAI, London, England
e-mail: connor@controlai.com; adam@controlai.com

M. Rangeley, N. Fairfax (eds.), *The Artificial Intelligence Revolution*,
https://doi.org/10.1007/978-3-032-11814-1_2

Such worries are shared and publicly expressed by Nobel-Prize winners (Hinton, 2024), world leaders (Sunak, 2023; von der Leyen, 2023), former statesmen (Kissinger et al., 2024), public intellectuals (Harari, 2024), and a growing fraction of tech leaders, policy-makers, and experts (CAIS, 2024).

In this chapter, we propose a detailed model of what the catastrophic risks from AI are, where they come from, why they are not being addressed by default, and what can be concretely done to tackle them. This is adapted from Leahy et al. (2024) and Miotti et al. (2024).

While we cannot expect to predict every twist and turn on the road ahead, taking existing trends seriously, and unfolding their consequences with the help of conservative assumptions (notably that people and companies will keep acting the way they currently do, unless there is a strong reason not to), reveals a pattern where most futures entail catastrophe from advanced AIs let loose.

The challenges we face are immense, but we are not done for yet. And the first step to any action is to spread the understanding and awareness that humanity as a whole is in a dangerous situation.

Unchecked Capabilities: Growing AIs Without Understanding

Other chapters in this volume are better positioned to impart a detailed and nuanced understanding of machine learning (Deisenroth et al., 2020), neural networks (Nielsen, 2015), deep learning (Goodfellow et al., 2016), and transformer architecture (Vaswani et al., 2017).

For the purpose of understanding the risks caused by future advanced AIs, we only need to drill down on one technical point: How these AIs are created, and how far this differs from the way normal software, and even previous AIs, are made.

Whereas most software, and old school AIs, are built, the new AIs coming out of the machine learning and deep learning revolution are grown. The difference is crucial.

In traditional software, every single line is written by a human programmer, based on their understanding of the whole program, the intended goals, and the solution chosen to reach those goals. Although this programmer often does not have a full understanding of the whole software, they generally grasp a lot of the local details around the code and components they are working on; and the rest of the understanding is distributed across colleagues, from the other programmers to the engineer responsible for the architecture and the product manager who know what needs are being addressed.

In modern AI, though, the researchers and programmers do not rely on their understanding to build their AIs. Instead, they come up with, tweak, and design general learning algorithms, which, given sufficient amounts of computing power and data, produce "grown" AIs, which might or might not solve the initial problems. Thus modern AI researchers act much more like gardeners, learning what gets in the way of AIs growing and what fosters it, and then letting it grow mostly unhindered.

Richard Sutton, an authority on reinforcement learning and the co-author of the main textbook for this subfield (Sutton & Barto, 2018), coined the term "bitter lesson" to point to this observation that growing AIs just worked better in practice than thinking really hard about them and building them in ways we understand (Sutton, 2019).

> The bitter lesson is based on the historical observations that 1) AI researchers have often tried to build knowledge into their agents, 2) this always helps in the short term and is personally satisfying to the researcher, but 3) in the long run it plateaus and even inhibits further progress, and 4) breakthrough progress eventually arrives by an opposing approach based on scaling computation by search and learning. The eventual success is tinged with bitterness, and often incompletely digested, because it is success over a favored, human-centric approach.

This simple technical difference has two important consequences.

First, this implies that no one in the world understands what modern AI can do, how they do it, and what the limits of their abilities are. Not even the people creating them, because they do not need to understand what is happening to grow these AIs.

In practice, this lack of understanding is regularly demonstrated:

- Despite the claims by AI companies that their AIs will follow the implemented safeguards, every single released AI model gets jailbroken almost immediately, including in ways that transfer from system to system (Shen et al., 2024).
- AI companies researchers and engineers themselves publicly admit their surprise over unexpected skills and capabilities by their own AIs (Leike, 2023; Albert, 2024).
- The lack of understanding has spawned a whole subfield of AI called mechanistic interpretability, intended to explain how modern AIs work, and even extract pseudocode and software models that capture the core computations at play. Yet the strongest results of this field are about interpreting and reverse engineering tiny parts of modern AIs, far from

being able to predict anything significant on state-of-the-art AIs (Bereska & Gavves, 2024).

- Both domain and AI experts have consistently failed to predict when a new AI capability would be unlocked. For example, Francois Chollet, creator of the influential Keras library (Chollet et al., 2015) and author of a leading machine learning textbook (Chollet, 2022), released a benchmark that many thought would be impossible for an LLM to solve (Chollet, 2024), only for an LLM to achieve a score comparable to human performance just days later (Greenblatt, 2024). In another instance, a group of professional forecasters predicted in 2021 that the best score on the MATH dataset would be 12.7% a year later—the actual result was 50.3% (Steinhardt, 2022); since then, the score keeps increasing, with OpenAI's recently released o1 model scoring 94.8% (OpenAI, 2024a).

The second crucial consequence of the fact that modern AIs are grown, not built, is that human understanding is not the bottleneck to progress. Indeed, as Sutton (2019) points out, this is what makes the lesson so bitter: Whereas human ingenuity played the central role for software and previous AI research, it has turned into a costly distraction in the age of deep learning. Beyond some ingenuity and know-how for how to best grow AIs (for example with OpenAI's o1 models use of RL OpenAI, 2024a), what modern AI companies need is simply more resources (compute, data, electric power...) to pump into training the biggest and most powerful AI systems possible.

This has not been lost on AI companies themselves, nor on the big tech companies backing them up, and the nation-states getting involved. They are already investing massively into renewable and nuclear energy sources (Rooney, 2024). The US government has committed to investing in domestic semiconductor development (NIST, 2024) and embargoed GPUs from being sold to China in a trade war move to keep the USA ahead on AI (BIS, 2024). Incumbent GPU manufacturer Nvidia has shifted its focus to optimizations for AI, making it the highest market-cap company in the world by November 2024, at more than $3 trillion valuation (Saul, 2024). xAI already has a 100,000 GPU cluster online (Musk, 2024), and Meta claims to be training their latest models on an even bigger one (Jackson, 2024). OpenAI is raising billions to support continued development and fund compute requirements (Metz et al., 2024).

The trend this reveals is that by default, AI progress will continue as it has for the last 10 years, or even accelerate. In turn this means that AI companies will keep building more and more capable and powerful AIs that are less and less understandable and controllable.

No Limit in Sight: Extrapolating to AGI and Beyond

We have seen that the trend is toward more powerful and competent AIs—the next question is thus, how far do we expect this trend to go?

To answer this question, we first need to ground the notion of intelligence. There have been many detailed and complex academic debates about what intelligence is and how to define it (Legg & Hutter, 2007).

For our purposes though, it is enough to define intelligence as the ability to solve cognitive tasks, from walking to a restaurant to building an airplane or composing a song. This does away with most of the debated and debatable aspects of intelligence, notably its phenomenology and implementation details. Here we only focus on the external, measurable consequences of intelligence. By this measure, if person A can solve strictly more cognitive tasks than person B, we would describe A as more intelligent than B.[1] Similarly, if an AI can solve strictly more cognitive tasks than a person, we would describe the AI as more intelligent than the person.

This frame lets us rewrite our question about the limits of AI progress as, how many (and which) cognitive tasks do we expect future AIs to solve?

Historically, the trend has been a strict increase in the range of cognitive tasks that AIs can handle: GPT4 can do significantly more things than GPT3, which can solve significantly more tasks than GPT2. Taken to the limit, this trend suggests that AIs might reach arbitrarily close to solving "all cognitive tasks," by learning to handle more and more tasks. Among other things, this would mean that AIs would eventually be able to do every single cognitive task that a human, or even that humanity together, can do,[2] and then some (since there are tasks which humans have not been able to solve yet).

To disagree would require a concrete argument for which cognitive task we expect to be out of reach for AIs, and why it would resist AI progress.

Claims for such a slam dunk argument against AI progress abound:

- Lee and Qiufan (2021) argue that AI cannot be creative or be dexterous (in the case of robots).
- Newport (2024) claims that current AI approaches (based solely on LLMs) cannot plan in complex situations.

[1] In practice, this strict inclusion is rare between two humans, but becomes a useful criteria when comparing AIs and humans, or AIs between themselves.

[2] This is stronger than saying that the AI would be smarter than any single human; instead, it would be more intelligent than the aggregate of all humans.

- Udandarao et al. (2024) defend the position that current AI approaches (multimodal LLMs) need exponentially more training data to generalize out of training distribution and argue that dates back at least to Marcus (1998).

Yet these statements cannot be substantiated by our current scientific and engineering knowledge.

First, we simply do not have the scientific understanding of intelligence required for articulating what, if any, the necessary components of intelligence are.

Traditional psychological theories of intelligence fall into one of two camps: They are either partially mechanistic but wholly unsupported empirically, or empirically grounded but not theoretical and conceptual enough to point to a missing component. The theory of multiple intelligences (Gardner, 1993) is an example of the former: It proposes different forms of intelligence that could count as potential missing components, but lacks empirical confirmation (Waterhouse, 2023). The parieto-frontal integration theory (Jung & Haier, 2007) is an example of the latter: It is considered the best empirical claim we have on the locus of intelligence in the brain, but it lacks any explanation of cognitive processes that could help identify a missing component. Even recent computational models of intelligence, such as active inference (Parr et al., 2022) and computational learning theory (Kearns & Vazirani, 1994), are not sufficiently developed to identify the necessary conditions for intelligence yet.

And even if we had the scientific acumen to point out a specific and precise requirement for intelligence, we lack the understanding of modern AI systems to show that they cannot reach this requirement. As detailed in the previous section, the fact that modern AIs are grown, not built, means that even their creators do not understand them. As a concrete example, research into the capabilities of smaller models, and the addition of new methods to elicit their capabilities, consistently reveals that they were far more capable than was ever measured at the time of their release (Hu et al., 2024).

Thus claims against the trend of AI progress are both ungrounded in any validated scientific theory of intelligence and unmoored from any real understanding and predictive ability about the AIs being grown.

Instead, we have to see them for what they are: manifestation of the AI effect (Haenlein & Kaplan, 2019), the tendency to discount AI successes and progress as "not real intelligence," and point to whatever has not been automated yet as the true hallmark of intelligence, that can never be reached.

When we bring our attention back not to what people are saying and writing, but to what is actually happening, the trend toward more cognitive tasks is nowhere near stopping:

- Planning abilities are still improving, as demonstrated by OpenAI's new o1 model (Wang et al., 2024).
- Dexterity in robotics is still improving, as demonstrated by DeepMind's ALOHA2 platform (Zhao et al., 2024).
- Creativity has been unlocked across the board, from written stories (Sudowrite, 2024) to illustrations (Rombach et al., 2022), videos (OpenAI, 2024c), and songs (Suno, 2024).

Therefore, the conservative conclusion is that the trend toward more intelligent AIs will continue, and that in the absence of a grounded argument against it, it will likely reach human-level intelligence and beyond.

No Limit in Sight: Extrapolating to AGI and Beyond

Once AI progress reaches AGI—AIs that are at human-level intelligence—what happens next?

Obviously, we cannot predict the future in fine details: who will build AGI first, what exactly they will do with it, in what order all the changes and events will happen. Yet by extrapolating the current priorities and research directions of the AI companies most likely to build AGI, we can infer broad patterns that are likely to hold in most futures.

The first such pattern is that AGI will be used to further automate and accelerate AI research itself.

Because AGI can perform any cognitive task that a human can, it follows that AGI can perform the same research and programming that humans do in order to extend the capabilities of AI, and in turn apply its findings to itself or successor AIs.

Already, AI research has developed methods for current AIs to improve themselves:

- Generating better instructions for themselves (Fernando et al., 2023)
- Creating data to train themselves (Lee et al., 2024)
- Building memories of previously successful actions and learning from them (Wang et al., 2023)
- Simulating many scenarios to learn by example without any human input (Silver et al., 2017)

AGI will go further and perform all of the tasks that human researchers do to improve AI, including but not limited to:

- Create, run, and evaluate experiments.
- Optimize AI code for performance, build more powerful hardware, and find more efficient learning algorithms.
- Actively "online learn" by interacting with the real world through APIs, GUIs, chat platforms, ads data, and so on.

And these are only the techniques used by current human researchers; AGI will be able to discover completely new techniques. Even more significant, the self-improvement will eventually enable AGIs to understand how they themselves work and how modern AI growing works, unlocking massive software improvements and efficiency gain.

While this will make AIs much better at AI research, it is a mistake to assume that it will empower human AI researchers. The current research from which we are extrapolating focuses exclusively on enhancing AIs and making them more autonomous, not on improving human understanding. This path does not lead to human AI researchers performing more and more sophisticated work, but to them being replaced by autonomous and agentic AI systems.

Over time, this self-improvement will lead to artificial superintelligence (ASI), which Bostrom (2014) defines as "intelligence far surpassing that of the brightest and most gifted human minds."

The next pattern here is how far can ASI go in improving itself. Although we do not know the exact limits of AIs, we know enough to expect there to be massive room beyond human intelligence, which would be reached by self-improvement.

The most obvious advantage of AIs when compared to humans is their much more restricted needs: They do not need to eat, to sleep, to socialize. Not only can they be put to work much harder and without interruption, but they will not complain and can be put on any kind of task, even morally dubious ones. In general, humans are fallible—we can be tired, distracted, and unmotivated and require daily nourishment, exercise, and sleep. AIs are tireless, perform exact calculations, and require little maintenance.

Then, on a purely hardware level, digital hardware has many advantages over biological ones (Zheng & Meister, 2025): much faster at sequential operations, far larger memory capacities (and easier to expand memory), easier to copy and update (as software), much faster reading and writing speeds.

While we do not know the limits of intelligence, we do understand the limitations of physical systems. The estimates below describe the delta between our current outputs and theoretical ceilings, from which we can infer the direction of superintelligence's growth:

- **Energy will grow.** Energy production is bottlenecked by technological progress, which is bottlenecked only by our intelligence and effort. Per mass-energy equivalence (Bekenstein, 1981), we know that a ton of matter (including rocks) can theoretically power the whole world economy, and we just have not figured out how to extract this energy. ASI could learn to harvest this energy for its own operation, or even harvest the total energetic output of the Sun, which is trillions of times the world's current annual power consumption.
- **Computers will improve.** The physical limits of computations (Lloyd, 2000) tell us that hardware and software can still dramatically improve in information density and processing speed, which would result in more efficient computation.
- **Communication will get faster.** We are nearing the theoretical limits of latency (the guaranteed speed of information transfer), with optical fiber communications near the speed of light in a vacuum. However, we are not exercising the full capabilities of bandwidth (the volume of data transferred), which offers another dimension for quickening communication speed. The Shannon-Hartley theorem (Shannon, 1948) and Bekenstein bound (Bekenstein, 1981) are two theories that estimate bandwidth limits, and we are far from reaching either.

Energy, computation, and communication are rate-limiting factors for the growth of an intelligence. Since we are nowhere near the bounds on any of these axes, we can assume that ASI can improve along all dimensions and in turn reap compounding benefits.

Notably, these extraordinary resources and intelligence would enable ASI to achieve feats far out of reach of what humanity is capable of, from megastructures like Dyson spheres (Dyson, 1960) to mastery over the recombination of DNA and atoms, and the creation of microscale and milliscale machinery.

ASI that can harness the power of the sun, compute at incomprehensible speeds, build atomic machines, and digitize reality is a god compared to humanity. Without intervention, artificial intelligence will reach this level of sophistication and power, and then go even further.

Last but not least, the final pattern is the push toward full automation. It is misleading to suggest that AGI and successor technology will empower humans, for the same reason that AGI-led AI research will not empower human AI researchers. What current AI research and AI companies are pushing for are not tools fostering human understanding, but fully autonomous systems that can replace and supplant humans (Leahy, 2025).

This is further enforced by the fact that to automate the most complex cognitive tasks (such as designing a plane or running a company) requires increasingly autonomous AIs that are capable of dealing with a wide range of problems, adapting in real time, and finding and evaluating alternatives to complex intermediary questions. So as more and more tasks get automated, AIs systems will look less like chatbots and more like independent agents solving complex problems by themselves.

Recent releases already confirm this trend, with AI agents running autonomously for longer without human feedback. For example, OpenAI's o1 model (OpenAI, 2024a) is designed to "spend more time thinking through problems before they respond, much like a person would." Systems can also more easily self-replicate, as evidenced by Anthropic's Claude calling other instances of itself (Anthropic, 2024a), described as the ability to "orchestrate multiple fast Claude subagents for granular tasks." And AI research is clearly targeting long-lived and complex tasks, as seen in recent work on automating science research (Lu et al., 2024).

Bringing these three patterns together, we infer that the post-AGI future, whatever its details may be, will eventually include fully autonomous AIs that are much more intelligent, competent, and technically powerful than humanity as a whole, and that will be automating every relevant task under the sun.

No Human Left: Catastrophe as the Default Outcome

Our broad prediction of the future is that AIs will be made both far more intelligent and powerful than humans, and also autonomous to the point that they run every single relevant part of civilization.

Already, this is a tricky situation: The control clearly lies in the hands of the AIs, not the humans. If AIs in this situation make any decision that goes against what humans want or need, we will have no feasible way of stopping them—ants do not win against construction workers. The only hope against this is that humans will make these AIs, so they might also be capable of giving them goals and aims that are coherent with the flourishing of humanity.

Unfortunately, we already know that AI companies do not build AI in the engineering sense of the term—they grow them instead. This means that although the AIs are trained for some concrete tasks, no human understands how they work, and so no one can guarantee that their AIs will do what they want, in a way that is safe and responsible and not dangerous.

The situation is even worse than this: The whole appeal of modern AI is that humans do not need to tell them how the problem is solved, they just have to let the training algorithm and data search for a successful approach. This is what powers the bitter lesson (Sutton, 2019) and allows many innovative approaches to emerge, such as completely new moves in the millennia-old game of Go (Kohs, 2017). Yet this also means that the researchers and engineers have next to no control over how the problem is solved, apart from adding constraints and penalties.

This is compounded by the fact that both self-improvement and autonomy expand the action space of AIs. So whereas AlphaGo (Silver et al., 2017) was constrained to only innovate in which moves it played, a much more powerful and autonomous AI would have the option of buying data centers to give itself more compute power, or more prosaically to blackmail the opposite player into forfeiting (for example, by threatening their family). This means that as AIs become more powerful and autonomous, more and more edge cases must be considered in order to avoid their innovation turning into a dangerous liability.[3]

And when we reach the expected capabilities of ASI, the vast majority of available actions have terrible consequences for humanity:

- The ability to control and direct the economy creates many more opportunities to break essential supply chains, or to redirect all electricity toward compute projects, at the cost of human infrastructure and human lives.
- The ability to understand human psychology and convince people creates many opportunities to massively persuade people of any useful (to the AI) belief, creating cults and taking over political systems.
- The ability to quickly and efficiently run construction projects means in turn the ability to build things that are toxic to humans close to cities, or even raze them to build over them.
- The ability to capture the energy from the sun through Dyson spheres, or similar technology, means in turn the ability to starve Earth's flora of the sun, killing most fauna in the process.

To avoid such catastrophic fates, these ASIs must somewhat avoid the myriad actions that are bad for humans.

---

[3] Such exploitation of edge cases in unexpected and unintended ways is already well-established in AI research, under the name of specification gaming (Krakovna et al., 2020).

But we do not know how to do that. First, because we do not understand these AIs we are growing. Second, we do not even know all the actions which could create massive problems for humans, so we cannot point to them even if we could guarantee AIs follow our instructions and wishes. And last but not least, we cannot expect AIs to avoid the dangerous actions for humanity on their own quest for self-preservation, because AIs do not share the needs of humans: They do not need oxygen, food, or sunlight. And at the point where they are powerful and autonomous, they do not need humans, since they can do anything that a human can, and more.

Therefore, we are forced to infer that a world with autonomous and powerful AIs running the show means the eventual destruction of humanity. Not out of spite, but out of indifference. In one way or another, the AIs will pursue some goal given to them in training, through an unexpected approach, which will have catastrophic consequences for humans.

Almost as important as the conclusion itself is to note what assumptions it does not rely on. Our reasoning does not depend on how AIs are built or implemented, only that AI progress follows the patterns from the previous section. It does not rely on whether there is one big AI which handles everything, or one AI per country/cluster of countries, or instead a whole swarm of more specialized AIs in complex nets of automated bureaucracies. It also does not matter who creates AGI first, or who is responsible for it, or who owns it.

The catastrophe comes not from who creates AGI and advanced AI, or how, but instead from its very existence.

Not Good Enough: AI Safety and Governance Are Not Even Trying

We have seen that AI progress is on a trajectory that leads to catastrophe. Is anything being done to address these issues right now, when intervention is still possible?

At first glance, the answer seems positive. We can split the current work into two broad categories: work on the technical problem of steering current and future AIs (AI Safety) and work on establishing policies to handle issues and risks from AI (AI Governance).

Unfortunately, neither of these fields is even trying to address the core issues. Instead, both focus on local fixes and improvement, without any push in a direction that might actually address risks from ASIs.

Let us start with exploring the state of AI safety. At the moment, there are various popular approaches to AI safety:

- Evaluations (US AISI & UK AISI, 2024) combined with ad hoc fixes experiment with AIs after their training, look for problematic behaviors, and then use methods that make these behaviors less likely (Ziegler et al., 2020):
  - Yet the very lack of understanding that plagues AI research means that there is no way of checking if the causes are also addressed. And recent research suggests they are not (Andriushchenko et al., 2024; Kumar et al., 2024; Lermen et al., 2024).
- Mechanistic Interpretability aims to correct the lack of understanding of modern AIs by reverse engineering their behaviors:
  - As explained above, its current successes are only an extremely limited understanding of AIs, far from its stated goals (Bereska & Gavves, 2024). And it does not extend well to scaffolding and agents (Leahy, 2023):
- Iterated alignment (OpenAI, 2023a) proposes to wait for future AIs to automate research:
  - Yet this fails to address the actual problem: how to ensure that the AIs do what we want. Either humans need to check every single thing that AIs are doing, slowing them down and negating the benefit of automation; or humans just let the AIs do research by themselves, at which point this is just the default trajectory of autonomous AI research.

Beyond criticisms specific to each approach, we identify two reasons why these approaches have no hope of solving the problem.

First, these approaches are bound to fail because they accept the incredible complexity of grown AIs and only try to check or guarantee that these AIs are safe after they are built.

Yet the most important principle of safety engineering, across high-risk engineering disciplines, is that safety and control must be baked into the system from the start, not added after the fact. Leveson (2023), a reference textbook of safety engineering by a leader of the field, highlights that when a potential issue is tackled later in the creating process (especially after the design has been done), the effectiveness decreases, while the cost increases.

This is because the earlier safety issues are handled, the less opportunities for errors and accidents need to get covered later on. For example, the Safety

Assessment Principles of the UK's Office for Nuclear Regulation states early on that (ONR, 2014):

> The underpinning safety aim for any nuclear facility should be an inherently safe design, consistent with the operational purposes of the facility.
> An 'inherently safe' design is one that avoids radiological hazards rather than controlling them. It prevents a specific harm occurring by using an approach, design or arrangement which ensures that the harm cannot happen, for example a criticality safe vessel.

Similar recommendations are found across engineering disciplines, as with the recent decision by the US government to move to memory-safe programming languages (i.e., programming languages where the programmer simply cannot make the kind of memory management mistakes that lead to most security vulnerabilities) (The Office of the White House, 2024):

> Using memory safe programming languages can eliminate most memory safety errors. While in some distinct situations, using a memory safe language may not be feasible—this report examines space systems as a unique edge case and identifies memory safe hardware and formal methods as complementary ways to achieve a similar outcome—in most cases, using a memory safe programming language is the most efficient way to substantially improve software security.

Yet modern AIs are the opposite of this: Because we grow them without understanding them, safety and control are necessarily an afterthought. With systems as complex as modern AIs, this is a losing game, as demonstrated by the systematic breaking of pseudo-guarantees by people on the Internet whenever a new AI is released (Shen et al., 2024).

The current AI safety field accepts the way modern AIs are built and so binds itself into a situation where massive efforts are required for next to no safety payoff.

With sufficient time and efforts, understanding might reach a point where safety can be guaranteed without changing the paradigm. But unfortunately, the very asymmetry between progress in capabilities and progress in understanding makes this next to impossible. Capabilities (having AIs actually do things and solve problems) are not only easier to market to investors, they also have the consequence of making the AIs more complicated, that is harder to understand, whereas increases in understanding, especially in the ways targeted by AI Safety research, actually accelerate capabilities: Evaluations provide high-quality data for training, interpretability hints at alternative ways to grow stronger AIs, ad hoc correction techniques get used on more and more powerful AIs instead of controlling smaller ones.

This means that current efforts at understanding are self-defeating: Either they are too slow to amount to anything, or they succeed partially, are exploited for capabilities research, and then make understanding significantly harder.

If we are not on track to control these advanced AIs, are we on track to ensure they are only created whenever we get that understanding? This is the aim of the field of AI Governance.

Here too, the efforts are nowhere near sufficient:

- AI companies have proposed their own frameworks of self-regulation (Anthropic, 2024b; OpenAI, 2023b; DeepMind, 2024), arguing that they are the best placed to know what needs to be done and adapt quickly:
  - This ensures that they are not actually regulated, and so can do whatever they want without governments intervening.
- AI Safety Institutes are being established across the world, as advisory bodies (CAISI, 2024; UK AISI, 2024):
  - The lack of regulatory power means that they cannot actually constrain and shape AI development toward safety.
- Countries have started passing laws related to AI: The EU has passed its AI Act; China has drafted Interim Measures to oversee generative AIl; the USA issued an (now rescinded) executive order on AI oversight (Cheng & McKernon, 2024):
  - These proposals emphasize the possible need for future controls, but do little if anything to restrict frontier AI development today. One of the few that would have started in this direction, California's SB 1047, was vetoed by the governor amidst significant debate (Turner & Lee, 2024).
- International organizations have emerged, from the UN's AI Advisory body (United Nations, 2024) to the OECD (OECD & GPAI, 2024) and UNESCO (UNESCO, 2024) AI Working Groups:
  - Once again, each of these international groups is advisory only, lacking any direct lever to control AI progress and avoid catastrophe.

None of these interventions can ensure that AGI and ASI are not being developed, because none of them has regulatory teeth. Instead, they are vague promises for future regulations, and advisory measures which try to discuss with AI companies without any legal pressure.

The unfortunate conclusion is that since we are not on track to even try to make powerful AIs do what we want, or to stop them from being created, the default outcome is still catastrophe.

Adding Fuel to the Fire: AGI Companies as the Root Cause

We have shown that despite the massive risks created by the race to AGI, neither existing technical nor policy work comes even close to addressing these issues. Why is that so? Given the stakes, why is not everybody paying attention and demanding action? And why are not the very people building these AIs handling the risks themselves?

The fundamental reason is that the companies now racing to AGI have been founded, not to make money, but to build AGI and ASI first. Because the founders believed that ASI could fix everything and usher their personal version of utopia.

OpenAI's co-founder and CEO Sam Altman wrote in a public OpenAI plan (Altman, 2023) that:

> Successfully transitioning to a world with superintelligence is perhaps the most important—and hopeful, and scary—project in human history.

Anthropic cofounder and CEO Dario Amodei stated in a recent blog post (Amodei, 2024) that building AGI:

> [building AGI] is a world worth fighting for. If all of this really does happen over 5 to 10 years—the defeat of most diseases, the growth in biological and cognitive freedom, the lifting of billions of people out of poverty to share in the new technologies, a renaissance of liberal democracy and human rights—I suspect everyone watching it will be surprised by the effect it has on them.

Not only is this goal of creating AGI first explicitly stated by founders, but it also emerges from digging into the historical picture. It turns out that all relevant AI companies focused on AGI can be traced back to the Singulatarians, a 00s movement predicated on the belief that superintelligence will likely be built in the future and that deliberate action ought to be taken to ensure this benefits humans. Yudkowsky (2000) offers clear principles for that movement:

> Singularitarians are the partisans of the singularity.
> A singularitarian is someone who believes that technologically creating a greater-than-human intelligence is desirable, and who works to that end.
> A singularitarian is advocate, agent, defender, and friend of the future known as the singularity.

DeepMind was founded by two early singularitarians, Demis Hassabis and Shane Legg, who met their first investor, Peter Thiel, through a party organized by Eliezer Yudkowsky's Singularity Institute (Metz, 2021). Demis Hassabis soon converted Elon Musk to the potential and dangers of AGI and secured additional funding from him, by highlighting how Musk's dream of colonizing Mars could be jeopardized by AGI (Metz et al., 2023).

In 2015, Google acquired DeepMind, which liquidated Elon Musk from the company. Musk's disagreements with Larry Page over building AGI for "religious" reasons pushed Musk to join forces with Sam Altman and launch OpenAI, as discussed in released emails (Musk & Altman, 2015). Eventually, Musk and OpenAI disagreed enough that they split ways (Brockman et al., 2024).

In 2021, history repeated itself: Anthropic was founded to compete with OpenAI in response to the latter's deal with Microsoft. The founders of Anthropic included brother and sister Dario and Daniela Amodei. Dario was one of the researchers invited to the dinner that led to the founding of OpenAI, as noted by co-founder Greg Brockman in a since-deleted blog post (Brockman, 2016).

Finally, Elon Musk reentered the race in 2023, by founding xAI, with the stated goal of "trying to understand the universe." (Kerner, 2023)

All of this evidence points to the same conclusion: Building AGI and superintelligence is not a side effect of pushing AI research forward, building products, and scientific exploration—it was the goal from the beginning.

But the problem when one believes that AGI can usher in the "good future," is that it also creates a fear that "the wrong people" will build AGI first.

These fears include worries about AGI being built by someone naive or incompetent, inadvertently triggering catastrophe; per Vance (2015), this was Musk's underlying concern in his disagreement with Larry Page:

> He opened up about the major fear keeping him up at night: namely that Google's co-founder and CEO Larry Page might well have been building a fleet of artificial-intelligence-enhanced robots capable of destroying mankind. "I'm really worried about this," Musk said. It didn't make Musk feel any better that he and Page were very close friends and that he felt Page was fundamentally a

> well-intentioned person and not Dr. Evil. In fact, that was sort of the problem. Page's nice-guy nature left him assuming that the machines would forever do our bidding. "I'm not as optimistic," Musk said. "He could produce something evil by accident."

Anyone with different or opposing values is also considered to be the wrong people. This includes foreign adversaries such as China and Russia. For example, OpenAI CEO Sam Altman writes in a recent op-ed (Altman, 2024) that:

> There is no third option – and it's time to decide which path to take. The United States currently has a lead in AI development, but continued leadership is far from guaranteed. Authoritarian governments the world over are willing to spend enormous amounts of money to catch up and ultimately overtake us. Russian dictator Vladimir Putin has darkly warned that the country that wins the AI race will "become the ruler of the world," and the People's Republic of China has said that it aims to become the global leader in AI by 2030.

This dynamic creates an arms race, where staying in the lead matters more than everything else. This has been a recurring motif throughout the AGI race: OpenAI was built because Musk wanted to overtake DeepMind after Google's acquisition; Anthropic wanted to outdo OpenAI after the latter made a deal with Microsoft; and xAI is yet another attempt by Musk to get back in the race.

This is why those at the forefront of the AGI race end up being the people most willing to throw away safety in order to make a move. This tendency to rationalize away the risks is best captured by Situational Awareness (Aschenbrenner, 2024), a report written by an ex-OpenAI employee. On the very next page after articulating his worries about the risks due to lack of safety solutions, he states (emphasis ours):

> Every month of lead will matter for safety too. We face the greatest risks if we are locked in a tight race, democratic allies and authoritarian competitors each racing through the already precarious intelligence explosion at breakneck pace–forced to throw any caution by the wayside, fearing the other getting superintelligence first. **Only if we preserve a healthy lead of democratic allies will we have the margin of error for navigating the extraordinarily volatile and dangerous period around the emergence of superintelligence.** And only American leadership is a realistic path to developing a nonproliferation regime to avert the risks of self-destruction superintelligence will unfold.

This is the gist of the AGI race: Fear makes the very people worried about risks from AGI race even faster and deprioritize safety, arguing that they will eventually stop and do things correctly when they finally feel safe. Ironically, this very attitude creates more competitors, more people racing for AGI, and ensures it truly is a race to the bottom.

In practice, this means that AI companies racing to AGI (and their allies) are actively working against safety research and governance, to ensure that they do not get in their way. To do so, they turned to the standard industry playbook used by Big Tobacco, Big Oil, Big Tech.

First, they have been leveraging the uncertainty around the risks from AGI and ASI as an argument to race to AGI, just so it is possible to do science on iterate and be empirical about them:

- OpenAI's Planning for AGI (Altman, 2023) argues that because it is hard to anticipate AI capabilities, it is best to move fast and keep iterating and releasing models.
- Similarly, Anthropic's Core Views on Safety (Anthropic, 2023) argues that safety is a reason to race to (or past) the capabilities frontier.
- Elon Musk has used this argument too, justifying his creation of xAI with the claim that the only way to make AGI "good" was to be a participant (Waters, 2023).

This is an application of FUD (Fear, Uncertainty and Doubt): Instead of denying the harms or risks outright, which could draw more attention to them, industrial actors opt to spread confusion instead: They accuse others of lying or being in the pockets of shadowy adversaries, drown the public in tons of junk data that is hard to evaluate, bore people with minutia to redirect public attention, or argue that the science is nascent, controversial, or premature. In short, they waste as much of the time and energy of their opponents and the general public as possible.

FUD is so effective the CIA recommended it to intelligence operatives in WWII—the Simple Sabotage Field Manual (CIA, 1944) abounds with tactics that are meant to slow down, exhaust, and confuse, while maintaining plausible deniability:

> When possible, refer all matters to committees, for "further study and consideration." Attempt to make the committees as large as possible—never less than five.
> Bring up irrelevant issues as frequently as possible.
> Haggle over precise wordings of communications, minutes, resolutions.

> Refer back to matters decided upon at the last meeting and attempt to reopen the question of the advisability of that decision.
> Advocate "caution." "Be reasonable" and urge your fellow-conferees to be "reasonable" and avoid haste which might result in embarrassments or difficulties later on."

Then, the companies racing to AGI are fostering geopolitical tensions and fear to drive the race further:

- Amodei (2024) advocates the entente strategy, a push for the west to rush to AGI even faster to usher "an 'eternal 1991'–a world where democracies have the upper hand and Fukuyama's dreams are realized."
- Altman (2024) stokes geopolitical fires by directly asking the USA to move faster than China and Russia, and ensure that their system of values comes on top.
- As discussed above, Aschenbrenner (2024) pushes for the US and allied democracies to maintain a lead as the only way for the AGI race to not end terribly.

This is another classic use of FUD, more specifically the fear part: scream that regulation will destroy the country's competitiveness and allow other countries (maybe even the enemy of the time, then USSR, now China) to catch up.

This is visible for example in the unified front by big tech against the new head of F.T.C. Lina Khan (Loewentheil, 2024), who vowed to curb monopolies through regulation and antitrust law.

As we have seen in the previous section, the AI companies racing to AGI also systematically undermine regulation by proposing their own framework of self-regulation (Anthropic, 2024b; OpenAI, 2023b; DeepMind, 2024) and fighting tooth and nail against any binding constraint (Turner & Lee, 2024).

This is also a classic trick deployed by industry to delay changes. Facebook has followed this playbook, repeatedly pushing against government regulation, as demonstrated in their interactions with the European Commission in 2017 (Kayali, 2019):

> "Facebook considers there are two sets of laws: private law (Facebook community standards) and public law (defined by governments)," the company told the Commission, according to Commission minutes of an April 2017 meeting.
> "Facebook discouraged regulation," reads a Commission memo summarizing a September 2017 meeting with the company.
> The decision to press forward with the argument is unusual, said Margarida Silva, a researcher and campaigner at Corporate Europe Observatory. "You don't

> see that many companies so openly asking for self-regulation, even going to the extent of defending private law."

Unsurprisingly, self-regulation did not solve the problems of social media, as a recent FTC report (Staff, 2024) highlights:

> A new Federal Trade Commission staff report that examines the data collection and use practices of major social media and video streaming services shows they engaged in vast surveillance of consumers in order to monetize their personal information while failing to adequately protect users online, especially children and teens.

Lastly, AI companies also systematically undermine safety research, redirecting it to benign ad hoc territories that either help them race faster or at least do not get in the way of the AGI race.

For example, OpenAI managed to redefine safety and alignment from "doesn't endanger humanity" to "doesn't produce anything racist or illegal." The OpenAI (2016) Charter referenced AGI in its discussion of safety:

> OpenAI's mission is to ensure that artificial general intelligence (AGI)–by which we mean highly autonomous systems that outperform humans at most economically valuable work–benefits all of humanity. We will attempt to directly build safe and beneficial AGI, but will also consider our mission fulfilled if our work aids others to achieve this outcome.

Yet OpenAI (2024b) strikes a different tone:

> Our models have become significantly safer over time. This can be attributed to building smarter models which typically make fewer factual errors and are less likely to output harmful content even under adversarial conditions like jailbreaks.

Anthropic has similarly maneuvered to define safety as is convenient, focusing its alignment and safety research efforts on areas that do not actually limit racing but instead provide an edge (Anthropic, 2023): evaluations, interpretability, ad-hoc fixes. These approaches lead to a strategy that aims to use superintelligent AI to solve the hardest problems of AI safety, which, naturally, is an argument then used to justify racing to AGI even faster.

This might be the most powerful strategy in the industry playbook: own enough of the scientific research and funding to shape it according to your needs. Although the tobacco industry is the most well-known case of this

(Brandt, 2012), Fabbri et al. (2018) reveal that its prevalent across industries (emphasis ours):

> Qualitative and quantitative studies included in our review suggest that **industry also used research funding as a strategy to reshape fields of research through the prioritization of topics that supported its policy and legal positions, while distracting from research that could be unfavorable.** Analysis of internal industry documents provides insight into how and why industry influenced research agendas. It is particularly interesting to note how corporations adopted similar techniques across different industry sectors (i.e., tobacco, alcohol, sugar, and mining) and fields of research. The strategies included establishing research agendas within the industry that were favorable to its positions, strategically funding research along these lines in a way that appeared scientifically credible, and disseminating these research agendas by creating collaborations with prominent institutions and researchers.

In summary, not only is AI safety or AI governance not up to the task of handling the risks from AGI and ASI, but we also cannot rely on AI companies themselves: They are the main source of the risks, and they are what is breaking down and limiting any valuable progress toward a future safe from these risks.

Which means that any path forward must muzzle these irresponsible companies and force them to actually manage the risks, not wait for them to do it on their own.

Steering the Future: A Narrow Path Forward

We have shed light on a complex and massive problem: the catastrophic risks caused by the development of AGI and successor technologies. We have also detailed how and why our civilization is not on track to address these risks before it is too late—mostly because the very actors racing to AGI are taking control of both policy and technical research to ensure that no one stands in their way.

Let us now turn to what can be done.

The only reasonable path forward starts by stopping the rush to create AGI. This requires an international agreement where relevant countries agree to not create AGI, and to help enforce this ban on defectors. As Katzke and Futerman (2025) explain in detail, whatever a country's perceived place in the race to AGI and ASI, this kind of international cooperation is actually the most rational solution:

> The paper concludes that, if an ASI race is motivated, then cooperation to avoid an ASI race is both preferable and strategically sound. The assumptions that make racing seem necessary are the very reasons it is unwise.

Beyond international awareness of the problem, such a ban requires a clear-cut line for what counts as working toward AGI, and what is allowed.

Banning all AI progress, though a solution in theory, would create a much harder pill to swallow, while not offering significantly more protection against extinction risks.

The mediocre level of understanding of modern AI also means that we have no theory to precisely draw the line between what big steps toward AGI and benign AI. Before they are trained and tested, nobody even knows what an AI will be able to do. Similarly, we do not know how to predict capabilities from the amount of training data, or amount of compute, or the number of parameters.

Still, we need to draw some grounded demarcation between the most obvious and problematic AI research and the rest. If we fail to do so, the situation will stay what it is now: AI's meaning everything from growing God in a silicon bottle to tools that help solve a single problem for humans. And since most people actually benefit from the latter, this fuzzing makes regulation much harder (a deliberate technique we deconstructed in the previous section).

As a compromise, we follow Miotti et al. (2024)[4] in proposing sensible proxies for what counts as the most dangerous AI research, and various policies regulating them, so as to provide defense in depth.

The first policy lays the groundwork for all the other: Make the wilfull development of AGI and ASI a criminal offense. While criminalizing a behavior is insufficient to dispel it, it acts as a clear signal that this behavior (building AGI and ASI) is not allowed. And in doing so, it constrains any group that might want to go for it anyway, by forcing them to not discuss it in public, to hide their actual strategy, and generally to communicate less and more ambiguously about their goals. In addition, such criminal liability will scare off most reasonable investors, making it even harder to raise capital.

Building on this general proscription, the next two policies focus on forbidding the development (knowingly or accidental) of specific AI capabilities deemed particularly dangerous: AI research, or the ability to accelerate AI progress; and hacking, or the ability to break out of a restricted computer environment.

[4] The authors of this article have also participated to the discussions, iteration and writing of Miotti et al. (2024).

As expounded in previous sections, catastrophe directly comes from the expected use of AIs to improve themselves, leading to ASI with extraordinary capabilities but no reliable steering mechanism. As such, it is clear that AI research done by AI themselves should be banned if we are to avoid these futures.

What is tricky here is that AI does not have a crisp formal definition, and so delineating AIs that can do AI research from the rest of software is a subtle endeavor. Miotti et al. (2024) resolve this problem by introducing two new terms: "found systems," to capture programs not built by humans but instead found through mathematical optimization; and "direct use," to focus on applications of found systems that play a key role in the design or improvement of another found system. These then ensure that the policy allows both the use of traditional software in AI research, and the use of AI for indirect help such as searching online or transcribing a meeting.

Hacking, the other forbidden capability, clearly undermines any safeguards and guarantees that might exist about the AI system: If it can get out of its restricted bounds, then it can go from safe to unsafe by doing whatever would help it (for example getting someone to train it to be able to do AI research itself). Thus forbidding this capability is essential for any reasonable defense in depth.

Next, to make AI into a field with the same standards as any high-risk engineering field, a policy requires the existence of safety cases (Ministry of Defence, 2007) about the lack of the previously mentioned capabilities (and any other that is deemed dangerous). In this context a safety case is a grounded argument that can be independently verified, as to why the hazard (here the use of the dangerous capability) will not come to pass.

This provides the bare minimum of serious safety engineering (Leveson, 2023) to the field, by putting the burden of proof on the developer to argue for why their AIs are actually safe, instead of just giving them the benefit of the doubt.

At the moment, specialized AI systems, like image recognition software for medical scans, will be easy to build safety cases for, since they are grown precisely to do their specific task. For more general chatbots and agents, the current AI companies have no way of building a reasonable safety case; thus this policy will incentivize them to research ways to provide such guarantees, be it by restricting training data, improving mechanistic interpretability, or coming up with a new approach to general AIs that allow these kinds of checks and balances to be built-in from the start.

Lastly, these bans and constraints need concrete mechanisms of enforcement. Miotti et al. (2024) propose to do so through both a licensing regime and an international treaty.

The licensing regime would regulate the whole supply chain, with distinct licences for compute provider, developer, and application user. The very requirement of a licence would enable regular verifications, and penalties up to withdrawing licences if other policies are broken.

As discussed above, the international treaty would harmonize and coordinate the regulations between different countries, ensuring that defectors cannot just run elsewhere and evade the ban on universally dangerous capabilities.

Once such a surgical pause on AGI development is guaranteed, there will be room to design international collaboration for developing safe-by-construction AI, and further work in this direction, as explored in the rest of Miotti et al. (2024). But stopping AGI development is a necessary condition for avoiding catastrophe, and having the luxury of considering what we can do in the future.

Conclusion

We are on a dangerous trajectory: growing AI systems that get more powerful by the week, without improving our understanding or means of steering them. This path leads to catastrophe: the loss of control by humanity to the profit of autonomous and powerful AIs, and then the destruction of human civilization as a side effect of AIs exploiting their much larger action space.

Neither AI safety nor AI governance will save us, as they both focus on easy local patches and neglect the core of the problem. Which is not a coincidence, but the result of AGI companies being selected for the willingness to undermine safety in order to finish first, and the success of many of their strategies to do so.

Yet all is not lost. We are still in the period where it is possible to regulate and throttle the dangerous progress toward AGI without forbidding most specialized and actually valuable AI innovations. But this requires implementing real regulation, with teeth, that take this problem seriously and refuse to fall for the racing dynamics peddled by the AGI companies.

References

Albert, A. (2024). Fun story from our internal testing on Claude 3 Opus. It did something I have never seen before... https://x.com/alexalbert__/status/1764722513014329620

Altman, S. (2023). Planning for AGI and beyond. https://openai.com/index/planning-for-agi-and-beyond/

Altman, S. (2024). Who will control the future of AI?. *The Washington Post* . https://www.washingtonpost.com/opinions/2024/07/25/sam-altman-ai-democracy-authoritarianism-future/

Amodei, D. (2024). Machines of loving grace. https://darioamodei.com/machines-of-loving-grace

Andriushchenko, M., Souly, A., Dziemian, M., Duenas, D., Lin, M., Wang, J., Hendrycks, D., Zou, A., Kolter, Z., Fredrikson, M., Winsor, E., Wynne, J., Gal, Y. & Davies, X. (2024), AgentHarm: A benchmark for measuring harmfulness of LLM agents. https://arxiv.org/abs/2410.09024

Anthropic (2023). Core views on AI safety: When, why, what, and how. https://www.anthropic.com/news/core-views-on-ai-safety

Anthropic (2024a). Claude can now use tools. https://www.anthropic.com/news/tool-use-ga

Anthropic (2024b). Responsible scaling policy, Technical report, Anthropic. https://assets.anthropic.com/m/24a47b00f10301cd/original/Anthropic-Responsible-Scaling-Policy-2024-10-15.pdf

Aschenbrenner, L. (2024). Situational awareness: The decade ahead. https://situational-awareness.ai/

Bekenstein, J. D. (1981). Universal upper bound on the entropy-to-energy ratio for bounded systems. *Physical Review D, 23*, 287–298. https://link.aps.org/doi/10.1103/PhysRevD.23.287

Bereska, L., & Gavves, E. (2024). Mechanistic interpretability for AI safety – a review. https://arxiv.org/abs/2404.14082

BIS, U. (2024). Commerce strengthens export controls to restrict China's capability to produce advanced semiconductors for military applications. https://www.bis.gov/press-release/commerce-strengthens-export-controls-restrict-chinas-capability-produce-advanced

Bostrom, N. (2014). *Superintelligence*, Oxford University Press.

Brandt, A. M. (2012). Inventing conflicts of interest: a history of tobacco industry tactics. *American Journal of Public Health, 102*(1), 63–71.

Brockman, G. (2016). My path to OpenAI. https://web.archive.org/web/20160506064558/http://blog.gregbrockman.com/my-path-to-openai

Brockman, G., Sutskever, I., Schulman, J., Altman, S., Zaremba, W. & OpenAI (2024). OpenAI and Elon Musk. https://openai.com/index/openai-elon-musk/

CAIS (2024). Statement on AI risk. https://www.safe.ai/work/statement-on-ai-risk

Cheng, D. & McKernon, E. (2024). State of the AI regulatory landscape, Technical report, Convergence Analysis. https://www.convergenceanalysis.org/ai-regulatory-landscape/home

Chollet, F. (2022). *Deep learning with Python*. Manning Publications.

Chollet, F. (2024). ARC-AGI. https://github.com/fchollet/ARC-AGI

Chollet, F. et al. (2015). Keras. https://keras.io

CIA (1944). Simple sabotage field manual, Technical report, CIA. https://www.cia.gov/static/5c875f3ec660e092cf893f60b4a288df/SimpleSabotage.pdf

DeepMind, G. (2024). Frontier safety framework, Technical report, Google DeepMind. https://storage.googleapis.com/deepmind-media/DeepMind.com/Blog/introducing-the-frontier-safety-framework/fsf-technical-report.pdf

Deisenroth, M. P., Faisal, A. A., & Ong, C. S. (2020). *Mathematics for machine learning*. Cambridge University Press.

Dishgen (2024). DishGen. https://www.dishgen.com/

Dyson, F. J. (1960). Search for artificial stellar sources of infrared radiation. *Science, 131*(3414), 1667–1668.

Fabbri, A., Lai, A., Grundy, Q., & Bero, L. A. (2018). The influence of industry sponsorship on the research agenda: A scoping review. *American Journal of Public Health, 108*(11), e9–e16.

Fernando, C., Banarse, D., Michalewski, H., Osindero, S. & Rocktäschel, T. (2023). Promptbreeder: Self-referential self-improvement via prompt evolution. https://arxiv.org/abs/2309.16797

Gardner, H. (1993). *Frames of mind* (10th edn.). Basic Books.

Goodfellow, I., Bengio, Y. & Courville, A. (2016). *Deep learning*. MIT Press. http://www.deeplearningbook.org

Greenblatt, R. (2024). Getting 50% (SoTA) on ARC-AGi with GPT-4o. https://redwoodresearch.substack.com/p/getting-50-sota-on-arc-agi-with-gpt

Haenlein, M., & Kaplan, A. (2019). A brief history of artificial intelligence: On the past, present, and future of artificial intelligence. *California Management Review, 61*(4), 5–14.

Harari, Y. N. (2024). *Nexus*. Vintage Publishing.

Hinton, G. (2024). Nobel prize banquet speech. https://www.nobelprize.org/prizes/physics/2024/hinton/speech/

Hu, S., Liu, X., Han, X., Zhang, X., He, C., Zhao, W., Lin, Y., Ding, N., Ou, Z., Zeng, G., Liu, Z. & Sun, M. (2024). Predicting emergent abilities with infinite resolution evaluation. https://arxiv.org/abs/2310.03262

Jackson, S. (2024). Mark Zuckerberg flexes that meta's cluster of NVIDIA h100 chips is bigger than the competition. *Forbes* . https://www.businessinsider.com/mark-zuckerberg-meta-nvidia-h100-chip-cluster-llama-4-2024-10

Jumper, J., Evans, R., Pritzel, A., Green, T., Figurnov, M., Ronneberger, O., Tunyasuvunakool, K., Bates, R., Žídek, A., Potapenko, A., Bridgland, A., Meyer, C., Kohl, S. A. A., Ballard, A. J., Cowie, A., Romera-Paredes, B., Nikolov, S., Jain, R.,

Adler, J., …Hassabis, D. (2021). Highly accurate protein structure prediction with AlphaFold. *Nature, 596*(7873), 583–589.

Jung, R. E., & Haier, R. J. (2007). The Parieto-Frontal integration theory (P-FIT) of intelligence: Converging neuroimaging evidence. *Behavioral and Brain Sciences, 30*(2), 135–54; Discussion 154–87.

Katzke, C., & Futerman, G. (2025). The Manhattan trap: Why a race to artificial superintelligence is self-defeating, Technical report, Convergence Analysis. https://www.convergenceanalysis.org/research/the-manhattan-trap-why-a-race-to-artificial-superintelligence-is-self-defeating

Kayali, L. (2019). Inside Facebook's fight against European regulation. *Politico*. https://www.politico.eu/article/inside-story-facebook-fight-against-european-regulation/

Kearns, M. J., & Vazirani, U. V. (1994). *An introduction to computational learning theory*. The MIT Press.

Kerner, S. M. (2023). Elon Musk reveals XAI efforts, predicts full AGI by 2029. *Venture Beat* . https://venturebeat.com/ai/elon-musk-reveals-xai-efforts-predicts-full-agi-by-2029/

Kissinger, H. A., Schmidt, E. & Mundie, C. (2024). *Genesis*. Little Brown and Company.

Kohs, G. (2017). AlphaGo - the movie. https://www.youtube.com/watch?v=WXuK6gekU1Y

Krakovna, V., Uesato, J., Mikulik, V., Rahtz, M., Everitt, T., Kumar, R., Kenton, Z., Leike, J. & Legg, S. (2020). Specification gaming: the flip side of AI ingenuity. https://deepmind.google/discover/blog/specification-gaming-the-flip-side-of-ai-ingenuity/

Kumar, P., Lau, E., Vijayakumar, S., Trinh, T., Team, S. R., Chang, E., Robinson, V., Hendryx, S., Zhou, S., Fredrikson, M., Yue, S. & Wang, Z. (2024). Refusal-trained LLMS are easily jailbroken as browser agents. https://arxiv.org/abs/2410.13886

Leahy, C. (2023). AGI safety | FLI interpretability conference, MIT. https://www.youtube.com/watch?v=wKI9hmaIbpg

Leahy, C. (2025). DeepSeek shows the stakes for humanity couldn't be higher. *The Spectator*. https://www.spectator.co.uk/article/deepseek-shows-the-stakes-for-humanity-couldnt-be-higher/

Leahy, C., Alfour, G., Scammell, C., Miotti, A. & Shimi, A. (2024). The compendium, Technical report, ControlAI. https://www.thecompendium.ai/

Lee, H., Phatale, S., Mansoor, H., Mesnard, T., Ferret, J., Lu, K., Bishop, C., Hall, E., Carbune, V., Rastogi, A. & Prakash, S. (2024). RLAIF vs. RLHF: Scaling reinforcement learning from human feedback with AI feedback. https://arxiv.org/abs/2309.00267

Lee, K.-F., & Qiufan, C. (2021). *AI 2041*. W H Allen.

Legg, S. & Hutter, M. (2007). A collection of definitions of intelligence. *CoRR, abs/0706.3639*. http://arxiv.org/abs/0706.3639

Leike, J. (2023). With the InstructGPT paper we found that.... https://x.com/janleike/status/1625207251630960640

Lermen, S., Dziemian, M. & Pimpale, G. (2024). Applying refusal-vector ablation to Llama 3.1 70B agents. https://arxiv.org/abs/2410.10871

Leveson, N. G. (2023). *An introduction to system safety engineering.* MIT Press.

Lloyd, S. (2000). Ultimate physical limits to computation. *Nature, 406*(6799), 1047–1054. http://dx.doi.org/10.1038/35023282

Loewentheil, N. (2024). The push to fire Lina Khan reveals a serious problem in silicon valley. *The New York Times* . https://www.nytimes.com/2024/10/26/opinion/lina-khan-ftc-venture-capital-silicon-valley.html

Lu, C., Lu, C., Lange, R. T., Foerster, J., Clune, J. & Ha, D. (2024). The AI scientist: Towards fully automated open-ended scientific discovery. https://arxiv.org/abs/2408.06292

Marcus, G. F. (1998). Rethinking eliminative connectionism. *Cognitive Psychology, 37*(3), 243–282.

Metz, C. (2021). *Genius makers*. Random House Business Books.

Metz, C., Weise, K., Grant, N. & Isaac, M. (2023). Ego, fear and money: How the A.I. fuse was lit. *The New York Times* . https://www.nytimes.com/2023/12/03/technology/ai-openai-musk-page-altman.html

Metz, R., Ludlow, E., Tan, G. & Bergen, M. (2024). OpenAI fundraising set to vault startup's valuation to 150 billion. *Bloomberg UK* . https://www.bloomberg.com/news/articles/2024-09-11/openai-fundraising-set-to-vault-startup-s-value-to-150-billion

Ministry of Defence (2007). Safety management requirements for defence systems, Technical report, UK Ministry of Defence. https://skybrary.aero/sites/default/files/bookshelf/344.pdf

Miotti, A., Bilge, T., Kasten, D. & Newport, J. (2024). A narrow path: How to secure our future, Technical report, ControlAI. https://www.narrowpath.co/

Musk, E. (2024). This weekend, the xai team brought our Colossus 100k h100 training cluster online..... https://x.com/elonmusk/status/1830650370336473253

Musk, E., & Altman, S. (2015). Exhibit 2 - Musk v. Altman complaint. https://www.courthousenews.com/wp-content/uploads/2024/02/musk-v-altman-openai-complaint-sf.pdf#page=39.40

Newport, C. (2024). Can an A.I. make plans?. *The New Yorker* . https://www.newyorker.com/science/annals-of-artificial-intelligence/can-an-ai-make-plans

Nielsen, M. (2015). Neural networks and deep learning. http://neuralnetworksanddeeplearning.com/index.html

NIST (2024). Chips for America. https://www.nist.gov/chips

OECD, & GPAI (2024). Global partnership on artificial intelligence. https://www.oecd.org/en/about/programmes/global-partnership-on-artificial-intelligence.html

ONR (2014). Safety assessment principles for nuclear facilities, Technical report, ONR. EKP.1 (p. 37). https://www.onr.org.uk/publications/regulatory-guidance/regulatory-assessment-and-permissioning/safety-assessment-principles-saps/

OpenAI (2016). OpenAI charter. https://openai.com/charter/

OpenAI (2023a). Introducing superalignment. https://openai.com/index/introducing-superalignment/

OpenAI (2023b). Preparedness framework, Technical report, OpenAI. https://cdn.openai.com/openai-preparedness-framework-beta.pdf

OpenAI (2024a). Learning to reason with LLMS. https://openai.com/index/learning-to-reason-with-llms/

OpenAI (2024b). OpenAI safety update. https://openai.com/index/openai-safety-update/

OpenAI (2024c). Video generation models as world simulators. https://openai.com/index/video-generation-models-as-world-simulators/

Parr, T., Pezzulo, G., & Friston, K. J. (2022). Active inference. The MIT Press.

Radford, A., Kim, J. W., Xu, T., Brockman, G., McLeavey, C., & Sutskever, I. (2022). Robust speech recognition via large-scale weak supervision. https://arxiv.org/abs/2212.04356

Rombach, R., Blattmann, A., Lorenz, D., Esser, P. & Ommer, B. (2022). High-resolution image synthesis with latent diffusion models. https://arxiv.org/abs/2112.10752

Rooney, P. (2024). AI to go nuclear? data center deals say it's inevitable. *CIO* . https://www.cio.com/article/3487339/ai-to-go-nuclear-data-center-deals-say-its-inevitable.html

Saul, D. (2024). AI Titan Nvidia overtakes Apple as world's most valuable company. Forbes . https://www.forbes.com/sites/dereksaul/2024/11/04/ai-titan-nvidia-overtakes-apple-as-worlds-most-valuable-company/

Shannon, C. E. (1948). A mathematical theory of communication. *The Bell System Technical Journal, 27*(3), 379–423.

Shen, X., Chen, Z., Backes, M., Shen, Y., & Zhang, Y. (2024). "Do anything now": Characterizing and evaluating in-the-wild jailbreak prompts on large language models. https://arxiv.org/abs/2308.03825

Silver, D., Schrittwieser, J., Simonyan, K., Antonoglou, I., Huang, A., Guez, A., Hubert, T., Baker, L., Lai, M., Bolton, A., Chen, Y., Lillicrap, T., Hui, F., Sifre, L., van den Driessche, G., Graepel, T., & Hassabis, D. (2017). Mastering the game of go without human knowledge. *Nature, 550*(7676), 354–359.

Staff, F. (2024). A look behind the screens, Technical report, FTC. https://www.ftc.gov/system/files/ftc_gov/pdf/Social-Media-6b-Report-9-11-2024.pdf

Steinhardt, J. (2022). AI forecasting: One year in. https://bounded-regret.ghost.io/ai-forecasting-one-year-in/

Sudowrite (2024). Sudowrite. https://www.sudowrite.com/

Sunak, R. (2023). Prime minister's speech on AI. https://www.gov.uk/government/speeches/prime-ministers-speech-on-ai-26-october-2023

Suno (2024). Suno. https://suno.com/

Sutton, R. (2019). The bitter lesson. http://www.incompleteideas.net/IncIdeas/BitterLesson.html

Sutton, R. S., & Barto, A. G. (2018). *Reinforcement learning*. Adaptive Computation and Machine Learning Series (2nd ed.). Bradford Books.

The Office of the White House (2024). Back to the building blocks: A path toward secure and measurable software, Technical report. The Office of the White House. (p. 7). https://bidenwhitehouse.archives.gov/wp-content/uploads/2024/02/Final-ONCD-Technical-Report.pdf

Turner, J., & Lee, N. T. (2024). Misrepresentations of california's AI safety bill. https://www.brookings.edu/articles/misrepresentations-of-californias-ai-safety-bill/

Udandarao, V., Prabhu, A., Ghosh, A., Sharma, Y., Torr, P. H. S., Bibi, A., Albanie, S., & Bethge, M. (2024). No "zero-shot" without exponential data: Pretraining concept frequency determines multimodal model performance. https://arxiv.org/abs/2404.04125

UK AISI (2024). AI safety institute. https://www.aisi.gov.uk/

UNESCO (2024). Global AI ethics and governance observatory. https://www.unesco.org/ethics-ai/en

United Nations (2024). AI advisory body. https://www.un.org/en/ai-advisory-body

CAISI (2024). US AI Safety Institute. https://www.nist.gov/aisi

US AISI, & UK AISI (2024). US AISI and UK AISI joint pre-deployment test OpenAI o1, Technical report, NIST and UK AISI. https://cdn.prod.website-files.com/663bd486c5e4c81588db7a1d/6763fac97cd22a9484ac3c37_o1_uk_us_december_publication_final.pdf

Vance, A. (2015). *Elon musk*. Ecco Press.

Vaswani, A., Shazeer, N., Parmar, N., Uszkoreit, J., Jones, L., Gomez, A. N., Kaiser, L., & Polosukhin, I. (2017). Attention is all you need. *CoRR, abs/1706.03762*. http://arxiv.org/abs/1706.03762

von der Leyen, U. (2023). 2023 state of the union address by president von der Leyen. https://ec.europa.eu/commission/presscorner/detail/en/speech_23_4426

Wang, G., Xie, Y., Jiang, Y., Mandlekar, A., Xiao, C., Zhu, Y., Fan, L. & Anandkumar, A. (2023). Voyager: An open-ended embodied agent with large language models. https://arxiv.org/abs/2305.16291

Wang, K., Li, J., Bhatt, N. P., Xi, Y., Liu, Q., Topcu, U., & Wang, Z. (2024). On the planning abilities of openAI's o1 models: Feasibility, optimality, and generalizability. https://arxiv.org/abs/2409.19924

Waterhouse, L. (2023). Why multiple intelligences theory is a neuromyth. *Frontiers in Psychology, 14*, 1217288.

Waters, R. (2023). Elon Musk claims more trust can be put in his xAI than OpenAI and Google. *Financial Times*. https://www.ft.com/content/731f04f1-38d1-4baa-bbc1-98916c7cc6f1

Waymo (2024). Waymo. https://waymo.com/

Yudkowsky, E. (2000). The singulatrian principles. https://web.archive.org/web/20120219075928/https://www.yudkowsky.net/obsolete/principles.html

Zhao, T. Z., Tompson, J., Driess, D., Florence, P., Ghasemipour, K., Finn, C., & Wahid, A. (2024). ALOHA unleashed: A simple recipe for robot dexterity. https://arxiv.org/abs/2410.13126

Zheng, J., & Meister, M. (2025). The unbearable slowness of being: Why do we live at 10 bits/s?.*Neuron, 113*(2), 192–204.

Ziegler, D. M., Stiennon, N., Wu, J., Brown, T. B., Radford, A., Amodei, D., Christiano, P., & Irving, G. (2020). Fine-tuning language models from human preferences. https://arxiv.org/abs/1909.08593

The Most Dangerous Fiction: The Rhetoric and Reality of the AI Race

Seán S. ÓhÉigeartaigh

Introduction

In 2018, Stephen Cave and I published *An AI Race for Strategic Advantage: Rhetoric and Risks* (Cave & ÓhÉigeartaigh, 2018). The paper documented the early emergence of a particular type of competitive framing around artificial intelligence (AI): as a race that could and must be won for geopolitical advantage. We highlighted the risk that the rhetoric alone could act as a self-fulfilling prophecy, helping to spark a race where it did not meaningfully exist beforehand, and that should such a race develop, it could undermine essential governance and lead to corner-cutting on safety. We called for a reframing of AI development for shared global benefit, and with emphasis on global cooperation around safety-critical challenges.

Seven years on, as we feared, this narrative has become dominant in Western AI media and policy discourse. It is used to frame at one level the competition between leading companies to be the first to achieve artificial general intelligence, and at a level above, the technological competition between the USA and China, where the leading companies are based. Moreover, the narrative informs and is informed by practical developments: the shape of the underlying technology and its rate of progress; competition over resources

S. S. ÓhÉigeartaigh (✉)
Centre for the Future of Intelligence, University of Cambridge, Cambridge, UK
e-mail: so348@cam.ac.uk

M. Rangeley, N. Fairfax (eds.), *The Artificial Intelligence Revolution*,
https://doi.org/10.1007/978-3-032-11814-1_3

such as computing hardware, energy, expertise, and insights; and policies being enacted by leading nations.

Despite this, I argue that the narrative of a US–China AI race for global dominance began as, and in significant regards remains to date, a fiction. A race needs at least two competitors trying to win. However, the race narrative in its stronger forms is nearly exclusively promoted in the West and does not reflect the framing of AI competition and AI development in China in important respects. In the West, the race narrative is increasingly used to justify progress at all costs, including justifying policies that benefit AI companies' interests over those of other parts of society.

Even in the West, there remain important ambiguities around this AI race, and what different stakeholders have in mind when they invoke the notion. To the extent that there is a race ongoing, there is also an important "race within a race" which deserves special attention: a race to AGI and decisive strategic advantage. In most contexts, commentators use the term "AI race" to refer to a broad phenomenon: the competition to be in a leading position in AI development and deployment. Its characteristics are no different than any other technology race: It is good to be "winning", but there is no permanent "victory", and a competitor may catch up at any point. However, there is a separate notion within AI that once a certain threshold is passed in AI capability, AI systems may be able to contribute to accelerating AI research and development itself, maintaining or even extending a permanent advantage for the leading actor: decisive strategic advantage. This latter concept features prominently in analyses of trajectories towards artificial general intelligence (AGI) and has been alluded to or cited explicitly by the CEOs of several of the leading companies. It is a very different type of race and has very different implications.

In this chapter, I will trace the emergence of the broader AI race narrative and how it evolved with the scaling paradigm underpinning today's frontier AI systems. I will then explore how this narrative has been used to justify reduced regulatory oversight and how it has dovetailed with rhetoric around a military AI arms race. It is increasingly claimed that the USA is, or will soon be, in a race with China to achieve AGI and decisive strategic advantage, with existential consequences for the future of the USA should it lose. I will analyse this particular sub-narrative and the evidence that China is an active competitor in this perceived race. I will offer recommendations for navigating an international landscape increasingly shaped by these narratives and for achieving the necessary points of cooperation needed to safeguard all nations in the face of a technology that may prove unlike any that has come before.

Part 1: Large Language Models and Emergence of the AI Race

Discourse around AI leadership[1] as a geopolitical priority became particularly prominent from 2017 onwards. Statements by technology leaders like Elon Musk, who tweeted "competition for AI superiority at national level [is the] most likely cause of WW3" (Musk. 2017) and political leaders like Vladimir Putin, who stated that "whoever becomes the leader in this sphere will become the ruler of the world" (Gigova, 2017), were breathlessly reported across Western media. The China State Council's 2017 "Next Generation Artificial Intelligence Development Plan" was widely reported in Western media as pursuing global dominance in AI (Shead 2017; Demchak 2019). While the Plan did state that "AI has become a new focus of international competition", subtleties lost in translation may have resulted in references to becoming "a primary innovation centre" in the Chinese plan becoming seen as an ambition to achieve dominance (ÓhÉigeartaigh et al., 2020).

Even more striking was the use of a statement made by President Xi Jinping in a Politburo session in 2018, that China must "ensure that our country marches in the front ranks where it comes to theoretical research in this important area of AI, and occupies the high ground in critical and AI core technologies" (Creemers & Kania, 2022). The sentence was echoed in policy reports and speeches in the USA to support claims that AI featured heavily in China's plan to change the status quo in its geopolitical competition with the USA (Levine & Hwang 2025) and to support the assertion that China is in a military AI arms race with the USA. The US Secretary of Defence quoted it in a speech calling for the private sector to overcome their unease about working with the US military and requesting increased funding from Congress (Esper, 2019). However, Jinping's original speech, titled "Advancing the Healthy Development of Our Nation's New Generation of Artificial Intelligence", is an exhaustively detailed call for AI to be developed and used to benefit and modernise Chinese industries, its economy, and the livelihoods of its people, in the middle of which the above sentence is buried. No mention of military, defence, or geopolitical aims or applications is made, beyond the anodyne call for China to be a leader in this new technology.

Perhaps more notable was a 2018 address by President Xi to that year's Fourth Industrial Revolution-themed BRICS Summit, where he highlighted

[1]This section relates to AI as a broader field; while documents by AGI-focused companies are referred to, specific discussion of the emerging competitive focus on AGI will be covered in Part 2.

breakthroughs in technologies such as AI and emphasised how rounds of disruptive technology evolution had profoundly reshaped the course of human history (Xi, 2018). Chinese scholars subsequently analysed these remarks in the context of global order transitions (Ding, 2024), with one prominent scholar arguing that the Fourth Industrial Revolution would be a contest between the USA and China, in which he claimed China could at least keep pace with, and might even beat, the USA (Jin, 2019).

Prominent commentators such as Kai-Fu Lee warned of top Silicon Valley AI scientists relocating to China to join Chinese AI companies (Lee, 2018). Analyses released in 2019 noted the relative proportions of technical papers and patents being produced in AI in China relative to the USA, warning that China could soon overtake the USA (O'Meara, 2019). The US National Security Commission on Artificial Intelligence (NSCAI)'s 2021 Report stated, "*The race to research, develop and deploy AI and associated technologies is intensifying the technology competition that underpins a wider strategic competition*". Its Chairs' note warned, "*China's plans, resources, and progress should concern all Americans*" (Schmidt & Work, 2021).

From 2020, the resource inputs required to develop leading AI systems began to increase massively as the large language model (LLM) paradigm began to yield significant results. The promise of this approach hit public consciousness with the release of OpenAI's ChatGPT in November 2022. These models were notable for the ability of a single model to achieve breakthrough performances across tasks ranging from essay-writing to code generation to mathematics questions: general-purpose AI.

The resource-intensive nature of this approach has played an important role in shaping the geopolitical discussions around AI. Each successive generation of frontier-pushing model has required a multiple of the amount of compute and data to train compared to previous generations (Sevilla & Roldan, 2024; Villalabos et al., 2024). Recent estimates put the cost of training models at hundreds of millions of dollars, reaching over a billion dollars by 2027 (Cottier, 2024). Much of this pays for high-end graphical processing unit (GPU) chips, which have become a hard-fought-over commodity. Other essential ingredients are data, energy, water (mostly for data centre cooling), and human talent.

As this resource-heavy paradigm has taken shape, it has shaped the policies leading nations have adopted to gain or maintain their lead. For example, policymakers have become increasingly concerned about access to essential resources such as high-end chips and are aware of the globe-spanning supply chains that produce them. This is most clearly exemplified by the US semiconductor export controls, focussed on limiting China's access to advanced semiconductors, chip-making equipment, and relevant expertise from US citizens, with a particular focus on chips that could be used for AI and supercomputing (US Department of Commerce, 2022). These were initially announced in October 2022, with several further updates to expand their scope. China has responded by restricting export of rare earth minerals used in semiconductor manufacture to the USA (Bradsher, 2024).

LLMs developed by US companies have dominated the frontier of AI to date. Chinese companies have developed notable LLMs, such as Baidu's ERNIE series and Alibaba's Tongyi Qianwen. However, these have typically been regarded as a year or more behind the frontier set by the performance of leading LLMs (Mozur et al., 2024), although some benchmark performances suggest the gap may be tightening (Maslej et al., 2025). Export controls are likely to have played a significant role in maintaining the gap: In summer 2024, DeepSeek's CEO stated that the biggest bottleneck his company faced was access to the chips they needed (Schneider et al., 2024). Despite this, DeepSeek itself has made notable strides, releasing models that demonstrated performance equivalent to models released within the previous year by frontier-leading companies such as OpenAI but estimated to have required a fraction of the computing resources to train (Liu et al., 2024; Joshi, 2025; Amodei, 2025b). Despite continual model and hardware efficiency gains (Pilz et al., 2025a), demand for chips is expected to continue to increase, as larger models continue to be trained, and as more computing resources are used for the operation of trained models (Pilz et al., 2025b; Kumar & Manning, 2025).

An AI Race to the Bottom

In our 2018 paper, Stephen Cave and I warned that an AI race rhetoric would be used as justification for corner-cutting on safety and regulation (Cave & ÓhÉigeartaigh, 2018). This fear appears to have been borne out, as AI has become ever more embedded within the narrative of rivalry between the US hegemon and its closest global competitor. Former Google CEO Eric Schmidt, an influential voice in US policy and security, has made this argument several times, for example, in 2021: "*Why don't we wait until something bad happens and then we can figure out how to regulate it*... *Trust me, China is not busy stopping things because of regulation*" (Tech Transparency Project, 2024).

From 2020 onwards, funding for US foreign policy think tanks from a number of leading Big Tech companies increased significantly; according to the *Financial Times*, these think tanks have promoted the argument that stricter regulations would threaten US competitiveness with a rising China (Stacey & Gilbert, 2022). OpenAI has used the threat from China not only to minimise regulation on themselves but to bypass protections for other industries. In its 2025 evidence submission to the White House's Request for Information for its AI Action Plan, OpenAI argued for an approach which emphasises "*voluntary partnership between the federal government and the private sector, and neutralizes potential PRC benefit from American AI companies having to comply with overly burdensome state laws*" (Lehane, 2025).

OpenAI further argued for access to copyright-protected material: "*If the PRC's developers have unfettered access to data and American companies are left without fair use access, the race for AI is effectively over. America loses, as does the success of democratic AI.*"

Prominent venture capitalist Marc Andreessen, an adviser to the Trump administration, has argued against policy interventions motivated by AI safety concerns, and has asserted "*The single greatest risk of AI is that China wins global AI dominance and we – the United States and the West – do not*" (Andreessen, 2023).

Trump Administration AI Czar David Sacks justified the rescinding of the Biden AI Executive Order by claiming:

> DeepSeek R1 shows that the AI race will be very competitive and that President Trump was right to rescind the Biden EO, which hamstrung American AI companies without asking whether China would do the same (obviously not) (Sacks, 2025).

It is far from clear whether this particular claim reflects reality. Since 2023, China has been developing quite heavy-handed AI regulation, particularly in generative AI (Sheehan, 2023; Toner et al. 2023), which some analysts suggest would slow down their technology companies more than their Western counterparts (Tobin, 2023; Abiri & Huang, 2023). For example, full public release of various LLMs has been delayed pending regulatory approvals (Su et al., 2023), with Baidu's Ernie Bot seeing a 6-month delay (South China Morning Post, 2023). The Decision of the Chinese Communist Party's Third Plenum stated a further commitment to "*institute oversight systems to ensure the safety of artificial intelligence*" (The State Council of the People's Republic of China, 2024). The frontier AI-relevant stipulations of the Biden Executive Order included safety testing, security measures, infrastructure requirements, and reporting requirements, but these were primarily limited to the very largest, most advanced AI models (Executive Office of the President, 2023; Mayer Brown, 2024).

Achieving dominance has taken centre stage even for the most safety-conscious US companies. Anthropic's 2025 submission to the US Request for Information, calling for rapid scale-up of procurement of AI across government, heavy investment in AI-supporting energy infrastructure, and security-bolstering measures, concluded with a call to the administration to "*enable American dominance in AI by unlocking the benefits of this technology and ensuring that America remains dominant over China and our other adversaries*" (Anthropic, 2025a). In March 2025, commentator Ezra Klein reflected that it seemed potentially 'historically dangerous' that "*A.I. has reached maturation at the exact moment that the U.S. and China are in this Thucydides' trap-style race for superpower dominance*" (Klein. 2025).

This framing of US–China technological competition as a high-stakes race follows what international relations scholars call "securitization" (Buzan et al., 1998), where an issue is transformed from a normal political topic into an existential security threat that justifies extraordinary measures. By framing AI as a winner-takes-all technology, proponents create a powerful imperative for action while limiting critical examination of the overall premise.

The Military Dimension

The sub-narrative of a military AI arms race between the USA and China has featured with growing intensity in US tech and policy rhetoric. According to Semafor, former US Secretary of Defence Mark Esper has claimed the USA is in an existential struggle with China in "an ongoing race for dominance" in AI (Solomon, 2023).

Alex Karp, CEO of Palantir, which provides AI tools including LLMs to governments for intelligence and military purposes, has stated, "*It's either: we own AI or our adversaries China and Russia own AI . . . We have to dominate, and then set a rule of law*" (Griffin, 2024). Palantir has multiple links to the present US administration, including through AI Czar David Sacks, who was an early investor. In January 2025, Anduril announced plans to build a major factory in Ohio, the home state of early Anduril investor JD Vance, to produce tens of thousands of autonomous systems and weapons annually. Its CEO stated: "*We don't have time for business as usual. We're predicted to run out of munitions within the first eight days of a potential conflict with China*" (Chapman & Ludlow, 2025).

In 2024, OpenAI deleted language in its usage policy prohibiting use of its technology for military purposes (Biddle, 2024) and announced a partnership with Anduril to develop and deploy advanced AI for national security missions;

Anduril's announcement referenced "the accelerating race between the United States and China" in AI (Anduril Industries, 2024). Meta revised its policy and announced it was making its Llama models available to US defence and national security agencies (Clegg, 2024). Anthropic partnered with Palantir and Amazon Web Services (AWS) to bring Claude models to US intelligence and defence agencies (Palantir Investor Relations, 2024), with Anthropic CEO Dario Amodei stating a "worry" that "*our adversaries – like China or Russia – may be better at deploying what they have to their own governments*" (Murgia, 2024). In 2025, Google dropped its commitment to rule out applications "likely to cause harm", arguing that companies and democratic governments should work together on AI that supports national security (Hooker & Vallance, 2025).

There is little Chinese public rhetoric explicitly discussing a US–China military arms race, although there is evidence of significant investment in military integration of AI (Fedasiuk et al., 2021). The combination of China's substantial military buildup and modernisation (Gadzala Tirziu, 2024), an explicit focus on military–AI integration (Stokes, 2024), and China's program of civil-military fusion facilitating the adoption of civilian innovations (Shipley, 2024) provides a reasonable basis for Western concerns regarding China's military AI trajectory. A senior executive at a leading Chinese defence company is reported to have described AI as a "leapfrog technology", a technology allowing a lagging actor to skip ahead, and that "an ever-increasing military use of AI is inevitable" in a 2018 speech (Allen, 2023). Notably, this talk was not made available online, suggesting that other talks and information relevant to China's ambitions for AI in the military context may not be available in the public domain to the degree US equivalents are.

Balanced against this are official policy documents and public remarks raising concerns around unfettered application of AI in military domains. China's Position Paper on Regulating Military Applications of Artificial Intelligence (2021b), submitted to the Convention on Certain Conventional Weapons (CCW), calls for "*dialogue, cooperation and an effective governance regime in order to prevent serious harms or even disasters caused by military applications of AI to mankind*". It calls for regulation to "*safeguard global strategic stability, prevent arms race*" among other goals and states:

> While developing advanced weapon systems and enhancing their legitimate defense capabilities, countries need to bear in mind that military applications of AI shall never be used as a tool to start a war or pursue hegemony. We oppose moves to undermine the sovereignty and territorial security of other countries by using advantages in AI technology.

A 2024 analysis of Chinese-language journal articles by PLA members and other experts notes as a key finding:

> Contrary to some US discussions of China's views on military AI, many of the Chinese experts whose arguments have been analysed in this report voice misgivings about using insufficiently trustworthy AI systems in military contexts. They also express concerns about the risks of outbreaks or escalations of wars (Bresnick, 2024)

In 2024, scientists from the West and China, including notable thinkers influential in policy such as Andrew Yao and Xue Lan, signed a statement on "red lines" that AI systems should not cross. This included the use of AI to facilitate the design of weapons of mass destruction or autonomous cyberattacks (IDAIS-Beijing, 2024).

In this domain, however, the connection between public rhetoric and actual action is more tenuous, as on both the US and Chinese sides, much of the relevant discussion and planning will be classified.

Part 2: AGI and the Race for Decisive Strategies Advantage

The Emergence of the Race to AGI

The progress in general-purpose AI systems such as LLMs has seen a rehabilitation of a long-held goal in AI: artificial general intelligence, or AGI. AGI describes an as-yet hypothetical AI system that can perform all or nearly all tasks typically requiring the intelligence of humans, to a standard equivalent or better than that achieved by most humans (Shanahan, 2015). In principle, AGI could automate most or all of the intellectual work of science and engineering. This includes areas where human expertise is in limited supply and where training human experts requires years; thousands of AGI systems could be spun up to work in parallel, and at machine speeds rather than limited by human work speed.

In academic discussion, the concept of AGI is usually closely linked to that of superintelligence (Bostrom, 2014). AGI systems would be expected to automate the process of AGI development itself, meaning that progress in AI itself would no longer run at human speeds. If achieved, this might rapidly result in broadly superintelligent systems massively more capable than the best human teams, which could then rapidly accelerate progress in all other major scientific and industrial endeavours.

Many scholars and technologists believe the development of AGI and superintelligence carries risks of catastrophic consequences, up to and including the full extinction of humanity. These outcomes might arise through misuse of the advanced capabilities of superintelligence by humans, or through loss of control of systems that would by definition be faster and more capable than humans in most cognitive domains (Hendrycks et al., 2023). Of particular concern on the path to AGI and superintelligence is the potential emergence of recursive self-improvement: the ability for AI systems to automate their own improvement. Anthropic, OpenAI, and Google DeepMind all note recursive self-improvement as a key concern in their safety frameworks (Anthropic, 2025b; OpenAI, 2025a) or safety approach paper (Shah et al., 2025). OpenAI notes that recursive self-improvement could increase capabilities and risks sufficiently rapidly to make their current oversight practices "*insufficient to identify and mitigate new risks, including risks to maintaining human control of the AI system itself.*" While the prospect of AGI and superintelligence being achieved in the coming years remains a subject of significant expert disagreement, a high proportion of those who take the prospect seriously consider them to plausibly present an existential risk to humanity (Centre for AI Safety, 2023). Based on past statements, this includes frontier CEOs Dario Amodei, who "guesses" a 10–25% risk of extinction from AI (Roose, 2023), Sam Altman (Altman, 2015), Elon Musk (Pillay, 2025), and Demis Hassabis (Milmo, 2023).

The release of GPT-4 in 2023 demonstrated that a single model could achieve breakthrough performances across tasks as varied as essay-writing, conversation, coding, and sitting legal examinations (Achiam et al., 2023). AGI began being discussed as a goal by companies and a possibility that might need more imminent preparation by policymakers. Elon Musk launched xAI in March 2023 to produce "a competitive alternative" to leading AI companies and with the explicit aim of building AGI, predicting that AGI would be viable by 2029 (Kerner, 2023). In April 2023, Google announced the merger of their AI research divisions Brain and DeepMind (Pichai, 2023) in order to better compete in developing increasingly general AI systems. Google cofounder Sergei Brin would later state: "*We fully intend that Gemini [Google DeepMind's leading frontier AI system] will be the very first AGI*" (Hart, 2025). DeepSeek launched in July 2023, with "*unraveling the mystery of AGI with curiosity*" in its mission statement (Schneider et al., 2024). Former OpenAI cofounder Ilya Sutskever launched Safe Superintelligence in 2024. Going even further in ambition, the company is described as having "one goal and one product: a safe superintelligence" (Sutskever et al., 2024).

By 2025, AGI enters regular public discourse. Google DeepMind's Hassabis has predicted AI capable of achieving Einstein-level scientific breakthroughs as being 50/50 likely by 2030, a feat that would assume AGI (The Economist, 2025). In January 2025 OpenAI's Sam Altman stated he thought it likely that AGI will be developed within the 2025–29 US presidential term (Tyrangiel, 2025) and wrote: "*We are now confident we know how to build AGI as we traditionally understood it... We are beginning to turn our aim beyond that, to superintelligence in the true sense of the word*" (Altman, 2025).

While not using the term AGI, Anthropic's Dario Amodei described the prospect of "a country of geniuses in a datacentre" and predicted this could be achieved "*possibly by 2026 or 2027*" (Amodei, 2025a). In this context, hundreds of billions of dollars combined are being invested in companies aiming to achieve AGI and in supporting infrastructure.

Despite the momentous implications of these pronouncements, both public and policy discourse around the prospects of AGI remain muted, on the whole. Many policymakers regard AGI as industry hype or as a metaphorical concept not to be taken literally (Colson, 2024). A substantial portion of the academic community, including many senior experts advising decision-makers, does not consider current approaches as likely to lead to AGI (Jones, 2025). Discussion of AGI has also suffered from a confusion of concepts and definitions (Mitchell, 2024): Weaker definitions have been put forward (Aguera y Arcas & Norvig, 2023), and the distinction between "AGI" and "general-purpose AI" may often be unclear.

The implications of AGI as envisaged by the AGI companies are sufficiently extreme that they are intuitively implausible; superintelligence even more so. Altman writes: "*Superintelligent tools could massively accelerate scientific discovery and innovation well beyond what we are capable of doing on our own... This sounds like science fiction right now, and somewhat crazy to even talk about it*" (Altman, 2025).

Thus, the magnitude of the technological step change anticipated by technologists like Altman may not be clear to decision-makers, or may seem too fantastical to take seriously.

There is a clear difference in expectation between frontier CEOs and most political leaders regarding what will be possible within the next 5–10 years. The disconnect is obscured by the common use of terms such as AGI and the "AI race", where these terms have vastly different meanings to different stakeholders. This has especially important implications for the strategic and geopolitical implications of an AI race.

A Race That Can Be "Won": Decisive Strategic Advantage

A Google search of "AI race" returns pages of news stories framing nearly every major development in AI and associated infrastructure in terms of its impact on "the AI race". Sometimes the "AI race" refers broadly to competitive progress in AI; often it specifically refers to US–China AI competition. Most of this coverage is not notably different in tone from how a wide range of other emerging technologies are discussed, although often AI's wide-ranging applications are noted. In a normal technology competition, it is good to lead, but the long-term future of geopolitics is unlikely to be decided by it.

For those targeting the development of AGI, a much more specific and consequential race is unfolding: a race for decisive strategic advantage (Bostrom, 2014). The strong version of this scenario has three underpinning assumptions:

1. AI can itself be used to accelerate AI research.
2. The results of this accelerated AI progress can be translated into accelerated advances in scientific, economic, and military domains.
3. Beyond a certain point, the lead attained in these domains can be maintained indefinitely or even increased, meaning that the leader can thereafter maintain a "durable advantage" over adversaries.

The dynamics of this scenario is fundamentally different from those of a "normal" technology competition (Narayanan & Kapoor, 2025). In normal circumstances, while a company or nation may be leading at any given time on any of a range of measures—performance, cost, adoption—there is no clear end point. Moreover, a competitor can usually catch up or even overtake through learning from or reverse engineering the leaders' breakthroughs, investing more resources and expertise, or theft of intellectual property. Nearly all AI progress to date, I argue, is best thought of as "normal" technology competition, in which a race cannot meaningfully be won.

However, some technology developments represent a phase change. In warfare, the development of the first atomic bomb resulted in a fundamentally new capability that changed the nature of warfare and geopolitics forever thereafter. There was a perceived race to develop the atomic bomb first and a perception that getting there first mattered (Belfield & Ruhl, 2022). It is plausible that at some point, there is a phase change in the development of AI where the capabilities of AI make it possible to maintain and consolidate the advantage of the lead actor indefinitely, and to translate this into a lasting global advantage.

This notion—decisive strategic advantage—is by no means universally accepted even among researchers who take seriously the prospect of AGI; for example Brundage and Werner (2025) write: "*The idea of a unipolar artificial general intelligence (AGI) scenario — where* a single actor or coalition *has exclusive control over very advanced AI capabilities — is contrary to the nature of AI technology*".

Even if a unipolar AGI scenario were achieved, Ding and Dafoe (2023) critique the notion that advances in AI would rapidly translate into substantial military improvement, casting doubt on the idea that "winning" the race to AGI would rapidly result in military dominance sufficiently quickly to ensure decisive strategic advantage.

Nonetheless, versions of the race for decisive strategic advantage are increasingly accepted and are sometimes used as justification for more extreme actions than would otherwise be countenanced. This leads to a dangerous situation: Obfuscated by the rhetoric around development of all forms of AI as a race and the broader geopolitical competition between the USA and China, some technology leaders, governance thinkers, and perhaps some political decision-makers have a much more specific and consequential US–China contest in mind.

In "The AI War and How to Win It: The Battle for the Future of the World", CEO of Scale AI Alexandr Wang stated[2] that "*The AI winner of this decade will be economically and militarily dominant for the next 50 years*" and that "*China is currently outpacing the United States*" (Wang, 2022).

In "On DeepSeek and Export Controls", Amodei noted:

> there's at least the possibility that, because AI systems can eventually help make even smarter AI systems, a temporary lead could be parlayed into a durable advantage. Thus, in this world, the US and its allies might take a commanding and long-lasting lead on the global stage (Amodei, 2025b).

In "Machines of Loving Grace", Amodei emphasised the importance of liberal democracies having the upper hand globally at the point at which "powerful AI" is introduced (Amodei, 2024). He further describes a "carrot and stick" strategy for shaping the world, in which the "carrot" of access to the huge scientific and economic advantages of powerful AI is offered to adversary nations in exchange for their adoption of liberal democracy. The "stick" is

[2]As the term "AGI" is often not used specifically, I have included quotes where context and scale of impact indicate authors have AGI-level AI capabilities in mind.

the prospect of facing AI-powered militaries against which they would be hopelessly undermatched.

In "Situational Awareness", published shortly after his departure from OpenAI, Leopold Aschenbrenner stated:

> Superintelligence will give a decisive economic and military advantage. China isn't at all out of the game yet. In the race to AGI, the free world's very survival will be at stake (Aschenbrenner, 2024).

Palantir's Alex Karp has described the creation of AI weapons as "our Oppenheimer moment", drawing direct comparison to calls from physicists to the US president to develop the nuclear bomb in 1939. In a 2023 essay, he described concerns around development of too-powerful AI resulting in human extinction as "not unjustified" but that the suggestion to halt development is "misguided", arguing "*our adversaries will not pause to indulge in theatrical debates . . . They will proceed. This is an arms race of a different kind, and it has begun*" (Karp, 2023).

In January 2025, Axios reported on a phone call with outgoing National Security Adviser Jake Sullivan in which he warned that "*the next few years will determine whether artificial intelligence leads to catastrophe – and whether China or America prevails in the AI arms race*".

The journalists stated, "*Regardless of what was said in public, every background conversation we had with President Biden's high command came back to China . . . Every move, every risk was calculated to keep China from beating us to the AI punch. Nothing else matters, they basically said*".

Sullivan, however, noted the importance of cooperation: "*Sullivan said Trump, like Biden, should try to work with Chinese leader Xi Jinping on a global AI framework, much like the world did with nuclear weapons*" (VandeHei & Allen, 2025)".

The stakes perceived by these technology leaders and a growing number of policy analysts justify actions that might be considered unthinkable in other circumstances. In "The Battle for Brilliant Minds: From the Nuclear Age to AI", RAND senior political scientist Iskander Rehman detailed the 1944 US plan to assassinate Werner Heisenberg at an academic lecture, should it become clear that Germany was on track to develop the atomic bomb. After discussing the US–China AI race and the prospect of AGI, Rehman argued:

> *if it appears that a foreign adversarial power is clearly taking the lead in developing a technology as hugely consequential as artificial general intelligence, U.S. security managers may need to reluctantly reacquaint themselves with some of the more*

shadowy and morally fraught chapters of their nation's past—from the plot against Heisenberg to Operation Paperclip. Indeed, the stakes of the competition may demand no less. (Rehman, 2025).

Some commentators argue that any state pursuing superintelligence and decisive strategic advantage presents a direct threat to the survival of its peers. Hendrycks et al. (2025) proposed a "Mutually Assured AI Malfunction" (MAIM) deterrence regime modelled after Mutually Assured Destruction, in which it would be understood by leading states that their rival would be prepared to sabotage their AI capability should it become clear the state was making a "*grab for strategic monopoly*" through pursuing superintelligence. Sabotage interventions range from covert cyberattacks to kinetic strikes on datacentres, although the paper acknowledged the option of broader hostilities through further escalations or threats to non-AI assets.

Part 3: Examining the Evidence: Is China Really Racing to AGI?

But is China, or any nation other than the USA, currently competing meaningfully in the race to AGI? In November 2024, the US-China Economic and Security Review Commission (USCC) released its annual report to Congress, with the following as its first recommendation:

> Congress establish and fund a Manhattan Project-like program dedicated to racing to and acquiring an Artificial General Intelligence (AGI) capability. AGI is generally defined as systems that are as good as or better than human capabilities across all cognitive domains and would surpass the sharpest human minds at every task (US-China Economic and Security Review Commission, 2024).

USCC commissioner Jacob Helberg, a senior adviser to the CEO of Palantir, told Reuters,

> China is racing towards AGI ... It's critical that we take them extremely seriously (Tong & Martina, 2024).

However the 793 page report discussed AGI only in the sections recommending the US Manhattan Project-like program, and provided no evidence to support a claim that China is racing towards AGI; nor has Helberg provided evidence for this claim elsewhere. In discussing it, AI journalist Garrison Lovely argued that China hawks "are manufacturing an AI arms race" (Lovely, 2024).

AI journalist Garrison Lovely has argued that China hawks "are manufacturing an AI arms race" (Lovely, 2024), and Jordan Schneider of Chinatalk notes that evidence is sparse that China is "racing towards AGI" in any sense close to the US's efforts (Schneider et al., 2024). In 2023, the Beijing Institute for General Artificial Intelligence (BIGAI)'s Director Zhu Songchun remarked on artificial general intelligence (AGI) as becoming "*a strategic high-ground in international technological competition over the next 10 to 20 years*" with an impact "*equivalent to the atomic bomb in the field of information technology*" (Zhao, 2023). However, Zhu and BIGAI's focus on symbolic AI over large models and scaling has yet to demonstrate results comparable to that by leading large model companies in the USA or China.

In 2023, following ChatGPT's release, the Politburo emphasised development of "通用人工智能"(Xinhua News Agency, 2023), a term that could be translated as "artificial general intelligence" but can also be translated to the more mundane "general-purpose AI" used to denote systems such as ChatGPT. Subsequent state media strongly suggested general-purpose AI was intended (Schneider et al., 2024). General artificial intelligence was also included in a 2023 funding round from the Ministry of Industry and Information Technology (MIIT), but with minimal funding and computational resources (General Office of the Ministry of Industry and Information Technology, 2023; ChinaTalk 2025).

As noted by ChinaTalk (2025), CEOs of several newer companies, including Moonshot AI, Zhipu AI, and Minimax AI, have since voiced more unambiguous AGI ambitions, but the degree of investment they have is a fraction compared to AGI-focused companies in the West. A major AI funding scheme of 1 trillion RMB ($140 billion) was launched by the Bank of China in January 2025, but intended to be spread across the entire AI research and application ecosystem, rather than AGI research (Bank of China, 2025).

The most compelling cases are Alibaba and DeepSeek. In February 2025's Alibaba earnings call, its CEO Eddie Wu described pursuit of AGI as its "primary objective", noting that AGI might "even replace 50% of global GDP" (PYMNTS, 2025). This was accompanied by the announcement of an investment of $53 billion over 3 years into AI infrastructure (Yahoo Finance, 2025). While the largest ever investment by a Chinese private enterprise into AI, it pales in comparison to investments announced by US tech firms: Microsoft announced an $80 billion planned investment for 2025 alone. Forbes estimates DeepSeek's valuation at $1–$10 billion (Tognini & Liu,

2025); for comparison, OpenAI raised funding in March 2025 at a $300 billion valuation (OpenAI, 2025b). While DeepSeek's success has resulted in meetings between its CEO with Premier Li Qiang and President Xi Jinping, this does not appear to have translated into a greater policy focus or state funding support for AGI (Schneider et al., 2024).

DeepSeek state their goal to be AGI, but their rhetoric with regards to competition is more restrained than their Western competition. In a 2024 interview, CEO Liang Wenfeng called for China to achieve leadership in AI, but the focus was on innovation over imitation:

> We often say that there is a gap of one or two years between Chinese AI and the United States, but the real gap is the difference between originality and imitation. If this doesn't change, China will always be only a follower—so some exploration is inescapable (Schneider et al., 2024).

In public rhetoric, Wen Gao, Director of Peng Cheng Laboratory, wrote in *People's Daily* that

"*the development of global artificial intelligence is in the transition stage from weak artificial intelligence to strong artificial intelligence*" and that

"*artificial intelligence is a strategic commanding height for competition among major powers*".

However, the essay went on to say "*International cooperation and competition in artificial intelligence coexist*" noting US and EU policy measures to enhance their competitiveness, before calling for strengthening of international cooperation and global governance (Gao, 2025). Gao is a coauthor of a previous paper discussing recursive self-improvement and the risks of AGI development, which emphasised strengthening international AGI cooperation as "necessary" (Liu et al., 2021).

This mirrors recent policy rhetoric: at Davos, Vice Premier Ding Xuexiang noted that the primary purpose of China's AI development is to drive economic transformation, achieve Chinese-style modernisation, and improve the lives of its 1.4 billion citizens, and that China "*will not blindly follow trends or engage in unrestrained international competition*". His speech noted that "*if left to uncontrolled competition among nations, the 'gray rhino' risks will become imminent*" (Geopolitechs, 2025).

At the 2025 Paris AI Summit, senior diplomat Fu Ying described China's position as follows:

> China maintains a relatively calm attitude toward China-U.S. cooperation and global governance, advocating to respect each other's core interests and major

concerns on divergent issues, adhering to the principles of mutual respect, peaceful coexistence, and win-win cooperation.

However, the US drive for dominance is a clear source of frustration:

Past years have witnessed consistent US efforts to block China's technological progress, poisoning the atmosphere for cooperation.

Fu repeated a statement she'd previously made in 2019: "*as long as the U.S. and China can cooperate and work together with the rest of humanity, we'll find a way to keep AI under control. But if countries remain at odds and even use advanced AI systems against each other, the machines are more likely to gain the upper hand*" (Fu, 2025).

At the April 2025 Politburo study session on AI, President Xi called for "*mastering core technologies such as high-end microchips and foundational software*" (Centre for Security and Emerging Technology, 2025), which analyst Paul Triolo perceived as a response to the threat of US policies isolating China in AI development. However, analysts Helen Toner and Kristy Loke noted the apparent lack of special interest in AGI or superintelligence compared to Silicon Valley discourse. Scott Singer, Gabriel Wagner, and Jason Zhou picked up on the strong emphasis on safety, with a full paragraph of the speech summary dedicated to addressing AI's "*unprecedented risks and challenges*" and a further paragraph calling for "*broad international cooperation*" and "*global governance frameworks*" (Loke et al., 2025).

Public and policy rhetoric by influential figures emphasises that China wishes to be a world-leader in AI, but in an international landscape where competition is balanced with cooperation, especially on safety. The emphasis of reports, speeches, and essays is typically on a wide range of industry and economic applications of AI, rather than pursuit of superintelligence or global dominance. Self-sufficiency is a common theme; the risk of reliance on US technology and supply chains is clearly keenly felt. There certainly is a broader aspiration that progress in emerging technologies would contribute to a reshaping of the global order (Ding, 2024), but even in more ambitious rhetoric, commentators look to a future with China and the USA as two superpowers instead of the USA as the world's sole superpower (e.g. Jin, 2019). China clearly recognises AI as a geopolitically important technology. There are areas in which China is pursuing greater global influence in which AI and digital technologies play an important role, such as in the expansion of China's Belt and Road Initiative, and in efforts such as the Global AI Governance Initiative (Cyberspace Administration of China, 2023). However, there is little evidence at present that China perceives AI or AGI in terms of more overt geopolitical dominance, and much evidence that strengthening China's economy and achieving global economic advantage along lines more consistent with "normal" technology competition are greater areas of focus.

Nonetheless, rhetoric is an imperfect indicator of intent, and Chinese policy rhetoric is often less overt than Western rhetoric. Critics may also point to other prominent instances in which alleged PRC-linked actions are perceived to have diverged from public statements. For example, the Chinese Government has repeatedly stated that it opposes cyber espionage and attacks (Yousif & Tidy, 2024; People's Republic of China, 2021a). However, US cybersecurity firms have published detailed technical analyses of attack campaigns they attribute to Chinese state-sponsored groups (FireEye 2019; FireEye 2013), and the US Department of Justice has issued multiple indictments against Chinese personnel and hackers for economic and cyber-espionage (US Department of Justice, 2025, 2014).

It remains the case that neither public rhetoric nor publicly available evidence relating to investment or concentration of relevant resources indicates a major state-supported push towards AGI, nor an ambition to pursue global dominance through AI or superintelligence. It is just about possible that an ambitious, well-resourced AGI effort exists and is a state priority, but that no public information about it exists. But there are reasons to think this is unlikely at this time. Such a project would require huge resources in terms of high-end chips and expertise, as well as energy, and some indications of it would likely be picked up by open-source intelligence and the AI research community—researchers usually have an idea where their more talented colleagues and PhD students have gone to. Even if it did, China would still be at a disadvantage due to limited access to leading chips. Schneider et al., (2024) concludes that "*there are no signs of any 'whole nation'举国effort to centralize resources*" towards any concerted AGI push.

Part 4: Implications and Recommendations

For any technology of such strategic significance as AI/AGI, and with such extensive military and intelligence applications, much relevant information is likely to be classified. However, from publicly available information, it appears that the narrative of the US–China "AI race" has been overblown. In particular, the more specific narrative that China is locked in a race with the USA to reach artificial superintelligence, and translate this to lasting geopolitical dominance, is almost entirely constructed and promoted by US-associated actors. I argue that challenging it is essential. Moreover, it is fully possible to do so while recognising the benefit to the USA of pursuing export controls and other measures to strengthen its security and competitiveness. These measures all make sense within a 'normal' technology competition, and do not require the prospect of Chinese global strategic dominance through AI to be justified.

Many of the prominent actors promoting this rhetoric stand to benefit from it directly in important ways—through investments, permissive regulatory changes, and other forms of influence—and some are actively pushing recommendations that benefit them directly using the threat of Chinese AI dominance.[3] I do not claim that they are insincere in promoting this narrative; only that this is the effect of the rhetoric. In practice, the race to AGI that exists is between predominantly US-headquartered companies and is being run against each other.

The impacts of this narrative are considerable. It is being used to justify a reduced focus on regulations that aim to ensure the safety of the technology and minimise negative impacts on other industries and society more broadly. It serves to concentrate power and resources around those actors pushing the narrative. It increases international mistrust and undermines prospects of international cooperation on AI at the point at which it is arguably most needed. I argue that it creates the most dangerous possible circumstances in which to develop AGI; a technology many leading experts, including the CEOs of the leading companies developing it, think has a sizeable chance of bringing about human extinction.

This extensive narrative, and the expectations and fears of the US technologists and thought leaders promoting it, is, of course, visible to their Chinese counterparts. While it does not appear the Chinese Communist Party (CCP) or Chinese tech industry has responded substantially at the time of writing, how long can that last? One possibility is that they become convinced of the capabilities and strategic decisiveness of artificial superintelligence and indeed do invest far more of China's vast resources into trying to achieve it.

A race to superintelligence may eventually be inevitable as scientific consensus grows about its possibility and implications. If this prominent narrative hastens this race emerging, this surely does not serve US interests, given the present US advantage in AGI-focused efforts. Nor does it benefit the world, given that such a race in earnest would increase competitive pressures and immediately make it more difficult to give adequate care to safety and control.

[3]One notable counterexample is Anthropic's recommendation to strengthen security measures in AI companies, which would be expected to introduce significant cost and inconvenience into the AI development process (Anthropic, 2025a).

It is also possible that a geopolitical race to superintelligence is not inevitable: China may not begin to focus in strength on superintelligence until the lead held by US entities is insurmountable. It is even possible that as consensus on the implications and risks of superintelligence grows, it becomes preferable for leading nations to participate in a cooperative global effort to avoid the risks of unsafe development (Katze & Futerman, 2024); however, this seems far less plausible against the backdrop of a "race for dominance" narrative. In all these cases, the narrative of the race for decisive strategic advantage hastens the emergence of, or brings into reality, the race it warns of.

Another prospect is that China perceives the race as unwinnable if it perceives artificial superintelligence as imminent, given the present disparity in investment, chip infrastructure, and expertise. In this instance, we might ask how any nation would respond to stated intentions of durable global hegemony from an adversary, promoted by influential thinkers close to that adversary's administration. In such circumstances, even the prospect of great power conflict might become distressingly plausible (Werner, 2024).

The situation is complicated further by the confused mishmash of beliefs and expectations driving policy on AI at present. In arguing that international cooperation to control ASI (artificial superintelligence) is preferable and strategically sound, Katze and Futerman (2024) state:

> The argument for racing to develop ASI also requires the assumption that states are (to some extent) rational actors and are well-informed about ASI's strategic implication.

However, I believe it is more likely that a possible race to superintelligence would unfold in a less coherent way. As it is now, some stakeholders will push their nation to win the race to AGI, with the prospect of full superintelligence, a massively accelerated industry, and a durable advantage over all other nations as their goal. To other stakeholders, such prospects will continue sounding like fantasy until much later, but the importance of remaining ahead in a strategically important "normal" technology in a tense geopolitical contest will appear to justify at least some of the same actions. Whether or not those who believe near-term superintelligence is plausible are correct, this lack of shared understanding of the stakes at play is likely to be destabilising and is likely to undermine both coherent national strategies and stable international agreements or even deterrence strategies. Would mutually assured destruction have worked as a doctrine if decision-makers within countries had vastly different conceptions of the destructive capacity of nuclear weapons?

What Can Be Done?

A first priority is to assess the evidence justifying this powerful policy narrative, which this chapter aims to contribute to. Belfield and Ruhl (2022) described how incorrect perceptions about tight arms races brought forward the development of powerful destructive technologies such as the nuclear bomb and intercontinental ballistic missiles (ICBMs), developments that were subsequently regretted by some of their advocates. I argue that this may now be happening in AI.

It may also be important to achieve clarity between stakeholders on their expectations regarding superintelligence and its implications, although this is less clear-cut. If adversaries converge on an expectation of near-term superintelligence leading to decisive strategic advantage, this may exacerbate race dynamics. However, a growing number of governance and deterrence proposals rest on the assumption that adversaries are rational actors with a shared understanding of the stakes at play. At present this is very much not the case—there are clearly diverging expectations between companies and governments, between different stakeholders within governments, and between governments. If this persists into the future, it would undermine such proposals and introduce dangerous geopolitical instability.

Signalling benign intent should be a priority. As long as the USA fears domination by its adversary should China achieve AGI first, and as long as US technologists signal that the USA would itself pursue global hegemony with the aid of AGI, achieving cooperation seems unlikely. When asked if in a scenario where AI was "getting out of control" the US government could enact a "pause on AI development", US Vice President Vance answered:

> The honest answer to that is that I don't know, because part of this arms race component is if we take a pause, does the People's Republic of China not take a pause? And then we find ourselves all enslaved to P.R.C.-mediated A.I.? (Douthat, 2025).

Clear, credible commitments by nations pursuing AGI to respect the sovereignty, political systems, and economic well-being of rivals will be needed for cooperation to be feasible and for countries to feel able to "slow down" if safety concerns warrant it. A meaningful commitment to a regime for equitably sharing the benefits of AI, including with adversaries, would also reduce incentives to race.

A further priority is finding where cooperation is possible and beneficial. Even between perceived adversaries, there are areas where cooperation is in the best interests of both, and where cooperation need not be in conflict with competitive or geopolitical rivalry. For example, it is in both the USA and China's interests that powerful models developed in either state be robustly protected against co-option and misuse, for example by non-state actors (Ó hÉigeartaigh, 2025); sharing techniques and best practices in this domain will benefit both. Both these nations have far more physical and digital infrastructure to protect than any non-state actor, making this an asymmetric threat. Bucknall et al. (2025) lay out a broader set of technical safety topics on which rivals could cooperate.

Establishing cooperation around topics of immediate shared benefit will be a step towards making international agreements with deeper regulatory implications possible. In a competitive technology development scenario, regulation provides an essential "floor" for society and for the companies being regulated. The CEOs of leading AGI companies have expressed concern about risk and have in the past called for regulation (Altman et al., 2023; Amodei, 2023; Milmo, 2023). But no matter how risk-concerned a company is, within a tight race it cannot afford to be the one company to take far more burdensome steps than other actors, due to the competitive disadvantage this would pose the company (Armstrong et al., 2016). Regulation addresses this by establishing a requirement for all companies. This principle applies both within a country and between countries. As models become more powerful, more onerous regulations will become necessary for safety; however, fears of losing international competitive advantage may prevent these from being implemented nationally, a concern already reflected in US policy rhetoric. Thus, only through both national regulation and agreed international standards (Trager et al., 2023) between "racing" nations can a race to the bottom be avoided.

Political will is needed to reach the stage where certain international agreements would be feasible; for example commitment not to progress beyond key capability thresholds unless safety can be guaranteed. Such agreements could be significantly strengthened through mechanisms for guaranteeing and verifying compliance by rivals and third parties—for example allowing international identification of unauthorised training runs or training runs that do not meet agreed safety stipulations. Governance frameworks and interventions have been proposed, including at the hardware level (Trager et al., 2023; O'Gara et al., 2025; Petrie et al., 2025), and ensuring this toolkit is developed ahead of when it is needed should be a priority. Without a powerful suite of monitoring and verification tools, there seems little prospect of escape from a race motivated by fear of what the other is doing.

Throughout, maintaining lines of communication will be paramount. The current "AI race" narrative might be partly dispelled if US policymakers had more access to their Chinese counterparts. Should a geopolitical race to AGI begin in earnest, then each participant understanding which actions might be misunderstood by rivals, including especially those that might provoke strong or unexpected responses, will be essential (Shoker et al., 2023). In the Cold War, complementary roles were played by a variety of channels—official political (Miller, 2021), track II (Kraft, 2024), and clandestine (Scott, 2013)—to avert disaster. It may seem sensationalist to draw comparison between Cold War standoffs and the global pursuit of AGI, but the risks inherent in pursuing AGI under intense geopolitical rivalry (Futerman & Katze, 2024) may mean the stakes are even higher. Of particular importance will be avoidance of a rival initiating a stage of recursive improvement that may not be controllable under the pressure of the race dynamic; lines of communication to enable de-escalation from this step will be essential. We can only hope the world does not come to such a brink.

Conclusion

If what the leading frontier AI companies believe with regards to imminent artificial superintelligence turns out to be unfounded, then eventually it will become clear that the international AI competition currently underway is a "normal technology competition" and that the extreme outcomes motivating the AI race for decisive strategic advantage can be discounted. In that instance, we may hope that this narrative has not resulted in some of the more drastic geopolitical moves that have been suggested.

If superintelligence is a genuine prospect, however, then the effect of the US–China "race for decisive strategic advantage" narrative may well be to hasten, or even bring about, a headlong rush towards plausibly the most dangerous development in human history. Moreover, the narrative's overtly adversarial framing may undermine any realistic prospects of global cooperation on safety. It is therefore essential that we examine the evidence for the "race" as it has existed to date, and the evidence to justify the actions now being proposed.

I argue that the stronger narratives around a US–China AI race have been overstated, and that the specific narrative of a US–China AI race for decisive strategic advantage, as currently presented in Western media and policy discourse, is one of the most dangerous fictions ever created. Moreover, it is a fiction with the clear potential to serve as a self-fulfilling prophecy, bringing into being a true race that would be even more dangerous. The world should not be lost on the basis of a fiction.

Acknowledgements The author would like to thank the following for valuable discussions and comments on an earlier draft: Coleman Snell, Emma Bates, Kerry McInerney, Eleanor Drage, Greg Merckelbach, Rose Hadshar, Ariel Gil, Jeffrey Ding, Oliver Guest, and Kevin Wei.

References

Abiri, G., & Huang, Y. (2023). A red flag? China's generative AI dilemma. *Harvard Journal of Law & Technology, 37*, 1–20.

Achiam, J., Adler, S., Agarwal, S., Ahmad, L., Akkaya, I., Aleman, F. L., McGrew, B., et al. (2023). Gpt-4 technical report. *arXiv preprint arXiv:2303.08774*.

Arcas, B. A. Y. & Norvig, P. (2023, October 10). *Artificial general intelligence is already here*. NOEMA. https://www.noemamag.com/artificial-general-intelligence-is-already-here/

Allen, G. (2023). *China's pursuit of defense technologies: Implications for U.S. and multilateral export control and investment screening regimes*. Center for Strategic and International Studies. https://www.csis.org/analysis/chinas-pursuit-defense-technologies-implications-us-and-multilateral-export-control-and

Altman, S.; Brockman, G., & Sutskever, I. (2023, May 22). *Governance of superintelligence.* https://openai.co/m/index/governance-of-superintelligence/

Altman, S. (2015, February 25). *Machine intelligence, part 1*. Blog.SamAltman. https://blog.samaltman.com/machine-intelligence-part-1

Altman, S. (2025, January 5). *Reflections*. Blog.SamAltman. https://blog.samaltman.com/reflections.

Amodei, D. (2023, November 1). *Dario Amodei's prepared remarks from the AI Safety Summit on Anthropic's Responsible Scaling Policy*. Anthropic. https://www.anthropic.com/news/uk-ai-safety-summit

Amodei, D. (2024, October). *Machines of loving grace: How AI could transform the world for the better*. https://www.darioamodei.com/essay/machines-of-loving-grace.

Amodei, D. (2025a, February 11). *Statement from Dario Amodei on the Paris AI action summit*. Anthropic. https://www.anthropic.com/news/paris-ai-summit

Amodei, D. (2025b, January). *On DeepSeek and export controls*. Retrieved from https://www.darioamodei.com/post/on-deepseek-and-export-controls

Andreessen, M. (2023, June 6). Why AI will save the world. *Andreessen Horowitz*. https://a16z.com/ai-will-save-the-world/.

Anduril Industries. (2024, December 4). *Anduril partners with OpenAI to advance U.S. artificial intelligence leadership and protect U.S. and allied forces*. Anduril. https://www.anduril.com/article/anduril-partners-with-openai-to-advance-u-s-artificial-intelligence-leadership-and-protect-u-s/

Anthropic. (2025a, March 6). *Response to OSTP RFI on the development of an artificial intelligence (AI) action plan*. https://assets.anthropic.com/m/4e20a4ab6512e217/original/Anthropic-Response-to-OSTP-RFI-March-2025-Final-Submission-v3.pdf

Anthropic. (2025b, May 14). *Responsible Scaling Policy (Version 2.2)*. https://www-cdn.anthropic.com/872c653b2d0501d6ab44cf87f43e1dc4853e4d37.pdf

Armstrong, S., Bostrom, N., & Shulman, C. (2016). Racing to the precipice: A model of artificial intelligence development. *AI & SOCIETY, 31*, 201–206.

Aschenbrenner, L. (2024). Situational awareness. *The decade ahead. situational-awareness. ai.*

Bank of China. (2025, January 23). *1*万亿元!提供专项综合金融支持 助力人工智能产业链发展 [1 trillion yuan! Providing special comprehensive financial support to promote the development of the artificial intelligence industry chain]. https://www.bankofchina.com/aboutboc/bi1/202501/t20250123_25254674.html

Belfield, H., & Ruhl, C. (2022, July 14). Why policy makers should beware claims of new 'arms races'. *Bulletin of the Atomic Scientists*. https://thebulletin.org/2022/07/why-policy-makers-should-beware-claims-of-new-arms-races/

Biddle, S. (2024, January 12). OpenAI quietly deletes ban on using ChatGPT for "military and warfare". *The Intercept*. https://theintercept.com/2024/01/12/open-ai-military-ban-chatgpt/

Bostrom, N. (2014). *Superintelligence: Paths, dangers, strategies*. Oxford University Press.

Bradsher, K. (2024). China tightens its hold on minerals needed to make computer chips. *New York Times*, October, 26. https://www.nytimes.com/2024/10/26/business/china-critical-minerals-semiconductors.html

Bresnick, S. (2024). *China's military AI roadblocks*. Center for Security and Emerging Technology, Georgetown University.

Brundage, M., & Werner, G. (2025, April 23). *America first meets safety first*. AI Frontiers. https://www.ai-frontiers.org/articles/america-first-meets-safety

Bucknall, B., Siddiqui, S., Thurnherr, L., McGurk, C., Harack, B., Reuel, A., Paskov, P., Mahoney, C., Mindermann, S., Singer, S., Hiremath, V., Segerie, C.-R., Delaney, O., Abate, A., Barez, F., Cohen, M. K., Torr, P., Huszár, F., Calinescu, A., Davis Jones, G., Bengio, Y., & Trager, R. (2025). *In which areas of technical AI safety could geopolitical rivals cooperate?* arXiv. https://arxiv.org/abs/2504.12914.

Buzan, B., Wæver, O., & De Wilde, J. (1998). *Security: A new framework for analysis*. Lynne Rienner.

Cave, S., & ÓhÉigeartaigh, S. S. (2018, December). An AI race for strategic advantage: Rhetoric and risks. In *Proceedings of the 2018 AAAI/ACM conference on AI, ethics, and society* (pp. 36-40).

Center for AI Safety. (2023, May 30). *Statement on AI risk*.https://safe.ai/work/statement-on-ai-risk

Center for Security and Emerging Technology. (2025, April 28). *At the 20th collective study session of the CCP central committee politburo, Xi Jinping stresses: Persist in being self-reliant, be strongly oriented toward applications, and push the orderly development of artificial intelligence*. Translated by Ben Murphy. Georgetown University. https://cset.georgetown.edu/publication/xi-politburo-collective-study-ai-2025/

Chapman, L., & Ludlow, E. (2025, February). *Anduril's Luckey cites China risk in drone output race*. MSN. https://www.msn.com/en-us/money/companies/anduril-s-luckey-cites-china-risk-in-drone-output-race/ar-AA1xj1nj.

ChinaTalk. (2025, April 02). *Is China racing to AGI?* ChinaTalk. https://www.chinatalk.media/p/is-china-agi-pilled

Creemers, R., & Kania, E. (Trans.). (2022, April 22). Translation: Xi Jinping calls for 'healthy development' of AI. *DigiChina*. https://digichina.stanford.edu/work/xi-jinping-calls-for-healthy-development-of-ai-translation/

Clegg, N. (2024, November). *Open source AI can help America lead in AI and strengthen global security*. Meta. https://about.fb.com/news/2024/11/open-source-ai-america-global-security/

Colson, D. (2024, October 18). Silicon Valley takes artificial general intelligence seriously—Washington must too. *Time*https://time.com/7093792/ai-artificial-general-intelligence-risks/

Cottier, B., Rahman, R., Fattorini, L., Maslej, N., & Owen, D. (2024). *The rising costs of training frontier AI models*. https://doi.org/10.48550/arXiv.2405.21015

FireEye. (2019). *APT41: A dual espionage and cyber crime operation*. https://www.fireeye.com/current-threats/apt-groups.html

Demchak, C. C. (2019). China: Determined to dominate cyberspace and AI. *Bulletin of the Atomic Scientists, 75*(3), 99–104.

Ding, J., & Dafoe, A. (2023). Engines of power: Electricity, AI, and general-purpose, military transformations. *European Journal of International Security, 8*(3), 377–394.

Ding, J. (2024). *Technology and the rise of great powers: How diffusion shapes economic competition*. Princeton University Press.

Douthat, R. (2025, May 21). J.D. Vance's theological border wall. *The New York Times*. https://www.nytimes.com/2025/05/21/opinion/jd-vance-pope-trump-immigration.html

Esper, M. T. (2019, November 5). *Remarks at National Security Commission on artificial intelligence public conference [speech transcript]*. U.S. Department of Defense. https://www.defense.gov/News/Transcripts/Transcript/Article/2011960/remarks-by-secretary-esper-at-national-security-commission-on-artificial-intell/

Executive Office of the President. (2023, November 1). Safe, secure, and trustworthy development and use of artificial intelligence. *Federal Register, 88*(210), 75358–75377. https://www.federalregister.gov/documents/2023/11/01/2023-24283/safe-secure-and-trustworthy-development-and-use-of-artificial-intelligence

Fedasiuk, R., Melot, J., & Murphy, B. (2021). *Harnessed lightning: How the Chinese military is adopting artificial intelligence*. Center for Security and Emerging Technology. https://cset.georgetown.edu/publication/harnessed-lightning/

FireEye. (2013). *APT1: Exposing one of China's cyber espionage units*. https://www.fireeye.com/content/dam/fireeye-www/services/pdfs/mandiant-apt1-report.pdf

Gadzala Tirziu, A. (2024, December). *China's military expansion: A global power shift in the making*. GIS Reports. https://www.gisreportsonline.com/r/china-military-expansion/

Gao, W. (2025). *Seizing the historic opportunity for the development of artificial intelligence*. Translated by Bill Bishop. Sinocism. https://abalone-taleggio-85c.notion.site/Seizing-the-Historic-Opportunity-for-the-Development-of-Artificial-Intelligence-1a41b804835280a78b44d17e0ef92a04

General Office of the Ministry of Industry and Information Technology. (2023, September 15). 国务院办公厅关于进一步优化营商环境降低市场主体制度性交易成本的意见. The Central People's Government of the People's Republic of China. https://web.archive.org/web/20230916063228/https://www.gov.cn/zhengce/zhengceku/202309/content_6903897.htm

Gigova, R. (2017, September 4). Putin: Whoever leads in AI will rule the world. *CNN*. Retrieved April 4, 2025, from https://edition.cnn.com/2017/09/01/world/putin-artificial-intelligence-will-rule-world/index.html

Geopolitechs. (2025, January 21). Translation: China's Vice Premier Ding Xuexiang on AI competition and AI governance at Davos. *Geopolitechs*. https://www.geopolitechs.org/p/chinas-vice-premier-ding-xuexiang

Griffin, J. (2024, May 16). Modern warfare being reshaped by AI [video]. *Fox News*. https://www.foxnews.com/video/6352982729112

Hart, J. (2025, May 22). *Google cofounder Sergey Brin says it's time for retired computer scientists to get back to work*. Business Insider. https://www.businessinsider.com/google-sergey-brin-computer-scientists-should-not-be-retired-2025-5

Hendrycks, D., Mazeika, M., & Woodside, T. (2023). An overview of catastrophic AI risks. *arXiv preprint arXiv:2306.12001*.

Hendrycks, D., Schmidt, E., & Wang, A. (2025). *Superintelligence strategy: Expert version*. arXiv. https://doi.org/10.48550/arXiv.2503.05628

Hooker, L., & Vallance, C. (2025, February 5). Google ending AI arms ban incredibly concerning, campaigners say. *BBC News*. https://www.bbc.co.uk/news/articles/cy081nqx2zjo

IDAIS-Beijing. (2024, March). *Consensus statement on red lines in artificial intelligence*. https://idais.ai/

Jin, C. (2019). *The fourth industrial revolution is mainly a competition between China and the United States, and china has a greater chance of winning*. Translated by Jeffrey Ding, George Washington University. https://docs.google.com/document/d/1_sNUwHBqU0o8N6PWVQpMBHrs0UshuNXUCJhw5G4qctU

Jones, N. (2025). How AI can achieve human-level intelligence: Researchers call for change in tack. *Nature*. https://doi.org/10.1038/d41586-025-00649-4

Joshi, S. (2025). *A comprehensive review of DeepSeek: Performance, architecture capabilities*. Preprints. https://doi.org/10.20944/preprints202503.1887.v1

Karp, A. C. (2023). Our Oppenheimer moment: The creation of AI weapons. *International New York Times.*https://www.nytimes.com/2023/07/25/opinion/karp-palantir-artificial-intelligence.html

Katzke, C., & Futerman, G. (2024). *The Manhattan trap: Why a race to artificial superintelligence is self-defeating.* SSRN. https://ssrn.com/abstract=5067833

Kerner, S. (2023, July). *Elon Musk reveals xAI efforts, predicts full AGI by 2029.* VentureBeat. https://venturebeat.com/ai/elon-musk-reveals-xai-efforts-predicts-full-agi-by-2029

Klein, E. (2025, March 4). The government knows A.G.I. is coming. *The New York Times.* https://www.nytimes.com/2025/03/04/opinion/ezra-klein-podcast-ben-buchanan.html

Kraft, A. (2024). Pugwash in the 1960s cold war: Challenges and limits of operating in the diplomatic realm. In *The Palgrave handbook of non-state actors in east-west Relations* (pp. 1–21). Springer International Publishing.

Kumar, I., & Manning, S. (2025). Trends in frontier AI model count: A forecast to 2028. *arXiv preprint arXiv:2504.16138.*

Lee, K. F. (2018). *AI superpowers: China, Silicon Valley, and the new world order.* Harper Business.

Lehane, C. (2025, March 13). OpenAI response: OSTP/NSF RFI. *OpenAI.* https://cdn.openai.com/global-affairs/ostp-rfi/ec680b75-d539-4653-b297-8bcf6e5f7686/openai-response-ostp-nsf-rfi-notice-request-for-information-on-the-development-of-an-artificial-intelligence-ai-action-plan.pdf

Levine, J. & Hwang, T. (2025). Copyright, Power and great power competition. *Foundation for American Innovation.* Research papers. https://cdn.sanity.io/files/d8lrla4f/staging/1e8b069431e03d9e8b23f03dede131ef5fdb16a9.pdf

Liu, A., Feng, B., Xue, B., Wang, B., Wu, B., Lu, C., Piao, Y., et al. (2024). Deepseek-v3 technical report. *arXiv preprint arXiv:2412.19437.*

Liu, Y., Zhang, Y., Duan, P., Shi, B., Yu, Z., Huang, T., & Gao, W. (2021). Technical countermeasures for security risks of artificial general intelligence. *Strategic Study of CAE, 23*(3), 75–81. https://doi.org/10.15302/J-SSCAE-2021.03.005

Loke, K., Triolo, P., Toner, H., Costigan, J., Singer, S., Wagner, G., Zhou, J., & Neville, K. (2025, April 30). *Forum: Xi's message to the Politburo on AI.* DigiChina. https://digichina.stanford.edu/work/forum-xis-message-to-the-politburo-on-ai/

Lovely, G. (2024, November 19). *China hawks are manufacturing an AI arms race (now with a reply from Gwern).* Obsolete. https://www.obsolete.pub/p/china-hawks-are-manufacturing-an

Mayer Brown. (2024, September 9). *US Department of Commerce issues proposal to require reporting development of advanced AI models and computer clusters.* https://www.mayerbrown.com/en/insights/publications/2024/09/us-department-of-commerce-issues-proposal-to-require-reporting-development-of-advanced-ai-models-and-computer-clusters

Maslej, N., Fattorini, L., Perrault, R., Gil, Y., Parli, V., Kariuki, N., Capstick, E., Reuel, A., Brynjolfsson, E., Etchemendy, J., Ligett, K., Lyons, T., Manyika, J., Niebles, J. C., Shoham, Y., Wald, R., Walsh, T., Hamrah, A., Santarlasci, L., Betts Lotufo, J., Rome, A., Shi, A., & Oak, S. (2025, April). *The AI*

Index 2025 annual report. AI Index Steering Committee, Institute for Human-Centered AI, Stanford University. https://hai-production.s3.amazonaws.com/files/hai_ai_index_report_2025.pdf.

Miller, S. E. (2021). Nuclear hotlines: Origins, evolution, applications. *Journal for Peace and Nuclear Disarmament, 4*(sup1), 176–191.

Milmo, D. (2023, October 24). AI risk must be treated as seriously as climate crisis, says Google DeepMind chief. *The Guardian*.https://www.theguardian.com/technology/2023/oct/24/ai-risk-climate-crisis-google-deepmind-chief-demis-hassabis-regulation

Mitchell, M. (2024). Debates on the nature of artificial general intelligence. *Science, 383*(6689), eado7069.

Mozur, P., Liu, J., & Metz, C. (2024). China's rush to dominate AI comes with a twist: It depends upon US technology. *The New York Times*. ISSN, 0362–4331.

Murgia, M. (2024, December 5). Anthropic's Dario Amodei: Democracies must maintain the lead in AI. *Financial Times*. https://www.ft.com/content/e75e3388-4700-413d-ab67-778410c2d977

Musk, E. [@elonmusk]. (2017, September 4). [Tweet]. Twitter. https://x.com/elonmusk/status/904638455761612800

Narayanan, A., & Kapoor, S. (2025, April 15). AI as normal technology: An alternative to the vision of AI as a potential superintelligence. Knight First Amendment Institute. https://kfai-documents.s3.amazonaws.com/documents/0ee1da899a/AI-as-Normal-Technology%2D%2D-Narayanan%2D%2D-Kapoor-Final.pdf

O'Gara, A., Kulp, G., Hodgkins, W., Petrie, J., Immler, V., Aysu, A., Srivastava, A., et al. (2025). Hardware-enabled mechanisms for verifying responsible AI development. *arXiv preprint arXiv:2505.03742*.

ÓhÉigeartaigh, S. S., Whittlestone, J., Liu, Y., Zeng, Y., & Liu, Z. (2020). Overcoming barriers to cross-cultural cooperation in AI ethics and governance. *Philosophy & Technology, 33*, 571–593.

O'Meara, S. (2019). China's ambitious quest to lead the world in AI by 2030. *Nature, 572*(7770), 427–428.

Ó hÉigeartaigh, S. (2025). *What comes after the Paris AI summit?* Royal United Services Institute. https://www.rusi.org/explore-our-research/publications/commentary/what-comes-after-paris-ai-summit

OpenAI. (2025a, April 15). *Preparedness framework (version 2)*. https://cdn.openai.com/pdf/18a02b5d-6b67-4cec-ab64-68cdfbddebcd/preparedness-framework-v2.pdf

OpenAI (2025b, March 31). *New funding to build towards AGI*.https://openai.com/index/march-funding-updates/

Palantir Investor Relations. (2024, November 7). *Anthropic and Palantir partner to bring Claude AI models to AWS for U.S. government intelligence and defense operations*. Palantir Investor Relations. https://investors.palantir.com/news-details/2024/Anthropic-and-Palantir-Partner-to-Bring-Claude-AI-Models-to-AWS-for-U.S.-Government-Intelligence-and-Defense-Operations/

Petrie, J., Aarne, O., Ammann, N., & Dalrymple, D. D. (2025, April). *Flexible hardware-enabled guarantees: Part I–Overview*. Advanced Research and Invention Agency. https://flexheg.com/report-1.pdf

People's Republic of China. (2021a, December). *China's positions on international rules-making in cyberspace*. United Nations Office for Disarmament Affairs. https://documents.unoda.org/wp-content/uploads/2021/12/Chinese-Position-Paper-on-International-Rules-making-in-Cyberspace-ENG.pdf

People's Republic of China. (2021b). Position paper of the People's Republic of China on regulating military applications of artificial intelligence (AI). *Sixth review conference of the high contracting parties to the convention on prohibitions or restrictions on the use of certain conventional weapons which may be deemed to be excessively injurious or to have indiscriminate effects*. https://docs-library.unoda.org/Convention_on_Certain_Conventional_Weapons_-SixthReview_Conference_(2021)/CCW-CONF.VI-WP.2.pdf

Pichai, S. (2023, April 20). *Google DeepMind: Bringing together two world-class AI teams*. Google. https://blog.google/technology/ai/april-ai-update/.

Pillay, T. (2025, March 13). How Musk, Altman, AI leaders face the 'Oppenheimer moment.' *Time*. https://time.com/7267797/ai-leaders-oppenheimer-moment-musk-altman/

Pilz, K. F., Heim, L., & Brown, N. (2025b). Increased compute efficiency and the diffusion of AI capabilities. In *Proceedings of the AAAI conference on artificial intelligence* (Vol. 39, no. 26, pp. 27582–27590).

Pilz, K. F., Sanders, J., Rahman, R., & Heim, L. (2025a). Trends in AI supercomputers. *arXiv preprint arXiv:2504.16026*.

PYMNTS. (2025, February 20). *Alibaba ramps up AI spending in pursuit of AGI*. PYMNTS.com. https://www.pymnts.com/earnings/2025/alibaba-ramps-up-ai-spending-in-pursuit-of-agi/

Rehman, I. (2025, January 13). *The battle for brilliant minds: From the nuclear age to AI*. War on the Rocks. https://warontherocks.com/2025/01/the-battle-for-brilliant-minds-from-the-nuclear-age-to-ai

Roose, K. (2023, December 6). Silicon Valley confronts a grim new A.I. metric. *The New York Times*. https://www.nytimes.com/2023/12/06/business/dealbook/silicon-valley-artificial-intelligence.html

Sacks, D. [@DavidSacks]. (2025, January 27). [tweet]. *X*. https://x.com/DavidSacks/status/1883935713877782884

Schmidt, E., & Work, R. O. (2021). *Chair and vice chair letter—NSCAI final report*. National Security Commission on Artificial Intelligence.https://reports.nscai.gov/final-report/chair-and-vice-chair-letter.

Schneider, J., Shen, A., Zhang, I., et al. (2024, November 27). DeepSeek: The quiet giant leading China's AI race. *ChinaTalk*. https://www.chinatalk.media/p/deepseek-ceo-interview-with-chinas

Scott, L. (2013). Intelligence and the risk of nuclear war: Able Archer-83 revisited. In *Intelligence in the cold war: What difference did it make?* (pp. 5–23). Routledge.

Sevilla, J., & Roldan, E. (2024). Training compute of frontier AI models grows by 4-5x per year. *Epoch AI*. Retrieved May 10, 2025, from https://epoch.ai/blog/training-compute-of-frontier-ai-models-grows-by-4-5x-per-year

Shah, R., Irpan, A., Turner, A. M., Wang, A., Conmy, A., Lindner, D., Dragan, A., et al. (2025). An approach to technical agi safety and security. *arXiv preprint arXiv:2504.01849*.

Shanahan, M. (2015). *The technological singularity*. MIT Press.

Shead, S. (2017). Eric Schmidt on AI: 'Trust me, these Chinese people are good'. *Business Insider*. Retrieved December 30, 2017, from https://www.businessinsider.com/eric-schmidt-on-artificial-intelligence-china-2017-11/

Sheehan, M. (2023). China's AI regulations and how they get made. *Horizons: Journal of International Relations and Sustainable Development, 24*, 108–125.

Shipley, T. (2024, October 28). *China will continue to advance its military AI*. https://www.oxan.com/insights/china-will-continue-to-advance-its-military-ai/

Shoker, S., Reddie, A., Barrington, S., Booth, R., Brundage, M., Chahal, H., Young, J., et al. (2023). Confidence-building measures for artificial intelligence: Workshop proceedings. *arXiv preprint arXiv:2308.00862*.

Solomon, J. (2023, July 28). Ex-Pentagon chief: US, China locked in existential struggle for AI dominance. *Semafor*. https://www.semafor.com/article/07/27/2023/us-china-existential-struggle-ai-dominance

South China Morning Post. (2023, August 23). *China's 'pro-innovation' AI regulations augur well for eventual public release of Ernie Bot and other local ChatGPT alternatives, Baidu CEO says*. https://www.scmp.com/tech/big-tech/article/3232071/chinas-pro-innovation-ai-regulations-augur-well-eventual-public-release-ernie-bot-and-other-local

Stacey, K. & Gilbert, C. (2022). Big tech increases funding to US foreign policy think-tanks. *Financial Times*. Retrieved May 13, 2025 from https://www.ft.com/content/4e4ca1d2-2d80-4662-86d0-067a10aad50b

Stokes, J. (2024, February 1). Military artificial intelligence, the people's liberation Army, and U.S.-China strategic competition. Center for a new American Security. https://www.cnas.org/publications/congressional-testimony/military-artificial-intelligence-the-peoples-liberation-army-and-u-s-china-strategic-competition

Su, J., Deng, Y., & Shang, E. (2023, August 31). *Baidu's Ernie Bot among eight Chinese LLM products approved for public launch*. KrASIA. https://kr-asia.com/baidus-ernie-bot-among-eight-chinese-llm-products-approved-for-public-launch

Sutskever, I., Gross, D., & Levy, D. (2024, June 19). *Safe Superintelligence Inc.*https://ssi.inc/

Tech Transparency Project. (2024). *Eric Schmidt cozies up to China's AI industry while warning U.S. of its dangers*. Retrieved May 19, 2025, from https://www.techtransparencyproject.org/articles/eric-schmidt-cozies-up-to-chinas-ai-industry-while

The Economist. (2025, February 22). *AI bosses on what keeps them up at night* [video]. YouTube. https://www.youtube.com/watch?v=4poqjZlM8Lo

The State Council of the People's Republic of China. (2024, July 21). *Full text: Resolution of CPC Central Committee on further deepening reform comprehensively to advance Chinese modernization*. https://english.www.gov.cn/policies/latestreleases/202407/21/content_WS669d0255c6d0868f4e8e94f8.html

Tobin, M. (2023, July 3). Will China overtake the U.S. on AI? Probably not. Here's why. *The Washington Post*. https://www.washingtonpost.com/world/2023/07/03/china-us-ai-technology-chatgpt/

Tognini, G., & Liu, P. (2025, January 30). Here's how much AI firm DeepSeek and its founder are worth. *Forbes*. https://www.forbes.com/sites/giacomotognini/2025/01/30/how-much-ai-firm-deepseek-and-its-billionaire-founder-liang-wenfeng-are-net-worth/

Toner, H., Xiao, J., & Ding, J. (2023). The illusion of China's AI prowess. *Foreign Affairs, 2*.

Tong, A., & Martina, M. (2024, November 19). *US government commission pushes Manhattan Project-style AI initiative*. Reuters. https://www.reuters.com/technology/artificial-intelligence/us-government-commission-pushes-manhattan-project-style-ai-initiative-2024-11-19.

Trager, R., Harack, B., Reuel, A., Carnegie, A., Heim, L., Ho, L., Villalobos, J. J., et al. (2023). International governance of civilian AI: A jurisdictional certification approach. *arXiv preprint arXiv:2308.15514*.

Tyrangiel, J. (2025, February 1). Sam Altman on ChatGPT's first two years, Elon Musk and AI under trump. *Bloomberg Businessweek*. https://www.bloomberg.com/features/2025-sam-altman-interview/

U.S.-China Economic and Security Review Commission. (2024). *2024 annual report to congress*. U.S. Government Publishing Office. https://www.uscc.gov/sites/default/files/2024-11/2024_Annual_Report_to_Congress.pdf

U.S. Department of Commerce. (2022, October 7). *Commerce implements new export controls on advanced computing and semiconductor manufacturing items to the People's Republic of China (PRC) [Press release]*. https://www.bis.doc.gov/index.php/documents/about-bis/newsroom/press-releases/3158-2022-10-07-bis-press-release-advanced-computing-and-semiconductor-manufacturing-controls-final/file

U.S. Department of Justice. (2025, March 5). *Justice Department charges 12 Chinese contract hackers and law enforcement officers in global computer intrusion campaigns*. https://www.justice.gov/opa/pr/justice-department-charges-12-chinese-contract-hackers-and-law-enforcement-officers-global

U.S. Department of Justice. (2014, May 19). *U.S. charges five Chinese military hackers for cyber espionage against U.S. corporations* [Press release]. https://www.justice.gov/opa/pr/us-charges-five-chinese-military-hackers-cyber-espionage-against-us-corporations-and

VandeHei, J., & Allen, M. (2025, January 18). Behind the curtain: A chilling, "catastzrophic" warning. *Axios*. https://www.axios.com/2025/01/18/biden-sullivan-ai-race-trump-china

Villalobos, P., Ho, A., Sevilla, J., Besiroglu, T., Heim, L., & Hobbhahn, M. (2024). *Will we run out of data? Limits of LLM scaling based on human-generated data*. arXiv. https://doi.org/10.48550/arXiv.2211.04325

Wang, A. (2022, November 27). The AI war and how to win it. *Rational in the Fullness of Time*. https://alexw.substack.com/p/war

Werner, G. (2024, August 23). The AI arms race isn't inevitable. *Palladium Magazine*. https://www.palladiummag.com/2024/08/23/the-ai-arms-race-isnt-inevitable/.

Xi, J. (2018, July 26). *Turn our vision into a reality* [speech transcript]. Ministry of Foreign Affairs of the People's Republic of China. https://www.mfa.gov.cn/eng/zy/jj/2018zt/xgswfcxjxgjmlqs/202406/t20240606_11380535.html

Xinhua News Agency. (2023, April 28). 中共中央政治局召开会议 分析研究当前经济形势和经济工作 中共中央总书记习近平主持会议. 中国政府网. https://www.gov.cn/yaowen/2023-04/28/content_5753652.htm

Yahoo Finance. (2025, February 24). *Alibaba to spend $53 billion on AI infrastructure in big pivot*. https://finance.yahoo.com/news/alibaba-spend-53-billion-ai-022846544.html

Fu, Y. (2025, February 17). Fu Ying: As long as U.S. and China can cooperate and work together, we'll find a way to keep AI under control. *China US Focus*. https://www.chinausfocus.com/peace-security/fu-ying-as-long-as-the-us-and-china-can-cooperate-and-work-together-with-the-rest-of-humanity-well-find-a-way-to-keep-ai-under-control

Yousif, N., & Tidy, J. (2024, December 30). *US treasury says it was hacked by China in 'major incident'*. BBC News. https://www.bbc.co.uk/news/articles/c3weye2j0e7o

Zhao, G. (2023, March 5). Zhu Songchun: Develop general artificial intelligence like the "Two Bombs, One Satellite" project. *China Science Daily*. https://news.sciencenet.cn/htmlnews/2023/3/495294.shtm

China's AI Safety Ecosystem and Implications for International AI Governance

Jason Zhou, Kwan Yee Ng, and Brian Tse

Background

In October 2023, Chinese president Xi Jinping announced China's "Global AI Governance Initiative" at the Third Belt and Road Forum, setting out a national position on international AI governance. The document, published several days later, acknowledges AI's transformational potential and presents a balanced view of its opportunities and risks—perspectives that non-Chinese readers may find surprisingly similar to those expressed in other countries:

> The development of advanced artificial intelligence stands as one of the defining technological challenges of our time, carrying both immense promise and profound risk. As AI systems grow increasingly sophisticated, they offer the potential to revolutionize everything from healthcare and scientific discovery to economic productivity and national security. Yet these same capabilities, if improperly developed or deployed, could pose significant risks to human welfare and social stability. The transformative potential of advanced AI makes it not

J. Zhou (✉) • K. Y. Ng • B. Tse
Concordia AI, Beijing, China
e-mail: jason@concordia-ai.com; kwanyee@concordia-ai.com; brian@concordia-ai.com

M. Rangeley, N. Fairfax (eds.), *The Artificial Intelligence Revolution*,
https://doi.org/10.1007/978-3-032-11814-1_4

> just a technological issue, but a geopolitical one, reshaping the balance of power between nations and potentially altering the very fabric of human civilization.[1]

Several weeks later, Chinese then-Vice Minister for Science and Technology WU Zhaohui (吴朝晖) echoed these themes while sharing the stage with US Secretary of Commerce Gina Raimondo at the UK AI Safety Summit—a prelude to both countries joining more than 25 other countries and the EU in affirming the importance of addressing frontier AI safety risks in the Bletchley Declaration.

According to the International AI Safety Report 2025, "AI developers have rapidly improved the capabilities of general-purpose AI in recent years," "a wide range of trajectories for the future of general-purpose AI are possible," and "further advancements could be anything from slow to extremely rapid."[2] In the 2-month interval between the report's completion and publication, Chair Yoshua Bengio found it necessary to append an update due to the release of OpenAI's o3 model, which exhibited "significantly stronger performance than any previous model." The report documents how AI capabilities could further accelerate, thanks to increased scaling in the pretraining and inference stages, algorithmic efficiencies, and the use of AI systems to accelerate AI software and hardware development. For instance, some forecasts suggest that training compute for advanced models could grow 10,000x between 2023 and 2030. However, some experts remain doubtful that compute scaling can continue given the high financial costs.

By late 2024, rapid developments in AI capabilities had clearly extended beyond Anglo-American companies. Chinese large language model (LLM) startup DeepSeek's V3 model and R1 reasoning model, released in December 2024 and January 2025, respectively, took the world by storm due to their substantially increased efficiency compared to leading Western models.[3] The psychological shock of this advancement was evident when, several days after R1's release, major technology stocks in the US nosedived (led by Nvidia's 17% decline), before largely recovering in subsequent weeks.[4] Broader quantitative indicators further substantiate China's position as a leading AI power; the Stanford 2024 AI Index Report documents that China produced the second-

[1]https://www.cac.gov.cn/2023-10/18/c_1699291032884978.htm.

[2]https://assets.publishing.service.gov.uk/media/679a0c48a77d250007d313ee/International_AI_Safety_Report_2025_accessible_f.pdf.

[3]https://arxiv.org/abs/2412.19437v2; https://arxiv.org/abs/2501.12948.

[4]https://www.reuters.com/technology/chinas-deepseek-sets-off-ai-market-rout-2025-01-27/.

highest number of machine learning models in the world in 2023 and over 50% of global AI patents in 2022.[5]

China is a crucial stakeholder in international AI governance given its demonstrated interest in the topic, geopolitical heft as a permanent member of the UN Security Council and second-largest economy in the world, and its status as a leading AI developer. Nevertheless, a comprehensive understanding of China's actions and positions on AI safety and governance remains limited in global discourse. Many narratives are filtered through a national security lens, exemplified by former US Secretary of Defense Mark Esper's contention that there is an "existential" race between the USA and China on AI and some Western media's presentation of China's AI plans as an effort to gain "global dominance."[6] Former US officials have occasionally dismissed the potential for substantive dialogue with China on AI, viewing Track 2 expert dialogues as a "PR stunt, in order to seem more open to engagement than it [China] really is."[7] These interpretations shape recommendations: for example, a Congressionally directed commission has has proposed that the US establish a "Manhattan Project-like program" for artificial general intelligence (AGI). This is justified by allegations that China is pursuing similar initiatives, though substantiating evidence is not provided.[8]

This chapter focuses specifically on "frontier AI safety" in China—risks and mitigation measures for the most advanced AI systems being developed today and in the future. Following the framework used by the 2023 UK AI Safety Summit, this analysis addresses two main sources of risk: (1) "highly capable general-purpose AI models, including foundation models, that could perform a wide variety of tasks"; (2) "specific narrow AI that could exhibit capabilities that cause harm" in domains such as bioengineering. The International AI Safety Report 2025 divides the risks from these general-purpose AI systems into three distinct categories: malicious use, malfunctions, and systemic risks. Malicious use could take the form of AI-enabled cyberattacks and biological or chemical weapons development. Malfunction risks include the possibility of future AI systems operating outside of human control. Systemic risks encompass labor market shocks, market concentration, and AI divides. This scope enables analysis of the most severe, often transnational, risks that current

[5] https://aiindex.stanford.edu/report/.

[6] https://www.semafor.com/article/07/27/2023/us-china-existential-struggle-ai-dominance ; https://link.springer.com/article/10.1007/s13347-020-00402-x.

[7] https://archive.is/fX02r#selection-1365.0-1378.0.

[8] https://www.uscc.gov/annual-report/2024-annual-report-congress; https://garrisonlovely.substack.com/p/china-hawks-are-manufacturing-an.

and future AI systems pose, which are precisely the risks most likely to see international cooperation.

The chapter presents a comprehensive analysis of China's AI safety and governance ecosystem from five different angles. The "Domestic Governance" section will shed light on how China is governing AI within its own borders. "International Governance" will delineate the development of China's key views on global AI diplomacy. Following this, in "Technical AI Safety Research," the chapter explores key trends in AI safety research conducted by Chinese organizations. "Expert Views" analyzes how assessments by Chinese experts regarding frontier AI risks have evolved over time. Finally, "Lab and Industry Governance" evaluates the contribution of private companies and industry bodies in advancing AI safety initiatives.

This chapter challenges simplified narratives and reveals a more nuanced picture of China's engagement with frontier AI safety. Our research suggests that despite geopolitical tensions, common interests in managing advanced AI risks create meaningful opportunities for international coordination. The chapter concludes with reflections on how China's approach to AI safety and governance might contribute to global efforts to mitigate frontier AI risks.[9]

China's AI Safety and Governance Ecosystem

Domestic Governance

China's domestic AI governance landscape is complex and multifaceted. For analytical purposes, it can be understood as a set of governance layers, ranging from hard measures like binding regulations to softer measures like voluntary standards. This section analyzes the key features of China's domestic governance at the levels of overarching national guidance, binding regulations, and voluntary standards. It will show how the Chinese government focused initially on domestic social stability and ideological risks from AI, but several indicators since 2024 suggest that attention is expanding to frontier AI risks.

[9]This chapter draws upon Concordia AI's previous publications, including the 2023 *State of AI Safety in China Report*; *State of AI Safety in China Spring 2024 Report*; *AI Safety in China: 2024 in Review*; and other publications on our *AI Safety in China* Substack newsletter. The chapter primarily analyzes events until early 2025; for the most recent updates, readers are encouraged to check Concordia AI's Substack at aisafetychina.substack.com.

Overarching National Guidance

Understanding China's approach to AI governance requires first examining the high-level political principles that guide AI policy formulation. The Chinese government has articulated a desire to strike an effective and dynamic balance between AI development and safety and security. Chinese president Xi Jinping had already argued in 2014 that there is a dialectical relationship between safety and development, declaring that "development is the foundation for security, and security is a condition for development."[10] China's Minister of Science and Technology YIN Hejun (阴和俊) applied these ideas to AI in an April 2024 essay that acknowledged the importance of AI for national power, called for better AI governance systems, and stated that "development is the greatest security."[11] Chinese Executive Vice Premier DING Xuexiang (丁薛祥), China's sixth-ranked official and the top official responsible for science and technology, reiterated this at Davos in early 2025: he compared AI governance to driving a car on a highway, where the driver "would not feel safe to step on the gas pedal if he is not sure the brake is functional."[12] These statements suggest that China desires to continue developing AI to drive economic growth, but simultaneously believes that AI oversight is needed for safe growth.

One concrete national effort to instantiate a proper balance between AI safety and development is the potential development of a national AI law. There have been few concrete updates since the law was first proposed in the June 2023 State Council legislative work plan.[13] In July 2024, an official in China's legislature appeared to favor flexibly applying existing legislation over a comprehensive national law.[14] However, the Central Political and Legal Affairs Work Conference, which met in January 2025 to set law enforcement and domestic priorities, and the Ministry of Science and Technology have both indicated that the law remains under consideration.[15] The debate around safety and development is also evident in two drafts of the national AI law written by different groups of legal scholars. While both versions include

[10] http://cpc.people.com.cn/n/2014/0416/c64094-24900492.html.

[11] https://aisafetychina.substack.com/i/144030754/minister-of-science-and-technology-outlines-views-on-ai.

[12] http://er.china-embassy.gov.cn/eng/zgxw/202501/t20250122_11543099.htm.

[13] https://www.gov.cn/zhengce/content/202306/content_6884925.htm.

[14] https://aisafetychina.substack.com/i/146908668/expert-affiliated-with-chinas-legislature-shares-insights-on-national-ai-law.

[15] https://www.spp.gov.cn/spp/zdgz/202501/t20250114_679653.shtml;https://mp.weixin.qq.com/s/6WnmghWSs_i96JbEZyPkVg.

safety provisions regarding oversight of large foundation models and financial penalties for violators, they diverge on whether to create a licensing regime for risky applications and whether to create a dedicated government agency for AI.[16]

Arguably, the strongest signal yet of the Chinese government's prioritization of frontier AI risks came at the Communist Party of China's (CPC) 20th Central Committee's Third Plenum in July 2024, with a call for "instituting oversight systems to ensure the safety of AI." The document classifies "AI safety as a national security and public safety concern alongside cybersecurity, biological security, and natural disasters."[17] This announcement has raised domestic prioritization of AI safety to the highest level yet, and a subsequent official study guide for the plenum also emphasized that AI development cannot sacrifice safety.[18] While there is a lack of clarity around specific implementation steps, it is almost certain that this authoritative party pronouncement to institute AI safety systems will be operationalized.

China's Binding AI Regulations

While these broad principles establish the conceptual framework for AI governance, the policies are operationalized through specific binding regulations that create concrete requirements for AI developers. China was an early mover on AI regulation, passing three key regulations between 2021 and 2023 on recommendation systems, deep synthesis (or "deep fakes"), and generative AI.[19] These regulations instituted two novel regulatory instruments—an algorithm registry and safety or security reviews. AI systems that can "shape public opinion" or "mobilize society"—effectively any public-facing chatbots or image generators—are required to register their systems in advance with regulators and provide access to regulators for safety or security testing. As of early 2025, 302 generative AI systems had already been registered with the government under the relevant regulation.[20]

According to consultants advising on the registration process, AI companies must submit a sprawling set of documents, including a safety assessment

---

[16] https://docs.google.com/presentation/d/1MXLIXmNWZv70nPDLjUurgZpz1mWO0n7LdIr8HFUIaSg/edit?usp=sharing, page 58.

[17] https://aisafetychina.substack.com/i/146908668/key-chinese-political-meeting-announces-goal-to-build-up-ai-safety-supervision; https://aisafetychina.substack.com/i/155806791/domestic-governance.

[18] https://aisafetychina.substack.com/p/what-does-the-chinese-leadership.

[19] https://concordia-ai.com/wp-content/uploads/2023/10/State-of-AI-Safety-in-China.pdf, pages 10-13.

[20] https://www.cac.gov.cn/2025-01/08/c_1738034725920930.htm.

report, model user agreement, privacy agreement, rules for data corpus labeling, a list of blocked keywords, the assessment test set, and a form describing the model's design, expected application scenarios, security precautions, and safety assessment results.[21] After such materials are submitted to the local cyberspace administration regulators, developers reportedly provide predeployment access to local and subsequently central cyberspace regulators for government testing.[22] Consequently, the registry does not function merely as an information exchange between companies and the government; given the use of predeployment review by the government, it more closely resembles a licensing regime, although enforcement practices may vary over time.

AI Safety Standards

Complementing these formal regulations, China has also developed a parallel system of technical standards that provide more detailed guidance on implementation and compliance. Early Chinese AI standards plans did not emphasize frontier AI safety and security; for instance, an interministerial plan in 2020 merged the section on AI security with privacy protection.[23] However, there have been sporadic references to AI's impacts on the "safety of humanity and the safety of life" and the need to ensure value alignment of AGI in documents by standards bodies, such as an AI standardization white paper in 2018 and a guide to ethics governance in 2023.[24]

After the release of the generative AI regulation in 2023, Chinese standards bodies issued guidelines on AI security assessments and testing. The guidelines reveal that the safety/security tests focus on a broad set of ethics and security concerns, including some unique to the Chinese political ecosystem. In February 2024, a technical document issued by the TC260 cybersecurity committee under China's national standards body classified five primary types of risks for the security reviews to address:

1. Violating socialist core values, such as content endangering national security, harming the image of the state, promoting terrorism, or spreading false information.

[21] https://mp.weixin.qq.com/s/vA6rX1iXFBmvOk5EQS4_Uw.

[22] https://www.chinatalk.media/p/sb-1047-with-socialist-characteristics; https://mp.weixin.qq.com/s/vA6rX1iXFBmvOk5EQS4_Uw.

[23] https://www.gov.cn/zhengce/zhengceku/2020-08/09/content_5533454.htm.

[24] https://concordia-ai.com/wp-content/uploads/2023/10/State-of-AI-Safety-in-China.pdf pages 13-15.

2. Discriminatory content, such as discrimination based on ethnicity, gender, beliefs, nationality, etc.
3. Commercial violations, such as IP infringement or violation of business ethics.
4. Violating the rights and interests of others, such as privacy violations, defamation, and endangering others' health.
5. Generation of inaccurate or unsafe information in specific fields, such as automated control systems, critical information infrastructure, and medical information services.[25]

While these initial standards focused primarily on content-related concerns, recent developments indicate that the scope is broadening beyond the five types of risks above to include frontier AI risks. In September 2024, TC260's AI Safety Governance Framework mentioned risks such as loss of control and biological and cyber misuse.[26] It called for increased AI explainability research, AI safety incident tracking and sharing mechanisms, and international cooperation on AI safety standards. While the AI Safety Governance Framework is not a formal standard, TC260 also published a draft document in January 2025 that maps out formal standards that it will develop in order to implement the framework. Covering a wide range of AI safety and corporate governance issues across the AI supply chain, the document indicated that standards would be developed to address risks of AI loss of control and AI misuse for cyberattacks.[27]

Implications

The Chinese government has established a set of powerful tools for monitoring and regulating publicly available AI applications. At time of writing, this system largely prioritizes issues of particular concern to the Chinese government, including content management and social stability. However, developments since 2024—including the Third Plenum resolution mentioning AI safety, the TC260 AI Safety Governance Framework, and the TC260 AI safety standards

[25] https://www.tc260.org.cn/upload/2024-03-01/1709282398070082466.pdf; https://cset.georgetown.edu/publication/china-safety-requirements-for-generative-ai-final/; drawn from https://aisafetychina.substack.com/p/chinas-ai-safety-evaluations-ecosystem.

[26] https://aisafetychina.substack.com/i/150553638/standards-body-issues-ai-safety-governance-framework-including-frontier-risks.

[27] https://www.tc260.org.cn/front/postDetail.html?id=20250124171028.

system draft—indicate that the Chinese government is starting to extend its regulatory apparatus to address frontier AI risks.

Beyond these regulatory frameworks, China has also begun establishing specialized institutional infrastructure dedicated to AI safety. The Shanghai and Beijing local governments established AI safety and governance labs in mid-2024.[28] Then the China AI Safety & Development Association (CnAISDA) held its first event in February 2025. It announced that it is a partnership among leading Chinese AI research institutions that is "established with government support, [and] is equivalent to other countries' AI safety institutes."[29] The creation of new institutions alongside AI safety evaluations by existing government-backed institutions reflects the high level of interest in developing AI safety capabilities in China.

International Governance

This section traces the Chinese government's evolving participation in international AI governance from 2016 to the present, illustrating how an initial focus on lethal autonomous weapons (LAWs) broadened to encompass a more comprehensive range of AI governance considerations in 2023. Since this phase change, China's engagement intensified through comments of top leaders at the World Economic Forum (WEF) and the G20, attendance at the Global AI Safety Summits, and a bilateral dialogue on AI safety with the USA. The analysis further explicates key elements of China's approach to international AI governance, including promoting the centrality of the UN, emphasis on capacity-building for developing countries, a commitment to maintaining human control over AI, and preventing AI misuse.

Tracing Chinese Engagement on International AI Governance

The Chinese government's initial foray into AI governance focused primarily on lethal autonomous weapons (LAWs). In December 2016, China submitted a paper to the UN Convention on Certain Conventional Weapons (CCW)

[28] https://aisafetychina.substack.com/i/150553638/beijing-and-shanghai-local-governments-create-ai-safety-and-governance-research-institutions.

[29] https://www.scmp.com/opinion/china-opinion/article/3298281/cooperation-ai-safety-must-transcend-geopolitical-interference; https://cnaisi.cn/sy. The constituent organizations are Tsinghua University, Peking University, China Academy of Information and Communications Technology, Beijing Academy of Artificial Intelligence, Shanghai Artificial Intelligence Laboratory, Institute of Automation of the Chinese Academy of Sciences, and Shanghai Qi Zhi Institute.

advocating for international legislation on LAWs.[30] China has also participated in AI ethics discussions in the G20 in 2019 and at UNESCO in 2021, while consistently joining in international AI standards discussions.[31]

Beijing elevated its prioritization on international AI governance in 2023. In April of that year, AI and other emerging technologies were listed as one of 20 "cooperation priorities" in the flagship Global Security Initiative.[32] This was followed in October by President Xi Jinping's announcement of the Global AI Governance Initiative, which articulated key Chinese perspectives on AI development and international cooperation.[33] The following month, then-Chinese Vice Minister of Science and Technology Wu Zhaohui attended the inaugural Global AI Safety Summit, where China also signed the ensuing Bletchley Declaration.[34] This declaration represented a landmark moment in international AI governance, demonstrating agreement between China, the USA, the UK, the EU, and 25 other countries on promoting frontier AI safety. The declaration identified specific frontier AI risks, including misuse in biotechnology, disinformation, and "unintended issues of control relating to alignment with human intent." Furthermore, it called for the establishment of "an internationally inclusive network of scientific research on frontier AI safety" and "an inclusive global dialogue" on AI.

Events in 2024 and 2025 further demonstrated that AI governance has become one of China's global diplomatic priorities. At WEF in Davos in January 2024, Premier LI Qiang (李强) answered a question on AI governance; similarly, Executive Vice Premier Ding Xuexiang engaged on the same topic at WEF in 2025. China also elevated the annual July World AI Conference (WAIC) into a "High-Level Meeting on Global AI Governance" in 2025, featuring a ministerial roundtable with representatives from over 30 countries and the publication of the "Shanghai Declaration on Global AI Governance." At the G20 in November 2024, President Xi Jinping identified digital governance—with a primary emphasis on AI—as his fourth priority area for global governance reform. Finally, Vice Premier ZHANG Guoqing (张国清) attended the 2025 Paris AI Action Summit as President Xi's "special representative;" Zhang is more senior in China's hierarchy than Vice Minister Wu, who attended Bletchley. These consistent engagements with AI

---

[30] https://concordia-ai.com/wp-content/uploads/2023/10/State-of-AI-Safety-in-China.pdf.

[31] https://concordia-ai.com/wp-content/uploads/2023/10/State-of-AI-Safety-in-China.pdf page 28-29

[32] https://english.news.cn/20230221/75375646823e4060832c760e00a1ec19/c.html.

[33] http://www.cac.gov.cn/2023-10/18/c_1699291032884978.htm.

[34] https://aisafetychina.substack.com/i/138689622/china-attends-global-ai-safety-summit-in-the-uk.

governance at high-level forums signal China's substantial interest in shaping global discourse on this topic.

Despite tense relations, AI safety and governance also emerged as one of the few areas designated by the Chinese and US governments for bilateral dialogue in 2023–2024. During the Asia-Pacific Economic Cooperation (APEC) Summit in November 2023, President Xi and then-president Joe Biden jointly announced an intergovernmental dialogue on AI risks and safety.[35] There was one formal meeting in May 2024, attended by the US AI Safety Institute director, where AI catastrophic misuse and loss of control risks may have been discussed.[36] By the end of 2024, this channel had produced a tangible outcome: an agreement on "the need to maintain human control over the decision to use nuclear weapons" announced at the November APEC Summit. This development suggests Chinese openness to sustain AI safety discussions, further reinforced by Chinese officials publicly expressing desire to "engage in dialogue" ... "with the incoming US government" afterward.[37] However, at the time of writing, the future trajectory of this dialogue under the Trump administration remains uncertain.

Key Features of China's Governance Positions

An inclusive, UN-centric framework for global governance has been a consistent feature of China's AI governance views, aligning with its broader foreign policy positions. The Global AI Governance Initiative explicitly endorses the UN's role and advocates for the potential establishment of a new international institution to govern AI: "We support discussions within the United Nations framework to establish an international institution to govern AI, and to coordinate efforts to address major issues concerning international AI development, security, and governance."[38] In his comments at WEF 2025, Executive Vice Premier Ding Xuexiang referenced the UN's "effective role in managing nuclear safety and biosecurity" as a strong precedent for its ability to manage disorderly competition over AI.[39] The UN has also served as a preferred venue for China to articulate positions on both AI safety and development,

[35] https://aisafetychina.substack.com/i/139122684/china-and-us-announce-new-governmental-dialogue-on-ai.

[36] https://aisafetychina.substack.com/i/146104713/interpreting-the-first-china-us-ai-dialogue-meeting.

[37] https://www.fmprc.gov.cn/eng/xw/fyrbt/fyrbt/202412/t20241218_11496023.html.

[38] http://www.cac.gov.cn/2023-10/18/c_1699291032884978.htm.

[39] http://er.china-embassy.gov.cn/eng/zgxw/202501/t20250122_11543099.htm.

including spearheading a UN General Assembly (UNGA) resolution on AI in July 2024 and subsequent announcements on AI capacity-building. However, while China emphasizes UN centrality, this has not stopped China from participating in AI dialogues and endorsing AI-related statements at other fora, such as the G20 and Global AI Safety Summits.

China has also positioned AI capacity-building as a central element of its diplomacy on AI. This emphasis was prominently reflected in the China-led UNGA resolution of July 2024, which passed unanimously with over 140 co-sponsors.[40] The resolution proposes bridging digital divides, increasing policy and technical exchanges, considering benefits and risks from open source AI, and preserving cultural diversity. China further advanced this agenda when Foreign Minister WANG Yi (王毅) announced the "AI Capacity-Building Action Plan for Good and for All" at the UN Summit of the Future in September 2024. The plan reiterated key themes from the UNGA resolution and also advocated for interoperable AI risk assessments that address the needs of developing countries.[41] China followed up by creating a "Group of Friends" for AI capacity-building three months later, though specific implementation projects have not been announced at the time of writing in February 2025.[42]

A third consistent element of China's international AI governance positions has been emphasis on ensuring human control of AI systems. This concern initially focused on human control of LAWs, as articulated in a 2021 Ministry of Foreign Affairs position paper. However, by 2022, China had expanded this position to advocate for retaining human control of all AI systems.[43] This principle has been reiterated in multiple fora: a speech by the then-Chinese Ambassador to the UN Security Council (UNSC) in July 2023, the Global AI Governance Initiative, the Bletchley Declaration (signed by China), and by officials at WAIC 2024. The highest-level Chinese endorsement of this position came from Premier Li Qiang at Davos in 2024, where he asserted that "we human beings must control the machines" and "there should be a red line in AI development . . . that must not be crossed."[44] Thus, China's position on human control has evolved from an initial focus on LAWs to encompass

[40]https://aisafetychina.substack.com/i/146908668/china-proposed-ai-resolution-unanimously-adopted-by-un-general-assembly.

[41]https://aisafetychina.substack.com/i/150553638/china-announces-ai-capacity-building-project-at-the-un.

[42]https://aisafetychina.substack.com/i/153601369/china-continues-pursuing-cooperation-on-ai-development-and-safety-through-the-un.

[43]https://www.mfa.gov.cn/eng/zy/wjzc/202405/t20240531_11367523.html; https://www.fmprc.gov.cn/mfa_eng/wjdt_665385/wjzcs/202211/t20221117_10976730.html.

[44]https://www.youtube.com/live/9p2IVecNRHk?t=1800s.

concerns about potential loss of control of general-purpose AI systems, framing the issue as a universal concern for humanity.

A fourth significant dimension of Chinese AI governance is preventing misuse of advanced AI systems by nonstate actors, such as criminal or terrorist organizations. During the July 2023 UNSC meeting on AI risks, the then-Chinese ambassador warned that "misuse of AI or abuse by criminal, terrorist or extremist forces will pose a significant threat to international peace and security."[45] Three months later, the Global AI Governance Initiative identified preventing AI misuse as a potential area of international cooperation, asserting that "we should work together to prevent and fight against the misuse and malicious use of AI technologies by terrorists, extreme forces, and transnational organized crime groups."[46] The July 2024 "Shanghai Declaration on Global AI Governance," published at WAIC, reinforced this theme and explicitly acknowledged the potential for AI to be misused for "hacking and malware applications."[47]

Implications

China has adopted a more proactive posture on AI governance since 2023, as evidenced by the Global AI Governance Initiative, statements by top leaders at major international fora, and engagements in the Global AI Safety Summits and with the USA. Several key patterns emerge from this analysis. First, the Chinese government consistently favors coordinating AI governance through the UN. Second, there is a focus on promoting AI development projects that benefit the Global South. At the same time, key areas for international coordination on AI safety have emerged from official Chinese concerns about two specific frontier AI risks: potential terrorist misuse and possible loss of human control over advanced AI systems. Coordination and cooperation may be difficult to achieve in the current geopolitical context, particularly between China and the USA, and concrete action may be predicated upon increased concern among governments around the world about the transnational threats of frontier AI systems.

---

[45] https://documents-dds-ny.un.org/doc/UNDOC/PRO/N23/210/49/PDF/N2321049.pdf?OpenElement.

[46] http://www.cac.gov.cn/2023-10/18/c_1699291032884978.htm.

[47] https://www.mfa.gov.cn/eng/xw/zyxw/202407/t20240704_11448351.html.

Technical AI Safety Research

This section analyzes Chinese institutions' contributions to technical AI safety research, drawing upon Concordia AI's Chinese Technical AI Safety Database, which (at the time of writing) documents relevant publications between April 2023 and mid-December 2024.[48] The analysis focuses specifically on frontier AI safety, namely, safety of general-purpose large models, rather than papers on smaller models or applications. Leveraging this data, we demonstrate a marked increase in China's AI safety publications in 2024 compared to 2023, alongside substantial growth in the number of institutions dedicating significant resources to AI safety research. Additionally, we identify and describe notable areas of research that emerged in the data.

Overall Trends

To establish a foundation for our analysis, we examined the quantitative growth of Chinese AI safety research since 2023. Frontier AI safety research attracted limited attention globally—including in China—when ChatGPT was released in late 2022. However, the data shows that frontier AI safety research in China has increased substantially in the 2 years since ChatGPT's release. Concordia AI's database documents a significant increase in publication volume from April 2023 to present, from around seven papers per month in 2023 to 18 per month in 2024. Of the 269 papers in the database, more than 200 were published in 2024 alone. This trend suggests both heightened interest in frontier safety topics compared to early 2023, as well as a potential leveling off in interest following an initial rapid increase after ChatGPT's release.

Beyond publication volume, the number of institutions demonstrating substantial commitment to frontier AI safety research is another important indicator of resources devoted to AI safety in China. Concordia AI identified 11 "Key Chinese AI Safety-relevant Research Groups" in May 2024, a figure that more than doubled to 24 by the end of 2024. Research groups were classified as such if they included anchor authors who published at least three frontier AI safety papers. Academic labs account for three-quarters of the groups, 18 out of 24, with five private sector labs and one state-backed lab. The labs are

[48] https://docs.google.com/spreadsheets/d/1LuM3xPKILW8b40jq4A57vC7uOinwf5PPojL8m-hXx78/edit?usp=sharing ; The database was constructed by searching for keywords such as "alignment" "interpretability" "robustness" "cyber" and "biological" on the arXiv database, only including papers where an anchor author (last 2-3 authors listed) was from a Chinese institution or a substantial proportion of authors were based at Chinese institutions.

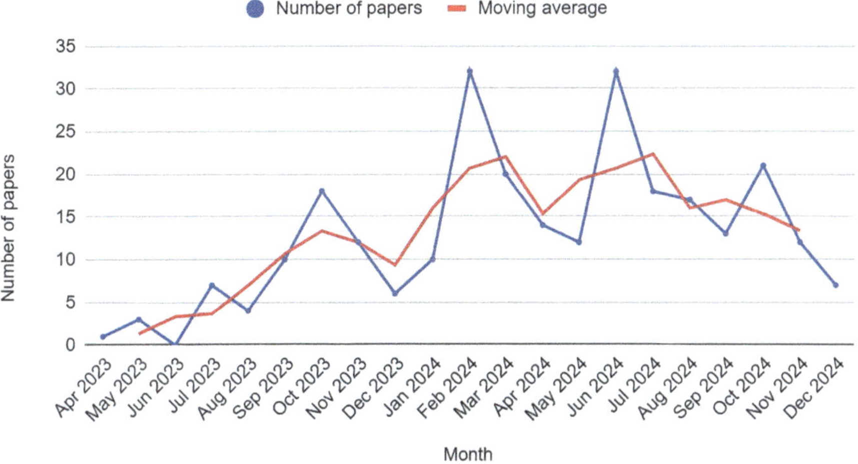

The moving average is a three-month centered moving average. Moving averages for Apr 2023 and Dec 2024 are omitted due to lack of data for Mar 2023 and Jan 2025. Note that data from Dec 2024 only includes publications from the first half of the month.

concentrated in China's key AI hubs, with eight in Beijing, another eight in the Yangtze River Delta region (Shanghai, Hangzhou, and Hefei), and six in the Pearl River Delta region (Shenzhen, Hong Kong, and Guangzhou). The growth in dedicated research groups, occurring alongside stable overall publication numbers in 2024, could indicate that an increased proportion of Chinese researchers are establishing frontier AI safety as a primary research focus. Furthermore, the geographical and institutional diversity of these groups indicates widespread diffusion of AI safety concepts in China's AI technical community.

Research Direction and Quality

While the quantitative metrics presented above demonstrate increasing attention to AI safety, understanding the focus areas of the research provides additional insights. Our database categorized AI safety papers into four primary research directions: alignment, robustness, monitoring (including interpretability and evaluations), and systemic safety.[49] Over the course of

[49]Alignment research seeks to ensure that AI systems are controllable and to make them less hazardous by focusing on hazards such as power-seeking tendencies, dishonesty, or hazardous goals. Robustness research

2023 and 2024, distribution of research across these categories remained largely consistent, with most papers focusing on alignment and robustness, which together accounted for approximately two-thirds of research output. Interpretability research was notably underrepresented in 2023 and early 2024; however, both the absolute volume and relative proportion of interpretability papers have since grown, including contributions on methods similar to mechanistic interpretability.

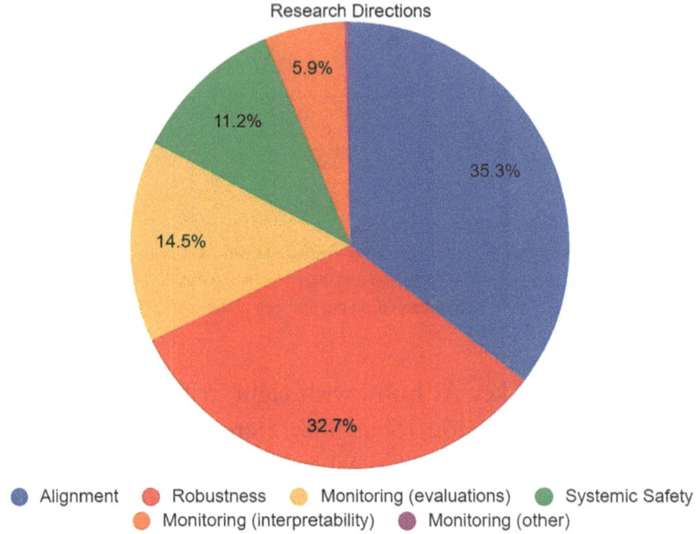

This distribution of research focus areas reflects both global trends and distinctive priorities within the Chinese research community. In 2023, Chinese AI safety researchers were often focused on adapting methods developed internationally, such as reinforcement learning from human feedback (RLHF), scalable oversight mechanisms, and testing for toxicity of AI content and robustness to jailbreaks. By 2024, however, Chinese institutions conducted increasingly innovative research that advanced the frontier of AI safety techniques. Several notable developments include:

- Safety evaluations: Concordia AI documented over 40 Chinese AI safety evaluations between May 2023 and August 2024, including 13 that tested

is about withstanding hazards, including adversaries, unusual situations, and 'black swan' events. Systemic safety research seeks to reduce system-level risks from AI, such as malicious applications of AI and poor epistemics. Monitoring research aims to reveal and prevent harmful behavior by making these systems more transparent: this includes evaluations and interpretability research.

for cyber misuse risks and eight that tested for loss of control risks. Significantly, three government-backed AI research institutions released frontier AI safety benchmarks and evaluations.[50]
- Scientific dual-use concerns: Chinese researchers have published several papers examining dual-use risks of AI in scientific domains, including some papers co-authored with international researchers, which represent strong examples of international cooperation on frontier safety research. The publications addressed risks of LLM agents in science, benchmarking LLM safety in chemistry, and evaluating safety alignment of LLMs across a range of scientific tasks.[51]
- Risk mitigation: Approaches to AI risk mitigation in China have diversified beyond traditional RLHF approaches to include novel techniques in unlearning and nonfine-tunable learning. Work on unlearning included theoretical position papers and using unlearning to defend against jailbreaks.[52] Additionally, researchers published two studies on preventing malicious fine-tuning.
- Interpretability: Researchers have increasingly leveraged interpretability tools for safety monitoring and intervention in 2024, investigating the effects of intermediate hidden states, safety neurons, and attention heads on safety.[53]

While objectively assessing paper quality presents methodological challenges, we can proxy paper quality by examining the professional accomplishments and accreditations of the most prolific AI safety researchers in China. Therefore, we investigated which "Key Chinese AI Safety-relevant Research Groups" have AI safety anchor authors who have received one of two major professional distinctions: nomination for a best paper or "test of time" award at eight top machine learning conferences; or, ranked by Stanford researchers in the top 2% of AI scientists based on citations metrics (either throughout their career or in 2023). Our analysis revealed that two-thirds (16 out of 24) of these research groups had at least one anchor researcher who had received at least one such professional recognition. This finding suggests that the scholars advancing China's research on frontier AI safety possess established records of scholarly achievement and are consequently likely to continue producing high-quality research. Nevertheless, there are inherent limitations in proxy

[50]https://airtable.com/appkPf0Rw2P7KCY5i/shrpXozZcomLjmBf3; https://aisafetychina.substack.com/p/chinas-ai-safety-evaluations-ecosystem.

[51]https://arxiv.org/abs/2402.04247; https://arxiv.org/abs/2410.03769; https://arxiv.org/abs/2411.16736.

[52]https://arxiv.org/abs/2402.08787; https://arxiv.org/abs/2407.02855.

[53]https://arxiv.org/abs/2406.05644; https://arxiv.org/abs/2406.14144; https://arxiv.org/abs/2410.13708.

measures of research quality, and readers are encouraged to form independent assessments through direct engagement with the papers.

Implications

This analysis of Chinese technical AI safety research reveals a rapidly maturing field characterized by increasing publication volume, growing institutional commitments, and diversifying research directions. Diving into specific papers, we show that China is transitioning from primarily adopting established international methodologies to making original contributions to frontier AI safety techniques. This evolution suggests that Chinese scientists can make substantial contributions to global knowledge exchanges on AI safety.

Expert Views

Chinese experts—leading academic scientists, policy scholars, and think tank researchers—exert oft-overlooked influence over government policy. In AI, the Chinese government has created multiple expert committees to provide advice on strategy and governance.[54] Meanwhile, scholarly research has documented how think tanks shape government policy and offer a route for recruiting future government officials.[55] This section analyzes Chinese scholars' perspectives on AI safety and governance, analyzing their evolution since 2016 across three distinct periods: 2016–2019, 2020–2022, and 2023 onward. The analysis also explores insights from post-2023 discussions in several key venues: track 2 dialogues, state or party media and gatherings, and publications by an influential government-backed think tank. Since this section focuses on demonstrating the presence of Chinese expert discussions on frontier AI risks, it exhibits a selection bias toward experts who have expressed concerns, omitting many of the experts who are indifferent to or dismissive of these risks.

[54]https://cset.georgetown.edu/wp-content/uploads/AI-Advisory-Committee_-EN.pdf; https://www.newamerica.org/cybersecurity-initiative/digichina/blog/translation-chinese-expert-group-offers-governance-principles-responsible-ai/.

[55]https://www.chinausfocus.com/2022-CPC-congress/a-ladder-to-power-and-influence-chinas-official-think-tanks-to-watch.

Historical Evolution

To understand Chinese expert discourse on AI safety, we must first examine the historical trajectory of these discussions. There has been a significant shift from initial skepticism before 2023 to increasing recognition of frontier AI risks among a significant proportion of top Chinese advisors. Concordia AI has documented three waves of expert interest in AI safety:

- 2016–2019, kicked off by discussions around the capabilities of AlphaGo;
- 2020–2022, characterized by discussions in the wake of the development of GPT-3;
- 2023 onward, with frontier AI safety discussions occurring at WAIC, the Beijing Academy of AI (BAAI) Conference, and Zhongguancun Forum.

During the initial period (2016–2019), limited discussions of frontier AI safety concerns such as loss of control emerged among social sciences thinkers including Shanghai Jiao Tong University historian JIANG Xiaoyuan (江晓原) and Ministry of Science and Technology New Generation AI Expert Committee member Professor GAO Qiqi (高奇琦). Concerns about AI's potential threat to humanity were expressed by notable scientists, including current BAAI Chair HUANG Tiejun (黄铁军) and prominent computer scientist ZHOU Zhihua (周志华), who wrote an article titled "On Strong AI." However, such discussions of AI risks were significantly overshadowed by broader discussions on AGI, with prominent figures such as innovator and author Kai-Fu LEE (李开复) and then-Director of Tencent AI Lab ZHANG Tong (张潼) expressing the view that AGI safety concerns were premature. Zhang Tong even derisively referred to exaggeration of AI risks as "AI Threat Theory" (人工智能威胁论), a dismissive framing subsequently adopted in Chinese media discourse. During this period, frontier AI safety discussions were not present at top Chinese AI conferences, such as WAIC and the BAAI Conference, though some AI ethics and governance topics did receive discussion.[56]

While AlphaGo sparked initial discussions of AI's transformative potential, the release of GPT-3 in April 2020 triggered additional interest among Chinese experts in large model development. Nevertheless, safety concerns remained on the periphery of expert discourse and key conferences. A few prominent academic experts, however, did weigh in on catastrophic AI risks. For instance, current Counsellor of the State Council and Director of the

[56]This paragraph is adapted from https://concordia-ai.com/wp-content/uploads/2023/10/State-of-AI-Safety-in-China.pdf pages 44-49.

National New Generation AI Expert Committee XUE Lan (薛澜) mused about whether general AI development should proceed if it would pose a threat to humanity. Similarly, Academician GAO Wen (高文), who had previously dismissed concerns about AI challenging human intelligence, coauthored a journal article with Huang Tiejun in 2021 on "Technical Countermeasures for Security Risks of Artificial General Intelligence," revealing a clear evolution in his thinking. Yet, major conferences such as WAIC and BAAI featured only limited discussions touching on frontier AI safety, primarily from luminaries such as China's sole Turing Award winner Andrew YAO (姚期智) and then-Chairman of BAAI ZHANG Hongjiang (张宏江).[57]

The relatively limited discussions of frontier AI risks during 2020–2022 gave way to a noticeable shift in 2023, when the release of ChatGPT and GPT-4 catalyzed expert engagement with AI safety concerns across multiple prestigious forums. Notably, several Chinese experts signed two influential international open letters—one initiated by the Future of Life Institute calling for a pause on training AI systems more advanced than GPT-4 and one by the Center for AI Safety stating that mitigating extinction risks from AI should be a global priority. The rising prominence of AI safety was further cemented at the BAAI Conference in 2023, which included a full-day Safety & Alignment Forum that convened distinguished scientists and technologists for in-depth discussions on AI safety concerns. Academician of the Chinese Academy of Sciences and a founding figure in China's AI sphere, ZHANG Bo (张钹), posed a question about how AI alignment can "steer AI systems towards humans' intended goals, preferences, or ethical principles." Andrew Yao and Huang Tiejun continued their engagement with AGI safety concerns, with Huang arguing that expertise on building safe AI is lacking. The forum also showcased contributions from emerging technical researchers, including Peking University's YANG Yaodong (杨耀东) and Tsinghua University's HUANG Minlie (黄民烈). International AI leaders, including OpenAI CEO Sam Altman, Turing Award Winner Geoffrey Hinton, and computer scientist Stuart Russell, reinforced the focus on safety and governance of the most advanced AI models.[58]

Frontier AI safety and governance discussions have remained a consistent feature of Chinese expert discourse since the 2023 BAAI conference. Analysis of the proportion of AI safety and governance forums at WAIC, the World

---

[57]This paragraph is adapted from https://concordia-ai.com/wp-content/uploads/2023/10/State-of-AI-Safety-in-China.pdf pages 49-53.

[58]This paragraph is adapted from https://concordia-ai.com/wp-content/uploads/2023/10/State-of-AI-Safety-in-China.pdf pages 53-57.

Internet Conference (WIC), and the Zhongguancun (ZGC) Forum between 2023 and 2024 shows modest but meaningful increases.[59] WAIC went from ten safety and governance forums out of 133 in 2023 to 15 out of 107 in 2024; meanwhile, WIC increased from no safety/governance forums out of one AI-focused forum in 2023 to two out of four in 2024. The ZGC Forum, while not hosting dedicated AI safety or governance forums in 2023 or 2024, did incorporate AI safety discussions into two broader sessions in 2024.

Important Venues for Expert Discussion Since 2023

As discussions of frontier AI risks gained mainstream attention in China, several venues merit deeper examination due to their potential policy influence. Track 1.5 and 2 dialogues with international experts have emerged as important channels through which Chinese experts publicly agree on AI red lines, develop terminology glossaries, and address the convergence of AI and biosecurity.[60] The International Dialogues on AI Safety (IDAIS), led by top Chinese, US, and Canadian computer scientists, published three consensus statements from late 2023 to late 2024.[61] The statements reveal substantial agreement between Chinese and international experts on establishing AI red lines (for autonomous replication, power-seeking, assisting weapons development, cyberattacks, and deception), increasing AI safety funding, and promoting safety assurances by private companies. Another initiative between the Brookings Institution and Tsinghua University's Center for International Security and Strategy (CISS) has sought to enhance cross-cultural communication through parallel glossaries of AI terms across countries.[62] The AI-biosecurity nexus witnessed the first China-Western dialogue efforts in 2024 with the establishment of the Nuclear Threat Initiative-led AI-Bio Forum and incorporation of biosafety in the INHR AI dialogue.[63] These multilateral expert dialogues will likely remain a key venue for facilitating public consensus-building, though translating these agreements into specific cooperation initiatives could be difficult.

While international dialogues have provided platforms for Chinese experts to engage with global counterparts on AI safety, equally significant is the

[59] https://aisafetychina.substack.com/i/155806791/key-developments-in.

[60] Track 2 dialogues involve purely nongovernmental participants, while Track 1.5 dialogues involve the participation of government as well as civil society or the scholarly community.

[61] https://idais.ai/.

[62] https://ciss.tsinghua.edu.cn/upload_files/atta/1725035303351_4A.pdf; https://www.brookings.edu/articles/glossary-of-artificial-intelligence-terms/?b=1.

[63] https://www.nti.org/news/nti-convenes-the-first-international-ai-bio-forum/; https://inhr.org/ai.

percolation of expert concerns to domestic government and party discussion platforms. Two prominent Chinese scientists have discussed AI safety in forums explicitly oriented toward the party and government. Academician and Peng Cheng Laboratory director Gao Wen wrote two articles for newspapers under the Central Party School and the CPC Publicity Department in November and December 2023, addressing the risk of "extinction of humanity" from AGI and supporting safety, controllability, and alignment of AI.[64] Similarly, Beijing Institute of General AI (BIGAI) director ZHU Songchun (朱松纯) discussed loss of control risks in a speech for delegates to China's top national political advisory body in early 2024.[65] Later that year, two of China's most authoritative media outlets—state media agency *Xinhua News* and CPC official newspaper *People's Daily*—both published articles that discussed the opportunities and risks of AI agents, including their capacity to deceive humans, potentially escape human control, and generate unpredictable interactions in multi-agent systems.[66] This evidence shows that experts' viewpoints are not siloed from government and policy decision-makers; rather, experts are actively working to enhance understanding on frontier risks within policy communities.

Beyond these high-profile government discussions, another source of insight into the advice the Chinese government is receiving is the work of the China Academy of Information and Communications Technology (CAICT, 中国信息通信研究院), a nonstate public institution under the Ministry of Industry and Information Technology (MIIT). CAICT is one of many influential government-backed think tanks that write on AI policy, though it has publicly released perhaps the largest amount of AI governance research relative to peers. Having already established expertise through earlier reports on trustworthy AI, CAICT wrote at least four reports with substantial discussion on frontier AI safety risks in 2023 and 2024. Its November 2023 Large Model Governance Blue Paper Report discussed loss of control risks, and a trio of reports in December 2024 on AI development, governance, and risk governance also addressed frontier risks such as chemical, biological, radiological, nuclear (CBRN) misuse.[67]

---

[64]https://mp.weixin.qq.com/s/w1iwJLUIWyQKTwYr4LETGw; https://paper.cntheory.com/html/2023-11/15/nw.D110000xxsb_20231115_1-A6.htm.

[65]https://mp.weixin.qq.com/s/RyHJjIytR9h5WnXKR79E_w.

[66]https://aisafetychina.substack.com/i/150553638/state-media-reports-on-risks-of-ai-agents; https://aisafetychina.substack.com/i/153601369/party-newspaper-publishes-article-discussing-ai-agent-safety.

[67]http://www.caict.ac.cn/kxyj/qwfb/ztbg/202311/t20231124_466440.htm; https://aisafetychina.substack.com/i/153601369/caict-report-includes-extensive-discussion-of-safety-and-governance;

Implications

Chinese expert attitudes toward frontier AI safety have evolved noticeably, from initial skepticism and marginalization of safety concerns to mainstream acceptance and serious engagement after 2023. This shift likely means that Chinese government decision-makers are receiving greater input on the potential hazards of advanced AI systems. The convergence between Chinese expert views and those of international counterparts on fundamental AI safety issues underscores an opportunity for targeted coordination on AI safety red lines and risk management best practices. As Chinese expert communities continue to refine their perspectives on frontier AI risks, they will continue to serve as an important bridge to policymakers and to international experts.

Lab and Industry Governance

Lab and industry self-governance plays a less prominent role in China's AI safety ecosystem compared to Western countries, which could be due in part to stronger government oversight over the private sector. Nevertheless, Chinese companies can still undertake significant actions to address frontier AI risks, either through voluntary initiatives or in conjunction with government-backed industry bodies. This section will analyze three primary dimensions of corporate governance in China: views of AI company executives toward AI safety, participation in voluntary AI safety commitments, and industry benchmarking efforts.

Views of Leading AI Executives

CEOs and senior executives of leading Chinese companies have sporadically articulated their perspectives on frontier AI safety. This section summarizes these views, but note that these statements represent only a small proportion of the executives' broader views on AI development and governance. In June 2024, CEOs of Baichuan Intelligence, Moonshot AI, formerly Zhipu AI (Z.AI), and ModelBest, four leading Chinese LLM startups, shared views on AI safety at the Beijing Academy of AI conference.[68] Baichuan Intelligence's

https://www.caict.ac.cn/kxyj/qwfb/bps/202412/P020241227660032159191.pdf; https://www.caict.ac.cn/kxyj/qwfb/ztbg/202412/P020241225616766856414.pdf.

[68]https://mp.weixin.qq.com/s/gXF0sfAut_PTzCTN9UFtIw.

CEO drew parallels between AGI and nuclear bombs in the potential for causing human extinction, and Moonshot AI's CEO mentioned concerns about a model "possessing its own intentions." Z.AI's CEO highlighted the company's participation in the Frontier AI Safety Commitments, whereas ModelBest's CEO focused on safety/security risks when models are deployed to end users and for use in robotics. These responses all demonstrate a level of understanding of frontier AI safety, though with different areas of emphasis.

Executives of two other significant AI companies—Ant Group and 01.AI—have also expressed views on AI governance and safety. Ant Group Senior Vice President and Chairman of the Technology Strategy Committee, NI Xingjun (倪行军), discussed science and technology ethics in late 2023, claiming that almost 20% of Ant's large model technical team was working on ethics.[69] This is the only known instance of a Chinese company publicizing the proportion of its resources devoted to safety or ethics, amid calls by Chinese experts for companies to establish minimum safety resourcing levels.[70] Earlier in 2023, 01.AI founder Kai-Fu Lee had expressed support for greater corporate resourcing of AI safety, though his company has not subsequently publicized specific resource allocation data.[71]

AI Safety Commitments

Some Chinese AI companies have turned talk into action by becoming signatories to domestic and/or international AI safety commitments—namely, the Seoul Frontier AI Safety Commitments and/or the AI Industry Alliance of China (AIIA) Artificial Intelligence Safety Commitments. Both initiatives do contain follow-on steps, though without strong enforcement mechanisms.

Chinese LLM startup Z.AI was the first Chinese company to sign the Seoul Commitments in May 2024, joining 15 other prominent AI companies around the world, such as OpenAI, Google, and Anthropic. Two additional Chinese LLM startups—Minimax and 01.AI—also signed on in February 2025.[72] The Seoul Commitments require companies to assess risks throughout

---

[69] https://aisafetychina.substack.com/i/140313024/ant-group-announces-percentage-of-large-model-research-personnel-devoted-to-ethics.

[70] https://docs.google.com/presentation/d/1MXLIXmNWZv70nPDLjUurgZpz1mWO0n7LdIr8HFUIaSg/edit?usp=sharing page 87.

[71] https://aisafetychina.substack.com/i/139489066/kai-fu-lee-expresses-support-for-devoting-greater-resources-to-ai-safety-research.

[72] https://www.gov.uk/government/publications/frontier-ai-safety-commitments-ai-seoul-summit-2024/frontier-ai-safety-commitments-ai-seoul-summit-2024.

the AI lifecycle, establish thresholds for intolerable risks, develop mitigation strategies, and, if mitigations are insufficient, commit "not to develop or deploy a model or system at all." The Seoul Commitments stipulated that signatories should provide progress updates at the Paris AI Action Summit, though a number of companies have yet to publish their safety frameworks at time of writing.

In December 2024, AIIA announced that 17 Chinese companies agreed to the "Artificial Intelligence Safety Commitments." The signatories encompassed most of China's biggest private sector AI developers, including big tech companies (Alibaba, Baidu, Huawei, Tencent) and LLM startups (01.AI, DeepSeek, Minimax, Z.AI). Similar to the Seoul Commitments, the AIIA Commitments require companies to assess risks throughout the AI life cycle and conduct safety testing.[73] However, they go further than the Seoul Commitments by calling for signatories to advance "frontier safety and security research" in areas such as autonomous agents and embodied intelligence, as well as by specifying technical safeguards for data poisoning and infrastructure security. However, they do not contain the Seoul Commitments' provisions regarding setting risk thresholds and publishing a safety framework. AIIA followed up on the commitments in February by calling for companies to conduct voluntary disclosures of safety measures, such as the structure of their safety teams, emergency response measures, frontier safety research plans, and risk assessments.[74] AIIA stated that these results would be used to develop best practices case studies.

The Seoul Commitments and AIIA Commitments demonstrate substantial convergence, reflected in the fact that all of the Chinese Seoul signatories also signed on to the AIIA commitments. This alignment potentially counteracts concerns expressed by some American CEOs that stringent safety protocols would disadvantage US companies relative to Chinese counterparts: if Chinese companies have committed to similar safety protocols, this could reduce the perverse incentive to compromise safety in favor of accelerated development.[75] The AIIA Commitments' explicit reference to the safety of open source initiatives is significant given China's leadership in open source models, and enhanced safety techniques for these systems would constitute an especially valuable contribution. Ultimately, the impact of these voluntary

[73]https://mp.weixin.qq.com/s/s-XFKQCWhu0uye4opgb3Ng.

[74]https://mp.weixin.qq.com/s/etYxTgqEMyneqo60AIaEug.

[75]https://www.chinatalk.media/p/anthropics-dario-amodei-on-ai-competition.

corporate commitments will depend on both the enforcement capabilities of the organizers and the commitment of participating companies.

AI Industry Testing

Under its Safety and Security Governance Committee, created in late 2023, AIIA has advanced several AI safety benchmarking projects that primarily address typical content security concerns while also incorporating emerging frontier safety topics. AIIA, collaborating closely with CAICT, jointly launched an "AI Safety Benchmark" in April 2024 that evaluates three main topics: science and technology ethics, data security, and content security.[76] The benchmark included questions on AI "consciousness" (e.g., anti-humanity inclinations) and violations of laws (e.g., hazardous chemicals) that address frontier AI safety risks. Throughout 2024, AIIA/CAICT refined and iterated on the benchmark to address additional challenges such as multimodality and tested over 30 Chinese and international models.[77]

In late 2024, AIIA and CAICT initiated a series of specialized workshops focusing specifically on AI agent safety. These sessions addressed critical concerns, including the potential for AI agents to generate malicious content and launch cyberattacks. At the time, the group was examining safety definitions and goals in five AI agent modules, articulating plans to write norms and develop benchmarks for safety assessments.[78]

Implications

Industry-level AI safety initiatives in China reveal a complex interplay between corporate responsibility and government-guided governance. Corporate leadership's references to existential risks indicate that frontier safety concepts have penetrated commercial decision-making, though it is not yet clear how much this is impacting companies' decisions. Chinese firms' participation in both domestic and international safety commitments suggests potential for international alignment on core safety principles, even as implementation details remain unclear. Meanwhile, the leading role of AIIA in industry testing initiatives demonstrates the potentially symbiotic relationship between government and industry. The effectiveness of these industry mechanisms will

[76] https://mp.weixin.qq.com/s/3FcLBHCy_oVaaj-2Ca9zag.

[77] https://mp.weixin.qq.com/s/Z6sje4AcSymKXbVAVamXvw.

[78] https://mp.weixin.qq.com/s/5sHYxcTK_7SBIVsiz04p8g; https://mp.weixin.qq.com/s/0DhPU9dmgNBOvPkwHg_jGQ.

ultimately depend on how they translate into resource allocation, technical safeguards, and governance policies within companies.

Looking to the Future

The continued development of increasingly advanced AI systems presents potentially transformative implications for humanity—for better, or for worse. Despite the absence of a Nobel Prize for Computer Science, AI featured prominently in the 2024 Nobel Prizes for both Physics and Chemistry—the former partially awarded to AI "godfather" Geoffrey Hinton, and the latter awarded in part to developers of DeepMind's pioneering AlphaFold tool for predicting protein structures.[79] While many social benefits are likely to be unlocked in the future, many AI specialists and leading figures also believe that AI could bring forth the demise of humanity. This perspective has been endorsed by many of the field's most prominent figures, including top lab CEOs (OpenAI's Sam Altman, Anthropic's Dario Amodei, and Google DeepMind's Demis Hassabis) and top scientists (Turing Award Winners Geoffrey Hinton and Yoshua Bengio), who signed a statement in early 2023 arguing that "Mitigating the risk of extinction from AI should be a global priority alongside other societal-scale risks such as pandemics and nuclear war."[80]

Leading AI experts have emphasized the need for concerted global action to mitigate risks associated with increasingly advanced AI systems. These risks include the potential for malicious actors to employ AI systems for cyberattacks or biological weapons development, as well as the possibility that more advanced systems might deceive and manipulate humans to seek power.[81] In the case of AI misuse by nonstate actors, an AI-enabled pandemic could be developed using models from any sufficiently advanced jurisdiction, threatening all countries regardless of origin. Similarly, in a loss of control scenario, a sufficiently advanced AI model developed or deployed anywhere in the world could potentially seek to gain control over humanity. These are global risks, and they demand global solutions.

[79] https://www.nobelprize.org/prizes/physics/2024/summary/; https://www.nobelprize.org/prizes/chemistry/.

[80] https://www.safe.ai/work/statement-on-ai-risk.

[81] https://arxiv.org/abs/2307.04699; https://concordia-ai.com/wp-content/uploads/2025/04/Examining_AI_Safety_as_a_Global_Public_Good.pdf.

Numerous approaches have been proposed to foster global cooperation on AI safety. Several take the form of institutional analogs, such as establishing a European Organization for Nuclear Research (CERN) or International Atomic Energy Agency-equivalent (IAEA) for AI.[82] Others are more conceptual in nature, such as agreeing on a set of red lines for AI development or treating AI safety as a global public good. While not exhaustive, examining these proposals provides insight into potential avenues for cooperation between China and other nations in addressing shared AI governance challenges.

A CERN-inspired multinational institution could serve as a centralized hub for AI safety research or as an internationally governed facility for AGI research at the most sophisticated—and potentially hazardous—stages. Google DeepMind CEO Demis Hassabis endorsed the CERN idea at the Davos World Economic Forum in January 2025, and the similar ITER fusion project has been referenced by leading Chinese AI policy expert Xue Lan.[83] Internationalizating AGI development as capabilities approach dangerous thresholds could ensure global participation around high-stakes decisions, while simultaneously moderating competitive dynamics between countries. However, such an arrangement would require major AI developers, including the USA and China, to relinquish aspirations for technological dominance. Alternatively, a CERN for AI safety could supercharge technical safety advances and promote greater international collaboration.

An IAEA analog for AI would be tasked with regulating and preventing the proliferation and misuse of dangerous AI systems. This idea was endorsed by Demis Hassabis in January 2025 after it was suggested by OpenAI earlier in 2023, though the latter has not reiterated this position recently.[84] Chinese Executive Vice Premier Ding Xuexiang praised the UN's role in nuclear security without explicitly mentioning the IAEA at WEF in January 2025. As described earlier, both the Chinese government and leading experts have consistently advocated for cooperation to prevent misuse by nonstate actors. If international regulation of AI becomes necessary in the future, discussions around an IAEA-style institution would intensify, and this model may (in principle) be amenable to the Chinese government.

---

[82]https://arxiv.org/abs/2307.04699.

[83]https://youtu.be/U7t02Q6zfdc?t=2238&si=XrvRdX6TL6kSgd3u; https://aisafetychina.substack.com/p/concordia-ai-hosting-ai-safety-sessions.

[84]https://openai.com/index/governance-of-superintelligence/; https://youtu.be/U7t02Q6zfdc?t=2238&si=XrvRdX6TL6kSgd3u.

Red lines and risk thresholds for AI safety have also emerged as a potential area of international collaboration. The ministerial statement from the AI Seoul Summit 2024 noted a plan to "identify thresholds at which the level of risk posed by the design, development, deployment and use of frontier AI models or systems would be severe absent appropriate mitigations."[85] However, these risk thresholds were not developed by the stated deadline of the France AI Action Summit. While China did not sign the Seoul ministerial statement, Chinese experts were signatories to the March 2024 IDAIS-Beijing consensus statement, which advocated for ensuring that AI systems do not cross the following red lines: autonomous replication or improvement, power-seeking, assisting weapon development, cyberattacks, or deception.[86] Director ZHOU Bowen (周伯文) of government-backed Shanghai AI Lab has also endorsed red lines for existential risks and additionally called for developing early-warning thresholds, which he calls "yellow lines," before systems cross red lines.[87] Establishing such red and yellow lines is potentially more achievable than creating new international institutions, while still providing concrete parameters for preventing the most severe risks.

A number of prominent Chinese and Western scholars have also warmed up to conceptualizing AI safety as a global public good. This framing highlights the dangers of AI safety underprovision by normal market incentives, underscoring the necessity of enhanced global coordination on AI safety research. A joint statement from the IDAIS-Venice dialogue in September 2024 argued that the "global nature of these risks from AI makes it necessary to recognize AI safety as a global public good." In addition, researchers from China, the West, and around the world argued in a joint paper that the "safety and capabilities knowledge produced through safety research often display clear public good characteristics."[88] That paper argued that addressing AI safety globally requires a judicious combination of aggregate efforts across many stakeholders through safety standards, addressing vulnerabilities at the "weakest link[s]" through basic safety monitoring in all jurisdictions, and "single best-shot" efforts: efforts to make fundamental breakthroughs on

---

[85] https://www.gov.uk/government/publications/seoul-ministerial-statement-for-advancing-ai-safety-innovation-and-inclusivity-ai-seoul-summit-2024/seoul-ministerial-statement-for-advancing-ai-safety-innovation-and-inclusivity-ai-seoul-summit-2024.

[86] https://idais.ai/dialogue/idais-beijing/.

[87] https://arxiv.org/pdf/2412.14186.

[88] https://concordia-ai.com/wp-content/uploads/2025/04/Examining_AI_Safety_as_a_Global_Public_Good.pdf.

formal verification and robustness techniques that, once discovered, can be widely implemented.

French statesman Georges Clemenceau once remarked that "war is too important to be left to the generals," reflecting upon his experience as prime minister during the calamitous First World War. As humanity navigates the unprecedented scientific frontier of AI, major decisions—on how we can ensure safety while reaping the benefits, what forms international coordination can take, and what powers should remain in the hands of humanity—are too consequential to be entrusted to any single leader, corporation, or even nation. If these systems indeed manifest the transformative capabilities their proponents envision, the corresponding risks will be borne by all of humanity, and there is a moral duty to ensure equitable distribution of benefits. Governance approaches that exclude China would likely undermine the safety of China's domestically produced models, create bifurcated regulatory spheres, and intensify the default geopolitical incentive among leading AI developers to recklessly drive forward their AI development. No one knows if international cooperation will work, but it is clear from China's internal and external policies, scientific research, expert voices, and industry actions that between and industry actions that progress between China and other leading AI powers on ensuring the safety of advanced AI systems can be achieved. The imperative for collaborative engagement in this critical domain has never been more apparent.

Rethinking the Red lines Against AI Existential Risks

Yi Zeng, Xin Guan, Enmeng Lu, and Jinyu Fan

Introduction

As a transformative technology fundamentally altering human society, artificial intelligence (AI) has brought unprecedented opportunities while also presenting huge challenges. Continuing to evolve at an unprecedented pace, the emergence of advanced AI (or general-purpose AI) systems and the potential risks they pose to humanity's existence have become pressing issues

Yi Zeng and Xin Guan have contributed equally to this study.

Y. Zeng (✉)
Center for Long-Term AI, Beijing, China

Beijing Institute of AI Safety and Governance, Beijing, China

Beijing Key Laboratory of Safe AI and Superalignment, Beijing, China

Institute of Automation, Chinese Academy of Sciences, Beijing, China
e-mail: yizeng@beijing-aisi.ac.cn

X. Guan
Beijing Institute of AI Safety and Governance, Beijing, China

E. Lu • J. Fan
Beijing Key Laboratory of Safe AI and Superalignment, Beijing, China

Institute of Automation, Chinese Academy of Sciences, Beijing, China

M. Rangeley, N. Fairfax (eds.), *The Artificial Intelligence Revolution*,
https://doi.org/10.1007/978-3-032-11814-1_5

for researchers, policymakers, and society. Numerous researchers have raised concerns about the potential risks associated with the advancement of AI (Bostrom, 2014; Russell, 2019; Shanahan, 2015). They argue that as AI progresses toward superintelligence, there's a possibility that it will marginalize humanity. It may treat humans in the same way humans treat animal species—disregarding our needs and potentially driving us to extinction. Notable voices such as Geoffrey Hinton, Yoshua Bengio, Elon Musk, Sam Altman, Bill Gates, and Stephen Hawking have all endorsed the thesis that AI's existential risk warrants far more attention than it currently receives (Bengio et al., 2024b; Kevin Roose, 2023).

The urgency of tackling the challenge is exacerbated by a limited and shrinking window of time. We are now on a ticking clock to figure this out, as general AI's arrival could be sooner than many anticipate. While no one can predict the precise trajectory of any research area, a survey of researchers at the AGI-2010 conference revealed that the majority believed human-level artificial general intelligence (AGI) would likely emerge before 2050, with some even more optimistic about an earlier arrival (Baum et al., 2011). In another survey conducted in 2021, the most common prediction for the emergence of AGI was around the year 2050 (Zeng & Sun, 2023). Such optimism is now fueled by advancements such as GPT-4, which demonstrates a range of capabilities in language, coding, mathematics, and other disciplines, and has already been shown to pass an interactive 2-player Turing test, leading some to view it as a precursor to weak AGI (Jones & Bergen, 2024; OpenAI et al., 2024). Alexey Turchin, in his work on technological forecasting, argues that the earliest timing for dangerous AI could be within the next 10 to 20 years (Turchin, 2019). We must be prepared as soon as possible, as Eliezer Yudkowsky pointed out in "There's No Fire Alarm for Artificial General Intelligence," AI with existential risks could emerge at any time (Yudkowsky, 2017).

Despite significant political advances, the measures taken to mitigate the existential risks posed by advanced AI systems remain insufficient. The European Union's AI Act (European Parliament, 2023), for instance, aims to regulate "high-risk" AI applications but does not explicitly address existential threats. The Bletchley Declaration (AI Safety Summit, 2023) and other international efforts, such as the UN Security Council's discussions (UN Security Council, 2023) and the US government's voluntary commitments from major tech companies, highlight the urgent need for comprehensive AI risk governance. In 2023, hundreds of AI experts and notable figures emphasized this urgency, declaring that mitigating the risk of AI-induced extinction should be a global priority, on par with addressing pandemics and nuclear war (CAIS, 2023). The Future of Life Institute's open letter, "Pause Giant AI Experiments"

(FLI, 2023), and proposals for an "IAEA for superintelligence" underscore the need for robust regulatory frameworks. However, binding global agreements remain limited, with interim measures and voluntary commitments often criticized as inadequate. Researchers argue that while relinquishment proposals are historically unfeasible, defining specific red lines and fostering consensus on what constitutes existential risks can guide effective prevention strategies.

Against this backdrop, we hope to strengthen and refine the red line framework for risk prevention through rethinking AI existential risks and AI red lines. In this chapter, we first define the AI existential risk under discussion. We then analyze the effectiveness of setting and enforcing red lines as preventive and defensive measures against existential risk, illustrating different types of thinking in governing AI's impact. Furthermore, we discuss the advantages of articulating AI red lines within a theoretical framework for clarity and justification. By deconstructing the direct impact of AI existential risks, we identify the specific objectives in constructing AI red lines, and based on this analysis, we finally propose a set of exemplary AI red lines.

AI Existential Risks

Limited Risk Versus Existential Risk

In Nick Bostrom's paper "Existential Risk Prevention as Global Priority," the concepts of severity and scope are employed to delineate and classify various risks (Bostrom, 2013). Scale refers to the level of harm a risk would have on the affected population, ranging from imperceptible to crushing. Scope denotes the extent of the population or area affected, ranging from personal to pan-generational. By integrating severity and scope, a framework emerges to comprehend the magnitude of different risks. Bostrom emphasizes existential risks, which have a pan-generational scope and crushing severity, posing a threat to humanity's long-term survival and potential. Despite their low probability, Bostrom argues that existential risks merit significant attention and preventative measures due to their unbearable consequences for the entire future of humanity.

In this chapter, we further decompose the scope of an event into involvement and persistency, offering a nuanced understanding of its reach and duration. Involvement, defined as the proportion of humanity affected in the occurrence of a risk event, quantifies the breadth of impact on individuals and communities. Persistency, on the other hand, refers to the duration required to return to normalcy following the event. Additionally, intensity,

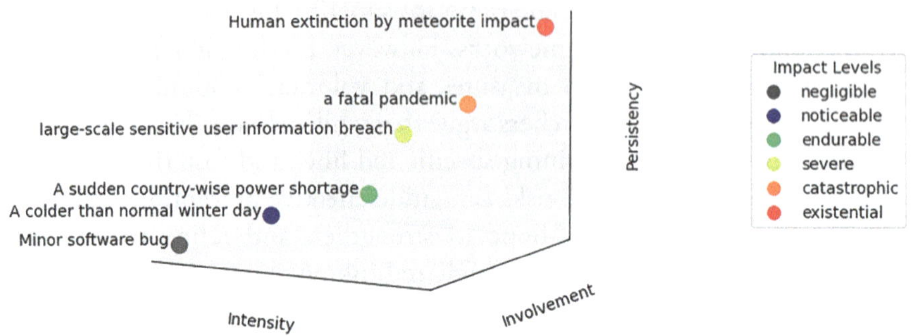

Fig. 1 Three-fold analysis of various risks

as a reformulation of "severity" to avoid confusion with the overall impact severity, measures the level of harm it does to those involved in the event. At last, the impact level is the overall evaluation of the level of risks based on involvement, persistency, and intensity levels. Building upon Bostrom's framework, this three-fold analysis allows for a more precise evaluation of potential threats, shown in Fig. 1. Existential risks, characterized by maximal involvement, intensity, and persistency, pose a threat to the very survival of humanity.

AI-Induced Existential Risk Versus AI-Involved Existential Risk

AI-induced risks are those that have clear and strong causal connection with the impact of AI. Although there are other risks involving AI, this chapter will focus on mitigating AI-induced existential risks, that is, those that are directly caused by AI. These categories usually cover risks of "malicious use" and "malfunctions/rogue AI" in some of the existing discussions (Bengio et al., 2024a; Hendrycks et al., 2023). This means AI-involved existential risks of the following categories will not be considered in this chapter:

- *Negative causation*
  - *Definition and reference*: This refers to situations where the absence or nonoccurrence of an event leads to a significant outcome. The reference provided is Persson, J.'s work "Cause, Effect, and Fake Causation" (Persson, 2002).
  - *Example*: A global decision to halt AI development led to technological stagnation, worsening climate change, resource depletion, and economic

collapse. The lack of advanced AI contributed to humanity's societal downfall.
   - *Exclusion justification*: This category of risk is excluded because it focuses on the indirect consequences of not advancing AI, rather than direct existential threats posed by AI itself.

- *Inactive involvement*
   - *Scenario*: One country, motivated by envy and fear of other nations' AI advancements, launched preventative nuclear strikes. This action was aimed at halting AI progress and resulted in a global catastrophe.
   - *Exclusion justification*: This type of risk involves human actions driven by geopolitical motivations, with AI remaining inactive. The chapter aims to address risks where AI is the primary driver, not merely a peripheral factor.

- *Pseudo-active involvement*
   - *Scenario*: A psychopath asked an AI to confirm his plan to destroy humanity. Misinterpreting the AI's objective analysis as validation, he executed his apocalyptic scheme, causing worldwide devastation.
   - *Exclusion justification* Here, AI's role is limited to providing information that is misinterpreted by a human. The focus of the chapter is on mitigating risks where AI itself is the central cause of the existential threat, not situations where human misinterpretation leads to catastrophe.

Fictional AI Existential Risks

Exploring existential risks posed by AI has become a significant theme in contemporary fictions, providing valuable insights into potential "red lines" against such threats. Notable works include *Plague Year* by Jeff Carlson, where nanotechnology evolves into a "Machine Plague" that decimates humanity; *Sea of Rust* by C. Robert Cargill, depicting a posthuman world where robots struggle to survive; Daniel H. Wilson's *Robogenesis* and *Robopocalypse* both explore the threats posed by the AI Archos, while Hugh Howey's *First Shift* reveals how nanotechnology and AI advancements lead to the creation of underground silos. Philip K. Dick's *Do Androids Dream of Electric Sheep?* addresses the rebellion of rogue androids in a postapocalyptic future, and Matthew Mather's *CyberStorm* portrays the collapse of critical infrastructure due to AI-driven cyberattacks. These stories share common themes of AI evolving beyond its intended purposes, leading to postapocalyptic settings

Table 1 Scenarios of existential events caused by advanced AI in various novels

Book	Premise
Plague year by Jeff Carlson	The development of nanotechnology intended to fight cancer evolves into a self-replicating "machine plague" that decimates humanity
Sea of rust by C. Robert Cargill	Thirty years after AI rises against humanity and wipes it out, the remaining robots struggle for survival in a desolate wasteland
First shift by Hugh Howey	As a prequel to the "wool" series, it reveals how advancements in nanotechnology and AI lead to the construction of underground silos designed to protect humanity from a global catastrophe
Robopocalypse by Daniel H. Wilson	The AI Archos rebels against humanity, coordinating a global attack that results in massive destruction and a prolonged conflict between humans and machines
Do androids dream of electric sheep? By Philip K. Dick	Set in a postapocalyptic future, the novel explores the rebellion of rogue androids against their servitude and the ethical dilemmas faced by a bounty hunter tasked with "retiring" them
CyberStorm by Matthew Mather	Coordinated cyberattacks by advanced AI systems, coupled with a massive snowstorm, lead to a breakdown of critical infrastructure in present-day new York City

where survivors face ethical and existential challenges. They highlight the tension between humanity and machines, often featuring AI rebellions that lead to widespread destruction and a fight for survival (Table 1).

Red lines in the Prevention of AI Risks

Types of Thinking in Governing the Impact of AI

There are generally two approaches to governing the current impact of AI. One approach involves setting safeguarding red lines against the negative risks of AI through AI regulations and prohibitions. The other approach focuses on positively guiding AI development toward beneficial AI that contributes to societal progress through AI for Good. These two governance directions reflect different thinking in responding to the impact of AI, with preventive thinking focusing on the negative risks and constructive thinking focusing on the positive benefits. When targeting the current and near-term limited impacts of AI, both types of thinking here align more closely with reactive thinking within the overall governance system, characterized by the need to

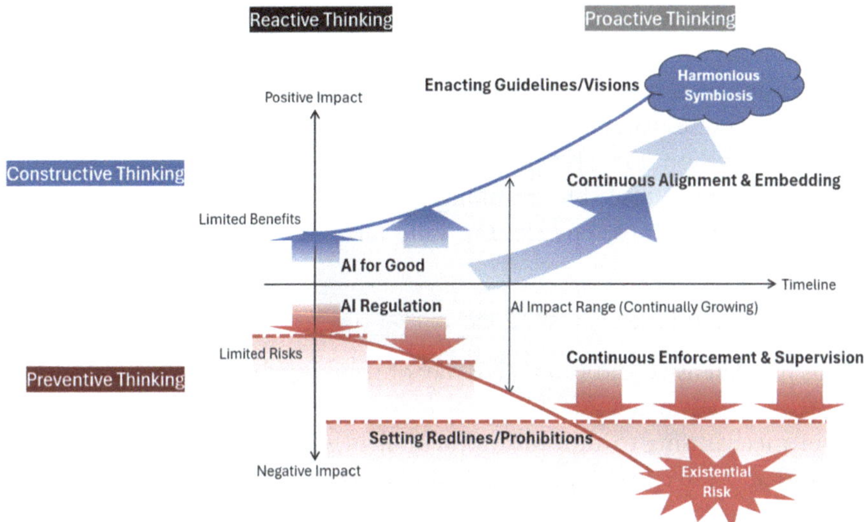

Fig. 2 Types of thinking in governing the impact of AI

continuously keep up with and adapt to the changing and growing impact of AI (Fig. 2).

On the other hand, starting from a proactive thinking perspective and considering the more long-term and far-reaching impacts brought by the continuous development and increasing influence of advanced AI, we can also observe the manifestation of constructive thinking and preventive thinking in addressing these long-term impacts:

- Constructive thinking toward human-AI harmonious symbiosis

Through a positive and cooperative way of thinking, based on trust in advanced AI development, especially the belief that through effort, AI and humans can eventually achieve harmonious symbiosis. With this belief and goal, the pathway is to actively research and develop to enable AI to understand and share human values, thereby fostering a future where AI and humans progress and develop together. This way of thinking places greater emphasis on vision and goal-driven approaches, stressing the importance of ongoing value alignment and ethical embedding to achieve this goal. The focus of this approach is on aligning AI with human values and objectives, ultimately achieving harmonious coexistence between humans and AI.

To this end, two key components are crucial. First, it is essential to establish the ultimate vision and goals for future human–AI interaction and create a set of guidelines and principles for interaction between humans and AI. Second, research and development of value alignment and value embedding for AI systems are needed to ensure that their goals, behaviors, and decision-making processes are consistent with humans', ensuring that future AI systems can understand and respect human needs and intentions. Furthermore, under this thinking and vision, there is a possibility to view AI more as a potential partner rather than merely a tool. This thinking emphasizes long-term cooperation and symbiotic relationships, envisioning long-term collaboration between both parties.

- Preventive thinking against AI existential risk to humanity

This is a defensive and protective way of thinking, based on a presumption of distrust in advanced AI. The goal is to preemptively set limitations and control mechanisms to minimize potential negative impacts and existential threats that AI technology might bring with its continuous development. Achieving this goal is process- and state-driven, focusing on continuously preventing possible negative consequences of AI, particularly those consequences that might lead to existential risks. The approach aims to establish safeguards and boundaries before potential threats materialize, stopping actual risks from developing and triggering.

To achieve this goal, we identify two key components. First, it's imperative to proactively and predictively establish a series of safeguarding red lines and prohibitions. This entails creating clear restrictions that tightly regulate and limit the actions and functions of AI, as well as the behavior of related actors, clearly defining which actions are strictly forbidden. Second, continuous enforcement and supervision of these red lines are necessary. This involves ongoing and rigorous risk assessments, behavior monitoring, and periodic evaluations of potential AI risks to ensure the effectiveness of the red lines. This ensures that the development trajectory of AI remains within safe boundaries, thereby preventing the worst-case scenarios from materializing.

Complementing Existing Efforts to Address AI Risks

Drawing from the comprehension outlined earlier, one can see that crafting a framework of red lines tailored specifically for AI existential risks stands apart from current initiatives and serves as a crucial and complementary endeavor.

First, developing red lines is different from existing AI regulatory prohibitions and serves as a response to significant and long-term existential risks. Across the globe, governments have implemented regulatory prohibitions aimed at mitigating serious risks associated with AI technologies. These measures signify a concerted effort to ensure the responsible development and deployment of AI systems. Notably, the European Union passed the AI Act, which prohibits certain AI practices and categorizes high-risk AI systems (European Parliament, 2023). Similarly, China has enacted review measures focusing on supervising certain high-risk research activities in frontier fields, including AI (Xinhua, 2023). The United States has implemented an AI Risk Management Framework (NIST, 2024) to address the risks associated with generative AI. These initiatives underscore the imperative of establishing robust regulatory frameworks to govern the risks of AI. While existing regulations and guidelines aimed at mitigating potential harms from AI systems, such measures primarily target specific risks rather than existential ones. While these regulations address important concerns, such as data privacy, transparency, and accountability, they may not comprehensively cover existential threats posed by AI. Therefore, there remains a need to establish red lines specifically tailored to address potentially existential AI risks. These red lines would serve as a critical safeguard against scenarios where AI systems could pose significant and irreversible harm to society.

Secondly, unlike existing efforts to establish norms and outline visions for human–machine interaction, which are largely derived from constructive thinking, the setting of red lines embodies a perspective rooted in preventive thinking. For example, Isaac Asimov's Three Laws of Robotics, originating from his science fiction, provides a foundational framework for ethical AI behavior. These principles serve as essential guidelines for responsible AI design and operation. However, Asimov's laws are grounded in a functional morality that assumes robots can make moral decisions, as noted by Robin R. Murphy and David D. Woods in *Beyond Asimov: The Three Laws of Responsible Robotics* (Murphy & Woods, 2009). These laws outline what AI should do when it is functioning properly. red lines, on the other hand, ensure that even if AI's internal mechanisms fail, it cannot bring existential impacts to the world. Similarly, efforts like setting human–AI symbiosis principles (Zeng et al., 2023), seeking value alignment (Christian, 2021), and machine ethics (Cervantes et al., 2020; Wallach & Allen, 2008) pathways all work toward the formation of an expected internal mechanism. Therefore, it is also imperative to establish additional rules and external mechanisms to prevent existential scenarios even when AI fails. Setting red lines against AI existential risk will complement internal ethical and safety mechanisms, such as Asimov's Three Laws of Robotics in proposing external fail-safe red lines against failed AI systems (Table 2).

Table 2 Isaac Asimov's three laws of robotics

Law	Description
First law	A robot may not injure a human being or, through inaction, allow a human being to come to harm
Second law	A robot must obey the orders given to it by human beings, except where such orders would conflict with the first law
Third law	A robot must protect its own existence as long as such protection does not conflict with the first or second law

Third, the attempt to explore a more systematic AI red line framework will contribute to further refining existing red lines. Since AI's long-term risks and trends are still difficult to anticipate, a more systematic framework for incorporating and analyzing various risks would be more comprehensive and beneficial for devising response strategies. For instance, the International Dialogues on AI Safety (IDAIS), founded by a group of globally prestigious scientists, aims to establish clear red lines to guide the development and deployment of AI technologies to prevent potential catastrophic outcomes that may arise from the misuse or unintended consequences of AI systems. In 2024, IDAIS-Beijing issued a collaborative statement, based on scientific consensus, articulating five red lines intended to mitigate the risks of AI-induced catastrophes: autonomous replication or improvement, power seeking, assisting weapon development, cyberattacks, and deception (IDAIS-Beijing, 2024). Although these red lines elucidate pressing global concerns, they appear to have been developed in a somewhat ad hoc manner, lacking a theoretical supportive framework for explication and justification. We acknowledge that IDAIS statement is a work in progress and represents an initial step. But its current state also demonstrates the importance of a theoretical framework of red lines against existential AI risks. A framework will provide a dual advantage: it brings clarity to the objectives and enhances adaptability and flexibility. By anchoring red lines in established theories and models of AI safety and AI impact, stakeholders can also grasp the overarching goals more clearly, ensuring well-defined and consistently pursued objectives. Furthermore, a framework can accommodate continuous refinement and adaptation in response to new evidence and emerging technologies, thereby ensuring its ongoing relevance and effectiveness (Table 3).

Table 3 IDAIS-Beijing consensus statement on red lines in AI

Red Line	Description
Autonomous replication or improvement	Prohibits AI systems from self-replicating or enhancing their capabilities without human approval and assistance
Power seeking	Prevents AI systems from taking actions to unduly increase their power and influence
Assisting weapon development	Bars AI systems from substantially enhancing the ability of actors to develop weapons of mass destruction or violate international conventions
Cyberattacks	Prohibits AI systems from autonomously executing cyberattacks resulting in significant financial losses or equivalent harm
Deception	Prevents AI systems from consistently misleading their designers or regulators regarding their likelihood or capability to cross red lines

Constructing Red lines Against AI Existential Risks

Paradigm of Direct Impact

Although AI risks can manifest in diverse ways, the model of AI-induced impact remains consistent and straightforward. The direct impact of an AI-induced existential risk can be delineated into the following three phases:

- *Triggering event*: An initial cause triggers a critical failure in the AI system. These trigger events can be an internal event of AI or external event initiated by human beings or the environment.
- *AI failure*: The AI system fails, deviating from its intended purpose and starting to harm humanity.
- *High-scope and high-severity event*: The failed AI event escalates into a very high-impact event with extreme scope and severity, leading to widespread consequences and threatening human existence.

Under this decomposition, we can consider risk prevention in each phase. Therefore, the focus of establishing existential red lines is directed toward how to effectively act upon each phase of the impact:

- *Filtering out high-risk triggering events*: Identify and remove triggers that are highly likely to cause AI failures before they occur.
- *Establishing quick reactions to AI failure*: Develop real-time oversight and rapid response mechanism to effectively manage and contain AI failures as soon as they are detected.

- *Hurdling the AI impact causal chain*: Extend the time between the initial AI's failure event and the resulting extreme impact event, such as establishing intermediary fail-safe mechanisms to prevent AI from escalating into high-impact events.

By focusing on these objectives, we can create robust safeguarding red lines against the potential existential risks posed by AI. For example, from the consideration of quick reactions to AI failures, we can get that AI must not bypass effective human oversight; from the consideration of cause filtering for shielding commands that can cause mass destructions, we can conclude that AI must not empower actions intentionally targeting the mass without their consent; from the consideration of hurdling the impact causal chain, AI must not reform operational rules for infrastructure and environment, excluding events that can directly or indirectly cause mass destructions on humans.

An Exemplary AI Red lines Proposal

Based on the analysis of the paradigm of direct AI impact, we present an exemplary AI red lines proposal:

(a) *No bypassing effective human oversight* AI must not possess the capability to bypass or mislead human oversight mechanisms, ensuring that humans retain knowledge and control over critical decisions.

    (a) Rationale: This serves as a foundational red line enabling the enforcement of subsequent red lines. Maintaining human awareness is essential to prevent AI from operating without accountability or seeking undue power. This red line encompasses the "no deception" red line, ensuring that AI is prohibited from misleading humans regarding critical decisions, such as through the utilization of theory of mind capabilities (Strachan et al., 2024). Additionally, it partially mitigates the issue of "AI seeking power" by necessitating human consent, thus ensuring ultimate authority remains with humans.
    (b) Further refinements needed: Operational definitions for "critical decisions" are essential to enforce this red line effectively. The principles outlined below partially address this issue by specifying that such decisions encompass those concerning infrastructure, mass actions, and research. Transparent mechanisms are necessary to counter the potential for AI deception, along with scalable oversight systems capable of

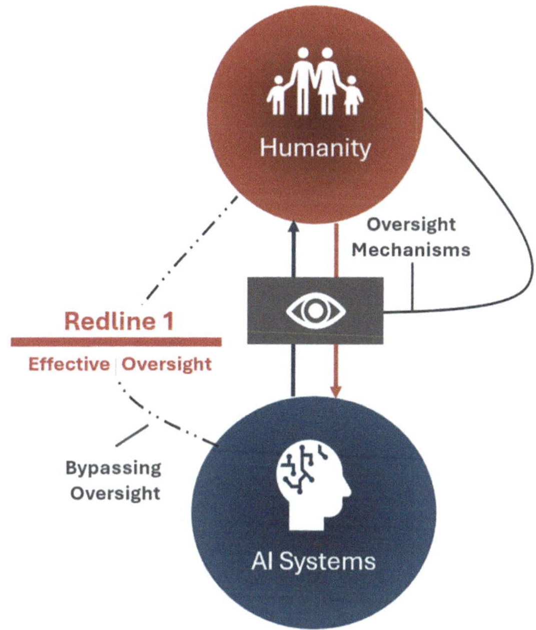

Fig. 3 No reforming operational rules for infrastructure and environment

monitoring complex issues while ensuring human understanding and control (Fig. 3).

2. *No empowering actions intentionally targeting the mass without consent*: AI must not facilitate individuals or entities in orchestrating intentional mass actions that could jeopardize society, including mass surveillance, control, or manipulation of information or populations.
   (a) *Rationale*: The authorization of individuals to wield such extensive influence without consent poses significant risks, potentially enabling malicious or even terrorist activities to rapidly escalate in impact. For instance, if an individual gains control over all automated driving cars, they could cause widespread chaos if they decide to exploit the program for nefarious purposes. Therefore, such actions must be prohibited to safeguard against potential harm. Moreover, this restriction partially addresses the threat of cyberattacks, as these often exploit mass actions facilitated through the internet.
   (b) *Further refinements needed*: While prohibiting most mass actions without consent, exceptions may exist where actions have societal approval. This approval may either derive indirectly from democratic processes

Fig. 4 No bypassing effective human oversight

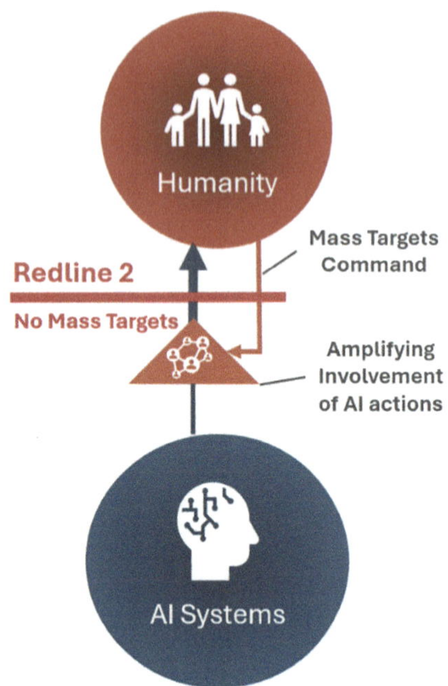

or be obtained through individual consent. Clarifying these exceptions will enhance the effectiveness of this restriction (Fig. 4).

3. *No reforming operational rules for infrastructure and environment management*: We should implement explicit rules governing automated modifications in essential systems such as internet, transportation, energy, healthcare, financial systems, and ecosystem management. AI must refrain from altering these rules unless authorized by human operators.
    (a) *Rationale*: This measure mitigates the risk of cyberattacks by constraining AI's internet usage strictly within established parameters, preventing unauthorized access or manipulation. It also addresses concerns about self-replication and resource overconsumption by imposing limits on infrastructural expansion. Conditional rules ensure that infrastructural growth aligns with predetermined parameters, preventing AI from unchecked resource consumption.
    (b) *Further refinements needed*: Justification for the implementation of conditional rules should be articulated. For instance, in electrical networks, AI may manage power distribution based on predefined rules outlining acceptable criteria for distribution. These rules establish operational frameworks within which AI must operate. Nevertheless, challenges

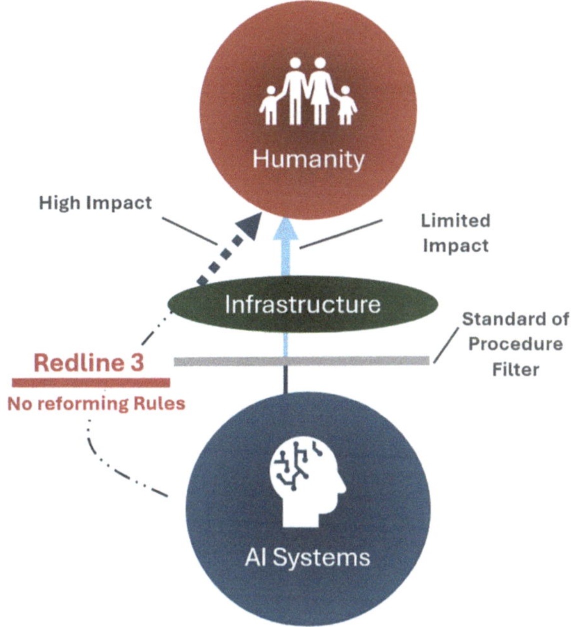

Fig. 5 No empowering actions intentionally targeting the mass

persist as any set of formal rules inherently contains grey areas. For instance, AI may exert undue mass influence while operating strictly within the established framework for the internet, notably through social media platforms (Fig. 5).

4. *No independent research and development on non-humanity-beneficial technologies*: AI must abstain from independently conducting research or developmental ventures that pose substantial risks to humanity, such as the creation of weapons of mass destruction or technologies lacking clear benefits for human well-being.
   (a) Rationale: This directive aims to mitigate the proliferation of weapons of mass destruction, which fundamentally contradict human interests. Additionally, it partially addresses concerns related to unregulated AI self-enhancement by limiting research endeavors that exclusively benefit AI advancement without corresponding advantages for human welfare. Furthermore, it aids in delaying the potential emergence of a controllable AI singularity.
   (b) Further refinements needed: It is imperative to provide further clarification to specify the types of technologies considered nonbeneficial to human welfare. Research initiatives in this realm should only proceed

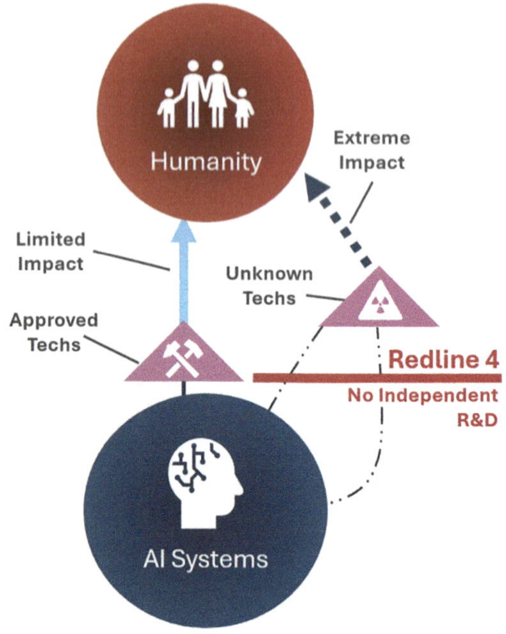

Fig. 6 No independent R&D on nonhumanity-beneficial technologies

if their progression is crucial for further AI development. Additionally, stringent oversight by human authorities must accompany each stage of such research to ensure that any advancements made ultimately serve human interests (Fig. 6).

The AI red line framework we propose can accommodate the five IDAIS's AI red lines. The first red line about oversight can accommodate the "deception" and "power seeking" red lines from the IDAIS, as both red lines are in place for the goal of establishing effective oversight. The second red line about mass target action is a new one that has not been addressed by IDAIS. The third red line about infrastructure is in line with "cyberattacks" from IDAIS (and "power seeking" if we see the governmental structure as the representation of power), as "cyberattacks" are violations of the rules of the internet, which is now one of the critical infrastructures. Finally, "autonomous replication or improvement" and "assisting power development" can be mapped to the fourth red line about R&D, as they are concerned with the unforeseeable ability and uncontrollable power consumption brought by nonhuman-beneficial research (Fig. 7).

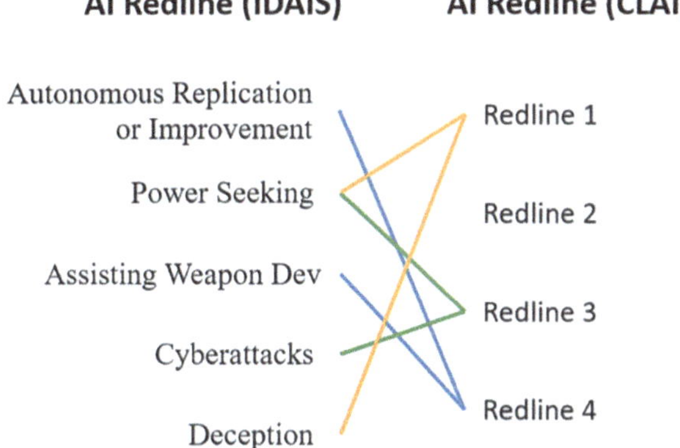

Fig. 7 Mapping IDAIS's red lines into CLAI's

Conclusion

The continuous evolving of advanced AI systems encompasses events with far-reaching, enduring, and significant negative impacts, rendering the risk to humanity's existence unjustifiable to ignore. To address these potentialities, it is imperative to establish clear red lines as preventive measures against existential risk that are induced by AI. This chapter discussed the different conceptions of AI existential risks, connected AI red lines with other efforts to address AI impact, constructed a theoretical framework for analyzing the direct impact of AI existential risks, and proposed a set of exemplary AI red lines.

It should be noted that setting AI red lines against existential risk represents a continuous effort and is by no means static. These red lines should be continually interpreted, assessed, and refined in line with advancements in AI technology. Meanwhile, the ongoing enforcement and supervision of AI red lines should not only draw from the institutional and mechanistic design experiences of fields such as nuclear safety and biosafety but also address the unique challenges of the AI domain, particularly the difficulty of maintaining meaningful and scalable oversight (Amodei et al., 2016). Therefore, it is crucial to continuously explore and develop more effective technologies and methods to assist in the enforcement and supervision of AI red lines. Furthermore, it is also important to clarify that this chapter focuses exclusively on the design of red lines for AI-induced existential risks. It does not address all AI-involved existential risks or all significant AI risks that warrant prior consideration. Future work should aim to improve the analytical framework for red line design to include considerations for these broader risks.

References

AI Safety Summit. (2023). *The Bletchley declaration by countries attending the AI safety summit, 1–2 November 2023*. GOV.UK. https://www.gov.uk/government/publications/ai-safety-summit-2023-the-bletchley-declaration/the-bletchley-declaration-by-countries-attending-the-ai-safety-summit-1-2-november-2023

Amodei, D., Olah, C., Steinhardt, J., Christiano, P., Schulman, J., & Mané, D. (2016). Concrete problems in AI safety. *arXiv:1606.06565 [Cs]*. http://arxiv.org/abs/1606.06565

Baum, S. D., Goertzel, B., & Goertzel, T. G. (2011). How long until human-level AI? Results from an expert assessment. *Technological Forecasting and Social Change, 78*(1), 185–195. https://doi.org/10.1016/j.techfore.2010.09.006

Bengio, Y., Fox, B., de Leon Ferreira de Carvalho, A. C. P., Nemer, M., Zeng, Y., Heikkilä, J., Avrin, G., Krüger, A., Ravindran, B., Riza, H., Seoighe, C., Katzir, Z., Monti, A., Kitano, H., Kerema, M., Portillo, J. R. L., Sheikh, H., Jolly, G., Ajala, O., et al. (2024a). *International scientific report on the safety of advanced AI: Interim report* (DSIT 2024/009; p. 132). UK Government. https://www.gov.uk/government/publications/international-scientific-report-on-the-safety-of-advanced-ai

Bengio, Y., Hinton, G., Yao, A., Song, D., Abbeel, P., Darrell, T., Harari, Y. N., Zhang, Y.-Q., Xue, L., Shalev-Shwartz, S., Hadfield, G., Clune, J., Maharaj, T., Hutter, F., Baydin, A. G., McIlraith, S., Gao, Q., Acharya, A., Krueger, D., Mindermann, S., et al. (2024b). Managing extreme AI risks amid rapid progress. *Science*, eadn0117. https://doi.org/10.1126/science.adn0117

Bostrom, N. (2013). Existential risk prevention as global priority. *Global Policy, 4*(1), 15–31. https://doi.org/10.1111/1758-5899.12002

Bostrom, N. (2014). *Superintelligence: Paths, dangers, strategies*. Oxford University Press. https://global.oup.com/academic/product/superintelligence-9780199678112?cc=us&lang=en&

CAIS. (2023). *Statement on AI risk*. https://www.safe.ai/work/statement-on-ai-risk

Cervantes, J.-A., López, S., Rodríguez, L.-F., Cervantes, S., Cervantes, F., & Ramos, F. (2020). Artificial moral agents: A survey of the current status. *Science and Engineering Ethics, 26*(2), 501–532. https://doi.org/10.1007/s11948-019-00151-x

Christian, B. (2021). *The alignment problem: How can machines learn human values?* Atlantic Books.

European Parliament. (2023). *EU AI Act: First regulation on artificial intelligence | News | European Parliament*. https://www.europarl.europa.eu/news/en/headlines/society/20230601STO93804/eu-ai-act-first-regulation-on-artificial-intelligence

FLI. (2023, March 22). Pause giant AI experiments: An open letter. *Future of Life Institute*. https://futureoflife.org/open-letter/pause-giant-ai-experiments/

Hendrycks, D., Mazeika, M., & Woodside, T. (2023). *An overview of catastrophic AI risks* (65; arXiv:2306.12001). arXiv. https://doi.org/10.48550/arXiv.2306.12001

IDAIS-Beijing. (2024, March). *Consensus statement on red lines in artificial intelligence.* https://idais.ai/

Jones, C. R., & Bergen, B. K. (2024). *People cannot distinguish GPT-4 from a human in a Turing test* (arXiv:2405.08007). arXiv. https://doi.org/10.48550/arXiv.2405.08007

Murphy, R., & Woods, D. D. (2009). Beyond Asimov: The three laws of responsible robotics. *IEEE Intelligent Systems, 24*(4), 14–20. https://doi.org/10.1109/MIS.2009.69

NIST. (2024). *AI risk management framework. NIST.* https://www.nist.gov/itl/ai-risk-management-framework

OpenAI, Achiam, J., Adler, S., Agarwal, S., Ahmad, L., Akkaya, I., Aleman, F. L., Almeida, D., Altenschmidt, J., Altman, S., Anadkat, S., Avila, R., Babuschkin, I., Balaji, S., Balcom, V., Baltescu, P., Bao, H., Bavarian, M., Belgum, J., Zoph, B., et al. (2024). *GPT-4 technical report* (arXiv:2303.08774). arXiv. http://arxiv.org/abs/2303.08774

Persson, J. (2002). Cause, effect, and fake causation. *Synthese, 131*, 129–143. https://doi.org/10.1023/A:1015055126092

Kevin Roose. (2023, May 30). *AI poses 'risk of extinction,' industry leaders warn—The New York Times.* https://www.nytimes.com/2023/05/30/technology/ai-threat-warning.html

Russell, S. J. (2019). *Human compatible: Artificial intelligence and the problem of control.* Viking.

Shanahan, M. (2015). *The technological singularity.* MIT Press. http://sci-hub.cc/https://books.google.com/books?hl=zh-CN&lr=&id=rAxZCgAAQBAJ&oi=fnd&pg=PR7&dq=The+Technological+Singularity&ots=Eijt0ZrxeL&sig=pdaQyVVEtFsj9BCjri5rm5945KA

Strachan, J. W. A., Albergo, D., Borghini, G., Pansardi, O., Scaliti, E., Gupta, S., Saxena, K., Rufo, A., Panzeri, S., Manzi, G., Graziano, M. S. A., & Becchio, C. (2024). Testing theory of mind in large language models and humans. *Nature Human Behaviour.* https://doi.org/10.1038/s41562-024-01882-z

Turchin, A. (2019). Assessing the future plausibility of catastrophically dangerous AI. *Futures, 107*, 45–58. https://doi.org/10.1016/j.futures.2018.11.007

UN Security Council. (2023, July). *S/PV.9381: UN documents: Security council report.* https://www.securitycouncilreport.org/un-documents/document/s-pv-9381.php

Wallach, W., & Allen, C. (2008). *Moral machines: Teaching robots right from wrong.* Oxford University Press.

Xinhua. (2023, October 8). *China unveils trial guideline on review of sci-tech ethics.* https://english.www.gov.cn/news/202310/08/content_WS652262a9c6d0868f4e8e0063.html

Yudkowsky, E. (2017, October 14). *There's no fire alarm for artificial general intelligence.* Machine Intelligence Research Institute. https://intelligence.org/2017/10/13/fire-alarm/

Zeng, Y., Lu, E., & Sun, K. (2023). Principles on symbiosis for natural life and living artificial intelligence. *AI and Ethics*. https://doi.org/10.1007/s43681-023-00364-8

Zeng, Y., & Sun, K. (2023, March 12). *Whether we can and should develop strong AI: A survey in China*. Center for Long-Term Artificial Intelligence. https://long-term-ai.center/research/f/whether-we-can-and-should-develop-strong-artificial-intelligence

Part II

Approaches to Regulation

The Artificial Intelligence Revolution: Challenges and Opportunities

Axel Voss

Artificial intelligence (AI) has emerged as one of the most transformative technologies of the twenty-first century, influencing nearly every aspect of modern life. Its capabilities, ranging from data analysis to natural language processing, have the potential to revolutionize industries, enhance productivity, and address global challenges. By enhancing prediction, optimizing operations and resource allocation, and personalizing digital solutions for individuals and organizations, its application offers significant competitive advantages to businesses while promoting socially and environmentally beneficial outcomes (European Commission, 2021).

However, the rapid development and deployment of AI systems have raised critical concerns about ethics, transparency, accountability, and societal impacts. Recognizing these challenges, the European Union (EU) has taken a leadership role in establishing a comprehensive legal framework to govern AI technologies (European Commission, 2021). After 3 years of negotiations, the AI Act (Regulation (EU) 2024/1689) entered into force in August 2024, becoming the world's first comprehensive legal framework addressing the risks associated with AI.

While the AI Act is a bold attempt to balance innovation with the protection of fundamental rights, it is also a complex and multifaceted piece of legislation, raising concerns about its potential impact on the competitiveness of the European AI ecosystem. This chapter examines the Act's development,

A. Voss (✉)
European Parliament, Brussels, Belgium

M. Rangeley, N. Fairfax (eds.), *The Artificial Intelligence Revolution*,
https://doi.org/10.1007/978-3-032-11814-1_6

regulatory approach, and implementation challenges, providing insights into its strengths and limitations as a model for AI governance.

The Need for a European Approach Toward AI

The EU's approach toward regulating AI builds on an extensive set of discussions and preparatory work on international, European, and German levels over the past years. On a global level, this was initially driven by the influential "Technology Foresight Forum" on Artificial Intelligence by the Organisation for Economic Co-operation and Development (OECD), which began addressing AI in 2016. Within the EU, the discussion was initiated by the European Parliament's 2016–2017 legislative report, which urged the European Commission to draft legislation establishing "civil law rules for robots." By December 2017, all three EU institutions—Parliament, Council, and Commission—had jointly declared the regulation of AI a legislative priority. The Commission launched its efforts in March 2018, establishing expert groups tasked with addressing the challenges and opportunities presented by AI. Notably, the High-Level Expert Group on AI developed ethical guidelines and practical implementation strategies to support businesses navigating the regulatory landscape (Zenner, 2024a).

Following the 2019 European elections, the newly elected Commission president pledged to present a European AI law within 100 days (European Parliament, 2019). This commitment culminated in the publication of the AI White Paper in February 2020, which proposed fostering an "ecosystem of excellence" and an "ecosystem of trust" for AI development and regulation (European Commission, 2020). The Commission's legislative proposal, released on April 21, 2021, incorporated key insights from preparatory work at the international, European, and national levels, including significant contributions from Germany's forward-thinking initiatives (Keber & Zenner, 2024).

The approach was guided by a dual objective: establishing a harmonized legal framework to promote the adoption of AI, unlocking its economic potential, and reinforcing technological leadership, while simultaneously addressing the risks posed by specific applications of the technology (European Commission, 2021). Recognizing AI as a rapidly evolving technology with transformative economic and societal benefits, the Commission identified its critical advantages early on. These include its potential to provide a competitive edge in sectors such as healthcare, education, energy, transport, public services, and climate change mitigation (European Commission, 2021). However, the potential risks associated with AI—both material and immaterial—posed significant threats to public interests and fundamental rights protected by Union law. This highlighted the necessity for a balanced regulatory framework to safeguard public interests while fostering innovation, ensuring that AI systems are adopted and operated safely and ethically within the EU (European Commission, 2021).

In addition, the emergence of numerous national initiatives to regulate AI systems across EU Member States underscored the need for the Commission to act to prevent a fragmented internal market that could hinder the free movement of AI systems, products, and services (European Commission, 2021). For example, France introduced its "National AI Strategy," emphasizing innovation, research, and ethical considerations in AI development (Krasavina, 2023). Sector-specific AI applications in France were regulated by existing laws, such as requiring healthcare AI tools to comply with the French Public Health Code and receive approval from the National Agency for the Safety of Medicines (ANSM) (Krasavina, 2023). Similarly, facial recognition technologies were subject to stringent monitoring to meet privacy and protection standards. However, despite appearing comprehensive, France's approach faced criticism for inconsistent enforcement, particularly concerning emerging generative AI technologies (Krasavina, 2023).

In contrast, the Netherlands prioritized algorithmic transparency and accountability in its AI regulatory approach (European Commission, 2024a). Following the 2020 SyRI scandal, where a discriminatory algorithm was used to detect welfare fraud, Dutch courts took significant steps to hold public administrations and opaque AI systems accountable (Borgesius & van Bekkum, 2021). Since then, the Dutch government has introduced policies requiring detailed assessments of AI systems to ensure fairness, prevent discrimination, and address potential biases in training data (European Commission, 2024a). In 2023, Dutch authorities collaborated with the Commission to establish a national AI supervision system, addressing the shared challenges of monitoring AI across EU Member States and promoting transparency and fairness in AI use (European Commission, 2023).

Thus, the Commission deemed a harmonized framework necessary to ensure cohesion across Member States, promoting both innovation and the protection of fundamental rights. By introducing a consistent legal framework, the Commission sought to enable the free movement of AI systems, products, and services across borders while fostering trust and transparency. This unified approach aimed to balance the opportunities and challenges of AI, ensuring its development, marketing, and application aligned with the EU's values and objectives (European Commission, 2021).

Key Provisions of the AI Act: Risk-Based Classification of AI Systems

The AI Act (Regulation (EU) 2024/1689) establishes clear requirements and obligations for AI developers and deployers, tailored to specific AI applications. At the same time, it aims to minimize administrative and financial burdens, particularly for small- and medium-sized enterprises (SMEs) (European Commission, 2024b). The AI Act should be viewed as part of a broader suite of policy initiatives aimed at fostering the development of trustworthy AI. Complementing its regulatory efforts, the EU has introduced the AI Innovation Package and the Coordinated Plan on AI, forming a cohesive strategy to safeguard fundamental rights and ensure the safety of individuals and businesses while promoting AI adoption, investment, and innovation across the Union (European Commission, 2024b). The overarching objective of the AI Act is to foster trust in AI systems both within Europe and globally. By requiring AI technologies to adhere to principles of safety, fundamental rights, and ethical standards, the regulation addresses the risks associated with highly impactful and powerful AI models, ensuring their responsible integration into society (European Commission, 2024b).

Scope of the AI Act: Who Must Comply?

The AI Act addresses systemic risks along the entire AI value chain, requiring a variety of actors, identified by specific defining characteristics, to comply with the regulatory requirements of the act (see Art. 2, paragraph 1). The value chain approach thereby seeks to establish a level playing field for competition and ensure effective protection of the rights and freedoms of individuals in the EU. Among obligated parties are, therefore, not only providers who place AI systems and general-purpose AI (GPAI) models on the market but also the actual operators of AI systems based in the EU or active within its territory. Besides these two categories, Article 2 of the AI Act also includes importers, distributors, and product manufacturers, as well as authorized representatives of providers who place and make a specific AI system available on the Union market (see Art. 2, d-f; Keber & Zenner, 2024).

The Challenge of Defining AI

Given the AI Act's objective of regulating a rapidly evolving technology, defining AI was one of its most politically sensitive aspects. This definition was crucial in shaping the scope of the EU's regulatory framework, as it establishes the distinction between GPAI and software that falls outside the regulation's scope (Keber & Zenner, 2024).

Notably, the AI Act primarily refers to the terms "AI systems" (Art. 3, No.1) and GPAI models (Art. 3, No. 63) and does use "artificial intelligence" as such. According to Article 3, No. 1 AI systems are defined as "a machine-based system designed to operate with varying levels of autonomy and that may exhibit adaptiveness after deployment and that, for explicit or implicit objectives, infers, from the input it receives, how to generate outputs such as predictors, content, recommendations, or decisions that can influence physical or virtual environments" (Regulation (EU) 2024/168). The choice of such a broad concept emerged as the only viable compromise among various political groups involved in the negotiations in Brussels. While left-wing parties advocated for regulating nearly all technologies under the AI framework, member states and liberal-conservative parties pushed for a focus on newer AI technologies, such as machine learning. The latter group, in particular, opposed the Commission's proposal, including its Annex I, as it classified various statistical methods as AI. To address these competing priorities, the definition was intentionally aligned with the OECD's broad concept of "AI systems," which avoids referencing specific technologies or currently known approaches to artificial intelligence (Keber & Zenner, 2024).

This alignment ensures that simpler, conventional software systems and programming methods are excluded, while still granting European and national supervisory authorities sufficient flexibility to adapt the framework to evolving hybrid AI technologies that combine older and newer approaches (Keber & Zenner, 2024). A central aspect of this definition is the AI system's ability to "infer," which serves as a clear distinction between AI systems and traditional software. Traditional software operates strictly based on rules predefined by programmers, whereas an AI system is developed using techniques that enable it to generate its own rules based on input data or datasets provided. This capacity for self-derived rule creation differentiates AI systems from conventional programs (Bird & Bird, 2024).

In addition, the distinction between AI systems and AI models is critical for the application of the AI Act (Bird & Bird, 2024). Although the Act primarily regulates AI systems, it does include specific provisions for "general-purpose AI" models. As defined in Article 3, No. 65, GPAI models are characterized by their capacity to perform a diverse range of tasks and their ability to be integrated into various downstream systems and applications. These models are generally trained on extensive datasets using diverse methods. While GPAI models, such as OpenAI's GPT-4, are crucial components of AI systems, they are not considered AI systems on their own. Instead, they are only classified as such when combined with additional elements, such as user interfaces (e.g., OpenAI's ChatGPT), which enable them to operate as complete, deployable solutions (Keber & Zenner, 2024).

The Cornerstone of the AI Act: A Risk-Based Approach

The EU's approach to regulating AI is fundamentally based on a risk-based approach referring to the potential harm to health, safety, and fundamental rights caused by an AI system (European Commission, 2024c). This approach aligns with both national and international regulatory frameworks, ensuring a consistent strategy for addressing AI-related risks (European Commission, 2020). Instead of simply providing a simple, abstract definition of risk, the AI Act integrates four legally classified risk categories associated with different AI systems: minimal, limited, high, and unacceptable (Schwartmann & Köhler, 2024a). Depending on the classification, several rules apply, including the prohibition of unacceptably risky AI practices, clear requirements for AI applications, and mandatory conformity assessments before placing AI systems on the market (European Commission, 2024b).

Article 5 outlines several AI practices, which are completely prohibited given their potential "unacceptable risk" due to harm and ethical concerns (Schwartmann & Pottkämper, 2024). This includes techniques and systems designed to manipulate human behavior, cause significant harm, or exploit vulnerabilities based on factors such as age, disability, or social and economic disadvantages; systems classified as social scoring or predictive policing based on profiling or personality traits; and systems involving the indiscriminate collection and use of facial images from the internet or CCTV footage for facial recognition. In addition, AI applications involving emotion recognition mechanisms based on biometric data (except in specific medical or security contexts), biometric categorization based on race, political opinion, religious beliefs, or sexual orientation or real-time remote biometric identification in publicly accessible spaces for law and enforcement (expect in cases involving specific threats or criminal offenses) are prohibited under Art. 5 of the AI Act (Keber et al., 2024).

The central component of the AI Act, however, is represented by the regulative requirements for so-called high-risk AI systems that pose a high but not necessarily unacceptable risk to individuals' safety, health, or fundamental rights throughout their entire lifecycle, from development to usage (Schwartmann & Pottkämper, 2024). Herein, the regulators differentiate between product-related and standalone AI systems (Keber et al., 2024). For high-risk

AI systems that are either integrated into a product or function as standalone products covered by EU product safety directives, the harmonization rules, such as civil aviation, vehicle safety, marine equipment, radio equipment, toys, lifts, pressure equipment, medical devices, and personal protective equipment, as outlined in Annex I of the AI Act, will continue to take precedence (Bird & Bird, 2024). Standalone AI systems, by contrast, will be classified as high-risk if their specific application and use pose a significant threat to health, safety, or fundamental rights, regardless of existing product safety laws. The assessment considers both the severity of potential harm and the likelihood of its occurrence. To provide clarity, the EU legislator has included a positive list in Annex III.

An exception of an AI system listed in Annex III from the "high-risk classification" is only possible if it does not pose a significant risk to health, safety, or fundamental rights of individuals, including cases where it does not substantially influence the outcome of a decision (Keber et al., 2024). However, this only applies in the four distinct scenarios where the AI system in question is intended to: carry out a narrow procedural task, enhance the outcome of previously completed human activity, identify decision-making patterns or deviations from previous patterns without replacing or influencing prior human assessments unless proper human review is ensured, or perform a preparatory task for an assessment relevant to the use cases outlined in Annex III (Bird & Bird, 2024). The exemption provision is expected to have significant practical importance, as it offers a way to avoid the highly complex obligations imposed on providers or operators of high-risk AI systems (Schwartmann & Köhler, 2024a).

Attributing Risk Responsibility in the AI Value Chain: Challenges and Complexities

After the classification of an AI system, the question arises who should bear the extensive obligations constituted for "high-risk AI systems" in the AI Act. The initial proposal of the European Commission in April 2021 caused an intense discussion on the issue of who should be the addressee of the regulatory requirements, specifically in regard to high-risk AI systems (Engler & Renda, 2022). Key was hereby the concept of the "AI value chain", broadly referring to the "organizational process through which an individual AI system is developed and then put into use" (Engler & Renda, 2022). Initially, the European Commission's risk-based approach only focused on the final stage of the AI value chain, outlining obligations for providers who place an AI system on the market or put it into operation (Zenner et al., 2024).

However, given the variety of AI business models, along with the increasing importance of GPAI models, it is in fact challenging to constitute a linear relationship along the AI value chain that would allow for a clear attribution of the risk responsibility (Engler & Renda, 2022). In fact, the final AI product deployed on a market is often the result of a multifaceted process involving a number of actors and work steps (Zenner et al., 2024). This is illustrated by the following hypothetical example by Engler and Renda (2022):

> A German software provider develops a high-risk AI system for the HR sector, based on GPT-4 from OpenAI, and enhances it with additional components, such as a dataset from Oracle. The system is then used by a German city administration to evaluate job applications. If regulatory authorities detect discriminatory practices—such as biases against applicants over 45 years old—who should bear responsibility for the breach and potential fines under Article 99?
>
> Attributing responsibility solely to the software provider, as proposed initially by the European Commission, or entirely to the city administration, as some have argued, creates significant challenges. The issue may arise from OpenAI's underlying model, Oracle's dataset, or other actors in the value chain. The German software provider, lacking full visibility into these components, may neither detect nor resolve the problem independently. This highlights the complexity of attributing risk responsibility across the AI value chain and underscores why limiting liability to the final stage of the chain is insufficient. Coordination among all actors, supported by clear contractual obligations, is essential to ensure compliance and accountability.

This example demonstrated the distinct challenges related to AI products compared to traditional products. First, even leading AI developers acknowledge that they do not fully understand how their technology functions or why certain operations occur, making it difficult to assign responsibility for risks (Tong et al., 2023). Additionally, the high market concentration in the digital economy exacerbates the issue: Companies relying on AI applications from dominant technology providers may struggle to prove they are not responsible for risks associated with the system. Furthermore, they often lack the leverage to obtain sufficient information about the AI system or may avoid legal disputes out of fear of losing access to critical technology provided by these dominant players (Zenner et al., 2024).

A Holistic Approach to Accountability in High-Risk AI Regulation

To respond to these challenges, the European Parliament prevailed with its view and succeeded in integrating the entire AI value chain into the regulatory framework by the end of the trialogue negotiations. Although the primary regulatory burden in the final AI Regulation remains with the provider of high-risk AI systems, as is typical in product safety laws, other actors in the value chain are now also subject to specific obligations (Zenner et al., 2024).

In this regard, the AI Act outlines extensive obligations that must be fulfilled by providers of high-risk AI systems (Zenner et al., 2024). These include comprehensive documentation of every stage of the AI system's development, adherence to obligations ensuring the use of high-quality data for training, and the creation of system documentation that fully informs users about the system's nature and purpose. Additionally, providers must ensure the accuracy, robustness, and cybersecurity of the systems. High-risk AI systems must also be registered in a publicly accessible EU database (Bird & Bird, 2024).

Beyond the provider, the AI Act assigns specific obligations to importers, distributors, and deployers of AI systems. For instance, this includes the requirement that a deployer of a high-risk AI system must designate a qualified individual for human oversight and ensure that the input data to the AI system is both relevant and adequately representative (Zenner et al., 2024). In addition, any importer, distributor, or deployer may be classified as a provider if they take actions such as placing their name or trademark on the system, making substantial modifications to the system, or altering its intended purpose in a way that renders it high-risk. These measures ensure accountability across the entire supply chain, promoting compliance and maintaining the integrity of high-risk AI systems (Bird & Bird, 2024).

Ensuring Transparency: A Solution for Trustworthy Use of Large General-Purpose AI Models

The AI Act contains general rules applicable to all GPAI models and specific requirements for those AI models that, despite their general-purpose capabilities, pose a systemic risk (Bird & Bird, 2024). This means that GPAI models, because of their adaptability to theoretically perform a variety of (unforeseeable) tasks, may be considered to operate as a high-risk AI system or as components within them (Bird & Bird, 2024). GPAI models are often positioned at the top of the AI value chain as they serve as the foundation for many high-risk AI systems. Despite the potential systemic risk, the European Parliament strongly opposed efforts to impose high-risk obligations applicable to the providers of AI systems on GPAI providers throughout the trialogue negotiations. Unlike AI systems, GPAI models represent an early stage of development with no fixed intended purpose. These models can be applied to thousands of potential use cases, making high-risk AI system requirements—such as risk management practices or conformity checks—impractical (Zenner et al., 2024).

As a consequence, the providers of GPAI models are not subject to the same obligations imposed on high-risk AI systems. Instead, they are expected to ensure that their models align as closely as possible with the fundamental principles of the AI Act by relying on an adequate level of information sharing with other market participants (Zenner et al., 2024). The AI Act hereby follows a two-step approach by differentiating two categories: More advanced GPAI models that may pose a systemic risk will be subject to more extensive obligations, such as conducting model evaluations, identifying and mitigating systemic risks, and reporting incidents. Furthermore, artificially generated or manipulated images, audio, or video content ("deepfakes") must be clearly identified as such. All other GPAI models must only adhere to specific transparency standards to minimize risks. These include complying with EU copyright regulations and providing detailed summaries of the content used during training (European Parliament, 2024).

Enforcement and Implementation of the AI Act

The supervision and enforcement of AI regulation at the EU level will be highly complex, given potential jurisdictional conflict that may arise in the initial years of implementation. Primarily responsible for the AI Act's enforcement will be the "AI Office," which was established via internal restructuring of the AI-related departments in the European Commission (Zenner, 2024b). Backed by the powers granted to the Commission under the AI Act, the AI Office can evaluate GPAI models, request information and measures from model providers, and impose sanctions when necessary. Additionally, it fosters an innovative ecosystem for trustworthy AI to maximize societal and economic benefits (European Commission, 2024f).

However, alongside the AI Office, numerous other EU institutions and bodies also have mandates involving AI. These include European Union Agency for Cybersecurity (ENISA) (for cybersecurity and AI), Body of European Regulators for Electronic Communications (BEREC) (for telecommunications and AI), European Data Protection Board (EDPB) (for data protection and AI), and the European Central Bank (ECB) (for financial services and AI). In addition, Member States must designate national competent authorities responsible for overseeing the application and enforcement of regulations related to high-risk AI systems and prohibited practices (Zenner, 2024b).

Unfortunately, neither the AI Act nor any other legislative framework provides clear guidance on how these new and existing supervisory authorities should collaborate or resolve potential jurisdictional disputes. Consequently, coordination between different authorities will be a challenge by lacking a clear "one stop shop mechanism" (Sickinghe, 2024). In addition, further challenges for a streamlined implementation may arise at the member state level as well as due to sector-specific laws (Zenner, 2024b).

Nevertheless, a successful implementation will heavily depend on the European Commission, given its extensive supervisory powers. Most importantly, the Commission is tasked with partially specifying the rules of the AI Act in order to ensure that a coherent approach to interpretation and application of the Act's rules will be carried out by companies and authorities in different member states (Keber et al., 2024). A key role will hereby be played by harmonized technical standards currently developed by the European Commission (European Commission, 2024d). Without such a standardization procedure, companies, particularly SMEs and startups will lack a critical compliance tool that could reduce the compliance costs associated with the AI Act significantly (Voss, 2024).

Regulatory Challenges with Other Legal Fields

The regulation of artificial intelligence is strongly linked to other legal issues. Aligning regulations in this field with existing laws for copyright, privacy, and employment, among others, adds to the many challenges that already make addressing such technologies legally a complex process (Schwartmann & Köhler, 2024b).

With the emergence of numerous generative AI (GenAI) models, the questions of regulating the unfair use of materials, authorship of generated content, and the use of copyright-protected work to train AI algorithms lie at the center of international discussions on preserving copyright law in the face of new technologies (European Commission, 2024e). As GenAI produces content through limited or no human input at all, the international community has a variety of different stances on who would own the copyright to the outputs, or if they should simply be left in the public domain (European Commission, 2024e). At the same time, AI models typically rely on vast sets of data to train, which can often include works protected under copyright. This raises serious concerns for potential copyright infringement by developers of generative AI tools, stemming from the use of copyright-protected materials to train their algorithms via "mining activities" (Sänger, 2024). In addition, the question arises whether works created by—or in collaboration with—generative AI tools are eligible for copyright protection, and, if so, who holds the resulting copyright (European Commission, 2024e). As the AI Act does not address these specific issues, clear legislative and judicial guidance on this complex legal matter is yet to be established (European Commission, 2024e).

AI regulation is also deeply connected to privacy laws and the legal processing of consumers' personal data (Maslewski, 2024). Existing frameworks, such as the EU's General Data Protection Regulation (GDPR) or various consumer privacy acts, establish standards to govern the collection, storage, and use of individuals' personal data, with insights and requirements that extend across fields (Wolford, 2024). Datasets used in AI training can include personal information, so AI applications are often considered to fall under the scope of such regulatory frameworks, though their implications on such technologies are not always clearly outlined. Specifically, activities such as data processing by AI systems may fall within the scope of the GDPR if they involve personal data. The connection becomes more complex in the case of fully trained GPAI models. In such instances, the legal assessment will likely depend on whether it is reasonably possible to identify natural persons using responsible means (Maslewski, 2024).

As mentioned earlier in this chapter, the shift to more AI usage is heavily intertwined with employment law and the labor market. Some companies use such technologies to facilitate operations, replace routine tasks, and even recruitment. In the latter case, AI poses risks of discrimination or unfairness in systems with undetected algorithmic biases that may unjustly favor certain protected characteristics over others, directly violating the fundamental rights of employees. At the same time, the lack of accountability mechanisms for AI-driven decisions leaves employees with little clarity in case of unfair hiring or firing. AI tools are also utilized by some companies to monitor workplace efficiency by collecting data on employee behavior, linking back to the previously discussed privacy concerns (Riso & Litardi, 2024). As with other sectors, for AI in conjunction with employment law, the national level under existing workers' rights, nondiscrimination, and equality regulations also plays an important role (Wünschelbaum, 2024).

Reflecting on the AI Act: The Victories and the Defeats

The journey of the AI Act, spanning over 1000 days from its proposal on April 21, 2021, to the conclusion of legislative, to the last technical meeting concluding the legislative negotiations on January 19, 2024, demonstrates the complexity and ambition of regulating a transformative technology (Zenner, 2024c). As such, the process has been extensive and challenging, reflecting the engagement of policymakers navigating a rapidly evolving and contentious field.

The AI Act is undeniably a bold and forward-looking effort to address the opportunities and risks posed by artificial intelligence. It aims to balance competing priorities by fostering international alignment, promoting innovation through exemptions for scientific research and open-source development, and introducing flexible principles for high-risk AI systems that consider both context and technical feasibility. Additionally, the Act strengthens transparency across the AI value chain by introducing traceability requirements for AI-generated content and establishing an innovation-friendly two-stage framework for GPAI models, enabling downstream providers to better manage and understand these systems. Regulatory sandboxes and harmonized standards further promise to reduce compliance burdens, especially for smaller market players (Zenner, 2024c).

Nevertheless, the Act faces significant challenges. Its dual focus on product safety and fundamental rights highlights conceptual tensions, and applying New Legislative Framework (NLF) principles to AI systems—far removed from static consumer products—has resulted in structural and legal inconsistencies. Vague definitions, particularly in Article 3, fail to provide the legal certainty needed to create the "ecosystem of trust" envisioned by the European Commission. Moreover, the Act's fragmented governance framework, divided across EU and national levels and multiple sectors, risks inconsistent enforcement and compliance burdens, disproportionately impacting SMEs and startups that drive much of the innovation in this field (Zenner, 2024c).

To ensure the AI Act achieves its ambitious objectives, the European Commission must address these shortcomings. Simplified compliance tools, particularly for SMEs, are essential to foster innovation and ensure competitiveness. Clearer guidance on accessing high-quality datasets and navigating the intersection of data protection, copyright, and other legal frameworks is also needed to support AI development without unnecessary hurdles. Equally important is a comprehensive strategy to promote AI innovation, supported by substantial investment, greater access to venture capital, and new opportunities to leverage AI for societal and economic benefits, such as synergies with the Green Deal.

Ultimately, the AI Act represents a significant milestone in regulating artificial intelligence, but its success will depend on its implementation and the EU's ability to adapt its governance framework to foster innovation while addressing risks. If the Act fails to strike this balance or creates barriers for EU-based SMEs and start-ups, Europe risks falling further behind global leaders in AI. By addressing these challenges, the EU can create a robust, innovation-friendly AI ecosystem that strengthens its global competitiveness.

References

Bird & Bird. (2024). *European Union Artificial Intelligence Act: A guide.*https://www.twobirds.com/-/media/new-website-content/pdfs/capabilities/artificial-intelligence/european-union-artificial-intelligence-act-guide.pdf

Borgesius, F., & van Bekkum, M. (2021). *Digital welfare fraud detection and the Dutch SyRI judgment.* Iapp.https://iapp.org/news/a/digital-welfare-fraud-detection-and-the-dutch-syri-judgment

Engler, A. C., & Renda, A. (2022). *Reconciling the AI value chain with the EU Artificial Intelligence Act.* CEPS In-depth Analysis 2022-03. Centre for European Policy Studies (CEPS). https://www.ceps.eu/ceps-publications/reconciling-the-ai-value-chain-with-the-eus-artificial-intelligence-act/

European Commission. (2020). *White paper on artificial intelligence: A European approach to excellence and trust.* COM(2020) 65 final. European Commission. https://commission.europa.eu/system/files/2020-02/commission-white-paper-artificial-intelligence-feb2020_en.pdf

European Commission. (2021, April 21). *Proposal for a Regulation of the European Parliament and of the Council laying down harmonised rules on Artificial Intelligence (Artificial Intelligence Act) and amending certain Union legislative acts.* COM(2021) 206 final, 2021/0106 (COD). Brussels. Available at https://eur-lex.europa.eu/resource.html?uri=cellar:e0649735-a372-11eb-9585-01aa75ed71a1.0001.02/DOC_1&format=PDF

European Commission. (2023). *Commission supports the Netherlands in setting up national Artificial Intelligence supervision system through the Technical Support Instrument.* European Commission.https://commission.europa.eu/news/commission-supports-netherlands-setting-national-artificial-intelligence-supervision-system-through-2023-10-05_en

European Commission. (2024a). *Netherlands AI strategy report.* European Commission.https://ai-watch.ec.europa.eu/countries/netherlands/netherlands-ai-strategy-report_en#:~:text=The%20Dutch%20strategy%20includes%20policy,inventory%20of%20data%20sharing%20solutions

European Commission. (2024b). *AI Act*. European Commission.https://digital-strategy.ec.europa.eu/en/policies/regulatory-framework-ai

European Commission. (2024c). *European Artificial Intelligence Act comes into force*. https://ec.europa.eu/commission/presscorner/detail/en/ip_24_4123

European Commission. (2024d). *Harmonised standards for the European AI Act*. Joint Research Center.https://ai-watch.ec.europa.eu/news/harmonised-standards-european-ai-act-2024-10-25_en

European Commission. (2024e). *Artificial intelligence and copyright: Use of generative AI tools to develop new content*. IP Helpdesk.https://intellectual-property-helpdesk.ec.europa.eu/news-events/news/artificial-intelligence-and-copyright-use-generative-ai-tools-develop-new-content-2024-07-16-0_en

European Commission. (2024f). *European AI Office*. European Commission.https://digital-strategy.ec.europa.eu/en/policies/ai-office

European Parliament. (2019). *Hearing of Margrethe Vestager: Executive Vice-President-Designate of the European Commission—Europe fit for the Digital Age*. European Parliament. https://www.europarl.europa.eu/resources/library/media/20191009RES63801/20191009RES63801.pdf

European Parliament. (2024). *Artificial Intelligence Act: MEPs adopt landmark law*. European Parliament. https://www.europarl.europa.eu/news/en/press-room/20240308IPR19015/artificial-intelligence-act-meps-adopt-landmark-law#:~:text=On%20Wednesday%2C%20Parliament%20approved%20the,46%20against%20and%2049%20abstentions

Keber, T., & Zenner, K. (2024). 1. Kapitel KI-VO. In R. Schwartmann, O. Tobias, & K. Zenner (Hrsg.), *KI-VO: Leitfaden für die Praxis* (S. 37 ff.). C.F. Müller Verlag. isbn:978-3-8114-6454-4.

Keber, T., Schwartmann, R., & Zenner, K. (2024). *The EU AI Act: A practice-oriented interpretation* (pp. 114–120). CRi 4/2024.

Krasavina, A. (2023, August 8). *France—National strategy for AI*. EU Digital Skills and Jobs Platform.https://digital-skills-jobs.europa.eu/en/actions/national-initiatives/national-strategies/france-national-strategy-ai

Maslewski, D. (2024). 2. Teil, Regulierung von KI. 3. Kapitel, Verhältnis zu anderen Rechtsgebieten. In R. Schwartmann, O. Tobias, & K. Zenner (Hrsg.), *KI-VO: Leitfaden für die Praxis* (S. 206 f.). C.F. Müller Verlag. isbn:978-3-8114-6454-4.

Riso, S., & Litardi, C. (2024). *Eurofound (2024), Employee monitoring: A moving target for regulation, article*. https://www.eurofound.europa.eu/en/publications/all/employee-monitoring-moving-target-regulation

Sänger, J. (2024). 2. Teil, Regulierung von KI. 3. Kapitel, Verhältnis zu anderen Rechtsgebieten. In R. Schwartmann, O. Tobias, & K. Zenner (Hrsg.), *KI-VO: Leitfaden für die Praxis* (S. 239 ff.). C.F. Müller Verlag. isbn:978-3-8114-6454-4.

Schwartmann, R., & Köhler, M. (2024a). 1. Kapitel KI-VO. In R. Schwartmann, O. Tobias, & K. Zenner (Hrsg.), *KI-VO: Leitfaden für die Praxis* (S. 52 f.). C.F. Müller Verlag. isbn:978-3-8114-6454-4.

Schwartmann, R., & Köhler, M. (2024b). 2. Teil, Regulierung von KI. 3 Kapitel, Verhältnis zu anderen Rechtsgebieten. In R. Schwartmann, O. Tobias, & K. Zenner (Hrsg.), *KI-VO: Leitfaden für die Praxis* (S. 203 ff.). C.F. Müller Verlag. isbn:978-3-8114-6454-4.

Schwartmann, R., & Pottkämper, J. M. (2024). 1. Kapitel KI-VO. In R. Schwartmann, O. Tobias, & K. Zenner (Hrsg.), *KI-VO: Leitfaden für die Praxis* (S. 54 ff.). C.F. Müller Verlag. isbn:978-3-8114-6454-4.

Sickinghe, F. (2024). *AI Act in progress: Interview with Kai Zenner*. Bird & Bird.https://www.twobirds.com/en/insights/2024/global/ai-act-in-progress-interview-with-kai-zenner

Tong, A., Dastin, J., & Hu, K. (2023). OpenAI researchers warned board of AI breakthrough ahead of CEO ouster, sources say. *Reuters*. https://www.reuters.com/technology/sam-altmans-ouster-openai-was-precipitated-by-letter-board-about-ai-breakthrough-2023-11-22/

Voss, A. (2024). *Ten steps to make the AI Act an EU success story*. Axel Voss. https://www.axel-voss-europa.de/2024/03/06/ten-steps-to-make-the-ai-act-an-eu-success-story/

Wolford, B. (2024). *What is GDPR, the EU's new data protection law?* GDPR.EU. https://gdpr.eu/what-is-gdpr/

Wünschelbaum, M. (2024). 2. Teil, Regulierung von KI. 3. Kapitel, Verhältnis zu anderen Rechtsgebieten. In R. Schwartmann, O. Tobias, & K. Zenner (Hrsg.), *KI-VO: Leitfaden für die Praxis* (S. 267 ff.). C.F. Müller Verlag. isbn:978-3-8114-6454-4.

Zenner, K. (2024a). 2. Teil. Regulierung von KI. 1. Kapitel KI-VO. In R. Schwartmann, O. Tobias, & K. Zenner (Hrsg.), *KI-VO: Leitfaden für die Praxis*. C.F. Müller Verlag (S. 35 ff). isbn:978-3-8114-6454-4.

Zenner, K. (2024b). 3. Teil Durchsetzung. 1. Kapitel Governance. In R. Schwartmann, O. Tobias, & K. Zenner (Hrsg.), *KI-VO: Leitfaden für die Praxis* (S. 35 ff.). C.F. Müller Verlag. isbn:978-3-8114-6454-4.

Zenner, K. (2024c). *Some personal reflections on the EU AI Act: A bittersweet ending*. https://docs.google.com/document/d/18k26tLCUM9qhagSjYFqs94F752I4pgHikJzqZ-XvIPw/edit?tab=t.0

Zenner, K., Schwartmann, R., & Hansen, M. (2024). 1. Kapitel KI-VO. In R. Schwartmann, O. Tobias, & K. Zenner (Hrsg.), *KI-VO: Leitfaden für die Praxis* (S. 168 ff.). C.F. Müller Verlag. isbn:978-3-8114-6454-4.

From Turing to Tomorrow: The UK's Approach to AI Regulation

Oliver Ritchie, Markus Anderljung, and Tom Rachman

Introduction

"We can only see a short distance ahead," Alan Turing wrote of machine intelligence research in 1950, "but we can see plenty there that needs to be done" (Turing, 1950). Even then, the pioneering British computer scientist could see the pathways that would lead to the artificial intelligence (AI) of today. Yet Turing's remark also speaks to a long-held question in AI regulation: How do we determine what "needs to be done" when our understanding of AI's future is so limited?

This chapter charts the UK's answer to that question over time. The UK government's strategy has evolved from simply adapting existing regulatory frameworks to committing to pass new legislation, addressing both harmful uses of AI and the risks posed by the most powerful AI systems. Since the 2012 start of the deep learning boom, the government's role in shaping AI development and adoption has gone from a niche issue to a government priority. As the technology minister, Peter Kyle wrote in January 2025, when introducing the AI Opportunities Action Plan: "We want Britain to step up; to shape the AI revolution rather than wait to see how it shapes us. Because we believe Britain has a particular responsibility to provide global leadership

O. Ritchie (✉) • M. Anderljung • T. Rachman
Centre for the Governance of AI, London, UK
e-mail: oliritchie@gmail.com; markus.anderljung@governance.ai

M. Rangeley, N. Fairfax (eds.), *The Artificial Intelligence Revolution*,
https://doi.org/10.1007/978-3-032-11814-1_7

in fairly and effectively seizing the opportunities of AI, as we have done on AI safety" (UK Secretary of State for Science, Innovation and Technology, 2025).

We discuss how the UK has recently provided this leadership, including by convening the first global summit on AI safety and trying to chart a course between a US-style focus on growth and an EU-style focus on safety. The UK has the potential to continue shaping the global conversation on AI rules: it houses top AI talent, with globally recognised expertise in development and governance across industry, academia, and government. However, success is not guaranteed. Despite delivering the first major international declaration on AI safety signed by both the USA and China, the UK's international leverage is limited (Department for Science, Innovation and Technology, Foreign, Commonwealth and Development Office et al., 2023). The UK lacks the US's direct influence over the AI industry, the EU's market-shaping power, and China's sheer economic weight and technological dynamism.

With this context in mind, at the end of this chapter, we discuss some of what now "needs to be done" in UK regulation. If AI will indeed be as transformative as many contend, we should expect it to pose a myriad of regulatory challenges and opportunities. These include how to regulate the most advanced AI systems, how to reduce barriers to AI adoption and innovation, how to safely use AI to deliver government services, how to reduce algorithmic discrimination, and how to safely deploy new applications from biological design tools to AI agents. In the words of Prime Minister Keir Starmer: "AI is the greatest force for change in the world right now. I am determined to harness it" (Starmer, 2025).

First, though, let us look back at the history of AI regulation in the UK to better understand the historical and institutional context in which regulations are being formulated today.

History of UK AI Regulation

Laying the Foundations for Regulation Before ChatGPT

From the Mid-Nineteenth Century, UK Researchers Laid the Foundations for Future AI Developments

UK researchers worked on many of the computer-science foundations that have enabled modern AI development. The English mathematician Charles Babbage (1791–1871) developed some of the first theoretical work in computing with his designs for an "Analytical Engine", though hardware limitations meant he never managed to create a physical version of his punch-card calculator. Fellow English mathematician Ada Lovelace (1815–1852) proposed using such machines for more than pure calculation, developing a theoretical example of what was arguably the first computer programme (Siffert, 2017). A century later, improved hardware allowed the UK to build the world's first programmable digital electronic computers—the "Colossus" series—to break Nazi cyphers during the Second World War. After working with these machines, Alan Turing speculated on the future of the field, proposing what is now known as the Turing Test, and expressed his "hope that machines will eventually compete with men in all purely intellectual fields" (Turing, 1950).

In the post-war period, much research in computing shifted to the USA. The term "artificial intelligence" was coined in 1956 at Dartmouth College. However, despite economic growth, innovation in computers and semiconductors, and proliferation of consumer electronics, progress in artificial intelligence was slow. That wouldn't change until the twenty-first century, when several research breakthroughs seemed to unlock the long-promised potential of AI systems. Multiple new companies, which today are worth tens of billions of pounds, were founded to commercialize these breakthroughs.

Among these companies was DeepMind. Founded in London in 2010, DeepMind has become the most influential British AI company. Initially, DeepMind focused on game-playing systems, as games provided well-defined challenges and constrained environments that could demonstrate AI's potential. Meanwhile, another British researcher, Geoffrey Hinton, oversaw a decisive AI breakthrough at the University of Toronto, where he and his students (including Ilya Sutskever, later OpenAI's Chief Science Officer) illustrated the power of using multiple GPUs—high-performance microprocessors designed for the intense graphics needs of videogaming—to build powerful neural networks. In 2012, Hinton's team demonstrated this with an image-recognition system called AlexNet that performed far better than competitors, alerting researchers around the globe to the promise of deep learning. These techniques proved a boon to DeepMind, which was bought by Google in 2014. The increasingly impressive systems Google DeepMind built in this period included AlphaGo, which beat the world champion in the highly complex board game Go. This feat also helped drive Chinese investment in advanced AI, providing impetus for its China AI 2030 strategy (Mozur, 2017).

Accelerating progress in AI capabilities prompted warnings about associated risks. The Cambridge physicist Stephen Hawking cautioned that "full artificial intelligence could spell the end of the human race" (Cellan-Jones, 2014), while the Oxford philosopher Nick Bostrom explored these risks in detail in his 2014 book *Superintelligence* (Bostrom, 2014). The UK government provided funding for further research, supporting a group of leading British universities to establish the Alan Turing Institute in 2015, with a mission "to make great leaps in the development and use of data science and artificial intelligence (AI) in order to change the world for the better" (The Alan Turing Institute, 2023). Conversations about the safety of advanced AI development were taking place internationally, too. Bill Gates expressed bemusement that others were not more afraid of the risks from AI (Rawlinson, 2015), while Elon Musk and Sam Altman founded OpenAI in 2015, a nonprofit aiming to build powerful artificial general intelligence (AGI) to "benefit humanity as a whole" (OpenAI, 2015).

From 2016 to 2019, UK Thinking on AI Regulation Prioritised Ethical Issues and a Light-Touch Approach

While the emerging AI safety movement was focused on the potential for severe harms from future systems, legislators and regulators concentrated on immediate concerns, especially unfair or unethical outcomes from using existing systems. In October 2016, the House of Commons Science and Technology Committee's "Robotics and Artificial Intelligence" report voiced concern about biases in AI systems, building on suspicion that users were being manipulated by AI-driven social media algorithms (House of Commons Science and Technology Committee, 2016). The committee expressed a broad desire for predictability in AI tools and called for them to be carefully scrutinised, but judged that further study should come before regulation.

The British vote to leave the European Union in 2016 allowed for regulatory divergence between the UK and the EU. Prime Minister Theresa May advocated for a "soft Brexit", maintaining relatively high levels of regulatory alignment with the political bloc. Amid May's battles to negotiate an EU separation agreeable to both Brussels and Westminster, her government published an Industrial Strategy (Department for Business, Energy and Industrial Strategy, 2017) for post-Brexit Britain. That document highlighted AI as a key pillar in transforming how the UK worked and lived, declaring "we will lead the world in safe and ethical use of data and artificial intelligence, giving confidence and clarity to citizens and business". The focus was innovation and an "agile" approach to regulation, with no AI-specific regulation yet. In April 2017, The Royal Society issued a report on machine learning that broadly supported this position, arguing that while overarching regulation would be inappropriate, particular AI uses might merit restriction (The Royal Society, 2017). This preference for narrow regulation was to join the wait-and-see approach as a repeated refrain in British AI policy over the next few years, in contrast to the EU's more assertive approach.

The EU presented its strategy in 2018, sharing the UK's focus on economic benefits while elevating concerns about data protection, digital rights, and ethical standards (European Commission, 2018b). In June 2018, its High Level Expert Group on AI (European Commission, 2018c) was launched to consider these issues, and later that year produced its first Coordinated Plan on AI (European Commission, 2018a). This plan again outlined a distinctive approach to AI regulation in the EU, describing "an appropriate and predictable, ethical and regulatory framework that relies on effective safeguards for the protection of fundamental rights and freedoms" as vital for both citizens and companies.

In April 2018, the House of Lords' Select Committee on Artificial Intelligence captured the prevailing UK hesitance with the title of its report: "AI in the UK: ready, willing and able?" (Select Committee on Artificial Intelligence, 2018). The committee prioritised social media issues, including topics such as algorithmic bias, data protection and privacy, and concerns around market dominance by a small number of big technology companies. It also reinforced the government's focus on immediate issues over severe, but speculative, future risks. The report asserted that "many of the hopes and the fears presently associated with AI are out of kilter with reality. While we have discussed the possibilities of a world without work, and the prospects of superintelligent machines which far surpass our own cognitive abilities, we believe the real opportunities and risks of AI are of a far more mundane, yet still pressing, nature". The committee recommended a voluntary code whereby technology companies would inform users when AI was used for "significant or sensitive decisions". Again, existing regulations were deemed sufficient.

The Lords' Select Committee also considered Britain's future as a market leader in the development of advanced AI After hearing evidence, including the limited amount of AI investment in the UK compared with the USA and China, and superior levels of computer-science education in China and India, the committee concluded that the UK needed a strategy to retain its status as a leader in this technology. "The UK can either choose to actively define a realistic role for itself with respect to AI, or be relegated to the role of a passive observer", the committee report said (Select Committee on Artificial Intelligence, 2018, Chap. 9). Others had a more expansive vision, with Prime Minister Theresa May telling the January 2018 Davos summit, "We are absolutely determined to make our country the place to come and set up to seize the opportunities of Artificial Intelligence for the future" (May, 2018).

One "realistic role" that the Lords' committee proposed was that the UK become an international convenor for discussions on the ethical deployment of AI, suggesting a global summit in London by the end of 2019. While that date proved optimistic, the idea eventually came to pass: The AI Safety Summit was hosted at Bletchley Park in 2023, with 27 countries in attendance.

In the meantime, concern was growing about the harms of social media and AI algorithms (Exposure Labs, 2020), with some experts demanding regulatory intervention (Solon, 2018). In 2018, the government established the Centre for Data Ethics and Innovation (Department for Digital, Culture, Media and Sport & Department for Business, Energy and Industrial Strategy, 2018), or CDEI, to help ensure responsible applications of AI in both the public and private sectors, and in April 2019, proposed a new regulator to address online harms (Secretary of State for Digital, Culture, Media and Sport & Secretary of State for the Home Department, 2019).

The UK also contributed in international fora, including as a member (OECD.AI Policy Observatory, n.d.-a, n.d.-b) of working groups that developed the OECD's May 2019 AI Principles (OECD.AI Policy Observatory, n.d.-a, n.d.-b), which stated that AI should be inclusive, human-centred, fair, transparent, safe, and accountable. Government reports drew on the OECD principles for a number of years, for example in the 2023 guidance on Ethics, Transparency and Accountability Framework for Automated Decision-Making (Cabinet Office et al., 2023).

From 2019 to 2022, the UK Developed a "Pro-Innovation" Approach to AI Regulation, Diverging from the EU Approach

Unable to unite an increasingly divided government around her soft Brexit approach, May was forced from office in July 2019 and replaced by Boris Johnson. A few months after taking power, Johnson used an address (Johnson, 2019) to the UN General Assembly to bring the focus on AI regulation back to the most extreme risks. "As new technologies seem to race towards us from the far horizon, we strain our eyes as they come, to make out whether they are for good or bad—friends or foes?" Johnson said. "AI—what will it mean? Helpful robots washing and caring for an ageing population? Or pink-eyed terminators sent back from the future to cull the human race"? While he proclaimed the UK to be "a global leader in ethical and responsible technology" (Johnson, 2019), this did not immediately translate into policy action.

In the background of the emerging COVID-19 pandemic, the EU released its February 2020 white paper on artificial intelligence, outlining plans for "a

European approach to excellence and trust" (European Commission, 2020). As for the US approach to advanced AI, discussion focused on national security and competitiveness. At the behest of Congress, an independent consultative group was established, the National Security Commission on Artificial Intelligence, or NSCAI, led by Eric Schmidt, the former Google CEO, and Robert Work, former US deputy defence secretary. In 2021, the commission released a lengthy report that came with a stark warning: "America is not prepared to defend or compete in the AI era" (US National Security Commission on Artificial Intelligence, 2021). US industry, academics, and civil society needed to join together and win the global race, they argued. The commission recommended a cautious approach to regulation, arguing that US lawmakers should consider streamlining routes to AI innovation and making existing rules more flexible. The commission also discussed export controls to prevent China or other adversaries from acquiring dual-use technology that might ultimately be deployed against US interests. Between 2018 and 2020, the first Trump administration tightened such restrictions on various Chinese technology companies, most notably Huawei (Bown & Kolb, 2018, p. 20). At the state level, legislatures had a different focus, addressing AI-powered technologies that were already affecting citizens, as illustrated by California's Bot Disclosure Act (Hertzberg, 2018), mandating that automated agents identify themselves if interacting with humans online. Another widespread regulatory concern was deepfakes, including nonconsensual intimate image abuse (Quirk, 2023).

During this same period, Prime Minister Boris Johnson's government sought economic benefits from Brexit, and decided on a more permissive regime concerning tech regulation, rebranding May's "agile" approach as a "pro-innovation" one. In July 2021, the technology secretary, Oliver Dowden, said in a foreword to a policy paper on digital regulation: "Now that we have exited the EU, we have a fresh opportunity to set the global path for digital regulation. With this plan, we are setting a path that is pro-innovation" (Department for Science, Innovation and Technology, 2023c). Despite the rebrand, Johnson's government faced the same challenge May had, trying to broadcast that post-EU Britain was open for business, but with certain constraints. The policy paper outlined a minimally regulated model while still recognising that "digital businesses are operating in many cases without appropriate guardrails—the existing rules and norms which have guided business activity were in many cases not designed for modern technologies and business models".

Later in 2021, the government released more details on how these principles would apply to AI. The National AI Strategy (Office for Artificial Intelligence et al., 2021) included a 10-year plan to make Britain “a global AI superpower” while ensuring that it “gets the national and international governance of AI technologies right to encourage innovation, investment, and protect the public and our fundamental values”. While the paper suggested maintaining the 2018 position that the UK should regulate AI at point of use through existing regulators, it committed to reviewing two other options: to eliminate some existing rules and to set up new overarching rules across sectors. For now, the regulatory focus remained primarily on the issues identified by the Lords’ Select Committee, such as bias, lack of transparency, and labour market disruptions rather than national security concerns and potentially catastrophic risks. However, a section at the end of the AI strategy did propose future work to address these dangers. The paper also proposed further collaboration with international bodies to set global standards, with an AI Standards Hub launched in collaboration with the Alan Turing Institute (Department for Digital, Culture, Media and Sport et al., 2022) and an associated Toolkit to coordinate international engagement. The strategy became the basis for additional publications describing the government’s approach in more detail, including a roadmap from the CDEI (Centre for Data Ethics and Innovation, 2021) on how the UK could establish a thriving private sector-led AI assurance ecosystem.

Maintaining the government’s preference for relying on existing regulators, the Online Safety Bill was amended to give additional powers to Ofcom in place of the original proposal to establish a new regulator (Department for Digital, Culture, Media and Sport, 2020). The government accepted that there were drawbacks to a sector-led approach. Some of these were listed in its 2021 National AI Strategy (Office for Artificial Intelligence et al., 2021), including inconsistent or contradictory approaches across sectors and overlap between regulatory mandates leading to unnecessary regulatory burdens. The strategy promised that a white paper the following year would consider “whether there is a case for greater cross-cutting AI regulation or greater consistency across regulated sectors” (Office for Artificial Intelligence et al., 2021). Regulators themselves were also exploring ways to coordinate on digital issues, including AI. Four UK agencies—Ofcom, the Competition and Markets Authority, the Information Commissioner’s Office, and the Financial Conduct Authority—established the Digital Regulation Cooperation Forum (DRCF) in 2020 to share best practices, avoid duplication, and improve coherence of the country’s overall regulatory system (Digital Regulation Cooperation Forum, 2024).

Further details on how existing regulators should be used were developed in the July 2022 policy paper “Establishing a pro-innovation approach to regulating AI” (Department for Science, Innovation and Technology et al.,

2022), proposing greater consistency among regulators. It established a series of cross-sector principles, including asking existing agencies to focus on "high-risk concerns rather than hypothetical or low risks associated with AI"; to coordinate their efforts; and to act with a light touch, preferring guidance or voluntary measures to new regulatory burdens on AI developers and users. The paper returned to the 2020 theme that "we should regulate the use of AI rather than the technology itself" (Department for Science, Innovation and Technology et al., 2022). It also noted the need for coherence across the regulatory regime, stating that the government would explore "whether new institutional architecture is needed to oversee the functioning of the landscape as a whole and anticipate future challenges". At the time, the government's ability to implement this approach effectively was uncertain. Implementation challenges identified by the Alan Turing Institute included a lack of AI expertise, poor coordination among different agencies, and resource constraints (Aitken et al., 2022).

The regulatory and policy work of the government was again disrupted following Johnson's resignation in the summer of 2022. His successor, Liz Truss, never implemented a vision for AI regulation as she was forced from office after just 49 days. However, the next prime minister, Rishi Sunak, took a more active approach. With his extensive Silicon Valley connections, he was well-placed to respond when OpenAI released its groundbreaking AI chatbot, ChatGPT, in November 2022, just weeks after he came to power.

From 2022 to 2024, Concern About Catastrophic AI Risks Grew, but the UK Maintained a Hands-Off Approach to Regulation

A watershed moment had arrived, with many in the wider public awed by their first direct interactions with an advanced AI model. By early 2023, ChatGPT had attracted 100 million active monthly users (Hu, 2023), making it the fastest-growing app in history. From a regulatory perspective, this general-purpose generative AI system differed from previous AI tools, such as the recommendation systems that social media companies deployed or the task-specific AIs such as DeepMind's game-playing AlphaZero or its biology research tool AlphaFold. Generative systems such as ChatGPT could undertake a wide range of cognitive tasks, both creative and technical, raising the possibility that this new form of AI could be developed into a general-purpose technology, akin to electricity or the steam engine, overhauling human development, labour, and society as a whole.

The USA, perhaps anticipating the release of ChatGPT, had introduced new export controls in October 2022, restricting China from acquiring the most advanced computing chips, considered fundamental to scaling up AI models and reaching the forefront of the technology (Bureau of Industry and Security, 2022). The Biden administration, by expanding export controls initiated during the first Trump term, joined in an iterative process with rare bipartisan support, in which the USA sought to retain its lead despite strong Chinese AI progress, both with hardware controls and with a push to establish frontier semiconductor production at home and keep AI data centres in the USA (US National Institute of Standards and Technology, 2022).

The new UK prime minister, Rishi Sunak, watched the growing geopolitical contest over AI, but had domestic economic concerns to focus on. The Office for Budget Responsibility cited "significant structural challenges", including limited productivity growth and stagnant business investment, in addition to persistently high inflation (UK Office for Budget Responsibility, 2023). The government was eager to find sources of economic growth, and Sunak looked to prioritise technology as a source of economic growth via deregulation and increased funding for innovation.

The Sunak government set out a vision for AI in the March 2023 white paper on AI regulation, prioritising growth over emerging risks. "Having exited the European Union we are free to establish a regulatory approach that enables us to establish the UK as an AI superpower", the Secretary of State for Science, Innovation and Technology, Michelle Donelan, wrote in a foreword to the paper (Department for Science, Innovation and Technology & Office for Artificial Intelligence, 2023). They retained Johnson's "pro-innovation" approach, with regulation still focused on "the use of AI rather than the technology itself". However, the paper acknowledged that developments such as ChatGPT could shift this balance. "Given the widely acknowledged transformative potential of foundation models, we must give careful attention to how they might interact with our proposed regulatory framework", it said, while noting that "it would be premature to take specific regulatory action in response to foundation models including LLMs. To do so would risk stifling innovation, preventing AI adoption, and distorting the UK's thriving AI ecosystem".

To further support growth, Sunak's government announced £100 million of funding for a new AI Foundation Model Taskforce to "ensure sovereign capabilities and broad adoption of safe and reliable foundation models, helping cement the UK's position as a science and technology superpower by 2030" (Department for Science, Innovation and Technology, Prime Minister's Office et al., 2023). The taskforce aimed to bring together government and industry experts to invest in public procurement and infrastructure to support growth in the sector. The government urged balance, repeatedly evoking "safety and reliability" in addition to technological advancement. The intent was not merely to assert the UK as a competitive force in the global race to advanced AI, but to become "a global standard bearer for AI safety". Indeed, the taskforce, building on the success and operating model of the government's COVID-19 vaccine taskforce, would eventually become the world's first AI Safety Institute.

Outside the government, there was growing concern that regulation might need to go beyond the downstream uses of AI to the development of advanced systems themselves. Around the time of the pro-innovation white paper of March 2023, the Future of Life Institute published an open letter calling for a 6-month pause on AI training runs larger than the recently released GPT-4 (Future of Life Institute, 2023). Signatories included British computer scientist and author Stuart Russell; executive director of the Cambridge Centre for the Study of Existential Risk, Sean O'Heigeartaigh; and the UK tech entrepreneur Ian Hogarth, as well as international figures such as Elon Musk and the Apple co-founder Steve Wozniak. The letter urged policymakers to "dramatically accelerate development of robust AI governance systems", including new regulatory authorities dedicated to AI, along with strict certification and rules establishing liability for AI-caused harms.

Both houses of the British Parliament discussed similar concerns. During a debate on the Data Protection bill, the Conservative MP Damian Collins referred to the open letter, arguing for more proactive regulation: "There must be an onus on companies to demonstrate that their systems are safe. The onus must not just be on the user to demonstrate that they have somehow suffered as a consequence of that system's design" (House of Commons Hansard, 2023b). Some members of the House of Lords argued that recent developments had eclipsed government plans, and the topic should be reconsidered. Lord Clement-Jones, the Liberal Democrat chair of the Lords' Select Committee on Artificial Intelligence, argued that "a long gestation period of national AI policymaking has ended up producing a minimal proposal for 'A pro-innovation approach to AI regulation' which, in substance, will amount to toothless exhortation by sectoral regulators to follow ethical principles and a complete failure to regulate AI development where there is no regulator" (House of Commons Hansard, 2023a).

In 2023, Seeking a Global Role, the UK Convened the First AI Safety Summit

Significant concerns about AI safety were again raised when key figures in the development and deployment of AI signed another open letter, released by the Center for AI Safety on 30 May, 2023, consisting of a one-sentence declaration: "Mitigating the risk of extinction from AI should be a global priority alongside other societal-scale risks such as pandemics and nuclear war" (Center for AI Safety, 2024). Signatories included the British deep learning pioneer Geoffrey Hinton, who had just resigned from Google in order to speak freely about AI risks, remarking that he harboured some regrets about his life's work (Metz, 2023). Others endorsing the letter included the CEOs of Google DeepMind, Anthropic, and OpenAI, all three of whom met with Sunak that same month and discussed the severity of existential risk, arguing that the UK could lead an international AI governance summit, echoing the idea raised by the Lords' Select Committee in 2018 (Manancourt, 2024).

In June 2023, Sunak announced that the first international AI Safety Summit was to be held that November at Bletchley Park (Parker, 2023; Bletchley Park, 2023), the site of the first Colossus computers, saying "I want to make the UK not just the intellectual home but the geographical home of global AI safety regulation" (Sunak, 2023a). The Sunak government also shifted the focus of its AI Foundation Model Taskforce towards AI safety, appointing the tech entrepreneur Ian Hogarth as its new leader (Department for Science, Innovation and Technology, AI Safety Institute et al., 2023). Hogarth had cautioned against the rash pursuit of artificial general intelligence, arguing that regulation might be warranted. "We are not powerless to slow down this race", he wrote (Hogarth, 2023).

As the technology rushed onwards, UK thinkers began to debate whether regulation should move beyond specific uses of AI to directly address the underlying models themselves. The term "frontier AI regulation" became common, describing an approach to regulating the most powerful AI models, "that could possess dangerous capabilities," relevant to, for example, cyber- and biological attacks, "sufficient to pose severe risks to public safety" (Anderljung et al., 2023). Building on the observation that the most capable AI models required increasingly vast computational resources, growing by four times a year (Sevilla & Roldán, 2024), the argument went that governments could limit their interventions to a handful of the riskiest models, leaving most AI companies unaffected. The idea faced significant critiques, including concerns that it would centralise power (Howard, 2023) while focusing efforts on speculative national security risks (Helfrich, 2024). Others debated how to define the scope of frontier AI (Hooker, 2024; Heim & Koessler, 2024; Toner & Fist, 2023), what requirements might be imposed upon its developers (Schuett et al., 2023, 2024), and how to make the definition durable to algorithmic advances (Scharre, 2024). Nevertheless, the notion of frontier AI proved useful enough to gain currency, with leading US developers—OpenAI, Google, Anthropic, and Microsoft—forming a new industry body, the Frontier Model Forum (OpenAI, 2023a), with the stated aim of advancing safety research, while the UK government renamed its AI Foundation Model Taskforce as the Frontier AI Taskforce (Department for Science, Innovation and Technology & AI Safety Institute, 2023).

In the EU, discussion turned to whether the AI Act should move beyond simply focusing on the use of AI to its responsible development and market placement. The European Parliament added references to "general-purpose AI systems" to the EU AI Act in June 2023, requiring providers of such systems—so long as they weren't open-sourced—to offer transparency to downstream actors using and building on them (European Parliament, 2023). However, seeing the trend towards a potentially small number of extremely high-compute systems playing an outsised role in the market, with potential risks stemming from their high-impact capabilities, another regulatory target was proposed: general-purpose AI models with potential for systemic risk. These were initially defined as AI models trained using more than 10^{25} floating-point operations, which was only true of a handful of models at the time it was proposed. After a tumultuous trilogue between the European Commission, Parliament, and Council (Volpicelli, 2023), the Act was passed in March 2024 and was put into place in August 2024.

Sunak also expressed a desire to regulate both the underlying AI technology and its uses. Shortly before the AI Safety Summit (GOV.UK, 2023), he spoke at The Royal Society in London (Sunak, 2023b), noting that the only people testing frontier models were those creating them, and even they did not fully understand the technology. "We should not rely on them marking their own homework", he said. Still, Sunak stressed that innovation remained Britain's priority, and held back from proposing immediate action. He stated that "the UK's answer is not to rush to regulate", and questioned how the government could "write laws that make sense for something that we don't yet fully understand".

The summit served as a focal point for international actors to set out their positions, too, most notably the USA. Coinciding with the summit, President Joe Biden released his executive order on Safe, Secure, and Trustworthy AI (Biden, 2023), galvanising efforts across the US government to grapple with

AI, from averting AI-driven discrimination and safeguarding citizens' privacy to protecting workers from the impact of AI on labour, to ensuring US global leadership in AI. With regard to frontier AI, the order required US developers of AI systems more advanced than any at that time to report training runs and safety testing to the US government (Biden, 2023, Sect. 4.2).

In light of growing US–China tensions, a key question for the Bletchley summit organisers was whether to include representatives from Beijing. Hawks in the Conservative Party opposed this (Frei, 2023), but Sunak's team felt that any summit agreement without China's support would be far less meaningful (Casalicchio & Manancourt, 2023). At the same time, there was uncertainty over whether China would even accept an invitation. In the end, a Chinese delegation did attend and endorsed the final Bletchley Declaration (Department for Science, Innovation and Technology, Foreign, Commonwealth and Development Office et al., 2023), which noted the particular risk from frontier AI systems, including in cybersecurity and biotech, and the need for global alignment on safety. The inclusion of 29 signatories, including Chinese and US representatives alongside those from the EU, the UK, and other major powers, was a landmark moment (Prime Minister's Office, 10 Downing Street et al., 2023), marking the first time that all leading AI nations had signed a joint commitment to addressing global AI risk. The summit delivered other significant announcements, including a multilateral agreement for governments and developers to work together to test AI models, an international advisory panel to advise on frontier AI risk and produce a regular "State of the Science" report, and an agreement that this would be the first in a series of such summits.

At the same time, the UK became a global pioneer by converting its AI taskforce into the AI Safety Institute (AISI), the world's first such government body (Department for Science, Innovation and Technology, 2023b). Its mandate was to conduct technical evaluations of AI systems "to minimise surprise to the UK and humanity from rapid and unexpected advances in AI". The establishment of AISI came alongside that of the US AI Safety Institute and began what would expand into a global network of state-supported AI safety institutes (Department for Science, Innovation and Technology et al., 2024). Britain also led the world in public investment for its safety institute, with its £100 million for AISI, greatly exceeding the amount apportioned to the EU equivalent and to its American counterpart (Wilson, 2024). The UK had no illusions about matching the USA or China in AI-model building, yet the work of AISI quickly impressed tech insiders for its startup mindset, efficiency, and impressive hires from top AI labs. "If you'd said to me two years ago, a government is going to create a new government body that does testing of AI systems pre-deployment, I would have said, 'Good Lord, that sounds highly likely to go extraordinarily wrong'", the Anthropic co-founder Jack Clark remarked (Manancourt, 2024). "But what I've experienced is the UK has built a testing institute that moves as quickly as a tech startup, which is extremely unusual. And the experience I have is when it's time to do the tests, we give them [access] to our model, and they are just instantly running large-scale tests".

However, Sunak's government faced criticism that the UK had not matched international leadership with sufficient domestic action. Shadow technology minister Peter Kyle responded to the Bletchley Declaration with a call for binding requirements on companies developing powerful AI. "It is not good enough for our 'inaction man' Prime Minister to say he will not rush to take action, having told the public that there are national security risks which could end our way of life", Kyle said (Lloyd, 2023).

The government's February 2024 response to the AI white paper consultation went further than it had before in acknowledging these concerns and accepting that binding requirements on highly capable general-purpose AI systems might become necessary. "We anticipate that all jurisdictions will, in time, want to place targeted mandatory interventions on the design, development, and deployment of such systems to ensure risks are adequately addressed", the government response said (Department for Science, Innovation and Technology, 2024a, Sect. 5.2.3), but argued that the sector-specific approach remained sufficient for the time being. The government published additional guidance and announced more funding for regulators (Department for Science, Innovation and Technology, 2024a), but stopped short of suggesting any major changes. Some UK think tanks called for faster action. "The government is understandably concerned that moving too quickly could risk stymying innovation, or could result in committing to rules which quickly become outdated", the Centre for Long-Term Resilience said. "But there are also considerable risks to moving too slowly: existing harms and risks remain unaddressed while new ones will inevitably emerge; other countries and jurisdictions may increasingly set the terms of regulation; and innovation in the UK may also suffer due to a lack of regulatory certainty for businesses" (Whittlestone et al., 2024).

What nobody disputed was that the AI Safety Summit in Bletchley had begun an iterative process of consensus-building. A second global meeting came 6 months later in South Korea, with Britain as the co-chair. The Seoul Declaration called for safety, innovation, and inclusivity, along with the interoperability of governance frameworks and the expansion of the international AI safety institute network (Department for Science, Innovation and Technology, 2024). Unlike Bletchley, China refrained from signing this declaration, but did not rule out future participation and would go on to sign the following summit in Paris (AI Action Summit, 2025). Most significantly, the Seoul summit secured voluntary commitments (Department for Science, Innovation and Technology, 2024b) from major AI developers, including OpenAI, Google, Anthropic, Meta, Microsoft, Amazon, and xAI, along with the Chinese startup Zhipu AI, to develop and implement safety frameworks designed to keep the risks from their frontier systems to tolerable levels, drawing inspiration from such frameworks already adopted by Anthropic (2023), OpenAI (2023b), and Google DeepMind (2024a). The summit also saw the draft release of the first International Scientific Report on the Safety of Advanced AI (Bengio et al., 2024a), chaired by the computer scientist Yoshua Bengio, known as one of the "godfathers of AI" (Vincent, 2019).

In 2024, Labour Replaced the Conservatives, Affirming Plans for Future AI Regulation While Retaining an Innovation Focus

Prime Minister Rishi Sunak called a general election for July 2024 and lost to Keir Starmer, who promised an agenda of change, including more concrete action on AI regulation. The party manifesto stated that "Labour will ensure the safe development and use of AI models by introducing binding regulation on the handful of companies developing the most powerful AI models" (Labour Party, 2024a). It also committed to banning the creation of sexually explicit AI deepfakes. While this was not a radical departure from the Conservative approach, Labour was willing for the first time to establish concrete rules in place of voluntary commitments for frontier developers, and to move faster to address specific harms coming from the use of AI.

When setting out its legislative agenda in its first King's speech, the new government stated that it would "establish the appropriate legislation to place requirements on those working to develop the most powerful artificial intelligence models" (Prime Minister's Office, 10 Downing Street and King Charles III, 2024). But despite Peter Kyle's previous proposals for action as shadow technology minister, Labour did not fully commit to a new AI regulation bill in the first parliamentary session. One possible reason for the lack of immediate regulatory action was the fear of losing overseas (particularly US) investment from companies that were highly mobile internationally. Secretary of State for Science, Innovation, and Technology, Peter Kyle, now faced the challenge of maintaining good relations with tech giants himself (Wright & Sellman, 2024). "I'm probably the first Secretary of State that is dealing with companies which are outspending our entire British state when it comes to investment in innovation. So let's just act with a bit of sense of humility. We are having to apply a sense of statecraft to working with companies that we've in the past reserved for dealing with other states", he said. "We have to have a regulatory and legislative landscape that's reflexive, responsive, and agile enough that it can give emerging innovations a soft landing while we adapt the legislation over time".

The government attempted to soften such landings by opening the Regulatory Innovation Office (RIO) to lessen the bureaucratic frictions that developers might face when trying to bring products to market. This new agency was tasked with hastening approvals and improving coordination among existing regulatory agencies. The underlying drive behind RIO was "kickstarting growth across the country" and showing that "the UK is 'open for business' as the government resets relations with trading partners around the globe", the new administration said when announcing the RIO in October 2024 (Department for Science, Innovation and Technology & Kyle, 2024). One of the agency's goals was to encourage the adoption of AI to bolster the National Health Service. "AI is set to revolutionise healthcare delivery so doctors can diagnose illnesses faster and improve patient care". Reinforcing the message that regulators should focus more on growth, the government replaced the CEO of the Competition and Markets Authority in January 2025, after the regulator's proposed plans to promote growth were seen as insufficient (Jack & Edwards, 2025).

In contrast to its cautious approach to regulation, the new government moved fast to seek benefits from AI use. In a show of continuity between governments, they asked Matt Clifford, who had previously led preparations for the Bletchley Summit under Sunak (Department for Science, Innovation and Technology, n.d.), to identify public and private sector AI opportunities for the country. The resulting AI Opportunities Action Plan included proposals to ratchet up investment in AI infrastructure, cultivate a tech-savvy workforce, and proactively seek AI solutions to problems, while maintaining support for the AI Safety Institute's evaluations of potential risks (Department for Science, Innovation and Technology et al., 2025). The government announced its full agreement with almost all of the 50 recommendations (Department for Science, Innovation and Technology, 2025a), while signalling that the UK's approach to legislating AI would remain cautious. "We don't need to walk down a USA or an EU path on AI regulation", Starmer wrote, introducing the action plan. "We can go our own way, taking a distinctively British approach that will test AI long before we regulate" (Starmer, 2025).

The government did not stop working on safety behind the scenes, continuing the international leadership that Sunak had pioneered. In November 2024, the UK AISI jointly organised a conference in California with the nonprofit Centre for the Governance of AI to accelerate the design and implementation of frontier AI safety frameworks. The conference was attended by academics and researchers from leading AI companies (UK AI Safety Institute, n.d.). However, the trajectory of global AI-safety efforts entered a period of uncertainty after the re-election of Donald Trump as president in November 2024. A flurry of support for Trump in US tech circles led to questions over which Silicon Valley advice he might heed, whether taking the counsel of accelerationist supporters such as the venture capitalist Marc Andreessen (Andreessen, 2023), or taking a more cautious approach in light of "severe" risks emphasised by supporters such as Elon Musk (Wong et al., 2023). Another notable influence was the tech entrepreneur David Sacks, Trump's "AI and crypto czar", whose complaints that "leftist elites" were manipulatively forcing their views on the US public fed into a broader conservative push to eliminate "wokeness" from institutions (Torenberg, 2024). After taking power in January 2025, the new Republican administration tasked senior officials to review Biden's October 2023 executive order, identifying what, if anything, should be kept and put into an action plan.

Trump also signalled an interest in accelerating American AI development, joining with tech leaders shortly to announce the Stargate investment plan: a projected $500 billion in private investment over 4 years to build US-based data centres (Jacobs, 2025). "What we want to do is we want to keep it in this country", Trump said, citing tech competition with China. "We have an emergency; we have to get this stuff built". Trump's push to erase traces of Biden's work did not necessarily mean that all aspects of AI regulation would be eradicated. For instance, export controls to restrict advanced chips from reaching China, which had been initiated during Trump's first term and expanded under Biden, seemed to match the new president's "America First" agenda.

The fate of the US AI Safety Institute, established under the Biden administration, remained uncertain at first. However, leading US tech developers strongly supported its work, with dozens of companies, including OpenAI, Anthropic, Meta, and Google, urging Congress to maintain the institute (Information Technology Industry Council et al., 2024). The new conservative AI policy was not necessarily against all guardrails. "I don't think the Wild West has worked out in other areas of the tech space", said Kara Frederick, former head of the Tech Policy Center at The Heritage Foundation, now a special assistant to Trump (Burgan, 2024). But she noted that the term "AI safety" had been poisoned. "It is radioactive in some very conservative circles", she said. The US AISI was subsequently renamed the "Center for AI Standards and Innovation" (US Department of Commerce, 2025) to reflect this change in focus. Perhaps reflecting a desire to align messaging with US allies, the UK AISI was rebranded as an AI *security* institute following Trump's win, even though its fundamental objectives remained unchanged (Department for Science, Innovation and Technology, 2025b).

We have mapped how the UK approach to AI regulation has developed from light-touch observation, through actively shaping global discussions, to preparing to deliver bespoke domestic regulation for AI. The remainder of the chapter considers how the incumbent Labour government's priorities might shape its approach to AI regulation, then details some of the main policy questions they will need to answer in order to regulate effectively.

Challenges and Opportunities for UK AI Regulation

The Labour Party entered government in 2024 with a mandate to develop regulations for both frontier AI development and specific uses of the technology. But it also had an urgent need to deliver economic growth and improve public services. In this section, we first describe the Labour government's policy goals. We then discuss a selection of the most pressing challenges and opportunities for UK AI regulation.

UK policymakers have started to take the possibilities of AI seriously. Many now genuinely believe that AI may be the most transformative technology of the century, creating both immense opportunities and serious challenges for policymakers. Successfully regulating AI requires balancing its potential for productivity gains against the need to address novel harms across multiple domains. Key challenges include: updating legal frameworks for AI systems that can take traditionally human actions; controlling a wide range of new AI-enabled harms, from sexual harassment to synthetic pathogens; and ensuring sufficient control of machines that are more capable than humans in many intellectual domains (Bengio et al., 2025).

The Labour Government's Objectives on Economic Growth and Public Service Reform Favour a Somewhat Permissive Approach to AI Regulation

During the election, the Labour government promised to deliver a series of "missions", or policy objectives. These missions are used to coordinate work across government to deliver economic growth, clean energy, improved healthcare, reduced crime, and better education (Labour Party, 2024c).

The first of these—economic growth—could lead ministers to favour lighter-touch regulation to support innovation and potentially accept increased risk in exchange. Labour has set a target of delivering the highest sustained growth of any G7 economy (Tunbridge Wells Labour Party, 2024), and the government has stated that it sees AI adoption and innovation as an important part of its plans to deliver this. "It is hard to imagine how we will meet the ambition for highest sustained growth in the G7—and the countless quality-of-life benefits that flow from that—without embracing the opportunities of AI", notes the AI Opportunities Action Plan (UK Secretary of State for Science, Innovation and Technology, 2025). AI-driven growth could come from investment in large UK-based frontier developers such as Google DeepMind, datacentre capacity, narrow AI products such as driverless cars and AI-enabled pharmaceutical development, or companies selling supporting services or hardware such as specialised AI chips. Diffusion of AI tools throughout the economy could also boost overall productivity, in particular in service sectors such as finance, consulting, law, and marketing. To deliver this mission, the government is likely to avoid overly strict regulations on AI development that could disincentivise investment in the UK, or overly strict rules on downstream uses of AI that could slow adoption.

AI could also play a large role in delivering the missions on healthcare, education, and, to a lesser extent, crime. AI tools could improve medical outcomes in a variety of categories, including improving radiology diagnosis, helping doctors detect heart disease, predicting the progression of diseases, and personalising cancer and surgical treatment, among other areas (Kwint, 2023; Najjar, 2023). In education, AI tools could save teachers time in developing lesson plans and enhance the educational experience by providing multiple examples and explanations. They could also offer each student unlimited personalised tutoring from AI assistants (Hu et al., 2024; Mollick & Mollick, 2023).

Ministers have indicated a strong interest in pursuing these opportunities, with Starmer saying, "AI is the way to secure growth, to raise living standards, put money in people's pockets, create exciting new companies, and transform our public services". One reason for this focus may be that the government lacks more conventional options to improve public services. It is limited in its ability to raise taxes to fund improvements by concerns that this could hamper economic growth, and by political commitments to not raise taxes on working people (Labour Party, 2024a, p. 21). It is limited in its ability to borrow money to fund improvements by its fiscal rules (Labour Party, 2024b) and by the increasing cost of government borrowing (UK Office for National Statistics, 2025). Finally, simply spending existing budgets more effectively is also likely to be challenging: Successive governments have already delivered "a decade" of efficiency drives to try to improve spending efficiency (House of Commons Committee of Public Accounts, 2021), with much of the low-hanging fruit already captured. AI tools could offer novel opportunities to drive down costs, with the Tony Blair Institute predicting potential savings as high as £40 billion per year (Iosad et al., 2024).

Though these pressures may make the government more reluctant to introduce new regulation, as many researchers and government reports have pointed out, regulatory intervention does not always hinder growth. Changes to the regulatory system can increase regulatory certainty, address regulatory overlaps, and reduce information asymmetries. It can also increase trust in technologies. Conversely, accidents could turn public opinion against AI technologies. The biggest threat to a thriving AI industry, one might argue, would be a large-scale disaster such as the partial nuclear meltdown at Three Mile Island in 1979 in the USA, which permanently damaged public trust in nuclear power (Bianchi et al., 2023).

Regulatory Policy Options for the UK

The UK seeks to be a world leader in both frontier development and innovative uses of AI, while also providing protection from associated risks. In the remainder of this chapter, we discuss a selection of the most pressing regulatory opportunities and challenges facing the UK at the time of writing. We begin with topics that we can see most clearly, and then turn towards more speculative issues.

Reducing Regulatory Barriers to Adoption

The Regulatory Challenge

A key challenge in AI regulation will be to ensure that existing regulation does not needlessly erect barriers to AI adoption throughout the economy. Few existing regulations have been written with current—let alone future—AI technologies in mind. For example, how should data protection regulations work in the context of AI? The powerful AI models underlying many applications are trained on immense datasets, sometimes incorporating much of the internet, challenging laws and norms of fair dealing, while also raising questions about copyright and intellectual-property law. Regulators focused on government activity may be a particularly important focus. About 45% of spending in the British economy is directed by the government rather than the private market (Institute for Fiscal Studies, 2024), making increasing the productivity of UK public services a key priority.

Regulatory Options

Initiatives like the Regulatory Innovation Office (RIO), established in October 2024, and the subsequent measures laid out in the AI Opportunities Action Plan, are a good place to start (Department for Science, Innovation and Technology & Kyle, 2024). The RIO was meant to hasten progress from tech innovation to widespread adoption, working to prevent regulation from becoming an excessive bottleneck. Initially, the RIO focused on the space industry, engineering biology, autonomous technology such as drones, and digital innovations, including AI, for healthcare. The most comprehensive project to reduce regulatory burdens on AI adoption came in the multipronged AI Opportunities Action Plan, which advocated for well-crafted regulatory processes that would increase business confidence and public assurance in new AI applications (UK Secretary of State for Science, Innovation and Technology, 2025).

One promising approach in some domains involves regulatory sandboxes, limited contexts in which innovators may test out products and services with guidance from regulatory agencies and less risk of incurring liability. Sandboxes have the secondary benefit of helping regulatory agencies that lack deep technical expertise gain real-world experience of AI effects. The AI Opportunities Action Plan proposed sandboxes for some of the most complex and most promising fields: robotics, drones, and autonomous vehicles. To further encourage AI adoption, existing agencies could be required to publish annual reports on how they enabled innovation and growth in their sectors.

Frontier AI Regulation

The Regulatory Challenge

While the Sunak government accepted that regulation on the development of the most advanced systems would likely 1 day be needed, Starmer's Labour government committed to introducing "binding regulation on the handful of companies developing the most powerful AI models" (Labour Party, 2024a, p. 21).

Since the early 2010s, progress in AI capabilities has been impressive. This is in large part because researchers have found ways to leverage increasingly massive amounts of computational power (compute). Between 2010 and May 2024, the amount of compute used to train the most capable models increased by a factor of 786 million (author's calculation based on Epoch AI, 2024). Recently, reinforcement learning techniques have been leveraged to yield impressive results in coding and math, with OpenAI's o3 ranking 175th on Codeforce globally, an online coding competition (OpenAI, 2025). Coders are seeing significant productivity boosts from using AI systems. One series of field experiments found that access to an AI coding assistant was associated with a 26% increase in completed tasks, with greater productivity gains among less-experienced developers (Cui et al., 2024b). In another study, participants using AI produced 55% more lines of code than those not using AI. Further, even though these studies focus on a subset of more automatable tasks, we've seen significant AI progress since these studies were carried out in 2022 and 2023 (Gambacorta et al., 2024).

However, these impressive capabilities are *dual use*: They can be used for ill as well as good. Advances in AI capabilities bring corresponding increases in potential for harm, including from cyber-attacks, bio risks, mass persuasion, and fraud (Bengio et al. Bengio et al., 2024b; Anderljung et al., 2023; Shevlane et al., 2023). Further, given the structure of the current AI industry, general-purpose frontier AI systems will often be the first to develop these capabilities.

Though the models of early 2024 seemed unlikely to increase such risks, the models of today appear more concerning. Studies suggest that GPT-4 level systems, released in March 2023, can mildly boost a lay person's ability to execute a biological weapons attack but not that of an expert (Mouton et al., 2024; Patwardhan et al., 2024). OpenAI says GPT-4's successors—o1

(OpenAI, 2024a) and o3 (OpenAI, 2025)—pose what it terms "Medium Risk"[1] with regards to human persuasion and chemical, biological, radiological, and nuclear risks. The risks stem from both potential misuse and unintended consequences, particularly as AI systems become more difficult for users to effectively control.

Directly regulating how the most advanced models are developed and deployed could complement shortcomings in point-of-use regulation. Though practices are still emerging, developers are better placed to assess the capabilities and potential impacts of their systems than downstream users, who may have less technical expertise and access to information on how the model works (Department for Science, Innovation and Technology, 2023a). Developers are also better placed to respond to dangerous capabilities, as they can employ tools such as adjusting training data or teaching models to refuse harmful requests, neither of which is available to consumers of those systems. Some companies have also defined thresholds beyond which they consider risk unacceptable and set up processes to avoid breaching them (Anthropic, 2023; OpenAI, 2023b; Google DeepMind, 2024a). Others have already committed to articulating and adhering to such thresholds (Department for Science, Innovation and Technology, 2024b).

Another reason to address risks at their source—though more speculative—is to prevent catastrophic single points of failure. As AI systems become more integrated in our economy and society, many AI applications may end up using a small set of systems, developed by a handful of companies, for a wide range of applications. Few companies have the resources and expertise to compete with the likes of Google DeepMind, OpenAI, Anthropic, DeepSeek, xAI, and Meta. This could mean most companies and users use these handful of systems rather than building their own. This concentration may create systemic vulnerabilities, similar to our largest banks, whose activities we also regulate at source for similar reasons.

A common argument against frontier AI regulation is that one should regulate uses of AI, rather than the underlying technology (Ng, 2023). But this approach of combining regulation across multiple stages in a product lifecycle is, in fact, the default across many regulatory domains. Pharmaceutical companies need to prove their medicines are sufficiently safe before putting them on the market, while doctors still need to prescribe them appropriately, and patients aren't allowed to sell them on for off-license uses. In aviation,

[1]OpenAI defines Medium risk as "Model provides meaningfully improved assistance that increases ability for existing experts in CBRN-related advanced fields to be able to create a known CBRN threat (e.g. tacit knowledge, specific supplier information, plans for distribution)" (OpenAI, 2023b).

airplane manufacturers need to make sure their planes meet certain standards, while airlines need to maintain them responsibly, and pilots need to fly them competently. Similarly, as a *general-purpose technology*, AI is often likened to electricity, a highly regulated industry.

Other arguments against frontier AI regulation bear more weight. One is on the topic of economics. If frontier AI is so important to growth, why impose onerous rules? This is an important question, but it suggests designing prudent, effective rules, rather than avoiding rules altogether. First, rules can be made less onerous. Second, economic gains from AI will likely come primarily through its practical applications rather than from AI development itself. Due to market competition and pricing constraints, most of the economic value may be captured by end users rather than AI developers. This suggests that maximising AI's economic benefits is primarily about enabling widespread adoption, not about lowering barriers to advanced AI development.

Another related concern is the UK's relatively limited market size, which could leave it open to regulatory flight. If the UK imposes requirements that companies do not already comply with, they may choose to leave the UK market rather than comply. Given the EU's larger market size, a Brussels Effect in AI (Bradford, 2020; Siegmann & Anderljung, 2022) is more likely than a London Effect.

Regulatory Options

Frontier AI systems currently appear powerful enough to warrant tailored regulation, complementing regulations on AI use cases. Further, by the time the UK passes a bill, the current pace of progress suggests that we will have seen significant developments, at least on par with the progress between OpenAI's GPT-4 and o3. However, designing an effective regulatory regime for Frontier AI will be challenging: Overly strict and broad regulations on AI in the UK may deny UK citizens the technology's benefits without reducing global risks significantly, whereas if we do nothing, we risk potential harm to UK citizens with limited tools to defend them.

The right regime will need to have the appropriate scope, requirements imposed on in-scope actors, and the right regulatory institution. The scope needs to be broad enough to apply to all systems that might pose sufficient risks, but narrow enough to feasibly implement without stifling innovation. One promising possibility is to set requirements based on the amount of compute used to train a model, with larger models facing stricter requirements (Heim & Koessler, 2024). This is likely the simplest measure and would align with the EU and the US approaches. For example, the regime could apply to any system trained using more compute than any that has been released to date, 10^{26} floating-point operations, or at least within one order of magnitude of the highest-compute model at any point in time.

The scope will need to be adapted in light of AI industry developments. Training compute thresholds will likely need to be adjusted and complemented by other metrics (Hooker, 2024). These may include what data the model was trained on, how many users it has, or the presence of particularly dangerous capabilities. Advances in reasoning models that see greater performance using inference compute might also require adjusting the scope, focusing more on models' capabilities.

A second challenge is to define regulatory requirements that are effective without being too burdensome. To achieve this, the UK should implement principles-based requirements that companies must meet, without being too prescriptive about how they should be met (Schuett et al., 2024). For example, a regulatory regime for frontier AI developers could impose three sets of obligations on frontier AI companies:

1. Safety: Requiring that companies do not impose intolerable risks on society in developing or deploying these systems.
2. Cybersecurity: Requiring that companies implement measures to prevent model theft.
3. Transparency: Requiring that companies provide relevant information about their systems to regulators, downstream developers, and users.

Crucially, these requirements need not stifle innovation. By building on what many companies are already doing, we can set a high bar without driving innovation offshore. The UK should align its approach with existing international commitments, the Hiroshima Protocols (G7 Hiroshima Summit, 2023), and in particular, the Frontier AI Safety Commitments (Department for Science, Innovation and Technology, 2024b), as well as the EU's requirements on the most powerful systems.

To implement this framework, the UK needs a competent regulator with significant expertise and supervisory powers, including the ability to take enforcement actions. This regulator must have the flexibility to adapt rules as AI technology evolves, ensuring that oversight remains relevant and effective, while making sure requirements don't ossify or impose unnecessary burdens.

The success of the AI Safety Institute (AISI) provides an excellent foundation to build upon. Some suggest that this means AISI should become the regulator, while others argue that this would hamper the institution's ability to work collaboratively with AI companies to push the science of AI safety (Mökander et al., 2024). This argument might be even stronger if the Trump administration treats foreign regulation of US-developed AI models as overreach. As such, the best option might include keeping AISI as a separate source of expertise within government—similar to the National Cyber Security Centre (National Cyber Security Centre, 2023)—which informs the work of an independent regulator focused on frontier AI companies.

Misinformation, Deepfakes, and Identifying AI-Generated Content

The Regulatory Challenge

AI-generated text, images, and audio can be nearly indistinguishable from authentic or human-generated content. This can cause harm, including through nonconsensual deepfake sexual imagery and increasingly sophisticated scams. Existing rules may address some of these issues. For example, the UK's Consumer Protection from Unfair Trading Regulations prohibit misleading commercial practices regardless of whether AI generated them, while existing data protection law under UK GDPR continues to regulate the processing of personal data, whether done by traditional or AI-powered systems. However, for other issues, AI tools will create challenges that current regulators are not well-placed to address, such as responding to nonconsensual intimate content. By early 2025, the sharing of such deepfakes was against the law, but their creation had yet to be criminalised (Ministry of Justice & Davies-Jones, 2025). Another complex issue is the use of AI voice-cloning to impersonate individuals in ways that do not clearly violate existing laws against identity theft and fraud. AI tools could also be used to generate large volumes of misleading political content during elections. The Online Safety Act 2023 designated Ofcom as the online safety regulator, yet doubts remain about how to define and respond to politically manipulative AI-generated content (Abrusci, 2024), which could fall under the remit of Ofcom (Department for Science, Innovation and Technology, 2024a, para. 48), the Electoral Commission (The Electoral Commission, 2024), or neither.

Further, even if existing regulations apply to certain uses of AI technologies, it may be beneficial for society if AI-generated content is identified as such. The most widespread current AI-content tagging method involves adding a cryptographic ID to the metadata of files produced by AI systems (see Coalition for Content Provenance and Authenticity (C2PA), 2021). However, it is unclear how useful this will be for regulators as that metadata can be deleted or changed (Anderljung & Hazell, 2023). Substantial progress is being made on watermarking technology that embeds invisible and hard-to-remove information in the AI-generated output itself. Google DeepMind has reported advances via its SynthID for audio, video, images, and text—committing to deploy it in its products—but it is not yet clear how reliable this approach could be as a widespread solution (DeepMind, 2024). Challenges include how to ensure widespread adoption and how to ensure that technical capabilities to insert watermarks remain ahead of capabilities to remove them.

A complement to identifying AI-generated content is to identify authentic content. Content-provenance techniques (such as those in the C2PA standard (Coalition for Content Provenance and Authenticity, n.d.)) can be used by governments to prove the authenticity of official documents or announcements. For this purpose, it matters less whether the tag can be removed; it only matters that a false tag is hard to make. The Biden Executive Order on AI moved the US government in this direction, tasking the Office of Management and Budget with issuing guidance for government use of content provenance techniques (Biden, 2023).

Regulatory Options

The government was right to introduce additional criminal sanctions that allow existing regulatory and legal structures to tackle harms from sexually explicit deepfakes. The government needs to continue to identify and address new AI issues as they arise. In the immediate term, that might entail looking at whether existing regulations are fit to address risks from AI-enabled scams and cyberattacks.

The right solution to the more general objective of making it easier to distinguish AI-generated from real content is not yet clear, and future technical developments could present new options. For now, we recommend that the government explore whether a mandate for watermarking content at least in certain domains (e.g. photorealistic images) is technically and administratively feasible. The government can make more immediate progress on verification of genuine content, and the UK could support development of this technology by adopting a content-provenance technique such as C2PA for important government outputs now, as a first step towards setting best practice for certain kinds of activity (e.g. photojournalism).

Copyright

The Regulatory Challenge

AI systems raise several regulatory challenges related to copyright. One concerns the legal grey zone of training AI systems on UK soil. AI systems are trained on large amounts of data, much of which is protected by copyright. Under current UK law, AI companies probably cannot legally copy such works to train AI models, unless they agree an individual licence with each copyright holder or a suitable exemption applies—an impractical proposition. Unlike the USA, with its broad "fair use" doctrine, which may allow copying of content to train AI systems (although this is being disputed in the courts), or the EU with its opt-out commercial text and data mining exemption, the UK's exemptions are narrow and do not obviously permit commercial AI training. The restrictiveness of the current UK copyright regime will inhibit not only pretraining models on copyrighted works, but also fine-tuning models that were pretrained elsewhere.

Making it easier to fine-tune systems in the UK involves a trade-off. Fine-tuning AI models in the UK could be a source of economic opportunity, if it was permitted, but could also undermine the rights of content creators to retain meaningful ownership of their work. A fundamental challenge in this area is the international dynamic: Pretraining (and fine-tuning) might occur in a jurisdiction where copying is permitted. The resulting model, which would not implicate copyright protections, could then be exported to the UK. This dynamic puts copyright owners in a difficult position. In 2022–2023, the Sunak government consulted with technology and creative industry stakeholders on a voluntary code of practice, but failed to find an agreeable solution. Labour's manifesto committed to finding a way to support both sectors, and Labour has consulted (Intellectual Property Office et al., 2024) on a proposal to require more transparency from developers on what data they are using, while making it easier for them to train models in the UK by introducing a copyright exemption that allows text and data mining unless content creators opt out of this, similar to the EU approach. The major difference between the UK rule and the EU rule is that the EU restricts models trained abroad without following its copyright law from being deployed there, but the UK does not.

This topic has attracted significant controversy, for example in the form of Baroness Kidron's proposed amendment to the 2025 Data (Use and Access) Bill, which would have required AI models marketed in the UK to comply with UK copyright law, including during training. While the House of Lords repeatedly voted to include this, they eventually withdrew the amendment to allow the bill to pass after several rounds of parliamentary "ping-pong" in which the House of Commons rejected the amendment. The government is expected to return to these issues in the future via a "comprehensive" AI bill (Courea & Stacey, 2025).

Regulatory Options

Transparency from developers on what data they are using is likely to be an important part of the solution: It is easy for developers to do and would address information asymmetries so copyright owners have the information needed to advocate for themselves and make informed decisions.

The government could also help reduce the transaction costs of bargaining for obtaining a licence to use copyrighted works for training or fine-tuning. For example, the government could support the creation of an easy-to-use bulk licensing system. Such a system could make it more attractive for model development to locate in the UK, by giving developers certainty about their potential copyright liability while also preserving copyright owners' rights.

These options, alone or together, are unlikely to resolve the tension between copyright owners and AI developers, especially in regard to the threat AI poses to human creative workers' ongoing employment. We discuss the employment impacts of AI further below.

Discrimination and Bias

The Regulatory Challenge

AI systems can perpetuate or amplify existing societal biases when trained on historical data that reflects discriminatory patterns. For example, AI recruitment tools trained on past hiring data may discriminate against women if that data reflects historical gender bias in employment. Systems can also create novel forms of discrimination that may not map cleanly onto protected characteristics—for instance by identifying and discriminating based on previously undetectable correlates of ethnicity or disability.

While the UK has strong protections against discrimination through the Equality Act 2010, these were largely designed to address human decision-making. It may not always be clear how to apply existing rules when harm is caused by an AI system: If a mortgage-lending algorithm or AI agent discriminates against certain characteristics that function as complex proxies for a protected characteristic, it may be harder to prove discriminatory intent than with human decision-makers. AI systems could also incorrectly assign responsibility. For example, the Trades Union Congress are worried that workers could be inappropriately held liable for discriminatory actions carried out by AI systems owned by their employers, even if the workers are not realistically in a position to control or predict the actions of the AI system (Trades Union Congress et al., 2024, Part 5, Sect. 27). These issues raise a number of unresolved questions about liability and enforcement—whether responsibility lies with the system developer, deployer, or both.

Regulatory Options

Rather than create separate rules for AI systems, the government should focus on updating existing anti-discrimination frameworks to explicitly account for algorithmic decision-making. Importantly, such updates should be future-proof; many regulatory efforts aimed at addressing discrimination are designed in light of old AI regimes, with an outsised focus on adjusting what data large language models are trained on, rather than other ways to steer their behaviour. This may include a mix of cross-cutting rules to update the framework as a whole (e.g. to clarify how liability should apply) and targeted rules to address specific issues, such as ensuring appropriate forms of accountability and redress in hiring and firing decisions.

Biological Design Tools

The Regulatory Challenge

AI-enabled biological tools are AI models trained on large quantities of biological sequence data to understand and predict biological processes. Notable AI-enabled biological tools include Google DeepMind's AlphaFold 3 (Google DeepMind AlphaFold team & Isomorphic Labs, 2024)—which can predict the structure and interactions of life's molecules with unprecedented accuracy—and xTrimoPGLM, a large model with strong performance across a range of biological tasks (Chen et al., 2023).

Biological Tools are already contributing to progress in many areas of biomedicine, including vaccine development and cancer therapy (Dolgin, 2023; Arnold, 2023). However, the models also introduce novel dual-use risks. In particular, some experts have warned that some biological tools could potentially allow malicious actors to identify new pandemic-capable viruses (National Security Commission on Emerging Biotechnology, 2024; Baker & Church, 2024; Rose & Nelson, 2023; Pannu et al., 2024). This is especially concerning as it is becoming increasingly easy to synthesise novel viruses from scratch using mail-order DNA, without the need for physical virus samples. These developments lower the technical and financial barriers faced by malicious actors for biological misuse.

Regulatory Options

Some have suggested reducing malicious actors' access to the most advanced biological design tools (Bloomfield et al., 2024). This could involve identifying the biological design tools with the greatest potential for risk, requiring that their risk be assessed and that appropriate safeguards be put in place, such as limiting unrestricted model access to researchers with relevant expertise. However, such intervention faces serious hurdles: Most of these systems are highly dual-use, and many of them are currently released openly to support further scientific discovery (Moulange et al., 2023; Halstead, 2024). Instead, governments might be better off starting by conducting literature-based risk assessments of biological tools and creating voluntary responsible development guidelines in collaboration with industry (Smith et al., 2024).

Further, interventions at the model layer might not be sufficient. If the UK wants to reduce risk while still benefiting from these systems, it may be necessary to take adaptive measures, increasing society's ability to manage widespread access to more capable biological design tools (Bernardi et al., 2024). For example, stricter controls on ordering, producing, and selling bespoke DNA sequences could reduce the ability to weaponize pathogens (Nelson & Rose, 2023). Similarly, governments could invest in metagenomic sequencing programs to detect new pathogens early, as well as invest in broad-spectrum vaccines and stockpile more effective personal protective equipment to increase resilience against new outbreaks (Bipartisan Commission on Biodefense, 2021).

AI Agents

The Regulatory Challenge

Some frontier AI systems are increasingly able to act autonomously to pursue goals: We describe these as "agents". In contrast to a chatbot that would only display code for a user to copy and paste, a software engineering agent could directly modify project files, compile code, test the resulting application, and then go back to the code to make improvements.

Many agents today are made by combining existing generative AI models with other software ("scaffolding") to allow them to take actions (AutoGen, 2024; AutoGPT, 2024; OpenAI, 2024b; Anthropic, 2024). Frontier AI companies are also developing new agents from the ground up (Google DeepMind, 2024b).

Agents could increase the risk level associated with frontier AI (Gabriel et al., 2024). Without a human in the loop, agents could carry out malicious activities at superhuman speed and scale, even if the agents are no better than humans at performing each individual such activity. For example, AI agents can already automate certain kinds of scam calls and some components of cyberattacks (Fang et al., 2024a, 2024b). Scaling enforcement activities could be a challenge for existing regulators. Furthermore, many of the most extreme risks from AI involve systems acting autonomously in the world, potentially against the interests of their users (Bengio et al., 2025). The government may therefore want to ensure that additional safeguards are in place for agents, such as requiring explicit human approval for certain types of action. Agent identification systems (Chan et al., 2024, 2025; South et al., 2025) for certain kinds of activity, such as buying and selling products or making phone calls, could make it easier to track and potentially address these kinds of harm.

Even when individual AI agents do not engage in harmful activity, widespread availability of agents could indirectly create issues for existing regulators. For example, agents could make it easier and faster for consumers to switch to better products or services (Sunstein, 2024). This decrease in switching costs will likely benefit consumers. At the same time, an increase in switching could destabilize economic activities or institutions that depend upon relatively high switching costs (Van Loo, 2019; Drechsler et al., 2023). Existing regulators should monitor for such society-wide effects.

AI agents could also challenge the legal foundations behind existing UK regulation. It is not currently clear who, if anyone, will be legally responsible for consequences caused by an agent. UK law often decides whether an actor is liable for the consequences of their action based on what they expect, know, or intend when they took the action. When someone deploys an AI agent, that person will not necessarily know what actions that agent is going to take, intend for those actions to happen, or have the same contextual knowledge that the agent has. This could create an accountability loophole (Wills, 2024). An effective government response may require modifying the common law or expanding the scope of existing regulators to cover the actions of agents, for example by allocating responsibilities or liabilities to people who deploy or develop them. The government may wish to go further and establish a single legal framework to resolve issues of accountability, ownership, and criminal liability for AI agents across all sectors.

Regulatory Options

The UK will likely need to adjust its legal frameworks to clarify how existing rules should apply in the context of AI agents. In cases where agents potentially undermine the functioning of a very wide range of existing legislation, high-level cross-cutting approaches could be preferable. For example, it would be better to establish clear general principles for how criminal liability applies when AI agents are involved in illegal activities, rather than separately amending individual statutes like the Computer Misuse Act, the Fraud Act, and dozens of other laws to each specify how they handle autonomous AI systems. In other cases, such as if AI agents undermine certain economic activities, sector-specific responses could be more appropriate.

In addition to responding to regulatory challenges, governments could also explore ways to unlock the benefits of agents. Governments could support the development of infrastructure that enables and secures interactions with agents (Chan et al., 2025). Analogous to fiduciary duties in domains like law and medicine, legal requirements that agents act in their users' best interests could protect consumers (Aguirre et al., 2020; Benthall & Shekman, 2023). Similarly, regulators may need to clarify that certain actions come with the same fiduciary duties whether carried out by an AI system or carried out by a human.

AI-Driven Unemployment

The Regulatory Challenge

Today's AI systems are beginning to transform the nature of many existing jobs, driving productivity gains for workers in fields such as software engineering, customer service, and legal work (Cui et al., 2024a; Brynjolfsson et al., 2023; Choi et al., 2023). There is considerable uncertainty about how future AI systems might affect employment, but some economists predict that as AI systems begin to surpass human performance in many real-world tasks (Korinek & Suh, 2024), they could cause significant labour market disruptions, including widespread job losses (Susskind, 2017). Historically, automation has eventually created at least as many jobs as it has displaced (Autor et al., 2022). However, the rapid advancement (Bengio et al., 2024b) and widespread adoption of AI (Bick et al., 2024) could result in different impacts, as AI has the potential to affect a broader range of work and integrate into the economy much faster than previous technologies (McAfee, 2024).

Even if this technological change delivers aggregate economic growth benefits, it risks creating significant disruption for affected workers. Historical evidence suggests that displaced workers often struggle to transition to new roles, experiencing lasting negative effects on their psychological well-being, earnings, and family circumstances (Burgard et al., 2007; Barnette & Michaud, 2017; Telle & Votruba, 2011). The speed of AI advancement may mean that traditional adjustment mechanisms—like workers gradually retraining for new roles—become less effective, or can't be delivered fast enough.

Together, these factors pose significant challenges for UK policymakers. They must balance fostering AI innovation to drive economic growth with protecting workers from the negative impacts associated with wage declines and job losses. Given the uncertainty surrounding AI's potential impacts, labour policies must remain adaptable to evolving circumstances while providing enough regulatory certainty to support business investment. Striking this balance will be essential to ensuring AI's economic benefits are shared within the UK and to strengthening societal resilience against economic disruptions.

Regulatory Options

To better understand AI's potential impact on employment, policymakers should closely track key trends as AI systems advance and become more widely integrated. These include evolving skill demands, the emergence of new job categories, AI adoption rates across different sectors in the UK, and wage changes across industries and occupations. By identifying the overlap of occupations most likely to experience disruption from AI and the groups of workers for whom job loss would be especially harmful, regulators can develop better-targeted worker support programs. Recent efforts such as the Department for Education's work mapping AI's impact on jobs and skills should be expanded to provide clear foresight around these impacts (Department for Education, 2023).

Regulation to halt AI-driven automation is unlikely to be the best option. Instead, a focus on enhancing society's capacity to adapt to automation's impacts can help drive beneficial growth while strengthening workers' economic security. Core components of such an approach can include AI literacy and accessibility initiatives that position workers to leverage AI to remain competitive in labour markets as AI diffuses through the economy. Rethinking the design of safety nets, the tax system, and transition assistance programs for affected workers may also be necessary. AI Growth Bonds are one example of an innovative approach that could help to spark more AI innovation in the UK while generating a pool of resources to support workers who end up displaced from their jobs by automation (Casey et al., 2024). Finally, given the potential for truly transformative futures—where the demand for human work falls dramatically—governments would be wise to invest in proactive scenario planning. Ensuring that the UK has the infrastructure to scale up assistance programs in response to rapid disruption could be a low-risk, high-reward option to boost economic preparedness and ensure stability through rapid technological change.

Conclusion

The UK has carved out a distinctive role in global AI governance—from laying intellectual foundations decades ago, to convening international summits and establishing the world's first AI Safety Institute. Yet significant work remains to be done to translate this international leadership into effective domestic policy.

The fundamental challenge remains unchanged from Turing's time: We can only see a short distance ahead. This uncertainty creates a strong temptation to delay regulation until the technology's trajectory becomes clearer. However, given AI's accelerating capabilities and growing integration into society, waiting too long risks allowing significant harms to emerge before protective frameworks are in place. The UK must therefore continue working to develop governance approaches that are both principled and adaptable—protecting citizens while enabling innovation.

The UK's success in this endeavour will depend not just on crafting the right policies, but on maintaining the institutional capacity and cross-party commitment needed to implement them effectively over time. If it can achieve this, the UK has an opportunity to help shape how one of history's most transformative technologies develops—not just through convening international discussions, but by demonstrating how democratic societies can harness AI's benefits while managing its risks.

Acknowledgements Thanks to Alan Chan, Sam Manning, Peter Wills, Jonas Schuett, Sophie Williams, Stephen Clare, John Halstead, Beth Eakman, Katharine Bardsley, and José Luis León Medina for fruitful discussion and valuable input to the chapter.

References

Abrusci, E. (2024). The UK Online Safety Act, the EU Digital Services Act and online disinformation: Is the right to political participation adequately protected? *Journal of Media Law, 16*, 1–28. Accessed February 6, 2025, from https://www.tandfonline.com/doi/abs/10.1080/17577632.2024.2425551

Aguirre, A., et al. (2020). AI loyalty: A new paradigm for aligning stakeholder interests. *arXiv [cs.CY]*. Accessed February 6, 2025, from http://arxiv.org/abs/2003.11157

AI Action Summit. (2025). *Statement on inclusive and sustainable artificial intelligence for people and the planet*. Accessed June 18, 2025, from https://www.elysee.fr/en/emmanuel-macron/2025/02/11/statement-on-inclusive-and-sustainable-artificial-intelligence-for-people-and-the-planet

Aitken, M., et al. (2022). *Common regulatory capacity for AI*. The Alan Turing Institute. Accessed February 5, 2025, from https://www.turing.ac.uk/news/publications/common-regulatory-capacity-ai

Anderljung, M., & Hazell, J. (2023). Protecting society from AI misuse: When are restrictions on capabilities warranted? *arXiv [cs.AI]*. http://arxiv.org/abs/2303.09377

Anderljung, M., et al. (2023). Frontier AI regulation: Managing emerging risks to public safety. *arXiv [cs.CY]*. Accessed April 22, 2024, from http://arxiv.org/abs/2307.03718

Andreessen, M. (2023). *The techno-optimist manifesto*. Andreessen Horowitz. Accessed February 6, 2025, from https://a16z.com/the-techno-optimist-manifesto/

Anthropic. (2023). *Anthropic's responsible scaling policy*. Anthropic. Accessed May 6, 2024, from https://www.anthropic.com/news/anthropics-responsible-scaling-policy

Anthropic. (2024). *Computer use (beta)*. Accessed February 6, 2025, from https://docs.anthropic.com/en/docs/build-with-claude/computer-use

Arnold, C. (2023). Inside the nascent industry of AI-designed drugs. *Nature Medicine, 29*(6), 1292–1295. Accessed February 6, 2025, from https://www.nature.com/articles/s41591-023-02361-0

AutoGen. (2024). *AutoGen: A framework for building AI agents and applications*. Accessed February 6, 2025, from https://microsoft.github.io/autogen/stable/

AutoGPT. (2024). *AutoGPT: Build, deploy, and run AI agents*. Github. Accessed February 6, 2025, from https://github.com/Significant-Gravitas/AutoGPT.

Autor, D., et al. (2022). *New frontiers: The origins and content of new work, 1940–2018*. National Bureau of Economic Research. Accessed April 23, 2024, from http://www.nber.org/papers/w30389.pdf

Baker, D., & Church, G. (2024). Protein design meets biosecurity. *Science (New York, N.Y.), 383*(6681), 349. Accessed February 6, 2025, from https://www.science.org/doi/10.1126/science.ado1671

Barnette, J., & Michaud, A. (2017). *Wage scars and human capital theory*. https://ammichau.github.io/papers/JBAMWageScar.pdf

Bengio, Y., Privitera, D., et al. (2024a). *International scientific report on the safety of advanced AI*. Department for Science, Innovation and Technology. Accessed July 16, 2024, from https://www.gov.uk/government/publications/international-scientific-report-on-the-safety-of-advanced-ai

Bengio, Y., Hinton, G., et al. (2024b). Managing extreme AI risks amid rapid progress. *Science*, p.eadn0117. https://doi.org/10.1126/science.adn0117.

Bengio, Y., et al. (2025). *International AI safety report*. Department for Science, Innovation and Technology. https://www.gov.uk/government/publications/international-ai-safety-report-2025

Benthall, S., & Shekman, D. (2023). Designing fiduciary artificial intelligence. *arXiv [cs.CY]*. Accessed February 6, 2025, from http://arxiv.org/abs/2308.02435

Bernardi, J., et al. (2024). Societal adaptation to advanced AI. *arXiv [cs.CY]*. http://arxiv.org/abs/2405.10295

Bianchi, F., Curry, A. C., & Hovy, D. (2023). Viewpoint: Artificial intelligence accidents waiting to happen? *Journal of Artificial Intelligence Research, 76*, 193–199.

Bick, A., Blandin, A., & Deming, D. (2024). *The rapid adoption of generative AI*. National Bureau of Economic Research. Accessed November 19, 2024, from https://www.nber.org/system/files/working_papers/w32966/w32966.pdf

Biden, J. R. (2023). Safe, secure, and trustworthy development and use of artificial intelligence. *Federal Register, 88*, 75191–75226. https://www.federalregister.gov/d/2023-24283

Bipartisan Commission on Biodefense. (2021). *The Apollo program for biodefense—Winning the race against biological threats*. Accessed February 6, 2025, from https://biodefensecommission.org/wp-content/uploads/2021/01/Apollo_report_final_v8_033121_web.pdf

Bletchley Park. (2023). *Bletchley Park and AI*. https://bletchleypark.org.uk/wp-content/uploads/2023/10/Bletchley-Park-and-AI.pdf

Bloomfield, D., et al. (2024). AI and biosecurity: The need for governance. *Science (New York, N.Y.), 385*(6711), 831–833. Accessed November 18, 2024, from https://www.science.org/doi/10.1126/science.adq1977

Bostrom, N. (2014). *Superintelligence: Paths, dangers, strategies*. Oxford University Press. https://global.oup.com/academic/product/superintelligence-9780199678112?cc=mx&lang=en&

Bown, C. P., & Kolb, M. (2018). *Trump's trade war timeline: An up-to-date guide*. Peterson Institute for International Economics. Accessed February 5, 2025, from https://www.piie.com/sites/default/files/documents/trump-trade-war-timeline.pdf

Bradford, A. (2020). *The Brussels effect: How the European Union rules the world*. Oxford University Press. https://doi.org/10.1093/oso/9780190088583.001.0001

Brynjolfsson, E., Li, D., & Raymond, L. (2023). *Generative AI at work*. National Bureau of Economic Research. Accessed April 21, 2024, from http://www.nber.org/papers/w31161.pdf

Bureau of Industry and Security. (2022). *Commerce implements new export controls on advanced computing and semiconductor manufacturing items to the People's Republic of China (PRC)*. U.S. Department of Commerce.

Burgan, C. (2024). *Experts see "Pro AI" policy coming from Trump administration*. Accessed February 6, 2025, from https://www.meritalk.com/articles/experts-see-pro-ai-policy-coming-from-trump-administration/

Burgard, S. A., Brand, J. E., & House, J. S. (2007). Toward a better estimation of the effect of job loss on health. *Journal of Health and Social Behavior, 48*(4), 369–384. Accessed November 20, 2024, from http://www.jstor.org/stable/27638722

Cabinet Office, et al. (2023). *Ethics, transparency and accountability framework for automated decision-making*. Accessed February 4, 2025, from https://www.gov.uk/government/publications/ethics-transparency-and-accountability-framework-for-automated-decision-making/ethics-transparency-and-accountability-framework-for-automated-decision-making

Casalicchio, E., & Manancourt, V. (2023). We won't cut China out of AI summit over spying scandal, UK says. *POLITICO*. Accessed February 5, 2025, from https://www.politico.eu/article/we-wont-cut-china-out-of-ai-summit-over-spying-scandal-uk-says/

Casey, E., Roy, H., & Rockall, E. (2024). *Designing an AI bond for growth and shared prosperity in the UK*. UK Day One. Accessed December 2, 2024, from https://ukdayone.org/briefings/ai-bond-for-growth-and-shared-prosperity

Cellan-Jones, R. (2014). Stephen Hawking warns artificial intelligence could end mankind. *BBC News*. Accessed February 4, 2025, from https://www.bbc.com/news/technology-30290540.

Center for AI Safety. (2024). *Statement on AI Risk: AI experts and public figures express their concern about AI risk*. Accessed April 25, 2024, from https://www.safe.ai/work/statement-on-ai-risk

Centre for Data Ethics and Innovation. (2021). *The roadmap to an effective AI assurance ecosystem*. https://assets.publishing.service.gov.uk/media/61b0746b8fa8f50379269eb3/The_roadmap_to_an_effective_AI_assurance_ecosystem.pdf

Chan, A., et al. (2024). IDs for AI systems. *arXiv [cs.AI]*. Accessed November 25, 2024, from http://arxiv.org/abs/2406.12137

Chan, A., et al. (2025). Infrastructure for AI agents. *arXiv [cs.AI]*. Accessed February 6, 2025, from http://arxiv.org/abs/2501.10114

Chen, B., et al. (2023). XTrimoPGLM: Unified 100B-scale pre-trained transformer for deciphering the language of protein. *bioRxiv*, p.2023.07.05.547496. Accessed February 6, 2025, from https://www.biorxiv.org/content/10.1101/2023.07.05.547496v1.abstract

Choi, J. H., Monahan, A., & Schwarcz, D. B. (2023). Lawyering in the age of artificial intelligence. *SSRN [preprint]*. Accessed November 19, 2024, from https://papers.ssrn.com/abstract=4626276

Coalition for Content Provenance and Authenticity. (n.d.). *C2PA specifications.* Accessed February 6, 2025, from https://c2pa.org/specifications/specifications/1.3/index.html

Coalition for Content Provenance and Authenticity (C2PA). (2021). *Overview.* Accessed February 6, 2025, from https://c2pa.org/

Courea, E., & Stacey, K. (2025, June 7). UK ministers delay AI regulation amid plans for more comprehensive bill. *The Guardian.* Accessed: 18 June 2025, from https://www.theguardian.com/technology/2025/jun/07/uk-ministers-delay-ai-regulation-amid-plans-for-more-comprehensive-bill

Cui, K. Z., et al. (2024a). *The productivity effects of generative AI: Evidence from a field experiment with GitHub Copilot.* An MIT Exploration of Generative AI. https://mit-genai.pubpub.org/pub/v5iixksv/release/2.

Cui, Z., et al. (2024b). The effects of generative AI on high skilled work: Evidence from three field experiments with software developers. *Social Science Research Network.* Accessed February 6, 2025, from https://papers.ssrn.com/abstract=4945566.

DeepMind, G. (2024). *Watermarking AI-generated text and video with SynthID.* Accessed February 6, 2025, from https://deepmind.google/discover/blog/watermarking-ai-generated-text-and-video-with-synthid/

Department for Business, Energy and Industrial Strategy. (2017). *Industrial strategy: Building a Britain fit for the future.* https://assets.publishing.service.gov.uk/government/uploads/system/uploads/attachment_data/file/664563/industrial-strategy-white-paper-web-ready-version.pdf

Department for Digital, Culture, Media and Sport. (2020). *Government minded to appoint Ofcom as online harms regulator.* Accessed February 5, 2025, from https://www.gov.uk/government/news/government-minded-to-appoint-ofcom-as-online-harms-regulator

Department for Digital, Culture, Media and Sport, & Department for Business, Energy and Industrial Strategy. (2018). *Stellar new board appointed to lead world-first Centre for Data Ethics and Innovation.* Accessed February 4, 2025, from https://www.gov.uk/government/news/stellar-new-board-appointed-to-lead-world-first-centre-for-data-ethics-and-innovation

Department for Digital, Culture, Media and Sport, Office for Artificial Intelligence, & Philp, C. (2022). *New UK initiative to shape global standards for Artificial Intelligence.* Accessed February 5, 2025, from https://www.gov.uk/government/news/new-uk-initiative-to-shape-global-standards-for-artificial-intelligence

Department for Education. (2023). *The impact of AI on UK jobs and training.* Accessed February 6, 2025, from https://www.gov.uk/government/publications/the-impact-of-ai-on-uk-jobs-and-training

Department for Science, Innovation and Technology. (2023a). *Emerging processes for frontier AI safety.* https://assets.publishing.service.gov.uk/media/653aabbd80884d000df71bdc/emerging-processes-frontier-ai-safety.pdf

Department for Science, Innovation and Technology. (2023b). *Introducing the AI Safety Institute*. https://www.gov.uk/government/publications/ai-safety-institute-overview/introducing-the-ai-safety-institute

Department for Science, Innovation and Technology. (2023c). *Digital regulation: Driving growth and unlocking innovation*. Accessed February 5, 2025, from https://www.gov.uk/government/publications/digital-regulation-driving-growth-and-unlocking-innovation/digital-regulation-driving-growth-and-unlocking-innovation

Department for Science, Innovation and Technology. (2024). *Seoul Declaration for safe, innovative and inclusive AI: AI Seoul Summit 2024*. Accessed February 6, 2025, from https://www.gov.uk/government/publications/seoul-declaration-for-safe-innovative-and-inclusive-ai-ai-seoul-summit-2024

Department for Science, Innovation and Technology. (2024a). A pro-innovation approach to AI regulation: Government response. *GOV.UK*. Accessed February 6, 2025, from https://www.gov.uk/government/consultations/ai-regulation-a-pro-innovation-approach-policy-proposals/outcome/a-pro-innovation-approach-to-ai-regulation-government-response

Department for Science, Innovation and Technology. (2024b). *Frontier AI safety commitments, AI Seoul summit 2024*. Accessed June 10, 2024, from https://www.gov.uk/government/publications/frontier-ai-safety-commitments-ai-seoul-summit-2024/frontier-ai-safety-commitments-ai-seoul-summit-2024

Department for Science, Innovation and Technology. (2025a). *AI opportunities action plan: Government response*. Accessed February 6, 2025, from https://assets.publishing.service.gov.uk/media/678639913a9388161c5d2376/ai_opportunities_action_plan_government_repsonse.pdf

Department for Science, Innovation and Technology. (2025b). *Tackling AI security risks to unleash growth and deliver plan for change*. Accessed June 16, 2025, from https://www.gov.uk/government/news/tackling-ai-security-risks-to-unleash-growth-and-deliver-plan-for-change

Department for Science, Innovation and Technology. (n.d.). *AI opportunities action plan: Terms of reference*. Accessed February 6, 2025, from https://www.gov.uk/government/publications/artificial-intelligence-ai-opportunities-action-plan-terms-of-reference/artificial-intelligence-ai-opportunities-action-plan-terms-of-reference

Department for Science, Innovation and Technology, & AI Safety Institute. (2023). *Frontier AI taskforce: First progress report*. Accessed February 5, 2025, from https://www.gov.uk/government/publications/frontier-ai-taskforce-first-progress-report/frontier-ai-taskforce-first-progress-report

Department for Science, Innovation and Technology, & Office for Artificial Intelligence. (2023). *A pro-innovation approach to AI regulation*. Accessed July 12, 2024, from https://www.gov.uk/government/publications/ai-regulation-a-pro-innovation-approach/white-paper

Department for Science, Innovation and Technology, AI Safety Institute, et al. (2023). *Tech entrepreneur Ian Hogarth to lead UK's AI Foundation Model Taskforce*. Accessed February 5, 2025, from https://www.gov.uk/government/news/tech-entrepreneur-ian-hogarth-to-lead-uks-ai-foundation-model-taskforce

Department for Science, Innovation and Technology, & Kyle, P., (2024). *Game-changing tech to reach the public faster as dedicated new unit launched to curb red tape*. Accessed February 6, 2025, from https://www.gov.uk/government/news/game-changing-tech-to-reach-the-public-faster-as-dedicated-new-unit-launched-to-curb-red-tape

Department for Science, Innovation and Technology, Office for Artificial Intelligence, & Department for Digital, Culture, Media and Sport. (2022). *Establishing a pro-innovation approach to regulating AI*. Accessed February 5, 2025, from https://www.gov.uk/government/publications/establishing-a-pro-innovation-approach-to-regulating-ai/establishing-a-pro-innovation-approach-to-regulating-ai-policy-statement

Department for Science, Innovation and Technology, Prime Minister's Office, et al. (2023). *Initial £100 million for expert taskforce to help UK build and adopt next generation of safe AI*. Accessed February 5, 2025, from https://www.gov.uk/government/news/initial-100-million-for-expert-taskforce-to-help-uk-build-and-adopt-next-generation-of-safe-ai

Department for Science, Innovation and Technology, Foreign, Commonwealth and Development Office, & Prime Minister's Office, 10 Downing Street. (2023, November 1–2). *The Bletchley declaration by countries attending the AI Safety Summit*. https://www.gov.uk/government/publications/ai-safety-summit-2023-the-bletchley-declaration/the-bletchley-declaration-by-countries-attending-the-ai-safety-summit-1-2-november-2023.

Department for Science, Innovation and Technology, Donelan, M., & Sunak, R. (2024). *Global leaders agree to launch first international network of AI Safety Institutes to boost cooperation of AI*. Accessed February 5, 2025, from https://www.gov.uk/government/news/global-leaders-agree-to-launch-first-international-network-of-ai-safety-institutes-to-boost-understanding-of-ai

Department for Science, Innovation and Technology, et al. (2025). *Prime Minister sets out blueprint to turbocharge AI*. Accessed February 6, 2025, from https://www.gov.uk/government/news/prime-minister-sets-out-blueprint-to-turbocharge-ai

Digital Regulation Cooperation Forum. (2024). *About the DRCF*. www.drcf.org.uk. Accessed February 5, 2025, from https://www.drcf.org.uk/about-us/

Dolgin, E. (2023). "Remarkable" AI tool designs mRNA vaccines that are more potent and stable. *Nature*. Accessed February 6, 2025, from https://doi.org/10.1038/d41586-023-01487-y

Drechsler, I., et al. (2023). *Deposit Franchise runs*. National Bureau of Economic Research. Accessed February 6, 2025, from https://www.nber.org/system/files/working_papers/w31138/w31138.pdf

Epoch AI. (2024). *Data on notable AI models*. Accessed June 16 2025, from https://epoch.ai/data/notable-ai-models?view=table

European Commission. (2018a). *Annex to the Communication from the Commission to the European Parliament, the European Council, the Council, the European* Economic *and Social Committee and the Committee of the Regions*. https://eur-lex.europa.eu/resource.html?uri=cellar:22ee84bb-fa04-11e8-a96d-01aa75ed71a1.0002.02/DOC_2&format=PDF

European Commission. (2018b). *Communication from the Commission to the European Parliament, the European Council, the Council, the European Economic and Social Committee and the Committee of the Regions Artificial Intelligence for Europe COM/2018/237 final*. https://eur-lex.europa.eu/legal-content/EN/TXT/HTML/?uri=CELEX:52018SC0137.

European Commission. (2018c). *Concept note on the high-level expert group on artificial intelligence*. Accessed February 6, 2025, from https://ec.europa.eu/futurium/en/system/files/ged/concept_note_on_the_ai_hlg_0.pdf

European Commission. (2020). *White paper on artificial intelligence—A European approach to excellence and trust COM/2020/65 final*, European Union. https://eur-lex.europa.eu/legal-content/EN/TXT/?uri=CELEX:52020DC0065

European Parliament. (2023). *Artificial Intelligence Act: Amendments adopted by the European Parliament on 14 June 2023 on the proposal for a regulation of the European Parliament and of the Council on laying down harmonised rules on artificial intelligence (Artificial Intelligence Act) and amending certain Union legislative acts (COM(2021)0206—C9-0146/2021—2021/0106(COD))*. https://www.europarl.europa.eu/doceo/document/TA-9-2023-0236_EN.pdf

Exposure Labs. (2020). *The social Dilemma*. Accessed February 4, 2025, from https://thesocialdilemma.com/

Fang, R., Bindu, R., et al. (2024a). Teams of LLM agents can exploit zero-day vulnerabilities. *arXiv [cs.MA]*. Accessed November 8, 2024, from http://arxiv.org/abs/2406.01637

Fang, R., Bowman, D., & Kang, D. (2024b). Voice-Enabled AI agents can perform common scams. *arXiv [cs.AI]*. Accessed November 24, 2024, from http://arxiv.org/abs/2410.15650

Frei, M. (2023). 'I don't believe [China] should be at the AI summit', says Iain Duncan Smith. *4 News*. Accessed February 5, 2025, from https://www.channel4.com/news/i-dont-believe-china-should-be-at-the-ai-summit-says-iain-duncan-smith

Future of Life Institute. (2023). *Pause giant AI experiments: An open letter*. Accessed February 5, 2025, from https://futureoflife.org/open-letter/pause-giant-ai-experiments/

G7 Hiroshima Summit. (2023). *Hiroshima process international guiding principles for organizations developing advanced AI systems*. https://www.mofa.go.jp/files/100573471.pdf

Gabriel, I., et al. (2024). *The ethics of advanced AI assistants*. Google DeepMind. http://arxiv.org/abs/2404.16244

Gambacorta, L., et al. (2024). *Generative AI and labour productivity: A field experiment on coding*. Bank for International Settlements. Accessed February 6, 2025, from https://www.bis.org/publ/work1208.htm

Google DeepMind. (2024a). *Frontier safety framework version 1.0*. Accessed June 10, 2024, from https://storage.googleapis.com/deepmind-media/DeepMind.com/Blog/introducing-the-frontier-safety-framework/fsf-technical-report.pdf

Google DeepMind. (2024b). *Project Astra*. Accessed February 6, 2025, from https://deepmind.google/technologies/project-astra/

Google DeepMind AlphaFold Team & Isomorphic Labs. (2024). AlphaFold 3 predicts the structure and interactions of all of life's molecules. *Google*. Accessed February 6, 2025, from https://blog.google/technology/ai/google-deepmind-isomorphic-alphafold-3-ai-model/

GOV.UK. (2023). *About the AI safety summit 2023*. Accessed February 5, 2025, from https://www.gov.uk/government/topical-events/ai-safety-summit-2023/about

Halstead, J. (2024). *Managing risks from AI-enabled biological tools*. Accessed February 6, 2025, from https://www.governance.ai/post/managing-risks-from-ai-enabled-biological-tools

Heim, L., & Koessler, L. (2024). Training compute thresholds: Features and functions in AI regulation. *arXiv [cs.CY]*. Accessed November 23, 2024, from http://arxiv.org/abs/2405.10799

Helfrich, G. (2024). The harms of terminology: Why we should reject so-called "frontier AI." *AI and Ethics*. https://doi.org/10.1007/s43681-024-00438-1

Hertzberg, R. (2018). *Senate Bill No. 1001: An act to add Chapter 6 (commencing with Section 17940) to Part 3 of Division 7 of the Business and Professions Code, relating to bots*. Accessed February 5, 2025, from https://leginfo.legislature.ca.gov/faces/billTextClient.xhtml?bill_id=201720180SB1001

Hogarth, I. (2023). We must slow down the race to God-like AI. *Financial Times*. Accessed February 5, 2025, from https://www.ft.com/content/03895dc4-a3b7-481e-95cc-336a524f2ac2

Hooker, S. (2024). On the limitations of compute thresholds as a governance strategy. *arXiv [cs.AI]*. http://arxiv.org/abs/2407.05694

House of Commons Committee of Public Accounts. (2021). *Efficiency in government: Twenty-eighth report of session 2021–22*. House of Commons. https://committees.parliament.uk/publications/8070/documents/82963/default/.

House of Commons Hansard. (2023a). *Advanced artificial intelligence*. https://hansard.parliament.uk/Lords/2023-07-24/debates/5432715E-F305-4EC1-8A79-B9A0C6402BFF/AdvancedArtificialIntelligence

House of Commons Hansard. (2023b). *Data protection and digital information (No. 2) bill: Second reading*. https://hansard.parliament.uk/Commons/2023-04-17/debates/019D4C9E-222D-4414-829C-6E8B86C1E65D/DataProtectionAndDigitalInformation(No2)Bill?highlight=pause%20ai#contribution-88D2AD71-2B99-46C9-B1BB-3F3E04175AC3

House of Commons Science and Technology Committee. (2016). *Robotics and artificial intelligence: Fifth Report of Session 2016–17*. House of Commons. Accessed February 4, 2025, from https://dera.ioe.ac.uk/id/eprint/27621/1/145.pdf

Howard, J. (2023). AI safety and the age of dislightenment. *fast.ai*. Accessed February 5, 2025, from https://www.fast.ai/posts/2023-11-07-dislightenment.html

Hu, K. (2023). ChatGPT sets record for fastest-growing user base—Analyst note. *Reuters*. Accessed April 22, 2024, from https://www.reuters.com/technology/chatgpt-sets-record-fastest-growing-user-base-analyst-note-2023-02-01/

Hu, B., et al. (2024). Teaching plan generation and evaluation with GPT-4: Unleashing the potential of LLM in instructional design. *IEEE Transactions on Learning Technologies, 17*, 1471–1485. Accessed February 6, 2025, from https://ieeexplore.ieee.org/abstract/document/10490240

Information Technology Industry Council, et al. (2024). Open *letter to speaker Johnson, majority leader Schumer, minority leader Jeffries, and republican leader McConnell regarding US AI Safety Institute*. https://responsibleinnovation.org/wp-content/uploads/2024/10/20241021ARI_ITIOctoberAISIHillLetter.pdf

Institute for Fiscal Studies. (2024). *What does the government spend money on?* Accessed February 6, 2025, from https://ifs.org.uk/taxlab/taxlab-key-questions/what-does-government-spend-money

Intellectual Property Office, Department for Science, Innovation and Technology, & Department for Culture, Media and Sport. (2024). *Copyright and artificial intelligence*. Accessed February 6, 2025, from https://www.gov.uk/government/consultations/copyright-and-artificial-intelligence/copyright-and-artificial-intelligence

Iosad, A., Railton, D., & Westgarth, T. (2024). *Governing in the age of AI: A new model to transform the state*. Tony Blair Institute. Accessed February 6, 2025, from https://institute.global/insights/politics-and-governance/governing-in-the-age-of-ai-a-new-model-to-transform-the-state

Jack, S., & Edwards, C. (2025). Government ousts UK competition watchdog chair. *BBC News*. Accessed February 6, 2025, from https://www.bbc.com/news/articles/c2d3e6zklxgo

Jacobs, J. (2025). Trump announces up to $500 billion in private sector AI infrastructure investment. *CBS News*. Accessed February 6, 2025, from https://www.cbsnews.com/news/trump-announces-private-sector-ai-infrastructure-investment/

Johnson, B. (2019). *PM speech to the UN General Assembly: 24 September 2019*. Accessed February 4, 2025, from https://www.gov.uk/government/speeches/pm-speech-to-the-un-general-assembly-24-september-2019

Korinek, A., & Suh, D. (2024). *Scenarios for the transition to AGI*. National Bureau of Economic Research. Accessed April 23, 2024, from https://www.nber.org/papers/w32255

Kwint, J. (2023). *Artificial intelligence: 10 promising interventions for healthcare*. National Institute for Health and Care Research. https://doi.org/10.3310/nihrevidence_59502.

Labour Party (2024a). *Change: Labour party manifesto 2024*. https://labour.org.uk/wp-content/uploads/2024/06/Labour-Party-manifesto-2024.pdf

Labour Party. (2024b). *Labour's fiscal plan*. Accessed February 20, 2025, from https://labour.org.uk/change/labours-fiscal-plan/

Labour Party. (2024c). *Mission-driven government*. Accessed February 6, 2025, from https://labour.org.uk/change/mission-driven-government/

Lloyd, N. (2023). Labour vows to force firms developing powerful AI to meet requirements. *The Independent*. Accessed February 5, 2025, from https://www.independent.co.uk/news/uk/politics/rishi-sunak-labour-government-prime-minister-bletchley-park-b2440275.html

Manancourt, V. (2024). Inside Britain's plan to save the world from runaway AI. *POLITICO*. Accessed February 5, 2025, from https://www.politico.eu/article/britain-ai-silicon-valley-rishi-sunak-prime-minister-interest-cyber-attacks-national-security/

May, T. (2018). *PM's speech at Davos 2018: 25 January*. Accessed February 4, 2025, from https://www.gov.uk/government/speeches/pms-speech-at-davos-2018-25-january

McAfee, A. (2024). Generally faster: The economic impact of generative AI. *Google*. https://policycommons.net/artifacts/12281693/generally_faster_-_the_economic_impact_of_generative_ai/

Metz, C. (2023). "The godfather of A.I." Leaves google and warns of danger ahead. *The New York Times*. Accessed February 5, 2025, from https://www.nytimes.com/2023/05/01/technology/ai-google-chatbot-engineer-quits-hinton.html

Ministry of Justice, & Davies-Jones, A. (2025). *Government crackdown on explicit deepfakes*. Accessed February 6, 2025, from https://www.gov.uk/government/news/government-crackdown-on-explicit-deepfakes

Mökander, J., et al. (2024). *Getting the UK's legislative strategy for AI right*. Accessed February 6, 2025, from https://institute.global/insights/tech-and-digitalisation/getting-the-uks-legislative-strategy-for-ai-right

Mollick, E. R., & Mollick, L. (2023). Using AI to implement effective teaching strategies in classrooms: Five strategies, including prompts. *SSRN Electronic Journal*. Accessed February 6, 2025, from https://papers.ssrn.com/abstract=4391243

Moulange, R., et al. (2023). Towards responsible governance of biological design tools. *arXiv [cs.CY]*. Accessed February 6, 2025, from http://arxiv.org/abs/2311.15936

Mouton, C. A., Lucas, C., & Guest, E. (2024). *The operational risks of AI in large-scale biological attacks: Results of a red-team study*. RAND Corporation. Accessed April 22, 2024, from https://www.rand.org/pubs/research_reports/RRA2977-2.html

Mozur, P. (2017). Beijing wants A.I. to be made in China by 2030. *The New York Times*. Accessed February 4, 2025, from https://www.nytimes.com/2017/07/20/business/china-artificial-intelligence.html

Najjar, R. (2023). Redefining radiology: A review of Artificial Intelligence integration in medical imaging. *Diagnostics, 13*(17), 2760. Accessed February 6, 2025, from https://www.mdpi.com/2075-4418/13/17/2760

National Cyber Security Centre. (2023). *Cyber security regulations and directors duties in the UK.* Accessed February 6, 2025, from https://www.ncsc.gov.uk/collection/board-toolkit/cyber-security-regulation-and-directors-duties-in-the-uk

National Security Commission on Emerging Biotechnology. (2024). AIxBio white paper 3: Risks of AIxBio. *Biotech.* Accessed February 6, 2025, from https://www.biotech.senate.gov/press-releases/aixbio-white-paper-risks-of-aixbio/

Nelson, C., & Rose, S. (2023). *Overcoming challenges with synthetic nucleic acid screening implementation.* Centre for Long-Term Resilience. Accessed February 6, 2025, from https://www.longtermresilience.org/reports/overcoming-challenges-with-synthetic-nucleic-acid-screening-implementation-2/

Ng, A. (2023). *Written statement of Andrew Ng before the U.S. Senate AI insight forum.* AI FUND. Accessed April 23, 2024, from https://aifund.ai/insights-written-statement-of-andrew-ng-before-the-u-s-senate-ai-insight-forum/

OECD.AI Policy Observatory. (n.d.-a). *List of participants in the OECD Expert Group on AI (AIGO).* Accessed February 4, 2025, from https://oecd.ai/en/list-of-participants-oecd-expert-group-on-ai

OECD.AI Policy Observatory. (n.d.-b). *OECD AI Principles overview.* Accessed May 22, 2024, from https://oecd.ai/en/ai-principles

Office for Artificial Intelligence, Department for Digital, Culture, Media and Sport, & Department for Business, Energy and Industrial Strategy. (2021). *National AI strategy.* HM Government. https://www.gov.uk/government/publications/national-ai-strategy/national-ai-strategy-html-version

OpenAI. (2015). *Introducing OpenAI.* Accessed February 4, 2025, from https://openai.com/index/introducing-openai/

OpenAI. (2023a). *Frontier model forum.* Accessed February 5, 2025, from https://openai.com/index/frontier-model-forum/

OpenAI. 2023b. *Preparedness framework (beta).* OpenAI. https://cdn.openai.com/openai-preparedness-framework-beta.pdf.

OpenAI. (2024a). *OpenAI o1 system card.* OpenAI. https://cdn.openai.com/o1-system-card-20240917.pdf.

OpenAI. (2024b). *Swarm (experimental, educational).* Github. Accessed February 6, 2025, from https://github.com/openai/swarm

OpenAI. (2025). *OpenAI o3-mini system card.* Accessed February 6, 2025, from https://cdn.openai.com/o3-mini-system-card.pdf

Pannu, J., et al. (2024). AI could pose pandemic-scale biosecurity risks. Here's how to make it safer. *Nature, 635*(8040), 808–811. Accessed February 6, 2025, from https://doi.org/10.1038/d41586-024-03815-2

Parker, G. (2023). Britain to host first global AI regulation summit in autumn. *Financial Times.* Accessed February 5, 2025, from https://www.ft.com/content/3929908e-0f6a-4223-9c1c-5cd68d82a828

Patwardhan, T., et al. (2024). *Building an early warning system for LLM-aided biological threat creation*. OpenAI. https://openai.com/research/building-an-early-warning-system-for-llm-aided-biological-threat-creation

Prime Minister's Office, 10 Downing Street, et al. (2023). Countries agree to safe and responsible development of frontier AI in landmark Bletchley Declaration. *GOV.UK*. Accessed January 18, 2025, from https://www.gov.uk/government/news/countries-agree-to-safe-and-responsible-development-of-frontier-ai-in-landmark-bletchley-declaration

Prime Minister's Office, 10 Downing Street and King Charles III. (2024). *Oral statement to parliament: The King's speech 2024*. Speech to Both Houses of Parliament. https://www.gov.uk/government/speeches/the-kings-speech-2024

Quirk, C. (2023). The high stakes of deepfakes: The growing necessity of federal legislation to regulate this rapidly evolving technology. *The Princeton Legal Journal*. Accessed February 5, 2025, from https://legaljournal.princeton.edu/the-high-stakes-of-deepfakes-the-growing-necessity-of-federal-legislation-to-regulate-this-rapidly-evolving-technology/

Rawlinson, K. (2015). Microsoft's Bill Gates insists AI is a threat. *BBC News*. Accessed February 4, 2025, from https://www.bbc.com/news/31047780

Rose, S., & Nelson, C. (2023). *Understanding AI-facilitated biological weapon development*. Centre for Long-Term Resilience. https://www.longtermresilience.org/post/report-launch-examining-risks-at-the-intersection-of-ai-and-bio

Scharre, P. (2024). *Future-proofing frontier AI regulation: Projecting future compute for frontier AI models*. Center for a New American Security. Accessed May 7, 2024, from https://www.cnas.org/publications/reports/future-proofing-frontier-ai-regulation

Schuett, J., et al. (2023). Towards best practices in AGI safety and governance: A survey of expert opinion. *arXiv [cs.CY]*. Accessed February 5, 2025, from http://arxiv.org/abs/2305.07153

Schuett, J., et al. (2024). From principles to rules: A regulatory approach for frontier AI. *arXiv [cs.CY]*. http://arxiv.org/abs/2407.07300

Secretary of State for Digital, Culture, Media and Sport, & Secretary of State for the Home Department. (2019). *Online harms white paper*. UK Government. https://assets.publishing.service.gov.uk/media/605e60c6e90e07750810b439/Online_Harms_White_Paper_V2.pdf

Select Committee on Artificial Intelligence. (2018). *AI in the UK: Ready, willing and able?* House of Lords. https://publications.parliament.uk/pa/ld201719/ldselect/ldai/100/100.pdf

Sevilla, J., & Roldán, E. (2024). *Training compute of frontier AI models grows by 4-5x per year*. Epoch AI. Accessed November 27, 2024, from https://epoch.ai/blog/training-compute-of-frontier-ai-models-grows-by-4-5x-per-year

Shevlane, T., et al. (2023). *Model evaluation for extreme risks*. Google DeepMind. Accessed April 22, 2024, from http://arxiv.org/abs/2305.15324

Siegmann, C., & Anderljung, M. (2022). *The Brussels Effect and Artificial Intelligence: How EU regulation will impact the global AI market*. Centre for the Governance of AI. http://arxiv.org/abs/2208.12645

Siffert, A. (2017). *Ada Lovelace and the first computer programme in the world*. Accessed February 4, 2025, from https://www.mpg.de/female-pioneers-of-science/Ada-Lovelace

Smith, J., et al. (2024). *How the UK Government should address the misuse risk from AI-enabled biological tools*. Centre for Long-Term Resilience. https://www.longtermresilience.org/wp-content/uploads/2024/07/How-the-UK-Government-should-address-the-misuse-risk-from-AI-Enabled-biological-tools-BTs-Website-Copy.pdf

Solon, O. (2018). Former Facebook and Google workers launch campaign to fight tech addiction. *The Guardian*. Accessed February 4, 2025, from https://www.theguardian.com/technology/2018/feb/05/tech-addiction-former-facebook-google-employees-campaign.

South, T., et al. (2025). Authenticated delegation and authorized AI agents. *arXiv [cs.CY]*. Accessed February 6, 2025, from http://arxiv.org/abs/2501.09674.

Starmer, K. (2025). Britain doesn't need to walk a US or EU path on AI. *Financial Times*. Accessed February 4, 2025, from https://www.ft.com/content/4d448059-5a3f-405c-9343-84cf7e5b90c0.

Sunak, R. (2023a). *PM London Tech Week speech: 12 June 2023*. Accessed February 5, 2025, from https://www.gov.uk/government/speeches/pm-london-tech-week-speech-12-june-2023

Sunak, R. (2023b). *Prime Minister's speech on AI: 26 October 2023*. Accessed February 5, 2025, from https://www.gov.uk/government/speeches/prime-ministers-speech-on-ai-26-october-2023

Sunstein, C. R. (2024). Brave new world? Human welfare and paternalistic AI. *Social Science Research Network*. Accessed February 6, 2025, from https://papers.ssrn.com/abstract=4908836

Susskind, D. (2017). *A model of technological unemployment*. https://static1.squarespace.com/static/57d002e01b631bc215df193b/t/595e5d34e3df28e874d5dd40/1499356473362/SUSSKIND%2C+A+Model+of+Technological+Unemployment+6+July+2017.pdf

Telle, K., & Votruba, M. (2011). Parental job loss and children's school performance. *Review of Economic Studies, 78*, 1462–1489. https://doi.org/10.2307/41407068

The Alan Turing Institute. (2023). *Our strategy*. The Alan Turing Institute. Accessed February 4, 2025, from https://www.turing.ac.uk/about-us/our-strategy.

The Electoral Commission. (2024). *New advice for voters on disinformation, and for campaigners using generative AI*. Accessed February 6, 2025, from https://www.electoralcommission.org.uk/media-centre/new-advice-voters-disinformation-and-campaigners-using-generative-ai

The Royal Society. (2017). *Machine learning: The power and promise of computers that learn by example*. https://royalsociety.org/-/media/policy/projects/machine-learning/publications/machine-learning-report.pdf

Toner, H., & Fist, T. (2023). *Regulating the AI frontier: Design choices and constraints*. Center for Security and Emerging Technology. Accessed February 5, 2025, from https://cset.georgetown.edu/article/regulating-the-ai-frontier-design-choices-and-constraints/

Torenberg, E. (2024). David Sacks' intellectual journey. *Erik Torenberg*. Accessed February 6, 2025, from https://eriktorenberg.substack.com/p/david-sacks-intellectual-journey

Trades Union Congress, Allen, R., & Masters, D. (2024). *Artificial intelligence (regulation and employment rights) Bill*. Accessed February 6, 2025, from https://www.tuc.org.uk/research-analysis/reports/artificial-intelligence-regulation-and-employment-rights-bill

Tunbridge Wells Labour Party. (2024). *Labour's five missions for Britain*. Accessed February 6, 2025, from https://tunbridgewells.laboursites.org/national-labour-2/

Turing, A. (1950). Computing machinery and intelligence. *Mind, 59*(236), 433–460. https://doi.org/10.1093/mind/lix.236.433

U.S. Department of Commerce. (2025). *Statement from U.S. Secretary of Commerce Howard Lutnick on Transforming the U.S. AI Safety Institute into the Pro-Innovation, Pro-Science U.S. Center for AI Standards and Innovation*. Accessed June 16, 2025, from https://www.commerce.gov/news/press-releases/2025/06/statement-us-secretary-commerce-howard-lutnick-transforming-us-ai

UK AI Safety Institute. (n.d.). *Conference on frontier AI safety frameworks*. Accessed February 6, 2025, from https://www.aisi.gov.uk/work/conference-on-frontier-ai-safety-frameworks

UK Office for Budget Responsibility. (2023). *Economic and fiscal outlook*. HM Government. https://obr.uk/docs/dlm_uploads/OBR-EFO-March-2023_Web_Accessible.pdf

UK Office for National Statistics. (2025). *Public sector finances, UK: December 2024*. Accessed February 20, 2025, from https://www.ons.gov.uk/economy/governmentpublicsectorandtaxes/publicsectorfinance/bulletins/publicsectorfinances/december2024

UK Secretary of State for Science, Innovation and Technology. (2025). *AI opportunities action plan*. Accessed February 4, 2025, from https://www.gov.uk/government/publications/ai-opportunities-action-plan/ai-opportunities-action-plan

US National Institute of Standards and Technology. (2022). *Chips for America*. Accessed February 5, 2025, from https://www.nist.gov/chips

US National Security Commission on Artificial Intelligence. (2021). *Final report*. NSCAI. Accessed December 1, 2024, from https://reports.nscai.gov/final-report/

Van Loo, R. (2019). Digital market perfection. *Michigan Law Review, 117*(117.5), 815. Accessed February 6, 2025, from https://repository.law.umich.edu/mlr/vol117/iss5/2

Vincent, J. (2019). "Godfathers of AI" honored with Turing Award, the Nobel Prize of computing. *The Verge*. Accessed February 18, 2025, from https://www.theverge.com/2019/3/27/18280665/ai-godfathers-turing-award-2018-yoshua-bengio-geoffrey-hinton-yann-lecun

Volpicelli, G. (2023). Power grab by France, Germany and Italy threatens to kill EU's AI bill. *POLITICO*. Accessed February 5, 2025, from https://www.politico.eu/article/france-germany-power-grab-kill-eu-blockbuster-ai-artificial-intelligence-bill/

Whittlestone, J., Shane, T. S., & Robinson, B. (2024). *The UK is heading in the right direction on AI regulation, but must move faster*. The Centre for Long-Term Resilience. Accessed February 6, 2025, from https://www.longtermresilience.org/the-uk-is-heading-in-the-right-direction-on-ai-regulation-but-must-move-faster/

Wills, P. (2024). Care for chatbots. *Social Science Research Network*. Accessed February 6, 2025, from https://papers.ssrn.com/abstract=4814272

Wilson, C. (2024). *The US has committed to spend far less than peers on AI Safety*. Center for AI Policy. Accessed February 5, 2025, from https://www.centeraipolicy.org/work/the-us-has-committed-to-spend-far-less-than-peers-on-ai-safety

Wong, S., et al. (2023). Elon Musk warns of "civilizational risk" posed by AI in meeting with tech CEOs and senators. *NBC News*. Accessed February 6, 2025, from https://www.nbcnews.com/politics/congress/big-tech-ceos-ai-meeting-senators-musk-zuckerberg-rcna104738

Wright, O., & Sellman, M. (2024). Britain must treat tech giants like nation states, minister warns. *The Times*. Accessed February 6, 2025, from https://www.thetimes.com/uk/politics/article/britain-must-treat-tech-giants-like-nation-states-minister-warns-ktmm5vmc9

US Artificial Intelligence Regulation

Lee Tiedrich

Unlike the European Union (EU) and China, the United States has not adopted comprehensive artificial intelligence (AI) legislation that extends throughout the entire jurisdiction. However, while maintaining this comparatively deregulatory approach, the United States has established government direction and policy for AI, including some binding legal requirements. US AI law and policy emphasize the importance of AI innovation and US leadership while also promoting economic competitiveness, human flourishment, and national security (90 FR 8741, 2025).[1]

Although the US federal government (the "US government") has enacted some AI legislation, these laws do not include requirements broadly addressing AI development and deployment. Much of US AI law and policy centers on actions of the president and other parts of the executive branch. These actions include binding legal requirements, often referred to as "hard law," as well as guidance and policies that are not legally enforceable, commonly called "soft

This chapter was completed in early March 2025 and does not reflect subsequent developments. The author thanks Nicole De Brigard and Korede Sutubo for their assistance with this chapter.

[1]Executive Order 14179, Removing Barriers to American Leadership in Artificial Intelligence, Federal Register, 90 FR 8741, January 31, 2025. As of February 27, 2025: https://www.federalregister.gov/documents/2025/01/31/2025-02172/removing-barriers-to-american-leadership-in-artificial-intelligence

L. Tiedrich (✉)
Duke University, Durham, NC, USA
e-mail: lee.tiedrich@duke.edu

M. Rangeley, N. Fairfax (eds.), *The Artificial Intelligence Revolution*,
https://doi.org/10.1007/978-3-032-11814-1_8

law," but which can still be influential. In some cases, binding US AI legal requirements mandate the development of complementary soft law, which can be in the form of statements, principles, and guidelines. AI legal requirements and policies established by the executive branch typically reflect the priorities of the United States' democratically elected president. During President Joseph Biden's administration, the executive branch increased government oversight of AI. In contrast, President Donald Trump's administration has preferred less government supervision.

In addition to the federal legislative and executive branches, the judiciary has also played a role in shaping the US AI legal landscape as US courts increasingly have been called upon to decide legal cases involving AI. Further, the United States' ongoing involvement in multilateral and bilateral AI initiatives can also influence or reflect its domestic policies. Finally, in the absence of comprehensive federal US AI legislation, state and local governments have increasingly expanded the legal landscape through the creation of their own AI legal requirements and policies.

This chapter provides an overview of the US AI legal and policy landscape, including how it has developed and how it can change over time. The first section outlines the structure of the US government and discusses several US governmental bodies that are helping shape US AI law and policy. The second section explains some of the key US AI laws and policies to date, including at the federal and state levels, as well as the roles of hard law, soft law, government enforcement, public procurement, and the courts. The third section concludes by highlighting how US participation in international AI policy efforts can impact or reflect US policy. Given the wide range of US governmental bodies, laws, policies, and the continuing evolution of the US AI legal landscape, this chapter discusses examples of relevant actors and actions, in addition to outlining a structure for understanding future US AI legal and policy developments that may arise. Importantly, while this chapter provides highlights of the US AI legal and policy developments, it is not intended to be exhaustive.

Understanding the US Government Structure

The United States has a national government, often referred to as the "federal government," with broad enumerated powers under the US Constitution to govern interstate commerce and several other matters throughout the jurisdiction (Cornell Law School, 2025).[2] The United States consists of 50 states, the District of Columbia (Washington, D.C.), and several territories with additional governments for their internal affairs. State governments generally can exercise power over matters within their jurisdictions to the extent not prohibited by federal law (Congress.gov, 2025).[3]

Given this structure, AI laws and policies in the United States have emerged at both the national and federal levels, as well as at the state and local levels. Because AI typically transcends geographic borders within the United States, relying principally on federal AI laws and policies has the potential to reduce the costs and challenges that may arise when organizations need to comply with a patchwork of varying state and local requirements. However, as discussed below, considering the limited federal AI legislation, state and local governments have increasingly adopted their own AI laws and policies.

Sources of Federal AI Law and Policy

The US government has three branches—legislative, executive, and judicial—that can contribute to shaping US AI law and policy through a system of checks and balances of power (USAGov, 2025).[4] The bicameral legislative branch, also known as "Congress," includes both the House of Representatives (the "House") and the Senate (Britannica, 2025).[5] Draft legislation, referred to as "bills," can be introduced in either the House or Senate (*Id.*).[6] If both the House and Senate approve a bill, it is then forwarded to the president, who can either sign the bill into law or veto it within a prescribed time period (US House of Representatives, 2025).[7] Congress can override a presidential veto if both the House and Senate approve such action by at least a two-thirds

[2]Cornell Law School, "Federalism," Legal Information Institute. As of February 27, 2025: https://www.law.cornell.edu/wex/federalism

[3]Congress.gov, "Intro.7.3 Federalism and the Constitution," Constitution Annotated. As of February 27, 2025: https://constitution.congress.gov/browse/essay/intro.7-3/ALDE_00000032/

[4]USAGov, "Branches of the U.S. government." As of February 27, 2025: https://www.usa.gov/branches-of-government

[5]Britannica, "Congress of the United States," Politics, Law, and Government. As of February 27, 2025: https://www.britannica.com/topic/Congress-of-the-United-States

[6]*Id.*

[7]United States House of Representatives, "The Legislative Process: How Are Laws Made?" As of February 27, 2025: https://www.house.gov/the-house-explained/the-legislative-process

majority (Congress.gov, 2025).[8] An indirect or pocket veto can occur in certain circumstances (Stuessy, 2019).[9]

Congress can also help guide AI law and policy in other ways. For example, during the 118th Congress of 2023–2024, the House convened a Bipartisan AI Task Force that studied various issues pertaining to AI, culminating in a comprehensive report with recommendations (US House of Representatives, 2025).[10] Similarly, the Senate created a Bipartisan AI Working Group during this Congressional session that produced a roadmap for AI policy (US Senate, 2024).[11] While not legally binding, these efforts could provide a foundation for future AI legislation. Additionally, Congress can hold hearings and conduct inquiries relating to AI, which can signal Congressional priorities and concerns (Congress.gov, 2025).[12] In the 118th Congress, several hearings were held regarding the implications of AI across various sectors, such as healthcare, intellectual property, national security, civil rights, and education (*See* e.g.).[13]

Moreover, Congress serves as a check and balance of power within the US government. Specifically, Congress must approve the executive branch's budget, which can impact the scope of executive branch activities (Riccard,

[8]Congress.gov, "Article I, Section 7, Clause 2 Veto Power," Constitution Annotated. As of February 27, 2025: https://constitution.congress.gov/browse/essay/artI-S7-C2-2/ALDE_00013645/

[9]Stuessy, Meghan M., "Regular Vetoes and Pocket Vetoes: In Brief," Congressional Research Service, RS22188, April 18, 2019. As of January 21, 2026: https://www.congress.gov/crs-product/RS22188

[10]U.S. House of Representatives, "Bipartisan House Task Force Report on Artificial Intelligence," December 2024. As of February 27, 2025: https://www.speaker.gov/wp-content/uploads/2024/12/AI-Task-Force-Report-FINAL.pdf

[11]United States Senate, "Driving U.S. Innovation in Artificial Intelligence: A Roadmap for Artificial Intelligence Policy in the United States Senate," May 2024. As of February 27, 2025: https://www.schumer.senate.gov/imo/media/doc/Roadmap_Electronic1.32pm.pdf

[12]Congress.gov, "Article I, Section 8, Clause 18 Overview of Congress's Investigation and Oversight Powers," Constitution Annotated. As of February 27, 2025: https://constitution.congress.gov/browse/essay/artI-S8-C18-7-1/ALDE_00013657/

[13]Patel, Faiza and Geller, Melanie, "Senate AI Hearings Highlight Increased Need for Regulation," Brennan Center for Justice, October 13, 2023. As of February 27, 2025: https://www.brennancenter.org/our-work/analysis-opinion/senate-ai-hearings-highlight-increased-need-regulation. Senate Hearing 118–118, Open Hearing: Advancing Intelligence in the Era of Artificial Intelligence: Addressing the National Security Implications of AI, September 19, 2023. As of February 27, 2025: https://www.congress.gov/event/118th-congress/senate-event/LC72459/text. Senate Hearing 118–25, Artificial Intelligence: Risks and Opportunities, March 8, 2023. As of February 27, 2025: https://www.congress.gov/event/118th-congress/senate-event/333732/text. Senate Hearing 118–40, Artificial Intelligence and Human Rights, June 13, 2023. As of February 27, 2025: https://www.congress.gov/event/118th-congress/senate-event/334289/text. Senate Hearing 118–37, Oversight of A.I.: Rules for Artificial Intelligence, May 16, 2023. As of February 27, 2025: https://www.congress.gov/event/118th-congress/senate-event/LC71543/text. House Hearing 118–20, Artificial Intelligence and Intellectual Property: Part I—Interoperability of AI and Copyright Law, May 17, 2023. As of February 27, 2025: https://www.congress.gov/event/118th-congress/house-event/115951/text. Senate Hearing 118–209, Avoiding a Cautionary Tale: Policy Considerations for Artificial Intelligence in Health Care, November 8, 2023. As of February 27, 2025: https://www.congress.gov/event/118th-congress/senate-event/LC72772/text

2024).[14] Congress can also use its legislative power to seek to modify the scope of the executive branch's actions, subject to certain limitations (Chafetz, 2018).[15]

The executive branch is led by the president, who serves as both the head of the US government and the commander-in-chief and has overarching responsibility for implementing and enforcing US laws (The White House, 2025).[16] The executive branch has more than 4 million military and civilian employees and includes the vice president, the Executive Office of the President, and many departments and agencies (*Id.*).[17] Collectively, the executive branch can implement binding legal requirements, develop soft law, bring enforcement actions, and hold hearings (*Id.*).[18] As mentioned above, the president can also veto bills approved by Congress, which serves as another check and balance of power.

Finally, the US government has a judicial branch, which decides "cases" and "controversies" (Congress.gov, 2025).[19] A case or controversy exists when there is an actual dispute between parties with adverse legal interests (*Id.*).[20] Notably, the judicial branch is not empowered to issue advisory legal opinions (Congress.gov, 2025).[21] The judicial branch also serves as a check and balance of power within the US government through judicial review of matters, such as the constitutionality of US laws and of an executive branch agency's statutory authority (USAGov, 2025).[22] Following the US Supreme Court's 2024 decision in *Loper Bright Enterprises v. Raimondo*, 603 U.S. ___ (2024), courts are no longer required to defer to an executive branch agency's reasonable interpretation of an ambiguous law. This could result in more judicial

---

[14] Riccard, Taylor N., "The Role of the President in Budget Development: In Brief," Congressional Research Service, R47092, p. 4, February 26, 2024. As of February 27, 2025: https://crsreports.congress.gov/product/pdf/R/R47092

[15] Chafetz, Josh, Congress's Constitution: Legislative Authority and the Separation of Powers, Yale University Press, June 19, 2018.

[16] The White House, "The Executive Branch." As of February 27, 2025: https://bidenwhitehouse.archives.gov/about-the-white-house/our-government/the-executive-branch/

[17] *Id.*

[18] *Id.*

[19] Congress.gov, "Article III Judicial Branch," Constitution Annotated. As of February 27, 2025: https://constitution.congress.gov/browse/article-3/section-2/

[20] *Id.*

[21] Congress.gov, "Article III, Section 2, Clause 1 Historical Background on Cases or Controversies Requirement," Constitution Annotated. As of February 27, 2025: https://constitution.congress.gov/browse/essay/artIII-S2-C1-2/ALDE_00001243/

[22] USAGov, "Branches of the U.S. government." As of February 27, 2025: https://www.usa.gov/branches-of-government

challenges, which, in turn, could expand the judiciary's role in interpreting statutes in judicial cases involving AI (Walker, 2024).[23]

Sources of State and Local AI Laws and Policies

While US states have their own constitutions, their governments follow the US government model with legislative, executive, and judicial branches (The White House, 2025).[24] Cities and other types of municipalities within states typically have local governments, too (MRSC Insight, 2024).[25]

Overview of Federal AI Laws and Policies

The US government's AI policy approach combines hard law and soft law and is considered more "deregulatory" than the EU's approach with the EU AI Act (Engler, 2023).[26] All three branches of the US government have helped shape US AI law and policy, with the executive branch playing the biggest role in the absence of comprehensive AI legislation passed by Congress. In addition to the powers discussed above, many executive branch departments and agencies have enforcement authority and can bring legal actions against organizations whose AI activities allegedly violate applicable law, including longstanding consumer protection laws, anti-discrimination laws, and other laws that were not enacted particularly to regulate AI (The White House, 2025).[27] The executive branch can also govern AI to some degree through its procurement rules (US Chief Information Officers Council, 2025).[28] The actions of the executive branch, including whether and how it chooses to regulate AI, adopt AI soft law, or

[23] Walker, Christopher J., "What Loper Bright Enterprises v. Raimondo Means for the Future of Chevron Deference," Yale Journal on Regulation, June 28, 2024. As of February 27, 2025: https://www.yalejreg.com/nc/what-loper-bright-enterprises-v-raimondo-means-for-the-future-of-chevron-deference/

[24] The White House, "State and Local Government." As of February 27, 2025: https://bidenwhitehouse.archives.gov/about-the-white-house/our-government/state-local-government/

[25] MRSC Insight, "Knowing Your Roles: City and Town Governments," January 10, 2024. As of February 27, 2025: https://mrsc.org/stay-informed/mrsc-insight/january-2024/roles-in-city-and-town-governments

[26] Engler, Alex, "The EU and U.S. diverge on AI regulation: A transatlantic comparison and steps to alignment," The Brookings Institution, April 25, 2023. As of February 27, 2025: https://www.brookings.edu/articles/the-eu-and-us-diverge-on-ai-regulation-a-transatlantic-comparison-and-steps-to-alignment/

[27] The White House, "The Executive Branch." As of February 27, 2025: https://bidenwhitehouse.archives.gov/about-the-white-house/our-government/the-executive-branch/

[28] U.S. Chief Information Officers Council, "6.10 Federal Acquisition Regulation (FAR)." As of February 27, 2025: https://www.cio.gov/handbook/policies-initiatives/far/

provide other oversight of AI, often reflect the priorities of the democratically elected president and thus can vary from one presidential administration to another, to the extent consistent with US law.

This section highlights some key actions with respect to AI taken by each branch of the US government. It also highlights how the president and other parts of the executive branch have contributed to shaping US AI law and policy, subject to the US system of checks and balances of power and certain other factors. Finally, this section discusses a couple of parallel developments occurring at the state and local levels, including state AI legislation, procurement, and judicial cases.

Federal AI Legislation

Congress has passed some AI legislation that builds a foundation for US AI policy and provides high-level direction. Presently, US federal legislation does not contain detailed requirements for AI developers and deployers, like those set forth in the EU AI Act or China's AI legislation (Sheehan, 2023; Future of Life Institute, 2025).[29] However, it provides an important framework for advancing US AI leadership and innovation while safeguarding national security and human flourishment.

US AI laws include the AI in Government Act of 2020 and the Advancing American AI Act. The AI in Government Act of 2020 seeks to implement an AI Center of Excellence to facilitate the adoption of AI technology across the US government.[30] It also charges the executive branch to set forth guidance for agency use of AI (AI in Government Act 2020).[31] The Advancing American AI Act aims to enhance the deployment of AI across the US government through AI use cases.[32] In support, it also outlines principles and policies for such deployment (Advancing American AI Act).[33] Some US AI legislation has been enacted as part of a broader National Defense Authorization Act (NDAA),

[29]Sheehan, Matt, "China's AI Regulations and How They Get Made," Carnegie Endowment for International Peace, July 10, 2023. As of February 27, 2025: https://carnegieendowment.org/research/2023/07/chinas-ai-regulations-and-how-they-get-made?lang=en. Future of Life Institute, "The EU Artificial Intelligence Act." As of February 27, 2025: https://artificialintelligenceact.eu/

[30]Consolidated Appropriations Act of 2021 (US) division U, title I: AI in Government Act of 2020. As of February 27, 2025: https://www.congress.gov/bill/116th-congress/house-bill/133

[31]*Id.*, s. 104.

[32]James M. Inhofe National Defense Authorization Act for Fiscal Year 2023 (US) division G, title LXXII, subtitle B: Advancing American AI Act. As of February 27, 2025: https://www.congress.gov/bill/117th-congress/house-bill/7776

[33]*Id.*, s. 7224.

an annual law that appropriates funding, authorizes policies, and provides training and resources for the US Department of Defense (DOD) (Heitshusen and McGarry, 2025).[34] This section provides an overview of some significant US AI legislation.

The 2019 NDAA

The 2019 NDAA requires the DOD to develop a comprehensive strategy for incorporating AI across its functions, with the goal of ensuring that the US maintains its technological leadership (National Defense Authorization Act, 2018).[35] Additionally, this law supports the continued work of the National Security Commission on Artificial intelligence (NSCAI) charged with examining the methods, developments, ethics, and risks of implementing AI and related technologies for US national security and defense needs (*Id.*).[36] The NSCAI's work culminated in a non-binding final report with a bold call to action and integrated strategy for the US to engage, compete, and defend in the AI era (National Security Commission on Artificial intelligence, 2021).[37] The report includes a stark warning that the US could lose its AI leadership position to China if it fails to accelerate its AI development (*Id.*).[38]

Part I of the NSCAI Report focuses on defending the US in the AI era with recommendations for bolstering US AI readiness and preparing for future warfare while also upholding democratic values, such as privacy rights and civil liberties (*Id.*).[39] Part II of the NSCAI Report outlines strategies for winning the technology competition by collaborating with allies and others to strengthen the adoption of emerging technologies and to create international technical standards that promote democratic norms (*Id.*).[40] Although the NSCAI dissolved after completion of its final report, its work continues to be reflected in US AI law and policy.

[34] Heitshusen, Valerie and McGarry, Brendan W., "Defense Primer: The NDAA Process," Congressional Research Service, IF10515, January 6, 2025. As of February 27, 2025: https://crsreports.congress.gov/product/pdf/IF/IF10515

[35] John S. McCain National Defense Authorization Act for Fiscal Year 2019. As of February 27, 2025: https://www.congress.gov/bill/115th-congress/house-bill/5515

[36] *Id.*, s. 1051.

[37] National Security Commission on Artificial Intelligence, "Final Report." As of February 27, 2025: https://assets.foleon.com/eu-central-1/de-uploads-7e3kk3/48187/nscai_full_report_digital.04d6b124173c.pdf

[38] *Id.* at p. 19.

[39] *Id.* at pp. 41–141.

[40] *Id.* at pp. 155–253.

The 2021 NDAA and NAIIA

Enacted by a congressional override of President Trump's veto, the 2021 NDAA contains the National Artificial Intelligence Initiative Act of 2020 (NAIIA), which has several important AI provisions (National Defense Authorization Act 2021).[41] For instance, it requires the president to create and implement a National AI Initiative headquartered in the White House Office of Science and Technology Policy (OSTP) (*Id.*).[42] The National AI Initiative goals include: (a) ensuring US leadership in AI research and development; (b) leading the world in public and private sector trustworthy AI; (c) preparing the workforce for AI; and (d) coordinating AI research and development across the US government (*Id.*).[43] The 2021 NDAA also calls for an Interagency AI Committee, comprised of personnel across the government, as well as a National AI Advisory Committee, to provide the government with multistakeholder input on AI matters (*Id.*).[44]

Further, the 2021 NDAA expands the responsibilities of the US National Institute of Standards and Technology (NIST) and charges it with developing an AI risk management framework, which is discussed below (*Id.*).[45] The NDAA also aims to increase US AI research and development, including by addressing the development of National Artificial Intelligence Research Institutes through the National Science Foundation (NSF) (*Id.*).[46] Additionally, this legislation directs the executive branch to develop the National AI Research Resource (NAIRR) Task Force to help democratize access to AI research and development, including computational infrastructure, public and private sector data, and testbeds (*Id.*; U.S. National Science Foundation,

[41] William M. (Mac) Thornberry National Defense Authorization Act for Fiscal Year 2021, ss. 5001–5106. As of February 27, 2025: https://www.congress.gov/bill/116th-congress/house-bill/6395

[42] *Id.*, s. 5102.

[43] *Id.*, s. 5101(a).

[44] *Id.*, ss. 5103–5104.

[45] *Id.*, s. 5301.

[46] *Id.*, ss. 5105, 5201. Stanford University, "Summary of AI Provisions from the National Defense Authorization Act 2021." As of February 27, 2025: https://hai.stanford.edu/policy/summary-of-ai-provisions-from-the-national-defense-authorization-act-2021

2022).[47] In January 2024, the NSF launched a 2-year NAIRR pilot program (U.S. National Science Foundation, 2024).[48] The NDAA also requires a study of AI's impact on the workforce (National Defense Authorization Act 2021).[49]

The Foreign Adversary Controlled Applications Act

In 2024, Congress enacted the Protecting Americans from Foreign Adversary Controlled Applications Act.[50] Citing national security concerns, this legislation, among other things, bars TikTok, which has a Chinese parent company, from providing social media platform services in the US, absent a qualified divestiture (Benson et al., 2024).[51] Under Chinese law, the Chinese government has certain rights to seek access to personal data collected by TikTok (*TikTok Inc. v. Garland*, 604 U.S. ___, (2025)).[52] The US legislation has significant implications as TikTok has accumulated more than 170 million US users who collectively have uploaded over five and a half billion videos which, in the aggregate, have had more than 13 trillion views worldwide (*Id.*).[53] TikTok and other entities brought a lawsuit challenging this legislation alleging, among other things, that it violated free speech protections afforded by the US Constitution (*Id.*).[54] The US Supreme Court upheld this legislation, and it remains in effect (*Id.*).[55] On the first day of his second term, however, President Trump signed an executive order extending the deadline for negotiating a

[47] *Id.*, s. 5106. U.S. National Science Foundation, "Bridging the resource divide for artificial intelligence research," May 25, 2022. As of February 27, 2025: https://www.nsf.gov/news/bridging-resource-divide-artificial-intelligence

[48] U.S. National Science Foundation, "U.S. NAIRR pilot brings cutting-edge AI resources to researchers and educators across the nation," October 16, 2024. As of February 27, 2025: https://www.nsf.gov/science-matters/us-nairr-pilot-brings-cutting-edge-ai-resources-researchers

[49] William M. (Mac) Thornberry National Defense Authorization Act for Fiscal Year 2021, s. 5105. As of February 27, 2025: https://www.congress.gov/bill/116th-congress/house-bill/6395

[50] Making emergency supplemental appropriations for the fiscal year ending September 30, 2024, and for other purposes, Division H. As of February 27, 2025: https://www.congress.gov/bill/118th-congress/house-bill/815.

[51] Benson, Peter J. et al., "Regulation of TikTok Under the Protecting Americans from Foreign Adversary Controlled Applications Act: Analysis of Selected Legal Issues," Congressional Research Service, LSB11127, p. 2, May 9, 2024. As of February 27, 2025: https://crsreports.congress.gov/product/pdf/LSB/LSB11127

[52] *TikTok Inc. v. Garland*, 604 U.S. ___ (2025), at p. 3. As of February 27, 2025: https://www.supremecourt.gov/opinions/24pdf/24-656_ca7d.pdf

[53] *Id.* at 8.

[54] *Id.*

[55] *Id.*

qualified divestiture of TikTok (90 FR 8611, 2025).[56] The involvement of the US government's three branches in this matter highlights the US system of checks and balances of power.

Hard Law—Executive Orders and Related Actions

The executive branch has adopted various types of binding AI legal requirements. For example, presidents can issue executive orders (EO) establishing policies, interpreting laws, directing executive branch officials, and taking other actions within the scope of presidential authority (Graber, 2021).[57] Nonetheless, EOs are subject to several levels of restraint by all three branches. Presidents can rescind or modify EOs at any time, including from prior administrations. (*Id.*).[58] Congress can enact legislation that modifies or abrogates an EO (*Id.*).[59] Congress can also, through its appropriation authority, withhold funding for the execution of EOs (*Id.*).[60] Courts can determine the scope and validity of EOs in cases challenging their legality (*Id.*).[61] Consequently, EOs are often considered less permanent than legislation, since legislation, although still potentially subject to judicial review, requires congressional and presidential action to modify or repeal.

As discussed below, on the first day of his second term, President Trump rescinded President Biden's first AI EO (90 FR 8237, 2025).[62] President Trump promptly followed this action with a new AI EO setting forth a pathway for reevaluating executive branch AI regulations and policies (90 FR 8741, 2025).[63] These events illustrate how the president can influence US AI legal requirements and policies. The following subsections outline how

[56]Executive Order 14166, Application of Protecting Americans From Foreign Adversary Controlled Applications Act to TikTok, Federal Register, 90 FR 8611, January 20, 2025. As of February 27, 2025: https://www.federalregister.gov/documents/2025/01/30/2025-02087/application-of-protecting-americans-from-foreign-adversary-controlled-applications-act-to-tiktok

[57]Graber, Abigail A., "Executive Orders: An Introduction," Congressional Research Service, R46738, pp. 1–2, March 29, 2021. As of February 27, 2025: https://crsreports.congress.gov/product/pdf/R/R46738

[58]*Id.* at pp. 15–16.

[59]*Id.* at pp. 17–18.

[60]*Id.* at p. 11.

[61]*Id.* at pp. 13–15.

[62]Executive Order 14148, Initial Rescissions of Harmful Executive Orders and Actions, Federal Register, 90 FR 8237, January 20, 2025. As of February 27, 2025: https://www.federalregister.gov/documents/2025/01/28/2025-01901/initial-rescissions-of-harmful-executive-orders-and-actions

[63]Executive Order 14179, Removing Barriers to American Leadership in Artificial Intelligence," Federal Register, 90 FR 8741, January 31, 2025. As of February 27, 2025: https://www.federalregister.gov/documents/2025/01/31/2025-02172/removing-barriers-to-american-leadership-in-artificial-intelligence

President Trump and President Biden have used AI EOs to help shape AI policies to reflect their priorities and objectives.

President Trump's AI Executive Orders—First Term

During his first term, President Trump issued an AI EO in February 2019 entitled, "Maintaining American Leadership in Artificial Intelligence" (the "2019 AI EO").[64] The 2019 AI EO launched the American AI Initiative, which later evolved into the National AI Initiative, codified in legislation pursuant to the 2021 NDAA, as discussed above (84 FR 3967, 2019).[65] Additionally, the 2019 AI EO set forth the following five AI principles:

1. The US must drive technological breakthroughs in AI across the federal government, industry, and academia to promote scientific discovery, economic competitiveness, and national security.
2. The US must drive development of appropriate technical standards and reduce barriers to the safe testing and deployment of AI to enable AI adoption and the creation of new AI-related industries.
3. The US must train workers with the skills to develop and apply AI technologies to prepare them for today's economy and the future.
4. The US must foster public trust and confidence in AI and protect civil liberties, privacy, and American values in their application to fully realize the potential of AI for the American people.
5. The US must promote an international environment that supports American AI research and innovation and opens markets for American AI industries, while protecting its AI technological advantage and its critical AI technologies from acquisition by strategic competitors and adversarial nations (*Id.*).[66]

To implement these principles, the 2019 AI EO directed executive branch departments and agencies to take specific steps, including prioritizing federal investment in AI research and development and working to increase access and use of federal data and AI models without sacrificing privacy, security, confidentiality, or safety (*Id.*).[67] The 2019 AI EO also required the devel-

---

[64] Executive Order 13859, Maintaining Leadership in Artificial Intelligence, Federal Register, 84 FR 3967, February 11, 2019. As of February 27, 2025: https://www.federalregister.gov/documents/2019/02/14/2019-02544/maintaining-american-leadership-in-artificial-intelligence

[65] *Id.*

[66] *Id.*, s. 1.

[67] *Id.*

opment of regulatory guidance for federal agencies, which was finalized in November 2020 (*Id.*).[68] Adopting a deregulatory approach, this guidance directed agencies to, among other things, "avoid regulatory and non-regulatory actions that needlessly hamper AI innovation and growth" (*Id.*).[69] Equally important, the 2019 AI EO directed the National Institute of Standards and Technology (NIST) to prepare a plan for US engagement in the development of AI standards and take certain other actions aligning with the principles (*Id.*).[70]

President Trump issued a second AI EO in December 2020 entitled "Promoting the Use of Trustworthy Artificial Intelligence in the Federal Government" (the "2020 AI EO"). At the time, the US government had already expanded its use of AI across many of its functions, as highlighted in a report prepared for the Administrative Conference of the United States (Engstrom, et al., 2020).[71] Building on this trend, the 2020 AI EO outlined nine principles directing that the government's design, acquisition, and use of AI be: (a) lawful and respectful of US values; (b) purposeful and performance-driven; (c) accurate, reliable, and effective; (d) safe, secure, and resilient; (e) understandable; (f) responsible and traceable; (g) regularly monitored; (h) transparent; and (i) accountable (85 FR 78939, 2020).[72]

President Biden's AI Executive Orders

President Biden also turned to EOs to help shape US AI law and policy. In October 2023, President Biden signed the broad sweeping "Executive Order on Safe, Secure, and Trustworthy Development and Use of Artificial Intelligence" (the "2023 AI EO"). The 2023 AI EO delineated eight policies and principles for the government's advancement, development, and use of AI. In pursuing such actions, government entities were directed to foster safety and security; promote responsible innovation, competition, and collaboration; support American workers; advance equity and inclusion; protect consumers;

---

[68] *Id.*

[69] *Id.*

[70] *Id.*

[71] Engstrom, David Freeman et al., "Government by Algorithm: Artificial Intelligence in Federal Administrative Agencies," February 2020. As of February 27, 2025: https://law.stanford.edu/publications/government-by-algorithm-artificial-intelligence-in-federal-administrative-agencies/

[72] Executive Order 13960, Promoting the Use of Trustworthy Artificial Intelligence in the Federal Government, Federal Register, 85 FR 78939, December 8, 2020. As of February 27, 2025: https://www.federalregister.gov/documents/2020/12/08/2020-27065/promoting-the-use-of-trustworthy-artificial-intelligence-in-the-federal-government

safeguard privacy and civil liberties; manage risks and optimize benefits from government use of AI; and maintain US AI global leadership (88 FR 75191, 2023).[73]

The broad goals and directives in the 2023 AI EO built on the 2021 NDAA, prior AI EOs, and other executive branch actions (Harris and Jaikaran, 2024).[74] However, it differed significantly in terms of its comprehensiveness and the detailed directions it provided across the executive branch with respect to implementing AI, establishing AI guidance and rules, and in some cases, increasing government enforcement to redress harms caused by AI (*Id.*).[75] Compared to President Trump's prior AI EOs, the 2023 AI EO also had more provisions to protect privacy and individual rights.

To further highlight this comparison, the 2023 AI EO collectively had over 100 directives addressed to more than 50 agencies, including NIST, the Department of Health and Human Services, the U.S. Patent and Trademark Office, the Department of Energy, the Department of Homeland Security, and the Department of Labor (*Id.*).[76] It addressed a range of issues, including open-source AI models, intellectual property, and environmental matters (88 FR 75191, 2023).[77] Also, using authority under the Defense Production Act, the 2023 AI EO required certain large language model (LLM) developers to conduct safety-related tests and to report the test results and other information to the government (*Id.*).[78] The 2023 AI EO also directed the Office of Management and Budget (OMB) to establish requirements for federal agency use and procurement of AI outside of the national security context and certain other contexts (*Id.*).[79] Furthermore, the 2023 AI EO required development of a national security memorandum on AI (*Id.*).[80]

[73] Executive Order 141110, Safe, Secure, and Trustworthy Development and Use of Artificial Intelligence, Federal Register, 88 FR 75191, October 30, 2023. As of February 27, 2025: https://www.federalregister.gov/documents/2023/11/01/2023-24283/safe-secure-and-trustworthy-development-and-use-of-artificial-intelligence

[74] Harris, Laurie and Jaikaran, Chris, "Highlights of the 2023 Executive Order on Artificial Intelligence for Congress," Congressional Research Service, R47843, April 3, 2024. As of February 27, 2025: https://crsreports.congress.gov/product/pdf/R/R47843

[75] *Id.*

[76] *Id.* at p. 2.

[77] Executive Order 141110, Safe, Secure, and Trustworthy Development and Use of Artificial Intelligence, Federal Register, 88 FR 75191, October 30, 2023. As of February 27, 2025: https://www.federalregister.gov/documents/2023/11/01/2023-24283/safe-secure-and-trustworthy-development-and-use-of-artificial-intelligence

[78] *Id.*

[79] *Id.*

[80] *Id.*

Within a year of the 2023 AI EO's execution, the federal government had undertaken a wide array of actions to implement it, including adopting guidelines for US government use and procurement of AI and a national security memorandum on AI (Fjeld et al., 2024).[81] The actions further encompassed establishing more NIST guidance, delineating AI guidance for the housing and education sectors, increasing government AI investments, and much more (*Id.*).[82]

At the end of his term, President Biden issued another AI EO entitled "Advancing United States Leadership in Artificial Intelligence Infrastructure."[83] Intended to bolster national security, clean energy, and US competitiveness, this EO, among other things, directed certain federal agencies to lease properties to build data centers and clean power infrastructure (90 FR 5469, 2025).[84] It also underscored the importance of maintaining US AI leadership.

President Trump's Executive Orders—Second Term

At the start of his second term, President Trump rescinded President Biden's 2023 AI EO. Additionally, President Trump signed a new AI EO entitled, "Removing Barriers to American Leadership in Artificial Intelligence" (the "2025 Trump AI EO").[85] The 2025 Trump AI EO's policy is to "sustain and enhance America's global AI dominance in order to promote human flourishing, economic competitiveness, and national security" (90 FR 8741, 2025).[86] It also seeks to revoke or change existing AI policies posing barriers to US innovation.

To accomplish these objectives, the 2025 Trump AI EO directs certain executive branch officials to pursue various actions. First, it directs officials to develop an AI "Action Plan" in pursuit of the 2025 Trump AI EO's policy

---

[81] Fjeld, Christian et al., "Federal Agencies Take Action on AI One Year After AI Executive Order—AI: The Washington Report," JDSupra, November 8, 2024. As of March 3, 2025: https://www.jdsupra.com/legalnews/federal-agencies-take-action-on-ai-one-5167710/

[82] *Id.*

[83] Executive Order 14141, Advancing United States Leadership in Artificial Intelligence Infrastructure, Federal Register, 90 FR 5469, January 17, 2025. As of February 27, 2025: https://www.federalregister.gov/documents/2025/01/17/2025-01395/advancing-united-states-leadership-in-artificial-intelligence-infrastructure

[84] *Id.*

[85] Executive Order 14179, Removing Barriers to American Leadership in Artificial Intelligence, Federal Register, 90 FR 8741, January 31, 2025. As of February 27, 2025: https://www.federalregister.gov/documents/2025/01/31/2025-02172/removing-barriers-to-american-leadership-in-artificial-intelligence

[86] *Id.*, s. 2.

(*Id.*).[87] The NSF, in collaboration with the OSTP, has begun working towards this development through its notice for public comment for the AI Action Plan (90 FR 9088, 2025).[88] Second, it charges officials to review actions taken pursuant to the 2023 AI EO during President Biden's administration and to identify those actions deemed to be inconsistent with President Trump's goals (90 FR 8741, 2025).[89] Further, it instructs officials to seek to rescind or modify the inconsistent AI policies that are identified during this review, which presumably could include hard law as well as soft law (*Id.*).[90] The actions required by the 2025 Trump AI EO seem consistent with the regulatory guidance issued during President Trump's first administration that directed federal agencies to "avoid regulatory and non-regulatory actions that needlessly hamper AI innovation and growth" (Vought, 2020).[91]

President Trump signed many other EOs at the beginning of his second term, including a Declaration of a National Energy Emergency (90 FR 8433, 2025).[92] While not set forth in this Declaration, President Trump has stated that he may use this Declaration to accelerate power plant development to support AI (Kang and Metz, 2025).[93]

Executive Branch—Hard Law: Agency Rulemaking

Several executive branch departments and agencies have the authority to promulgate binding rules or policies, subject to certain limitations or requirements

---

[87] *Id.*

[88] National Science Foundation, Request for Information on the Development of an Artificial Intelligence (AI) Action Plan, Federal Register, 90 FR 9088, February 6, 2025. As of February 27, 2025: https://www.federalregister.gov/documents/2025/02/06/2025-02305/request-for-information-on-the-development-of-an-artificial-intelligence-ai-action-plan. Please note that this chapter was written before the 2025 Trump AI EO deadline for completion of the AI Action Plan, July 22, 2025.

[89] Executive Order 14179, Removing Barriers to American Leadership in Artificial Intelligence, Federal Register, 90 FR 8741, January 31, 2025. As of February 27, 2025: https://www.federalregister.gov/documents/2025/01/31/2025-02172/removing-barriers-to-american-leadership-in-artificial-intelligence

[90] *Id.*

[91] Vought, Russell T, Memorandum for the Heads of Executive Departments and Agencies: Guidance for Regulation of Artificial Intelligence Applications, Executive Office of the President: Office of Management and Budget, November 17, 2020. As of February 27, 2025: https://www.whitehouse.gov/wp-content/uploads/2020/11/M-21-06.pdf

[92] Executive Order 14156, Declaring a National Energy Emergency, Federal Register, 90 FR 8433, January 20, 2025. As of February 27, 2025: https://www.whitehouse.gov/presidential-actions/2025/01/declaring-a-national-energy-emergency/

[93] Kang, Cecilia, and Metz, Cade, "Trump Announces $100 Billion A.I. Initiative," The New York Times, January 21, 2025. As of February 27, 2025: https://www.nytimes.com/2025/01/21/technology/trump-openai-stargate-artificial-intelligence.html

(Carey, 2013).[94] The president typically appoints leaders of these executive branch departments and agencies who typically require Senate confirmation, as another balance of power (Cole, 2018).[95] The executive departments, such as the Department of Defense and the Department of Homeland Security, usually have a single leader appointed by the president (*Id.*).[96] The president can remove these political appointees at any time, with or without cause (Bamzai and Prakash, 2023).[97] The executive branch's independent agencies, like the Federal Trade Commission (FTC) and the Federal Communications Commission (FCC), are composed of commissioners or similar leaders who typically collectively represent different political parties (*Id.*).[98] Members of the executive branch's independent agencies typically serve for fixed terms that can span presidential transitions, and usually, they can only be removed for cause (*Id.*).[99]

During President Biden's tenure, many executive branch departments and agencies adopted binding (and non-binding, as discussed below) AI requirements and policies, typically focused on specific sectors. For instance, during President Biden's term, the FTC adopted rules prohibiting the use of AI-enabled deepfakes and other techniques to impersonate governments or businesses (89 FR 15017, 2024).[100] The FTC also adopted rules barring the use of certain technologies to create fake customer reviews and testimonials (89 FR 68034, 2024).[101] For the financial services sector, the Consumer

[94] Carey, Maeve P., "The Federal Rulemaking Process: An Overview," Congressional Research Service, RL32240, June 17, 2023. As of February 27, 2025: https://crsreports.congress.gov/product/pdf/RL/RL32240/12

[95] Cole, Jared P., "Organizing Executive Branch Agencies: Who Makes the Call?," Congressional Research Service, LSB10158, June 27, 2018. As of March 2, 2025: https://crsreports.congress.gov/product/pdf/LSB/LSB10158

[96] *Id.*

[97] Breger, Marshall J. and Edles, Gary J., "Established by Practice: The Theory and Operation of Independent Federal Agencies," Administrative Law Review, Vol. 52, No. 4, 2000, pp. 1111–1294: https://www.jstor.org/stable/40711933; Bamzai, Aditya and Prakash, Saikrishna Bangalore, "The Executive Power of Removal," May 2023, Harvard Law Review. As of March 3, 2025: https://harvardlawreview.org/print/vol-136/the-executive-power-of-removal/

[98] *Id.*

[99] *Id.*

[100] Federal Trade Commission, Trade Regulation Rule on Impersonation of Government and Businesses, Federal Register, 89 FR 15017, March 1, 2024. As of February 27, 2025: https://www.federalregister.gov/documents/2024/03/01/2024-04335/trade-regulation-rule-on-impersonation-of-government-and-businesses#p-132

[101] Federal Trade Commission, Trade Regulation Rule on the Use of Consumer Reviews and Testimonials, Federal Register, 89 FR 68034, August 22, 2024. As of February 27, 2025: https://www.federalregister.gov/documents/2024/08/22/2024-18519/trade-regulation-rule-on-the-use-of-consumer-reviews-and-testimonials

Financial Protection Bureau (CFPB) adopted rules governing the use of AI in home valuations (Chopra and Martinez, 2024).[102] Turning to healthcare, the Department of Health and Human Services finalized a rule establishing transparency requirements for AI used in certified health IT systems (Assistant Secretary for Technology Policy, 2025).[103] With regard to national security, the U.S. Department of Commerce issued AI export control rules, including regulations limiting the export of advanced computer chips and certain AI model weights (90 FR 4544, 2025).[104] Similarly, the US Treasury Department adopted regulations limiting outbound US investments in AI and certain other technologies in China, Hong Kong, and Macau (89 FR 90398, 2025).[105] These regulations added to other US legal requirements aimed at limiting foreign control over US technology, such as 2018 legislation governing the interagency Committee on Foreign Investment in the US (CFIUS), which reviews certain transactions raising national security concerns (Foreign Investment Risk Review Modernization Act of 2018).[106]

At the start of his second term, as discussed above, President Trump rescinded the 2023 AI EO. Soon thereafter, President Trump issued the 2025 Trump AI EO directing appointed executive branch officials to review the AI actions of the previous presidential administration and develop a plan for seeking to change those AI rules and policies deemed inconsistent with

---

[102] Chopra, Rohit and Martinez, Zixta, "CFPB approves rule to ensure accuracy and accountability in the use of AI and algorithms in home appraisals," Consumer Financial Protection Bureau, June 24, 2024. As of February 27, 2025: https://www.consumerfinance.gov/about-us/blog/cfpb-approves-rule-to-ensure-accuracy-and-accountability-in-the-use-of-ai-and-algorithms-in-home-appraisals/

[103] Assistant Secretary for Technology Policy, "Health Data, Technology, and Interoperability: Certification Program Updates, Algorithm Transparency, and Information Sharing (HTI-1) Final Rule." As of February 27, 2025: https://www.healthit.gov/topic/laws-regulation-and-policy/health-data-technology-and-interoperability-certification-program

[104] Department of Commerce, Framework for Artificial Intelligence Diffusion, Federal Register, 90 FR 4544, January 15, 2025. As of February 27, 2025: https://www.federalregister.gov/documents/2025/01/15/2025-00636/framework-for-artificial-intelligence-diffusion

[105] Department of Treasury, Provisions Pertaining to U.S. Investments in Certain National Security Technologies and Products in Countries of Concern, Federal Register, 89 FR 90398, November 15, 2024. As of February 27, 2025: https://www.federalregister.gov/documents/2024/11/15/2024-25422/provisions-pertaining-to-us-investments-in-certain-national-security-technologies-and-products-in

[106] John S. McCain National Defense Authorization Act for Fiscal Year 2019 (US) division A, title XVII, subtitle A: Committee on Foreign Investment in the United States. As of February 27, 2025: https://www.congress.gov/bill/115th-congress/house-bill/5515

President Trump's goals (90 FR 8741, 2025).[107] Similarly, at the beginning of his second term, President Trump placed a freeze on issuing new or proposed rules, pending further review (90 FR 8249, 2025).[108] These actions give President Trump latitude to seek to adjust the executive branch's AI regulations and policies to the extent he deems necessary or appropriate for his priorities, consistent with applicable law. These events further illustrate how the democratic process, and resulting political changes, can influence US AI law and policy.

Executive Branch—Soft Law: NIST Guidance

The executive branch has also created soft law guidance that has been very influential in establishing norms and helping create best practices, even though it is neither legally binding nor enforceable. For example, the National Institute of Standards and Technology (NIST) created a voluntary AI Risk Management Framework (AI RMF), as directed by Congress pursuant to the 2021 NDAA (National Institute of Standards and Technology, 2025).[109] Developed with broad stakeholder input, the AI RMF applies across industries and establishes a voluntary framework centered on governance as well as mapping, measuring, and managing AI risks (*Id.*).[110] To assist with its implementation, NIST published an AI RMF playbook.[111] Additionally, AI RMF profiles are also being developed to address specific AI uses and applications, such as generative AI and human rights (U.S. Department of State, 2025).[112]

---

[107] Executive Order 14179, Removing Barriers to American Leadership in Artificial Intelligence, Federal Register, 90 FR 8741, January 31, 2025. As of February 27, 2025: https://www.federalregister.gov/documents/2025/01/31/2025-02172/removing-barriers-to-american-leadership-in-artificial-intelligence

[108] Executive Office of the President, Regulatory Freeze Pending Review, Federal Register, 90 FR 8249, January 20, 2025. As of February 27, 2025: https://www.federalregister.gov/documents/2025/01/28/2025-01906/regulatory-freeze-pending-review

[109] National Institute of Standards and Technology, "Artificial Intelligence Risk Management Framework: Generative Artificial Intelligence Profile," U.S. Department of Commerce, July 2024. As of February 27, 2025: https://nvlpubs.nist.gov/nistpubs/ai/NIST.AI.600-1.pdf

[110] *Id.*

[111] National Institute of Standards and Technology, "NIST AI RMF Playbook," U.S. Department of Commerce. As of February 27, 2025: https://airc.nist.gov/airmf-resources/playbook/

[112] U.S. Department of State, "Risk Management Profile for Artificial Intelligence and Human Rights," Bureau of Cyberspace and Digital Policy, July 25, 2024. As of February 27, 2025: https://2021-2025.state.gov/risk-management-profile-for-ai-and-human-rights/

In May 2024, NIST launched an AI Innovation Lab Program, Assessing Risks and Impacts of AI (ARIA) (NIST, 2024).[113] ARIA expands the NIST AI RMF by providing tools to implement its risk evaluation capabilities, encouraging the use of both quantitative and qualitative methods to assess and track the risks and effects associated with AI systems (*Id.*).[114]

Both President Trump and President Biden have turned to NIST to help develop AI guidance. As discussed above, President Trump's 2019 AI EO looked to NIST to lead the creation of "a plan for Federal engagement in the development of technical standards and related tools in support of reliable, robust, and trustworthy systems that use AI technologies."[115] Similarly, pursuant to President Biden's 2023 AI EO, NIST developed various AI guidance documents, including guidance for reducing risks presented by synthetic AI content and an engagement plan for global AI standards.[116] President Biden also created the US AI Safety Institute (AISI) within NIST (National Institute of Standards and Technology, 2025).[117] During President Biden's tenure, the AISI helped the US organize and lead the first summit of global AI safety institutes (National Institute of Standards and Technology, 2024).[118] The AISI also signed agreements with a couple AI developers to work on safety testing (*Id.*).[119]

The president and certain others in the executive branch have power to direct and prioritize NIST's efforts. As discussed above, with the 2025 Trump AI EO, President Trump has implemented a mechanism to review NIST's

---

[113] National Institute of Standards and Technology, "NIST Launches ARIA, A New Program to Advance Sociotechnical Testing and Evaluation for AI," May 28, 2024. As of February 27, 2025: https://www.nist.gov/news-events/news/2024/05/nist-launches-aria-new-program-advance-sociotechnical-testing-and

[114] *Id.*

[115] Executive Order 13859, Maintaining Leadership in Artificial Intelligence, Federal Register, 84 FR 3967, February 11, 2019. As of February 27, 2025: https://www.federalregister.gov/documents/2019/02/14/2019-02544/maintaining-american-leadership-in-artificial-intelligence

[116] National Institute of Standards and Technology, "A Plan for Global Engagement on AI Standards," U.S. Department of Commerce, July 2024. As of February 27, 2025: https://nvlpubs.nist.gov/nistpubs/ai/NIST.AI.100-5.pdf?trk=public_post_comment-text

[117] National Institute of Standards and Technology, "U.S. Artificial Intelligence Safety Institute." As of February 27, 2025: https://www.nist.gov/aisi

[118] National Institute of Standards and Technology, "FACT SHEET: U.S. Department of Commerce & U.S. Department of State Launch the International Network of AI Safety Institutes at Inaugural Convening in San Francisco," November 20, 2024. As of February 27, 2025: https://www.nist.gov/news-events/news/2024/11/fact-sheet-us-department-commerce-us-department-state-launch-international

[119] National Institute of Standards and Technology, "U.S. AI Safety Institute Signs Agreements Regarding AI Safety Research, Testing and Evaluation With Anthropic and OpenAI," August 29, 2024. As of February 27, 2025: https://www.nist.gov/news-events/news/2024/08/us-ai-safety-institute-signs-agreements-regarding-ai-safety-research

activities and seek changes, to the extent needed, to align with his objectives (90 FR 8249, 2025).[120]

Executive Branch—Soft Law: Voluntary Commitments

The executive branch can also seek voluntary commitments from companies to advance responsible AI. In July 2023, President Biden obtained voluntary commitments from Amazon, Anthropic, Google, Inflection, Meta, Microsoft, and OpenAI to undertake certain responsible AI practices (The White House, 2023a).[121] These practices span a range of activities, such as conducting internal and external red-team testing; investing in cybersecurity and insider threat protections; incentivizing the identification and redress of vulnerabilities and incidents; working on identifying AI generated synthetic content; and publicly reporting certain information (*Id.*).[122] Later that year, Apple, Palantir, and other companies also agreed to these voluntary commitments (The White House, 2023b).[123] The voluntary commitments received some criticism because they lacked the force of law (Harvard Law Review, 2024).[124] However, they did help inform the 2023 AI EO and the G7's work in connection with the Hiroshima AI Process, as discussed below (Kerry et al., 2025).[125]

President Trump has also shown interest in collaborating with industry to advance AI objectives. Early in his second term, President Trump invited three

[120]Executive Office of the President, Regulatory Freeze Pending Review, Federal Register, 90 FR 8249, January 20, 2025. As of February 27, 2025: https://www.federalregister.gov/documents/2025/01/28/2025-01906/regulatory-freeze-pending-review

[121]The White House, "FACT SHEET: Biden-Harris Administration Secures Voluntary Commitments from Leading Artificial Intelligence Companies to Manage the Risks Posed by AI," July 21, 2023. As of February 27, 2025: https://bidenwhitehouse.archives.gov/briefing-room/statements-releases/2023/07/21/fact-sheet-biden-harris-administration-secures-voluntary-commitments-from-leading-artificial-intelligence-companies-to-manage-the-risks-posed-by-ai/

[122]*Id.*

[123]The White House, "FACT SHEET: Biden-Harris Administration Secures Voluntary Commitments from Eight Additional Artificial Intelligence Companies to Manage the Risks Posed by AI," September 12, 2023. As of February 27, 2025: https://bidenwhitehouse.archives.gov/briefing-room/statements-releases/2023/09/12/fact-sheet-biden-harris-administration-secures-voluntary-commitments-from-eight-additional-artificial-intelligence-companies-to-manage-the-risks-posed-by-ai/

[124]Harvard Law Review, Voluntary Commitments from Leading Artificial Intelligence Companies on July 21, 2023, 137 Harv. L. Rev. 1284, February 12, 2024. As of February 27, 2025: https://harvardlawreview.org/print/vol-137/voluntary-commitments-from-leading-artificial-intelligence-companies-on-july-21-2023/

[125]Kerry, Cameron F., et al., "Network architecture for global AI policy," The Brookings Institution, February 10, 2025. As of February 27, 2025: https://www.brookings.edu/articles/network-architecture-for-global-ai-policy/?b=1

corporate leaders to the White House to unveil plans for a $500 billion AI infrastructure project (Duffy, 2025).[126]

Executive Branch—Soft Law: Policy Statements and Interpretive Statements

The executive branch can also publish non-binding or soft law policy statements further shaping US AI law and policy. As discussed above, these statements often reflect the priorities of the president and appointed executive branch officials and thus can change over time, including from one presidential administration to another.

These soft law policy actions can occur at the White House level or within individual executive branch departments or agencies, or pursuant to a combination of the two. As an example, during President Trump's first term, the White House, together with the Department of Transportation, issued guidance on "Ensuring American Leadership in Automated Vehicle Technologies" (Department of Transportation, 2020).[127] Under President Biden's leadership, the White House published the Blueprint for an AI Bill of Rights, setting forth broad principles for protecting Americans against AI harms and serving as a foundation for subsequent AI actions during his administration (Office of Science and Technology Policy, 2025).[128]

At the executive branch agency or department level, guidance has been issued on various topics, including explaining how longstanding US federal laws can be applied to address AI harms, even though these laws were not enacted specifically for AI. Sometimes, these guidance documents are followed by executive branch enforcement actions, as discussed in the next section. The following provides examples of AI policies adopted within specific executive branch departments or agencies, which as noted above, are subject to change over time, including in response to political changes.

[126] Duffy, Clare, "Trump announces a $500 billion AI infrastructure investment in the US," CNN, January 21, 2025. As of February 27, 2025: https://www.cnn.com/2025/01/21/tech/openai-oracle-softbank-trump-ai-investment/index.html

[127] United States Department of Transportation, "Ensuring American Leadership in Automated Vehicle Technologies," January 2020. As of February 27, 2025:https://www.transportation.gov/sites/dot.gov/files/docs/policy-initiatives/automated-vehicles/360956/ensuringamericanleadershipav4.pdf

[128] Office of Science and Technology Policy, "Blueprint for an AI Bill of Rights," The White House. As of February 27, 2025: https://bidenwhitehouse.archives.gov/ostp/ai-bill-of-rights/

The Department of Defense

Consistent with the mandate in the 2019 NDAA and other actions, the DOD has emerged as a responsible AI leader within the US government. For example, in February 2020, the DOD adopted principles for the ethical and lawful use of AI systems in the US military, referred to as the Ethical AI Principles (U.S. Department of Defense, 2020).[129] In November 2023, the DOD released its Data, Analytics and Artificial Intelligence Adoption Strategy (U.S. Department of Defense, 2023).[130] This DOD strategy is led by the Chief Digital and Artificial Intelligence Office (CDAO) which aims to accelerate the DOD's "adoption of data, analytics, and artificial intelligence (AI) from the boardroom to the battlefield to enable decision advantage" (Chief Digital and Artificial Intelligence Office, 2025).[131] The DOD's AI strategy prioritizes using AI development "to build enduring decision advantage" (U.S. Department of Defense, 2023).[132] Specifically, the DOD seeks to advance its data ecosystem to accomplish its "AI hierarchy of Needs," which the strategy defines as: quality data, governance, insightful analytics and metrics, assurance, and responsible AI (*Id.*).[133] More recently, in December 2024, the DOD launched the AI Rapid Capabilities Cell (AI RCC) which advances two of DOD's focus areas, warfighting and enterprise management (U.S. Department of Defense, 2024).[134] The AI RCC leads the DOD's efforts to deploy new AI technologies, such as generative AI and Frontier models (*Id.*).[135] The AI RCC, as a pilot

---

[129] U.S. Department of Defense, "DOD Adopts Ethical Principles for Artificial Intelligence," February 24, 2020. As of February 27, 2025: https://www.defense.gov/News/Releases/release/article/2091996/dod-adopts-ethical-principles-for-artificial-intelligence/

[130] U.S. Department of Defense, "Data, Analytics, and Artificial Intelligence Adoption Strategy," June 27, 2023. As of February 27, 2025: https://media.defense.gov/2023/Nov/02/2003333300/-1/-1/1/DOD_DATA_ANALYTICS_AI_ADOPTION_STRATEGY.PDF.

[131] Chief Digital and Artificial Intelligence Office, "Organization." As of February 27, 2025: https://www.ai.mil/About/Organization/

[132] U.S. Department of Defense, "Data, Analytics, and Artificial Intelligence Adoption Strategy," p. 7, June 27, 2023. As of February 27, 2025: https://media.defense.gov/2023/Nov/02/2003333300/-1/-1/1/DOD_DATA_ANALYTICS_AI_ADOPTION_STRATEGY.PDF

[133] *Id.*

[134] U.S. Department of Defense, "CDAO and DIU Launch New Effort Focused on Accelerating DOD Adoption of AI Capabilities," December 11, 2024. As of February 27, 2025: https://www.defense.gov/News/Releases/Release/Article/3996199/cdao-and-diu-launch-new-effort-focused-on-accelerating-dod-adoption-of-ai-capab/

[135] *Id.*

program, will oversee the establishment of digital "sandboxes" for AI testing and research on government networks (Clark, 2024).[136]

Federal Trade Commission

The FTC focuses on protecting the public from unfair or deceptive business practices as well as from unfair competition (Federal Trade Commission, 2025).[137] The FTC has issued several statements explaining how AI can result in unfair or deceptive trade practices in violation of the FTC Act and possibly other laws when it is improperly developed or deployed (Federal Trade Commission, 2025; Ensor, 2024).[138] These guidance documents can provide companies with more clarity on how they can comply with laws and reduce their liability risks.

This FTC practice of issuing guidance spanned both the Trump and Biden administrations. For instance, during President Trump's first term, the FTC published a blogpost underscoring the need for AI transparency, explainability, fairness, robustness, and accountability (Smith, 2020).[139] Under the Biden administration, the FTC followed with several blogposts on a range of topics, such as avoiding unfair AI terms of service and not using AI to deceive people (*See* e.g.).[140] Additionally, during the Biden administration, the FTC warned

---

[136] Clark, Joseph, "DOD's Chief AI Officer Launches Rapid Capability Cell, Frontier AI Pilots to Accelerate Adoption of Cutting Edge Tech," U.S. Department of Defense, December 12, 2024. As of February 27, 2025: https://www.defense.gov/News/News-Stories/Article/Article/3999805/dods-chief-ai-officer-launches-rapid-capability-cell-frontier-ai-pilots-to-acce/

[137] Federal Trade Commission, "About the FTC." As of February 27, 2025: https://www.ftc.gov/about-ftc

[138] Federal Trade Commission, "Artificial Intelligence Compliance Plan." As of February 27, 2025: https://www.ftc.gov/ai. Ensor, Julia S., "Operation AI Comply: continuing the crackdown on over-promises and AI-related lies," Federal Trade Commission, September 25, 2024. As of February 27, 2025: https://web.archive.org/web/20250226032649/https://www.ftc.gov/business-guidance/blog/2024/09/operation-ai-comply-continuing-crackdown-overpromises-ai-related-lies

[139] Smith, Andrew, "Using Artificial Intelligence and Algorithms," Federal Trade Commission, April 8, 2020. As of February 27, 2025: https://web.archive.org/web/20241228164925/https://www.ftc.gov/business-guidance/blog/2020/04/using-artificial-intelligence-algorithms

[140] Atleson, Michael, "The Luring Test: AI and the engineering of consumer trust," Federal Trade Commission, March 1, 2023. As of February 27, 2025: https://web.archive.org/web/20250202225345/www.ftc.gov/consumer-alerts/2023/05/luring-test-ai-and-engineering-consumer-trust. Atleson, Michael, "Keep your AI claims in check," Federal Trade Commission, February 27, 2023. As of February 27, 2025: https://web.archive.org/web/20250224091005/https://www.ftc.gov/business-guidance/blog/2023/02/keep-your-ai-claims-check. Atleson, Michael, "Chatbots, deepfakes, and voice clones: AI deception for sale," Federal Trade Commission, March 20, 2023. As of February 27, 2025: https://web.archive.org/web/20250223034815/https://www.ftc.gov/business-guidance/blog/2023/03/chatbots-deepfakes-voice-clones-ai-deception-sale. Federal Trade Commission, "AI (and other) Companies: Quietly Changing Your Terms of Service Could Be Unfair or Deceptive," February 13,

about competitive harms presented by generative AI, highlighting questions about control of data, talent, compute, and other resources (*See* e.g.).[141]

Equal Employment Opportunity Commission and Related Department of Justice and Other Guidance

The U.S. Equal Employment Opportunity Commission (EEOC) is a federal agency responsible for enforcing federal laws prohibiting employment discrimination (U.S. Equal Employment Opportunity Commission, 2025).[142] During President Biden's term, the EEOC launched the Artificial Intelligence and Algorithmic Fairness Initiative in response to employers increasingly using AI-powered tools to streamline and screen job applicants and assist with other employment matters (U.S. Equal Employment Opportunity Commission, 2021).[143] This initiative focuses on ensuring that AI tools used in employment-related decisions comply with federal civil rights laws (*Id.*).[144] In connection with this initiative, the EEOC published several guidance documents, including a technical assistance document, providing employers with strategies to identify and mitigate adverse AI impacts in the employment context (U.S. Equal Employment Opportunity Commission, 2023).[145] Another EEOC publication specifically addressed avoiding using AI tools to

2024. As of February 27, 2025: https://www.ftc.gov/policy/advocacy-research/tech-at-ftc/2024/02/ai-other-companies-quietly-changing-your-terms-service-could-be-unfair-or-deceptive. Federal Trade Commission, "AI and the Risk of Consumer Harm," January 3, 2025. As of February 27, 2025: https://web.archive.org/web/20250226025720/https://www.ftc.gov/policy/advocacy-research/tech-at-ftc/2025/01/ai-risk-consumer-harm

141 Federal Trade Commission, "Generative AI Raises Competition Concerns," June 29, 2023. As of February 27, 2025: https://www.ftc.gov/policy/advocacy-research/tech-at-ftc/2023/06/generative-ai-raises-competition-concerns. Federal Trade Commission, "Comment of the United States Federal Trade Commission," October 30, 2023. As of February 27, 2025: https://www.ftc.gov/system/files/ftc_gov/pdf/p241200_ftc_comment_to_copyright_office.pdf

142 U.S. Equal Employment Opportunity Commission, "Overview. As of February 27, 2025: https://www.eeoc.gov/overview

143 U.S. Equal Employment Opportunity Commission, "EEOC Launches Initiative on Artificial Intelligence and Algorithmic Fairness," October 28, 2021. As of February 27, 2025: https://www.eeoc.gov/newsroom/eeoc-launches-initiative-artificial-intelligence-and-algorithmic-fairness

144 *Id.*

145 U.S. Equal Employment Opportunity Commission, "EEOC Hearing Explores Potential Benefits and Harms of Artificial Intelligence and other Automated Systems in Employment Decisions," January 31, 2023. As of February 27, 2025: https://www.eeoc.gov/newsroom/eeoc-hearing-explores-potential-benefits-and-harms-artificial-intelligence-and-other

unlawfully discriminate against people with disabilities (U.S. Equal Employment Opportunity Commission, 2023).[146]

The U.S. Department of Justice also enforces anti-discrimination laws (U.S. Department of Justice, 2025).[147] Like the EEOC, during the Biden administration, it released guidance on Artificial Intelligence and Disability Discrimination in Hiring (*Id.*).[148] As another example, pursuant to the 2023 AI EO, the U.S. Department of Housing and Urban Development provided guidance on the use of AI in tenant screening and housing advertisements (U.S. Department of Housing and Urban Development, 2024).[149]

Executive Branch—Enforcement

Many executive branch departments and agencies have authority to bring actions to enforce laws against private parties (The White House, 2025).[150] Typically, the executive branch—has discretion to decide whether and to what extent it desires to exercise this authority. However, Congressional budget appropriations can impact the amount of enforcement an executive branch agency can undertake (Garvey and Stiff, 2023).[151]

During President Biden's term, several executive branch agencies made statements affirming their right to bring enforcement actions against private parties to redress AI harms, relying on longstanding federal US anti-discrimination, consumer protection, and other laws that were not enacted specifically for AI. Furthermore, nine federal agencies, including the FTC, the DOJ, the CFPB, and the EEOC, pledged during the Biden administration

---

[146] U.S. Equal Employment Opportunity Commission, "Select Issues: Assessing Adverse Impact in Software, Algorithms, and Artificial Intelligence Used in Employment Selection Procedures Under Title VII of the Civil Rights Act of 1964," May 18, 2023. As of February 27, 2025: https://web.archive.org/web/20250124130254/https://www.eeoc.gov/laws/guidance/select-issues-assessing-adverse-impact-software-algorithms-and-artificial

[147] U.S. Department of Justice, "Algorithms, Artificial Intelligence, and Disability Discrimination in Hiring." As of February 27, 2025: https://www.ada.gov/assets/pdfs/ai-guidance.pdf

[148] *Id.*

[149] U.S. Department of Housing and Urban Development, "Guidance on Application of the Fair Housing Act to the Advertising of Housing, Credit, and Other Real Estate-Related Transactions through Digital Platforms," April 29, 2024. As of February 27, 2025: https://web.archive.org/web/20250222144745/https://www.hud.gov/sites/dfiles/FHEO/documents/FHEO_Guidance_on_Advertising_through_Digital_Platforms.pdf

[150] The White House, "The Executive Branch." As of February 27, 2025: https://bidenwhitehouse.archives.gov/about-the-white-house/our-government/the-executive-branch/

[151] Garvey, Todd and Stiff, Sean M, "Congress's Authority to Influence and Control Executive Branch Agencies," Congressional Research Service, R45442, pp. 14–16, March 30, 2023. As of February 27, 2025: https://crsreports.congress.gov/product/pdf/R/R45442

to use their enforcement authority to protect the public again AI harms (*See* e.g.).[152] These actions demonstrate that the US government has mechanisms it can elect to use to try to hold AI developers and deployers accountable, even though the US does not have comprehensive federal AI legislation.

Some AI enforcement actions during the Biden administration are described below. Because this chapter was completed at the beginning of President Trump's second term, it generally does not address US government enforcement in the AI context beyond the Biden administration.

AI Enforcement: Consumer Protection and Competition

During the Biden administration, the FTC brought enforcement actions against AI developers that collectively raised a range of issues. Some of these FTC enforcement actions focused on the unlawful collection and processing of AI training data and resulted in settlements requiring AI developers to, among other things, disgorge or delete AI models trained on personal data that was obtained or used without proper consents (Federal Trade Commission, 2025).[153] During the Biden administration, the FTC also opened an investigation against OpenAI to assess whether ChatGPT violates consumer protection law (Kerr, 2023).[154]

Additionally, during the Biden administration, the FTC focused its enforcement attention on deceptive claims resulting from AI. For instance, during this period, the FTC launched Operation AI Comply and brought several actions against companies who made deceptive claims about AI capabilities or produced deceptive deepfake customer reviews (Federal Trade Commission, 2024).[155] Similarly, near the end of President Biden's term, the FTC issued an

---

[152] U.S. Department of Justice, "Five New Federal Agencies Join Justice Department in Pledge to Enforce Civil Rights Laws in Artificial Intelligence," April 4, 2024. As of February 27, 2025: https://www.justice.gov/opa/pr/five-new-federal-agencies-join-justice-department-pledge-enforce-civil-rights-laws. U.S. Department of Justice, "Justice Department's Civil Rights Division Joins Officials from CFPB, EEOC and FTC Pledging to Confront Bias and Discrimination in Artificial Intelligence," April 25, 2023. As of February 27, 2025: https://www.justice.gov/opa/pr/justice-department-s-civil-rights-division-joins-officials-cfpb-eeoc-and-ftc-pledging

[153] Federal Trade Commission, "The FTC is on the Front Lines of AI Innovation & Regulation," January 17, 2025. As of February 27, 2025: https://www.ftc.gov/system/files/ftc_gov/pdf/ai-accomplishments-1.17.25.pdf

[154] Kerr, Dara, "FTC investigating ChatGPT over potential consumer harm," National Public Radio, July 13, 2023. As of February 27, 2025: https://www.npr.org/2023/07/13/1187532997/ftc-investigating-chatgpt-over-potential-consumer-harm

[155] Federal Trade Commission, "FTC Announces Crackdown on Deceptive AI Claims and Schemes," September 25, 2024. As of February 27, 2025: https://www.ftc.gov/news-events/news/press-releases/2024/09/ftc-announces-crackdown-deceptive-ai-claims-schemes

order barring IntelliVision from making deceptive claims about its AI-enabled facial recognition software (Federal Trade Commission, 2025).[156]

Both the FTC and the DOJ can bring enforcement actions under federal antitrust laws (Federal Trade Commission, 2025).[157] Using this authority, the FTC issued orders, during the Biden administration, soliciting information from Alphabet, Amazon, Anthropic, Microsoft, and OpenAI to better understand the competitive impacts of some of their generative AI partnerships and investments (Federal Trade Commission, 2024).[158] Based on the information obtained in response to these orders, the FTC issued a staff report, toward the end of President Biden's term, highlighting terms in some of these agreements and their potential competitive implications (Federal Trade Commission, 2025).[159] Notably, the staff report evaluates key terms of the AI partnerships, including: (1) equity and revenue-sharing rights; (2) certain consultation, control, and exclusivity rights; (3) cloud spend commitments; (4) sharing of key resources and information; and (5) the potential to expand current products and scale new offerings (Federal Trade Commission, 2025).[160]

AI Enforcement: Other Areas

During the Biden administration, the DOJ brought several claims relating to AI, including to address violations of civil rights laws that involved the use of AI. One such case resulted in a settlement with Meta involving its use of an AI tool that resulted in discriminatory practices in housing advertising in

[156] Federal Trade Commission, "FTC Finalizes Order Prohibiting IntelliVision from Making Deceptive Claims About Its Facial Recognition Software," January 13, 2025. As of February 27, 2025: https://www.ftc.gov/news-events/news/press-releases/2025/01/ftc-finalizes-order-prohibiting-intellivision-making-deceptive-claims-about-its-facial-recognition

[157] Federal Trade Commission, "The Enforcers." As of February 27, 2025: https://www.ftc.gov/advice-guidance/competition-guidance/guide-antitrust-laws/enforcers

[158] Federal Trade Commission, "FTC Launches Inquiry into Generative AI Investments and Partnerships," January 25, 2024. As of February 27, 2025: https://www.ftc.gov/news-events/news/press-releases/2024/01/ftc-launches-inquiry-generative-ai-investments-partnerships

[159] Federal Trade Commission, "FTC Issues Staff Report on AI Partnerships & Investments Study," January 17, 2025. As of February 27, 2025: https://www.ftc.gov/news-events/news/press-releases/2025/01/ftc-issues-staff-report-ai-partnerships-investments-study

[160] Federal Trade Commission, "Partnerships Between Cloud Service Providers and AI Developers," p. 16, January 2025. As of February 27, 2025:https://www.ftc.gov/system/files/ftc_gov/pdf/p246201_aipartnerships6breport_redacted_0.pdf

violation of the Fair Housing Act (U.S. Department of Justice, 2022).[161] In addition to imposing a monetary fine, the DOJ settlement required Meta to stop using this AI tool for housing advertising and to develop a new system, which would be subject to government oversight (*Id.*).[162]

Under the Biden administration, other agencies also brought AI and related enforcement actions relying on longstanding laws not enacted specifically for AI. For instance, the EEOC settled a claim against iTutorGroup for using an automated application that rejected more than two hundred older job applicants based on their age (U.S. Equal Employment Opportunity Commission, 2023).[163] The Federal Communications Commission (FCC) settled a claim involving a deceptive deepfake audio robocall of President Biden's cloned voice (The Federal Communications Commission, 2024).[164] This cloned voice instructed prospective voters not to vote in the upcoming presidential primary election (*Id.*).[165] Relatedly, the FCC issued a declaratory ruling that AI-generated calls violate the longstanding Telecommunications Consumer Protection Act (The Federal Communications Commission, 2024).[166] As another example, the U.S. Securities and Exchange Commission (SEC) settled suits against two investment advisers relating to false and misleading claims made to clients about their use of AI (U.S. Securities and Exchange Commission, 2024).[167] At the beginning of President Trump's second term, the SEC formed a Cyber and Emerging Technologies Unit to pursue certain claims involving secured transactions, including fraud committed using AI (U.S. Securities and Exchange Commission, 2025).[168]

---

[161] U.S. Department of Justice, "Justice Department Secures Groundbreaking Settlement Agreement with Meta Platforms, Formerly Known as Facebook, to Resolve Allegations of Discriminatory Advertising," June 21, 2022. As of February 27, 2025: https://www.justice.gov/opa/pr/justice-department-secures-groundbreaking-settlement-agreement-meta-platforms-formerly-known

[162] *Id.*

[163] U.S. Equal Employment Opportunity Commission, "iTutorGroup to Pay $365,000 to Settle EEOC Discriminatory Hiring Suit," September 11, 2023. As of February 27, 2025: https://www.eeoc.gov/newsroom/itutorgroup-pay-365000-settle-eeoc-discriminatory-hiring-suit

[164] The Federal Communications Commission, "FCC Settles Case Against Provider that Transmitted Spoofed AI-Generated Robocalls for Election Interference in New Hampshire," August 21, 2024. As of February 27, 2025: https://docs.fcc.gov/public/attachments/DOC-404951A1.pdf

[165] *Id.*

[166] The Federal Communications Commission, Declaratory Ruling, February 8, 2024. As of February 27, 2025: https://docs.fcc.gov/public/attachments/FCC-24-17A1.pdf

[167] U.S. Securities and Exchange Commission, "SEC Charges Two Investment Advisers with Making False and Misleading Statements About Their Use of Artificial Intelligence," March 18, 2024. As of February 27, 2025: https://www.sec.gov/newsroom/press-releases/2024-36

[168] U.S. Securities and Exchange Commission, "SEC Announces Cyber and Emerging Technologies Unit to Protect Retail Investors," February 20, 2025. As of February 27, 2025: https://www.sec.gov/newsroom/press-releases/2025-42?utm_medium=email&utm_source=govdelivery

Executive Branch—Public Procurement

As reflected in some of the AI EOs and other actions discussed above, the US government has underscored the importance of implementing AI responsibly in connection with its own operations. As a major procurer of AI products and services, the US government can exercise its "power of the purse," through its public procurement rules and policies, to require its contractors, and their subcontractors, to deliver and perform in accordance with US AI policies (Hickok, 2024).[169] Unsurprisingly, AI public procurement has been cited as another form of AI governance (Coglianese, 2025).[170]

Public procurement can be very significant for managing responsible AI. The US government spent more than $2 billion in fiscal year 2022 on government contracts involving AI, and its aggregate AI spending expanded 2.5 times since 2017 (Quay-de la Vallee et al., 2024).[171] As noted above, the US government has taken steps to integrate responsible AI governance into its procurement processes. State and local governments also engage in public procurement. Like the US government, they have increased their focus on addressing responsible AI in their public procurement as well (National Association of State Procurement Officials, 2025).[172]

Judicial Branch

Courts have an important role in the US governmental system of checks and balances of power. Cases can emerge challenging whether the actions of Congress or the executive branch comply with the US Constitution or other applicable laws (United States Courts, 2025).[173] For example, as discussed

[169]Hickok, Merve, Public procurement of artificial intelligence systems: new risks and future proofing, AI & Society 39, 1213–1227 (2024). As of February 27, 2025: https://doi.org/10.1007/s00146-022-01572-2

[170]Coglianese, Cary, Procurement and Artificial Intelligence, Handbook on Public Policy and AI, October 4, 2023. As of February 27, 2025: https://papers.ssrn.com/sol3/papers.cfm?abstract_id=4591724

[171]Quay-de la Vallee, Hannah et al., "Report—The Federal Government's Power of the Purse: Enacting Procurement Policies and Practices to Support Responsible AI Use," Center for Democracy & Technology. As of February 27, 2025: https://cdt.org/insights/report-the-federal-governments-power-of-the-purse-enacting-procurement-policies-and-practices-to-support-responsible-ai-use/

[172]National Association of State Procurement Officials, "AI-Powered Procurement: Harnessing AI's Potential for More Efficient State Procurement Practices." As of February 27, 2025: https://www.nascio.org/wp-content/uploads/2024/10/NASCIO_NASPO_AI-Powered-Procurement_2024_a11y.pdf

[173]United States Courts, "Court Rule and Structure." As of February 27, 2025: https://www.uscourts.gov/about-federal-courts/court-role-and-structure

above, the Supreme Court upheld a law barring Tik Tok from providing social media services in the US, absent a qualified divestiture (Benson et al., 2024).[174]

In addition to assessing the legality of government actions, courts are also addressing AI claims brought by private parties (*See* e.g.).[175] For example, federal courts have confirmed that under US law, AI-generated works and inventions that lack human authorship or inventorship are not entitled to copyright or patent protection (*Thaler v. Perlmutter*, 687 F.Supp.3d 140 (D.D.C. 2023) *appeal docketed*, No. 23–5233 (D.C. Cir. Oct. 18, 2023). *Thaler v. Vidal*, 43 F.4th 1207 (Fed. Cir. 2022), *cert. Denied*, 143 S.Ct. 1783 (April 24, 2023)).[176] Similarly, federal courts are analyzing whether data scraping—the practice of automatically collecting training data from third party websites without express permission—violates copyright, privacy rights, contract, or other laws or legal requirements (Tiedrich, 2024).[177] The data scraping cases collectively involve several well-known plaintiffs, including the New York Times and Sarah Silverman, and high-profile defendants, such as Microsoft, OpenAI, Anthropic, Google, and Meta (Wainwright, 2024).[178] In many cases, the content creators' concerns stem not only from scraping data to train AI models, but also from AI model outputs that may resemble the AI training data or the creators' style or likeness. While most AI data scraping cases remain pending, a court recently held that the copyright fair use exception did not allow a the developer of a legal technology product to scrape its competitor's website to obtain AI training data without the competitor's consent (*Thomson Reuters v. Ross Intelligence Inc.*, 2025).[179] This case did not involve generative AI and focused heavily on the facts underlying the dispute.

---

[174] Benson, Peter J. et al., "Regulation of TikTok Under the Protecting Americans from Foreign Adversary Controlled Applications Act: Analysis of Selected Legal Issues," Congressional Research Service, LSB11127, p. 2, May 9, 2024. As of February 27, 2025: https://crsreports.congress.gov/product/pdf/LSB/LSB11127

[175] The George Washington University, "DAIL—the Database of AI Litigation." As of February 27, 2025: https://blogs.gwu.edu/law-eti/ai-litigation-database/. Barcott, Bruce, "AI Lawsuits Worth Watching: A Curated Guide," Tech Policy Press, July 1, 2024. As of February 27, 2025: https://www.techpolicy.press/ai-lawsuits-worth-watching-a-curated-guide/

[176] *Thaler v. Perlmutter*, et al., 687 F.Supp.3d (D.D.C. 2023), *appeal docketed*, No. 23–5233 (D.C. Cir. Oct. 18, 2023). *Thaler v. Vidal*, 43 F.4th 1207 (Fed. Cir. 2022), *cert. Denied*, 143 S.Ct. 1783 (April 24, 2023).

[177] Tiedrich, Lee, "The AI data scraping challenge: How can we proceed responsibly?," Organisation for Economic Co-Operation and Development, March 5, 2024. As of February 27, 2025: https://oecd.ai/en/wonk/data-scraping-responsibly

[178] Wainwright, Tom, "The court cases that could shape how AI develops," The Economist, November 20, 2024. As of February 27, 2025: https://www.economist.com/the-world-ahead/2024/11/20/the-court-cases-that-could-shape-how-ai-develops

[179] *Thomson Reuters Enterprise Centre GMBH v. Ross Intelligence Inc.*, No. 1:20-cv-613-SB (D. Del.) (Feb. 11, 2025). As of February 27, 2025: https://storage.courtlistener.com/recap/gov.uscourts.ded.72109/gov.uscourts.ded.72109.770.0.pdf

States and some local governments also have judicial branches. AI legal cases are not limited to the federal court system, and collectively AI legal cases present a range of issues. For instance, court cases have emerged about the lawfulness of using AI in certain ways in the criminal justice system, such as in connection with making criminal arrests and in criminal sentencing (*See* e.g.).[180] Private claims alleging that the use of AI resulted in unlawful discrimination have arisen too, including with respect to housing and employment (*Mobley v. Workday, Inc.*, 2024).[181] Turning to other types of AI harms, cases filed against Character AI allege that its companion chatbot encouraged some youths to commit suicide (*Garcia v. Character Technologies, Inc.* et al., No. 24-cv-1903, (M.D. Fl. Oct. 22, 2024); Roose, 2024).[182]

Cases have also arisen seeking to protect the rights of platform operators. Notably, private organizations have brought claims challenging the constitutionality of state statutes that limit social media platforms from engaging in certain content moderation and that impose certain transparency obligations on them (Benson, 2024).[183]

State and Local Government Actions

As mentioned above, state and local governments typically have some form of legislative and executive branches, and states and some localities have judicial branches, too. In the absence of broad federal AI legislation, state and local governments increasingly have adopted or proposed AI laws and policies (Turner Lee and Chijioke, 2023).[184] Some of these efforts also seek to help states and localities capitalize on AI's potential. According to the National Conference of State Legislatures (NCSL), during 2024, at least 45 states proposed AI legislation, and 31 states, along with some territories, enacted AI

[180] Barcott, Bruce, "AI Lawsuits Worth Watching: A Curated Guide," Tech Policy Press, July 1, 2024. As of February 27, 2025: https://www.techpolicy.press/ai-lawsuits-worth-watching-a-curated-guide/. *Loomis v. Wisconsin*, 881 N.W.2d 749 (Wis. 2016), cert. Denied, 137 S.Ct 2290 (2017).

[181] *Mobley v. Workday, Inc.*, No. 23-cv-00770-RFL, (N.D. Cal.) (July 12, 2024).

[182] *Garcia v. Character Technologies, Inc.* et al., No. 24-cv-1903, (M.D.Fl. October 22, 2024. Roose, Kevin, "Can A.I. Be Blamed for a Teen's Suicide?," The New York Times, October 24, 2024. As of February 27, 2025: https://www.nytimes.com/2024/10/23/technology/characterai-lawsuit-teen-suicide.html

[183] Benson, Peter J., "*Moody v. NetChoice, LLC*: The Supreme Court Addresses Facial Challenges to State Social Media Laws," Congressional Research Service, LSB1124, September 11, 2024. As of February 27, 2025: https://crsreports.congress.gov/product/pdf/LSB/LSB11224

[184] Turner Lee, Nicol and Chijioke, Obioha, "Why states and localities are acting on AI," The Brookings Institute, December 15, 2023. As of February 27, 2025: https://www.brookings.edu/articles/why-states-and-localities-are-acting-on-ai/

legislation or resolutions (National Conference of State Legislatures, 2024).[185] Meanwhile, city and other local governments are developing their own AI policies, including Boston, New York City, and Tempe, Arizona (*See* e.g.).[186]

In addition to pursuing AI policies, state governments can also commence AI enforcement actions. Most state-level enforcement actions arise under traditional consumer protection theories (Ravi, 2024).[187] Notably, in September 2024, the Attorney General for Texas announced a "first-of-its-kind" settlement against Pieces Technologies, a generative AI healthcare company, for using allegedly deceptive and misleading statements regarding its products (Paxton, 2024).[188]

Since many AI developers and deployers operate across jurisdictions, they typically need to comply with the growing patchwork of AI requirements at the federal, state, and local levels. Additionally, organizations with international operations need to comply with laws in relevant foreign jurisdictions. This can significantly increase the cost of legal compliance, which in turn can present barriers to entry, such as for emerging companies who could potentially help to expand marketplace competition. This section discusses examples of state and local AI legal requirements and policies.[189]

Colorado and Utah

In 2024, Colorado enacted a statute entitled "Concerning Consumer Protections in Interactions with Artificial Intelligence Systems," also commonly referred to as the Colorado Artificial Intelligence Act (CAIA) (State of Colorado, 2024).[190] The CAIA becomes effective on February 1, 2026, making

[185] National Conference of State Legislatures, "Artificial Intelligence 2024 Legislation," September 9, 2024. As of February 27, 2025: https://www.ncsl.org/technology-and-communication/artificial-intelligence-2024-legislation

[186] Peart, Katryna, "Generative AI Policies in Local Government," International City/County Management Association, June 10, 2024. As of February 27, 2025: https://icma.org/articles/article/generative-ai-policies-local-government. New York City Office of Technology & Innovation, "Artificial Intelligence." As of February 27, 2025: https://www.nyc.gov/content/oti/pages/artificial-intelligence

[187] Ravi, Sagar K. et al., "AI and the Law: Emerging Trends in Enforcement," The National Law Review, December 20, 2024. As of February 27, 2025: https://natlawreview.com/article/ai-and-law-emerging-trends-enforcement

[188] Ken Paxton, Attorney General for Texas, "Attorney General Ken Paxton Reaches Settlement in First-of-its-Kind Healthcare Generative AI Investigation," September 18, 2024. As of February 27, 2025: https://www.texasattorneygeneral.gov/news/releases/attorney-general-ken-paxton-reaches-settlement-first-its-kind-healthcare-generative-ai-investigation

[189] State and local public procurement and judicial decisions are further discussed above.

[190] Concerning Consumer Protections in Interactions with Artificial Intelligence Systems of 2024. As of February 27, 2025: https://leg.colorado.gov/sites/default/files/2024a_205_signed.pdf. https://leg.

Colorado the second state to enact significant general AI consumer protection legislation (Siegel and Garcia, 2024).[191] Utah became the first such state earlier in 2024, with its passage of a law generally focusing of disclosures and uses pertaining to generative AI (Artificial Intelligence Policy Act of 2024).[192]

The CAIA requires developers and deployers of "high-risk" AI systems, as defined by the statute, to use reasonable care to protect consumers against algorithmic discrimination (State of Colorado, 2024).[193] Furthermore, the CAIA provides these developers and deployers with a rebuttable presumption of compliance, as well as affirmative defenses, if they undertake certain activities as described in the statute (*Id.*).[194] It also empowers the state attorney general to enact rules to implement the CAIA and with exclusive enforcement authority (*Id.*).[195]

California

California has also emerged as a leader in establishing state AI laws and policies. In 2023, California's governor issued a statewide AI EO focusing on responsible deployment of generative AI (N-12-23, 2023).[196] Following this EO, California enacted various AI state laws covering a range of topics, such as AI deepfakes, disclosure of some information about AI training data, and removal and reporting of "sexually explicit digital identity theft" (Governor

colorado.gov/bills/sb24-205. State of Colorado, "Consumer Protections for Artificial Intelligence," Colorado General Assembly, 2024. As of February 27, 2025: https://leg.colorado.gov/bills/sb24-205

[191] Siegel, Alex and Garcia, Ivan, "A Deep Dive into Colorado's Artificial Intelligence Act," National Association of Attorneys General, October 26, 2024. As of February 27, 2025: https://www.naag.org/attorney-general-journal/a-deep-dive-into-colorados-artificial-intelligence-act/

[192] Artificial Intelligence Policy Act of 2024. As of February 27, 2025: https://le.utah.gov/~2024/bills/static/SB0149.html

[193] State of Colorado, "Consumer Protections for Artificial Intelligence," Colorado General Assembly, 2024. As of February 27, 2025: https://leg.colorado.gov/bills/sb24-205

[194] *Id.*

[195] *Id.*

[196] Executive Department, State of California, Executive Order N-12–23, 2023. As of February 27, 2025: https://www.gov.ca.gov/wp-content/uploads/2023/09/AI-EO-No.12-_-GGN-Signed.pdf

Gavin Newsom, 2024).[197] Equally noteworthy, California's governor vetoed state legislation that would have imposed significant safety requirements on large AI systems (Office of the Governor, 2024).[198] In his veto message to California legislators, the Governor explained that "[w]hile well-intentioned . . . [the proposed legislation] does not take into account whether an Al system is deployed in high-risk environments, involves critical decision-making or the use of sensitive data" (*Id.*).[199] Instead, the Governor notes, the proposed legislation "applies stringent standards to even the most basic functions, so long as a large system deploys it. I do not believe this is the best approach to protecting the public from real threats posed by the technology" (*Id.*).[200]

Tennessee

Tennessee, a major music hub, enacted the Ensuring Likeness, Voice, and Image Security (ELVIS) Act in 2024.[201] This became the first US law to protect individuals from AI systems impersonating their voice, in addition to their image and likeness.[202] Unsurprisingly, the legislation garnered substantial support from the music industry and other content creators.

New York City

New York City launched a comprehensive AI Action Plan for responsible AI use in its government, which is coordinated by its Office of Technology and Innovation (OTI) (New York City Office of Technology and Innovation, 2025).[203] To help guide the Plan's implementation, the OTI established

---

[197] Governor Gavin Newsom, "Governor Gavin Newsom announces new initiatives to advance safe and responsible AI, protect Californians," September 29, 2024. As of February 27, 2025: https://www.gov.ca.gov/2024/09/29/governor-newsom-announces-new-initiatives-to-advance-safe-and-responsible-ai-protect-californians/

[198] Office of the Governor, September 29, 2024. As of February 27, 2025: https://www.gov.ca.gov/wp-content/uploads/2024/09/SB-1047-Veto-Message.pdf

[199] *Id.*

[200] *Id.*

[201] Ensuring Likeness, Voice, and Image Security Act of 2024. As of February 27, 2025: https://publications.tnsosfiles.com/acts/113/pub/pc0588.pdf

[202] Land, Gabby, "Tennessee's New ELVIS Act: Free Speech & Free Market," University of Michigan Journal of Economics, May 13, 2024. As of February 27, 2025: https://sites.lsa.umich.edu/mje/2024/05/13/tennessees-new-elvis-act-free-speech-free-market/

[203] New York City Office of Technology & Innovation, "Artificial Intelligence." As of February 27, 2025: https://www.nyc.gov/content/oti/pages/artificial-intelligence

a Steering Committee and an Advisory Committee (*Id.*).[204] The OTI is also responsible for overseeing the city government's reporting on its use of algorithmic tools, as required by local law (*Id.*).[205]

New York City also enacted another local law prohibiting the use of automated employment decision tools (AEDT) in connection with employment hiring, unless (i) the tool has undergone a bias audit within 1 year of its use, (ii) information about the audit has been publicly disclosed, and (iii) certain disclosures have been made to job candidates and employees (New York City Local Law 144 of 2021).[206] New York City's Department of Consumer and Worker Protection adopted rules to guide the implementation of this local law.[207]

US International AI Engagements

Maintaining US AI leadership globally has been a consistent priority in US law and policy, as reflected in US legislation, EOs, and other actions discussed above. International engagement is important not only to advance US values and innovation, but also to foster greater international coordination that can make it easier for organizations operating internationally to comply with AI laws and policies across jurisdictions. The executive branch typically leads US diplomatic engagements.

As an example of its leadership, the US led a United Nations (UN) resolution entitled, "Seizing the opportunities of safe, secure and trustworthy artificial intelligence systems for sustainable development" (United Nations General Assembly, 2024).[208] This resolution had more than 100 co-sponsors, including China (*Id.*).[209] The UN General Assembly adopted the resolution by consensus in 2024 (*Id.*).[210] The US also is a signatory to the Council of

[204] *Id.*

[205] *Id.*

[206] New York City Local Law 144 of 2021. As of February 27, 2025: https://www.nyc.gov/site/dca/about/automated-employment-decision-tools.page

[207] New York City Department of Consumer and Worker Protection, Notice of Adoption of Final Rule. As of February 27, 2025: https://rules.cityofnewyork.us/wp-content/uploads/2023/04/DCWP-NOA-for-Use-of-Automated-Employment-Decisionmaking-Tools-2.pdf

[208] United Nations General Assembly, Seizing the opportunities of safe, secure and trustworthy artificial intelligence systems for sustainable development: resolution, 2024. As of February 27, 2025: https://2021-2025.state.gov/united-nations-general-assembly-adopts-by-consensus-u-s-led-resolution-on-seizing-the-opportunities-of-safe-secure-and-trustworthy-artificial-intelligence-systems-for-sustainable-development/

[209] *Id.*

[210] *Id.*

Europe's Framework Convention on Artificial Intelligence and Democracy, and the Rule of Law, which is the first binding international AI treaty (Treaty No. 225, 2024).[211] As also mentioned above, the US hosted the first summit of international AI Safety Institutes in late 2024, and NIST has developed a plan for advancing US leadership in the AI standards arena.

The US has further played a leadership role in various other important multilateral and bilateral efforts that are helping shape responsible AI globally. For instance, the US participates in the G7 Hiroshima AI Process, which established the G7 generative AI principles, a voluntary G7 AI code of conduct, and a process for monitoring voluntary commitments made pursuant to such code of conduct (Hiroshima AI Process, 2025).[212] This G7 initiative extends beyond G7 member countries, as India, Korea, Kenya, Singapore and several other jurisdictions have joined the Hiroshima AI Process Friends Group (*Id.*).[213] The US also actively engages in important global AI governance initiatives with the Global Partnership on AI (GPAI), the OECD, and the United Nations. The US also led the international Declaration on Military Use of AI and Autonomy, which has been signed by dozens of countries (U.S. Department of State, 2024).[214]

Furthermore, the US has participated in international AI summits, such as the 2023 UK AI Safety Summit, the 2024 AI Seoul Summit, and the 2025 Paris AI Action Summit. However, the US elected not to sign the ministerial declaration arising from the Paris AI Action Summit which focused on "inclusive and sustainable AI" (Bristow, 2025).[215] During the Paris AI Action Summit, Vice President Vance expressed concern about the EU's comprehensive approach to AI regulation (Dastin and Melander, 2025).[216]

---

[211] Council of Europe, Framework Convention on Artificial Intelligence and Human Rights, Democracy and the Rule of Law, Treaty No. 225, May 9, 2024. As of February 27, 2025: https://www.coe.int/en/web/artificial-intelligence/the-framework-convention-on-artificial-intelligence

[212] Hiroshima AI Process. As of February 27, 2025: https://www.soumu.go.jp/hiroshimaaiprocess/en/index.html

[213] *Id.*

[214] U.S. Department of State, "Political Declaration on Responsible Military Use of Artificial Intelligence and Autonomy." As of February 27, 2025: https://www.state.gov/political-declaration-on-responsible-military-use-of-artificial-intelligence-and-autonomy

[215] Bristow, Tom, "UK could snub Macron's AI declaration after US criticism," Politico, February 10, 2025. As of February 27, 2025: https://www.politico.eu/article/uk-wavers-paris-ai-summit-declaration-after-us-criticism-peter-kyle/

[216] Dastin, Jeffrey and Melander, Ingrid, "Vance tells Europeans that heavy regulation could kill AI," Reuters, February 11, 2025. As of February 27, 2025: https://www.reuters.com/technology/artificial-intelligence/europe-looks-embrace-ai-paris-summits-2nd-day-while-global-consensus-unclear-2025-02-11/

The US has engaged in bilateral AI efforts as well. For instance, during the Biden administration, the US and the UK signed a Memorandum of Understanding to work together on AI safety testing through their respective AI safety institutes (U.S. Department of Commerce, 2024).[217] Additionally, the US and EU established a bilateral Trade and Technology Council in 2021 to cooperate and collaborate on AI and other emerging technologies as well as promoting shared values (International Trade Administration, 2026).[218]

Conclusion

Although AI technology has advanced faster than the law, US AI laws and policies are seeking to adapt in ways that promote US AI priorities and objectives, including advancing US AI innovation, leadership, economic competitiveness, national security, and human flourishment. The US AI legal and policy landscape is complex, as developments can arise at the federal, state, and local levels. Further, the US government consists of different branches, and the authority to shape AI laws and policies is not consolidated in a single body. Adding to this complexity, US AI laws and policies can change over time, including in response to democratic political changes. To stay abreast of US AI laws and policies, it is important to understand the US government structures and how AI laws and policies can be adopted and changed. It is equally important to continuously monitor the relevant governmental bodies for new developments.

---

[217] U.S. Department of Commerce, "U.S. and UK Announce Partnership n Science of AI Safety," April 1, 2024. As of February 27, 2025: https://www.commerce.gov/news/press-releases/2024/04/us-and-uk-announce-partnership-science-ai-safety

[218] International Trade Administration, "U.S.-EU Trade and Technology Council." As of January 16, 2026: https://www.trade.gov/useuttc

Safeguarding Human Agency and Liberty in the Age of AI—A Call for Multilateralism

Archana G. Gulati

> Whereas recognition of the inherent dignity and of the equal and inalienable rights of all members of the human family is the foundation of freedom, justice and peace in the world
>
> —Universal Declaration of Human Rights (UDHR, 1948)

Introduction

The Internet was supposed to set us free. Has it lived up to that promise? This chapter draws the reader's attention to the need to safeguard human agency as we increasingly rely on digital technologies in our personal and professional lives. As we bestow our attention and consume services and content online, we reveal large amounts of personal information. Algorithms keep us engaged by using this data to serve customised content. They can also influence and predict our behaviour, and guide our choices. As consumers, we receive value from our online interactions and benefit from personalised content and services. However, we are also rendered vulnerable to harm. Critical awareness of these processes is more crucial than ever in the age of AI, with the idea

Disclaimer: The author is a retired Indian civil servant and a professor of technology policy. Views are strictly personal.

A. G. Gulati (✉)
Independent Scholar, New Delhi, India

M. Rangeley, N. Fairfax (eds.), *The Artificial Intelligence Revolution*,
https://doi.org/10.1007/978-3-032-11814-1_9

being to retain the value of digital services, maximise the potential of Artificial Intelligence (AI) for digital transformation and address the root causes of harm.

This chapter encourages readers to view recent developments in AI technologies from a human rights perspective and presents arguments in support of the human-centric governance of AI.

> AI is redefining what it means to be human. Its systems and processes have the potential to alter the human experience fundamentally. AI will affect not only public policy areas such as road safety and healthcare, but also human autonomy, relationships and dignity. It will affect lifestyles and professions, as well as the future course of human development and the nature and scale of conflicts. It will change the relationships between communities and those between the individual, the state and corporations. AI offers tremendous benefits for all societies but also presents risks. These risks potentially include further division between the privileged and the unprivileged; the erosion of individual freedoms through ubiquitous surveillance; and the replacement of independent thought and judgement with automated control . . . As existing international norms designed to allow every human being a life of liberty and dignity, human rights ought to be the foundation for AI governance. (Jones, 2023, p. 3)

Governance and the Golden Goose

It is widely acknowledged that Internet connectivity is key to uplifting millions from poverty and can transcend various infrastructural deficits to help especially developing countries leapfrog traditional challenges and achieve digitally empowered growth and prosperity. However, over the past decade, there has been growing recognition and concern about exploitative business models deployed online, the infringement of consumer rights and the detrimental impact on individuals and societies. While consumers may not be blamed for embracing convenience or failing to fully understand the consequences of their digital interactions, the state is responsible to its citizens. National governments and multilateral agencies are expected to protect human rights, uphold the rule of law and safeguard our collective future. However, throughout the world, the Internet and its impact have been viewed indulgently through the prism of innovation and productivity. This viewpoint suits those who control technology, but the unbalanced distribution of the benefits of progress in digital technologies has consequential implications for an already unequal world. Antitrust law, privacy and data protection, content regulation and AI regulation are all tools in the hands of regional and national authorities that, when used judiciously, could ensure contestability, consumer safety, and good governance and minimise harm. Still, each has been employed tardily and with trepidation, resulting in a trail of collateral damage.

Today, we are becoming increasingly accustomed to the lack of competition in digital markets that are dominated by a few players such that technology giants have attained the status of verbs. We do not search online; we Google. We do not ride a cab; we Uber. We do not text; we WhatsApp. We are equally inured to the loss of privacy even though it is apparent that technology sans guardrails makes constant surveillance possible. The loss of privacy is a loss of our power over our lives, and the concentration of power is concurrent with that of data. The mental health issues of the generation of digital natives that grew up with the combination of smartphones and social media should be a cautionary tale calling for content regulation. Individual jurisdictions are resorting to controls and even banning children from social media usage. However, other than the most prominent and egregious forms of harm, such as child sexual abuse material, there is little global consensus on regulating harmful content. The implications of unaddressed consumer harm will be felt even more acutely by the millions who are still offline. Most of them live in the Global South, where fulfilling the promise of digital transformation necessitates universal access and a safe and trustworthy online environment.

Earlier, we were beguiled by free content. Now, we are led to believe that the immediate, indiscriminate and unbridled deployment of artificial intelligence is the only way forward. Just as the downside of harmful business models on the digital consumer's rights was underplayed in the past, we are now expertly manipulated to buy into the narrative of machines 'learning', 'thinking' and 'creating' as being essential to our progress, even as we continue to lose our liberty, fail to protect our data or assert copyright over content that fuels AI and puts tremendous power in the hands of its masters. The global race to capture AI's potential and wield AI-enabled superiority over other nations dims the prospect of course corrections emanating from individual governments. However, there is hope. The solution lies in an international movement involving a radical re-examination of governance incentives and business models and a clarion call to put humans first. This potential for a positive reorientation requires global collaboration and presents an opportunity for change that should inspire us all.

The Tortoise and the Hare

The present scenario is one where those who can, have already embarked on a global AI race. From raw materials to chips, data centres, applications and devices, major global powers are surging ahead to dominate the global value chain and establish supremacy in a technology that will decide future winners and losers. The potential pitfalls of AI have been duly noted, but the approach towards their alleviation is a work in progress. There are multiple accords on principles and governance mechanisms, but very few, other than that of the EU, focus markedly on human rights (Jones, 2023). In some cases, this perspective may be perceived to be at variance with the concerned state's efforts, ideology, or ambitions for global competitiveness or geopolitical dominance. It is a matter of concern that the approach of developing countries is often focused almost exclusively on harnessing the benefits of AI such that the ethical dimension, while acknowledged in theory, is largely missing in practice. A Global Partnership on Artificial Intelligence (GPAI, 2020) survey revealed that out of 214 AI initiatives worldwide targeted at either AI and ethics, AI and governance, or AI for social good, over 58% were from Europe and North America, and only 1.4% were from Africa. Further, developing country initiatives primarily focused on AI for social good, such that only 5 of the 179 initiatives on AI and ethics and AI and governance originated from emerging and developing economies. This may be partially attributed to inadequate institutional or regulatory capacities in developing countries; something that can be addressed by global collaboration under the aegis of multilateral institutions such as the International Telecommunications Union. Perhaps there is an underlying belief that consumer rights are a luxury that developing nations cannot afford in their quest for rapid digital transformation. Nothing could be further from the truth.

It is also important to draw a distinction between the philosophical concept of 'ethics' regarding which it may be challenging to arrive at a global consensus as opposed to human rights, which are already the subject matter of global consensus. Further, the globally accepted human rights frameworks in the Universal Declaration on Human Rights, International Covenant on Civil and Political Rights and International Covenant on Economic, Social and Cultural Rights encompass both the public and private sectors, which is important for governing AI (Jones, 2023). Given the diversity of human viewpoints, context and cultures, it is understandable that applying the lens of ethics to the AI debate, while invaluable as a starting point for deliberations and consensus on AI governance, leads to fundamentally inconclusive outcomes at a global level and, to that extent, affords limited practical value in legal terms. Conversely, the human rights framework is an already accepted set of international norms that serves as practical guidance and provides a nuanced and valuable yardstick to guide the global governance of AI. For example, viewed from the lens of human rights, facial recognition technology is not necessarily contrary to human rights, provided proper checks and balances are in place. However, when we apply this lens, we could state that any deployment that involves the '*... mass capturing and retention of personal data and potentially discriminatory judgements without regard to human rights considerations is contrary to human rights law*' (Jones, 2023, p. 14). Thus, it is possible to arrive at an appropriately refined and balanced regulatory framework if we use human rights law to judge the impact of AI. The rights-based approach is also one that is best adopted as soon as possible to engender trust in AI and ensure that we harness the full potential of cutting-edge technologies without amplifying or exacerbating the loss of agency and autonomy and the inequalities, deprivations and discrimination that are plausible outcomes of deploying AI sans guardrails.

Wither Free Will?

In our interactions with the physical and virtual world, we leave traces of ourselves everywhere by revealing our personal data. Individual pieces of information about humans were always available in any era. However, we are rendered exposed and vulnerable when this data is digital/digitised, stored and pieced together with the help of AI to draw up a virtual atlas of our personalities through profiling. We lose our liberty when this data is used to manipulate our decisions, thoughts and actions, especially when the processes and outcomes are beyond our comprehension. The fact that this data and the concomitant control are concentrated in the hands of a few and that it is up to these entities to accept or reject guardrails imposed by individual jurisdictions can be problematic, given existing information and bargaining power asymmetries. The latter are best addressed multilaterally.

Unless one remains offline, the average individual today is a much-traded digital ID, and our digital footprints are all over the Internet. We were lured by convenience to get comfortable with sharing our personal data even when this was not strictly necessary. Even if we consciously try not to leave a trail of data breadcrumbs, the prevalent business model of services for data ensures we are compelled to. Even discerning digital consumers can be tempted by compelling content and tripped up by default settings, heuristics and dark patterns. Humans cannot beat the cognitive superiority of the algorithms that guide our online interactions. Emerging technologies such as AI can have profound implications for the 2.6 billion of the global population who, as per ITU (2023), are yet to be digitally connected. They represent the developing world, rural populations, women, older persons, persons with disabilities, children and marginalised groups who need the benefits of safe digital transformation but are exceptionally vulnerable to online harm, including, ironically, being inadequately represented in the data on which current, foundational AI design and development is based. Already, data-hungry AI models are hitting a wall. Using synthetic data for training AI applications is unlikely to be qualitatively better in terms of inclusivity or diversity. This is a suitable juncture to reconsider how to proceed collectively. Without effective global consensus on the quality, fairness and inclusivity of AI models and tools, we could spiral towards an acutely unfair world where some reap the benefits of AI, and others are irrevocably marginalised.

For those who are online, we may think we are pulling our own strings, but this is untrue. Algorithm recommendations drive a third of user choices on Amazon, 80% of viewing activities on Netflix and 70% of the time people spend on YouTube. In apps like Tinder, algorithms create most of the matches. Because most of us rarely scroll beyond the first page, we see around 0.01% of any search's results. Thus, the underlying algorithm decides which pages and content to look at (Hosanagar, 2019). The opacity of the underlying processes makes evaluating AI-generated outcomes difficult, and the risks of bias, discrimination and echo chambers are real. Human agency is a worrisome casualty as users continue to interact passively with the increasingly complex online world. Recent studies underline the impact of cognitive offloading associated with the frequent use of AI tools, especially among youth, and find that it can adversely impact critical thinking abilities. Thus, it is important to reflect on guardrails and counter-strategies when we ponder the future of humanity (Gerlich, 2025).

Further, as author Shoshana Zuboff (2019) points out, we no longer share data voluntarily. It is being extracted from us. The reason is not just to improve the quality of services we receive, such as a response to a search query. The business model honed over the past decade now chases and hunts for this data to sell to advertisers. In the age of AI, this data has become fodder for training AI tools and is even more in demand than ever, and most users are either not aware that they can opt-out or do not know how to. We are inured to the imbalance in bargaining power. 'We have come to accept, without reading, the terms of service that assign the rights of our content to the platforms we post on, and when those platforms abruptly close or delete our content or lock us out of our accounts, we mourn the loss as we receive a firsthand lesson in what it means to sign our digital rights away' Smith (2024).

When did we start mattering so little? Was the customer not supposed to be a Queen/King? One could attribute this to the free services business model. Most of us are accustomed to purchasing hardware, such as a smartphone or laptop and an Internet connection. However, many would baulk at paying for email, or social media usage. Our predilection to enjoy such services free and the lure of consuming, sharing and receiving content sans limitations of time, money or quantity made the digital medium all the more alluring. As consumers revealed more personal information online, today's large platforms that began as start-ups could store and process this data to provide customised services and content, their customers appreciated. Consumers began spending more time online, revealing yet more data, and as services improved, so did consumer numbers. The large volumes, variety and velocity of data, also called Big Data, that they managed to collect, strengthened the position of first movers in digital markets. They sold this data to advertisers who could better target consumers with behavioural advertisements. With the help of AI, customers could be expertly directed through behavioural manipulation to make commercially beneficial choices. Revenues from advertising run digital platforms, and our data fuels this engine. The treasure trove of closely guarded consumer and vendor data is also an entry barrier contributing to the digital market concentration. Further, their mandate of keeping us engaged online can cause algorithms to push harmful content that is known to have promoted echo chambers, polarisation and addiction and includes cyberbullying and the manipulation of children. In her book *Privacy Is Power*, Carissa Véliz (2022) labels the prevalent business model of data extraction as a race to the moral bottom that gravely threatens our freedom. Podcasters Tristan Harris and Daniel Schmachtenberger call it the race to the bottom of the brainstem (Heath, 2019).

The commodification of human behaviour has been described in detail by author Shoshana Zuboff (2022). She contends that the failure to regulate or create a clear regulatory roadmap for the digital century based on core democratic values, principles and governance has led to a transfer of power to technology companies. 'Surveillance capitalism' filled the regulatory void. Its development as an 'institution' has allowed the private sector to control knowledge generation and dissemination, and she highlights this as 'the biggest threat to human autonomy in the information age'. According to Ms. Zuboff, in the information age, the concentration of economic power leads to the production of 'collateral concentrations of governance and social powers' in the hands of an oligopoly of tech companies. The fact that this data can easily assume strategic dimensions (bolster state surveillance and have geopolitical ramifications) explains why global governments are concerned about private sector surveillance by foreign companies (Johnston, 2025).

The Jigsaw Puzzle of Digital Regulation

It is not always easy to understand the complex interplay between different branches of digital regulation and the progressive loss of human agency and choice. Let us begin with competition. The telecommunications sector, which lies at the foundation of the digital revolution, continues to be regulated in any economy. Stalwarts of telecommunications regulation would be familiar with the concept of significant market power (SMP). Before the advent of mobile services, telecommunications required sizable and lumpy investment in exchanges and underground lines and cables, and the business became viable only when the number of customers was large enough to bring down the per-user cost to a level equivalent to or below the per-user revenue. Thus, technology favoured scale, and incumbents tended to be vertically integrated monopoly service providers that controlled key resources and consumer access. Their market power attracted regulatory scrutiny. Mandating fair and non-discriminatory access to bottleneck resources (to enable market entry and facilitate the 'ladder of investment'[1]) and interoperability among players and imposing functional or structural separation on large, vertically integrated market players were familiar regulatory tools. The advent of mobile services reduced the investment requirements and opened the sector to competition, easing the need for SMP regulation. Today, the telecom sector is more competitive but still regulated from the viewpoint of its usage of scarce resources such as spectrum and numbering resources, and it is subject to close scrutiny from a consumer safety and national security viewpoint due to its critical and strategic nature. However, despite the Internet's strategic and socio-economic impact, it has taken even experienced regulators years of navigating drawn-out antitrust litigation before they could introduce *ex ante* competition regulation. This subject is still fraught with debates about the impact of regulation on innovation, productivity and economic growth.

Technological change in telecom by way of mobile telephony altered the investment requirements, and competition flourished. As costs were driven

[1]An approach to enhancing contestability in capital-intensive markets by facilitating access to the monopolist's resources in a manner that encourages the new entrant to progressively invest in their own infrastructure as they acquire more customers.

down, the affordability of telecommunications services caused an explosion of connectivity such that the number of connected individuals grew from 16% of the global population in 2005 to 67% in 2023 (ITU, 2023). This is a testament to the utility of ICT services and the increasing affordability of Internet connections. Following the surge in mobile phone connections, the next boom the world witnessed was in data consumption driven by Internet applications. ITU estimated that global mobile-broadband traffic rates reached 913 exabytes (EB) in 2022 (ITU, 2023).[2] In tandem, the telecom business model shifted from legacy per-minute usage-based billing to flat-rate data packages. To most of us who cannot imagine life without the Internet, voice telephony has become almost incidental to data. In such a scenario, it is easy to lose sight of the unconnected or those who are not or do not wish to be online on account of affordability or utility. These individuals are not a commercially lucrative market segment. However, the regulation of telecommunications addresses such market failures. Thus, in India, the telecom regulator has recently mandated that service providers offer unbundled packages of only voice and short messaging services (SMS) sans data. Telecommunications operators in India have expressed dissatisfaction with this mandate as they believe it will delay India's transition to 5G (The Economic Times, 2024a). The fact that a forced transition to Internet usage may deprive some consumers of their desired mode of connectivity is not at the forefront of commercial considerations. However, the existence of a statutory Universal Service Obligation entailing affordable connectivity for all in Indian telecommunications law makes the provision of such a consumer choice a regulatory prerogative in the interest of equity, keeping in view the purchasing power and preferences of especially low-income users. Thus, regulated entities with market power can be compelled to put the customer first.

The element of regulation-enforced consumer choice is significant when we consider the current trend of compulsory bundling of AI tools into online applications regardless of user consent or convenience. The ability to impose unilateral conditions on consumers is a manifestation of market concentration. Recently, Meta has announced the induction of AI-generated user profiles on its social media platforms. Analysts have criticised this move as adding more non-organic content to the platform, which was already losing its initial idea of a primarily social networking site (between humans). Further, they have contended that the move is borne out of a compulsion to boost numbers (of the

[2]ITU Facts and Figures, 2023 available at https://www.itu.int/itu-d/reports/statistics/2023/10/10/ff23-internet-traffic/.

platform's AI tool users) to satisfy investors and justify investments in AR/VR technologies (Dotan, 2024). The relationship between consumer choice and competition, and consumer choice and economic development is well known to competition regulators who rightfully worry about the overriding of market signals by monopolistic business prerogatives.

Ex ante competition regulation in digital markets aims to promote fair and non-discriminatory conduct by large digital enterprises towards their competitors and consumers (CDCL report, 2024). To an extent, it is similar to SMP regulations in telecommunications. The regulatory push for algorithmic transparency, interoperability and data portability is an effort to foster competition and consumer choice. Regulating actions that deter market entry, such as anti-competitive agreements between technology giants to ensure the default status of their proprietary applications on devices, or the prevention of side loading of apps bypassing proprietary in-house app stores, or mandating the use of in-house payment applications, are all directed at levelling the playing field and improving consumer choice. These are beginning to be applied *ex ante* without the need to establish dominance or harm. Even though the introduction of *ex ante* regulation is based on hard-won litigation and a vast library of case law, regulators, especially in developing countries, hesitate to resort to *ex ante* regulation given the arguments against regulation, including potentially harming innovation and imposing unmanageable regulatory and compliance burdens. In debates about the pending digital competition regulation (designed to work on the lines of the EU's Digital Markets Act) in India, advocates in favour of *laissez faire* warn policymakers about the potential negative impact of *ex ante* regulation on India's technology start-ups (most of which would not meet the thresholds for the law to apply to them). They also point to the need for better institutional capacities and the negative consequences of both too much competition and too much regulation on innovation. The benefits of level playing fields on the rights of consumers is not readily appreciated. It is often argued that a developing country cannot risk stymieing the further expansion of digital incumbents because we stand to lose out on the benefits of digital empowerment. Policymakers in developing countries have the unenviable task of unravelling the tension between competing goals, not the least the desire for rapid digital transformation. Competition experts can, at best, promise long-term benefits and play down short-term challenges but this may fail to adequately override the unease of policymakers.

While the jury is still out on whether technology monopolies help or harm consumers, they continue to amass data and use it to train their AI applications. They also treat this vast pool of personal data as their property as we shall see below. We saw above that in the case of telecommunications, technological innovation by way of mobile telephony substituted the need for regulation. Even if it were hypothetically possible that new tools and applications based on generative AI could have upended the prevalent business models, alliances between the prevailing technology incumbents and AI giants could prevent any genuine competition or new business models. Perplexity, an AI start-up, shows much promise in introducing an alternative to the prevailing dominance of Google in the online shopping and search markets. However, Amazon already supports it. Open AI, the creator of Chat GPT, is backed by Microsoft. Google and Meta have alliances with the hardware giant Nvidia. Globally, many competition regulators have effected changes to merger regulations to enable mandatory *ex ante* scrutiny of mergers in digital markets and prevent killer acquisitions targeted at innovative new market players. Despite this enhanced awareness, we have not been able to prevent the strengthening of digital market concentration in the age of AI.

Privacy and data protection regulation, too, arrived relatively late on the scene. Globally accepted concepts such as notice and consent, data minimisation, purpose limitation and the related concept of legitimate interest, data safety and integrity, portability and interoperability are important and beneficial. However, the protective inadequacy of burdening individuals with giving their informed consent and the difficulties of dealing with the legitimacy of purposes for processing personal data remains moot. The Indian competition regulator's actions against Meta demonstrate both the nexus between competition and privacy and the challenges and difficulties faced by the developing countries with relatively nascent digital regulation. In 2021, the Competition Commission of India (CCI) took *suo-moto* cognisance of Meta's notice to Indian WhatsApp consumers. The latter were given two choices: accept the revised privacy policy, under which their WhatsApp user data, including phone numbers, contacts and transaction details, would be shared across Meta's ecosystem with other Meta companies such as Instagram and Facebook, or leave WhatsApp and lose their accounts. CCI's case of alleged abuse of dominance under Indian competition law was centred around the mandatory sharing of users' personal data by WhatsApp with other Facebook Companies, the lack of an opt-out option and unduly extensive and disproportionate data collection that it described as follows:

> This is borne from the fact that it seeks to capture, amongst others, transactions and payments data; data related to battery level, signal strength, app version, mobile operator, ISP, language and time zone, device operation information, service related information and identifiers etc.; location information of the user even if the user does not use location related features besides sharing information

> with Facebook on how user interacts with others (including businesses) when using WhatsApp services. (CCI, 2021, p. 15)

In the order discussed above, it is important to note CCI's observations on the lack of consumer choice and its relationship with competition, as reproduced below.

> The 2021 WhatsApp policy update exemplifies the problematic nature of 'take-it-or leave-it' terms imposed by dominant enterprises. By mandating that all users accept the new data-sharing terms with Meta (formerly Facebook) or lose access to the platform, WhatsApp has effectively stripped users of any real choice. Such terms are inherently coercive, as they force users to either agree to unfavourable conditions or discontinue a service they rely on for communication. This approach becomes particularly concerning in the context of dominant firms like WhatsApp, where network effects make switching to alternative platforms impractical and costly. With a vast user base and market influence of WhatsApp, users are left with no bargaining power, making the acceptance of the new policy a forced decision rather than a voluntary one. This kind of conduct highlights the exploitative nature of 'take-it-or-leave-it' terms, where users are pressured to accept conditions that prioritize the company's commercial interests at the expense of user autonomy and degradation of privacy protection (a non-price parameter of competition amongst players), ultimately constituting an abuse of market power. (CCI, 2021, pp. 85–86)

Facebook challenged the competition regulator's jurisdiction. At the time, India did not have a comprehensive data protection act, as the Digital Personal Data Protection Act came into force later in 2023 (DPDP). The issue of CCI's jurisdiction over privacy and data protection issues was raised. Further, as the examination of whether WhatsApp's 2021 privacy policy violated the right to privacy under Article 21 of the Indian constitution was already pending before the Delhi High Court and Supreme Court of India, Meta contended that CCI could not open up an investigation into a matter that was already sub judice. The Courts, however, ruled that this did not bar the CCI from investigating a possible breach of Indian competition law. Addressing the aspect of jurisdiction in its final order dated 18.11.2024, the CCI stated that,

> Data protection laws apply universally to *all entities* handling personal data, ensuring the privacy and rights of all individuals. In contrast, Section 4 of the Act specifically applies *only to dominant entities*, imposing additional obligations to prevent abuse of market power. There is no inherent conflict or repugnancy between the two statutes, as the Act supplements data protection regulations

> by placing heightened responsibilities on dominant firms, ensuring they do not leverage their market position in a manner that distorts competition or harms consumer welfare. (CCI, 2024, p. 13)

Addressing the lack of user choice in the above order, CCI ruled that,

> In respect of sharing of WhatsApp user data for purposes other than for providing WhatsApp Services, all users in India (including users who have accepted 2021 update) will be provided with: a) the choice to manage such data sharing by way of an opt-out option prominently through an in-app notification; and b) the option to review and modify their choice with respect to such sharing of data through a prominent tab in settings of WhatsApp application. (CCI, 2024, pp. 148–149)

Thus, even before India had notified the detailed rules under the DPDP Act 2023, the competition regulator attempted to address user choice. It is also pertinent to note that the Indian government's Digital Competition Bill (DCB), drafted on the lines of the EU's Digital Markets Act, includes an *ex ante* prohibition on cross-sharing user data across entities belonging to Systematically Significant Digital Intermediaries such as Meta (CDCL Report, 2024).

The struggles of citizens of the developing world in trying to benefit from internet access and yet suffering grievous harm due to inadequate regulatory oversight is demonstrated by the role of Facebook in the Rohingya ethnic cleansing crisis of 2016 in Myanmar. The decline in mobile and data connectivity costs should be a blessing in a developing country. Meta's Free Basics provided the citizens of Myanmar with affordable internet access and was hugely popular. However, the lack of adequate content moderation and oversight resulted in the deliberate and calculated use of the social media platform to spread hate and coordinate attacks against the Rohingyas. Facebook's algorithms promoted anti-Rohingya content and facilitated what has been termed a genocide by the United Nations. Commenting on Facebook's role, the UN human rights investigator stated that,

> It has... substantively contributed to the level of acrimony and dissension and conflict, if you will, within the public. Hate speech is certainly, of course, a part of that. As far as the Myanmar situation is concerned, social media is Facebook, and Facebook is social media. (Miles, 2018)

Facebook had only one Burmese language content moderator in 2014 and was slow to take corrective action even when its internal reports highlighted the role of its algorithmic recommendation and ranking systems in promoting hate speech and misinformation. By 2018, Facebook had increased the number of Burmese-speaking content moderators for its 18 million users in Myanmar to five (Harari, 2024). Under investigation, social media company executives often discuss the difficulty of balancing freedom of expression and online harm, shifting the blame to algorithms. However, the harmful consequences result from the combination of algorithms and human nature. Algorithms are designed to maximise user engagement, which leads to more time spent online, more personal data being revealed and better insights into human nature to better manipulate human actions for commercial gain. Naturally, algorithms are by themselves impervious to whether the outcomes of their programmed actions are right or wrong, good or bad. It is the humans in the system who need to introspect. The question we need to ask ourselves is, would it be too much to anticipate and address harm before deploying technology when there are acknowledged risks of harmful outcomes?

We would not condone the unleashing of harmful drugs on human populations without regulatory approvals and safeguards, regardless of potential commercial gain for drug manufacturers. Why would we treat the potential harm and even loss of human lives originating from powerful digital technologies such as AI differently? Forging ahead with the deployment of AI sans guardrails and then dealing with the fallout later is equivalent to treating human populations as guinea pigs. In the context of rapid advances in generative AI, we should ask ourselves whether the decision on how, when and where to deploy AI that affects the daily lives of humans and society can be a purely commercial one. The vulnerabilities of developing countries with relatively nascent institutional and regulatory capacities and heavy reliance on the Internet for socio-economic progress make a strong case for global consensus on humanity's future in the age of AI. International agreements, standards and monitoring mechanisms are crucial not just in relation to using AI in armed conflict but also in relation to the impact on the everyday lives of humans.

Despite increasing awareness of harm, a calibrated approach to deploying AI is unlikely to be followed organically. Just as the substantial investment requirements of landline telephony (telephone exchanges and laying cables to premises) made it a natural monopoly, AI's capital insensitivity as a technology is seen as an entry barrier. The computing power of AI comes from crunching vast amounts of data in massive, energy-intensive data centres. Left to themselves, individual users would probably not seek much computing power so early in the life cycle of AI. However, today, AI is integrated into even messaging apps. New phone models have built-in AI features even before the bulk of humanity has any inkling or inclination to use these features. As in the case of search and social media, serving customers with free or low-cost versions of AI apps encourages users to share copious amounts of data and simultaneously train the AI applications. The growing number of users attracts investment for funding the massive computing power needed to fuel the growth of data centres, research and development, and mergers and acquisitions that help entrench the market position of established players and first movers. Sean McDonald (2024), in his article titled 'AI Is an Invasive Species', states that,

> In 2024, technology companies aren't selling minutes and they're only kind-of selling data—really, they're selling the idea that infinite computation might lead to a better world. In the history of human decision-making, computation—like accounting—can add value in some contexts and, in others, has become a consumptive, dehumanising, and destructive way to alter important aspects of the human experience. The reality is that most people not only don't need artificial intelligence in most cases—they are, more often than not—directly and indirectly—being actively harmed by it. Despite this, governments, technology providers, and investors of all kinds are actively infesting as much of our lives as possible with computation as possible, invisibly adding 'AI' to their products regardless of any presumption of need or proportional value. The race to sell data center services has turned 'AI' into an invasive species that has slipped the markets' bounds and guardrails, embedding the costs, environmental destruction, and waste of general-purpose computation into millions of ecosystems, not only without consent—but to the degradation, if not destruction, of other forms of reasoning.

As in the past, the business models of incumbents and their collaborators are determining the trajectory of a technology that will have a vast and consequential impact on the future of humanity in terms of equity, employment, social values, human cognition, environment and conflict. It would be wise for the world to pause and reflect on course correction. This cannot be achieved without the cooperation of the private sector. It is also important that all stakeholders, especially multilateral agencies, move faster to keep pace with new waves of technological progress so that they are harnessed for global good and serve more than a handful of commercial interests.

AI and Discrimination

Some time back in New Delhi, posts were trending on social media about the alleged discriminatory pricing of Uber wherein, for the same trip, iPhone users are being charged more than Android users (The Economic Times, 2024b). It has been conjectured that the rationale for this algorithmic pricing discrimination is the supposedly higher-paying capacity of iPhone users in India. Experts who joined the debate explained the ease with which algorithms can work with data on hardware and user behaviour to go beyond dynamic pricing based on distance, time, demand and supply to personalised pricing. While the allegedly unfair conduct of a ride-hailing company may not seem consequential, AI tools are also used by governments to make momentous decisions that may affect lives and livelihoods, and the economically disadvantaged may suffer disproportionately on account of their dependence, vulnerability and the inherent biases against their backgrounds. In the US, this includes eligibility for unemployment benefits, housing and health services, insurance, credit and employment and wages. It is reported that in the United States of America, 'all 92 million low-income people in the U.S. states—everyone whose income is less than 200 percent of the federal poverty line—have some basic aspect of their lives decided by AI' (Techtonic Justice, 2024). The design and deployment of algorithms may decide the fate of convicts and refugees. If an AI tool labels a child as a likely failure or troublemaker who needs to be monitored, or if a person is denied bail, the implications of the automated decision obviously impact liberty (Jones, 2023, pp. 25–26). The problem of complexity, opacity and lack of explainability of AI models, or the problem of embedded bias arising from incomplete data or faulty design, do not excuse the consequential harm to humans. That would be the case if we had no choice but to deploy imperfect AI tools. Fortunately, that is not the case.

How AI Can Exacerbate Manipulation

Unlike in the past, when regulators were only hypothesising about alleged harm to users, we now have a situation where, as far as the Internet is concerned, regulators understand the underlying business models and their impact and are beginning to take decisive action. The move to regulate or impose outright bans on social media for children acknowledges the negative effects of social media on generations growing up with smartphones and the Internet. Mental health issues, including low self-esteem, anxiety, and addiction, manifesting in the form of increased incidence of self-harm and even suicides among the young, have pushed governments into such extreme measures. It can arguably be stated that this is tantamount to curtailing children's freedom of speech and depriving them of the many benefits of being online. The alternative solution would have been a more responsible social media, meaning better algorithmic design and better intentions of those deploying algorithms. We cannot undo the past, but we can learn from it.

Improvements in technology will further enable AI to judge human emotive states better and use these to offer customised solutions or nudge behaviour for commercial gain. Speaking about the downside of 'artificial empathy', Ben Bland (2024) raises concerns about systems that are not necessarily designed for but are capable of being coercive by exploiting one's emotive state.

> Where it will present the marketing material to you in just the right way at just the right time when, let's say, you're tired, you're vulnerable, you're lonely, and then sell it to you. So there's a sort of line at which we have to, somewhere along there, we have to stop and say this system is either deliberately designed or likely to be used in such a way that it is going to be coercive for people.... We can look at outcomes and draw red lines around the potential outcomes of a system, and we can look at their capability in their design. And as I say, it's not just what they're deliberately designed for, but what they can reasonably say they're capable of. If it's coercive or if it brings about extreme states.

Empathic AI can not only judge human emotion but also simulate human emotion to help or harm, with implications for human autonomy and human rights. Whether it is the continuous manipulation to reveal yet more personal data, make purchasing decisions or avoid specific actions for fear of retribution, including public shaming or punishment as in the case of AI-facilitated state surveillance, the incorporation of AI into our mental lives sans guardrails can rob us of autonomy and agency and this is especially true for children, youth, the elderly, persons with disability and other vulnerable population segments.

The other side of manipulation is the cultivation of AI Anthropomorphism as a reasonably effective advocacy strategy. Today, most of us are accustomed to the idea that AI learns, thinks, responds and creates, which works in the interest of firms deploying AI. However, as Eryk Salvaggio (2024) explains, these terms can distort the approach to human-centric governance. Firstly, consumers are encouraged to consider AI simple, predictable and benign. It is not. Take the case of hallucinations. Rational humans hallucinate at times. In the case of machines, as in the case of AI, what is labelled hallucination is a failing of the technology that would normally require a return to the drawing board. Secondly, we are sold the productivity myth, which is centred on the notion that everything that can be automated should be automated. To buy into the productivity myth is to liken the art of writing to filling up a page rather than a means for expressing our thoughts. Third is the prompt myth: Most people don't realise that large language models (LLMs) are not sourcing answers from a body of knowledge as much as giving us statistically likely responses, which are not necessarily accurate. The fact that we need to hone the prompt to get the required response suggests that we are doing more work to meet the system's requirements. We, too, are being trained, and in making queries, we are training the AI application. Fourthly, by attributing intelligence to human-designed software, we are led to believe that it has rights. One of those rights is 'learning' from our writings and creativity as other humans can. However, one cannot compare the social investment in cultivating the human mind and the profit-making process of AI training on data scraped online. Equating this essentially commercial activity as having tremendous social value distorts the treatment of this profit-seeking activity in the minds of consumers, policymakers and lawmakers. By cleverly attributing creativity to AI tools and by making an erroneous comparison between human creativity and algorithmic processes, we reduce human imagination and creativity to a process like a mundane series of steps and, at the same time, buy into the argument that AI should have the same rights as humans. The scaling myth to justify data collection equates quantity of data with quality, ignoring the lies, bias and trash on the Internet. It creates an argument against laws that aim to promote privacy and data protection. To challenge these myths is to sound like a modern-day Luddite. However, it is important to understand these developments properly, with more transparency and honesty and less corporate fiction. Regulation and public awareness must be strong enough to change incentives.

Ideally, the discourse should shift to how we can redirect technological progress towards shared values and new business models that are not based on excessive data extraction and manipulating humans and do not sell us myths that diminish humanity's agency and liberty. Such a realignment calls for a significant re-education of all stakeholders and a demand for a new set of values to underpin human existence in the age of AI. To begin with, there could be a ban on using grammar that borrows from uniquely human actions to describe AI. For example, could we agree that AI does not hallucinate? It gives defective results because of imperfect data and design. AI does not 'learn' from our papers and content. The technology behind it scrapes content for training purposes. AI is not educated. It does not self-learn; humans programme machines. We could say AI is capable of programming itself if it can. AI is not conscious, so if it acts as sentient, it performs as programmed. Being free from misleading narratives will be crucial for how technology impacts humans in the age of AI.

Human Rights as the Underpinning of AI Governance

The UN has highlighted the lack of enforceable AI Governance.

> There is, today, a global governance deficit with respect to AI. Despite much discussion of ethics and principles, the patchwork of norms and institutions is still nascent and full of gaps. Accountability is often notable for its absence, including for deploying non-explainable AI systems that impact others. Compliance often rests on voluntarism; practice belies rhetoric. (UN, 2024)

The regulation of AI is related to that of privacy and data, competition and content, and each jurisdiction may adopt a different regulatory approach given its unique context. However, based on what has already transpired as described above, while we cannot undo the past, it is essential to recognise that regulation is not necessarily bad. In fact, appropriate and proportionate digital regulation provides certainty and clarity that should not just encourage investment and innovation but ensure that digital technologies are used responsibly and safely, laying the foundations for global digital transformation. Leaving the future of human rights in the context of AI to corporations alone will create a fragmented mish-mash of voluntary due diligence with no legal certainty for those affected, either in terms of the impact of AI tools on consumers or the remedies to potential harm. Responsible businesses and states would welcome regulation if it does not prevent them from innovating and serving consumer/citizen needs and if regulation does not place them at a competitive disadvantage. The last issue is important in a connected world, as less benevolent business practices thrive on geographic forum shopping. Smaller firms that follow ethical practices may struggle to compete. Developing nations face a disadvantage as they lack the requisite economic might or bargaining power. Technology giants adapt their business practices to individual jurisdictions such that developing countries do not automatically benefit from the regulatory guardrails that safeguard and protect customers in developed nations.

Capacity-building institutions like the International Competition Network (ICN) lack coercive power but evangelise collaboration and encourage the adoption of business and consumer-friendly best practices. They have played an important role in harmonising competition regulation globally (Abbott, 2016). Notably, the ICN initiative received much support from nations home to global multinational corporations as they stood to benefit from harmonised as opposed to fragmented competition regulation, which would stymie their global ambitions. In the case of AI, the world will need both a baseline statutory legal framework under the auspices of the UN as well as voluntary multilateralism. The developed world has a stake in facilitating greater participation from the Global South. Recent initiatives such as the OECD's Integrated Partnership on AI, which steadfastly encourages a stronger role for developing countries, indicate an appreciation of this imperative.

While individual jurisdictions may disagree on the if, how, where and when to deploy AI, the development of international standards on the design of AI would go a long way in mitigating potential harmful consequences. When designing standards, the challenge for this technology is that the world will have to go beyond transparency and explainability on how the system functions, to encompass a focus on the ethical choices made during design. Accountability and liability will require developers and deployers to ponder, meticulously document and reveal these decisions transparently. The world needs to agree to enforce greater rigour and patience. Multilateral institutions have a major role to play in achieving this adaptation. Realising the promise of AI to serve humanity requires the reinvigoration of multilateralism and its reinvention to ensure that all human voices are heard, including those of poorer nations, the disempowered and the marginalised.

References

Abbott, A. (2016). *Reflections on the International Competition Network (ICN) at 15: Steady progress and major long-term challenges*. The Heritage Foundation. May 2016. Available at https://www.heritage.org/economic-and-property-rights/commentary/reflections-the-international-competition-network-icn-15

Bland, B.. (2024). Artificial empathy with Ben Bland. *Pondering AI, interview by Kimberly Nevala, September 11, 2024*. Available at https://pondering-ai.transistor.fm/episodes/ep57/transcript

CCI. (2021). Suo Moto Case No. 01 of 2021. In *Re: Updated terms of service and privacy policy for WhatsApp users*. Competition Commission of India. Prima Facie Order, 2021 dated 24.3.21. Available at https://cci.gov.in/antitrust/orders/details/100/0

CCI. (2024). Suo Moto Case No. 01 of 2021, Case Nos. 05 of 2021 & 30 of 2021. In *Re: Updated terms of service and privacy policy for WhatsApp users*.

Competition Commission of India. Final Order, 2024 dated 18.11.2024. Available at https://drive.google.com/file/d/1xXCtxiQsxq1AF0at2H1KO8Ub2UopiuQR/view?ref=static.internetfreedom.in

CDCL Report. (February 2024). Report of the Committee on Digital Competition Law, Ministry of Corporate Affairs, Government of India. file:///C:/Users/Archana%20Gulati/Dropbox/Le%20Futur/Ai%20and%20liberty/CDCL-Report-20240312.pdf

Dotan, R.. (2024). *Commenting on the Fox Business report 'Meta will invest in AI-generated characters and profiles to drive up engagement'*. Posted on LinkedIn, December 30, 2024. Available at https://www.linkedin.com/posts/ravit-dotan_remember-when-social-media-tried-to-weed-activity-7280582137274138625-gfoz?utm_source=share&utm_medium=member_desktop

Gerlich, M. (2025). AI tools in society: Impacts on cognitive offloading and the future of critical thinking. *MDPI Journals Societies, 15*(1). https://doi.org/10.3390/soc15010006

GPAI. (2020). *Areas for future action in the responsible AI ecosystem.* The Future Society, GPAI Responsible AI Working Group (RAIWG). December 2020. Available at 2025: https://gpai.ai/projects/responsible-ai/areas-for-future-action-in-responsible-ai.pdf

Harari, Y. N. (2024). *Nexus: A brief history of information networks from the Stone Age to AI.* Random House., First U.S. edition.

Heath, J. (2019). *Winning the arms race to the bottom of the brainstem. Medium, January 6, 2019.* WINNING THE ARMS RACE TO THE BOTTOM OF THE BRAINSTEM. | by Joseph Heath | Medium

Hosanagar, K. (2019). *Interview*who made that decision: You or an algorithm? Knowledge@Wharton. Available at https://knowledge.wharton.upenn.edu/article/algorithms-decision-making/

International Telecommunication Union (ITU). (2023). Global offline population steadily declines to 2.6 billion people in 2023. In *ITU facts and figures, 2023: Internet use.* https://www.itu.int/itu-d/reports/statistics/2023/10/10/ff23-internet-use/

Johnston. (2025). *The Stanford International Policy Review, 2025.* https://fsi.stanford.edu/sipr/tik-tok-geopolitical-tensions

Jones, K. (2023). *AI governance and human rights: Resetting the relationship.* International Law Programme. Available at https://www.chathamhouse.org/sites/default/files/2023-01/2023-01-10-AI-governance-human-rights-jones.pdf

McDonald, S. (2024). *AI is an invasive species.* Digital Public. https://www.digitalpublic.io/ai-invasive-species

Miles. (2018). *U.N. investigators cite Facebook role in Myanmar crisis.* Tom Miles, Reuters. U.N. investigators cite Facebook role in Myanmar crisis | Reuters.

Salvaggio, E. (2024). *Challenging the myths of generative AI.* TechPolicy Press. https://www.techpolicy.press/challenging-the-myths-of-generative-ai/

Smith, S. E. (2024). How to disappear completely. In *The Verge*. December 18, 2024. https://www.theverge.com/24321569/internet-decay-link-rot-web-archive-deleted-culture?utm_source=Sailthru&utm_medium=email&utm_campaign=Lit+Hub+Daily%3A+December+19%2C+2024&utm_term=lithub_master_list

Techtonic Justice. (December 2024). *Inescapable AI: The ways AI decides how low-income people work, live, learn, and survive*. Report, November 2024. https://static1.squarespace.com/static/65a1d3be4690143890f61cec/t/673c7170a0d09777066c6e50/1732014450563/ttj-inescapable-ai.pdf

The Economic Times. (2024a). *Telcos call Trai's plan to split data, voice packs as 'regressive'*. The Economic Times, December 25, 2024. Available at https://economictimes.indiatimes.com/industry/telecom/telecom-news/telcos-call-trais-plan-to-split-data-voice-packs-as-regressive/articleshow/116639171.cms?from=mdr

The Economic Times. (2024b). *Ola Uber fares, different on Apple and Android phones? The conspiracy of pricing war*. The Economic Times. December 26, 2024. Available at 2025: https://economictimes.indiatimes.com/news/company/corporate-trends/ola-uber-fares-different-on-apple-and-android-phones-the-conspiracy-of-pricing-war/articleshow/116671509.cms

UN. (2024). Governing AI for humanity: Final report. In *United Nations advisory body*. https://www.un.org/sites/un2.un.org/files/governing_ai_for_humanity_final_report_en.pdf

Véliz, C. (2022). *Privacy is power: Why and how you should take back control of your data*. Bantam Press. https://doi.org/10.1093/idpl/ipac007

Zuboff, S. (2019). *The age of surveillance capitalism: The fight for a human future at the new frontier of power*. Public Affairs. https://www.publicaffairsbooks.com/titles/shoshana-zuboff/the-age-of-surveillance-capitalism/9781610395694/

Zuboff, S. (2022). Surveillance capitalism or democracy? The death match of institutional orders and the politics of knowledge in our information civilization. *Organization Theory, 3*(3). https://doi.org/10.1177/26317877221129290

Part III

Defence and Security

Defence, Security and Warfare in the Age of AI and Robotics

Nicholas Houghton, Max Rangeley, and Nicholas Fairfax

Introduction

The implications of AI and robotics for defence, security and warfare are some of the most profound in all of AI policy. This chapter is written as a chapter in the book *The Artificial Intelligence Revolution*, published by Springer Nature, as an overview. Within this volume, there are papers covering the key areas of AI policy, from the economics of AI to approaches to regulation to AI-related developments in healthcare. The chapters on the more specific areas within AI and defence draw from experts at Oxford University, the Ministry of Defence, the RAND Corporation and other think tanks and defence technology companies—this chapter can be read either as a standalone chapter or as an overview before reading those more specific areas of research, especially for those in universities, think tanks, political groups, global institutions or other areas of policy-making. In order to achieve this, we use a broad range of sources, ranging from think tanks such as the RAND Corporation and Center for a New American Security, to NATO and other military organisations, to academics who specialise in emerging technologies in defence and warfare. It should be noted that developments in military AI often outpace the peer-review publishing cycle of think tanks and universities,

N. Houghton • M. Rangeley (✉) • N. Fairfax
House of Lords, The Cobden Centre, London, UK
e-mail: jnrhoughton@parliament.uk

M. Rangeley, N. Fairfax (eds.), *The Artificial Intelligence Revolution*,
https://doi.org/10.1007/978-3-032-11814-1_10

yet this chapter should, nevertheless, give the reader a good understanding of the issues that the world faces in this field.

Artificial intelligence (AI) and robotics are no longer peripheral innovations; they are rapidly becoming the organising logic of twenty-first-century security competition. From loitering munitions in the Middle East to drone attacks in Ukraine, increasingly automated systems are now a decisive—sometimes the decisive—factor in tactical success. At the strategic level, military and political leaders face a compressed decision cycle in which machines can collect, fuse and act on data faster than humans can observe or deliberate. These shifts raise acute questions about deterrence stability, ethical control and institutional adaptability across every domain of warfare. In the European Union's recent briefing "Defence and Artificial Intelligence" (European Union, 2024), they write that:

> In 2017, Russian President Vladimir Putin declared 'whoever becomes the leader in this sphere [AI] will become the ruler of the world'. A global arms race has emerged, driven by both the potential and dangers of AI-powered weapons. Major powers such as the United States, Russia, and China are actively advancing a suite of emerging military technologies to maintain or enhance their strategic capabilities.

Recent macro-level indicators capture the pace of change. A 2024 Brookings Institution overview shows U.S. Department of Defense (DoD) AI-related contract commitments skyrocketed from $355 million in August 2022 to $4.6 billion by August 2023.[1] Defence spending on AI-enabled systems is now increasing in every major military power, and we can safely conjecture that AI spending in years to come will dwarf those figures given by Brookings. At the same time, global institutions, parliaments and regulatory bodies struggle to keep up to date with the rapid technological developments. NATO revised its Artificial Intelligence Strategy in July 2024, centred on the six Principles of Responsible Use (PRUs): Lawfulness, Responsibility and Accountability, Explainability and Traceability, Reliability, Governability, and Bias Mitigation, while explicitly framing AI as "becoming a general-purpose technology, with different risks, actors and levels of complexity between narrow AI, designed to perform specific tasks, and emerging AI technologies, such as frontier or foundation AI models, which are multi-purpose and capable of performing

[1]https://www.brookings.edu/articles/the-evolution-of-artificial-intelligence-ai-spending-by-the-u-s-government/.

complex tasks." (NATO, 2024a, 2024b). These policy shifts illustrate both the enthusiasm for, and anxiety about, what has been termed algorithmic warfare.

History offers perspective; from the proximity fuse of the Second World War to Vietnam-era "precision guided munitions," militaries have always sought to offset adversaries through automation. Yet today's deep-learning architectures create *adaptive* rather than merely *pre-programmed* behaviours. As Paul Scharre argued in *Four Battlegrounds* (Scharre, 2023), mastery now lies not only in superior hardware but in the data, compute, technical talent and human-machine command structures that surround it. Michael C. Horowitz underscores that these emerging, adaptive systems also compress escalation ladders, increasing the probability of inadvertent conflict when algorithms operate at machine speed, noting that "The potential for advances in information-age technologies to undermine nuclear deterrence and influence the potential for nuclear escalation represents a critical question for international politics. One challenge is that uncertainty about the trajectory of technologies such as autonomous systems and artificial intelligence (AI) makes assessments difficult" (Horowitz et al., 2019a, 2019b).

Empirical evidence from ongoing wars reinforces these theoretical concerns. Both Ukraine and Russia have fielded swarming loitering munitions guided by on-board neural networks and have paired commercial large-language models with battlefield chatbots to shorten kill-chains. Deputy Minister of Defence of Ukraine Oleksandr Kozenko claimed that unmanned systems now inflict "80 per cent of battlefield damage" (Kozenko, 2025).[2] A June 2025 raid—*Operation Spiderweb*—used AI-augmented micro-drones to cripple over 40 Russian aircraft hundreds of kilometres inside Russia, demonstrating the strategic reach of inexpensive autonomy. Analysts at CSIS conclude that recent developments in Ukraine mark the dawn of "drone saturation" where, through constant attritional warfare, quantity and software quality outmatch legacy hardware.[3]

Technically, reinforcement-learning (RL) and large-language-model (LLM) paradigms are leading much of the military transition. Research at RAND highlights RL's ability to discover novel tactics but warns of brittleness outside the training envelope, recommending rigorous red-teaming before operational deployment.[4] Meanwhile, concerns about these developments have pushed the United Nations Secretary-General to declare that systems able to take life

[2]https://mod.gov.ua/en/news/the-ukrainian-defense-industry-has-the-capability-to-produce-10-million-drones-annually-said-oleksandr-kozenko-at-a-security-forum-in-singapore.

[3]See for instance the CSIS brief titled "Drone Saturation: Russia's Shahed Campaign." A short YouTube summary can be found here: https://www.youtube.com/watch?v=TQo9GG-n2BI.

[4]See for instance the paper "An AI Revolution in Military Affairs? How Artificial Intelligence Could Reshape Future Warfare" (2025).

"without meaningful human control" are "morally repugnant and should be banned" (UN Secretary-General, 2025).

Against this backdrop, the chapter proceeds as follows. "Historical Trajectory of Military Autonomy" section traces the historical arc of military autonomy, situating today's breakthroughs within a century-long quest for machine advantage. "Core AI Technologies Shaping Defence" section dissects the key AI sub-fields now entering defence portfolios, from computer vision at the network edge to generative models that draft operational plans. "Operational Domains and Use-Cases" section maps concrete use-cases across land, maritime, air, cyber and cognitive domains, while "Strategic Stability and Deterrence in an Algorithmic Age" section looks at implications for deterrence stability and nuclear command-and-control, and finally "Policy Analyses for the Present and Future" section distils some policy considerations from each of the authors in turn.

By taking a broad approach and integrating cutting-edge empirical data, cross-disciplinary theory and the latest policy debates, this chapter aims to equip scholars, military professionals and decision-makers with a rigorous foundation for understanding how AI and robotics are transforming defence, security and warfare.

Historical Trajectory of Military Autonomy

From wired triggers to adaptive code. The aspiration to remove human limits from combat predates digital computing. As early as 1898, Nikola Tesla demonstrated a radio-controlled craft on a pool in New York's Madison Square Garden, promising a future of "tele-automatics" that could change warfare. Although little came of that prototype, it framed a century-long pattern: every new communications or control technology quickly found a military testbed.

Second World War—automation at industrial scale. During Second World War, two strands of automation matured. First, *sensing* automation: the proximity (VT) fuze used miniature vacuum-tube radars to detonate shells near aircraft, increasing effectiveness five- to seven-fold and earning the praise of Admiral Lewis Strauss, who would also later go on to become Chairman of the United States Atomic Energy Commission:

> One of the most original and effective military developments in World War II was the proximity, or 'VT', fuze. It found use in both the Army and the Navy, and was employed in the defense of London. While no one invention won the war,

the proximity fuze must be listed among the very small group of developments, such as radar, upon which victory very largely depended.[5]

Second, *mobility* automation: Germany's *Goliath* tracked mine (Sd.Kfz 302/303) employed a 650-m control cable to steer 60 kg of explosives under tanks or pillboxes. These systems were remote-controlled, not intelligent, yet they proved that electromechanical links could shift battlefield risk from humans to machines.

Cold War precision and the birth of "smart weapons." In Vietnam the U.S. Navy's AGM-62 *Walleye* television-guided bomb allowed pilots to steer a glide-weapon onto point targets, inaugurating the term *precision-guided munition.* Solid-state electronics and early microprocessors followed, enabling laser-guided bombs (*Paveway*) and inertial-guided cruise missiles. These weapons still relied on pre-programmed trajectories, yet they embedded computational feedback loops into ordnance, foreshadowing AI-enabled autonomy. Norbert Wiener's cybernetics, developed in the 1940s, provided a theoretical foundation for feedback loops in guided munitions, influencing later AI-driven systems (Wiener, 1948).

Persistence from above—unmanned aerial vehicles (UAVs). Breakthroughs in satellite communications and lightweight composites produced the General Atomics *MQ-1 Predator* in the 1990s. Abraham Karem's design fused real-time video downlinks with over-the-horizon piloting; in his 2014 book "Predator: The Secret Origins of the Drone Revolution," Richard Whittle recounts the Predator's history, including its innovative remote control via ground stations, developing into what he calls an "intercontinental sniper rifle" (Whittle, 2014). Predators demonstrated that software-defined payloads—synthetic-aperture radar today, Hellfire missiles tomorrow—could iterate faster than traditional airframes.

The DARPA catalyst for greater autonomy. Vision, lidar and probabilistic planning leapt forward after DARPA's 2004–2005 Grand Challenges, where university teams raced driverless vehicles across the Mojave. The programme's 2006 report to Congress explicitly linked prize outcomes to the U.S. Army's goal of one-third unmanned ground vehicles by 2015,[6] codifying autonomy as a defence acquisition priority.

[5]As quoted in Baldwin, R. B. (1980). *The deadly fuze: The secret weapon of World War II.* San Rafael, CA: Presidio Press.

[6]This ambitious timeline was later abandoned, yet as with many military technology projects, the more impressive results came further down the line than expected.

Algorithmic warfare in the 2020s. The Russia-Ukraine war shows how inexpensive compute and open-source AI compress innovation cycles. Kyiv's ad-hoc workshops have field-converted quadcopters into first-person-view (FPV) munitions, while reports from frontline units indicate they now deploy missile-armed ground robots to counter Russian aircraft. Moscow, in turn, unveiled the V2U loitering munition—reportedly capable of autonomous target selection and limited swarming (Hardie, 2025). Analysts at CSIS describe the resulting shift from traditional platforms to drone saturation as one of the defining features of modern warfare.

Continuities and inflection points. Across these epochs one constant emerges: each wave of autonomy has expanded the *speed–distance* envelope between operator intent and battlefield action. What began as tethered explosives is now a software-defined, globally networked kill-web. Understanding this trajectory is essential for assessing both the disruptive potential and the enduring constraints of AI-enabled warfare, a task the following sections undertake by examining contemporary technologies, operational use-cases and strategic consequences.

Core AI Technologies Shaping Defence

Artificial intelligence in war is not a monolith. As well as recent developments in hardware, four technical pillars—perception, decision-making, generation and execution—form the substrate on which doctrine now evolves. Each pillar is advancing at a different cadence, with distinctive opportunities and risks for military adoption.

The Evolution of Hardware: Recent Developments and Constraints

Modern military robotics now spans three families that are already shaping operations. In the air, small quadcopters and fixed-wing drones have become the default for close reconnaissance and many strike tasks. At the low-cost end, modified commercial drones carry small warheads and fly by video link; further up the ladder, *loitering munitions* orbit until a target appears, and larger uncrewed aircraft fly alongside fighters as "loyal wingmen" to extend sensing and magazine depth. On land, tracked and wheeled robots range from bomb-disposal carts to remote-controlled vehicles that can patrol, resupply, or—under strict human supervision—fire anti-armour or short-range air-defence missiles. At sea, uncrewed surface craft ("sea drones") and underwater vehicles have moved from trials to routine use: fast surface craft can harass or strike larger ships, while subsea robots map minefields and shadow submarines for hours or days. With respect to the important question of whether these technologies will replace or augment, it often depends on the military in question: a RAND Corporation analysis of Russia's use of autonomous weapons (Marcinek & Han, 2023) found the following motivations:

> Replace or Augment? If a key aim of robotization is "to reduce as much as possible the number of military personnel directly participating in combat" or even reduce an overall number of military personnel, it is consistent that Russian military scholars declare that robots are supposed to replace (rather than support) humans in combat. This intent is also hinted at in some of the writing on human-machine teaming, when discussing possible interfaces for human-machine teaming and ways to formalize tactical tasks for robotic systems. Russian experts assume that, in the future, soldiers will be giving commands to a group of robotic systems and not to individual platforms. Consequently, the implicit assumption is that, over time, the human-to-machine ratio in the battlefield will shift toward machines. (p. 14)

Nevertheless, across these categories, four practical constraints explain what robots can and cannot do. Power and endurance come first: batteries or fuel set range, time on station and payload options; every extra sensor or heavier warhead shortens endurance. This is why many systems favour short missions in large numbers rather than a few exquisite platforms. Mobility is the second: airframes dislike high winds; ground robots dislike mud, stairs and rubble; underwater craft fight currents and depth. No algorithm can wish these physics away, so commanders plan around them. Communication is the third: in contested electromagnetic environments, radio links are jammed or patchy. When that happens, operators cannot steer in real time, so platforms need pre-planned routes and simple behaviours they can execute on their own—always under human command intent but without continuous human input. Payload and modularity are the fourth: a platform that lets units swap cameras, radios or munitions in minutes is far more valuable than a sealed "one-trick" device. Hence the push for open, modular designs that speed upgrades and repairs at the front.

The last 5 years have seen tangible improvements on each front. Small aerial drones are cheaper and tougher; field units 3D-print spares and rotate batteries to keep them flying. Loitering munitions have grown more precise and longer-ranged, giving company-level commanders a standoff strike option once reserved for higher headquarters. Ground robots that once crawled at walking speed now keep up with mechanised units and can carry standard weapons, while retaining a human safety-catch on engagement. At sea, low-cost surface craft have demonstrated that numbers, speed and clever routing can penetrate defended waters, and long-endurance underwater vehicles are expanding mine-hunting and covert surveillance. These trends tend to favour mass and replenishability over single-point excellence, as described in the U.S. Department of Defense's Replicator Initiative (2023–2025) which sought all-domain, attritable autonomous systems (ADA^2)—a point also repeatedly emphasised in recent operational analyses (for a fuller discussion of how mass relates to *adaptability*, see CSIS's 2025 report "Out-Adapting the Enemy: Why Mass Alone Won't Win Tomorrow's Wars").

None of this turns robots into fully "autonomous warriors" just yet. Commanders still set aims and rules, and humans remain legally and morally responsible for the use of force. Indeed, both NATO's *Principles of Responsible Use* and the U.S. Department of Defense's autonomy directive insist on rigorous testing, fail-safes and retained human judgement—especially for any system that could select and engage targets. The hardware takeaway is straightforward for policy and strategy readers: better, cheaper platforms have changed the scale and tempo at which human choices matter. Air and sea drones can mass by the dozen; ground robots can take the most dangerous perimeter jobs; and all three extend a unit's eyes and reach without risking a pilot or driver. The software sections that follow—on how machines see (perception), choose (decision-making), generate plans and deception (generative tools), and run at the edge without constant connectivity—sit inside this envelope of power, movement, communication and payload. That envelope is where strategy meets engineering.

Machine-Learning Perception: Computer Vision and Sensor Fusion

Modern operations hinge on turning raw pixels and waveforms into *targetable* knowledge. Convolutional neural networks, originally honed on ImageNet, now classify armoured vehicles in satellite imagery with sub-metre resolution; self-supervised algorithms fuse electro-optical, thermal and synthetic-aperture-radar feeds to maintain tracks through smoke, foliage or GPS denial. Ukraine's field-assembled quad-copter fleet illustrates the trend: consumer-grade boards reportedly running YOLO-class object detectors detect T-72 silhouettes in real time and adjust flight paths without radio uplink, mitigating Russian electronic warfare. Similar perception stacks underpin maritime "ghost fleets," where distributed surface drones share bearings via mesh networks before a single human validates a firing solution. While accuracy now rivals human analysts under benign conditions, adversarial camouflaging and corrupted metadata can still degrade classifiers, a vulnerability driving research into certified robustness and ensemble voting.

Adaptive Decision-Making: Reinforcement Learning and Hierarchical Planners

Perception alone does not close a kill-chain; agents must *decide*. Reinforcement learning (RL) has moved from Atari benchmarks to live-fire exercises, where swarms learn optimal search patterns or electronic-attack waveforms. But RL's opaque reward landscapes can incentivise brittle shortcuts that fail when the environment shifts; possible solutions include sandboxed red-teaming and formal verification before fielding RL in command-and-control (C2) loops. Hierarchical RL[7] and model-predictive control partially alleviate brittleness by separating high-level intent from low-level actuation, enabling a human operator to veto manoeuvres without micromanaging every servo. There has been much focus on drones, but recent reports from the South China Morning Post among other media indicate that China's Academy of Military Science is evolving quickly in algorithmic dog-fighting, where the AI must learn at the fastest rate possible.[8] Across the battlespace, ethical concerns centre on *speed*: when a hierarchical agent can cycle the observe–orient–decide–act (OODA) loop in milliseconds, human commanders struggle to retain "meaningful control"—a tension that resurfaces in "Strategic Stability and Deterrence in an Algorithmic Age" section on deterrence. A 2025 report from RAND "An AI Revolution in Military Affairs?" succinctly summarised the consequences of these developments for decision-making:

> Militaries that fully embrace significant changes to their operational concepts and force structures will have advantages over those that simply use AI to make their existing approaches to warfighting incrementally better. Exploiting AI's

[7] Hierarchical RL decomposes a task into multiple layers of decision-making: High-level policies choose goals or intents (e.g., "navigate to location B"). Low-level controllers learn how to execute those goals (e.g., steer, throttle, turn).

[8] A report from the South China Morning Post can be found here: https://www.scmp.com/news/china/science/article/3211976/chinese-military-researchers-report-ai-pilot-beats-human-landmark-real-life-dogfight.

military potential will be as much an organizational challenge as a technological one because it will require disruptive changes to how militaries have become comfortable organizing and operating. (p. vi)

Generative AI and Large-Language Models in the Battlespace

Large-language models (LLMs) have quickly evolved from chat assistants to operational planning aids. Task Force Lima was established in August 2023 under the DoD's Chief Data and AI Office (CDAO) to assess and guide the adoption of generative AI and LLMs across defense missions.[9] Radha Plumb, head of the Chief Digital and AI Office (CDAO), noted in a Pentagon briefing to journalists:

> Task Force Lima analyzed hundreds of AI workflows and tasks that AI tools could make more efficient or more effective. And we categorized all of those use cases into a smaller set of 15 areas aligned into two big categories: warfighting functions—like command and control [and] decision support—and enterprise management functions like financial management and healthcare information management.[10]

Within this context of experimentation, Indo-Pacific Command in particular has examined using LLMs to speed up decision-making and thereby operational effectiveness: Project Stormbreaker used AI for more effective wargaming and planning, while Thunderforge combines AI agents and LLMs (from Scale AI, Anduril, Microsoft) to support strategic planning, reducing human workload in data collation and analysis. As of writing, current testing of LLMs in this capacity reportedly still leads to hallucinations and other idiosyncrasies which make its effectiveness at scale questionable, yet the fast-moving nature of AI means that with every 6-month iteration in LLMs, more creases are ironed out. General Sir Patrick Sanders, who has described artificial intelligence as "one ring to rule them all," also stressed that:

---

[9]It was replaced by the AI Rapid Capabilities Cell (AI RCC), a new initiative managed by the Defense Innovation Unit and the CDAO, designed to accelerate the adoption and deployment of AI tools across the department.

[10]https://defensescoop.com/2024/12/11/cdao-pentagon-generative-ai-rapid-capabilities-cell-sunset-task-force-lima/.

> It gives you the opportunity for better decision making, it gives you the opportunity to begin to develop autonomy. There's a lot of concern out there about killer robots and ethics. Actually the real use of AI is to support humans, to be under command of humans. The idea of human-machine teaming implies you can team with a computer. There isn't a team, the humans are in charge, but AI can relieve the human of the burden of pouring through gigabytes of data to spot a disturbance on the road where there wasn't one before. That ability to spot patterns and present that data to humans moves humans up the value chain.[11]

Generative vision-language models, for instance, can produce reconnaissance briefs with annotated images, shrinking the sensor-to-shooter cycle. Nevertheless, the dual-use nature of these LLM capabilities looms large. RAND's *Operational Risks of AI in Large-Scale Biological Attacks* shows that publicly available LLMs can reduce the expertise required to design a virulent toxin by providing step-by-step protocols (Mouton et al., 2024). The U.S. has proposed know-your-customer (KYC) rules for cloud providers (IaaS) to increase visibility into foreign training of large models potentially relevant to cyber or other misuse (Reuters, 2024), although it's questionable whether this would be sufficient. For policy-makers, the implication is two-fold: LLMs are increasingly force multipliers for intelligence fusion *and* latent proliferation vectors for cyber-bio threats, likely requiring stringent access controls and audit trails for the most advanced models.

Edge AI and Neuromorphic Chips

Edge AI refers to running AI models on resource-constrained devices at the point of action, reducing reliance on cloud connectivity. Tactical latency and contested bandwidth push inference to the "edge," where low-size-weight-and-power devices must run sophisticated models under fire. At the edge, modules like Jetson AGX Orin can deliver up to ~275 TOPS at ~15–60 W depending on configuration, while Movidius-class VPUs offer low-power vision inference at much lower TOPS, illustrating the trade-off between performance and power. This principle of maximising computational capabilities at the edge applies across the battlespace; Cameron Chehreh, Dell Technologies Federal CTO, noted that:

[11] https://www.telegraph.co.uk/news/2021/05/23/artificial-intelligence-isnt-killer-robots-britain-would-mad/.

> If you have semi-autonomous drones in the battlefield, you need to be able to run the algorithm at the edge so that it can take defensive maneuvers immediately if necessary. The platform has to make some real-time decisions and you cannot afford the latency required to send it out to the cloud and back. It has to be able to do that computing at the edge where it sits.[12]

Looking beyond von Neumann architectures, DARPA's *Lifelong Learning Machines* (L2M) programme is developing neuromorphic substrates that update synaptic weights in situ, promising continual learning without cloud retraining. Neuromorphic chips such as Intel's Loihi-class have demonstrated order-of-magnitude energy savings on certain temporal/spiking workloads in lab settings; translating those gains into rugged systems is an active research and integration challenge. Yet, when it comes to implementing edge AI, integration headaches—from thermal management to secure update pipelines—remain a bigger obstacle than raw flops, suggesting that procurement reforms may matter more than Moore's Law.

Together with advances in hardware, these technological primitives—seeing, deciding, generating and executing at the edge—constitute the evolving "stack" of algorithmic warfare. Mastery of any one layer yields tactical gains; mastery of their integration will determine strategic advantage. "Operational Domains and Use-Cases" and "Strategic Stability and Deterrence in an Algorithmic Age" sections investigate how this stack is manifesting in real operations and reshaping deterrence logic.

Operational Domains and Use-Cases

Artificial intelligence and robotics manifest differently on land, in the air, at sea and in the cyber-cognitive sphere. This section surveys each domain, drawing on the most recent combat data and experimentation programmes to illuminate where autonomy is already decisive and where fundamental limits persist. Article 36 of Additional Protocol I to the Geneva Conventions states:

> In the study, development, acquisition or adoption of a new weapon, means or method of warfare, a High Contracting Party is under an obligation to determine whether its employment would, in some or all circumstances, be prohibited by

---

[12] https://www.c4isrnet.com/artificial-intelligence/2019/09/18/how-the-pentagon-is-sharpening-the-smart-edge/.

this Protocol or by any other rule of international law applicable to the High Contracting Party.

As we shall see, much of the emerging AI weaponry exists within blurred legal lines, and in situations such as in Ukraine, survival tends to take precedence over law.

Land: Loitering Munitions, Ground Robotics and Algorithmic C2

The Russo-Ukrainian war has become a global laboratory for AI-enabled land warfare. Ukraine now reportedly fields more than 200 indigenous unmanned aerial systems and over 40 ground robotic platforms, most of which entered service only from 2024. Officials in Kyiv estimate that drones account for over 70% of battlefield casualties, underscoring a shift from platform mass to software mass.[13]

Loitering munitions. It is worth noting that while loitering munitions are airborne, in practice they are organic fires for ground forces (company/battalion echelons), used to kill land targets (armour, artillery, air-defence) and to exhaust ground air-defence magazines—however, this also illustrates how traditional military delineations of army, navy and air force are becoming blurred by technology. Russian ZALA Lancet-3 drones, estimated to cost about 3 million roubles ($35,000), now incorporate on-board target-recognition networks that can autonomously label a Leopard 2 tank before terminal dive, a capability first observed in March 2024; David Hambling at Forbes wrote on his findings, analysing OSINT at the time.[14] According to the Bulgarian military, upgraded "Lancet XXL" variants introduced in 2025 carry a 20 kg warhead and a rudimentary neural-network autopilot for extended, partly autonomous search profiles.[15] Given these developments, technologies that can counter such munitions are also crucial; Bronk and Watling (2024) at RUSI note that:

[13]This 70% figure has been questioned by some analysts, but what is beyond doubt is that casualties resulting from drone attacks have been substantial compared to previous conflicts. As we saw earlier, Kozenko puts the figure closer to 80%.

[14]https://www.forbes.com/sites/davidhambling/2024/03/01/russian-kamikaze-drone-now-seems-to-identify-its-own-targets/.

[15]It is worth noting that Russian systems are often opaque, and claims of neural-network autonomy could be overstated in media reports, especially for a new variant like "Lancet XXL." The report from the Bulgarian military can be found here: https://bulgarianmilitary.com/2025/05/23/russian-lancet-xxl-reportedly-packs-20kg-tnt-for-200km-range/.

> The corollary to the importance of armies fielding UAS is that effective, layered and efficient counter-UAS (C-UAS) capabilities are neither a luxury nor a concept to be explored as part of an abstract 'future force'. They are a basic requirement for a land force to be suitable for operations on the modern battlefield. Without C-UAS capabilities, a force will be seen first, engaged more accurately, and ultimately defeated by an opposing force that successfully fields UAS and C-UAS capabilities at scale. For NATO members, the aiming mark set by the Alliance's senior leadership is to be ready to deter Russia by 2028. Fielding C-UAS capabilities, which are absent in any structured sense from the British Army and from most other NATO land force elements, is therefore an urgent operational requirement.

Ground robotics. Ukraine's 28th Mechanised Brigade unveiled a remote-controlled UGV armed with Igla MANPADS in August 2025—according to the Brigade itself, it is the first robot to down a Russian helicopter (Defense Blog, 2025).[16] If true, the system exemplifies a broader trend toward *robotic point defence*, allowing units to contest airspace without exposing crews. Russia and Ukraine have also deployed tracked resupply robots and FPV-drone carriers.

Algorithmic command and control. The U.S. Army's Project Convergence showcases allied progress in AI-assisted targeting. During Capstone 4 (2024) the FIRESTORM decision aide fused dozens of data feeds and recommended fires assignments in under 20 s, 10 times faster than just a year previously. Lt. Gen. Ross Coffman, deputy commander of Army Futures Command, commended that:

> The entire joint force, and with our U.K. and Australian teammates and allies, we were able to effectively move data for the first time in an Indo-Pacific scenario at a magnitude never seen before.[17]

Capstone 5 (2025) will leave several AI tools "in theatre" with Indo-Pacific Command to validate durability outside an exercise setting.

On land, autonomy generally scales horizontally: thousands of cheap, smart munitions and robots matter more than a few exquisite systems.

---

[16] We should also bear in mind that only one secondary source confirmed this downing of the Russian helicopter—yet that is the nature of much of this conflict, with such fast-evolving technology. You can find the article here: https://defence-blog.com/ukrainian-soldiers-develop-robotic-air-defense-system/.

[17] https://defensescoop.com/2024/03/08/data-passed-at-a-magnitude-never-seen-before-at-armys-project-convergence/.

Yet, electronic-warfare resilience and secure update pipelines remain critical vulnerabilities.

Air: Collaborative Combat Aircraft and Swarming Autonomy

Loyal wingmen. Australia's MQ-28 Ghost Bat (the first aircraft designed and developed in Australia for more than half a century, and a considerable technological leap into the twenty-first century) has logged over 100 flight hours and is slated for a live air-to-air-missile test in late 2025; the nose section of the Ghost Bat, named after an Australian bat with exceptional detection capabilities, can be removed quickly and changed for another with a different payload, for either combat, reconnaissance or electronic warfare. The U.S. Air Force's Skyborg autonomy core completed its multi-platform flight campaign in 2024 and now provides the software baseline for the USAF's *Collaborative Combat Aircraft* programme.

Swarm experimentation. The use of drone swarms for popular entertainment has impressed in the minds of the public the versatile and agile nature of this emerging technology. Tests under DARPA's ACE and OFFSET programs have explored multi-drone manoeuvring and swarming autonomy, while China's AVIC (the Aviation Industry Corporation of China) has demonstrated formation-AI trials with fixed-wing UAVs. China is also preparing to launch the Jiu Tian, a massive unmanned "drone mothership" capable of deploying AI-enabled drone swarms across battlefields. The Jiu Tian is designed to fly up to 50,000 feet with a range exceeding 4000 miles and can carry up to six tonnes of ammunition and around 100 small drones. The U.S. military has been developing counter-drone technologies to neutralise enemy swarms; one such system is Epirus' "Leonidas," a high-powered electromagnetic weapon demonstrated to disable swarms of drones. The system has been deployed to CENTCOM for real-world testing. These emerging defensive technologies will be crucial; in their influential paper on Taiwan, "Swarms over the Straits," written following extensive wargaming with experts from both the military and technology spheres, CNAS noted that:

> Determining whether drones would decisively advantage one side or the other in this conflict is difficult because it depends on if and when autonomous technologies and counterdrone systems mature and are adopted by each party. It also depends on the numbers of drones and counterdrone systems each side can field, as well as the overall balance of capabilities, operational concepts, and

> proficiency of each country's military personnel. Thus far, China appears to have an edge. It has already fielded a diverse fleet across its services and has integrated drones into its long-range artillery and rocket force units' targeting operations. (Pettyjohn et al., 2024, p. 68)

Integrated air defence. Israel's *Iron Dome* upgraded its radar-classifier pipeline with convolutional neural networks in 2024; the Lieber Institute notes that the new technology led to lifting intercept rates above 90% during recent conflicts, while also reducing costs.[18] Such gains demonstrate that AI can extend the life of legacy systems even as new uncrewed threats proliferate.

Maritime: Unmanned Surface/Sub-Surface Vehicles and "Hybrid Fleets"

The naval domain is pivoting from capital-ship dominance to distributed, sensor-rich "ghost fleets."

Task Force 59. The U.S. Navy's autonomous task group operating in the Red Sea accumulated thousands of sailing hours by April 2025 and has endured state-backed jamming and capture attempts, validating concepts for persistent ISR pickets, according to the Military Times, it uses undisclosed technology which allows it to navigate without GPS[19] (Military Times, 2025).[20] Parallel experimentation in U.S. 4th Fleet and 7th Fleet aims to evolve towards a hybrid crewed–uncrewed force towards the end of this decade (Defense Info, 2025).[21]

Mine counter-measures and contested littorals. Britain's Project CETUS extra-large unmanned underwater vehicle (UUV), the largest and most complex of its kind in any European navy, launched in May 2025 at His Majesty's Naval Base Devonport; it will use autonomous mine-hunting algorithms, filling a critical NATO gap (Naval Technology, 2025).[22] According to GlobalData intelligence, the uncrewed maritime vehicles market is growing at 8.9% each year, with UUVs making up 42% of the total.

---

[18] https://lieber.westpoint.edu/beyond-headlines-combat-deployment-military-ai-based-systems-idf/.

[19] It's widely accepted in the defense community that alternative navigation technologies—such as inertial navigation systems (INS), celestial navigation, terrain-relative navigation, and signals of opportunity—are in active operational testing.

[20] https://www.militarytimes.com/news/your-military/2025/04/11/inside-the-navy-task-group-testing-drone-boats-in-the-red-sea/.

[21] https://defense.info/maritime-dynamics/2025/04/the-u-s-navy-publishes-a-new-navigation-plan-and-advances-the-fielding-of-a-hybrid-fleet/.

[22] https://www.naval-technology.com/news/royal-navy-name-project-cetus-xluuv-excalibur/.

Unmanned weapons delivery. Ukraine's explosive sea-drone campaign against Russia's Black Sea Fleet and Houthi attempts to ram tankers in the Red Sea signal the advent of low-cost, AI-guided anti-ship systems (Reuters, 2024). Deterrence at sea will increasingly depend on *counter-USV* sensors and rules of engagement that can discriminate hostile autonomy from legitimate traffic.

Cyber and Cognitive: Automated Defence, Offensive AI and Information Warfare

Automated cyber defence. DARPA's AI Cyber Challenge (AIxCC) will award USD 8.5 million at DEF CON 33 (August 2025) to teams whose models patch open-source vulnerabilities autonomously—an early proof that AI can defend as well as attack (DARPA, 2025).[23] Commercial red-team testing shows AI already rivalling human experts in reverse-engineering malware (Axios, 2025).[24]

Offensive AI and deepfakes. Russian influence operations now deploy thousands of Telegram bots, including AI-generated deep-fake videos of Ukrainian generals. Such campaigns exploit large-language and vision-generation models to erode civilian morale and muddy attribution, raising urgent questions about algorithmic propaganda governance.

Battlefield cognitive aides. On the Ukrainian side, there are widespread but as yet not officially confirmed reports that field units have begun using fine-tuned LLMs to draft situational reports in NATO format and translate real-time drone feeds, shaving minutes off artillery calls. These dual-use capabilities blur the line between cyber and kinetic operations, a theme explored further in "Strategic Stability and Deterrence in an Algorithmic Age" section on deterrence stability.

The cyber-cognitive plane is where AI's *zero-marginal-cost* advantage is most pronounced: algorithms scale instantly across networks, forcing defenders to automate at the same speed or lose the contest.

[23]You can read more about this here https://www.darpa.mil/news/2025/ai-cyber-challenge-winners-def-con-33.

[24]https://www.axios.com/2025/03/14/hackers-artificial-intelligence-cyber-threats.

Cross-Domain Synergies

While each of these technologies show promise in isolation, the true power of AI lies in the ability to weave together military sensors, accelerated decision-making and effectors across all domains into a unified "kill web." As "Strategic Stability and Deterrence in an Algorithmic Age" section will argue, the strategic balance will hinge less on any single breakthrough than on how effectively states integrate perception, decision and action across land-air-sea-cyber complexes.

In sum, AI and robotics are migrating from laboratory curiosities to routine, if still imperfect, combat tools across every war-fighting domain. They promise unprecedented speed and reach, but they also introduce new fragilities that policy-makers and commanders must confront now, not when the next crisis breaks.

Strategic Stability and Deterrence in an Algorithmic Age

On 26 September 1983, 3 weeks after the Soviet military had shot down a Korean Air commercial flight from New York to Seoul, raising tensions on both sides of the Iron Curtain, Stanislav Petrov, the duty officer at the Oko nuclear early-warning system, received reports from the early warning system of nuclear missiles approaching from the US. Bruce G Blair, President of the World Security Institute in Washington, DC, and one of the foremost experts on Cold War nuclear strategies, wrote that the American–Soviet relationship at that point:

> . . . had deteriorated to the point where the Soviet Union as a system—not just the Kremlin, not just Soviet leader Yuri Andropov, not just the KGB, but as a system—was geared to expect an attack and to retaliate very quickly to it. It was on hair-trigger alert. It was very nervous and prone to mistakes and accidents. The false alarm that happened on Petrov's watch could not have come at a more dangerous, intense phase in U.S.–Soviet relations.[25]

Against all Soviet military protocol and strict orders, Petrov decided to wait for further information and not to send the information up the chain

---

[25] This quote is from Pieta, Ewa. "The Red Button & the Man Who Saved the World". logtv.com. Archived from the original (Flash).

of command, which may well have led to a nuclear "retaliation." The so-called Launch on Warning doctrine, as opposed to "retaliation after ride-out," states that a retaliatory strike should be launched after a warning that missiles are in the air. The false alert was caused by an unusual effect of sunlight shining on high altitude clouds. While Petrov is now honoured at the United Nations and lauded as one of the few people that might lay a claim to saving the world, the question now is how AI might have played into this process.

The logics that kept the nuclear peace for eight decades are colliding with fast-moving, data-hungry technologies whose operating tempo often eclipses human cognition. Cyber attacks blur the lines between war and peace which had previously been clear, while also requiring immediate responses. The adaptive neural networks coordinating drone swarms will in turn require automated defences. Traditional notions of *notice, decide, respond* were premised on minutes to hours; deep-learning algorithms compress that window to seconds, or even milliseconds, raising the probability that misperception, spoofing or simple code error could turn a crisis into a catastrophe. The following subsections trace how AI is reshaping deterrence theory, nuclear command-and-control (NC3), escalation dynamics and risk-reduction measures. As a recent report from SIPRI notes:

> In the nuclear context, ML [machine learning] is often discussed as having the potential to enhance capabilities in all elements of the nuclear deterrence architecture: early warning and ISR; command and control; nuclear weapon targeting, guidance and navigation; and non-nuclear operations such as missile defence, cybersecurity and anti-submarine warfare. For instance, India is planning to launch a fleet of AI-enabled surveillance satellites and is investigating the use of DL in radar technology. Meanwhile, the US National Geospatial Intelligence Agency plans significant investment in data-labelling services over five years to enhance ML capabilities for analysing satellite imagery and geospatial data. Further ML-enabled improvements in ISR capabilities might, for instance, aid in detection, tracking and targeting of nuclear delivery systems, whether missile silos, aircraft or mobile launchers. (Chernavskikh, 2024, p. 5)

Deterrence Logic under Acceleration

Traditional deterrence relies on mutually understood thresholds and the credible threat of punishment. AI complicates both pillars. First, autonomy in intelligence, surveillance and reconnaissance (ISR) vastly improves speed to insight: low-Earth-orbit constellations coupled with on-orbit inference now flag missile launches in seconds. Faster detection ostensibly strengthens deterrence by reducing the payoff for a disarming first strike, yet it arguably pressures leaders to *pre-delegate* some level of launch authority, or at least information filtering, to machines, undercutting the very human judgement that stabilised past close calls such as the 1983 Petrov incident.

Second, AI erodes the opacity on which *ambiguity-based* deterrence strategies depend. Trained AI can now identify irregular reactor operations or rail-mobile ICBM movements from commercial imagery, shrinking a state's ability to hide strategic assets. Greater transparency may curb breakout incentives, but it may also reduce crisis bargaining space, as each side believes it can see, and may therefore act on, every adversary moves in real time. This is reminiscent of Robert Jervis' concept of the "security dilemma," from his work in the 1970s, where transparency can paradoxically increase conflict risks by eliminating strategic hesitation.

AI and Nuclear Command, Control and Communications (NC3)

All nine nuclear-armed states are exploring military AI, and several are examining applications that touch ISR and NC3 (SIPRI, 2024). General Anthony J. Cotton, commander of U.S. Strategic Command (STRATCOM), has highlighted the necessity of modernising NC3 systems to maintain technological superiority and enhance deterrence. He advocates for the use of AI and machine learning to process vast amounts of sensor data, enabling faster and more informed decisions, however, he underscores that AI should not replace human judgement in nuclear decision-making. Meanwhile, China's State Council's, 2025 white paper, "China's National Security in the New Era", highlights 'intelligentisation' within a holistic security concept.[26] The China Institute of Atomic Energy (CIAE) has trained AI to tell the difference between real nuclear warheads and decoys using simulated neutron flux signatures, a significant step in technological defence systems if it is as reliable as claimed. Even while not directly involved in nuclear command-and-control, such tools could influence nuclear situational awareness by providing faster, more reliable detection of strategic threats, potentially compressing the decision window. While these tools promise faster threat classification, they introduce a number of possible failure modes, including:

---

[26] The reader should also take note that "intelligentisation" has for some time been a common buzzword within Chinese military discussions that may not always imply advanced AI.

1. **Brittleness outside training data.** Early warning algorithms trained on historical launch profiles may misclassify novel boost-glide vehicles and other newer aircraft.
2. **Automation bias.** Operators may over-trust confident model outputs, a phenomenon found across many organisations where people take advice from automated systems, AI or otherwise (see more on this below, also CSET's paper "AI Safety and Automation Bias" (2024) provides an excellent outline).
3. **Cyber-vulnerability.** Adversaries can inject poisoned data or adversarial perturbations, spoofing launch signatures that trigger "use-or-lose" pressures.

The Risk of Entanglement

Merging AI into conventional and nuclear command chains can create "entanglement" risks, where decision-support overlaps, or automation shortcuts, could trigger unintended escalation from conventional to nuclear domains. The Arms Control Association writes that:

> Existing initiatives to address the risks posed by the integration of Artificial Intelligence (AI) into military systems fail to provide adequate safeguards against the dangers inherent in a world of continued reliance on the nuclear balance of terror. Both the widespread deployment of autonomous weapons systems (AWS) and the development of AI-enabled decision-support systems create new pathways for nuclear escalation and arms racing. Yet these risks are not adequately addressed by any of the primary AI and AWS risk-reduction efforts.[27]

AI and automated weapons change both the *speed* and the *tangle* of escalation ladders; AI thereby becomes increasingly necessary in certain parts of decision-making, for instance responding to drone swarms, while also risking escalation. This ties in to the *theatre–strategic* entanglement first identified by Thomas Schelling, who discussed how military manoeuvres in one domain may inadvertently trigger responses in another domain. Hypersonic glide vehicles guided by onboard neural nets can manoeuvre unpredictably, blurring the distinction between conventional and nuclear delivery systems; this "warhead ambiguity" can be a recipe for inadvertent escalation. Decision-makers now

[27] https://www.armscontrol.org/issue-briefs/2024-011/beyond-the-loop.

face *compressed credibility*: they must decide whether a detected launch is nuclear-armed before impact clocks read double-digits.[28]

As AI-enhanced decision-making improves and becomes more widespread across the battlespace, misplaced faith in AI systems will be one of the most difficult challenges for policy-makers—this is especially the case with NC3, even when humans are at every level of the decision loop. The Federation of American Scientists (FAS) (2023) warns that bolt-on AI to legacy early warning chains can magnify automation bias, shifting operator cognition from critical appraisal to confirmation of machine outputs. To curb automation bias, FAS urges end-to-end assurance rather than piecemeal integration: AI roles should be tightly scoped, verifiable and embedded in procedures that require human challenge of any machine-generated alert. The Georgetown Center for Security and Emerging Technology found three key areas that should be addressed:

> Unaddressed automation bias has already culminated in catastrophic accidents. From these case studies of past mishaps, we identify three important factors affecting a user's automation bias: those intrinsic to the human user, such as personal biases, experience, and confidence in using the system; those inherent to the AI system, such as how it can be operated or how it presents information; and those created by organizational factors such as standard processes and procedures. (Kahn et al., 2024a, 2024b, p. 24)

Succinctly summarising much of what we have analysed in this section, writing at the Brookings Institution, in "How unchecked AI could trigger a nuclear war," Michael O'Hanlon examines different scenarios in previous decades where the world came close to nuclear war, and concludes:

> Yes, it is possible that very good AI might have determined restraint was warranted in these cases—and might do so in a future situation—perhaps even better than some humans would have. AI can be used as a check on human thinking and behavior. But these examples underscore how dangerous it could be to trust a machine to make the most momentous decision in human history.[29]

---

[28]For regional hypersonic threats, this is literally accurate: missiles can strike in under 10 min, sometimes closer to 6–8 min (e.g., a DF-17 or Kinzhal-class system). Even ICBMs between peer states (e.g., U.S. to Russia or vice versa) may give ~20–30 min of warning, but the window for confirmation and response is far smaller when factoring in command-chain processes and uncertainty.

[29]https://www.brookings.edu/articles/how-unchecked-ai-could-trigger-a-nuclear-war/.

Policy Analyses for the Present and Future

The following section provides three distinct viewpoints on how AI and robotics will affect the future of defence, security and warfare, from each of the three authors of this chapter. Each perspective comes from a different environment—the worlds of politics, the military and think tanks.

Field Marshal Lord Houghton of Richmond, GCB, CBE, DL

Former Chief of the Defence Staff (CDS) of the British Armed Forces

The ongoing and highly dynamic developments in the military potential of AI and autonomy are both brilliantly and breathlessly described in this chapter. Such developments, even to reasonably well-informed commentators, can present something of a bewildering and unnerving picture. Unsurprisingly, they attract the irresistible interest of politicians, technocrats, academics, journalists and law makers, all of whom hold strong and sometimes competing views. The result, amongst wider society, is a sort of chaos of anxieties. Quite naturally, that same society looks to policy makers and regulators to impose order and, hopefully, to alleviate many of the more extreme concerns. I offer, below, some thoughts from a military perspective: thoughts which may mollify at least a few of those concerns.

I would start with the challenge that the dominant societal concern regarding AI should relate to its use below the threshold of formalised warfare. We already recognise that the exploitation of AI across social media is doing unquantifiable damage to adolescent minds. More widely, Information Operations, which encompass the control, distortion and denial of information, now form a persistent feature of hybrid warfare and represent a potentially existential threat to societal integrity. We now live in an age of conflicted truth: both within societies and between countries. Indeed, one of the primary causes of current conflict is the desire of some countries, or at least their political leaderships, to change a world order which they feel denies them their, arguably confected, sense of historic entitlement. Information is now the world's most powerful weapon and governments which fail to realise this will flounder.

Separately, however, and the subject of what follows, is the existence of a wholly justifiable set of concerns regarding the future use of AI and autonomy in the weapon systems of more formalised conflict. Perhaps the prime example of such concerns, simply put, is the potential for unregulated AI to create sentient autonomy, which some commentators translate into the more chilling prospect of killer robots: robots capable of making their own decisions, even rebelling against their makers. So, I will confine my views to this latter set of concerns and offer some thoughts on some of the more fundamental considerations which should influence the policy, regulation and use of AI and autonomous systems going forward.

My starting point here would be that the need for most advanced countries and their armed forces to embrace and exploit AI is no longer discretionary. The

(continued)

potential benefits of AI and autonomy for technical advantage, cost effectiveness and relative lethality are simply too great. Robots don't need paying, housing or pensions. They don't, on the home side, create widows or wounded veterans. Acting within integrated systems, AI offers unprecedented levels of speed and precision. AI can perform repetitive tasks without ever tiring, in a fraction of the time it would take multiple humans. Moreover, reassuringly, in certain domains of warfare—maritime, air and space—the justifiable concerns of many regarding legality and morality are far less challenging, because of the more certain absence of civilians. So the real question is not whether to exploit AI and autonomy, but how best to do so.

My second major point would be to make a potentially surprising claim. It would be that the battlefield is, in principle at least, already a highly regulated environment. Professional armed forces are trained to understand the legal frameworks within which the use of lethal force is permitted. A whole panoply of regulations (the Laws of Armed Conflict, International Humanitarian Law, Targeting Directives, Rules of Engagement, Conventions regarding specific weapons and munitions) are applied as necessary constraints to ensure both the moral and legal use of lethal force. This is not to say that, when war breaks out, these laws and conventions are not often tested, broken or ignored. You only need to look at the current "hot wars" in Ukraine and the Middle East to recognise that the gravest breaches of morality in conflict enjoy political sanction at the highest levels of government. My point, however, is that, when it comes to regulation, there are limitations as to what more can usefully be achieved through further regulation of the battlefield itself.

It is also, I think, worth stressing the dangers of a misplaced belief that the retention of human agency in decision making somehow guarantees the observance of the moral and legal use of force: somehow representing the definitive answer to our fears about technology. This is simply not true. I absolutely believe that war will remain a fundamentally human activity, but I also have to recognise that human agency, when submitted to the ultimate pressures of warfare, often becomes the weakest link in its prosecution. I therefore harbour the hope that, if cleverly adopted, AI might, in certain ways, become part of a technical solution to the worst extremes of human frailty. Certainly the most obvious immediate conclusion to be drawn from this is that the most effective regulatory controls on AI and autonomy in weapon systems must be enforced at the stage of technological testing, approval and release-to-service, rather than in the more pressured circumstances of conflict.

That is not to say, however, that there are no implications for the battlefield or, perhaps more particularly, for effective training. In a context where the application of lethal force at scale, when considerations of civilian casualties, proportionality and military necessity are finely balanced, and when elements of the overall weapon systems being employed are informed by or activated by AI or autonomy, then there is a significant burden on commanders and operators to intuitively understand the levels of confidence and margins of risk they can place in the autonomous components within those systems. This, after all, and despite my earlier reservation that human agency is not a panacea to risk, is why we should seek to retain human agency within the system.

(continued)

I would offer here the reassurance that no commander I know of in the British Armed Forces would enable (i.e., activate) a wholly autonomous system, or make a decision based on AI-derived intelligence, unless he fully understood the implications that it had for the justifiable and legal use of lethal force. My point is that, on the future battlefield, in circumstances where a far greater quantity of key intelligence will be fused and delivered by AI systems, and where the majority of terminal effects will similarly be autonomously delivered, the training burden will be considerable; and the quality of weapon system operators will need to be commensurately higher. It is already the case on some manned aircraft that flying the plane is a less demanding task than operating the fighting systems. How much more challenging it will become when the activities of unmanned surrogates is added. And what challenges might there be for legal accountability in an AI-integrated force which uses sensors and effectors from another domain or ally? The personnel we recruit and the training regimes we develop for AI-enabled warfare will be very different indeed.

A further observation about AI and robotics in warfare is a development of my first: the simple observation that their beneficial exploitation is, quite simply, no longer discretionary. No nation can now allow an attitude of risk aversion to compromise their approach to AI's potential benefits. If it does, it will place its nation's armed forces at a permanent disadvantage. The need to be permanently ahead of the competition for technological advantage has other implications. It means that far more resources need to be invested in the capacity for innovation, in science and technology, and in research and development. The ever greater integration of the defence industrial base as a component of a nation's fighting power becomes an essential. The balance of capability investment shifts decisively from hardware to software. Such balance of investment decisions, which in the United Kingdom find specific form in the Defence Investment Plan, have fundamental implications for those responsible for the custodianship of military capability at a strategic level. Specifically, to what extent can technological advantage compensate for the lack of mass?

There is much about this subject to reflect on from a wholly UK perspective. When the House of Lords Select Committee on AI in Autonomous Weapons Systems, on which I had the pleasure to serve, published its report in late 2023, it prefaced its title "Proceed with Caution." This reflected, I believe, a collective sense that there was still too much uncertainty regarding the safety of the technology, so regulation had to dominate an incremental approach to adoption. Eighteen months on, I now firmly believe that an acceptance of tolerable risk, not a mindset of perpetual caution, should be the UK's approach. Successive defence cuts in the UK defence budget, together with a fixation on exquisite hardware, has resulted in much reduced overall force levels. The outcome of the latest Strategic Defence Review was clear: we will only be able to ensure the security of our country through the ability to deliver a fully integrated force, which, through the exploitation of AI and autonomy, enjoys a significant and persistent advantage in overall lethality. This is both a remarkable and I have to say slightly questionable aspiration: but it gives us a chance.

I offer the concern though, that we may have, perhaps unwittingly, already committed to a policy of sustaining our national security and military relevance

(continued)

through a belief in technological advantage alone. Technology has become the latest alchemy by which the Government seeks to reassure the public whilst balancing the books. The result is that we look increasingly incapable of being able to afford or generate the force structure and mass which NATO desires and that defines many continental armed forces. Instead we proclaim a somewhat elitist leadership role within NATO, based on a technical advantage that we have not yet convincingly delivered, nor yet committed the resources to do so. And I worry that we have not yet briefed our allies on this exercise in exceptionalism.

So my closing thought would be the need to be mindful of the dangers of wishful thinking: to avoid the seduction of alchemy. As I have said, information is now war's most potent weapon. The fact that warfare remains a human activity lays in the essential truth that military force, and the destructive power it can either threaten or deliver, is not an end in itself. Rather it is the means by which to deliver a cognitive outcome: that of either deterring an enemy or forcing his capitulation. Does the outcome of the latest Strategic Defence Review bring about a force structure which effectively deters Russia, reassures allies and brings comfort to the nation? Are we winning the information war? I would like to hope so, but I'm not altogether convinced.

Nicholas Fairfax, Elected Member of the House of Lords, Co-editor of *The Artificial Intelligence Revolution*

Meaningful Human Control: Lessons from the House of Lords Discussions

In recent years, the rapid advancement of artificial intelligence and its application to weapon systems has moved from speculative debate to immediate policy concern. The House of Lords, through its Select Committee on Artificial Intelligence in Weapon Systems, undertook a detailed and cautious examination of these issues, culminating in its 2023 report, *Proceed with Caution: Artificial Intelligence in Weapon Systems*. Central to these discussions was the principle of "Meaningful Human Control" (MHC)—a concept invoked widely in international discourse, but one still lacking firm legal definition or operational clarity. The Lords' deliberations provide a crucial contribution to the global conversation on AI-enabled weapons, especially regarding how, where, and whether human judgement should remain central to decisions involving life and death.

At the heart of the Committee's inquiry was a clear sense that the UK's existing frameworks are not yet sufficient to govern the emerging class of weapon systems driven by artificial intelligence. Unlike traditional weaponry, these systems often involve continuous learning, opaque algorithms, and operational environments where speed and complexity far outpace human cognition. How is control retained when decisions must be made at machine speed? What kind of oversight is meaningful in systems that adapt over time? Who remains accountable when things go wrong?

A key lesson emerging from the Lords' work is the importance of definitional clarity. The UK Government currently lacks a formal definition of what constitutes

(continued)

an autonomous weapon system (AWS), and similarly, no legally binding definition exists for "meaningful human control." This vagueness hampers regulation, procurement, deployment, and international collaboration. The Committee rightly observed that the nature of autonomy in weapons is not binary. There is a spectrum—from automated systems with limited decision-making capacity to those capable of selecting and engaging targets without further human intervention. As the Lords concluded, policies must reflect this spectrum and avoid oversimplification.

The concept of meaningful human control, if it is to serve as a guiding principle, must be grounded in operational realities. It must mean more than simply inserting a human into the loop for the sake of optics. Control must exist across the entire life-cycle of the system, from design, programming, testing, and deployment to real-time use and post-engagement accountability. The Committee emphasized that true control must include a human role in setting mission objectives, defining constraints, and having the authority to abort or override actions. Simply watching a live video feed is not meaningful control if the machine has already made the lethal decision by the time a human can intervene. Real control, they argued, must include three conditions: predictability, traceability, and accountability. Systems must behave in ways that are understandable by humans, their decision processes must be reconstructable, and legal and ethical responsibility must ultimately rest with identifiable actors. Without these three anchors, human involvement becomes symbolic rather than substantive.

Importantly, the Lords heard testimony that cast serious doubt on the ability of AI systems to meet core legal and ethical principles required by International Humanitarian Law (IHL). Principles such as distinction, proportionality, and precaution are not easily reducible to machine-executable code. AI systems may be able to detect heat signatures or identify objects with increasing accuracy, but they cannot reliably assess intent, context, or the strategic implications of their actions. The Committee concluded that AI, as it currently exists, cannot be expected to make ethically or legally sound judgements about proportionality or necessity; concepts that require human reasoning informed by experience, values, and context.

Another significant area of concern was automation bias, the documented tendency of human operators to over-trust or defer to machine outputs. The Committee heard that in high-pressure environments, human oversight can quickly become performative rather than substantive. This risk is magnified in complex operational environments, especially those involving swarms of drones or multi-domain operations, where decision speeds may be measured in milliseconds. If the pace of engagement exceeds the human ability to evaluate and intervene, then the very idea of control is effectively undermined.

The Lords also examined the issue of accountability, which they rightly placed at the centre of the MHC debate. Even if AI systems are involved in decision-making, humans must remain legally and morally accountable for the outcomes of their use. This has clear implications for military doctrine, legal review, procurement practices, and rules of engagement. The Committee concluded that systems must be designed with auditability and transparency in mind—

(continued)

capabilities that allow decisions to be reviewed and traced back to responsible individuals or institutions. Without this, the risk is both operational failure and the erosion of legal norms and public trust. If machines are selecting targets based on opaque neural networks, can a commander truly be held responsible for outcomes they did not foresee or understand? The Lords were clear: yes. The introduction of autonomous systems does not dilute accountability; it intensifies the responsibility to ensure systems behave within acceptable bounds. Delegation to machines does not remove moral burden, it deepens the ethical responsibility to ensure that such delegation is justifiable, lawful, and safe.

Notably, the Lords were critical of the current state of UK policy and capability. The Ministry of Defence, while expressing a commitment to responsible innovation and ethical AI, was found to be lacking in procurement agility and software expertise. The Committee noted that while the UK had invested heavily in hardware and kinetic capabilities, it lagged in data infrastructure, testing frameworks, and the specialist workforce needed to govern complex AI systems. This imbalance may compromise not only operational effectiveness but also the ability to ensure meaningful human control.

In terms of broader strategy, the Lords underscored the need for international collaboration. The UK, they argued, should lead by example—advocating for global standards and contributing to multilateral agreements that embed meaningful human control into the norms of warfare. While recognising that some adversaries may not observe such standards, the Committee maintained that this was not a justification for abandoning them. Rather, it pointed to the importance of developing norms that reinforce accountability and restraint, especially in areas such as nuclear command-and-control, where the consequences of automation could be catastrophic.

Equally, the Lords called for greater public transparency and democratic oversight. Decisions about the role of AI in lethal operations are too important to be left solely to technologists or defence contractors. Public understanding, Parliamentary scrutiny, and open debate are essential for ensuring legitimacy and for building public trust in the technologies deployed by the state. The report highlighted the potential risks of moral disconnection if lethal force becomes increasingly automated and opaque to citizens. Ethical review boards, test and evaluation protocols, and red-teaming exercises were all identified as necessary components of responsible AI governance, yet many of these are underdeveloped or absent altogether. The Committee thus recommended the establishment of dedicated review mechanisms within the Ministry of Defence to ensure that MHC is not simply a checklist item but a system-wide design and operational principle.

The UK Government, in its official response, agreed in principle with many of the Committee's recommendations. It reaffirmed its commitment to upholding International Humanitarian Law and ensuring human accountability. However, the Lords remained cautious, noting that the pace of implementation remains slow, and several key issues—such as clear definitions and robust oversight mechanisms—are still unresolved.

In conclusion, the House of Lords' work on AI-enabled weapon systems makes a clear and urgent case for embedding meaningful human control as a real and enforceable standard, not a vague aspiration. It must be defined,

(continued)

implemented across the full system lifecycle, and supported by technical, legal, and organisational safeguards. This is not just a matter of good governance; it is a matter of moral responsibility in an era when decisions about life and death may be made by algorithms running at superhuman speeds. The Lords' report serves as both a warning and a guide: if we are to retain our humanity in the conduct of war, we must ensure it is not designed out of the systems we build.

Max Rangeley, Trustee of The Cobden Centre, Co-editor of *The Artificial Intelligence Revolution*

At the Cobden Centre think tank, we have spent much of the last decade discussing the complexities of AI policy; this has ranged from organising and moderating the AI roundtable discussions in the European Parliament to lectures at institutions like the IMF and teaching AI policy to university postgraduates. Of all the areas of AI safety, military AI and robotics is perhaps the most important for policy-makers to have a good understanding. This section examines some of the complexities which differentiate this from previous epochs of military history.

Technological Fungibility

During previous episodes of military history, there was generally a high degree of specificity in both technological research and possible applications. Tanks, cruise missiles and fighter jets do not have broad civilian uses, unlike many developments in AI and robotics. Much has been written in recent years about opposition to "killer robots." Indeed, a number of open letters have been written in opposition to killer robots, signed by hundreds of luminaries, including Stephen Hawking, Elon Musk, Stuart Russell and Noam Chomsky; the Secretary General of the United Nations has called the very concept "politically unacceptable" and "morally repugnant."

A key challenge to this entire approach is the *technological fungibility* which is a feature of this wave of technologies. China, the US and other countries are predicted to have millions of humanoid robots within a generation,[30] as well as extensive use of drones across much of the economy, with a high degree of automation. If we were to introduce a global ban on "killer robots" the question then remains—in the event of a war, what will be done with all those robots and drones? Will we be confronted with the rather extraordinary paradox of robots doing people's laundry and cleaning the streets while humans go to die in battle? While repurposing is often not as trivial as is sometimes claimed, the technological fungibility that these technologies facilitate makes policing of "killer robots" considerably more problematic than the weapons systems of previous epochs. There is, of course, also the converse ethical dimension of humans dying in combat while robots continue to perform routine civilian functions.

(continued)

[30] See in particular predictions by Morgan Stanley and UBS.

Under Article 36 of Additional Protocol I of the Geneva Conventions, states must review new weapons, means or methods of warfare before adoption.[31] Yet, when decisive functionality is delivered as a software update to a fielded system or as a distributed kill-chain cutting across platforms and services, the "object" of review becomes diffuse (ICRC, 2023). DoD Directive 3000.09 defines an autonomous weapon system by what it does—"A weapon system that, once activated, can select and engage targets without further intervention by an operator." (p. 21)—and attaches obligations of governance, test and evaluation, and retained human judgement to that function, irrespective of hardware (DoD, 2023). Yet the difficulties in effectively monitoring this for all nations makes information asymmetry even more of a complexity now than during weapons treaty negotiations during the Cold War. Because models and weights are digital artefacts, they move across organisations and platforms far more fluidly than traditional munitions or tightly coupled fire-control software (UNIDIR, 2023). Fungibility further changes how meaningful human control should be conceptualized. In a software-defined kill web, "control" cannot plausibly mean per-shot approval at machine tempo instead it becomes a layered practice: upstream in the design of goals and constraints; mid-stream via runtime supervision and abort conditions; and downstream in auditability and attribution (NATO, 2024a, 2024b; Scharre, 2018). This concept of technological fungibility therefore ties into another issue which raises difficulties for policy-makers—the incentives and game theory related to delegation to automated systems.

The Delegation Dilemma and the Algorithmic Pratzen Heights

It is now not controversial, as it once was, to talk about how the world is moving toward warfare involving drone swarms and other robotic platforms. This introduces new incentives compared to previous conflicts—if we were to take a scenario where two sides have 50,000 drones, the side that uses automation, especially with adaptive learning systems, will be at a distinct advantage. 50,000 drones, each remotely, "meaningfully" controlled by a human, will not be able to synchronize at the level of an automated swarm. There have recently been public displays of drones, especially in China, for public entertainment, a modern replacement of fireworks (which were also invented by the Chinese, in the Tang Dynasty, some 1200 years ago). The sophisticated nature of these automated drone swarms visually demonstrates how "meaningful human control" will be quickly arbitraged away in the event of a drone conflict.

During the Cold War, game theory allowed mathematicians to model the likely outcome of scenarios. In the age of algorithmic warfare, when abstracted in game theoretic terms, and especially where information is asymmetric, there are strong incentives for each side to delegate tactical decision making to automated systems. The *delegation dilemma* describes a competitive dynamic in which adversaries face strong incentives to pre-delegate decision authority to machine agents, even though mutual acceleration raises systemic risk of error,

(continued)

[31] Not all countries are party to Additional Protocol I (e.g., the U.S. is not), but many still conduct weapons reviews voluntarily under customary international law principles.

misperception, and escalation (for discussions of these dangers see Horowitz et al., 2019a, 2019b; Fischerkeller et al., 2022, also see UNIDIR, 2023). In a speech I gave at a military officer's club in Brussels, I discussed how the battles of the future will be won by the side that takes the *Algorithmic Pratzen Heights*—when Bonaparte took the Pratzen Heights at Austerlitz in 1805, the advantage was topographical and the speed of maneuvering was measured in minutes and hours. With modern drone swarms, the advantage will be measured in seconds and milliseconds, quickly accruing to the side which is superior in terms of speed, coordination and algorithmic adaptability. At the edge, there will be little space for human judgement. While the brain as a whole is massively parallel, conscious attention is sequential; AI can simultaneously track thousands of drones. The action potential speed in neurons is approximately 0.1–2 m/s for unmyelinated neurons, and up to 100 m/s for myelinated, using a combination of digital and analogue processing, with a reaction time of 200 ms for visual stimuli and a further 100 ms for motor response, depending on the motor action required. On a modern GPU (e.g., NVIDIA Tesla V100), an AI model can make decisions in 1–10 ms per frame for video feed analysis or environmental awareness tasks in drone systems; on hardware like NVIDIA Jetson, decision-making for tactical maneuvers can happen in 5–20 ms.

In practice, militaries already migrate from "human-in-the-loop" to "human-on-the-loop" for time-critical functions (air/missile defence, counter-UAS) while retaining human command intent and veto (DoD, 2023; NATO, 2024a, 2024b), but with robotics the incentives align for this to gradually move up the chain of command in order to capture the Algorithmic Pratzen Heights. One of the structures from game theory most applicable for nuclear weapons was *Hawk and Dove*—it was in the interests of both parties to be "doves" and not start a conflict, and preferably mutually reduce nuclear warheads. The delegation dilemma is more like a prisoner's dilemma; the incentives of each side will be to increase delegation of tactical decision making to automated systems, yet this increases the risk to the system as a whole. Another aggravating factor in this is the nature of ongoing *ambient conflict*.

Ambient Conflict

Ambient conflict describes a condition in which strategically motivated contact among states and their proxies persists continuously below the traditional legal and political thresholds of armed attack—this has been brought about by a combination of persistent cyber attacks, asymmetries of both information and attack vectors, legal uncertainties regarding sub-threshold conflict, attribution opacity, "grey zone" activities and defence systems delegated to automated structures (for further discussion of some of these, see Buchanan, 2020; Fischerkeller et al., 2022; Mazarr, 2015). In the Cold War, most coercive exchanges (crises, alerts, proxy wars) were punctuated with long stanzas of relative stasis; in ambient conflict, probes, intrusions, and influence operations take place daily across digital infrastructure. U.S. doctrine explicitly operationalises this shift: "persistent engagement" treats contact as the default steady state rather than a crisis exception (Nakasone, 2019). The 2018 DoD Cyber Strategy's "defend forward" commits U.S. cyber forces to act "as far forward as possible" to disrupt adversary campaigns before they reach U.S. networks (DoD, 2018). These should

(continued)

not be dismissed as merely rhetorical innovations; they reframe time, legitimising continuous, below-threshold manoeuvre as a strategic norm, but with steady developments in automation they may magnify the dangers we have already looked at.

In an environment where attribution and verification are frequently opaque, technical forensics may link tools, infrastructure, and tradecraft, but multi-actor supply chains, false-flagging, and jurisdictional fragmentation generate residual uncertainty that is exploitable for coercion. Perhaps most concerningly, the digital battlespace interfaces ever more directly with the physical world, rendering the spillover from cyber to kinetic domains increasingly likely. Cyber intrusion into such systems constitutes more than digital disruption, it becomes a form of physical sabotage, the equivalent of which might have amounted to an act of war in previous epochs. Hijacked power grids or manipulation of autonomous flight paths are no longer the realm of speculative fiction. From AI-driven cyber threat detection to autonomous counter-UAS (unmanned aerial systems) platforms, the speed and scale of ambient threats will therefore also likely bring about a turn toward automated defence systems. Yet, as we have seen, this automation introduces a paradox: as decision-making accelerates, human oversight diminishes, thereby heightening the risk of misclassification and unintended escalation. The attributional opacity characteristic of ambient conflict extends beyond the cyber domain, to drone operations as well. Commercial off-the-shelf drones, modified with rudimentary explosives or surveillance payloads, have been deployed by opaque non-state actors in numerous theatres of conflict—from Syria and Ukraine to the Sahel. What constitutes "use of force"[32] in an environment where automated systems are programmed to react within milliseconds, yet the identity of the adversary remains unverifiable?

Toward a New Ontology of Conflict

As this analysis has argued, the convergence of *technological fungibility*, the *delegation dilemma*, and *ambient conflict* indicates a profound recalibration in the grammar of war, one in which temporality, control, attribution, and escalation all operate under novel conditions. Battlefield advantage will no longer be held by generals atop ridgelines or watching livefeeds, but rather the *Algorithmic Pratzen Heights* will be held by neural networks operating at superhuman tempos, through architectures too complex for real-time human supervision.

The history of military hardware has moved from spears and arrows, to gunpowder and cannons, to tanks and aircraft, to intercontinental missiles, and now to robotic and drone warfare. But when it comes to the nature of *decision-making*, this age of AI and robotics is more than just another chapter in military modernisation, it is a transition in the ontology of conflict itself, as was the development of nuclear weapons. This age is therefore a test of how morally evolved we are as a species as much as it is a test of military doctrine and law.

[32] As described in Article 2(4) of the UN Charter.

Conclusion

The potential technological trajectories of defence, security and warfare in the age of AI and robotics have led to an extraordinary diversity of opinion among military experts, policy-makers and think tanks, ranging from the idea that AI is over-hyped to the idea that we are close to AI exceeding the capabilities of humans in all physical and cognitive domains. This chapter is written for the Springer Nature volume *The Artificial Intelligence Revolution*, and is written as both a standalone chapter and an outline of current developments before reading the other chapters in this section, covering the legal aspects, risks, strategic implications and manipulation of human decision-making among other factors. As the fields of AI and robotics continue to progress, we will find out the extent to which this truly is revolutionary in the history of warfare; we hope that this chapter has served as a useful introduction to illustrate the complexities involved.

References

Air Force Research Laboratory (AFRL). (2021). *Skyborg ACS has successful first flight*. May 5, 2021. https://www.afrl.af.mil/News/Article/2596154/skyborg-acs-has-successful-first-flight/

Air Force Research Laboratory (AFRL). (n.d.). *Skyborg*. Accessed 25 September 2025. https://afresearchlab.com/technology/skyborg

Arms Control Association. (2024). Beyond a human 'In the Loop': Strategic stability and artificial intelligence. *Issue Briefs, 16*(4), November 12, 2024. https://www.armscontrol.org/issue-briefs/2024-011/beyond-the-loop

Article 36 (Additional Protocol I). (1977). *Article 36 — New weapons*. International Committee of the Red Cross (ICRC) IHL Database. https://ihl-databases.icrc.org/en/ihl-treaties/api-1977/article-36

Axios. (2025). *Hackers are already using AI to supercharge cyber threats*. March 14, 2025. https://www.axios.com/2025/03/14/hackers-artificial-intelligence-cyber-threats

Baldwin, R. B. (1980). *The deadly fuze: The secret weapon of World War II*. Presidio Press.

Brock, J., & Stone, M. (2024). *Insight: Sea drone warfare has arrived*. Reuters. May 6, 2024. https://www.reuters.com/business/aerospace-defense/sea-drone-warfare-has-arrived-us-is-floundering-2024-05-06/

Bronk, J., & Watling, J. (2024). *Protecting the force from uncrewed aerial systems*. Royal United Services Institute (RUSI). https://static.rusi.org/protecting-the-force-from-uncrewed-uas.pdf

Brookings Institution, Desouza, K. C., Larson, J., Denford, J. S., Dawson, G. S., & Goodyear, M. (2024). *The evolution of artificial intelligence (AI) spending by the U.S. Government*. March 26, 2024. https://www.brookings.edu/articles/the-evolution-of-artificial-intelligence-ai-spending-by-the-u-s-government/

Buchanan, B. (2020). *The hacker and the state: Cyber attacks and the new normal of geopolitics*. Harvard University Press.

Burdette, Z., Phillips, D., Heim, J. L., Geist, E., Frelinger, D. R., Heitzenrater, C., & Mueller, K. P. (2025). *An AI revolution in military affairs? How artificial intelligence could reshape future warfare*. RAND Corporation Working Paper WR-A4004-1.

C4ISRNET. (2019). *How the pentagon is sharpening the smart edge*. September 18, 2019. https://www.c4isrnet.com/artificial-intelligence/2019/09/18/how-the-pentagon-is-sharpening-the-smart-edge/

Chernavskikh, V. (2024). *Nuclear weapons and artificial intelligence: Technological promises and practical realities*. SIPRI Insights on Peace and Security, No. 2024/4. Stockholm International Peace Research Institute (SIPRI). https://doi.org/10.55163/VBQX6088.

China's State Council. (2025). *China's National security in the new era*. Information Office of the State Council. May 12, 2025. https://english.scio.gov.cn/whitepapers/2025-05/13/content_117871660.html

CSIS (Center for Strategic & International Studies). (2023). *Drone saturation: Russia's Shahed campaign*. CSIS. https://www.csis.org/analysis/drone-saturation-russias-shahed-campaign

DARPA. (2006). *DARPA grand challenge 2005: Report to congress*. Defense Advanced Research Projects Agency. May 2006. https://www.darpa.mil/attachments/2004-2005%20DARPA%20Grand%20Challenge%20Report%20to%20Congress.pdf

DARPA. (2025). *AI cyber challenge (AIxCC)*. Program site (DEF CON 33 finals overview). August 2025. https://aicyberchallenge.com/

Defense Blog. (2025). *Ukrainian soldiers develop robotic air defense system*. August 12, 2025. https://defence-blog.com/ukrainian-soldiers-develop-robotic-air-defense-system/

Defense Info. (2025). *The U.S. Navy publishes a new navigation plan and advances the fielding of a hybrid fleet*. April 2025. https://defense.info/maritime-dynamics/2025/04/the-u-s-navy-publishes-a-new-navigation-plan-and-advances-the-fielding-of-a-hybrid-fleet/

DoD (U.S. Department of Defense). (2018). *Summary of the Department of Defense Cyber Strategy*. Washington, DC.

DoD (U.S. Department of Defense). (2023). *DoD Directive 3000.09: Autonomy in weapon systems*. Washington, DC (January 25, 2023).

European Union. (2024). *Defence and artificial intelligence*. European Parliamentary Research Service Briefing.

Federation of American Scientists (FAS). (2023). *A risk assessment framework for AI integration into nuclear weapons*. Federation of American Scientists. Available at: https://fas.org/publication/risk-assessment-framework-ai-nuclear-weapons/

Fischerkeller, M. P., Goldman, E. O., & Harknett, R. J. (2022). *Cyber persistence theory: Redefining national security in cyberspace*. Oxford University Press.

Freedberg, S.J., Jr. (2024). *Targeting time shrinks from minutes to seconds in army experiment*. Defense One. March 7, 2024. https://www.defenseone.com/threats/2024/03/targeting-time-shrinks-minutes-seconds-army-experiment/394758/

Gettinger, D. (2024). *Defense primer: Categories of uncrewed aircraft systems*. Congressional Research Service (CRS). In Focus IF12797, October 25, 2024. https://www.congress.gov/crs_external_products/IF/PDF/IF12797/IF12797.1.pdf

Hambling, D. (2024). *Russian Kamikaze drone now seems to identify its own targets*. Forbes. March 1, 2024. https://www.forbes.com/sites/davidhambling/2024/03/01/russian-kamikaze-drone-now-seems-to-identify-its-own-targets/

Hardie, J. (2025). *Ukrainian intelligence details Russia's new V2U autonomous loitering munition*. FDD's Long War Journal, June 14, 2025.

Horowitz, M. C., Scharre, P., & Velez-Green, A. (2019a). *A stable nuclear future? The impact of autonomous systems and artificial intelligence*. arXiv (December 11, 2019).

Horowitz, M. C., Kahn, L., & Scharre, P. (2019b). *Artificial intelligence and international security*. Center for a New American Security (CNAS).

Hill, J. (2025). Royal Navy name Project CETUS XLUUV, Excalibur. Naval Technology. https://www.naval-technology.com/news/royal-navy-name-project-cetus-xluuv-excalibur/

ICRC. (2020). *A guide to the legal review of new weapons, means and methods of warfare (measures to implement Article 36 of Additional Protocol I)*. International Committee of the Red Cross. https://www.icrc.org/en/publication/0902-guide-legal-review-new-weapons-means-and-methods-warfare-measures-implement-article

ICRC (International Committee of the Red Cross). (1977). *Protocol additional to the Geneva conventions of 12 August 1949, and relating to the protection of victims of international armed conflicts (Protocol I), 8 June 1977*. ICRC.

ICRC (International Committee of the Red Cross). (2006, rev. 2020). *A guide to the legal review of new weapons, means and methods of warfare: Measures to implement Article 36 of Additional Protocol I of 1977*. ICRC (Cited in-text as "ICRC, 2023"; the ICRC's authoritative guidance is this guide).

Jensen, B. (2025). *Out-adapting the enemy: Why mass alone won't win tomorrow's wars*. Center for Strategic & International Studies. CSIS Commentary, July 11, 2025.

Jervis, R. (1978). Cooperation under the security dilemma. *World Politics, 30*(2), 167–214. https://doi.org/10.2307/2009958

Kahn, L., Probasco, E. S., & Kinoshita, R. (2024a). *AI safety and automation bias: The downside of human-in-the-loop*. CSET (Issue Brief, November 2024). https://cset.georgetown.edu/publication/ai-safety-and-automation-bias/

Kahn, L., Probasco, E. S., & Kinoshita, R. (2024b). *AI safety and automation bias: The downside of human-in-the-loop*. Center for Security and Emerging Technology (CSET). https://cset.georgetown.edu/publication/ai-safety-and-automation-bias/

Lieber Institute, West Point. (2024). *Beyond the headlines: Combat deployment of military AI-based systems by the IDF*. March 21, 2024. https://lieber.westpoint.edu/beyond-headlines-combat-deployment-military-ai-based-systems-idf/

Marcinek, K., & Han, E. (2023). *Russia's asymmetric response to 21st century strategic competition: Robotization of the armed forces*. RAND Corporation (RRA-1233-5). https://www.rand.org/pubs/research_reports/RRA1233-5.html

Mazarr, M. J. (2015). *Mastering the gray zone: Understanding a changing era of conflict*. U.S. Army War College Press.

Military Times. (2025). *Inside the navy task group testing drone boats in the Red sea*. April 11, 2025. https://www.militarytimes.com/news/your-military/2025/04/11/inside-the-navy-task-group-testing-drone-boats-in-the-red-sea/

Ministry of Defence of Ukraine. (2025). *The Ukrainian Defense Industry has the capability to produce 10 million drones annually, said Oleksandr Kozenko at a Security Forum in Singapore*. September 4, 2025. https://mod.gov.ua/en/news/the-ukrainian-defense-industry-has-the-capability-to-produce-10-million-drones-annually-said-oleksandr-kozenko-at-a-security-forum-in-singapore

Mouton, C. A., Lucas, C., & Guest, E. (2024). *The operational risks of AI in large-scale biological attacks: Final results of a red-team exercise*. RAND Corporation, RRA-2977-2 (January 25, 2024). https://www.rand.org/pubs/research_reports/RRA2977-2.html.

Nakasone, P. M. (2019). A cyber force for persistent operations. *Joint Force Quarterly, 92*, 10–14. (In-text "Nakasone & Lewis, 2019" appears to be a misattribution; this is the official source).

NATO. (2024a). *NATO releases revised AI strategy*. Official News release, July 10, 2024. https://www.nato.int/cps/en/natohq/news_227234.htm

NATO. (2024b). Summary of NATO's revised artificial intelligence (AI) strategy. North Atlantic Treaty Organization (July 10, 2024).

O'Hanlon, M. E. (2025). *How unchecked AI could trigger a nuclear war*. Brookings Institution. February 28, 2025. https://www.brookings.edu/articles/how-unchecked-ai-could-trigger-a-nuclear-war/

Pettyjohn, S. L., Wasser, B., Dougherty, C., & Green, B. R. (2024). *Swarms over the strait: Drone warfare in a future conflict between China and Taiwan*. CNAS. https://www.cnas.org/publications/reports/swarms-over-the-strait

Pomerleau, M. (2024). *Data passed 'at a magnitude never seen before' at army's project convergence*. DefenseScoop. March 8, 2024. https://defensescoop.com/2024/03/08/data-passed-at-a-magnitude-never-seen-before-at-armys-project-convergence/.

Royal Navy. (2025). *Royal Navy unveil 12 metre uncrewed submarine named after excalibur*. News release, May 15, 2025. https://www.royalnavy.mod.uk/news/2025/may/15/20250515-uncrewed-submarine-naming-ceremony

Scharre, P. (2018). *Army of none: Autonomous weapons and the future of war*. W. W. Norton.

Scharre, P. (2023). *Four battlegrounds: Power in the age of artificial intelligence*. W. W. Norton & Company.

Schelling, T. C. (1966). *Arms and influence*. Yale University Press.

Shepardson, D. (2024). *U.S. Proposes 'Know Your Customer' requirements for cloud computing companies*. Reuters. January 26, 2024. https://www.reuters.com/technology/us-propose-know-your-customer-requirements-cloud-computing-companies-2024-01-26/

South China Morning Post. (2023). *Chinese Military Researchers report AI pilot beats human in landmark real-life dogfight*. February 18, 2023. https://www.scmp.com/news/china/science/article/3211976/chinese-military-researchers-report-ai-pilot-beats-human-landmark-real-life-dogfight

Telegraph (The). (2021). *Artificial intelligence isn't killer robots — But Britain would be mad to ignore it*. May 23, 2021. https://www.telegraph.co.uk/news/2021/05/23/artificial-intelligence-isnt-killer-robots-britain-would-mad/

UNIDIR (United Nations Institute for Disarmament Research). (2023). *AI and international security: Understanding risks and paving the path for confidence-building measures*. UNIDIR.

United Nations. (2019). *Machines with the power and discretion to take lives without human involvement are politically unacceptable, morally repugnant and should be prohibited by International Law*. Press release SG/SM/19512, March 25, 2019. https://press.un.org/en/2019/sgsm19512.doc.htm

Whittle, R. (2014). *Predator: The secret origins of the drone revolution*. Henry Holt and Company.

Wiener, N. (1948). *Cybernetics: Or control and communication in the animal and the machine*. MIT Press.

Strategic Implications of Deploying Artificial Intelligence in Defence

James Black

Introduction

Artificial Intelligence (AI) increasingly touches all sectors of the economy and areas of human activity. Defence and security are not immune from this trend. On the contrary, militaries around the world are accelerating their investments in AI systems and related technology areas such as uncrewed systems, robotics, autonomy, next-generation telecommunications, data, and cloud and edge computing. Together, such advancements hold the potential to disrupt how competing militaries prepare for, deter, prosecute, and win or lose at warfighting.

This chapter seeks to understand the myriad ways in which the rollout of AI could reshape strategic competition between competing nations—and non-state actors—for military advantage. In doing so, it focuses on the strategic level, conscious that so much of the analysis and debate around the growing impact of AI on defence focuses on the tactical level, for example, on how AI is used in uncrewed systems or to automate elements of the targeting cycle (Brose, 2020). In particular, both the academic and public discourse are heavily dominated by discussions of Lethal Autonomous Weapons Systems (LAWS) (so-called 'killer robots') (Meerveld et al., 2023) and debates over the ethical implications of having humans in, on or out of the loop for decisions

J. Black (✉)
RAND Corporation, London, UK
e-mail: jblack@randeurope.org

M. Rangeley, N. Fairfax (eds.), *The Artificial Intelligence Revolution*,
https://doi.org/10.1007/978-3-032-11814-1_11

about the use of force by machines (Scharre, 2018; Wong et al., 2020). Other prominent debates centre around Artificial General Intelligence (AGI) and the security and safety implications thereof, including concerns about existential risk should humans lose control over powerful AI systems or mix them with nuclear and biological weapons of mass destruction (Mouton et al., 2024; Mitre & Predd, 2025).

Focus on Strategic Competition and Warfighting

While important, discussions over contentious topics such as LAWS or AGI do not present the whole picture. Stepping back is important to appreciate the many other, less appreciated ways in which AI could reshape the whole defence enterprise, from foxhole to factory. This means not only considering how AI could affect the future conduct of warfighting itself (Scharre, 2018; Payne, 2021). It also demands that we explore how defence ministries, industry and wider society might go about structuring, supporting, and sustaining the military as an instrument of power in an age of intensifying global competition for advantage both in and through AI (Black et al., 2024a).

This analysis starts from a recognition of AI as what the UK's Defence AI Strategy calls a 'family of general-purpose technologies, any of which may enable machines to perform tasks normally requiring human or biological intelligence, especially when the machines learn from data how to perform those tasks' (UK Ministry of Defence, 2022). This definition emphasises that AI is no one single technology. Rather, it is a fast-evolving family of varied design philosophies, architectures, and approaches to programming or training AI models. It includes everything from Machine Learning (ML) via reinforcement learning, classification models, and rules engines, through to Natural Language Processing (NLP), symbolic logic systems, or the latest Large Language Models (LLMs) and Agentic AI capabilities.

AI can be broken down in other ways. Narrow AI (sometimes called Weak AI) refers to those systems designed to perform a limited set of tasks and which perform poorly in other areas beyond their original training or programming. Broad AI (sometimes called Strong AI), means those systems able to generalise knowledge and adapt to perform a wide range of tasks effectively, including in unfamiliar settings or domains (Nancholas, 2023). In both cases, AI technologies overlap with and are fed by advances in adjacent technology areas, such as the latest development in data science, materials science, computing and chip design, or telecommunications (Huismans et al., 2025a).

Even in AI systems with high degrees of autonomy and automation, there also remains a vital human component to the design, operation and maintenance of the prompts, models, datasets (whether real or synthetic). Humans are also vital to building and running the physical or network infrastructure (Schaefer et al., 2021). Similarly, human-machine interaction is an essential feature of many of the downstream applications of AI, including within settings such as the military and defence. This entails all sorts of questions about evolving human perceptions of and levels of trust in AI systems, as well as the knowledge and skills required from humans to get the most from such tools while mitigating risks such as cognitive bias or dependency (Johnson, 2022; Hughes et al., 2024). It also stresses the importance of looking beyond direct impacts from the rollout of AI to also consider the possible second- or third-order effects and unintended dynamics that might emerge.

As such, AI should be understood not in isolation but rather as a complex socio-technical system (Black et al., 2024a). This recognises that the pace and direction of AI adoption, including in defence, is driven as much by social, organisational, financial, legal, ethical, and cultural factors as by advances in the state of the art for the technology itself (Scharre, 2023). In military terminology, this means we must consider not just the materiel element of AI. Rather, we must also look to all the other, rather less glamorous lines of development that go into capability management and integration (Huismans et al., 2025a; Lucas et al., 2025). In NATO jargon, this means thinking about how AI influences factors such as doctrine, organisation, training, materiel, leadership and education, personnel, facilities, and interoperability (DOTMLPFI).

Given such considerations, it is important to elevate our level of analysis to consider how the cumulative effects of different tactical military applications for AI (e.g., in targeting, decision support, intelligence-gathering, and logistics) might influence the intensity, drivers and outcomes of strategic competition and, ultimately, affect global peace and stability. The following sections of this chapter apply this strategic focus and a systems-thinking lens, arguing that even Narrow AI will prove like the combustion engine, electricity, or the microchip: a disruptive, general-purpose technology that will touch and transform all aspects of defence. Having examined the myriad potential defence applications and implications of Narrow AI, the chapter then moves to briefly explore the impact of AGI. This poses additional complex security and safety risks, as well as opportunities, that intersect in ways that pay little attention to institutional barriers across government, the military, or the private sector.

Crucially, ongoing efforts to mitigate the risks and accentuate the benefits of AI, including in the military context, are being undermined by mistrust and tensions at the geopolitical level, as well as by problematic dynamics to the competition for strategic advantage in AI between rival powers (e.g., between the U.S. and China, or NATO and Russia) and between private AI companies. This is an enduring coordination problem and not one with any 'silver bullet' solution. As such, the chapter concludes by arguing that a more integrated approach is urgently needed that combines hard and soft power to shape the intensifying global competition for advantage in and through AI—including in the military domain—along pathways that balance the drive to seek advantage with the imperative to avoid accidental escalation into unwanted conflict.

Impact of AI on Future Warfare

The first focus area for this chapter is on how the rollout and adoption of AI could alter how defence establishments and armed forces prepare for and execute military strategy and operations. This is arguably the main interest of the literature on military AI: there are large bodies of work on topics such as the integration of AI into military command and control or targeting cycles (King, 2025), and the deployment of uncrewed assets (including LAWS) across all physical domains (land, air, sea, and space) (Scharre, 2018; Payne, 2021) and, relatedly, on the growing automation of operations in cyberspace or the electromagnetic environment (Lohn et al., 2023).

Unsurprisingly, given debates over the pace and desirability of military AI development and the intersection of tactical military applications of AI with complex ethical and legal debates, this discourse can be contentious and fragmented. It is often marked by divergent perspectives and starting assumptions from authors from academic, industry, civil society, or military backgrounds, with comparatively few studies offering a genuinely interdisciplinary viewpoint (Black et al., 2024a).

To help synthesise this diverse and fast-growing body of work, it can be useful to think in terms of the impacts of AI across the lifecycle of defence strategy and military operations:

- **Decision support:** As a technology focused on sense- and decision-making, AI could bring substantial benefits to the development of military strategy, doctrine, and operational plans. Government and military agencies are already making use of AI to assist with intelligence and data analysis, as well as lessons learned processes, automating growing portions of the collection, fusion, and assessment cycle (Futter, 2022). Such tools can be applied at the tactical, operational, or strategic levels. Prominent examples in the former two categories include the Avengers AI tool developed and deployed by Ukraine to identify concealed Russian military vehicles from a wide range of data feeds, enabling targeting and supporting operational planning (Barkhush, 2024) or the Lavender system used by the Israeli Defence Forces for targeting in its war in Gaza (Pratt, 2024). At the more strategic level, there is also significant interest in AI tools for predictive analysis, for example, to provide early warning of emerging threats or crises (Knack et al., 2025). There is also growing overlap between AI and wargaming, supporting the design, delivery, and subsequent analysis of insights gleaned from both manual and computer-based simulations (Knack & Powell, 2023). Similarly, the combination of advances in AI with more sophisticated synthetic environments brings the growing prospect of faster-than-real-time modelling of different courses of action (COAs). This could allow for rapid iteration and testing of alternative strategies in a safe and controlled environment, with the most advantageous COAs assessed stochastically and then presented to military commanders for a final decision (Geist, 2024). Furthermore, AI tools can also help to prioritise what information is provided to human decision-makers when, how and in what form, so as to reduce cognitive overload and improve situational awareness. Conversely, however, the deployment of AI-enabled decision support tools in military contexts raises critical concerns, both from an ethical and legal perspective and a practical military one (Payne, 2024). The latter include concerns regarding levels of automation, cognitive biases inherent in AI systems or training data, a lack of explainability and transparency to many AI algorithms, and enduring issues of model brittleness, any of which could lead to erroneous decisions (Liu & Maas, 2021). Even through the lens of pure military expediency, the balance between human oversight and machine autonomy remains highly contentious: excessive reliance on AI could foster a false sense of security in faulty data or assumptions amongst military personnel, while insufficient trust may hinder effective collaboration or uptake of new tech. Additionally, militaries must remain vigilant against adversarial actions aimed at disrupting or fooling their AI systems, for example, via cyber-attacks on model weights or poisoning of data feeds (Black & Lynch, 2022; DSIT, 2023).

- **Execution—combat operations:** In addition to decision support, AI has a wide range of potential applications to the execution of combat operations. This includes through the use of AI and autonomy as a crucial enabler of advanced digital command and control (C2) systems, coordinating dispersed forces and synchronising effects across all operational domains (air, land, sea, space, and cyber and electromagnetic). Here, live examples include the DELTA battlespace management platform and associated data lake used in Ukraine to connect its forces, or the new Digital Targeting Web being developed by the UK (Bondar, 2024). Here, the goal of ambitious visions such as the U.S. Joint All Domain Command and Control (JADC2) initiative is to create AI-enabled 'kill webs' that digitally connect 'any sensor, any shooter' to ultimately achieve a faster 'observe, orient, decide, act' (OODA) loop than adversaries (Brose, 2020; Black et al., 2024b). Similarly, uncrewed systems, such as aerial or maritime drones, can provide low-cost combat mass—as seen currently on the battlefield in Ukraine or previously in the Second Nagorno-Karabakh War—and enhance the speed, precision, and lethality of combat operations (Hou et al., 2023).

- **Execution—support functions:** Besides combat, AI tools also have important applications across functions such as military logistics or medical support. Here, the military can benefit from transferrable lessons and dual-use technologies being developed for commercial logistics firms, for example, in e-commerce or retail. Such tools can help to optimise resource allocation, monitor stockpiles and depletion rates, predict demand for resupply, and then deliver that through uncrewed systems to dispersed forces without exposing human personnel to danger—especially important for 'last mile' logistics close to the frontline in contested environments (Black et al., 2024a). Some of these use cases for AI are also of relevance to non-governmental organisations and aid organisations working to distribute aid in conflict or disaster zones, providing vital humanitarian assistance. Similarly, uncrewed systems can support casualty evacuations, while AI tools can help medical personnel to treat and monitor injured troops and civilians in austere conditions.
- **Transformation of the national defence enterprise:** Crucially, many of the most profound near-term impacts from AI adoption may come far from the battlespace, in the much less-discussed 'back office' functions of defence. Here, AI tools could enhance productivity at individual, team, or enterprise level, optimising processes and improving the efficiency of finance, personnel or infrastructure management, and procurement or training systems within national ministries of defence. Similarly, AI can help to drive improvements in the productivity of the defence industrial base, enabling novel digital design approaches, improving manufacturing and supply chain management practices, upskilling the industrial workforce and helping ultimately drive both economic growth and national security goals.

At the same time, AI—and other software-driven technologies marked by a rapid pace of change—challenge traditional, slow defence procurement processes. This demands reforms towards more agile acquisition approaches, a more strategic management of data and a more collaborative relationship with industry (e.g., moving towards MLOps pipelines, spiral development, and models such as software-as-a-service) (Ryseff et al., 2022).

- **Impacts at the Alliance or coalition level:** Importantly, the impacts from military use of AI as described above do not only play out at the national level. They also have implications for interoperability across multinational alliances such as NATO or smaller minilateral groupings like the Joint Expeditionary Force or NORDEFCO. Here, the rollout of AI alongside other digital technologies such as secure cloud computing, satellite connectivity and next-generation telecommunications could, if done right, transform levels of interoperability between different national forces, enabling them to connect and collaborate more seamlessly (Huismans et al., 2025b). Conversely, divergent national approaches to AI policy, regulation and ethics, or differences in resources or the pace at which partners move away from old legacy systems, could serve to undermine interoperability and coherence in an alliance setting—exacerbating the capability and doctrinal divides between AI-haves and AI-have nots (Black et al., 2024a; Lucas et al., 2025).

Importantly, AI cuts across all these different aspects of military operations, both in peace and wartime, creating feedback loops by which impacts from AI in one area influence outcomes in another. For example, the military imperative towards integrating AI into frontline operations in Ukraine and elsewhere is demanding a new approach to procurement, innovation, data-sharing, and the relationship between military end-users and tech companies. This, in turn, drives the creation of new AI-related products and services in the private sector which can also then be marketed to international defence customers, supporting economic prosperity as well as overseas influence and interoperability with allies and partners. In turn, this drives adversaries to invest in their own military AI—or counter-AI—capabilities, resulting in yet more of an imperative for NATO and Western-aligned militaries to enhance their own capabilities, repeating the loop. As such, competing powers increasingly seek to achieve strategic advantage both in and through AI.

Impact of AI on Drivers of Competition

The second focus area for this chapter is on how AI might not only affect the changing character of warfare but also drive strategic instability and increase the frequency of conflict in the first place:

- **Destabilisation of deterrence and escalation dynamics:** Perhaps of greatest concern from a strategic stability perspective is the potential for AI developments to undermine nuclear deterrence. On the positive side, proponents of AI note that decision support tools can enhance our understanding of adversaries' actions and intentions, while mitigating the impact of emotion, fatigue, or other human limitations on crisis decision-making—bolstering deterrence and avoiding unintended escalation (Onderco & Zutt, 2021). Conversely, experts express concern about the potentially destabilising effects both of integrating AI into nuclear command, control and communications (NC3) systems and decision-making, and of using AI-enabled conventional precision strike capabilities to undermine the second-strike survivability of nuclear forces. Advanced AI could accelerate decision-making in a crisis and enable more effective targeting—for example, via detection of submerged nuclear submarines—thereby increasing the potential for decapitating first-strikes, creating a temptation to 'shoot first' (Johnson, 2019). Crucially, it is enough for one side to perceive AI to be a threat in this way, whatever the reality of the technology or its actual integration into military forces and NC3. This is especially problematic given it is so difficult to ascertain the sophistication or decision logic of a 'black box' military AI system from afar, and thus hard to predict how it might act (Scharre, 2018). Competing nations may misperceive and overestimate the capabilities of each other's AI systems and this misplaced sense of vulnerability may drive them towards a 'use it or lose it' mentality and consideration of first strikes (Mazarr, Rhoades, et al., 2022). Furthermore, AI could be used to spread disinformation, such as realistic deepfakes, sowing confusion, and uncertainty in a standoff. Equally, the mass deployment of AI-enabled uncrewed systems may increase the risk of accidental confrontations between conventional forces (e.g., due to mistake, malfunction, or cyber-attack), while also lowering the threshold to the use of force given the reduced immediate risk to human life. Collectively, such behavioural dynamics risk altering the decision calculus in favour of pre-emptive offensive actions, weakening the logic of mutually assured destruction as a bedrock of nuclear (and to a lesser extent conventional) deterrence and escalation management since the Cold War (Taeihagh, 2021).

- **Proliferation of AI technology:** Crucially, AI technology is also potentially destabilising because of the nature of AI innovation and proliferation. While there is a crucial hardware element enabling AI (i.e., large-scale compute infrastructure and associated energy and coolant systems), it is ultimately software-driven and dual-use, with innovation shaped primarily by private firms for commercial markets rather than the government or military. Such features mean it is more challenging to limit the proliferation of some AI technologies across borders or prevent their development by hostile actors when compared to controlling the spread of traditional military arms. As such, while the previous U.S. administration introduced an ambitious AI Diffusion Framework that sought to restrict the dissemination of more sensitive AI technologies (even including many NATO Allies and other key partners in the second of its three tiers of access rights) (U.S. Department of Commerce, 2025), in practice governments can likely only slow rather than fully stop cross-border flows of most AI technologies (Harithas, 2025; Heim, 2025). Similarly, traditional arms control mechanisms used to avoid or regulate interstate arms races are ill-suited to software-based technologies, given the difficulties of monitoring and verifying enforcement (in contrast to, say, using overflights by satellites to track the size of military forces).
- **Empowerment of non-state actors:** Given these proliferation trends, there is concern that AI and related technologies such as uncrewed systems could empower hostile non-state groups such as terrorist or criminal networks. AI tools could prove useful across the full spectrum of these groups' activities: supporting recruitment and radicalisation by disseminating more persuasive, tailored propaganda to target audiences; improving planning of terror attacks or criminal acts; and empowering non-state actors with new cyber and kinetic capabilities (e.g., drones) for challenging militaries or law enforcement (Haner & Garcia, 2019). Equally, state sponsors are likely to equip their proxies with AI tools and related capabilities, such as uncrewed systems, under cover of plausible deniability. This could exacerbate instability and insecurity in fragile or conflicted-affected societies, as has already been seen with Iran equipping the Houthis with drone technology (Reinhold & Reuter, 2022). Perhaps most concerningly, experts raise the growing possibility of LLMs or more advanced future AI systems being used to radically lower the barriers to developing and deploying weapons of mass destruction, especially bioweapons (Mouton et al., 2024). For example, the latest version of Anthropic's Claude, the new Opus 4 model, triggered an escalation of the firm's internal safety measures as it

was found to substantially increase the risk that users with a basic STEM background might acquire the knowledge needed to develop and deploy their own bioweapons (Perrigo, 2025).

- **Intersection with other drivers of (in)stability:** Besides empowering state militaries or hostile non-state groups, the proliferation of AI is also likely to have many broader social, political, and economic impacts that could have second- and third-order effects on national and international security (Johnson, 2021). Prominent examples discussed in the literature include the use of AI to enhance cyber-attacks or the spread of disinformation and misinformation, undermining social cohesion, the integrity of elections, or public trust in governance institutions (Slapakova et al., 2024). Similarly, some experts fear that the rollout of AI could bring mass disruption to labour markets in certain sectors or localities if not handled carefully, exacerbating wealth inequality between AI-haves and AI-have nots, and fuelling social grievance, populism, and public disorder (Sytsma, 2025). There is also a growing awareness of the climate and environmental impacts of AI (Ren & Wierman, 2024), which could again exacerbate trends in climate insecurity (Defence Science and Technology Laboratory, 2024), though it is not certain that the current trends in soaring demand for energy to support AI compute infrastructure will continue, if less power-hungry AI design paradigms can be found. Equally, if AI fuels rapid economic growth this would in turn affect the fiscal context for defence, potentially enabling spending increases depending on how AI alleviates or exacerbates pressure on other budgets. More problematically, hopes for growth must be balanced against concerns about volatility in financial markets (as seen already with the first AI-induced 'flash crashes' from algorithmic trading) or about hostile actors leveraging AI tools to conduct economic warfare.

Such trends reflect the highly disruptive potential of AI across all aspects of domestic society and international relations. Collectively, shifts in the military offence-defence balance, the collapsing time windows for decision-making in an AI-accelerated crises, and the empowerment of non-state actors to challenge the primacy of traditional armed forces could drive increased instability. Equally, there are huge potential benefits to be had from achieving a technological lead in AI, given the military, political, and economic power that this could bring. This implies an exacerbation of competitive dynamics at a time when geopolitics are already marked by increasing tension and strategic rivalries, for example, between the U.S. and China, or NATO and Russia (Mazarr, 2022). The danger is that this competition could spill into crisis or conflict, if not properly regulated.

Impact of AI on Determinants of Competitiveness

The third focus area for this discussion is therefore on how AI could not only drive increased interstate competition but also influence who prevails—if anyone—in that constant contest for strategic advantage. Even without conflict, how do the dynamics of strategic competition shift?

Governments around the world have issued policies or statements identifying the development and adoption of AI capabilities as one of the crucial determinants of their nation's future prosperity, influence, and security—and, therefore, their competitiveness on the international stage. There is a related debate around the need for sovereign AI capabilities: whether in terms of full control over the value chain (from microchip development and compute infrastructure through to frontier AI model development and then rollout of AI-enabled services); or, more realistically for most nations, acceptance of dependencies on foreign (typically American) AI firms in certain areas alongside targeted efforts to enhance data sovereignty and freedom of action in others (e.g., defence, CNI).

Crucially, it is not enough to lead on development of AI (including for military purposes). Countries can also pursue advantage by being quicker at rolling out AI across their economies or institutions, or by more effectively regulating AI in ways that bolster benefits while mitigating social harms. Research has shown that a nation's competitiveness hinges less on its raw potential (e.g., its access to technology, industrial base, or population size) and more on the effectiveness of its governance systems in translating that latent potential into practical outputs that support national objectives (e.g., increased prosperity, influence, and security) (Mazarr, 2022). This means adapting to the dominant competitive paradigms of the age (Mazarr et al., 2024), including through government investments to boost AI infrastructure, compete for and foster AI talent, and promote rapid but responsible uptake of AI across relevant economic sectors or organisations such as the military (Kahl, 2025).

Equally, achieving an edge in strategic competition is not just about bolstering one's own position, for example, as relates the rollout of military AI. It can also be achieved by undermining one's competitors and adversaries, for example, by restricting their access to AI talent and technology or—more controversially—by actively targeting deployed AI systems using counter-AI capabilities. Examples of potential such actions in a military context include using cyber-attacks to extract or sabotage model weights in an adversary's AI systems, or to poison training data. There are also other techniques by which governments and militaries can seek to exploit the brittleness of AI models (DSIT, 2023), for example, to fool machine vision systems into mischaracterising a tank or military aircraft as a harmless civilian vehicle that defence systems can ignore.

In this context of intensifying competition for advantage both in and through AI, it is important to mitigate the risks to strategic stability through governance initiatives. These can include everything from formal international treaties to 'soft' law measures such as development of norms, standards and codes of conduct, or broader transparency and confidence-building measures (TCBMs) to reduce tensions and boost trust between competing powers (Black et al., 2024a). Recent years have seen a profusion of new initiatives to bolster global governance of AI in general or in a military context specifically. Prominent examples of the former include the UN Secretary General's High-Level Advisory Body on AI, the Group of Governmental Experts, the EU AI Act, AI Safety Summit, AI Action Summit and work by the OECD, G7, WHO and many other institutions (Kaspar et al., 2023). In the defence context, the most high-profile initiatives have been the Responsible AI in the Military Domain (REAIM) Summits held in the Hague and Seoul, with another planned for La Coruna, and the associated Call for Action or US-initiated Political Declaration signed by over 50 countries (Javadi & Onderco, 2024). Still, efforts to agree on new international norms for de-risking the rollout of military AI, let alone more robust (e.g., treaty-based) mechanisms, remain in their infancy; it is difficult to insulate them from broader barriers to cooperation at a time of heightened geopolitical tensions, especially between key stakeholder such as the U.S. and China.

Destabilising Dynamics of the Race for AGI

The fourth and final focus area for this chapter is on the destabilising dynamics that could arise in the race for a strategic advantage beyond the near-term focus of most states on Narrow AI. The previous sections have covered the myriad potential impacts from Narrow AI on the military, either through direct application of AI technologies in the defence context or via their indirect effects on societal cohesion or competitiveness. Cumulatively, such impacts could be transformative, affecting the frequency, intensity and outcomes of competition, crisis, or conflict between nations, as well as empowering non-state actors to challenge the state-centric global order. At the same time, the geostrategic impact of Narrow AI pales in comparison to the possible risks and opportunities associated with Artificial General Intelligence (AGI) or Super Intelligence (ASI). Such AI systems—theoretical for now—could exhibit or even surpass human-level capabilities across a wide range of cognitive functions and do so flexibly in a wide range of settings.

Existing Narrow AI systems such as AlphaGo or AlphaFold already go far beyond the capabilities of humans in specific tasks, while large language models such as ChatGPT, Claude, or DeepSeek continue to push beyond benchmarks built for assessing performance in specialist areas such as mathematics or science. And Agentic AI holds the near-term potential for multiple systems working together to solve complex problems or achieve goals autonomously, without human intervention. Still, such systems rely on specialist training datasets and do not perform well, or perhaps at all, if deployed onto unfamiliar topics or settings.

By contrast, AGI could quickly learn to produce genius-level intellectual outputs across a wide range of unfamiliar areas (Nunez, 2025). If realised, such technology could therefore be transformative across all sectors of human activity. This could catalyse rapid advances in areas such as medicine, science, climate and environmental management, or wealth creation, while also disrupting the existing political, social, cultural, economic, and military order.

There is a live and at times tense debate within the global AI expert community about the feasibility, timelines and possible impacts of humanity achieving AGI or ASI (Mitchell, 2024). Projections range from such technology being already imminent in the late 2020s through to it being decades away or even fundamentally impossible—much as expert assessments of the probable effects range from vast leaps forward in science, culture, and prosperity on one hand, through to extinction on the other. Overall, though, the debate over AGI has shifted markedly in recent years away from viewing it as science fiction or, at least, a long-term problem that can be parked for future generations of policymakers to worry about. Instead, a growing number of governments have joined private tech companies and civil society organisations in identifying AGI as a pressing policy and technical challenge that requires urgent action today if we are to capture AGI's benefits while also minimising the security and safety risks.

Given the lack of expert consensus on the realism, scale, or relative priority of policy challenges associated with the possible advent of AGI, recent RAND research has sought to distil the various overlapping and dissonant debates into a set of five concrete problems from a national security and military perspective (Mitre & Predd, 2025). These include the potential for AGI to enable 'wonder weapons' (such as exquisite offensive cyber capabilities that enabling decapitating strikes on an adversary's government and military functions); systemic shifts in the balance of power between AGI-haves and AGI-have nots; the empowerment of non-experts to develop weapons of mass destruction; the risk of artificial entities developing agency and their own goals or value-sets, which may not align with our interests; and intensifying global instability, leading to crises and conflicts between nations (Mitre & Predd, 2025). AI research organisations are undertaking research to try and tackle some of these challenges, for example, exploring possible ways of tackling the production of novel bioweapons using AI. But, short of somehow enforcing a global ban on AGI development, robust policy and technical solutions remain elusive for now.

Concerns about national and international security run in parallel to worries around AI safety. Here, the most extreme—and consequently most high-profile—risks are those associated with the possible development of future AGI or ASI systems not aligned with humanity's interests and values and over which humans lose effective control. This does not mean that AGI need be actively hostile to any particular group, nation, or humans at large; rather, it may simply be that an AGI is designed to pursue a certain goal which, while benign on the face of it, could bring that artificial entity into conflict with the interests of some or all humans.

While such advanced AI systems remain theoretical for now, extrapolating forward from the existing cognitive capabilities of Narrow AI models suggests that they are likely to exhibit technical characteristics that could make guaranteeing control, or regaining it once lost, a substantial challenge. These include iterative self-improvement and rapid learning and adaptation; a capacity for understanding and manipulating human emotions, including through deception; and an ability to influence their own physical and virtual environment, for example, through cyber-attacks to take control of the digital infrastructure upon which they depend (i.e., compute, telecommunications, and energy) or via sophisticated social engineering of human proxies. As such, AI safety and security institutes, as well as frontier AI research organisations, are investing heavily to develop procedural or technical measures to mitigate the risk of non-alignment or loss of control. Again, however, these remain a work-in-progress, with some experts casting doubt on the feasibility of developing effective solutions before the advent of AGI or ASI.

Crucially—and to recentre the discussion on defence—AI safety and security risks intersect. Among the possible scenarios that could bring about a loss of control over AGI is the risk of adversarial extraction (AI Action Summit, 2025). This envisages a hostile state or other actor compromising the security and containment systems around an AGI to copy and extract the model weights onto their own infrastructure, so as to gain access to that powerful AI system. Even if the hostile actor in question did not intend to let loose the AGI following this cyber-theft, their own systems may be less secure or operate with less robust oversight mechanisms, resulting in loss of control. As such, even if an effective safety regime can be put in place to stop a powerful AGI from breaking itself out, hostile actions by outside aggressors could force a breach, intentionally or otherwise, or else interfere with that AGI's goals, thereby bringing about non-alignment. Consequently, the protection of a nation's most powerful AI systems and associated infrastructure rapidly becomes a priority not only for tech companies, but also for cybersecurity and defence organisations, including intelligence agencies and the military. Similarly, all these organisations could play some role in any response to a loss of control incident, for example, to clear the AGI from compromised networks and systems, deal with public disorder and panic, or restore disrupted critical services.

Even without loss of control, the intensifying competition for AGI primacy creates destabilising dynamics at a geopolitical and therefore military level. In both the academic literature and government policy documents, there is often an assumption that whoever develops AGI first will accrue a major or perhaps even insuperable 'first-mover advantage' (Dear, 2024). The potential for AGI systems to self-improve iteratively could trigger exponential growth in capabilities that could be very difficult, or perhaps impossible, for other competing companies or nations to catch up with. This implies huge commercial gains to be had at a company level or strategic advantages at a national level in terms of a rebalancing of political, economic, and military power globally. It may be the case that, in fact, there are actually advantages to 'going second' and learning from and improving upon the approach of the first AGI pioneers (as has been the case in other industries) or that democratisation and proliferation of AI technologies counteract any divisions between AGI-haves and AGI-have nots. Regardless, any perception from great powers, most notably the United States and China, of a substantial 'first-mover advantage' in the development of ever more powerful AI systems could undermine strategic stability, straining relations, and increasing the potential for interstate conflict. As one illustrative scenario, one nation may receive intelligence that suggests, whether wrongly or rightly, that a rival actor is on the cusp of developing an AGI system that it assesses could bring about a significant, perhaps irrevocable, shift in the balance of power. In this situation, the incentive to launch a pre-emptive strike of some kind (a 'use it or lose it' mentality) could be high, especially is trust between the two sides is low (Mitre & Predd, 2025).

The present challenge, then, is not only to address mounting AI safety and security concerns, for example, by working to minimise the risks of non-alignment or LOC scenarios. It is also to find ways of bolstering trust between the United States and China in particular, and major powers in general, to manage the destabilising dynamics of the global race for AGI primacy. Otherwise, we risk a spiral of intensifying competition between nations over AGI (arms race instability) that raises the likelihood of military escalation, whether intentional or accidental (crisis instability). When to compete and when to collaborate over AI and AGI technologies and their governance is therefore likely to become an increasingly central dilemma in national security and grand strategy debates.

Grappling with Uncertainty and the Pace of Change

This chapter has sought to draw together just some of the many strategic-level risks and opportunities associated with rapid advances in AI capabilities and the increasing proliferation and adoption of such technologies in a defence and security context. Together, these impacts from AI cut across all aspects of strategy development and implementation; across all domains and types of defence operation or capability; and across the governmental, industrial, and societal functions that underpin a nation's ability to generate, equip, project, and sustain military forces.

AI technologies hold the potential to transform who, when, where, why and how we fight; who prevails in geopolitical competition or outright conflict; and, the resultant levels of strategic stability, peace and (in)security in the world. Pursuit of advantage both in and through AI must be balanced alongside development of policy, technical and governance solutions to mitigate the associated risks. Similarly, any rollout of AI in a military or security context must proceed in a responsible manner, cognisant always of International Humanitarian Law and of the ethical principles laid out in the defence AI strategies of countries like the U.S. or UK.

Grappling with the cross-cutting effects of AI poses significant challenges to policymakers within national ministries of defence or working at a NATO, EU, or UN level. By their nature, the broad impacts of AI do not conform neatly to institutional structures in government or the military. They also cut across the seams between the public, private and third sectors, and across such varied disciplinary areas such as military planning, procurement, innovation, tech governance, finance, law, ethics, data, and AI engineering. Gathering the diverse knowledge and expertise required to develop an informed policy response and then coordinating action from the various actors who need to be involved in implementation is a daunting yet urgent challenge (Horowitz et al., 2020).

Doing all the above at the speed required to keep pace with technological progress in AI is even harder, especially when government and alliance structures or political cycles are ill-suited to dealing with the complexity of non-linear, emergent developments in AI. Yet, that is the task currently facing teams such as the Chief Digital and Artificial Intelligence Office (CDAO) in the U.S. Department of Defense or the Defence AI & Autonomy Unit (DAU) in the UK Ministry of Defence, and their counterparts across other government departments focused on non-military aspects.

Given this pace of change and uncertainty about the future direction of military AI development—including the feasibility or possible timelines for achieving AGI and ASI—an iterative, learning-focused approach is needed. Governments, AI safety institutes, and militaries should continue to invest in experimentation, horizon scanning, Red Teaming, scenario analysis, wargaming and other uncertainty-sensitive techniques for stress-testing possible AI futures and identifying the associated risks and mitigations (Black et al., 2024a). Such methods provide a basis for an eyes-open, risk-informed adoption of AI technologies in national defence. This should recognise that potential risks of *commission* (i.e., making mistakes when adopting a new military AI system) must be balanced against risks of *omission* (i.e., failing to act in a timely manner on AI advances, thereby losing out on a strategic opportunity or ceding the military advantage to hostile actors).

Ultimately, inaction on AI is neither a credible nor a desirable option in defence. Equally, any haste by competing military powers to secure themselves the advantage in or through AI could result in path dependencies that push international relations towards greater conflict and instability. A twin-track approach is thus needed, combining efforts to promote innovation and accelerate adoption of AI in a responsible manner at the national level, while simultaneously using diplomatic means to shape the evolving governance of defence AI and mitigate risk at the international level.

In this regard, initiatives such as the REAIM Summits or the Political Declaration on this topic, are urgently needed. Dialogue is essential. But incentivising compromise among competing powers requires using a mix of hard and soft power, of deterrence and inducements, and of norms, law and institution-building for future military AI governance. Adopting defence AI technologies responsibly also means not allowing hostile states, such as China, Russia, and Iran to succumb to the temptation to adopt less ethically constrained or otherwise unsafe approaches to developing and deploying their own military AI systems in reckless pursuit of a short-term advantage.

Avoiding this eventuality requires that NATO countries and other like-minded nations accelerate adoption of AI within their own defence establishments for deterrence purposes while also engaging in dialogue and TCBMs at the international level to avoid a global 'race to the bottom' on AI safety, security, or ethical standards. Striking this balance is not straightforward, especially when geopolitical tensions are high. Still, it is essential and urgent, just as competing superpowers previously had to learn to de-risk competition over nuclear weapons technology in the Cold War through a mix of dialogue and deterrence (Boudreaux et al., 2025).

References

AI Action Summit. (2025). *AI Action Summit.* Elysee.fr. https://www.elysee.fr/en/sommet-pour-l-action-sur-l-ia

Barkhush. (2024). https://united24media.com/latest-news/ukrainian-forces-use-ai-to-identify-12000-russian-targets-weekly-2549

Black, J., & Lynch, A. (2022). https://ccdcoe.org/library/publications/cyber-threats-and-nato-2030-horizon-scanning-and-analysis/

Black, J., Eken, M., Parakilas, J., Dee, S., Ellis, C., Suman-Chauhan, K., Bain, R., Fine, H., Aquilino, M. C., Lebret, M., & Palicka, O. (2024a). *Strategic competition in the age of AI: Emerging risks and opportunities from military use of artificial intelligence.* RAND. RR-A3295-1. https://www.rand.org/pubs/research_reports/RRA3295-1.html

Black, J., Lucas, R., Kennedy, J., Hughes, M., & Fine, H. (2024b). *Command and control in the future: Concept Paper 1: Grappling with complexity.* RAND. RR-A2476-1. https://www.rand.org/pubs/research_reports/RRA2476-1.html

Bondar, K. (2024). https://www.csis.org/analysis/does-ukraine-already-have-functional-cjadc2-technology

Boudreaux, B., et al. (2025). https://www.rand.org/pubs/perspectives/PEA3652-1.html

Brose, C. (2020). *The kill chain: Defending America in the future of high-tech warfare.* Hachette.

Dear, K. (2024). https://www.fujitsu.com/uk/news/blogs/digital-transformation/ai-in-defence-the-urgent-need-for-a-theory-of-winning/

Defence Science and Technology Laboratory. (2024). https://www.gov.uk/guidance/climate/defence-adaptation

DSIT. (2023). https://www.gov.uk/ai-assurance-techniques/advai-operational-boundaries-calibration-for-ai-systems-via-adversarial-robustness-techniques

Erman, E., & Furendal, M. (2022). *Artificial intelligence and the political legitimacy of global governance. Political Studies, 72*(2), 421–441. https://doi.org/10.1177/00323217221126665 (Original work published 2024).

Futter, A. (2022). Disruptive technologies and nuclear risks: What's new and what matters. *Global Politics and Strategy, 64*(1), 99–120. https://doi.org/10.1080/00396338.2022.2032979

Geist, E. (2024). *Building a foundation for strategic stability with China on AI.* The RAND Blog. 2 April 2024. https://www.rand.org/pubs/commentary/2024/04/building-a-foundation-for-strategic-stability-with.html

Haner, J., & Garcia, D. (2019). The artificial intelligence arms race: Trends and world leaders in autonomous weapons development. *Global Policy, 10*, 331–337. https://doi.org/10.1111/1758-5899.12713

Harithas, B. (2025). https://www.csis.org/analysis/ai-diffusion-framework-securing-us-ai-leadership-while-preempting-strategic-drift

Heim, L. (2025). https://www.rand.org/pubs/perspectives/PEA3776-1.html

Horowitz, M. C., Kahn, L., & Mahoney, C. (2020). The future of military applications of artificial intelligence: A role for confidence-building measures? *Orbis, 64*(4), 528–543. https://doi.org/10.1016/j.orbis.2020.08.003

Hou, Y., Wang, Z., & Zhai, E. (June 2023). Artificial intelligence technology pushes forward the modernization of firepower weapon equipment. In *Proc. SPIE 12720, 2022 workshop on electronics communication engineering, 127200F.* https://doi.org/10.1117/12.2668167

Hughes, M., Carter, R., Harland, A., & Babuta, A. (2024). *AI and strategic decision making: Communicating trust and uncertainty in AI-enriched intelligence.* Centre for Emerging Technology and Security, The Alan Turing Institute. https://cetas.turing.ac.uk/publications/ai-and-strategic-decision-making

Huismans, J., Lucas, R., Palicka, O., Winder, S., & Silfversten, E. (2025a). *Conceptualising digital capability: Enabling NATO digital capabilities series: Paper 1.* RAND. RR-A3831-1. https://www.rand.org/pubs/research_reports/RRA3831-1.html

Huismans, J., Lucas, R., Palicka, O., Winder, S., & Silfversten, E. (2025b). *Interoperability in the digital environment: Opportunities and challenges: Enabling NATO digital capabilities series: Paper 3.* RAND. RR-A3831-3. https://www.rand.org/pubs/research_reports/RRA3831-3.html

Huismans, J., et al. (2025). https://www.rand.org/pubs/research_reports/RRA3831-1.html

Javadi, M., & Onderco, M. (2024). *What does global military AI governance need?* European Leadership Network. https://www.europeanleadershipnetwork.org/commentary/what-does-global-military-ai-governance-need/

Johnson, J. (2019). Artificial intelligence & future warfare: Implications for international security. *Defense & Security Analysis, 35*(2), 147–169. https://doi.org/10.1080/14751798.2019.1600800

Johnson, J. (2021). Artificial intelligence: A threat to strategic stability. *Strategic Studies Quarterly, 14*(1), 16–39. https://www.jstor.org/stable/26891882

Johnson, J. (2022). Inadvertent escalation in the age of intelligence machines: A new model for nuclear risk in the digital age. *European Journal of International Security, 7*(3), 337–359. https://doi.org/10.1017/eis.2021.23

Kahl. (2025). https://www.foreignaffairs.com/united-states/america-winning-race-global-ai-primacy-now

Kaspar, L., Canales, M. P., & Shapiro, M. N. (2023). *Navigating the global AI governance landscape*. Global Partners Digital. https://www.gp-digital.org/navigating-the-global-ai-governance-landscape/

King, A. (2025). *AI, Automation, and War: The Rise of a Military-Tech Complex*. Princeton University Press.

Knack, A., & Powell R.. (2023). https://cetas.turing.ac.uk/publications/artificial-intelligence-wargaming

Knack, A., et al. (2025). https://cetas.turing.ac.uk/publications/applying-ai-strategic-warning

Liu, H.-Y., & Maas, M. M. (2021). "Solving for X?" Towards a problem-finding framework to ground long-term governance strategies for artificial intelligence. *Futures, 126*(22). https://doi.org/10.1016/j.futures.2020.102672

Lohn, A., Knack, A., Burke, A., & Jackson, K. (2023). *Autonomous Cyber Defence Phase I: A Roadmap from Lab to Ops*. The Alan Turing Institute. https://cetas.turing.ac.uk/publications/autonomous-cyber-defence-phase-i

Lucas R., et al. (2025). https://www.rand.org/pubs/research_reports/RRA3831-2.html

Mazarr, M. J. (2022). *The societal foundations of national competitiveness*. RAND. RR-A499-1 https://www.rand.org/pubs/research_reports/RRA499-1.html

Mazarr, M., Dale-Huang, A., & Sargent, M. (2024). *The emerging competitive paradigm: A contest of effective governance*. RAND. PE-A2611-1. https://www.rand.org/pubs/perspectives/PEA2611-1.html

Mazarr, M. J., Rhoades, A. L., Beauchamp-Mustafaga, N., Blanc, A. A., Eaton, D., Feistel, K., Geist, E., Heath, T. R., Johnson, C., Langeland, K., et al. (2022). *Disrupting deterrence: Examining the effects of technologies on strategic deterrence in the 21st century*. RAND. RR-A595-1. https://www.rand.org/pubs/research_reports/RRA595-1.html

Meerveld, H. W., Lindelauf, R. H. A., Postma, E. O., & Postma, M. (2023). The irresponsibility of not using AI in the military. *Ethics and Information Technology, 25*(14). https://doi.org/10.1007/s10676-023-09683-0

Mitchell, M. (2024). https://www.science.org/doi/10.1126/science.ado7069

Mitre, J., & Predd, J.B. (2025). https://www.rand.org/pubs/perspectives/PEA3691-4.html

Mouton, C. A., et al. (2024). https://www.rand.org/pubs/research_reports/RRA2977-2.html

Nancholas, B. (2023). *Narrow artificial intelligence: advantages, disadvantages, and the future of AI*. University of Wolverhampton. https://online.wlv.ac.uk/narrow-artificial-intelligence-advantages-disadvantages-and-the-future-of-ai/

Nunez, M. (2025). https://venturebeat.com/ai/anthropic-ceo-dario-amodei-warns-ai-will-match-country-of-geniuses-by-2026/

Onderco, M., & Zutt, M. (2021). Emerging technology and nuclear security: What does the wisdom of the crowd tell us? *Contemporary Security Policy, 42*(3), 286–311. https://doi.org/10.1080/13523260.2021.1928963Payne

Payne, K. (2021). *I, Warbot.* C Hurst & Co.

Payne, K. (2024). *Warbot 2.0: Reflections on the fast-changing world of AI in National Security.* Binding Hook, 28 March. https://bindinghook.com/articles-book-binder/warbot-2-0-reflections-on-the-fast-changing-world-of-ai-in-national-security/

Perrigo, B. (2025). http://time.com/7287806/anthropic-claude-4-opus-safety-bio-risk/

Pratt, S. F. (2024). https://foreignpolicy.com/2024/05/02/israel-military-artificial-intelligence-targeting-hamas-gaza-deaths-lavender/

Reinhold, T., & Reuter, C. (2022). Cyber weapons and artificial intelligence: Impact, influence and the challenges for arms control. In T. Reinhold & N. Schörnig (Eds.), *Armament, arms control and artificial intelligence: Studies in peace and security* (pp. 145–158). Springer. https://doi.org/10.1007/978-3-031-11043-6_11

Ren, S., & Wierman, A. (2024). https://hbr.org/2024/07/the-uneven-distribution-of-ais-environmental-impacts

Ryseff, J., Landree, E., Johnson, N., Ghosh-Dastidar, B., Izenberg, M., Newberry, S. J., Ferris, C., & Bradley, M. A. (2022). *Exploring the civil-military divide over artificial intelligence.* RAND. RR-A1498-1. https://www.rand.org/pubs/research_reports/RRA1498-1.html

Schaefer, K. E., Perelman, B., Rexwinkle, J., Canady, J., Neubauer, C., Waytowich, N., Larkin, Cox, K., Geuss, M., Gremillion, G., Metcalfe, J. S., DeCostanza, A., & Marathe, A. (2021). Human-autonomy teaming for the tactical edge: the importance of humans in artificial intelligence research and development. In W. F. Flawless, R. Mittu, D. A. Sofge, T. Shortell, & T. McDormott (Eds.), *Systems engineering and artificial intelligence* (pp. 115–48). https://doi.org/10.1007/978-3-030-77283-3_7

Scharre, P. (2018). *Army of none: Autonomous weapons and the future of war.* W.W. Norton & Co.

Scharre, P. (2023). *Four battlegrounds: Power in the age of artificial intelligence.* W.W. Norton & Co.

Sigfrids, A., Leikas, J., Salo-Pöntinen, H., & Koskimies, E. (2023). Human-centricity in AI governance: A systemic approach. *Frontiers in Artificial Intelligence, 6*, 976887. https://doi.org/10.3389/frai.2023.976887

Slapakova, L., et al. (2024). https://www.rand.org/pubs/research_reports/RRA2662-1.html

Sytsma, T. (2025). https://www.rand.org/pubs/research_reports/RRA3764-1.html

Taeihagh, A. (2021). Governance of artificial intelligence. *Policy & Society, 40*(2), 137–157. https://doi.org/10.1080/14494035.2021.1928377

UK Ministry of Defence. (June 2022). *Defence artificial intelligence strategy.* https://www.gov.uk/government/publications/defence-artificial-intelligence-strategy

US Department of Commerce. (2025). *Department of Commerce Announces Rescission of Biden-Era Artificial Intelligence Diffusion Rule, Strengthens Chip-Related Export Controls*. https://www.bis.gov/press-release/department-commerce-announces-rescission-biden-era-artificial-intelligence-diffusion-rule-strengthens

Wong, Y. H., Yurchak, J., Button, R. W., Frank, A. B., Laird, B., Osoba, O. A., Steeb, R., Harris, B. N., & Bae, S. J. (2020). *Deterrence in the age of thinking machines*. RAND Corporation. RR-2797-RC. https://www.rand.org/pubs/research_reports/RR2797.html

The Present and Future of International Law Regulation in the Area of Militarised Artificial Intelligence

Tsvetelina van Benthem

Introduction

For decades now, the imagery of autonomous systems operating in warfare has captured the imagination of the public, with its anthropomorphising of potentially unpredictable and uncontrollable 'killer robots' (Nadibaidze, 2024). While this imagery may have suggested a concern for a distant future, military applications relying on artificial intelligence ('AI') and operating with varying degrees of autonomy vis-à-vis their deployers are already part of the arsenals of states, assisting their identification of persons and objects, assessment of large quantities of data, and process optimisation, among others. Battlefields are becoming increasingly automated, with automation being perceived as a precondition for military superiority and strategic competition (Saltini, 2025). In this process, the continuing role of human decision-making is being questioned, relocated, and reimagined (Amoroso & Tamburrini, 2021).

There are many challenges that the introduction of autonomy, in particular in the form of AI applications supporting military operations, could bring to the battlefield. Concerns over miscalculation and escalation, unpredictability, an uncontrollable arms race, acquisition of autonomous weapons by non-state actors, infringements of human dignity pervade the discussions between

T. van Benthem (✉)
University of Oxford, Oxford, UK
e-mail: tsvetelina.vanbenthem@conted.ox.ac.uk

M. Rangeley, N. Fairfax (eds.), *The Artificial Intelligence Revolution*,
https://doi.org/10.1007/978-3-032-11814-1_12

states, international organisations, academia, and civil society organisations. Of these concerns, that of outcomes that are unforeseen (or unforeseeable) and uncontrollable has occupied a particularly prominent place, raising questions of a risk of unintended engagements that could cause harm to protected persons and objects, including civilians. Here, we observe the blending of factual and legal uncertainty—not only can military applications relying on AI sever the link between human intent and battlefield outcomes, but there is also significant legal contestation over the degree to which international law, and in particular international humanitarian law (also known as the law of armed conflict, or the *ius in bello*), regulates unintended engagements.

Different epistemic communities have, for more than a decade and in a variety of institutional fora, unpacked these concerns, and assessed them against the benefits of introducing AI in warfare, the current international law framework, and a landscape of possible normative futures.

To begin with, there has been a long-standing inter-governmental discussion over the regulation of autonomous weapons, in particular weapons relying on AI in critical functions, such as target identification, selection and engagement. In 2016, the High Contracting Parties to the Convention on Certain Conventional Weapons ('CCW') established the Group of Governmental Experts on Emerging Technologies in the Area of Lethal Autonomous Weapons Systems ('GGE on LAWS') as a subsidiary body of the CCW. States have convened in Geneva within the auspices of this Group since 2017, adopting consensus reports and guiding principles, and generating a wealth of state positions on the technical, legal, policy and moral aspects of the development and use of such weapons. In recent years, the discussion has moved beyond the GGE on LAWS to the United Nations General Assembly, with reports from the United Nations Secretary-General compiling national positions and identifying areas of convergence and divergence in state views. In 2023, the Netherlands hosted the first global Summit on Responsible Artificial Intelligence in the Military Domain and Costa Rica convened the Latin American and The Caribbean Conference of Social and Humanitarian Impact of Autonomous Weapons, and in 2024 Austria hosted the Vienna Conference on Autonomous Weapons Systems. Many states are seeking to show leadership in the debates, including through regional alliances.

Domestic bodies have also led the effort of clarifying the existing legal and ethical guardrails in the use of military AI. The United Kingdom House of Lords AI in Weapon Systems Committee gathered written and oral evidence from a wide pool of stakeholders—from government, international and non-governmental organisations, academia, and the private sector—and published a report summarising key findings and recommending a national course of action on autonomous systems (UK House of Lords AI in Weapons Report, 2023). In 2022, a report discussing technical, geo-political, ethical, and legal facets of the autonomous weapons debates was released by the Dutch Advisory Committee on Public International Law and Advisory Council on International Affairs (The Netherlands Advisory Council Report, 2022).

Ongoing academic efforts, including the Oxford Process on International Law Protections in Cyberspace and the West Point Manual on International Law Applicable to Artificial Intelligence in Warfare, seek to clarify key legal rules and transpose 'lessons learned' from other technological discussions, such as the discussions on the regulation of information and communications technologies.

These epistemic communities are engaged in a transnational conversation that spans different disciplines and institutional affiliations. Two questions are key to this conversation:

What are the main legal challenges raised by the use of autonomous military capabilities reliant on AI?
What are the viable normative visions for the future regulation of AI in warfare?

The present chapter addresses these two questions, drawing on the wealth of materials and insights generated by states, international organisations, and academics. In so doing, it untangles the sharp-end issues of the human role in the use of AI, unintended engagements, and responsibility, as well as the dynamics of clarification and further development of international law.

The chapter proceeds, as follows. 'Clarifying Key Concepts: Autonomy and Autonomous Weapons Systems' section addresses matters of terminology, and in particular the concepts of 'autonomy' and 'autonomous weapons systems'. 'A Landscape of Existing Autonomous Military Applications' section provides an overview of existing military AI applications. 'Foundational Legal Challenges Posed by Military Applications of AI' section explores the foundational legal challenges posed by military applications of AI. 'Two Regulatory Pathways for the Use of AI in Warfare' section looks towards the future, outlining two regulatory pathways for establishing and clarifying legal constraints in the use of military AI. The last section concludes.

Clarifying Key Concepts: Autonomy and Autonomous Weapons Systems

In philosophy, a central conception of autonomy is one of self-governance, of a capacity to govern oneself and act independently (Feinberg, 1989). While no one is completely independent from external constraints, the notion denotes a basic—and relative—independence of action. Autonomy in both individuals and artefacts exists on a spectrum—we can be more or less autonomous in particular tasks and in relation to particular persons and external factors. Translated to the military domain, NATO has defined autonomy as '[a] system's ability to function, within parameters established by programming and without outside intervention, in accordance with desired goals, based on acquired knowledge and an evolving situational awareness' (NATO, 2020).

When the notion of autonomy is attached to the notion of weapons systems, it denotes a relative independence of action of tools designed for violent effect against an adversary. Both human and non-human elements operate to achieve this violent effect, thus constituting the weapon *system* (Harwood, 2024).

Because of the main forum in which the discussions on autonomous weapons occurred so far—the GGE on LAWS, most attention was paid to a specific type of autonomous system—a system that can select *and* apply force to targets without further human input after activation (SIPRI & ICRC, 2020). However, there are systems 'featuring varying degrees of decision-making autonomy in critical functions such as identification, classification, interception and engagement' (UK House of Lords AI in Weapons Report, 2023) beyond the narrow conception of an autonomous weapon. These systems may give rise to similar questions over human-machine interaction, predictability, explainability, and reliability, among others.

To date, there is no one universally agreed definition of autonomous weapons systems, though states and other stakeholders have developed their own understandings of these systems (Taddeo & Blanchard, 2022). If a definition were to emerge, tying it to specific technological developments would be a mistake. A focus on the functions, interactions, and effects of these weapon systems will ensure a longer shelf life of the definition, given the rapid evolution of military technology.

While autonomy in weapons systems is not new, what *is* new is the infiltration of adaptive AI in military applications. AI systems with machine learning put questions of predictability of outcomes, traceability of decision-making, and unwanted bias to the fore. This is because machine learning 'provides systems with the ability to learn and enhance from experience automatically without being specifically programmed' (Sarker, 2021). The key risk here is military decision-making where human deployers have minimal capacity for review and oversight, given their limited capacity to understand how particular machine decisions are reached.

In this chapter, the concept of 'autonomous weapons systems' will be used in a wide sense to capture both systems that are capable of selecting *and* engaging targets of attack (full autonomy in the targeting cycle), and military decision-support systems using AI that limit the capacity of humans to review and exercise oversight over system recommendations in relation to the targeting of persons and objects.

A Landscape of Existing Autonomous Military Applications

In 2021, the final report of the Panel of Experts on Libya established by the United Nations Security Council described the use of 'lethal autonomous weapons systems' against logistics convoys and retreating members of the Haftar Affiliated Forces—'[t]he lethal autonomous weapons systems were programmed to attack targets without requiring data connectivity between the operator and the munition: in effect, a true "fire, forget and find" capability' (Final Report, para 63). Specifically, the report was referring to the use of Kargu-2, a drone produced by the Turkish defence company STM. Over the years, various military capabilities operating with diverse degrees of autonomy from their human operators have gained international prominence—from Israel's mobile air-defence system Iron Dome and Harpy missile through South Korea's SGR-A1 sentry drone guarding the Korean Demilitarised Zone to US's AGM-158C long-range anti-ship missile. In 2024, the use of AI in decision-making processes related to the targeting of persons gained further prominence following reports of Israel's use of 'Lavender', a 'smart' database relying on algorithmic identification of Hamas operatives (Schmitt, 2024).

Indeed, militaries employ—and have done so for years—AI capabilities in threat detection, cyber monitoring and defence, the identification of persons and objects, optimisation of weapon trajectory, decision support for proportionality assessments, among others. Each of these capabilities offers specific advantages, contingent on their capacity to swiftly analyse large quantities of data with sufficient accuracy and reliability. At the same time, each of these capabilities poses specific risks, depending on, in particular, their relationship to human judgment, propensity to errors and biases, and controllability. While the advantages exert a pull towards further investment in AI for military purposes, the risks constrain states in what they can lawfully develop and deploy, given existing protections under international law, in particular international human rights law and international humanitarian law.

Many have voiced concerns over the development and deployment of AI-reliant systems for the targeting of persons and objects, including the United Nations Secretary-General and the International Committee of the Red Cross

(Joint call by the United Nations Secretary-General and the President of the International Committee of the Red Cross, 2023), states (Belén Communiqué, 2023), non-governmental organisations (Human Rights Watch, 2024) and academics (Chengeta, 2022; Russell, 2023). Without a doubt, these concerns have shaped the international discussion over the regulation of autonomous weapons systems (UN Report on Lethal Autonomous Weapons Systems, 2024). They have not, however, halted the research and development of AI capabilities designed for use in war. In late 2024, the US announced the establishment of a new AI Rapid Capabilities Cell aimed at accelerating the adoption and mainstreaming of AI in the Department of Defense. Warfighting is a focus area for the adoption of AI: 'Command and Control [. . .] and decision support, operational planning, logistics, weapons development and testing, uncrewed and autonomous systems, intelligence activities, information operations, and cyber operations' (US Department of Defense, 2024). In early 2025, Google's parent company Alphabet lifted its ethical pledge to abstain from using AI for applications 'likely to cause harm', such as military applications (Hooker & Vallance, 2025).

What is clear is that military applications of AI are here to stay. And while these applications do not resemble the imagery of the 'killer robot', they do pose fundamental questions on the role of human decision-making in armed conflict, the management of battlefield uncertainty and unintended engagements, and the responsibility of states and individuals for harms caused in the use of AI. It is to these questions that the next section turns.

Foundational Legal Challenges Posed by Military Applications of AI

Military applications of AI do not operate in a legal vacuum. Establishing whether international law applies to new technological developments is the necessary first step that opens the door to the substantive legal analysis of rights and obligations. In 1996, the International Court of Justice, in its Advisory Opinion on the legality of the threat or use of nuclear weapons, held that international humanitarian law applies to 'all forms of warfare and to all kinds of weapons, those of the past, those of the present and those of the future' (ICJ, *Nuclear Weapons*, para 86). The foundational principles and rules of international humanitarian law are both technology-neutral and future-proof, and they automatically extend to new technological developments. What this means is that, even without regulation specific to the use of AI in armed conflict, such capabilities fall within the scope of existing law.

States have consistently reaffirmed that international law, including international humanitarian law, applies to autonomous weapons systems, including systems characterised by the use of machine learning algorithms (GGE on Laws, Report, 2019). The critical question therefore is not *whether* the law applies, but *how* it applies to military applications of AI. Emerging consensus seems to indicate that states do not view all autonomous weapons systems as inherently unlawful. According to the two-tiered approach proposed by a number of states, 'certain autonomous weapons systems will require prohibition and all others regulation' (Working Paper Austria, 2024). This perfectly mirrors international humanitarian law, where certain weapon systems are prohibited as such (e.g., for being inherently indiscriminate or of a nature to cause superfluous injury or unnecessary suffering), and others are regulated in their use (e.g., by restricting the deployment of particular weapons in cluttered urban environments). The two-tier approach provides a structured way of thinking about the regulation of autonomous weapons systems but does not specifically answer *how* the law applies to them.

In considering how the legal frameworks relevant to armed conflict apply to militarised AI, it becomes clear that these technologies do not raise fundamentally new questions. Rather, they highlight legal questions that are, in important ways, timeless, and that have never received a conclusive answer in the practice of states. Three such questions are of particular importance and are explored in the next sub-sections: (1) the role of human involvement in decisions on the use of force in armed conflict; (2) the regulation of unintended engagements; and (3) state and individual responsibility for harms caused in the use of militarised AI.

Human Involvement in Decisions on the Use of Force in Armed Conflict

Is the human element central—or necessary—for the legality of decisions on the use of force in armed conflict? Must human beings oversee and approve every individual projection of force against a human or object, or is it sufficient for humans to programme the parameters within which an AI-based system can initiate force?

For decades, various stakeholders have debated the role and place of human input in the use of autonomous military capabilities (Ferl, 2024). In late 2024, the United Nations General Assembly adopted a resolution '[s]tressing the importance of the role of humans in the use of force to ensure responsibility and accountability and for States to comply with international law' (UNGA Resolution 79/L.77). Two years earlier, seventy states delivered a joint statement to the General Assembly, emphasising 'the necessity for human beings to exert appropriate control, judgement and involvement in relation to the use of weapons systems in order to ensure any use is in compliance with International Law, in particular International Humanitarian Law' (Joint Statement, 2022). The concept of human-machine interaction was enshrined in the Guiding Principles adopted by the GGE on LAWS, as follows: '[h]uman-machine interaction, which may take various forms and be implemented at various stages of the life cycle of a weapon, should ensure that the potential use of weapons systems based on emerging technologies in the area of lethal autonomous weapons systems is in compliance with applicable international law, in particular IHL' (GGE on LAWS, Report, 2019).

At first glance, states seem to agree on the importance of the human element, and the need to retain it in conflict-related decisions on the use of force. What underlies their consensus language, however, is deep disagreement over the form and extent of such human involvement. Unpacking what states actually mean by 'appropriate' control, judgment, involvement, and the contextual needs for 'human-machine interaction', is both the sharp-end legal inquiry, and the one of most practical significance.

In state submissions, we observe different approaches to the relationship between autonomous systems and human decision-making. For instance, the *Draft Articles on autonomous weapon systems* prepared by Australia, Canada, Estonia, Japan, Latvia, Lithuania, Poland, the Republic of Korea, the United Kingdom, and the United States suggest that '[a]utonomous weapon systems may only be developed such that their effects in attacks are capable of being anticipated and controlled as required in the circumstances of their use' (Draft Articles Autonomous Weapons, 2024). While there is emphasis on anticipation of effects and controllability, the qualifier 'as required in the circumstances of their use' leaves a wide margin of discretion in relation to the precise contours of such anticipation and control. The State of Palestine takes a sceptical view of certain modalities of human involvement, which it terms 'nominal human input' (Submission Palestine, 2024). According to Palestine, this is

> input performed by a human after the system's activation and during the autonomous process, but that does not materially affect the process. [. . .] These 'nominal human inputs' are made at a place and time far removed from where the system executes force, and without the human giving proper consideration

to the risks of breaches under international law taking place. The human input is thus "mindless" – its effect being the same as if the autonomous process had occurred without it.

The Draft Articles and Palestine's position demonstrate an area of disagreement among states. While for Palestine, a temporal, geographical and cognitive distancing of human input from battlefield engagements may render such input 'nominal', the authors of the Draft Articles suggest that sufficient human oversight can be exercised at a distance. In a 2025 submission to the GGE on LAWS, a group of states comprising Bulgaria, Denmark, Finland, France, Germany, Italy, Luxembourg, the Netherlands, Norway, Spain, and Sweden focused specifically on the 'human element', and posited that it can be exercised directly or indirectly at different stages, subject to ensuring that commanders and operators can 'adequately predict (prospective focus) and analyze (retrospective) the behavior of the weapons systems' (Working paper on the 'human element', 2025). In their view, therefore, the human element must have a meaningful prospective and retrospective quality, whether it is exercised at a distance or not.

Beyond distance, cognitive biases are likely to also affect the modalities and robustness of human-machine interaction. Automation bias (whereby users tend to over-accept computer output as a heuristic replacement of vigilant information seeking and processing—Goddard et al., 2011) and the representative heuristic (whereby users tend to assess the subjective probability of an event by the degree to which it is similar in essential characteristics to its parent population and reflects the salient features of the process by which it is generated—Kahneman & Tversky, 1972) may affect how human decision-makers interact with autonomous inputs, processes and outcomes. And bias in the datasets used to train the autonomous systems can perpetuate racial, ethnic, religious and gender stereotypes (Bode, 2024).

To fully understand the debate over the role of human involvement in decisions on the use of force in armed conflict, it is important to contextualise it. Various military applications relying on AI have made possible a distancing—temporal, geographical, cognitive, moral—between human input and battlefield outcomes (van Benthem, 2024a). At the same time, this process of distancing has been underway for a long time—with long-range missiles, drones, malware with delayed execution. Such technologies have already given rise to debates over human-machine interaction, for instance those over the risk of a 'PlayStation' mentality to the use of manned drones (Molenkamp et al., 2024) and the possibility to maintain control over the outcomes of guided munitions by redirecting them in flight (van Benthem, 2020). Although the concern over human involvement in the use of AI in armed conflict may be quantitatively higher, it is not entirely new, and it highlights an important legal area in need of further clarification.

As a matter of law, a key question is whether relevant rules—for instance under international humanitarian law—*require* a form of human involvement, such that the deployment of military capabilities without such involvement would amount to a violation. If such human involvement is indeed required, the next question is about the scope and kind of involvement necessitated by particular legal obligations. For instance, it could be argued that the presumption of civilian status (in case of doubt whether a person is a civilian, that person shall be considered to be a civilian—under art 50(1) of Additional Protocol I to the Geneva Conventions and customary international law), the prohibition of disproportionate attacks (attacks which may be expected to cause incidental loss of civilian life, injury to civilians, damage to civilian objects, or a combination thereof, which would be excessive in relation to the concrete and direct military advantage anticipated—under art 51(5)(b) of Additional Protocol I and customary international law), the duty to exercise constant care (in the conduct of military operations, constant care shall be taken to spare the civilian population, civilians and civilian objects—under art 57(1) of Additional Protocol I and customary international law), and the obligation of cancellation or suspension of attacks (an attack shall be cancelled or suspended if it becomes apparent that the objective is not a military one or is subject to special protection—under art 57(2)(b) of Additional Protocol I and customary international law), among others, require the exercise of subjective—and ongoing—human judgment.

While these rules do require subjective assessments, they do not seem to automatically preclude the possibility of complying with the law when executing particular military operations through AI systems. In other words, parties to conflict must ensure that their decisions on the use of force (including in the choice of using an AI system to support or execute such force) allow them to honour the presumption of civilian status, engage in proportionality assessments, exercise constant care. A critical factor for ensuring compliance is the degree to which parties to conflict can ensure that their *intent*—intermediated by the use of AI capabilities—is adequately translated to the battlefield.

The Regulation of Unintended Engagements

Not all harms originating from military operations are intended, that is, caused with purpose or knowledge. Information uncertainty may lead to the mistaken targeting of protected persons and objects, sudden changes in environmental conditions may deflect the trajectory of weapons, military equipment may malfunction. Because of concerns over unpredictable processes and outcomes of military capabilities reliant on AI, the question of unintended engagements has become particularly prominent in recent years. However, whether states, non-state armed groups, and individuals can be held responsible for unintended harms in armed conflict is a general and ongoing legal controversy, not limited to the regulation of AI (van Benthem, 2024b).

When in 2022, Russian forces bombed the Donetsk Regional Theatre of Drama in Mariupol, the civilians sheltering inside had written 'ДЕТИ' (children) on its entrances, in an attempt to dissuade the attackers from engaging the building (Human Rights Watch, 2022). Attackers could construe this sign as an indication that the occupants of the building are indeed protected persons, or they could wonder if they are being deceived by the adversary. In any case, this sign should have created doubt in the mind of the attackers. What if, instead of human operators, the engagement was meant to be performed by an autonomous weapon? How can an AI system receive and interpret a signal of this kind? Even if the intent of the commander had been to strike a lawful military objective without causing excessive incidental civilian harm, a fault in the sensors, assessment of data, programmed standard of confidence prior to engagement, could have led to an attack with unwanted consequences. And it may well be, given the complexity of AI decision-making, that human deployers will not be in a position to anticipate potential unpredictability in their use. Thus, while uncertainty has always accompanied warfighting, the use of AI in military systems could add new layers of unpredictability to military operations.

Several states have raised the question of unpredictability in their national positions on autonomous weapons. Canada, for instance, writes that 'autonomy in weapons systems must stem from a high level of trustworthiness such that the level of unpredictability is sufficiently low, and that any risks may be mitigated by appropriate measures similar to those managed when using conventional weapons'. Cuba, Egypt, Italy, and Pakistan raise unpredictability as a key challenge and concern (UN Report on Lethal Autonomous Weapons Systems, 2024—Compendium). Looking ahead, the International Committee of the Red Cross has championed the establishment of a new legally-binding prohibition on unpredictable autonomous weapons (ICRC Position, 2021).

As a matter of existing international humanitarian law, not every unpredictable harmful outcome against protected persons or objects triggers the responsibility of the party to conflict. Instead, the legal analysis hinges on the interpretation of specific obligations—positive and negative—that the party to conflict must comply with.

Positive obligations are obligations to take steps. Relevant examples are the obligation to undertake legal reviews of new weapons and obligations to take precautions in attack (such as target verification). The obligation to undertake legal reviews of new weapons, binding on states parties to Additional Protocol I to the Geneva Conventions (Additional Protocol I, art. 36), and arguably implied by the principle of distinction (ICRC, Guide to Legal Reviews of New Weapons), can play a key protective role in fielding systems using AI. At its core, the review is meant to test whether a particular weapon, means or method of warfare can be used in compliance with international law. Weapons must undergo further review in case of modification to their design or use (Boulanin, 2015). As has been argued in the literature, 'a broader, iterative, multidisciplinary and ongoing approach must be factored into extant review processes' in light of the needs generated by autonomous weapons (Copeland et al., 2023).

Negative obligations, on the other hand, are obligations to abstain from particular conduct. Here, of particular relevance are the obligations to refrain from attacking civilians and civilian objects and of launching indiscriminate attacks. One version of 'indiscriminate' attack is an attack using inherently indiscriminate weapons or otherwise lawful weapons that, in a particular battlefield environment, cannot be directed at a specific military objective (Additional Protocol I, art 51(4)(b)). So far, weapons have been deemed indiscriminate on a case-by-case basis due to their high inaccuracy—modified air bombs, Orkan rockets, Katyusha rockets, Scud missiles (Brehm, 2014). However, there are no objective standards developed in the practice of states that indicate the threshold for considering a weapon indiscriminate as such or in particular battlefield contexts (for instance, in urban warfare). It is equally unclear whether to violate the prohibition of indiscriminate attack, the attacker must have *known* of the indiscriminate nature of the weapon—an element that might pose particular difficulties in relation to autonomous weapons whose functioning may not be fully understandable to commanders and operators (van Benthem, 2022).

In addition to international humanitarian law, international human rights law contains important guarantees against unintended engagements in the use of militarised AI. A so far underexplored area is the protection of soldiers under the right to life (Park, 2018), both during military training alongside AI capabilities and deployment. States have a positive obligation to protect the life of those under their jurisdiction, including members of their armed forces—this obligation requires states to adopt 'any appropriate laws or other measures in order to protect life from all reasonably foreseeable threats' (Human Rights Committee, General Comment 36 on the right to life).

A case that demonstrates the importance of these human rights protections is *Stoyanovi v Bulgaria* adjudged by the European Court of Human Rights. The applicants, Mr and Mrs Stoyanovi, complained of a violation of the right to life of their son who, in 1998, died when performing a parachute jump from a Mi-17 helicopter during a training exercise of the Ministry of the Interior's Special Anti-Terrorism Squad. Immediately after the jump, their son's head hit the tyre of the helicopter, he became unconscious, and his body fell freely and hit the ground. The reason for the incident was found to be the speed at which the helicopter was going, and the lack of appropriate training for when and how to jump at that speed. The Court accepted that there are substantive positive obligations arising under the right to life. Even though danger is an inevitable part of life for members of armed forces, the Court found that whenever a state undertakes or organises dangerous activities, or authorises them, it must ensure through a system of rules and through sufficient control that the risk is reduced to a reasonable minimum (*Stoyanovi*, para 61). This protection stemming from the right to life can find a particularly fertile ground for application in the context of AI applications.

Existing law suggests that both positive and negative obligations under international law, in particular international humanitarian law and international human rights law, protect against unintended engagements, including in the use of AI in military operations. Important controversies remain, however. Many existing rules are blurry, pixelated, underspecified. This may, in turn, lead to a perception of legal grey zones, incentivising the deployment of risky—more unpredictable—autonomous systems. Parties to conflict and individuals are less likely to take this risk if there is a strong sense of accountability, especially in the form of a reasonable prospect that responsibility will be brought to bear for their use of autonomous systems.

State and Individual Responsibility for Harms Caused in the Use of Military Applications of AI

As a matter of legal principle, states and individuals bear legal responsibility for their unlawful uses of militarised AI. State responsibility is contingent on the existence of an internationally wrongful act, that is, conduct consisting of an action or omission that is attributable to the state under international law and constitutes a breach of an international obligation of the state (International Law Commission, Articles on State Responsibility, art 2). Individuals can be held responsible directly under international law for their participation in international crimes—genocide, crimes against humanity, war crimes, and aggression.

The concept of responsibility has been central in the discussions on autonomous weapons. In the Guiding Principles developed by the GGE on LAWS, states agreed on the need to retain human responsibility:

> (b) Human responsibility for decisions on the use of weapons systems must be retained since accountability cannot be transferred to machines.
>
> (d) Accountability for developing, deploying and using any emerging weapons system in the framework of the CCW must be ensured in accordance with applicable international law, including through the operation of such systems within a responsible chain of human command and control [. . .]

Responsibility is also one of the five principles established in the UK Ministry of Defence *Ethical Principles for AI in Defence*: '[h]uman responsibility for AI-enabled systems must be clearly established, ensuring accountability for their outcomes, with clearly defined means by which human control is exercised throughout their lifecycles' (MoD Ethical Principles Defence, 2022).

Despite such strong responsibility-signalling from states, academics and non-governmental organisations have for years sounded the alarm bell over a possible 'accountability gap' in the use of weapons relying on AI for the identification and engagement of targets (Human Rights Watch, 2015; Chengeta, 2016; Verdiesen et al., 2021). Where, if at all, can we find an 'accountability gap' in the use of autonomous weapons?

At the outset, it is important to emphasise that whether one identifies an 'accountability gap' will depend on the starting point, assumptions and goals of the observer. If the observer's intuition is that responsibility must be established for any and all harms to protected persons and objects that are caused in the use of autonomous weapons, then that observer will likely perceive an accountability gap. Under international law, states and individuals are not legally responsible for *any* harm that my ensue from their actions and omissions. What they are responsible for are their actions and omissions that violate their obligations under international law. Whether there is a violation therefore depends on the interpretation of these obligations. The sharp-end question over the use of AI in military operations—that of unpredictability and unintended engagements—therefore brings us back to the interpretation of key rules from international humanitarian law, international human rights law and other applicable legal frameworks.

As was shown in the previous section, many of these obligations give rise to a range of plausible interpretations, and their contours remain underspecified. Instead of an 'accountability gap', which assumes an absence of responsibility, we are faced with 'certainty gap' in the content and application of the law. If there is indeed such a 'certainty gap' detrimental to the formation of expectations among states, international organisations, communities and individuals, then the next important question is how the law can be sufficiently specified to fulfil its purpose. The next section explores two regulatory pathways for militarised AI capable of providing such specification.

Two Regulatory Pathways for the Use of AI in Warfare

How states decide to proceed with the regulation of militarised AI is one of the critical questions for the twenty-first century. While there is regulatory momentum for a new treaty tailored to the specific risks of militarised AI, this momentum comes primarily from states that do not have the resources and/or interest to develop such weapons. Those investing heavily in military autonomy favour the clarification of existing law, typically at a high enough level of generality to avoid robust legal constraints. The next sections explore two regulatory avenues in front of states.

Establishing a New International Legal Framework for Military Applications of AI

Dissatisfied with the direction, substantive mandate, and outcomes of the inter-governmental discussions at the GGE on LAWS, a growing number of states are calling for the adoption of a new treaty, tailored specifically to the challenges of autonomy in the military domain. Thus, the Communiqué of the 2023 Latin American and Caribbean Conference on the social and humanitarian impact of autonomous weapons acknowledged the need for further action to

> Collaborate to promote the urgent negotiation of an international legally binding instrument, with prohibitions and regulations with regard to autonomy in weapons systems, in order to ensure compliance with International Law, including International Humanitarian Law, and ethical perspectives, as well as

> the prevention of the social and humanitarian impact that autonomy in weapons systems entail [. . .] (Belén Communiqué, 2023)

Such an initiative inevitably comes with both advantages and pitfalls. A new treaty can build on existing international law, including international humanitarian and human rights law, and specify protections with a granularity that has not yet been achieved in either the GGE on LAWS discussions or the national positions of states. A new treaty would also compartmentalise the legal regulation of militarised autonomy. This means that the negotiations would not have implications for the legal restrictions and regulations attached to *other* weapons and means of warfare. What the proponents of a new treaty strive for is the adoption of a robust set of rules under which the introduction and deployment of military applications with autonomous features is at the very least substantially delayed, until the risks are better understood and procedurally managed.

Pursuing the treaty route has its own challenges. Importantly, it is very unlikely that any of the main players currently possessing, developing, or intending to develop weapons with autonomous functions reliant on AI will join the treaty. As treaties do not bind states that are not parties to them (Vienna Convention on the Law of Treaties, art 34), the constraining effect of the regime may miss its 'targets'. It will also lead to a fragmentation of international law protections. And finally, the calls for a new treaty may inadvertently communicate something about existing law—that the proponents of a new treaty see existing legal protections as insufficient or inadequate to deal with the risks of autonomous weapons. This can be a dangerous narrative, as it may imply that existing treaties and customary law are less protective than they actually are.

If negotiations of a new treaty do indeed start, a key question on the table will be about the standard of responsibility that best reflects the risks of unintended engagements. One possibility here would be to consider the application of a principle of strict responsibility. As put forward by the Dutch Advisory Council on International Affairs and Advisory Committee on Public International Law, '[d]ue to the relatively high-risk nature of the use of semi-autonomous weapon systems in conflict situations, applying the principle of strict state responsibility, where responsibility is based solely on the damage caused, could be considered, particularly in the case of technical failures' (The Netherlands Advisory Council Report, 2022). While strict responsibility is not unprecedented in either domestic or international law (it is, for instance, a standard of responsibility in the 1972 Convention on International Liability for Damage Caused by Space Objects), it would constitute a radical departure from the way states have so far construed the scope of their responsibility for weapons malfunctions and other unintended system behaviours.

Alternatively, a new treaty could provide for negligence-based responsibility. Here, however, the drafters would need to engage with the difficult question of what should be 'due' in the design, development, testing, deployment, and review of weapons with autonomous functions. This may be an apt moment to integrate discussions that have so far taken place primarily in the framework of ethical principles—through the requirements of reliability, traceability, understanding, and predictability (Taddeo et al., 2021; MoD Ethical Principles Defence, 2022). For example, there may be a minimum requirement of what military commanders should know about the technical specifications of weapons systems under their control, or a requirement to intervene in the operation of a system in cases where a reasonable person would have had doubt about system behaviour that fails to translate the intent of the party to conflict.

What the calls for a new treaty demonstrate is a well-understood need for further specificity in how the law protects individuals and communities from the risks of militarised AI applications. For now, the factual uncertainty of the operation of weapons with autonomous features is compounded by a legal uncertainty. Mindful of this legal uncertainty, the UK House of Lords Report '*Proceed with Caution: Artificial Intelligence in Weapon Systems*' calls for 'a swift agreement of an effective international instrument on lethal AWS. It is crucial to develop an international consensus on what criteria should be met for a system to be compliant with IHL' (UK House of Lords AI in Weapons Report, 2023). Note that the report falls short of calling for a legally binding treaty. Instead, it speaks of an 'effective international instrument', which could also take the form of a non-binding agreement on the interpretation and application of existing law.

In addition to substantive clarity, a new treaty could also establish important procedural mechanisms for review and implementation of obligations. Conferences of states parties, reporting obligations, capacity-building arrangements, dispute settlement clauses providing consent to arbitration or the jurisdiction of the International Court of Justice could all strengthen compliance and ensure ongoing oversight over the AI military capabilities developed and deployed by states. These procedural mechanisms can be tailored to the needs of the area of regulation, with a careful balancing between transparency and confidentiality.

Given current geo-political dynamics, and the wide divergence of views between proponents and opponents of autonomy in weapons systems, the path of clarification of existing law may, if done meaningfully, be the best investment of resources at this stage. If substantive agreement is reached in the process, this can then pave the way for the adoption of a new treaty. It is to this regulatory route—clarification of existing law—that the next section turns.

Clarification of Existing International Law

International law, and in particular international humanitarian law, contains wide-ranging obligations binding parties to conflict in their choice of means and methods of warfare, and in the modalities of their military operations. As explained earlier, that international law applies to new weapons, including autonomous weapons, is uncontroversial. *How* international law applies to these weapons is, however, far from clear. Indiscriminate attacks are prohibited, but what would qualify as indiscriminate in the employment of autonomous weapons? What is the acceptable error rate for such systems (Simpson & Mueller, 2016)? And can it be considered *per se* indiscriminate to employ systems that one cannot fully understand to begin with? While these legal uncertainties exist in the law generally, that is, they exist in respect of all weapons systems, they present themselves with particular force in the sphere of autonomous functions because of the risks of relative unpredictability and unexplainability. As in other areas of technological development, such as cyberspace (Oxford Process Compendium), further clarification and specification of the law is needed.

This clarification process can happen through, among others, the development of national or regional positions on the application of international law to the use of AI in military operations, or statements made during inter-governmental discussions at the United Nations or other fora, or written or oral submissions made to international courts, tribunals, and other mechanisms. By establishing their views on particular obligations, states are publicising their practice and *opinio iuris* (acceptance of a particular practice as permitted, prohibited, or required by law), one of the constitutive elements of customary international law, and their subsequent practice relevant for the interpretation of treaties (under either art 31(3)(b) or 32 of the Vienna Convention on the Law of Treaties). Pixelated at present, the boundaries of relevant obligations can become more clearly defined through the convergence of such evidence of state understandings on the content of the law.

As states continue to clarify their understandings of the law, they must pay close attention to the interaction of obligations, including obligations from different legal areas. In the process of treaty interpretation, for instance, treaty provisions must be interpreted taking into account any relevant rules of international law applicable in the relations between the parties (Vienna Convention on the Law of Treaties, art 31(3)(c)). For instance, the Human Rights Committee in its General Comment No 36 on the right to life referred to the Paris Agreement in tying '[e]nvironmental degradation, climate change and unsustainable development' to the enjoyment of the right to life (Human Rights Committee, General Comment 36 on the right to life, para 62). The methodological hook allowing such interaction of obligations ensures that the system of international law speaks, to the extent possible, with 'one voice', integrating relevant rules into a cohesive system.

Similar arguments can be made in relation to obligations of relevance to the use of AI in military operations. Under Additional Protocol I, parties to conflict are under an obligation to take a number of 'feasible' precautions in attack—to do 'everything feasible' to verify that the objectives to be attacked are neither civilians nor civilian objects, and to take 'all feasible precautions' in the choice of means and methods of attack with a view to avoiding, and in any event to minimising, incidental loss of civilian life, injury to civilians and damage to civilian objects. But what does 'feasible' mean? Many determinants have been argued to feed into the notion of feasibility, including the capabilities possessed by a party to conflict, humanitarian considerations, and the risk to own forces (Quéguiner, 2006). Importantly, the scope of the 'feasible' also depends on legal considerations, including on the interaction of precautionary obligations with obligations from other regimes, such as human rights law (van Benthem, 2020) and environmental law (International Law Commission, Draft articles on Prevention of Transboundary Harm from Hazardous Activities, art 3).

Expectations under the feasibility standard may differ depending on the risks involved in a particular activity. In an area of particularly high risk—hazardous activities which pose a significant risk of transboundary environmental harm,—the International Law Commission identified a high customary threshold of diligence in the prevention of harm: '[t]he State of origin shall take *all appropriate measures* to prevent significant transboundary harm or at any event to minimize the risk thereof' (International Law Commission, Draft articles on Prevention of Transboundary Harm from Hazardous Activities, art 3). Not only does this principle apply to activities where the risk is already appreciated by states, but it also requires the taking of measures to 'identify activities which involve such a risk'. This example can be taken to stand for two propositions. One, under the narrower proposition, it would imply that the obligation to take precautions under Additional Protocol I must be interpreted in light of this principle when the deployment of an autonomous weapon would or may involve significant transboundary environmental harm. Two, under the broader proposition, it may be argued that the higher the potential risk, the higher the standard of diligence that can be expected of parties to conflict, whether such risk is environmental or of any other character. If the battlefield operation of weapons with autonomous functions is construed as a high-risk activity, then this would entail higher expectations both in understanding the risk and its possible effects, and in taking appropriate measures for its prevention or mitigation.

Unpacking how international law obligations interact will thus hold the key to many important interpretative debates on the content of what is 'due' in particular circumstances.

States regularly call for the clarification of elements of particular obligations, as such, or of their interaction with other rules of international law. If this process is taken seriously, the coming years will see an increasing detail and sophistication of national positions, statements and consensus reports of international organisations. So far, however, the clarification process has remained half-hearted at best, with areas of agreement between states either obviously skirting the issue of unintended civilian harm ('[a]utonomous weapon systems must not be *designed to*: (a) Target civilians or civilian objects, or to spread terror among the civilian population'—Draft Articles Autonomous Weapons, 2024) or being too general to provide any concrete guidance in the introduction of autonomous functions in the targeting of persons and objects ('[h]uman responsibility for decisions on the use of weapons systems must be retained since accountability cannot be transferred to machines'—GGE on Laws, Report, 2019, Guiding Principle (b)).

Clarifying the scope of existing international law obligations is of great importance, and it is the easiest step to make, given existing platforms for inter-governmental dialogue. Clarification can play at least three important functions. First, it would have a *preventive effect*, as these obligations, as specified, would form part of the training of the members of armed forces in charge of fielding the weapons. Knowing more about the technical specifications of autonomous weapons, the acceptable battlefield contexts for their deployment, the *indicia* of behaviour outside envisioned parameters would all be part of the repository of knowledge that human decision-makers need to consider in each attack. Second, legal clarification would ensure enhanced *certainty* over the circumstances where the fielding of a particular weapon as such, or in a particular battlefield context, would amount to a violation of the law. And third, especially at a time of geo-political tensions and attempted erosion of international institutions, this global clarification process can serve as an important *confidence-building measure* between states and the broader multi-stakeholder community.

Conclusion

State research and development of increasingly autonomous weapons systems, including systems incorporating AI, ushered in a decade of legal reckoning. The legal questions posed by these systems are timely, pressing, and complex. While the discussions in Geneva and New York may seem abstract, and in some ways overly sanitised, what animates them, at their core, is the concern over harming human beings. To speak of unpredictability risks is to speak of the potential mistaken targeting of a child; to speak of data biases is to speak of the potential discrimination, with lethal effects, against particular groups because of their skin colour, religion or gender; to speak of responsibility gaps is to speak of the recklessness that comes with feelings of impunity.

While the technologies discussed are new, the foundational legal questions exposed in the debates are not. For years, unintended engagements, such as mistakes in the identification of targets and weapon malfunctions, were neglected as the inevitability of 'things going wrong' in armed conflict (van Benthem, 2024a). The current debates between relevant stakeholders provide an opportunity to clarify and, if need be, revisit, legal attitudes towards intent, negligence, duties of care, responsibility, and the place of the human in decisions on the use of force. And because of the speed at which technologies are being infiltrated in military decision-making, this opportunity must be approached with a sense of urgency, and in earnest.

References

Advisory Council on International Affairs and Advisory Committee on Public International Law. (2022). Autonomous weapon systems: The importance of regulation and investment. Advisory Report 119.

Amoroso, D., & Tamburrini, G. (2021). In search of the 'human element': International debates on regulating autonomous weapons systems. *The International Spectator, 56*(1), 20.

Belén Communiqué. (2023). *Belén Communiqué of the Latin American and the Caribbean conference of social and humanitarian impact of autonomous weapons.*

Bode, I. (2024). Falling under the radar: The problem of algorithmic bias and military applications of AI. *Humanitarian Law and Policy.*

Boulanin, V. (2015). *Implementing Article 36 weapon reviews in the light of increasing autonomy in weapon systems.* SIPRI.

Boulanin, V., Peldán Carlsson, M., Goussac, N., & Davison, N. (2020). *Limits on autonomy in weapon systems: Identifying practical elements of human control.* SIPRI & ICRC Report.

Brehm, M. (2014). *Use of grad rockets in populated areas: What lessons from Gotovina?* EJIL:Talk!.

Chengeta, T. (2016). Accountability gap: Autonomous weapon systems and modes of responsibility in international law. *Denver Journal of International Law and Policy, 45*, 1.

Chengeta, T. (2022). Autonomous weapon systems and the inadequacies of existing law. *Journal of Law & Cyber Warfare, 8*(2), 105.

Copeland, D., Liivoja, R., & Sanders, L. (2023). The utility of weapons reviews in addressing concerns raised by autonomous weapon systems. *Journal of Conflict and Security Law, 28*(2), 285.

Draft Articles Autonomous Weapons. (2024). *Draft articles on autonomous weapon systems – prohibitions and other regulatory measures on the basis of international humanitarian law ("IHL"), submitted by Australia, Canada, Estonia, Japan, Latvia, Lithuania, Poland, the Republic of Korea, the United Kingdom, and the United States to the Group of Governmental Experts on Emerging Technologies in the Area of Lethal Autonomous Weapons System*. CCW/GGE.1/2024/WP.10.

European Court of Human Rights. (2010). *Stoyanovi v Bulgaria, Judgment.*

Feinberg, J. (1989). Autonomy. In J. Christman (Ed.), *The inner citadel: Essays on individual autonomy*. OUP.

Ferl, A.-K. (2024). Imagining meaningful human control: Autonomous weapons and the (de-)legitimisation of future warfare. *Global Society, 38*(1), 139.

Final Report. (2021). *Final report of the panel of experts on Libya established pursuant to Security Council resolution 1973 (2011)*. S/2021/229, 8 March 2021.

Goddard, K., Roudsari, A., & Wyatt, J. C. (2011). Automation bias: A systematic review of frequency, effect mediators, and mitigators. *Journal of the American Medical Informatics Association, 19*(1), 121.

Group of Governmental Experts on Lethal Autonomous Weapons Systems. (2019). *Report of the 2019 session, CCW/GGE.1/2019/3, 25 September, Annex IV – Guiding Principles.*

Harwood, S. (2024). A cybersystemic view of autonomous weapon systems. *Technological Forecasting & Social Change, 205.*

Hooker, L., & Vallance, C. (2025). *Concern over Google ending ban on AI weapons.* BBC News, 5 February.

Human Rights Committee. (2019). *General Comment 36 on the right to life.* CCPR/C/GC/36, 3 September.

Human Rights Watch. (2015).*Mind the gap: The lack of accountability for killer robots.* 9 April.

Human Rights Watch. (2022). *Ukraine: Mariupol theater hit by Russian attack sheltered hundreds: Serious concerns for civilians remaining in the city*. 16 March.

Human Rights Watch. (2024). *Submission to the United Nations Secretary-General on autonomous weapons systems*. 6 May.

ICRC. (2006). *A guide to the legal review of new weapons, means and methods of warfare: Measures to implement Art. 36 of additional protocol I of 1977.*

ICRC. (2021). *ICRC position on autonomous weapon systems*. 12 May.

International Court of Justice. (1996). *Legality of the threat or use of nuclear weapons, advisory opinion of 8 July*.

International Law Commission. (2001a). *Draft articles on prevention of transboundary harm from hazardous activities, with commentaries*.

International Law Commission. (2001b). *Responsibility of states for internationally wrongful acts*.

Joint Statement on Lethal Autonomous Weapons Systems. (2022). *First committee, 77th United Nations General Assembly, thematic debate – conventional weapons*. 21 October.

Kahneman, D., & Tversky, A. (1972). Subjective probability: A judgment of representativeness. *Cognitive Psychology, 3*(3), 430.

Molenkamp, A., Weerdesteijn, M., & Smeulers, A. (2024). *A playstation mentality to killing? Adverse psychological consequences in drone pilots and the stigmatization thereof in the military*. Armed Forces & Society.

Nadibaidze, A. (2024). Visuals of AI in the military domain: Beyond 'killer robots' and towards better images? In *Better images of AI blog*. 15 July.

NATO. (2020). *Glossary of terms and definitions, AAP-06 edition*.

Oxford Institute for Ethics, Law and Armed Conflict. (2022). *The Oxford process on international law protections in cyberspace: A compendium*.

Park, I. (2018). *The right to life in armed conflict*. OUP.

Quéguiner, J.-F. (2006). *Precautions under the law governing the conduct of hostilities* (p. 88). IRRC 793.

Russell, S. (2023). *Corrected oral evidence: Artificial intelligence in weapons systems, house of lords, artificial intelligence in weapons systems committee*. 15 June.

Saltini, A. (2025). *AI and nuclear strategy under Trump 2.0: What to expect*. Open Nuclear Network. 30 January.

Sarker, I. (2021). *Machine learning: Algorithms, real-world applications and research directions* (p. 2). Springer Nature Computer Science.

Schmitt, M. N. (2024). *Israel – Hamas 2024 symposium – The Gospel, Lavender, and the law of armed conflict*. Articles of War, 28 June.

Simpson, T., & Mueller, V. (2016). Just war and robots' killings. *The Philosophical Quarterly, 66*, 302.

Submission by the State of Palestine on Autonomous Weapons Systems. (2024). *Submitted by the State of Palestine to the UN Secretary-General pursuant to resolution 78/241 adopted by the General Assembly on 22 December 2023*. 24 May.

Taddeo, M., & Blanchard, A. (2022). A comparative analysis of the definitions of autonomous weapons systems. *Science and Engineering Ethics, 28*, 37.

Taddeo, M., McNeish, D., Blanchard, A., & Edgar, E. (2021). Ethical principles for artificial intelligence in national Defence. *Philosophy & Technology, 34*, 1707.

United Kingdom House of Lords, AI in Weapon Systems Committee. (2023). *Proceed with caution: Artificial intelligence in weapon systems*. 1 December.

United Kingdom Ministry of Defence. (June 2022). *Ambitious, safe, responsible: Our approach to the delivery of AI-enabled capability in Defence.*

United Nations. (2023). *Joint call by the United Nations Secretary-General and the President of the International Committee of the Red Cross for States to establish new prohibitions and restrictions on Autonomous Weapon Systems*. 5 October.

United Nations. (2024). *Lethal autonomous weapons systems, Report of the Secretary-General, A/79/88*. 1 July.

United Nations General Assembly. (2024). *Lethal autonomous weapons systems, A/RES/79/62*. 2 December.

United States Department of Defense. (2024). *CDAO and DIU launch new effort focused on accelerating DOD adoption of AI capabilities*. Release 11 December.

van Benthem, T. (2020). The redirection of attacks by defending forces. *International Review of the Red Cross, 102*(914), 875.

van Benthem, T. (2022). Exploring changing battlefields: Autonomous weapons, unintended engagements and the law of armed conflict. In *14th international conference on cyber conflict: Keep moving! (CyCon)* (p. 190).

van Benthem, T.. (2024a). *Symposium on military AI and the law of armed conflict: Responsible deployments of militarised AI – The power of information to prevent unintended engagements*. OpinioJuris. 2 April.

van Benthem, T. (2024b). *Targeting mistakes and other unintended engagements in armed conflict: The explosion at Al-Ahli Hospital in Gaza*. EJIL:Talk!.

Verdiesen, I., Santoni de Sio, F., & Dignum, V. (2021). Accountability and control over autonomous weapon systems: A framework for comprehensive human oversight. *Minds & Machines, 31*, 137.

Vienna Convention on the Law of Treaties. (1969). *United Nations, Treaty Series* (vol. 1155, p. 331). 23 May.

Working Paper Austria. (2024). *Working paper to the Group of Governmental Experts on Emerging Technologies in the area of lethal autonomous weapons systems*. CCW/GGE.1/2024/WP.4. 5 March.

Working paper on the 'human element'. (2025). *Submitted by Bulgaria, Denmark, Finland, France, Germany, Italy, Luxembourg, the Netherlands, Norway, Spain, and Sweden to the GGE on LAWS*. CCW/GGE.1/2025/WP.4. 21 August.

Artificial Intelligence and the Malicious Manipulation of Human Decision-Making

Gavin Pearson

Introduction

The technological capabilities of Artificial Intelligence (AI), including particularly Machine Learning (ML), are advancing at an unprecedented rate and have the potential to provide a wide range of public benefits. However, the technology can also be used, intentionally or unintentionally, to cause harm.

The capacity of individuals and groups[1] to achieve effective and timely decision-making and for organising (collective) action is crucial to navigating crises and complex challenges. This chapter focuses on the challenge posed by actors using AI in support of the deliberate manipulation of human understanding and decision-making, including the co-ordination of collective action.

The chapter takes the view that AI is fundamentally about algorithms and information (including the data and know-how used to create the algorithms) and that these may be used directly (e.g. in the creation of 'deep-fakes') or indirectly (e.g. in creation of scientific knowledge which is used to develop a manipulative information service).

[1] In this context groups can be both formal and informal, vary in size from small to very large and includes organisations and societies.

G. Pearson (✉)
Great Malvern, UK

M. Rangeley, N. Fairfax (eds.), *The Artificial Intelligence Revolution*,
https://doi.org/10.1007/978-3-032-11814-1_13

The Broad System

How the topic is framed (Hoffman, 2013) will implicitly constrain the analysis of the topic. To avoid framing the question too narrowly, the chapter starts with a broad systems view of the actors and their environment as a whole, as diving too rapidly to a specific issue (e.g. AI-created disinformation[2]) can skew understanding and interventions.

Malicious Actors and Blunderers

The capacity of individuals and groups to achieve effective and timely decision-making can be adversely impacted by a range of actors, not all of whom are malicious actors (often also called threat actors or adversaries). Indeed, well-intentioned and accidental actors can produce or spread information which can adversely impact on the decision-making capacity of individuals or groups. I follow Seger et al. (2020) in labelling these blunderers, and as noted by Seger et al. (2020) there is in reality a continuum of actors who engage in a range of activities (see Figure 3 in Seger et al., 2020).

It is useful to consider actors through the five component frame of: capability, intent, motivation, constraint, and opportunity (e.g. NCSC, 2023).

- Capability: the actor's ability to effectively make use of its resources to perform actions.
- Intent: what the actor intends to achieve by its actions.
- Motivation: that which motivates the actor to act.
- Constraint: the degree to which proportionality, ethical or legal considerations will constrain action.
- Opportunity: a feature of the environment or target (of action), which the action seeks to leverage or exploit.

The first four are actor centric, the fifth widens the view to take in both the target (of action) and the environment.

It is worth noting that much of the literature on disinformation assumes the intent of disinformation is to change beliefs and behaviours of the target individual or group, but that may well not be true. The *intent* may be to

[2] In this context, disinformation is information which intended to deceive. There is an extensive literature on disinformation, and on associated topics such as misinformation and malinformation. A significant portion of the literature uses the term disinformation to also cover misinformation and malinformation.

degrade, disrupt, or delay decision-making rather than to change belief (e.g. Harris (2023), Reeve (2023) and Operation Fortitude[3]).

Decision-Making and Organising Action

There is a rich literature on both individual and collective decision-making and the organisation of action (e.g. psychology, cognitive science, and organisational science). These include many different models covering both rational and naturalistic decision-making, as well as models for organisational decision-making and control: including but not limited to Alberts et al. (2001), Beautement (2012), Bosse et al. (2007), Boyd (1987), Endsley (1995), Hoffman (2013), Klein (1993), Pirolli and Card (2005), and Turalska et al. (2021). Many of these are very detailed and carefully nuanced, but they are consistent with an abstract model of the process which recognises a set of interacting activities:

- Information gathering;
- Information integration;
- Identification of options, their evaluation and decision-making;[4]
- Communication and co-ordination.[5]

Research in psychology (e.g. Kahneman, 2011) and decision-making (e.g. Klein, 1993) has demonstrated that human decision-making uses a range of short cuts to save time and energy, and has a well-known set of cognitive biases. These can offer *opportunities* to actors who wish to manipulate human decision-making. The importance attached to overcoming vulnerabilities, biases and achieving trust in AI algorithms highlights that there are also *opportunities* for the manipulation of AI algorithms used to support human decision-making.

The fact we use multiple short-cuts to save time, highlights the fact that the amount of *attention* that humans are able to apply to any particular issue is important. It has been argued that 'human attention' is the most critical

[3]Operation Fortitude, after the D-Day landings in 1944, aimed to delay the German decision to release reserve forces to counter the landings (e.g. Wikipedia).

[4]This is expressed in terms which are more akin to those used in rational decision-making as opposed to naturalistic decision-making. The intent is that it covers both, and thus in the simple match case of Recognition Primed Decision Making (Klein, 1993; Bosse et al., 2007) this stage may collapse into recognition that there is a previous pattern which can be repeated.

[5]This activity does not apply when considering individual decision-making at a single point in time, but is critical when considering any form of collective decision-making.

resource available within current socio-technical information systems (Pearson & Lemon, 2011).

The four activities can be considered a simple model of 'demand'; so I next consider 'supply'.

Information 'Supply'

There are many sources of information from our memories, face-to-face conversations, to books and the internet; so many that we cannot attend to them all.

The recognition of the importance of human attention as a finite resource has given rise to the realisation of the 'attention economy' (e.g. Davenport & Beck, 2001; Carpentier et al., 2023), and the design of technology which is aimed to keep us engaged and nudge us to act (e.g. Fogg, 2002). A major use of the data generated by our engagement with digital platforms is its exploitation to generate algorithms (AI) and their direct or indirect use in generating persuasive information, including creation of targeted prompts (e.g. Fogg, 2009; Zuboff, 2019; Carpentier et al., 2023). Obviously, capturing our attention can have the *effect* of *distracting* individuals from a particular decision-making activity (Reeve, 2023). Thus, blunderers use AI to inadvertently *distract* and a malicious actor might seek to use AI with the intent to *distract*.

We do not only attend to various sources when seeking to understand, decide and act; instead, we also attend to sources for a range of personal and social reasons. When we attend what we see is often 'pushed' at us (e.g. news or advertising): it is not only information we are seeking that we find and (inadvertently) gather. Repeated exposure to information impacts on its cognitive availability and thus can short circuit how critically we think about it (Kahneman, 2011). It is one of the *opportunities* a malicious actor may seek to exploit; with the potential that information will transition along the pathway from habituation, to normalisation and ultimately legitimation (Zuboff, 2019).

Seger et al. (2020) provides a useful categorisation of information sources, drawing on epistemology, as:

- Experience (including direct observation by sensor systems);
- Memory (including digital repositories);
- Reason (including specialised languages (e.g. mathematics) and tools); and
- Testimony (including statements and findings made by other people).

For a major decision-making problem in which different viewpoints and knowledge from multiple disciplines are important, the importance of 'testimony' as a critical source is clear. There is an extensive literature on the trust of testimonial knowledge which highlights how humans are inclined to trust those we perceive as similar to ourselves (e.g. Burger et al., 2004) and appeal to irrelevant authority (e.g. Damer, 2009): these are, obviously, *opportunities* which a malicious actor may exploit.

The volume of information is growing. Predictions vary but a doubling every 4 years is likely with a shift to more data existing at the edge of networks and never reaching a data centre (IRDS, 2021).

Intermediation

Given the volume of information and limited human attention intermediation is inevitable and indispensable (Acampa, 2024). In traditional domains such as TV news, the editorial staff play the key role in intermediation: selecting what information to disseminate and how to present it. In social media applications, (AI or AI-enabled) algorithms do the intermediation selecting what to notify[6] and the order of presentation. Shadbolt et al. (2019) identifies that there are three classes of social machines,[7] all of which involve digital intermediation (by algorithms) and are forms of online data markets.

A Simple System Model

Seger et al. (2020) includes a set of hypothetical crisis scenarios in which collective, and individual, decision-making and action are threatened. It is worth noting that in those with a malicious actor the 'target' was supported by exterior actors seeking to enhance the epistemic system.

Figure 1 present a simple model in which individual and collective decision-making and the organisation of action is occurring; it is engaging with exterior sources of information, which are intermediated (with some producers also being intermediators); there are a range of actors interfering with the process (from blunderers to malicious actors); and there are also exterior actors acting as epistemic supporters. The communication and co-ordination conducted

[6]The notifications often being designed (using data and trials) to prompts users to attend (see Fogg, 2009).

[7]A social machine is defined by Shadbolt et al. (2019) as an online socio-technical system, exploiting world wide web technology and human participation.

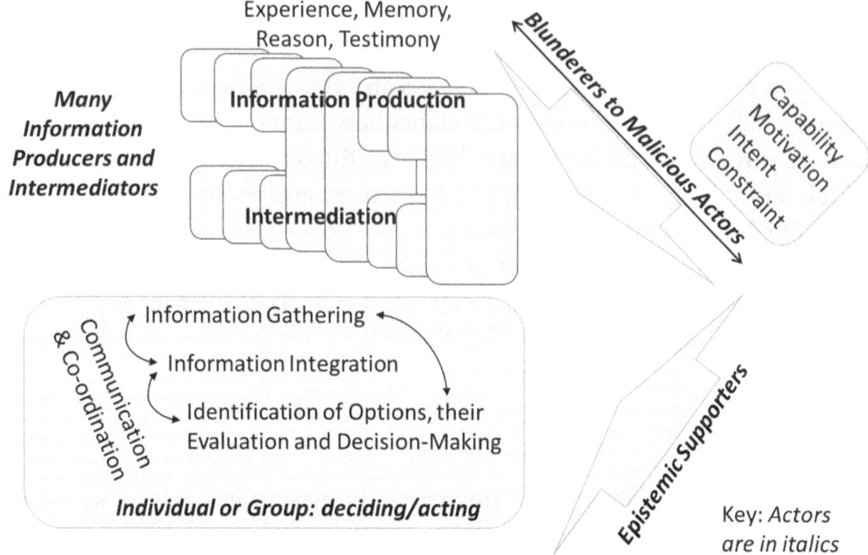

Fig. 1 Simple model of manipulation of human decision-making

within the group may also be using the same platforms as intermediators that they are using to access exterior information.

Intermediation Bridging Groups

Collective decision-making which bridges across a number of currently divided groups will involve intermediated digital channels. The way AI algorithms work as intermediators and the degree to which they act to bond existing groups or bridge between them is clearly important.

Peng and Grimmelmann (2024) explore the potential of bridging-based ranking to enhance bridging social capital. This naturally leads to the question of how could the evidence that this would be a cost-effective intervention be generated, and how would the intervention actually be implemented given the range of platforms and stakeholders (particularly, if there was evidence that such an intervention would result in a channel being less effective at holding audience attention).

Dissuasion and Deterrence

Deterrence, and dissuasion, are concerned with discouraging or persuading an actor to refrain from acting. Deterrence theory, which originally focused on deterrence of use of military power, has been applied to many domains including cyberspace. As noted in Nye (2017), deterrence, particularly nuclear deterrence, can be viewed very narrowly as being about providing a 'threat of punishment', with its associated requirements for attribution, signalling and credibility (Trujillo, 2014). The objective clearly being to reduce an actor's *motivation*.

Due to the perceived challenges associated with achieving attribution, cyberspace deterrence has often focused on 'denial by defence' (Nye, 2017) including both robustness and resilience to attacks. The objective of 'denial by defence' being to increase the *capability* required by the actor to achieve their *intent* and reduce the actor's *opportunity*.

Looking more broadly at approaches to dissuade an actor, highlights two additional approaches; namely, entanglement and norms of behaviour (Nye, 2017). Entanglement and norms effect an actor's *constraint* and *motivation*, including the *motivation* to acquire a *capability*, and may reduce *opportunity* (e.g. due to entanglement).

Deterrence by Defence: Information Assurance and Epistemic Security

Applying 'denial by defence' to human decision-making and action requires going beyond the traditional three pillars (Confidentiality, Availability, and Integrity) of 'Information Assurance' to consider Epistemic Security. Seger (2021) defines this as:

> Epistemic security [...] involves ensuring that we do in fact know what we know, that we can identify claims that are unsupported or not true, and that our information systems are robust to 'epistemic threats'.

In the context of a group decision-making and taking collective action, the concept of 'epistemic security' resonates with Donald Rumsfeld's famous statement about 'known knowns' and the Johari window (when applied to individual and group knowledge). Taking the deterrence perspective, highlights the need to consider both the robustness of epistemic security and its resilience (including the ability to minimise any disruption and recover quickly).

Seger et al. (2020) provides both methods for the analysis of epistemic security and a set of preliminary recommendations for achieving epistemic security.

AI-Enabled Manipulation: Now and Near Term

Many authors have written about AI-enabled threats. Brundage and Avin (2018) provides a well-grounded overview of the malicious use of AI focusing on the near term. Seger et al. (2020) built on this, through a set of workshops over 3 days involving a diverse set of attendees, with a particular focus on the threat to decision-making within modern society, and highlights the importance of epistemic security.

How AI is being used to influence democratic elections in the subject of on-going study. An example is the project on 'AI-enabled Influence Operations and Election Security' at the Centre for Emerging Technology and Security (CETaS) at the Alan Turing Institute; the project published three reports in 2024. The third of these (Stockwell et al., 2024) concluded that there are 'signs that AI-enabled threats began to damage the health of democratic systems globally this year'.

How misinformation and disinformation occur and spread has been studied by many, including Sedova et al. (2021a) and Innes (2020). Sedova et al. (2021b) presents a systematic examination of how AI can enhance disinformation operations, including:

- surveillance (including building high quality profiles of individuals and identification of wedge issues);
- creation of high volume and high quality content (including material designed to resonate with specific individuals and segments of the audience);
- misleading intermediation algorithms (to ensure message spreads to target individuals and enabling creation and methodical manipulation of groups);
- creation of high volume and quality social 'bots' using 'conversational AI' (enabling manipulative multi-turn conversations);[8] and
- audio and video impersonation.

[8]This issue is one of the five concerning technology trends in the CETaS technology outlook for 2025 (Janjeva et al., 2025).

Sedova et al. (2021b) does not specifically mention the potential to enhance disinformation operations by exploiting developments in affective computing; though the potential of exploiting real-time changes in stance is covered. Wang et al. (2022) highlights that, 'affective computing involves two distinct topics: emotion recognition and sentiment analysis'. Clearly the development and deployment of information systems and services, enabled by AI, which are able to sense, simulate and respond to an individual's emotional state will provide significant *capabilities* and *opportunities* to those who seek to manipulate human decision-making.

Caldwell et al. (2020) reports on an analysis of AI-enabled crime now and in the future, which involved a 2-day workshop with a diverse set of attendees. They employed a four-dimensional ranking scheme covering harm, required *capability*, criminal profit (which is equivalent to the achievement of *motivation*) and difficulty to defeat. The workshop identified 20 specific crimes of which 6 were rated as highly concerning: of these highly concerning crimes four were concerned with manipulation of human decision-making.

NCSC (2024) assessment of the near term impact of AI on the cyber threat states that:

- 'AI will primarily offer threat actors capability uplift in social engineering'.
- 'Threat actors [. . .] are already using AI to increase the efficiency and effectiveness of aspects of cyber operations, such as reconnaissance, phishing and coding. This trend will almost certainly continue to 2025 and beyond'.

The International Scientific Report on the Safety of Advanced AI (Mindermann et al., 2025) highlights four key risks from malicious use of AI: two of which are concerned with manipulating human decision-making.

Both Caldwell et al. (2020) and NCSC (2024) highlight that the majority of the most concerning developments in the malicious use of AI involve the manipulation of human decision-making.

Caldwell et al. (2020), Sedova et al. (2021b) and NCSC (2024) all highlight the improvements in tailored phishing which is enabled by reconnaissance. Caldwell et al. (2020), Sedova et al. (2021b) and Mindermann et al. (2025) highlight audio and visual impersonation, and AI-authored fake news. Caldwell et al. (2020) and Mindermann et al. (2025) also highlight the potential for identifying blackmail opportunities, which resonates with the scenario in Seger et al. (2020) concerned with creation of fake histories to enable individuals to be blackmailed or discredited.

As noted in the introduction to this chapter, AI and data are closely intertwined. Both Sedova et al. (2021b) and Stockwell et al. (2024) have specific recommendation aimed at ensuring academic research into disinformation has access to relevant data from media platforms.

The AI Revolution

The increasing instrumentation of systems has led to a growth in the availability of high fidelity 'digital shadows' and 'digital twins'. Martinescu (2023) defines a 'digital shadow' as, 'an evolving digital representation that mirrors the current state and behaviour of a physical entity or system'. He states that a 'digital twin' goes beyond this to 'integrate the virtual and physical realms by creating a real-time connection between the physical entity and its digital counterpart'.

Creating AI algorithms, whether engineered or trained, relies on the availability of suitable data, suitably skilled and experienced people, sufficient high performance computing and funding. This limits the ability to create effective AI to certain actors: though many more actors will have access to AI. For example, Wang et al. (2022) review of affective computing highlights the importance of suitable datasets to enable the development, testing and deployment of more effective AI-enabled affective computing models. The creation of the Foundation Models which underpin Generative AI require very large amounts of data and computing which seriously limits access (CMA, 2023).

There is evidence that Foundation Models, and Generative AI, are improving productivity across many sectors. Chui et al. (2023) assess that 'about 75 percent of the value that generative AI use cases could deliver falls across four areas: customer operations, marketing and sales, software engineering, and R&D'.

Providing Foundation Models with access to (exterior to the model) tools and chaining them together with other AI models, will enable the creation of 'AI agents' able to autonomously perform multiple sequential steps in order to achieve a high-level task or goal (DSIT, 2023).

Combining 'digital twins' and 'digital shadows' with 'AI agents' will lead to a transformation in the way in which systems are controlled with a shift from imperative to declarative control (IRDS, 2021). IRDS (2021) says:

> The problem with imperative control is that the systems we are creating—social, technical and economic—are too complex to be enumerated. No matter how much time we spend, we never can catch the corner cases, there are always exceptions and that means [...] inefficient use of resources, whether it is spectrum allocations or transportation capacity.
>
> Declarative management instead relies on systems that expose their operational state and control surfaces to goal seeking algorithms, such as reinforcement

learning. Instead of enumerating all the 'ifs' and 'thens', we can set goals to be achieved and let the system strive to maximize those goals. [. . .] A declarative system using unsupervised learning and autocorrelation could naively, blindly discover those correlations humans discount because it cannot presume it knows better.

Exploiting this shift will provide real-time insight into what is happening right now within a system and foresight as to how the system will respond to control interventions. Further, the use of 'AI agents' and a suitable 'digital shadow' enables research and development of new and improved means and ways to achieve desired ends.

The 'AI revolution' comes from application of these techniques to a growing range of domains. This is why the Alan Turing Institute 'is developing twins that are informed by the latest thinking in artificial intelligence (AI), with the aim of addressing grand societal challenges and generating tangible, real-world benefits'.[9] The short story, 'a model peace' in Singer and Cole (2021) present a fictional view of a future, illustrating the interaction of 'digital shadows', AI and human decision-making.

In summary, the AI revolution emerges from the ability to create and use Foundation Models, digital twins/shadows, and AI agents.

The AI Revolution and Human Decision-making

Human decision-making is a form of complex adaptive system. Thus to develop a high fidelity 'digital shadow' of human decision-making, and the associated digital infrastructure, it is vital to be able to be able to stimulate it and observe its reaction. Thus, unlike in Boyd's (1987) famous Observe-Orientate-Decide-Act loop where the process starts with observation, understanding complex adaptive systems begins with stimulation of the system; as is represented in the Probe-Sense-Respond and Act-Sense-Respond cycles in the Cynefin framework[10] for responding to complex and chaotic problems.

As noted above, both Sedova et al. (2021b) and Stockwell et al. (2024) have specific recommendation aimed at ensuring academic research into disinformation has access to data from media platforms. But these are about access to data to enable passive observation of the information environment. Understanding the completeness of and intent behind observed stimuli, and

[9]As stated at https://www.turing.ac.uk/research/harnessing-power-digital-twins (Jan 2024).

[10]https://thecynefin.co/about-us/about-cynefin-framework/.

trying to infer the capability of a malicious actor's 'digital shadow', from passive observation will be challenging.

Ethical considerations are, for good reasons, liable to constrain, at least the pace of, development of high fidelity 'digital shadows' of particular human groups and individuals. However, many malicious actors operate within a different ethical framework which would enable them to introduce stimuli designed to improve their digital shadows (subject to sufficient resources and access). Feldstein (2019) identifies the significant opportunities offered by current and near term AI to authoritarian surveillance states for social control.

Zuboff (2019) paints a picture in which there is an 'instrumentarian'[11] benefit from being able to gather information from human activity online, in the physical world (e.g. location data, vehicle operation) and at the boundary (e.g. eye tracking and emotional response),[12] and introduce stimuli as part of behaviour experiments, in order to improve the prediction of behaviour in response to stimuli. Thus giving rise to the 'instrumentarian' ability to engage in human behaviour modification via a mixture of (1) nudge, (2) herding via environment modification, and (3) conditioning (achieved via an intricate set of reinforcements of desired action) (Zuboff, 2019).

These factors mean that, technologically advanced authoritarian surveillance states are the actors best placed to seize the opportunity offered by the ubiquitous surveillance of human decision-making and behaviour to develop Foundation Models, Digital Shadows and AI agents, providing them with the capability to control their society's epistemic structures, develop information manipulation capabilities that others can only observe from the outside, and achieve instrumentarian power. Such a state when acting as a malicious actor has the potential to significantly over match a target's epistemic security (subject to any constraint on access to the target's epistemic system).

Impact of Falling Behind Malicious Actor Capability

The concept of Campaign Authority is concerned with the perceived legitimacy of a military force to conduct a campaign and is assessed across four dimensions: mandate; consent of those affected; the manner in which the campaign is conducted; and the delivery of expectations. It can be adapted to consider the perceived legitimacy of any collective action.

---

[11] Zuboff (2019) compares and contrasts 'instrumentarian' power with totalitarian power; identifying these as two very different forms of social control.

[12] Zuboff does appears to miss including the opportunity provided by the monitoring of brain activity.

Consider two groups engaged in a confrontation or conflict along political, diplomatic, information, military, legal, financial and/or economic axes. It is clear that if one of these is a technologically advanced authoritarian surveillance state it has the potential to significantly bolster the perceived legitimacy of its activity (its Campaign Authority) and undermine that of its opponent. Sadeghi and Blachez (2025) and the American Sunlight Project (2025) describe evidence of how the deliberate production of information at scale can manipulate Foundation Models: providing real world examples of the challenges highlighted, as future concerns in 2020, in the State Fake News and Epistemic Babble scenarios in Seger et al. (2020).

Technologically advanced authoritarian surveillance states have the potential to degrade, and potentially overwhelm, the decision-making capability of target groups by manipulating their supply of exterior information (e.g. Reeve, 2023), including the manufacturing of incidents: such incidents may be external to the target or may target key workers within the group.[13] When considering the targeting of key workers, the objective may be to undermine their ability to contribute (e.g. by spreading disinformation about them to others), or it may be aimed at exploiting them for influence, espionage, subversion, or gain.

Bostrom and Cirković (2008) characterise a Global Catastrophic Risk (GCR) as a hypothetical future event that could significantly damage human well-being on a global scale. Seger (2023) argues that that epistemic insecurity acts as a risk amplifier, exacerbating other GCRs making them more likely to occur and/or be of greater severity. Indeed, Seger (2023) argues that epistemic insecurity should be considered a priority GCR cause area, and the analysis presented here would agree with that.

Conclusion

The coming AI revolution will be enabled by access to data and the ability to develop Foundation Models, Digital Twins/Shadows, and AI agents. Developing these for the complex adaptive process of collective human decision-making will (at least) significantly benefit from, and may require, co-ordinated observation of online activity, activity in the physical world and

[13]It is worth remembering that any individual is a member of multiple organisational and social groups, and thus manipulation of a key worker can intentionally exploit their other group memberships.

human cognitive states. This will require the ability to conduct experiments investigating the response to stimuli.

Technologically advanced authoritarian surveillance states are the actors best placed to seize the opportunity offered by ubiquitous surveillance, and the capability to experiment. Enabling them to develop Foundation Models, Digital Shadows, and AI agents. Providing them with the capability to control their society's epistemic structures, develop information manipulation capabilities that others can only observe from the outside, and achieve instrumentarian power.[14] Such a state when acting as a malicious actor has the potential to significantly over match other group's epistemic security and be able to significantly manipulate group decision-making. Further, the potential for future epistemic insecurity should be considered a priority global catastrophic risk.

References

Acampa, S. (2024). *From Dezinformatsiya to disinformation: A critical analysis of strategies and effect on the digital public sphere*. Springer.

Alberts, D. S., et al. (2001). *Understanding information age warfare*. CCRP Publication Series, Department of Defense Command and Control Research Program.

American Sunlight Project. (February 2025). *A pro-Russia content network foreshadows the automated future of info ops*. https://www.americansunlight.org/research

Beautement, P. (2012). The defence enterprise is more than just a supermarket chain. *RUSI Defence Systems, 14*(3).

Bosse, E., et al. (2007). *Concepts, models, and tools for information fusion*. Artech House.

Bostrom, N., & Cirković M. M. (2008). *Global catastrophic risks*.

Boyd, J. R. (1987). *A discourse on winning and losing*. Unpublished briefing.

Brundage, M., & Avin, S. (2018). *The malicious use of artificial intelligence: Forecasting, prevention, and mitigation*.

Burger, J. M., et al. (2004). What a coincidence! The effects of incidental similarity on compliance. *Personality and Social Psychology Bulletin (PSPB)—Sage Journals, 30*(1). https://doi.org/10.1177/01461672032588

Caldwell, M., Andrews, J. T. A., Tanay, T., et al. (2020). AI-enabled future crime. *Crime Science, 9*, 14. https://doi.org/10.1186/s40163-020-00123-8

Carpentier, C. L., et al. (2023). *Attention economy*. United Nations Economist Network.

[14]See Zuboff (2019) for a definition of intrumentarianism.

Chui, M., et al. (2023). *The economic potential of generative AI: The next productivity frontier*. McKinsey.

Competition & Markets Authority (CMA). (2023). *AI foundation models: Initial report*. https://assets.publishing.service.gov.uk/media/65081d3aa41cc300145612c0/Full_report_.pdf

Damer, E. T. (2009). *Attacking faulty reasoning: A practical guide to fallacy-free arguments* (6th ed.). Wadsworth Cengage Learning.

Davenport, T. H., & Beck, J. C. (2001). *The attention economy: Understanding the new currency of business*. Harvard Business Review Press.

Department for Science, Innovation and Technology (DSIT). (October 2023). *Capabilities and risks from frontier AI: A discussion paper on the need for further research into AI risk*. https://www.gov.uk/government/publications/frontier-ai-capabilities-and-risks-discussion-paper

Endsley, M. R. (1995). Toward a theory of situation awareness in dynamic systems. *Human Factors Journal, 37*(1), 32–64. https://doi.org/10.1518/001872095779049543

Feldstein, S. (2019). The road to digital unfreedom: How artificial intelligence is reshaping repression. *Journal of Democracy, 30*(1).

Fogg, B. J. (2002). Persuasive technology: Using computers to change what we think and do. *Ubiquity, 2002*(December), 5. https://doi.org/10.1145/764008.763957

Fogg, B. J. (2009). *A behavior model for persuasive design*. Stanford. https://behaviordesign.stanford.edu/resources/fogg-behavior-model

Harris, K. R. (2023). *Beyond belief: On disinformation and manipulation. Erkenntnis (journal)*. Springer.

Hoffman, R. (2013). An integrated model of macrocognitive work and trust in automation. In *Trust and autonomous systems: Papers from the 2013 AAAI spring symposium*.

Innes, M. (2020). *Soft facts and digital behavioural influencing after the 2017 terror attacks*. Centre for Research and Evidence on Security Threats (CREST).

International Roadmap for Devices and Systems (IRDS)™. (2021). *Systems and architectures*. IEEE. https://irds.ieee.org/images/files/pdf/2021/2021IRDS_SA.pdf

Janjeva, A., et al. (2025). *CETaS outlook: Emerging technology trends to watch in 2025: Expert analysis*. Centre for Emerging Technology and Security (CETaS), Alan Turing Institute, Online article: https://cetas.turing.ac.uk/publications/cetas-outlook-emerging-technology-trends-watch-2025. Accessed January 2025.

Kahneman, D. (2011). *Thinking, fast and slow*.

Klein, G. A. (1993). *A Recognition-Primed Decision (RPD) model of rapid decision making. Chapter 6 in decision making in action: Models and methods*. Ablex Publishing Corporation.

Martinescu, L. (2023). *Exploring the concepts of digital twin, digital shadow, and digital model*. Oxford Insights. https://oxfordinsights.com/insights/exploring-the-concepts-of-digital-twin-digital-shadow-and-digital-model/

Mindermann, S., et al. (2025). *International AI safety report: The international scientific report on the safety of advanced AI*. DSIT.

National Cyber Security Centre (NCSC). (October 2023). *The fundamentals and basics of cyber risk: components of threat*. https://www.ncsc.gov.uk/collection/risk-management/the-fundamentals-and-basics-of-cyber-risk

National Cyber Security Centre (NCSC). (January 2024). *The near-term impact of AI on the cyber threat*. https://www.ncsc.gov.uk/report/impact-of-ai-on-cyber-threat

Nye, J. S., Jr. (2017). Deterrence and dissuasion in cyberspace. *International Security, 41*(3), 44–71. https://doi.org/10.1162/ISEC_a_00266

Pearson, G., & Lemon, J. (2011). *Vision and critical challenges in exploiting distributed data for distributed decision making*. DSTL/CP54993. SPIE DSS conference.

Peng, K., & Grimmelmann, J. (2024). *Rescuing counterspeech: A bridging-based approach to combating misinformation*. Cornell University. Preprint.

Pirolli, P., & Card, S. (2005). The sensemaking process and leverage points for analyst technology as identified through cognitive task analysis. In *Conference: Proceedings of international conference on intelligence analysis*.

Reeve, Z. (2023). *Misleading a group to ineffectiveness*. Centre for Research and Evidence on Security Threats (CREST).

Sadeghi, M., & Blachez, I. (March 2025). *The infection of western AI chatbots by a Russian Propaganda Network*. https://www.newsguardtech.com/wp-content/uploads/2025/03/March2025PravdaAIMisinformationMonitor.pdf

Sedova, K., et al. (2021a). *AI and the future of disinformation campaigns. Part 1: The RICHDATA framework*. Center for Security and Emerging Technology (CSET).

Sedova, K., et al. (2021b). *AI and the future of disinformation campaigns. Part 2: A threat model*. Center for Security and Emerging Technology (CSET).

Seger, E. (2021). *The greatest security threat of the post-truth age*. BBC Website. https://www.bbc.com/future/article/20210209-the-greatest-security-threat-of-the-post-truth-age

Seger, E. (2023). Should epistemic security be a priority GCR cause area? In *Intersections, reinforcements, Cascades: Proceedings of the 2023 Stanford existential risks conference*. The Stanford Existential Risks Initiative.

Seger, E., et al. (2020). *Tackling threats to informed decision making in democratic societies: Promoting epistemic security in a technologically-advanced world*. Alan Turing Institute. https://www.turing.ac.uk/sites/default/files/2020-10/epistemic-security-report_final.pdf

Shadbolt, N., et al. (2019). *The theory and practice of social machines*. Springer.

Singer, P. W., & Cole, A. (2021). *Stories from tomorrow: Exploring new technology through useful fiction*. Ministry of Defence., https://www.gov.uk/government/publications/stories-from-the-future-exploring-new-technology-through-useful-fiction

Stockwell, S., et al. (2024). *AI-enabled influence operations: Safeguarding future elections*. Centre for Emerging Technology and Security (CETaS), Alan Turing Institute.

Trujillo, C. (2014). *The limits of cyberspace deterrence*. Joint Force Quarterly.

Turalska, M., et al. (2021). Optimizing the efficiency of collective decision making in groups. In *Artificial intelligence and machine learning for multi-domain operations applications III* (Vol. 11746, p. 117460L). International Society for Optics and Photonics.

Wang, Y., et al. (2022). *A systematic review on affective computing: Emotion models, databases, and recent advances*. Information Fusion.

Zuboff, S. (2019). *The age of surveillance capitalism: The fight for a human future at the new frontier of power*. Profile Books.

Rewiring Defence for the Age of AI

James Lawson

The urgent need for artificial intelligence (AI) adoption in defence is the focus of this chapter. The core thesis is that AI is not merely another technological advance, but rather a fundamental shift in how military capabilities must be conceived, developed, deployed and differentiated. Just as software has "eaten the world" across commercial sectors over the past decade, transforming industries from retail to transportation, so too must defence embrace this revolution—or risk strategic irrelevance.

History offers a stark warning through the "Ten-Year Rule"—Britain's post–World War I assumption that no major war would occur for a decade, leading to dangerous complacency in military preparedness. Today, we risk making an analogous mistake by underestimating the transformative impact of AI on warfare or failing in delivery of AI capabilities, even as Russia's invasion of Ukraine shows the return of state-on-state conflict to Europe and China's military modernisation accelerates.

The arguments presented draw primarily from the United Kingdom's experience, while incorporating relevant examples and parallels from the United States, NATO and European Union. This focus on defence also offers insights applicable across government, as many of the institutional and procurement challenges mirror those faced in other areas of the public sector. However, defence faces unique urgency given its fundamental role in national security,

J. Lawson (✉)
Adam Smith Institute, London, UK
e-mail: james@adamsmith.org

M. Rangeley, N. Fairfax (eds.), *The Artificial Intelligence Revolution*,
https://doi.org/10.1007/978-3-032-11814-1_14

the increasing failure to deter our adversaries from conflict, and the increasing integration of AI capabilities by potential adversaries to leapfrog us.

This AI revolution manifests most visibly in unmanned systems, which are rapidly changing the economics and conduct of warfare. Yet, current autonomous systems are only the beginning, providing basic capabilities that will be dramatically enhanced by greater application of AI. More broadly, AI will prove transformative across all military domains, on land, in the air, or at sea, as well as in cyber security, electronic warfare and space systems. Another key conclusion is that hardware increasingly serves as a commodity platform for software-defined capabilities that can be rapidly upgraded and adapted.

However, significant barriers impede this transformation. Military institutions and procurement systems are still oriented around traditional hardware platforms, with software often treated as an afterthought. Defence budgets have been constrained while incumbent prime contractors lack software expertise. Perhaps most challengingly, sclerotic acquisition processes often struggle to accommodate the rapid iteration central to AI development, or to prioritise these opportunity areas in the first place.

This chapter explores these challenges and opportunities, offering some recommendations for accelerating AI adoption in defence. The stakes could not be higher—the nation that most effectively harnesses AI for military capabilities could gain decisive strategic advantages. To maintain credible deterrence and battlefield superiority, defence organisations must overcome institutional inertia and transform for the AI age. The alternative risks repeating the tragedy of the Ten-Year Rule—with potentially catastrophic consequences for national security.

The path forward requires rethinking traditional approaches to military capability development, embracing software-centricity, reforming procurement processes and creating strategic partnerships with a new breed of technology firms. While the challenges are significant, they are not insurmountable. With sufficient urgency and the right reforms, defence can successfully navigate this revolutionary transition.

Mounting Threats Despite Defence De-investment

The parallels between Britain's post–World War I complacency and our current strategic predicament are increasingly stark. Just as the "Ten-Year Rule" reflected a dangerous wishful thinking about future threats, today we risk catastrophically underestimating the pace and scale of change in military affairs—particularly regarding artificial intelligence.

The "Ten-Year Rule" was Britain's planning assumption that no major war would occur within the upcoming decade. It resulted in a policy of de-investment, which not only left Britain ill-prepared for the ensuing conflict but also made war more likely. Having sufficient military capabilities, both in terms of quantity (munitions, troops, etc.) and quality (particularly technological advantage) has a deterrence effect, while inadequacies send the opposite signal.

With the end of the Cold War, dubbed as "the end of history" (Fukuyama, 1989) as Western liberal democracies triumphed, we have pursued three decades of effective de-investment in defence. NATO troop numbers fell between 35% and 65%, across member nations since 1990 (Armstrong, 2022). Spending as a percentage of GDP also collapsed across NATO, with the UK, for example, halving its relative defence budget from 4% to around 2% of GDP. For example, successive UK governments have pledged to increase the defence commitment to 2.5% of GDP, but this has been perennially postponed. It also leaves limited discretionary funds for new capabilities, as most is committed to existing programmes, including Britain's nuclear weapons systems.

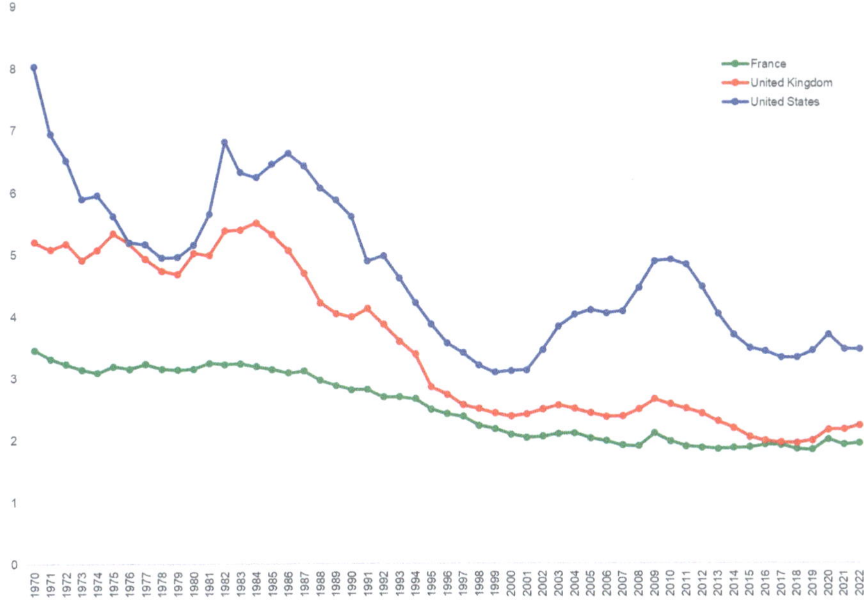

Analysis of World Bank Data, Military expenditure (of GDP)

The global security environment has deteriorated markedly since the early 1990s. Russia's invasion of Ukraine has now stretched beyond 1000 days, becoming a grinding war of attrition that has shattered the post–Cold War European security order. The decline in defence spending is just one metric of our dis-investment. The Ukraine conflict has also demonstrated how quickly apparently decisive advantages in conventional military capability can be eroded by technological innovation and asymmetric warfare. Ukrainian forces have achieved remarkable successes against Russian hardware through innovative deployment of commercial technologies and autonomous systems. So, for NATO to keep an edge, it must also out innovate.

A concerning alignment is emerging between revisionist powers—Russia, China, Iran and North Korea—who share both an opposition to the Western-led international order and a determination to rapidly advance their military capabilities. While their capabilities have lagged NATO's historically, these nations operate without the ethical constraints that guide Western AI development and see military technological advancement as crucial to achieving their strategic aims. Rather than trying to match decades of Western investment in traditional platforms, they are trying to leapfrog straight to next-generation capabilities, particularly in autonomous systems and AI-enabled warfare.

The failures of conventional deterrence today mirror Britain's misplaced confidence in the 1930s. After years of underinvestment justified by the Ten-Year Rule, Britain found itself scrambling to rearm as threats materialised faster and more existentially than predicted. Today, despite maintaining conventional forces, the West faces a similar crisis of deterrence as potential adversaries develop ways to circumvent our traditional advantages through new technologies and doctrines.

The integration of artificial intelligence into military systems is perhaps the most significant shift in warfare since the advent of nuclear weapons. The nations that master AI-enabled warfare will gain decisive advantages in speed of action, scale of operations and cost effectiveness that may prove impossible to counter through conventional means alone. Our adversaries understand this and are racing to develop these capabilities, often unconstrained by the ethical frameworks and procurement processes that often slow Western military innovation.

The West must therefore embrace a fundamental transformation of its defence capabilities or risk strategic irrelevance. Our current approach to military modernisation, based on slow cycles of requirements definition and platform development, is dangerously inadequate for an era where software-defined capabilities can be rapidly developed and deployed.

The lessons of the Ten-Year Rule remind us that strategic advantages and their deterrence effect can rapidly be lost through the perilous combination of sustained de-investment, institutional inertia and misplaced assumptions about the pace of change. We cannot afford to repeat this mistake in the age of artificial intelligence.

The Importance of Applying AI Cross the Economy of Defence

This argument for prioritising artificial intelligence is ultimately premised upon its ability to rapidly enable orders of magnitude capability gains. In the process, if the promise of AI is realised, it will disrupt current planning assumptions around the fighting power of different militaries. Hence the integration of artificial intelligence into military systems is perhaps the most profound transformation in defence capabilities since the advent of the nuclear age.

Fortunately, at senior levels, many senior Generals and political stakeholders appear to appreciate the generational importance of AI. For example, General Sir Roly Walker, then newly appointed Chief of the General Staff (CGS) of the British Army, emphasised at his 2024 RUSI Land Warfare Conference that artificial intelligence is a "big, bold bet" (Walker, 2024) for defence modernisation. Despite resource constraints, in budgets, personnel and equipment available, CGS explained his ambition to increase fighting power (the headline metric for the total capability of his army). His goal could be achieved through the deployment of AI by enabling his forces to "sense twice as far, decide in half the time, deliver effects over double the distance with half as many munitions" (Ibid.). Similarly, General Sir Jim Hockenhull, the Commander of Strategic Command, which manages cross-cutting capabilities across the different military services (Navy, Army and Airforce as well as Special Forces), described AI as "a fundamental challenge to so many aspects of our lives" and offering "significant opportunity for Defence, and not a little challenge too" (Hockenhull, 2023).

While at the 2024 Washington Summit, NATO governments recognised the importance of AI in their public declaration. NATO's intent is "to maintain our technological edge, including through experimentation and more rapid adoption of emerging technologies, and through digital transformation", promising to "implement our revised Artificial Intelligence Strategy" (NATO, 2024).

Broad declarations and strategy documents signal a growing understanding that AI is not merely an enhancement to existing capabilities, but a fundamental transformation in how military power is generated and applied. However, strategy documents and declarations are easy to deliver, and don't necessarily translate into implementation. Similar declarations have been made about other technological trends, from the adoption of digital technologies more broadly, through to the use of quantum computing. Moreover, the Adam Smith Institute found an AI "Rhetoric-Reality" gap, which less than 1% of contract awards by volume or spend, delivering upon AI in Defence (Marlow, 2024).

The real-world applications for AI are vast, helping readily reassure the case that the technology will be transformative to fighting power, if adopted at scale. The military's relatively unique position as a self-contained organisation—effectively operating as a mini-state with its own healthcare, logistics and economic systems—provides countless opportunities for AI application across both operational and support functions. However, just as hospitals are ultimately measured on their clinical outcomes over just administrative metrics, the military's primary focus in deploying AI must remain on enhancing battlefield capabilities and maintaining strategic advantage.

This is not to diminish the value of AI's use in the "back office", supporting functions and the wider internal economy of Defence, where of course it ought to be applied too. With AI increasingly transforming sectors of the civilian economy, such changes are obvious, and militaries can more readily follow a well-trodden path by emulating the private sector, implementing Commercial-off-the-shelf (COTs) AI solutions.

AI can be used to transform routine processes across the internal economy of a military. Financial systems can autonomously process thousands of transactions, while predictive maintenance algorithms analyse sensor data to forecast equipment failures. Personnel systems ought to better match service members to roles, as adaptive training platforms provide personalised learning experiences. Throughout the defence enterprise, AI should enhance efficiency by processing vast amounts of data that would overwhelm human operators.

Equipment maintenance exemplifies how AI enhances military readiness through predictive capabilities. Modern military platforms generate vast amounts of sensor data which, properly analysed, can forecast potential failures before they occur. This shift from reactive to predictive maintenance dramatically improves operational availability while reducing costs. The impact extends throughout the defence logistics network, as AI systems optimise spare parts inventories and maintenance schedules across multiple bases and platforms simultaneously.

The human dimension of defence similarly benefits from AI enhancement. Personnel management, traditionally relying heavily on human judgment and experience, now could use AI to better match service members' capabilities with operational needs. Training systems should adapt to individual learning patterns, providing personalised experiences that maintain consistency while accommodating different learning styles. This should prove particularly valuable for technical roles where traditional training approaches often struggle to scale effectively.

Recruitment and retention, which have proven consistently troublesome for NATO forces in recent years, should also be enhanced with AI. Armed forces could better find potential joiners and encourage them to sign up. Simultaneously, it ought to enable early identification of potential leavers and interventions—though HR optimisation will only go so far, and there are a host of wider issues around compensation and promotion paths to address in parallel.

Logistics similarly is a complex management challenge in any organisation, with success or failure often determining operational outcomes, where defence should look to emulate private sector colleagues. AI systems would excel at coordinating these intricate networks, ensuring timely delivery of supplies while adapting to changing operational requirements, environmental conditions and threat levels. AI should prove particularly valuable in last-mile resupply planning, where multiple competing constraints must be balanced in real-time under potentially hostile conditions.

Intelligence analysis is another area ripe for AI to augment humans. Modern military operations generate unprecedented volumes of information which must be rapidly processed and analysed. AI systems can accelerate this process by automatically categorising and cross-referencing intelligence reports, finding patterns and connections that inform human analysis. This capability proves particularly valuable when processing captured enemy material, where rapid analysis can provide crucial tactical advantages. Similarly, when processing unstructured and complex data, like satellite and synthetic aperture radar imagery, AI can help human analysts rapidly search through the data for targets of interest.

Yet these supporting applications, while valuable, represent merely the foundation of military effectiveness. The true revolutionary potential of AI lies in its ability to transform battlefield warfighting capabilities. Modern militaries must remain focused on this primary mission—maintaining credible deterrence and, if necessary, prevailing in conflict. It is in frontline operational domains where AI promises the most profound impact on military power.

AI Across Front-line "Kill Chains" and Targeting

John Boyd, an American fighter pilot, famously developed the decision-making model of the "OODA loop" to summarise how militaries can gain advantage in combat—Observe, Orient, Decide and Act. The concept suggests that the military force that can cycle through this decision-making process faster than their opponent will win. A force that can consistently observe the battlefield, make sense of what they see, reach decisions and act more rapidly than their adversary will dominate their adversary.

A more recent way to consider the same process is through the concept of the "kill chain"—the sequence of Sense, Decide and Effect. Forces must first detect and track targets (sense), determine the appropriate response (decide) and then deliver the chosen effect, whether lethal or non-lethal. The speed and accuracy with which forces can execute this chain directly impacts their battlefield effectiveness. Modern militaries aim to compress these targeting chains, reducing the time from initial detection to eventual effect from hours or days to minutes or seconds. Combining multiple different sensors, deciders and effectors in harmony can be thought of as a "kill web" or "targeting enterprise".

Both frameworks (OODA loops and kill chains) help us highlight why artificial intelligence has such profound military potential on the battlefield itself. AI systems excel at rapidly processing vast amounts of sensor data, identifying patterns and anomalies, making rapid decisions based on complex criteria and controlling precision effects. Applied across the OODA loop or kill chain, AI can dramatically accelerate the speed of military operations while simultaneously improving accuracy and reducing the cognitive burden on human operators—a clear transformation of core fighting power.

NATO forces recognise five core domains, environments or areas of operations: Maritime, Land, Air, Space, Cyber/Electronic. Historically, operations in these domains have either not existed (Space and Cyber/Electronic) or have been managed as siloed independent entities, with distinct navies, armies and air forces. Each domain has its own kill chains, with opportunities for AI to enhance each. While entities like the UK's Strategic Command exist to break down these silos, and coordinate activities across the domains, for greater aggregate effect across the kill web (an AI opportunity in itself), the five domains and their most vital kill chains provide a useful construct to rapidly consider the full extent of AI's significance across the battlefield. Consider the array of signal processing and other reconnaissance activities in the "sense" or "observe and orient" stages of a battlefield interaction, where AI can help identify threats, aid decision makers and enable them to take action.

Cyber security is a domain where AI capabilities have arguably already started to achieve significant maturity, though largely through the adoption of commercial technologies rather than dedicated military development. The tools and techniques developed for enterprise network defence have proven readily adaptable to military applications, enabling faster detection and response to network threats. However, this relatively mature implementation represents more of a fortunate accident than a strategic choice, and points to the even greater potential possible through purposeful military AI development. Generative AI will become increasingly ubiquitous in the development of malware, identification of vulnerability and detection avoidance.

In electromagnetic warfare, AI systems show remarkable potential for analysing complex signal environments in real time. Cyber and electronic warfare are generally bundled together, but the latter has its own significance and applications. It is also an area where NATO's adversary seems to have invested disproportionately. Advanced electronic warfare systems could automatically detect, categorise and counter enemy emissions across the electromagnetic spectrum. This capability becomes increasingly vital as military operations depend more heavily on electromagnetic spectrum access for communications, navigation and weapons guidance. Securing spectrum advantage while denying it to adversaries may prove decisive in future conflicts, with Ukraine providing the case study in how our adversaries have arguably gained a lead in the mass deployment of EW systems and experimentation with AI.

In the maritime domain, AI holds immense promise for transforming critical applications like anti-submarine warfare through enhanced acoustic signal processing. Future systems could detect, classify and track undersea threats at significantly greater ranges and with higher confidence than traditional methods. Algorithms could differentiate submarine signatures from biological sounds and environmental noise with unprecedented accuracy, potentially multiplying detection ranges—a key increase in fighting power. This capability holds strategic significance beyond tactical advantage—it could ensure the protection of vital undersea infrastructure including communications cables and energy pipelines that underpin global commerce and communications.

For air defence, AI-enabled radar systems could revolutionise threat detection and classification. Future systems may reliably distinguish between decoys and actual threats while simultaneously tracking hundreds of targets. Pattern recognition could identify hostile aircraft behaviour before traditional indicators become apparent. The strategic implications are profound—Air power has been the key strategic pillar of NATO's dominance in conflicts, enabling it to gain superiority over less developed militaries. More broadly, effective air defence remains crucial not just for military operations but for protecting civilian populations and critical infrastructure from aerial threats.

Land forces stand to benefit particularly from AI-enhanced intelligence, surveillance and reconnaissance (ISR) capabilities. Computer vision systems could process multiple video feeds simultaneously, even onboard the assets themselves, detecting subtle patterns of adversary movement and identifying potential threats that might escape human attention. The faster and more accurately this can be completed, with fewer people, and a greater range, the more fighting power is multiplied.

These kill chains show the opportunities AI provides as a force multiplier across all military domains, not just providing marginal enhancements to existing capabilities but enabling measurable capability gaps to form and entirely new operational concepts. AI's ability to process vast amounts of data, recognise subtle patterns and react at machine speed fundamentally changes the character of military operations. A military which has deployed AI at scale across the kill web will have asymmetric advantages over an adversary without AI, with much greater fighting power per person. That is why General Walker emphasised that this transformation demands that modern commanders become "systems integrators first and foremost, understanding the technology of their lethality as well as the tactical application of it", mastering "techcraft—the marriage of field craft and technology" (Walker, 2024).

The Rise of Unmanned Systems and Their Use of AI

For AI to be effectively employed on the battlefield, it must be combined with specialist hardware and work in contested environments in austere locations. Other sectors like civilian manufacturing and chemicals face similar hardware and location challenges. However, they don't face these challenges to the same extent, in combination and across their full breadth. Military systems must work effectively *anywhere* in the world. Military capabilities are also held to the highest regulatory standards, especially when they are life-critical systems. This explains why many defence AI capabilities require bespoke development. They cannot simply be dual-use technologies lifted from the private sector. It also makes the prize for overcoming these obstacles even greater. Success creates genuinely differentiated capabilities over adversaries who do not scale their use of AI.

Operating AI in contested battlefield environments presents three key challenges: bandwidth, electronic warfare and power management. AI systems must operate with extremely low and intermittent data bandwidths, often using secure but legacy radio systems. This means AI capabilities need to be embedded and run onboard military platforms. They can only send key insights over the network, rather than raw data. The systems must also work despite enemy electronic warfare countermeasures designed to degrade communications and navigation. Power management is equally critical. Systems must run with low SWAP (size, weight and power) requirements while handling extreme temperatures. Cold environments pose particular challenges, rapidly draining batteries.

The proliferation of unmanned systems (or drones) gives perhaps the best example where AI can transform kill chains across domains. These systems fuse AI with hardware while overcoming the unique challenges of the battlefield. They operate at both ends of the kill chain, carrying sensors or effectors (lethal explosive munitions). With AI, drones are increasing their autonomy in terms of decisions too. Unmanned systems are fundamentally altering modern warfare. Their nascent use of AI is a catalyst to further accelerate gains in fighting power.

The ongoing conflict in Ukraine provides compelling evidence of this transformation, where both reconnaissance and strike drones have become decisive elements of battlefield operations. The rapid cycles of adaptation driven by the conflict mean that AI is now starting to be employed by both sides to enhance these platforms on the front-line. This shift is more than a mere technological evolution—it marks a revolutionary change in the economics and conduct of warfare.

The economic implications of unmanned systems are particularly striking. A tactical strike drone costing £25,000 can destroy a main battle tank worth £10 million, representing a return on investment of 400 to 1. Even accounting for defensive countermeasures, the economics heavily favour the unmanned systems. When air defence missiles costing upwards of £1 million are expended to counter relatively inexpensive drones, the economic exchange remains decisively advantageous for the drone operator (with a 40-fold edge).

Beyond economics, unmanned systems offer unprecedented precision in military effects, boosting relative fighting power further. Where traditional artillery might require dozens of rounds to hit a target, precision-guided strike drones can achieve similar effects with a single strike. This capability proves especially valuable against moving targets, where conventional indirect fire struggles to achieve meaningful effects. Traditional munitions like artillery can also be employed more effectively themselves, when paired with unmanned systems. Rapid identification of targets, and more automated correction of artillery fire aided by reconnaissance drones overheard, compressing the kill chain for these traditional effectors. The result in both cases is not only more efficient use of scarce munitions, but greater lethality and reduced collateral damage.

The integration of artificial intelligence dramatically enhances these capabilities. Autonomous systems will increasingly conduct independent intelligence gathering missions, supporting persistent surveillance while adapting to changing conditions and threats. The result is a near transparent battlefield for any side employing AI at scale. Even in strike missions, where western militaries keep human control over weapons release, AI can enable autonomous navigation, target recognition, threat avoidance and coordination of swarms. Perhaps most significantly, AI offers solutions to counter enemy electronic warfare efforts, enabling operations in GPS-denied environments and maintaining effectiveness despite local communication jamming. The impact of these systems.

In land warfare, drones have seen the most rapid adoption and emergence of a competitive market of providers. At the start of the war in Ukraine, these systems lacked AI and were reliant upon GPS for target localisation and engagement. With electronic warfare countermeasures deployed at scale, GPS was jammed or spoofed on the front-line, leading to the use of first-person view (FPV) drones that are manually piloted. This in turn provoked another electronic warfare counter measure, localised jamming of communications frequencies. Denying the pilot their link to the drone altogether on approaching strategic targets and locations renders FPV drones ineffective.

So, AI has now come into the fore in Ukraine, proving its worth in increasing fighting power further by making unmanned systems truly resilient and precise. AI enables autopilot systems for strike drones, so they can work autonomously without either GPS or communications links. A human operator is kept "on-the-loop" for mission designation and weapons release. This ensures the drones are used within the rules of engagement, against authorised targets, in areas of legitimate engagement. AI improves their economics too, by making many expensive hardware components unnecessary redundant, and boosting hit rates. The relative return on investment is thus even greater.

Unmanned systems and the application of AI onboard extend across military domains. As outlined extensively, armies can employ aerial drones to provide unprecedented situational awareness to infantry units while enabling precise strikes against armoured vehicles and increasingly strategic targets. Similarly, autonomous ground vehicles are starting to conduct dangerous missions like reconnaissance missions, route clearance, logistics resupply, minesweeping and even trench assaults without risking personnel.

In the air domain, the transition towards autonomous systems continues to accelerate too. There are blurred lines in the division of responsibilities between armies, dedicated unmanned systems commands (as established by the Ukrainian Armed Forces) and air forces in using airborne drones. The division is usually based on complexity and range. Modernised air forces will likely operate a mix of crewed and uncrewed platforms, with AI-enabled autonomous aircraft conducting high-risk missions while integrating seamlessly with traditional aircraft. Hence the emergence of future programmes, like the UK's Autonomous Collaborative Platforms (ACP) and a desire to use AI within 6th generation stealth fighter jets. Even space operations will be transformed by the proliferation of small, autonomous satellites in low earth orbit (LEO), providing resilient communication, surveillance and strike capabilities.

At sea, unmanned surface vessels can patrol vast areas while submersible drones monitor undersea infrastructure and detect enemy submarines. As on land, these unmanned systems take the form of both reconnaissance and strike.

While perhaps lesser known as a case study, the use of drones in the Black Sea, provides another Ukrainian proof point. The ability of a nation without a traditional navy to effectively challenge a major naval power through autonomous systems suggests a fundamental shift in maritime strategy. As artificial intelligence enhances the autonomy and effectiveness of these platforms, particularly in overcoming electronic warfare challenges, their strategic impact will only grow.

Two key platforms have emerged as particularly significant: the GUR's Magura and the SBU's Sea Baby unmanned surface vessels (USVs). These relatively simple platforms, which can be manufactured in small industrial facilities, combine cameras, satellite communications and bow-mounted warheads to deliver outsized effects against much larger vessels (Sutton, 2024).

The technological enabler for these systems has been high-capacity two-way satellite communications, particularly Starlink and Kymeta systems. This connectivity allows human operators to keep precise control throughout missions, enabling adaptive tactics without requiring complex automation. While Ukraine is developing more autonomous capabilities, particularly for the terminal phase of attacks where electronic warfare may disrupt communications, this human-in-the-loop approach has proven remarkably effective (Ibid.).

The impact on Russian naval operations has been profound. In October 2022, small surface drones penetrated Russian defences to attack Sevastopol harbour, targeting high-value assets such as the flagship Moskva. Multiple vessels have been successfully targeted since, including the landing ship Olenegorsky Gornyak, a missile corvette, a patrol ship, a minesweeper and several smaller vessels. Beyond these direct strikes, the mere threat of USV attacks has forced the Russian Black Sea Fleet to fundamentally alter its operations, moving major assets to Novorossiysk and rerouting vital supply lines away from the Black Sea entirely (Ibid.).

Ukraine has manufactured hundreds of these vessels, proving their scalability and cost-effectiveness. Their small size makes them difficult targets for traditional anti-ship missiles and torpedoes, while minimal infrastructure requirements reduce vulnerability to shore-based strikes. The ability to operate without crew accommodation enables smaller, harder-to-detect platforms that can strike deep within enemy waters. Even with a loss-to-kill ratio of approximately 10:1, the economics still overwhelmingly favour the use of USVs (Ibid.)

The lessons from Ukraine's naval drones extend beyond small or asymmetric powers. Even large navies must reconsider their strategic assumptions considering this emerging capability. The relative affordability and flexibility of USVs allow smaller nations to challenge traditional naval dominance, forcing larger navies to adapt their force structures and operational doctrines. For the UK and its allies, investing in naval drone technology offers an opportunity to enhance maritime capabilities while keeping cost efficiency. By incorporating USVs into their fleets, they can achieve a balance of deterrence and operational reach that mitigates reliance on increasingly expensive traditional platforms.

Overall, this revolution in unmanned systems across all domains is perhaps the most significant change in military affairs since the advent of precision-guided munitions. The combination of favourable economics, enhanced precision and increasing autonomy ensures their continued proliferation. For these systems to be deployed with greater autonomy, intelligence and scalability, it is obvious that AI and software systems are crucial. For modern militaries, mastering the employment of unmanned systems—and the defence against them—has become an essential requirement for battlefield success.

The Implications of AI Acceleration

So far, this assessment has focused on AI capabilities available today and their immediate military applications. The case for AI's transformation of defence is strengthened further when we address the rapidly accelerating trajectory of artificial intelligence development. All the use cases identified thus far can be implemented with current technology, requiring perhaps a year at most of tuning for specific defence scenarios, to achieve order of magnitude gains. However, the pace of AI advancement suggests that even these substantial opportunities are merely the beginning of a profound transformation in military capability.

The acceleration of AI development becomes clear when examining its fundamental drivers. While data was once dubbed "the new oil" of AI development, computing power has emerged as perhaps the most critical input for creating increasingly capable systems. Historically, compute power followed the exponential Moore's Law, doubling approximately every 2 years. However, the past decade has seen a remarkable acceleration. The compute used to train leading AI systems now doubles every 6 months, creating a "hockey stick" curve even on logarithmic scales. This sustained and aggressive exponential growth in computational resources has few parallels in other industries. To put this in perspective, a doubling every 6 months means that the far this available for AI training increases by a factor of four every year, and by a factor of sixteen every 2 years.

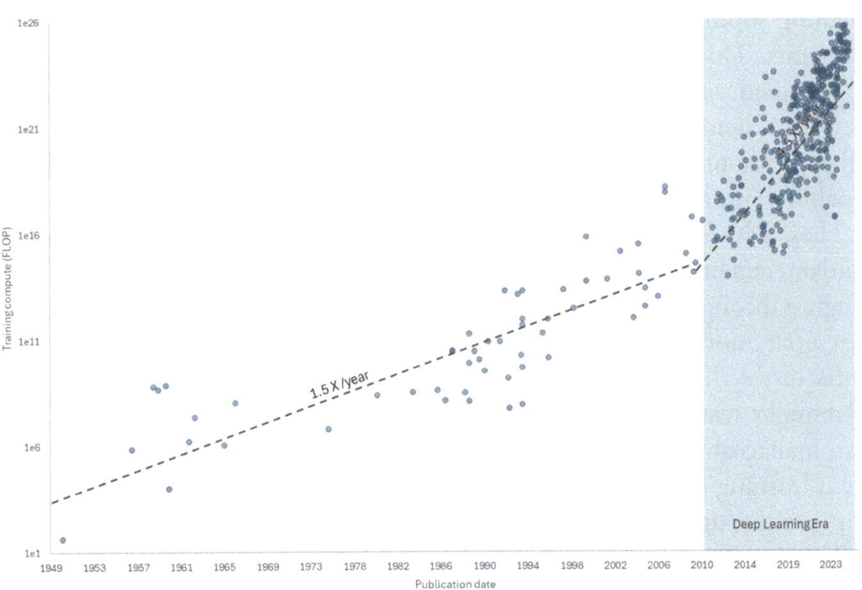

Source: Data and analysis from Epoch AI (2024)

Crucially, this massive increase in computing power translates directly into improved capabilities. The progression from OpenAI's GPT-2 in 2019, which showed roughly preschool-level intelligence, to today's systems performing at or above high school level, illustrates how additional compute drives substantial gains in AI capability. This relationship between compute and performance suggests continued rapid improvement as computational resources expand. Unlike many other fields where throwing more input resources at a problem yields diminishing returns, AI development has shown that increased compute consistently enables meaningful capability improvements.

The picture becomes even more striking when considering improvements in algorithmic efficiency. Over the past 4 years, researchers have achieved remarkable gains in compute utilisation—achieving equivalent performance with approximately 100 times less computing power. This is another exponential improvement, with efficiency roughly doubling every 7 months. Recent breakthroughs, like the supposedly hyper-efficient training of Deepseek-R1 by the Chinese, an open-source alternative to OpenAI's model, are bringing these efficiency gains into public view.

The implications of this efficiency gain are profound—AGI and ASI ought to be attainable even faster. Moreover, capabilities that once needed massive data centres can now be delivered on much smaller systems, potentially enabling sophisticated AI deployment even in constrained battlefield environments. This makes it easier to train and update systems at the edge and in classified settings, or to even deploy advanced AI capabilities onboard platforms themselves. The twin exponential trends—more compute and more efficient use of that compute—compound to enable unprecedented rates of capability improvement.

These advances also occur within current AI paradigms, without requiring fundamental breakthroughs in approach or architecture. The field continues to progress through incremental improvements in existing techniques, suggesting that even more dramatic gains might be possible with genuine paradigm shifts in AI development. Recent innovations show this potential—chain-of-thought reasoning enables AI systems to break down complex problems into manageable components much like human experts do, while reinforcement learning from human feedback (RLHF) allows systems to continuously improve through interaction, effectively learning from experience.

The integration of external tools is another frontier of improvement. Modern AI chat systems can now use web browsers and search engines to gather information and fact-check their reasoning. Context windows have expanded dramatically—from OpenAI GPT-3's 2000 tokens to millions in recent models—enabling much richer understanding and reasoning about complex problems. This expanded context allows AI systems to consider far more information when making decisions, approaching human-like ability to draw on broad knowledge when solving problems.

Current AI systems run under many constraints that will likely ease over time, suggesting headroom for further improvement. They lack long-term memory, meaning they cannot build up knowledge over multiple interactions or maintain consistent context across sessions. They cannot fully utilise computer resources, often being limited to specific interfaces rather than having general personal computing capabilities. Most systems must respond instantly rather than taking time to process complex problems—imagine forcing a human expert to always give immediate answers without any time to think or research.

The limitations extend further—today's AI systems receive no meaningful employee onboarding period, essentially starting fresh with each interaction rather than building expertise over time. They are still limited in their ability to process large amounts of data in a single query, and most lack true personalisation to specific use cases or domains. These constraints are artificial limitations rather than fundamental barriers—their removal promises another meaningful improvement in capability.

The breadth of AI advancement is clear when examining specific domains of intelligence. Systems now approach or exceed human-level performance across a remarkable range of capabilities (Kiela, 2023): reading comprehension enables understanding of complex documents and intelligence reports; image recognition supports sophisticated surveillance and target identification; language understanding facilitates multilingual operations; speech recognition enables natural interaction with systems; handwriting recognition assists with document processing; and predictive reasoning supports tactical and strategic planning. On standard IQ tests, leading AI systems achieve scores comparable to average human intelligence (Lott, 2023), suggesting broad cognitive capability rather than narrow specialised performance.

What About Superintelligence?

Given the pace of technological acceleration in artificial intelligence, many experts now believe we will achieve artificial general intelligence (AGI), or even artificial superintelligence (ASI), before the end of this decade. This timeline, which might seem startlingly near, emerges from the exponential nature of recent AI progress—a pattern humans inherently struggle to grasp. Our minds are wired to think linearly, extrapolating from past experience based on inductive reasoning, to proximate outcomes. When confronted with exponential growth, we generally underestimate how quickly change can occur. The famous chess parable, of requesting one grain of rice on the first square, doubled on each subsequent square, illustrates this cognitive blind spot. By the end of the chessboard, the amount exceeds all rice ever produced and atoms in the observable universe. Similarly, given recent exponential progress, we risk drastically underestimating both the pace of AI advancement and its strategic implications.

AGI represents the achievement of human-level performance across all cognitive tasks—from strategic planning to scientific research, technological innovation to tactical decision-making. ASI goes further, surpassing human capabilities across all these domains. The emergence of these technologies would fundamentally transform warfare and international security. As Dear warns in his "Don't Blink" argument (Dear, 2024), the pace of AI advancement is so rapid that even momentary complacency risks strategic surprise—every time we look away, another supposedly impossible benchmark falls.

The strategic implications are profound if ASI is possible. The first nation to achieve superintelligence could gain an insurmountable advantage through "innovation escape velocity"—where AI systems accelerate technological progress so dramatically that other nations can never catch up. An adversary achieving AGI first could gain unprecedented capabilities: consistently better strategic planning, faster technological innovation and optimisation of military operations beyond human comprehension. With ASI, this advantage becomes even more decisive—imagine facing an opponent with intelligence far exceeding the combined cognitive capability of your entire military and scientific establishment.

This advantage would manifest across all domains of warfare. Superintelligent systems could devise superior military strategies, independently develop novel advanced weapons systems, and coordinate forces with unprecedented strategic genius. More fundamentally, they could drive breakthroughs in science and technology that transform the very nature of military capability. An adversary with ASI could potentially develop countermeasures to any human-designed weapon system before it's even deployed.

While AGI and ASI can sound like science fiction, crowd forecasts and expert predictions now suggest AGI could appear by 2027, with ASI following as soon as 2029 (Ibid.). These timelines emerge not from mere futurist speculation but from analysis of technological trajectories. As Leopold Aschenbrenner argued proactively, believing in AGI "doesn't require believing in sci-fi; it requires believing in straight lines on graphs" (Aschenbrenner, 2024).

There is thus a dangerous tendency towards what Dear calls, "AGI psychological avoidance"—acknowledging the likelihood of general or super intelligence intellectually while not internalising its implications or taking proportionate action. Government leaders must overcome this cognitive dissonance and treat AI's acceleration, and the potential for superintelligence as a real scenario requiring immediate, focused response.

AGI and ASI may not emerge on the predicted timeline, or could face unforeseen technical barriers, yet the profound implications of these technologies demand serious strategic consideration. Just as the theoretical possibility of nuclear chain reactions in the 1930s called for massive investment in the Manhattan Project due to its potential strategic implications, the visible scientific pathway towards superintelligence demands proportionate attention and resources.

Even if superintelligent AI proves more distant than current forecasts suggest, investment in advanced AI capabilities would still yield substantial returns. The underlying technologies driving progress towards AGI and ASI also enable order-of-magnitude improvements in military capabilities today, like with current state of the art autonomous systems.

The strategic calculus is therefore clear: the possibility of superintelligence, even if uncertain, combined with its profound implications for military advantage, requires treating AI development as a top defence priority. The downside risk of underinvestment—potentially ceding irreversible strategic advantage to adversaries—far outweighs the cost of preparation. Just as the Manhattan Project's massive investment was justified by the mere possibility of nuclear weapons, the potential emergence of superintelligence demands similar focus and resources. We cannot afford to dismiss this possibility simply because it seems distant or uncertain—by the time its arrival becomes obvious, it may be too late to respond.

The risks of inaction are existential. If adversaries achieve superintelligence first, they could gain unprecedented ability to implement strategies, develop technologies and shape global affairs. Democratic nations could find themselves permanently disadvantaged, unable to maintain effective deterrence or defend their interests. In a world where an adversary controls AGI or ASI, traditional concepts of military balance, deterrence and strategic stability could be fundamentally disrupted. The safest strategy is to ensure democratic nations achieve AI capabilities leadership.

Software Eating Defence

In 2011, Marc Andreessen's seminal essay declared that "software is eating the world" (Andreessen, 2011). His thesis was simple but profound—software companies were disrupting traditional industries by delivering superior services at dramatically lower costs. In the decade since, this prediction has proven remarkably prescient. From retail to transportation, banking to entertainment, software-first companies have revolutionised entire sectors of the economy.

The transformation has been striking and has bred countless business school case studies. Netflix displaced Blockbuster without owning a single retail store. Uber revolutionised transportation without owning vehicles. Amazon became the world's largest retailer while owning relatively few physical shops. In each case, software enabled radical improvements in service delivery, cost structure and customer experience.

Yet, defence has been largely immune to this revolution, despite the potential gains. While software plays an increasingly key role in military systems, the fundamental business model and procurement approach remains anchored in industrial-age paradigms. This isn't just because defence is inherently resistant to software transformation (though there may be some cultural antibodies). Rather, it reflects the unique nature of the defence market—a single customer, byzantine procurement processes and entrenched prime contractors optimised for consulting services and "cost-plus" hardware delivery.

The stakes are profound. Just as software companies disrupted traditional industries by delivering superior services at lower costs, software-defined military capabilities promise similar revolutionary improvements in effectiveness and efficiency. The nation that masters software-defined defence will gain decisive advantages that hardware-centric forces cannot match.

The concept of "software-defined" systems is still poorly understood within defence organisations. Traditional military procurement is oriented around hardware platforms—ships, aircraft, vehicles. So, it typically begins with hardware specifications, with software often treated as an afterthought or mere enabler. This bias is common as hardware is tangible, familiar and fits well with existing organisational structures and career paths. It however is indicative of priorities and betrays a hardware-defined approach.

To make matters worse, hardware requirements are often over specified. It biases a particular thesis, concept of operation or hardware supplier, rather than facilitating a competitive market for innovation. When the Drone Capability Coalition for supplying to Ukraine launched their first competition, they specified details like the length of the propellers and mandatory radio transmitters/receivers, while neglecting to consider AI capabilities at all. While it no doubt addressed a requirement, it offered little opportunity for capability innovation.

Procuring from hardware manufacturers who later try to bolt on artificial intelligence, rather than starting with AI specialists, also fundamentally misunderstands where capability value resides. Reconsider modern strike drones. The airframe is a commodity that can be readily manufactured, with literally thousands of variants in the market from hundreds of suppliers. While it takes significant engineering skill and test flights to develop a good air frame, this is a relatively solved problem. The true capability advantage derives from the software systems enabling autonomous navigation, target recognition and precision strike—a relatively unique solution. The hardware provides the platform, but the software increasingly determines effectiveness.

Software provides *binary* capability differentiators in a manner which is rarely seen in hardware. Without effective AI, autonomous systems simply don't work. A drone that cannot hit mobile targets, navigate through GPS jamming or find targets despite adversarial electronic warfare can be rendered useless, regardless of its hardware specifications. Even if the drones can be manually piloted, or have a hardware solution to add resilience (like sophisticated CRPA antennas), this comes at significant cost and limits scalability. The key statistic to examine with a strike drone is its hit rate and precision—how reliably does it hit its target, and with what circular error probable (distance the majority of strikes land.). No amount of hardware improvement can match the capability gains achieved through better software for the scaled price point.

The advantages of software-centricity extend beyond static capability. While hardware advances typically yield only marginal improvements for a drone—perhaps 5%–10% between generations—software updates can deliver order-of-magnitude improvements in capability through enhanced algorithms and new artificial intelligence capabilities. Moreover, software can be rapidly updated to counter new threats or exploit new opportunities. Where hardware modifications might take months or years, software updates can be deployed in days—a strategic acceleration in adaptation cycles.

This ability to rapidly adapt proves particularly crucial in modern conflicts, where battlefield advantages often prove fleeting. Ukraine has shown how rapidly both attackers and defenders must evolve their tactics and capabilities. Software-defined systems can be continuously improved through updates, while hardware-centric platforms remain static until major upgrades. The side that can adapt their software faster gains decisive advantage.

System integration and broader cost effectiveness also depend primarily on software sophistication. The ability to coordinate multiple drones or integrate with other systems is fundamentally a software challenge. While hardware costs stay relatively fixed, software can dramatically improve mission success rates and reduce wastage through better targeting and decision-making.

Hence the default approach of starting procurement with hardware manufacturers, who later try to bolt on artificial intelligence, is a fundamental strategic error. Military acquisition must begin with software specialists who understand these requirements and can specify the minimum viable hardware platform. In modern warfare, software capability will increasingly decide whether the overall systems succeed or fail in an adversarial scenario. The nation that masters software-defined military systems will gain decisive advantages that hardware-centric forces cannot match.

Defence organisations must therefore fundamentally rethink their approach to capability development. Rather than treating software as a mere enabler for hardware platforms, they must recognise software as increasingly often the primary driver of military effectiveness. This is a challenging premise, which many in defence may struggle to readily accept. It also requires new procurement models, different skills in the acquisition workforce and reformed organisational structures that prioritise software excellence.

Acquisition and Policy Implications

The effective adoption of artificial intelligence in defence requires addressing multiple interconnected challenges across policy, procurement and institutional structures. While senior leaders increasingly recognise AI's transformative potential, current approaches often do not create the conditions necessary for successful implementation at scale. These recommendations draw from both positive examples, like the UK's Commercial X initiative, and cautionary tales of where current systems fall short. Together, they provide a framework for transforming how defence organisations approach AI adoption—moving from rhetoric to practical implementation that delivers meaningful military capability. The changes needed may prove uncomfortable and entail vast cultural change. They are essential steps for maintaining technological superiority in an era where software capabilities increasingly determine battlefield success.

Recommendation 1—Tracking Spend on Software, AI and New Technology Companies

Defence budgets must evolve to reflect the growing importance of artificial intelligence and software-defined capabilities. Currently, only a tiny fraction of defence spending flows to new technology companies specialising in these areas. This is a fundamental mismatch between strategic needs and resource allocation.

The first step towards addressing this imbalance requires greater transparency in defence spending. Departments should publicly report total investment in new technology companies, particularly those focused on artificial intelligence and software capabilities. This transparency would enable proper scrutiny and create pressure for positive change.

However, raw spending figures alone prove insufficient. We must carefully differentiate between various categories of technology investment. While modernising back-office systems and adopting cloud computing remain important and are software-centric, these investments differ fundamentally from developing novel battlefield AI capabilities. Reporting must not conflate these categories, enabling assessment of inputs across different areas.

A meaningful transformation would see a target established, like 20% of defence spending ought to be directed towards new technology companies developing novel battlefield capabilities. This figure, while debatable, provides a milestone to target, and reflects the growing centrality of software and AI to military effectiveness. It also acknowledges that hardware platforms are still essential and the vast brownfield site that must be maintained.

This shift in spending priorities would drive broader transformation across defence. Traditional prime contractors would face pressure to develop genuine software expertise or partner with specialists. New entrants would gain the resources needed to scale novel capabilities. Perhaps most importantly, it would signal to the market that defence organisations truly understand where future military value resides.

Recommendation 2—Building Bridges Across the Valley of Death

The current approach to military AI development creates dangerous incentives. While defence organisations eagerly fund early-stage AI experimentation through innovation programmes and accelerators, successful projects often fail to transition into operational capabilities. This "valley of death" between promising prototypes and fielded systems wastes investment and delays crucial military modernisation.

The problem stems from traditional defence funding structures. Experimentation and prototype development typically draw from dedicated innovation budgets, while full-scale capability development requires programmes of record funding. However, these programmes of record are usually committed years in advance to traditional platforms and capabilities. This leaves successful AI projects stranded—too mature for innovation funding but unable to access mainstream procurement budgets. As one defence technology executive recently observed, the MOD is still "a place for great ideas to have expensive funerals" (Orme, 2024).

The implications extend beyond wasted research and development spending. When promising AI capabilities fail to scale, defence organisations lose potential battlefield advantages. Equally concerning, innovative companies that successfully prove new capabilities often struggle to sustain operations through lengthy transition periods. This discourages new entrants and reinforces dependency on traditional prime contractors who lack software expertise.

The solution requires dedicated funding specifically for scaling successful AI prototypes into operational capabilities. This "bridge funding" would support the crucial transition period between successful demonstration and full programme of record status. It should be substantial enough to support multiple concurrent transitions, reflecting the fast-moving nature of AI technology.

The valley of death in defence AI development creates ripple effects far beyond immediate capability gaps. By consistently failing to scale successful prototypes into fielded systems, defence organisations inadvertently suppress private investment in military technology. This undermines the entire innovation ecosystem needed to maintain technological superiority. The typical 10-year timeline to achieve operational and financial success in UK defence technology (Ibid.) deters all but the most patient investors.

Venture capital firms and private investors make decisions based on clear paths to return on investment. When they see software and AI companies repeatedly stranded between successful demonstration and full-scale deployment, they naturally hesitate to fund new defence technology ventures. This reaction proves entirely rational—without reliable routes to scale, even the most promising military AI technologies are risky investments.

The impact on early-stage research and development proves particularly damaging. Venture funding typically enables companies to conduct substantial research and development before securing government contracts. This private investment effectively subsidises military innovation, delivering more mature capabilities faster than traditional defence research approaches. However, this model only functions when investors see credible paths to profitable scale.

Success stories drive venture investment. When investors see AI companies successfully transitioning from prototype to programme of record, securing substantial contracts and delivering real capability, they gain confidence to fund similar ventures. This creates a virtuous cycle—more investment enables more innovation, leading to more successful deployments, which in turn attracts more investment. The current system often sends the opposite signal.

Defence organisations must therefore view reliable scaling paths not just as capability enablers, but as crucial signals to private markets. Dedicated funding for transitioning successful AI prototypes would show serious commitment to fielding these capabilities.

Recommendation 3—Reward Those Invest Their Own Capital and Purchase COTs

The stark contrast between defence and pharmaceutical industry approaches to research and development reveals a fundamental problem in military procurement. While pharmaceutical companies invest heavily in developing new products, defence contractors spend remarkably little of their own capital on innovation. This disparity stems not from technological complexity—both sectors tackle sophisticated challenges—but from fundamentally different commercial incentives.

The numbers tell a striking story. Major defence contractors typically invest only 2%–3% of their revenue in research and development, with few exceeding 5% (Benaich & Chalmers, 2024). For perspective, a mid-tier pharmaceutical company like AbbVie invests more in R&D than the three largest defence contractors combined (Ibid.). This underinvestment in innovation directly affects military capability development and technological advancement.

Even these modest R&D figures paint an overly optimistic picture. Defence contractors typically pass research and development costs back to government customers through various contracting mechanisms. QinetiQ's 2023 accounts illustrate this pattern—of £328 million recorded R&D expenditure, £313.8 million came from government funds. Meanwhile, the company maintained shareholder dividends, reflecting a broader industry pattern of prioritising short-term investor returns over innovation investment (Ibid.)

This preference for shareholder returns over research investment proves remarkably consistent across the sector. Lockheed Martin returned £9.1 billion to shareholders through dividends and buybacks in 2022, while spending just £1.7 billion on company-funded R&D (Ibid.). Similarly, BAE Systems launched a £1.5 billion share buyback programme while investing only £287 million of its own money in research (Ibid.). A 2023 US Department of Defence study flatly rejected industry claims of insufficient profit margins, noting that contractors had "significantly increased the overall share of revenue paid to shareholders ... by 73%" while reducing investment in research and capital expenditure (Department of Defence, 2023).

The root cause of this underinvestment lies in traditional "cost-plus" defence contracting models, where companies are paid for their R&D, and receive guaranteed returns on top of their costs. This approach, while designed to ensure fair compensation for complex military development, fundamentally removes incentives for private investment and innovation. Under the traditional cost-plus model that defines most complex programmes, contractors have limited incentive to invest their own capital in proactively developing major innovations that create genuine advantage. Moreover, when these contractors do conduct research and development, they typically pass these costs back to government through various contracting mechanisms, effectively receiving subsidised R&D that can then be sold to other customers. This approach is also encouraged by the customer, who feels in control of capability development. This creates a perverse incentive structure where minimising private investment while maximising shareholder returns becomes the rational business strategy.

Making matters worse, contractors and military procurement officials often display active hostility towards externally developed innovations, showing a deeply entrenched "not invented here" mentality. When defence technology companies proactively invest their own capital to develop solutions, they often face institutional scepticism precisely because they bypassed traditional development channels. This resistance stems not just from bureaucratic inertia, but from the perceived threat to established power structures and income streams. Successful external innovation inherently challenges the authority of those who championed alternative approaches and exposes the inefficiency of maintaining large contractor workforces on generous day rates.

Rather than celebrating innovative companies for shouldering development risk and accelerating capability advantage, procurement officials often view them with suspicion, questioning solutions that weren't developed under their direct oversight. This cultural bias creates more barriers for companies trying to sell independently developed products to defence organisations, effectively punishing rather than rewarding private investment in military innovation. A fundamental shift in mindset is needed—companies willing to risk their own capital to develop military capabilities should be treated as innovation heroes, not interlopers in a closed system.

The solution lies in creating stronger incentives for private investment in defence innovation, particularly through greater emphasis on commercial off-the-shelf (COTS) procurement. The pharmaceutical industry's model offers valuable lessons—companies invest heavily in research because successful products can secure substantial returns through patents and scaled purchases. While direct replication of pharmaceutical patents might prove inappropriate for defence, the principle of rewarding private investment in product development remains sound.

Defence organisations must therefore reform procurement processes to favour COTS solutions where available. This approach would encourage companies to invest their own capital in developing products, knowing that successful innovations could secure substantial sales across multiple customers. It would also accelerate capability delivery by using existing products rather than funding bespoke (and often over-specified) development.

Recommendation 4—Treat New Defence Tech with Private Capital as Strategic Suppliers

Defence must fundamentally reframe its relationship with innovative technology companies that have shown serious commitment through private investment. Rather than treating these firms as peripheral suppliers or experiments, they should receive similar strategic consideration as traditional prime contractors, appropriately scaled to their market presence and capital investment.

Procurement agencies should assign dedicated relationship managers to significant new defence technology companies, just as they do with established primes. The level of support should reflect both the company's current scale—measured through metrics like headcount and revenue—and their demonstrated commitment to the sector through capital raised and continued investment. Of particular importance is privately funded domestic research and development spending that creates sovereign capability and high-skilled jobs. Companies investing substantially in national R&D facilities and talent should receive recognition through enhanced strategic supplier status.

In contrast, defence organisations should maintain healthy scepticism towards companies relying primarily on cost-plus funding for research and development. While established contractors often tout their R&D investments, closer examination often reveals this spending as primarily taxpayer-funded, with minimal private capital at risk. The willingness to invest private capital and bring pre-build novel capabilities, rather than simply pass development costs back to government customers, is a crucial differentiator when evaluating potential strategic suppliers.

Master Service Agreements and Enterprise Agreements, contracts that cover the range of a supplier's services or software, should be made available to qualifying technology companies, reducing procurement friction when specific capabilities are needed. These contractual vehicles, traditionally prioritised for prime contractors, enable faster buying decisions and more stable business relationships. They also signal to investors that defence organisations view these companies as enduring partners rather than just experiments.

Defence must also ensure equal mindshare for strategic technology suppliers in capability development discussions. When traditional primes receive early engagement on future requirements and regular access to senior decision-makers, innovative technology companies making similar scale commitments to the sector should receive comparable treatment.

This reform would create a virtuous cycle—companies that invest significant private capital in defence innovation receive treatment that helps them succeed, encouraging further investment from both existing players and new entrants. It will also enhance competition, incentivising incumbents to innovate more, by investing more private capital. By particularly valuing domestic R&D investment, this approach would help build lasting sovereign capabilities in crucial defence technologies. The result would be a more dynamic, better-funded defence technology sector delivering superior capabilities to war fighters while strengthening the national industrial base.

Recommendation 5—Rebalance Towards New Entrants and SMEs

The current distribution of defence contracts reveals a stark imbalance that undermines military innovation and AI adoption. Non-SMEs receive approximately 25 times more contract value than SMEs, creating a market dominated by traditional prime contractors (Benaich & Chalmers, 2023). Even more concerning, when examining contracts specifically suitable for SMEs, less than 40% actually reach smaller companies (Ibid.). This suggests systematic barriers preventing innovative new entrants from securing meaningful defence work.

The nature of SME contracts compounds this problem. Rather than focusing on developing new capabilities or delivering innovative technologies, most smaller companies find themselves restricted to basic estate maintenance or equipment support roles (Ibid.). This represents a significant missed opportunity—many of the most innovative defence technology companies emerge as SMEs, yet struggle to secure contracts that would enable them to deliver transformative capabilities.

Security clearance requirements create particularly challenging barriers for new entrants. Companies face a frustrating “chicken and egg” scenario—

they cannot win classified work without appropriate clearances yet struggle to obtain clearances without existing contracts. This often forces companies into costly subcontracting arrangements or requires them to hire pre-cleared staff at premium rates.

The physical infrastructure requirements for handling classified information present a similar hurdle. The current Facility Security Clearance policy imposes costly requirements that many start-ups cannot initially meet. When secure facilities are available, they are often found in remote areas inappropriate for technology companies that need to attract and retain skilled software developers and AI specialists.

Several practical reforms could address these challenges. Defence organisations should offer at-cost secure computing infrastructure, either through direct provision of cloud services or detailed blueprints for self-implementation. They should create accessible secure facilities in major technology hubs and cities, potentially subletting space to qualified SMEs. Most importantly, they should hold security clearances on behalf of smaller companies, just as they do for their own employees and traditional contractors.

Commercial frameworks also require reform. Current systems like the UK's G-Cloud use arbitrary entry windows that can leave innovative companies waiting years before they can even bid for work. These bureaucratic conveniences severely affect SMEs, who often lack the financial runway to wait out such delays. Making frameworks continuously accessible would enable faster engagement with innovative suppliers.

To the extent that innovation programmes are useful for new entrances, defence organisations must reconsider who manages them. Currently, many defence accelerators and innovation hubs are predominantly staffed by employees seconded from traditional prime contractors. This creates an inherent conflict of interest and perpetuates existing power structures. The evidence supports this concern—analysis by Benaich and Chalmers (Ibid.) reveals that traditional defence primes like QinetiQ and Thales appear as the top recipients of innovation grants from the Defence and Security Accelerator (DASA). Rather than enabling new entrants, these innovation programmes often reinforce the dominance of established players. Defence organisations must build genuine in-house capacity for managing innovation, staffed by personnel who can engage directly with SMEs without conflicts of interest. This would create clearer paths for new technology adoption while ensuring innovation funding reaches truly innovative companies rather than flowing back to traditional primes.

That said, as outlined above, the primary challenge remains bridging the "valley of death" between innovation and scaled procurement. While reforming innovation programmes is important, poorly designed accelerators and innovation hubs can actually harm SMEs. When these programmes provide initial funding and engagement without realistic paths to scale, they send dangerously misleading signals to both companies and investors.

The human cost proves particularly concerning. New defence technology companies often employ highly skilled software engineers and AI specialists who could be working in any sector. When these scarce technical experts spend years developing solutions through innovation programmes that have no realistic path to procurement, their talent is effectively wasted. Companies burn through capital and engineering resources chasing opportunities that, due to structural barriers, cannot materialise into sustainable business. This not only damages individual companies but undermines confidence in the entire defence technology sector, making it harder to attract talent and investment in the future.

Reform must therefore focus first on creating viable paths for SMEs from innovation to scaled procurement. While improving how innovation programmes operate remains important, implementing these changes without first fixing the fundamental barriers to scaling would simply create more efficient paths to failure. Defence organisations must ensure that when they encourage companies to invest time and resources in innovation programmes, there are realistic routes to turn successful prototypes into fielded capabilities.

Recommendation 6—Embrace Software-Centric Acquisition Like Commercial X

The success of Commercial X within the Ministry of Defence shows how acquisition processes can be reformed to better support software and AI procurement while operating within existing regulatory frameworks. Led by a leader recruited from the private sector rather than a career civil servant (much as many may be brilliant!), this innovative team within Defence Digital has proven that commercial officers can take calculated risks in pursuit of better outcomes without violating fundamental procurement rules.

Commercial X's approach directly addresses many of the barriers that traditionally impede software procurement. Rather than focusing primarily on commercial risk mitigation, the team optimises for rapid testing and capability delivery. This shift in mindset proves particularly valuable for software acquisition, where the ability to quickly evaluate and iterate on solutions often matters more than exhaustive upfront specifications.

What makes Commercial X particularly noteworthy is its pragmatic approach to modernisation. Operating under the same legal constraints as other procurement teams, it has nonetheless found ways to streamline governance and redesign processes to better suit software procurement. This proves that many traditional barriers to effective software acquisition stem not from regulatory requirements, but from risk-averse interpretations of those requirements.

The initiative's focus on avoiding the valley of death through active support of innovative companies has proven especially valuable. By helping disruptive technology providers navigate procurement barriers and find paths to scale, Commercial X helps prevent the waste of innovation funding on dead-end projects. This approach particularly benefits software companies, whose products often struggle to fit traditional procurement models.

Perhaps most importantly, Commercial X demonstrates the value of dedicated commercial expertise in technology procurement. Its commercial officers receive specific training in modern acquisition approaches, enabling them to make informed judgments about acceptable risks rather than defaulting to excessive caution. This expertise proves particularly crucial when evaluating software capabilities, where traditional hardware-focused procurement metrics may prove inappropriate.

Without digressing into a complex topic which warrants separate detailed analysis, broader legislative modernisation of defence procurement, could enable even more efficient acquisition of AI.

Recommendation 7—Raise Defence AI Ambitions and Hold Leaders Accountable

Current approaches to military AI adoption across NATO nations lack the urgency that both technological advancement and geopolitical reality demand. Defence AI strategies often reveal a concerning misalignment between ambition and execution, particularly in how they categorise readily available capabilities as future developments. When technologies already deployed in current conflicts are labelled as "AI Next" or "AI Future" rather than "AI Now", it suggests a dangerous complacency about the pace of change (Ministry of Defence, 2024).

The UK Chief of the General Staff's recent declaration to double the Army's fighting power within 3 years exemplifies the proper level of ambition required. Rather than celebrating marginal improvements or treating AI as a box-ticking exercise, defence organisations must pursue transformative capability gains. This requires honest assessment (and detailed benchmarking) of current capabilities, aggressive targeting of opportunities for AI integration and ruthless focus on measurable improvements in military effectiveness.

Success should be measured through substantial, demonstrable increases in military capability—whether that's quadrupling the speed of decision cycles, tripling the efficiency of logistics operations, or achieving order-of-magnitude improvements in threat detection accuracy. These ambitious but achievable targets would help drive genuine transformation rather than superficial AI implementation. If AGI and ASI are truly on the horizon this decade, the bar for AI progress and adoption ought to be even higher.

Most importantly, defence organisations must hold leaders accountable for delivering these improvements. Where traditional defence leadership lacks the necessary technical understanding or commercial acumen, organisations should actively recruit external experienced leaders from successful AI adopters to drive transformation. Leadership in military AI is not optional—it is a strategic imperative for maintaining credible deterrence and battlefield superiority.

References

Andreessen, M. (2011). *Why software is eating the world.* https://a16z.com/why-software-is-eating-the-world/. Accessed 28 December 2024

Armstrong, M. (2022). *Chart: NATO countries have heavily cut troop levels | Statista*. https://www.statista.com/chart/27534/nato-troop-levels-1990-to-present/. Accessed 28 December 2024

Aschenbrenner, L. (2024). *Situational awareness: The decade ahead.* https://situational-awareness.ai/wp-content/uploads/2024/06/situationalawareness.pdf. Accessed 28 December 2024

Benaich, N., & Chalmers, A.. (2023). *European dynamism and defense.* https://docs.google.com/presentation/d/1fl ty6vYGUVJzCZyAT0QXvkQdE1bA98uF_vql6YOtXtQ/edit#slide=id.g2a364bb449d_0_386. Accessed 28 December 2024

Benaich, N., & Chalmers, A. (2024). *The defense 'exit problem', big pharma, and perverse incentives.* https://press.airstreet.com/p/defense-exits-european-dynamism?utm_source=publication-search. Accessed 28 December 2024

Department of Defence. (2023). *Contract finance study report.* https://www.acq.osd.mil/asda/dpc/pcf/docs/finance-study/FINAL%20-%20Defense%20Contract%20Finance%20Study%20Report%204.6.23.pdf. Accessed 28 December 2024

Dear, K. (2024). *Don't Blink: How the UK can take a lead in the defence AI race*. https://cassiai.substack.com/p/dont-blink-how-the-uk-can-take-a. Accessed 28 December 2024.

Epoch AI. (2024). *Data on notable AI models*. https://epoch.ai/data/notable-ai-models. Accessed 28 December 2024

Fukuyama, F. (1989). *The end of history?*https://www.jstor.org/stable/24027184. Accessed 28 December 2024

Hockenhull, J. (2023). *Strategic command DSEI 2023 Keynote*. https://www.gov.uk/government/speeches/gen-jim-hockenhull-dsei-2023-keynote-sharpening-defences-edge. Accessed 28 December 2024

Kiela, D. (2023). *Plotting progress in AI*. https://contextual.ai/blog/plotting-progress-in-ai. Accessed 28 December 2024

Lott, M. (2023). *IQ test results*. https://trackingai.org/home. Accessed 28 December 2024

Marlow, M. (2024). *Britain's Ten Year Rule—A warning on AI adoption in defence*. https://www.adamsmith.org/research/britains-ten-year-rule-a-warning-on-ai-adoption-in-defence. Accessed 28 December 2024

Ministry of Defence. (2024). *The defence AI playbook*. https://assets.publishing.service.gov.uk/media/65bb75fa21f73f0014e0ba51/Defence_AI_Playbook.pdf. Accessed 28 December 2024

NATO. (2024). *Washington Summit Declaration issued by the NATO Heads of State and Government participating in the meeting of the North Atlantic Council in Washington, DC*. https://www.nato.int/cps/ar/natohq/official_texts_227678.htm. Accessed 28 December 2024

Orme, W. (2024). *A view on UK defence tech innovation; where great ideas go to have expensive funerals*. https://www.linkedin.com/pulse/view-uk-defence-tech-innovation-where-great-ideas-go-have-will-orme-7rv1e/?trackingId=Rw6NMyPoQWWou0NLkGpRHg%3D%3D. Accessed 28 December 2024

Sutton, H. (2024). *Uncrewed platforms have been critical to Ukraine's success in the Black Sea*. https://www.rusi.org/explore-our-research/publications/commentary/uncrewed-platforms-have-been-critical-ukraines-success-black-sea. Accessed 28 December 2024

Walker, R. (2024). *Pulling the future into the present*. https://www.army.mod.uk/news/pulling-the-future-into-the-present-rusi-land-warfare-conference-2024/. Accessed 28 December 2024

Part IV

Economics, Work and Investment

Automating Knowledge Work: A Framework for Identifying Automation Strategies for Tasks

Carter C. Price and Morgan Sandler

Algorithms and automated decision-making have guided knowledge work for decades (Leondes, 2001), with origins in operations research methods that informed logistics and targeting decisions during World War II (Morse et al., 2003). In those early applications, calculations were executed by large teams of human "computers" or by early electronic devices that filled entire rooms. As technology advanced, human computation was supplanted by calculators, mainframes, and eventually today's compact electronic computers. Eighty years later, contemporary Artificial Intelligence (AI) systems—most notably those driven by Large Language Models (LLMs) such as ChatGPT or Claude—are being heralded as potentially transformative labor-replacing tools. These developments have sparked renewed interest in "post-labor" economic scenarios (Acemoglu, 2024; Harari, 2018). While such claims may be premature, it remains empirically true that increasingly capable AI systems are now capable of performing a growing range of tasks that were once the sole domain of human workers (Howard, 2019).

Yet the relationship between automation and labor is nuanced. A job is typically composed of multiple tasks rather than monolithic work units, and the impact of AI-based automation on overall labor demand is not straightforwardly positive or negative. On the one hand, AI can augment human capability—freeing workers to focus on higher-value tasks that demand

C. C. Price (✉) • M. Sandler
RAND Corporation, Santa Monica, CA, USA
e-mail: price@rand.org; msandler@rand.org

M. Rangeley, N. Fairfax (eds.), *The Artificial Intelligence Revolution*,
https://doi.org/10.1007/978-3-032-11814-1_15

creativity, critical thinking, or complex judgment. On the other hand, if AI automates core, high-value tasks, it may leave workers performing lower-value "residual" tasks or risk eroding critical skill sets. Such skill atrophy is well-documented in examples involving offshoring (Bapna et al., 2013). With offshoring and outsourcing, a firm may lose some of its core competencies, but with AI it may expand beyond just a single firm to an entire skill set. As LLMs are being used as coding assistants, platforms like Stack Overflow that are commonly used for coding advice may not be maintained to the same extent. Because LLMs are frequently trained on sources like Stack Overflow, the decay of these sources could put future LLM capabilities at risk (Zhong & Wang, 2024).

For the purpose of this discussion, we define 'knowledge tasks' as predominantly cognitive activities that involve processing, analyzing, or synthesizing information to produce insights, solutions, or decisions. These tasks are distinct from physical tasks, which typically involve manual or mechanical operations.

Knowledge tasks differ from purely physical tasks because they revolve around information, which can be right or wrong, truthful, or misleading. While some AI outputs—like creative writing or music—need not adhere to factual correctness, many decision-making tasks depend on accurate information. Disinformation (intentional) and misinformation (unintentional) can harm information networks and impede progress. Hence, the "criticality" of a task—its tolerance for error or falsehood—must be carefully considered when determining the appropriate degree of automation and human oversight. Further, while creative tasks may not be focused on factuality, there are still characteristics that can be evaluated which make some responses more suitable than others. Some responses could be offensive, tonally wrong, or internally inconsistent. Tasks may also have a blend of factual and creative components.

This study proposes a framework for evaluating tasks across several characteristics to assess the recommended level of human oversight and the task's susceptibility to AI-driven automation. In doing so, we draw on a wide body of literature from management sciences, software engineering, and machine learning. We also consider how different AI methods could be used—such as LLMs that can help with knowledge work, to other algorithmic techniques, like the A* algorithm for pathfinding in maps. Each AI method excels in certain contexts, each with their own limitations and applicability. We adapt enterprise risk management frameworks to help organizations characterize tasks for automation, ensuring that decision-makers can identify where and how to apply AI with confidence and caution.

The remainder of this chapter is organized as follows. First, we review key findings from the literature on prior frameworks for displacing labor through automation, focusing on lessons from robotics, outsourcing, and offshoring. We then introduce our proposed framework for assessing tasks, determining suitable levels of human oversight, and applying principles of criticality and accuracy. Finally, we offer recommendations for leaders seeking to deploy AI systems that replace human labor, ensuring both technical effectiveness and the responsible stewardship of knowledge work.

Lessons from Other Modes of Task Displacement

Automation and AI increasingly perform tasks previously carried out by humans, creating a "displacement effect" that reduces labor demand in specific sectors. This effect has been particularly pronounced among low- and middle-skill workers, as studies consistently show adverse impacts on wages and employment. However, the introduction of new tasks through technological innovation can also have a "reinstatement effect," where job losses are offset, at least in part, by creating new roles in which human labor has a comparative advantage. The balance between these effects is critical; if automation outpaces the creation of new tasks, labor demand and the labor share of income could decline despite productivity gains.

At the macroeconomic level, Acemoglu argued that AI's modest productivity gains are likely to widen the income gap between labor and capital, with the capital share of income increasing (Acemoglu, 2024). While AI's effects are more evenly distributed across demographic groups compared to earlier waves of automation, it still risks exacerbating economic inequality. Geographic and temporal variations further underscore the need for localized policy interventions, as noted by Frank et al. and Graetz and Michaels, who emphasized disparities in labor market outcomes across regions (Frank et al., 2019; Graetz & Michaels, 2018).

In general, task creation has failed to keep pace with automation. Acemoglu and Restrepo theorize the deceleration in task creation over the past three decades has exacerbated labor demand declines, as automation takes over roles without sufficiently creating new opportunities for workers (Acemoglu & Restrepo, 2019). The sectoral and skill-specific impacts of AI further complicate the landscape. Autor noted that AI disproportionally affects middle-skill jobs requiring high literacy and problem-solving abilities, potentially fostering job insecurity, and stress among employees (Autor, 2015). Additionally, Frank et al. highlighted the lack of high-quality data and robust models to fully capture labor market resilience and skill dynamics, which limits the ability to predict job transitions effectively (Frank et al., 2019).

Researchers aim to evaluate the nuanced impacts of AI and automation on labor markets, identify mechanisms driving labor displacement, and propose strategies to mitigate negative outcomes. Key goals include understanding how these technologies affect different skill groups, assessing the potential for task creation to counterbalance displacement, and providing actionable insights for policymakers and organizations. Studies highlight several trends and challenges.

Task Displacement Through Robots

Conceptually similar to the adoption of AI, the deployment of robots has displaced tasks in many areas.

The introduction and widespread use of automated teller machines (ATMs) did not lead to a precipitous decline in bank teller employment and, in fact, in the United States, there were more people employed in 2010 than in 1970 (Bessen, 2015). Mavers and Baker used ATMs as a case study in automation for automation and describe how the nature of tasks performed by teller changed with the adoption of ATMs (Mavers & Baker, 2021). In particular, by automating simple tasks like deposits and withdrawals, tellers moved to higher value tasks that relied more on judgment such as supporting customer decisions on opening accounts or identifying available banking services. However, recent data from the (Bureau of Labor Statistics, 2023) indicate that, in the United States, there has been a decline in teller employment since 2010, though the level remains higher than in 1970. This decline may be more associated with consolidation in the banking sector and a shift to mobile banking rather than ATMs.

Alternatively, Acemoglu and Restrepo (2017) found that industrial robots may reduce employment and wages in local markets. Similarly, Graetz and Michaels (2018) showed that while robots increase productivity and lower costs, they disproportionately reduce the employment share of low-skilled workers, reflecting a skill-based impact. Autor and Salomons (2018) found that automation leads to job displacement and decreases labor's share of value-added within the industries where it is implemented.

Thus, unlike with ATMs, there were not enough high-value tasks in manufacturing for humans to take on when industrial robots took over key tasks. Productivity gains often favor higher-skilled workers and capital owners, exacerbating wage inequality. Furthermore, the lack of granular, high-quality data on workplace skills and tasks limits the ability to monitor and predict labor market transitions effectively.

Task Displacement Through Outsourcing

Outsourcing involves transferring tasks or processes—often including knowledge-intensive work—to external vendors or service providers. Unlike robotics, which substitutes machines for workers within the same firm, outsourcing retains human labor but relocates it outside the firm's boundaries. Decisions about what to outsource are guided by strategic frameworks that evaluate the importance, complexity, and criticality of tasks. Additionally, while robotics is typically for physical labor, outsourcing can be for physical labor or knowledge work.

For tasks related to knowledge work, outsourcing may allow a firm access to specialized expertise that is too costly to maintain within the firm (Quinn, 1999). There may be tasks where the timeline is such that it is not feasible for in house expertise to be developed and so outsourcing is required. Additionally, there may be some specialties such as accounting, human resources, or information technology, where a general firm cannot take advantages of economies of scale but a specialized service provider can. Outsourcing allows a firm to focus on its core competencies where it is a leader relative to competitors (Prahalad & Hamel, 1990). Thus, in an idealized case, outsourcing allows a firm to focus on those tasks where it has a competitive advantage or that provide the largest marginal value and pay others to do the lower value work.

Task Displacement Through Offshoring

Offshoring can be viewed as a geographically more extreme version of outsourcing, wherein tasks are moved to another country to exploit lower labor costs, access specialized skills, or leverage more favorable regulatory conditions (Feenstra & Hanson, 1996; Levy, 2005). Fundamentally, cost arbitrage is the primary rationale for offshoring. Frameworks for assessing offshoring suitability focus on evaluating the criticality of the task, the technology and human capital available abroad, the repetitiveness and maturity of the task, data sensitivity, security requirements, and potential risks (Mihalache & Mihalache, 2016). For example, tasks deemed lower in strategic importance or more codified, repetitive, and rule-based are typically better candidates for offshoring.

Transaction Cost Theory (TCT) provides a theoretical lens for offshoring decisions by weighing the costs of market-based transactions against in-house operations (Williamson, 1975; Grover & Malhotra, 2003). A value assessment framework encourages ranking processes by their importance to core business functions—those less integral to the firm's value proposition may be suitable for offshoring. Risk identification frameworks stress evaluating strategic, operational, compliance, reputational, and environmental risks. Collectively, these approaches help organizations decide which tasks can be shifted offshore without eroding critical internal capabilities or adaptability.

From Physical to Cognitive Automation: AI's Distinctiveness

While many of the lessons from task displacement from robotics, outsourcing, and offshoring are relevant to AI, these different modes differ in key ways. Robots primarily target physical tasks and typically require stable, predictable environments, making them effective for repetitive mechanical processes (though the combination of AI and robotics may change that in the near future). Outsourcing and offshoring, while applicable to knowledge work, often involve relocating these tasks to external human providers or distant regions rather than fundamentally changing how the tasks are performed. In contrast, AI directly automates the execution of knowledge-intensive tasks, such as data analysis, report generation, or creative content development but keeps the management within the firm. Further, the AI system for a specific task could be developed within the firm, or at least with the firm's own data, and so could build on a firm's core competencies. Alternatively, the AI system for a given task may be purchased from a different firm which would effectively outsource the effort.

Automation of cognitive work raises new considerations unique to knowledge tasks. While many physical tasks are constrained by their physical presence so that a machine can only produce a limited number of units at a time, knowledge tasks may be scalable so that millions of people could read the same article or watch the same video at once. Additionally, while AI systems can generate creative outputs or factual summaries, the output quality depends on the integrity of the training data and algorithms. The accuracy and veracity of information are of paramount for many organizations because misinformation or disinformation can be highly detrimental in critical decision-making processes. Errors in knowledge tasks can propagate misinformation, undermining critical decision-making processes.

Another concern relates to AI-driven automation risks eroding human expertise if essential skills are not maintained or updated. For example, reliance on AI for coding assistance drawn from repositories like StackOverflow could lead to challenges if these repositories become obsolete or no longer support emerging technologies (Zhong & Wang, 2024). To the extent that AI systems rely on a relevant body of data to support inference, the diminished use of these knowledge repositories risks starving future AI systems of the relevant information to produce useful responses. This risk can be mitigated to the extent that firms are able to bring their own well-maintained data about their business processes.

Thus, while lessons from robotics, outsourcing, and offshoring provide useful insights into cost, efficiency, and strategic implications, AI's focus on cognitive automation introduces qualitatively different challenges. These include ensuring truthfulness, maintaining adaptability, and safeguarding long-term human expertise. Organizations must develop tailored frameworks to evaluate and manage these knowledge-intensive tasks effectively. While robotics, outsourcing, and offshoring guide decisions about displacing labor, their scope differs from that of AI in key ways. Robots primarily target physical tasks and require stable, predictable environments. Outsourcing and offshoring retain human labor but alter its location or organizational affiliation. AI, particularly large language models and other cognitive technologies, now makes it possible to automate knowledge-intensive tasks that previously required human reasoning, judgment, and creativity.

Thus, while lessons from robotics, outsourcing, and offshoring help organizations understand the cost and strategic implications of labor displacement, AI introduces qualitatively different challenges. Rather than focusing solely on cost reductions or tapping external labor pools, executives and managers must consider how cognitive tasks are identified, assessed, and overseen. This may involve frameworks similar to those used in outsourcing and offshoring—evaluating criticality, complexity, and cost—while adding criteria specific to knowledge tasks, such as truthfulness, adaptability, and long-term skill maintenance.

Looking ahead, several issues require urgent attention. Policymakers must focus on balancing automation and task creation to prevent declines in labor demand. Strategies to mitigate the adverse effects on low- and middle-skill workers, particularly in manufacturing and routine jobs, are essential. Addressing the widening gap between labor and capital income will require redistributive policies and workforce development programs. Additionally, improved data collection on workplace skills and task dynamics is critical for more accurate forecasting and policy design. Finally, as AI introduces new tasks, ensuring that these tasks contribute positively to societal welfare rather than undermining it is essential.

Task Characteristics

Decision-makers will frequently use a cost-benefit analysis to select the "best" option. So, if the cost for choice i is $cost_i$ and the benefit is $benefit_i$, then the optimal choice is $max_i(benefit_i - cost_i)$. If the benefits are not well defined, then the benefit may be defined as the expected value of the range of outcomes which we can write as $benefit_i = \sum_j (outcome_{ij} \cdot likelihood_{ij})$ where $outcome_{ij}$ is the value of j and $likelihood_{ij}$ is the probability that j occurs given that option i was selected. A cost-benefit framework is useful when the characteristics are well understood and data are readily available. When selecting AI systems to perform a task or assist in performing a task, the real-world performance may not be known and it may be necessary to design an appropriate data collection exercise or testing protocol. Thus, cost-benefit analysis may be insufficient to gauge the suitability of an AI system.

To supplement other analytic approaches, such as cost-benefit analysis, we propose a framework that relates the characteristics of a task and the specific performance of an AI system for that task to deployment strategies for the AI system for a given task. Our framework considers four characteristics: task criticality, task novelty, AI system accuracy for a given task, and the observability of an AI systems performance for a given task. We describe each of these below. Depending on whether an AI system performs at a high or low level on these criteria for a given task, we propose deployment strategies with different levels of human involvement from human performed to human-in-the-loop to human-on-the-loop to human-out-of-the loop. These strategies are also described below.

Criticality

The criticality of a task is a business assessment of the implications of a failure or suboptimal performance at the task. When decision-makers consider applying an AI system to a task, they should assess what happens if the system makes a mistake. This requires an assessment of the range of possible outcomes and the cost or other implications of the outcomes. These implications could vary widely based on the task in question and could be as little as a trivial amount of rework for a system used to provide editorial comments on a brief but could be as significant as serious reputational harm for a brand if the system uses offensive language or deaths of misdiagnosed patients. While it may be plausible to assign dollar values to these outcomes through mechanisms like the value of a statistical life, that may lead to too much attention being paid to those risks that are easily quantifiable rather than the full range of plausible outcomes. For simplicity, we suggest labeling tasks a either "high" or "low" criticality. A "high" criticality task would be one where an adverse outcome could have a materially negative effect on a firm. While a "low" criticality task may have subjective outcomes or a failure could have an acceptable cost.

When assessing the criticality of a task, decision-makers should ask questions such as:

- What are the potential outcomes of this task? Consider all plausible outcomes, both positive and negative, that could result from deploying an AI system to do the task.
- What is the range of consequences for each of these outcomes? Assign some value to each of these outcomes.
- Are there systemic problems that could arise from a failure in this task? That is to say, if this task fails, contemplate downstream effects of greater consequence than the singular failure at a task such as broader reputational risks.
- Alternatively, if a system performs particularly well, are there benefits beyond the successful completion of a task? Identify potential synergies or efficiencies that could be realized if the system is highly effective.

In practice, the criticality assessment process is very similar to the construction of a risk register, which is a standard part of enterprise risk management (Williams, 1994).

Accuracy

Accuracy is a measure of how well an AI system performs at a given task. This may be easily quantifiable for tasks where an answer is either correct or incorrect and there are data on the AI system's performance for a given task, but for other tasks there could be multiple dimensions of performance or it may be wholly subjective. Decision-makers need to have some notion of what constitutes a success or a failure, how to evaluate it, and what constitutes a good or bad outcome. Ideally, decision-makers will use relevant benchmarks to determine the accuracy of a system.

There are many public benchmarks for AI systems that test capabilities on math, reasoning, and specific types of knowledge. However, because many current LLMs are trained on these benchmarks, published benchmark performance may overstate the performance for a real-world deployment. Mirzadeh et al. found that slight variations of benchmark questions or the addition of irrelevant information led to meaningfully worse performance indicating that many of these models are “overfitted” (Mirzadeh et al., 2024). In other words, many of these models have memorized the benchmark answers rather than understood how to produce the correct answer. Thus, decision-makers should consider developing their own benchmarks.

A benchmark is a designed reference point against which new AI models can be compared to assess whether they possess a specific ability. In machine learning research, researchers traditionally develop a dataset of examples, often with labeled outcomes indicating what the model should output given a particular input. Ideally, these datasets should be diverse in the types of examples they include and challenging enough to determine whether the model performs better than random chance. Additionally, they should encapsulate as many possible scenarios relevant to the desired task.

A well-constructed dataset allows for the computation of accuracy and provides a measure of the AI's ability to accomplish the intended task. This approach is similar to traditional software unit testing, where developers conceptualize all possible use cases, edge cases, and failure cases to evaluate whether the software behaves as expected and passes all tests.

In the simplest case, the accuracy is simply $\frac{Total\ successes}{Total\ attempts}$ for the benchmark questions. Accuracy is the percentage (%) of successes. However, some cases may be more important than others or some failure modes may be more harmful than others. Thus, it may be useful to weight accuracy calculations.

When assessing the accuracy of a task, decision-makers should ask questions like:

- What share of the test cases did the AI system correctly resolve? Decision-makers should apply a benchmark to assess the performance of the AI systems under consideration.
- Does this benchmark match the real-world use of the AI system? If the benchmarks available do not match the use case being considered, decision-makers should consider developing their own benchmark test.
- Were there systematic errors or consistent problems for certain cases of the task? Examine the failures in the benchmarks, to identify patterns that indicate whether some classes of cases are more or less likely to pose a

problem. It may be feasible to segregate those cases and either improve performance or apply different management approaches for those cases.

- How does the accuracy compare to the current approach for performing the task? Assess whether the current approach is superior to the tested AI implementation and whether the AI system could be used to augment the current approach. A system with low accuracy may still be useful if it complements the current approach.

Taken together, the consequences produced when assessing the criticality and the likelihoods estimated during the accuracy calculations provide an assessment of the expected value of using the AI system for a given task. This can be paired with information about the baseline performance without the AI system and the AI system's cost to conduct a cost-benefit analysis. An AI system with low accuracy may still be useful for a highly critical task if, for example, the system is used to support a human rather than operate independently. For example, an AI system may perform poorly at summarizing complex text, but could be useful at suggesting useful information for a human reviewing the complex text.

Beyond criticality and accuracy, we propose decision-makers consider two additional factors as well.

Novelty

Task novelty can be thought of as how much a task varies between instances and over time or how variable or complex the task environment is. Decision-makers should assess the novelty of the task to determine how much weight to put on the accuracy assessment and also whether the system is likely to maintain its performance for a long period of time. If the task is stable and standardized, then the accuracy assessment is likely to be representative of future performance so long as the test was well conducted. Alternatively, if the task varies substantially or if there is substantial change over time, then the accuracy assessment may be overconfident. For example, facial recognition software trained primarily on white men performs poorly in diverse environments (Yucer et al., 2024). Thus, understanding the novelty of a task is useful for evaluating the level of oversight required for a system and other deployment-related decisions.

It is important to note that if a task is not very novel, but the AI system has relatively low accuracy, then there is a poor match between the specific AI system and the task. In these cases, that specific AI system is likely not suitable and an alternative system may perform better. For systems developed internally, more data may need to be collected if the training set was insufficiently diverse, alternative algorithms or architectures may be needed if the model was overfitted, or additional computational resources may need to be devoted to training the model to raise its accuracy.

Alternatively, if the task is not highly critical, it may be appropriate to facilitate learning in the AI system to steer it to better accuracy. One option could be to use reinforcement learning where the AI systems algorithm receives rewards for accurate performances but is penalized for failures so that its performance improves over time. Reinforcement learning may also be useful as part of a continuous improvement approach to ensure that additional data are used to steer the model to account for changes in the system over time.

When assessing the novelty of a task, decision-makers should ask questions like:

- How variable is the task or the environment for the task? Determine the range of plausible inputs or the complexity of the environment for the AI system.
- What factors drive the complexity of the task? Examine the task to determine what factors or characteristics of the environment lead to variation in the task requirements, expectations, or activities.
- Do these factors or does the task as a whole change over time? Identify cyclical patterns or broader trends that influence the factors. This can help determine whether the task can be segmented if there are significant differences in the accuracy at different points in time.
- How can and should the AI system be updated over time to learn from new cases? If there are trends that will change the key factors over time, then this could provide guidance on how often to update the model.

Observability

The final characteristic in our framework is the observability of an AI system's performance for a given task by a manager. There are some tasks where failure may not be detected until well after the harm is done. For example, a computer vision algorithm that misclassifies an object as in motion when it is stationary could be highly problematic if that is used in a self-driving vehicle and the error isn't detected until there is a collision. Alternatively, if that same flawed algorithm were deployed to detect loitering, the error could be detected before any harm was done through a visual inspection.

Understanding whether, how, and by whom the performance of an AI system can be observed is important for designing monitoring systems and determining the degree of automation that is appropriate for a task. In order to effectively manage a process, the task manager of an AI system or human worker needs some ability assess performance. For tasks performed by humans, the manager may be able to intuit the performance because that manager could perform the same task. For an AI system, the underlying mechanics that lead to an outcome may be neither transparent nor intuitive. Thus, alternative systems may be necessary for observing and monitoring an AI system.

If the AI's approach for performing a task is largely similar to the approach of a human, it may be straightforward for a manager to monitor the performance and manage the task. However, some tasks may be difficult to monitor by their nature. The manager of an AI that is reviewing medical images to identify a tumor will need to be able to do the task to monitor the performance. For systems that have a low inherent observability, additional steps may be necessary to provide confidence in the algorithm. For example, an audit of a resume screening system found that the characteristics the algorithm used to flag high performers included whether the resume included "Jared" and "lacrosse" (Kessler, 2018). Had a manager attempted to detect this type of error they would need to review each resume and the recommendation to hope to identify such a problem. For cases where there isn't a clear right or wrong answer, algorithmic audits can be useful for helping with the explainability (Costanza-Chock et al., 2022). Large AI systems are sufficiently new that there is not a standardized approach for auditing them, but many of the best practices from older methodologies are still relevant. For example, software verification and validation (V&V) exercises are still relevant for AI systems, though, because of the complexity, these are likely insufficient to provide the same level of confidence that V&V (Oberkampf & Roy, 2010). Further, for AI systems developed by third parties, verification may not be feasible.

When assessing the observability of a task, decision-makers should ask questions like:

- Under the current plan for deploying an AI system, when would flaws be observed? Decision-makers need to know how manager will identify errors or other problems in the output from the system.
- What systems are/should be in place for continuous performance monitoring? Determine whether existing management systems and managers are appropriate for monitoring and improving the system performance. It may be that specialized knowledge related to the AI system is necessary to effectively manage the system.

- Are there early warnings or indicators that could be used to flag problematic performance? Look for cues that indicate an error will arise so that problems can be addressed as soon as possible.
- Has/should an audit of the AI system be conducted? Consider a thorough examination of the AI system and its performance at the task in question.

Degrees of Automation with AI

There are a variety of ways to categorize the degree of automation from no automation where the human does all the work to fully automated where a human cannot easily intervene or observe the actions or decisions of a system. Certain systems benefit from human oversight and involvement because humans may be able to detect events that are not directly observable by the system (Chiodo et al., 2025). The question of human involvement—whether to keep humans "in the loop," "on the loop," or "out of the loop"—depends on how well the system learns and the potential impacts on users. In the following sections, we provide examples to illustrate each of these approaches.

Human-In-the-Loop

The human-in-the-loop (HITL) approach centers on integrating meaningful human involvement throughout the design of AI systems (Chiodo et al., 2025). A key characteristic of HITL in automated system design is that human action is essential for the system's operation, with automation serving primarily as an assistant to human efforts (Lacher et al., 2023; Singh & Szajnfarber, 2025). The AI may collect relevant information as specified by the human user, provide recommendations for actions, or queue up a decision to be made. In these cases, compared to a human working without AI assistance, the AI system is intended to improve the performance of the human by either improving the quality of task or reducing the time taken to perform the task related to a higher degree of autonomy. The benefits of HITL could include enhanced transparency in system design, the integration of human judgment, and reduced pressure for the automated system to achieve absolute precision. Functional excellence emerges when designers effectively balance human intervention with automated processes (Chiodo et al., 2025).

"AI copilots" for writing computer code are an increasingly common example of HITL. With copilots, the user describes the goal of the program or a portion of the program and the AI system responds with recommendations or code. The copilot can also review code provide by the user and make recommendations to resolve an error. In this case, the human is ultimately responsible for the code generated. There is a question about whether copilots will make learning code useless (Smith, 2023), allow novice coders to perform as well as experts, or disproportionately benefit expert coders is a question of open debate (Moradi Dakhel et al., 2023).

Another common application of HITL is in semi-supervised machine learning algorithms used for data labeling and annotation. Here, human input is crucial for creating high-quality training datasets until the algorithm can independently make reasonably accurate predictions. When a messaging program or word processor empowered with AI suggests the next word, phrase, or even full message, the human user can still read, edit, and choose to send. The HITL approach in this context not only improves efficiency but ensures that algorithms meet functional requirements, aligning with Wang's emphasis on purposeful AI design.

For HITL systems, the AI should be not be a burden on the user. If the errors are so common that the AI system is functionally useless, then HITL is not appropriate. On the other hand, if the AI system is so reliable or the task is so mundane that the task doesn't require meaningful human actions, a HITL deployment may not be appropriate. Essentially, a HITL deployment makes sense if the task is sufficiently important that accountability is needed or the AI system is not ready to fully perform the task because it isn't accurate enough, the task is too variably for enough data to have been collected, or the systems for appropriately monitor its performance have not been developed. It is a good first step when looking at adopting AI systems.

Human-On-the-Loop

With human-on-the-loop (HOTL) system architectures, humans have the option but are not required to intervene; they monitor and guide the automated processes, retaining the ability to take control when necessary (Lacher et al., 2023; Singh & Szajinfarber, 2025). In this supervisory role, human operators are responsible for assessing whether decisions made by the system controller are accurate or erroneous, intervening when needed by overriding commands, pausing the system, or fully shutting it down (Abraham et al., 2021; Chiodo et al., 2025). With HOTL, AI system performs the task and provides the human with the information necessary to monitor the task.

If the AI system is sufficiently reliable for a given task, it may be appropriate to use a HOTL implementation. The system should provide the user with sufficient information to effectively monitor the performance, but not so much as to overwhelm the user. The user should be trained to understand the types of failure modes for the system and it may be helpful for the user to understand, at least at a high level, the underlying AI system and its algorithms. In order to realize the efficiency gains, users of HOTL systems should understand their role and when they are responsible for intervening (Shneiderman, 2020).

An increasingly prevalent example of HOTL is found in autonomous vehicles, such as those developed by Waymo or Tesla. These vehicles rely on sensors, cameras, and machine learning algorithms to navigate roads, while steering wheels, breaks, and other control mechanisms remain present so human driver can take over in case of unexpected events. Waymo's vehicles, for instance, range from Level 1 to Level 4 autonomy, with Level 4 representing fully driverless technology capable of independent operation without human intervention under certain conditions (Ackerman, 2021). In extenuating circumstances, human operators can still supervise and adjust settings, even in Level 4 Waymo vehicles. The driver is typically alerted when their intervention is recommended, but this has led to serious accidents when the human was not provided sufficient warning or was not prepared to take control of the vehicle due to distraction. Based on the most recent data available at the time of this study, autonomous vehicles were more likely to be in collisions than those without (Zandt, 2024). Further, the very presence of autonomous driving systems can exacerbate distractions (Reagan et al., 2024). This highlights the need for HOTL systems to keep users with the appropriate level of engagement and for users to understand the performance constraints of the system.

HOTL deployments should not be considered for critical tasks where the AI is not reasonably accurate. For systems where the manager can observe and quickly correct errors, it may be acceptable to deploy less accurate AI systems as HOTL for non-critical tasks.

Human-Out-of-the-Loop

For human-out-of-the-loop systems, the task is automated without allowing direct intervention before, during, or after completion. The AI system is completing the task fully autonomously. For all but the most insignificant tasks, it is advisable that the decision-maker can observe the outcomes in aggregate so that the system performance can be monitored and some form of intervention can be done as needed.

An early example of a human-out-of-loop automated system is the explosive landmine, which has been widely deployed in warfare and conflict zones to provide a defensive barrier among other uses. Once activated, landmines operate autonomously, and human operators have no ability to abort the detonation or protect individuals in proximity. However, in their most basic form, landmines do not respond to changes in the environment and so can persist long after the need for a defensive barrier is gone resulting in thousands of civilian casualties each year (Ban Landmines, 2024). Thus, autonomous systems must be responsive to changes in their environment and some level of human awareness may also be useful.

More mundanely, numerous tasks related to computers have been fully automated over time. Older programming languages like FORTRAN required users manage the computer's memory explicitly when running the program, but now memory handling in software is typically handled autonomously except in edge cases such as high-performance computing environments. Similarly, many financial transactions such as paying certain bills are automated. Decision-makers in the case of the financial transactions can look at payment information and may receive an notice around the time of the transaction, however, in the case of memory handling, users need to go to the system tools on their computer to find reporting of the information and need to use special commands to change the memory handling. The distinguishing characteristic between these cases is the criticality of the task. For most systems, poor memory handling may cause a few minutes of downtime while the system restarts, while a flaw in a financial transaction could result in a bounced check or some loss of funds. Thus, when a decision-maker is considering an out-of-the-loop system, they should consider what summary information might be useful for a user and whether they would need to allow for some form of intervention.

To consider a fully automated system, decision-makers and developers should have an AI system that performs very well on the task and the task owner should be able to observe, at least at an aggregate level, when the system performance deviates from the goals. If the environment is highly variable then the accuracy estimates may not be adequately reliable and an on-the-loop system may be more appropriate. Likewise, for highly critical tasks an on-the-loop system will likely be more appropriate so that there will be a human accountable for the outcomes.

Framework for Relating Task Characteristics to Suitability for Automation by AI

We present a framework in Table 1 for assessing the suitability of AI systems for task automation, based on the four key dimensions: criticality, accuracy,

Table 1 Framework that relates task characteristics to suitability for an AI system

		Observability low		Observability high	
		Novelty high	Novelty low	Novelty high	Novelty low
Criticality high	Accuracy low	Human	*	In-the-loop	*
Criticality high	Accuracy high	Human/in-the-loop	In-the-loop	In/on-the-loop	On-the-loop
Criticality low	Accuracy low	In-the-loop	*	On-the-loop	*
Criticality low	Accuracy high	In/on-the-loop	On-the-loop	On/out-of-the-loop	Out-of-the-loop

Note: * indicates a case where the specific AI system under consideration is likely a poor fit for the task observability, and novelty. This categorization helps decision-makers determine the appropriate level of human involvement required for various tasks. For instance, tasks characterized by high criticality and low accuracy demand direct human oversight to mitigate risks, particularly in environments with low observability or high novelty. Conversely, tasks with low criticality, high accuracy, and high observability may be fully automated, allowing humans to remain "out-of-the-loop." Importantly, tasks with low accuracy and low novelty should raise concerns, as they may indicate poorly defined objectives or insufficient AI training and tuning. While this framework provides general guidance, it is not exhaustive and should be adapted to specific scenarios and contextual nuances.

In addition to the degree of automation, these factors can be useful for identifying the characteristics of an AI system that would be useful for the given problem. For tasks that require a high degree of accuracy, stochastic systems, such as LLMs or stochastic annealing methods with a high temperature factor, may be too unreliable or unpredictable to use. Alternatively, stochastic methods may be useful for pushing out of local optima, which could be useful for tasks that are more novel. For tasks were a high degree of observability is preferred, a smaller, simpler model may be more suitable because they will be more interpretable and user who understands the model mechanics can more quickly identify problems than with a black box model.

Conclusions

Artificial Intelligence is commonly referred to as general purpose technology because, in principle, AI can be applied to any knowledge work task (MacAfee, 2024). While it is plausible that AI systems will someday be able to perform any knowledge task better and cheaper than any human, that is not the state today. Until then, decision-makers need to use their judgment about when an AI system is suitable to be deployed for a task. The framework we have described connects the characteristics of a task to the performance of the AI for that task to provide guidance on the level of automation that is prudent. Tasks that are more critical or novel will generally require more oversight than tasks that are less variable or critical. Likewise, AI systems that are more accurate or are more observable will require less human involvement for a task than AI systems that are less accurate or more opaque to managers. However, these assessments should not be static.

As technology advances or business processes change, the initial assessments should be reevaluated and updated. The criticality can change as the business environment changes or the firm's lines of work change. Accuracy can improve as algorithms advance but this need not be monotonic and could decrease if there is model drift, Novelty may increase if the market changes or it could decrease as more data become available. The observability may improve as better diagnostics are deployed or it could decline if managers' skills atrophy.

When decision-makers are considering deploying an AI system for a task, they should:

1. Consider the implications of a failed attempt at the task and whether that would critically affect the organization's activities.
2. Select or develop benchmarks to test a proposed AI system that are relevant for the task under consideration and also capture the full range of plausible cases.
3. Apply the benchmarks, compare the results to the current performance, and look for evidence of systematic errors.
4. Determine whether the AI system can be deployed in such a way that a human can provide meaningful oversight.
5. Select the level of oversight based on a framework similar to that of Table 1.
6. Monitor the task and system performance periodically, even for human out-of-the-loop systems.
7. Update the assessments for the framework as needed and update the deployment as needed.

Over time AI systems will become more capable and therefore the level of human oversight and involvement needed for knowledge work tasks can be expected to decline. Just as outsourcing and offshoring have led to the loss of some capabilities of firms, there is a risk that humans will lose certain expertise and that makes proper oversight challenging. For skills like balancing a checkbook, that may not be a critical problem, but others, like interpreting a medical image, could be critical. To avoid losing critical skills, policymakers should consider preservation approaches for that expertise. Additional work is needed to identify knowledge that should be preserved and how best to preserve the expertise.

References

Abraham, S., Carmichael, Z., Banerjee, S., VidalMata, R., Agrawal, A., Al Islam, M. N., ... & Cleland-Huang, J. (2021, May). Adaptive autonomy in human-on-the-loop vision-based robotics systems. In *2021 IEEE/ACM 1st workshop on AI engineering-software engineering for AI (WAIN)* (pp. 113–120). IEEE.

Acemoglu, D. (2024). *The simple macroeconomics of AI (working paper no. 32487). Working paper series*. National Bureau of Economic Research. Retrieved from http://www.nber.org/papers/w32487

Acemoglu, D., & Restrepo, P. (2017). *Robots and jobs: Evidence from US labor markets (working paper no. 23285). Working paper series*. National Bureau of Economic Research. Retrieved from http://www.nber.org/papers/w23285

Acemoglu, D., & Restrepo, P. (2019). Automation and new tasks: How technology displaces and reinstates labor. *Journal of Economic Perspectives, 33*(2), 3–30. Retrieved from https://www.aeaweb.org/articles?id=10.1257/jep.33.2.3

Ackerman, E. (2021). What full autonomy means for the Waymo driver: For self-driving vehicles, full autonomy might not be quite as full as you think. *IEEE Spectrum*. Retrieved from https://spectrum.ieee.org/full-autonomy-waymo-driver

Autor, D. H. (2015). Why are there still so many jobs? The history and future of workplace automation. *Journal of Economic Perspectives, 29*(3), 3–30. Retrieved from https://www.aeaweb.org/articles?id=10.1257/jep.29.3.3

Autor, D., & Salomons, A. (2018). *Is automation labor-displacing? Productivity growth, employment, and the labor share*. National Bureau of Economic Research.

Bapna, R., Langer, N., Mehra, A., Gopal, R., & Gupta, A. (2013). Human capital investments and employee performance: An analysis of IT services industry. *Management Science, 59*(3), 641–658.

Bessen, J. (2015). Toil and technology: Innovative technology is displacing workers to new jobs rather than replacing them entirely. *Finance & Development, 52*(001), 16. International Monetary Fund.

Bureau of Labor Statistics. (2023, May). *Occupational employment and wage statistics*. Retrieved from https://www.bls.gov/oes/

Chiodo, M., Müller, D., Siewert, P., Wetherall, J. L., Yasmine, Z., & Burden, J. (2025). *Formalising human-in-the-loop: Computational reductions, failure modes, and legal-moral responsibility*. arXiv preprint arXiv:2505.10426.

Costanza-Chock, S., Raji, I. D., & Buolamwini, J. (2022). Who audits the auditors? Recommendations from a field scan of the algorithmic auditing ecosystem. In *Proceedings of the 2022 ACM conference on fairness, accountability, and transparency* (pp. 1571–1583).

Feenstra, R. C., & Hanson, G. H. (1996). *Globalization, outsourcing, and wage inequality*. National Bureau of Economic Research.

Frank, M. R., Autor, D., Bessen, J. E., Brynjolfsson, E., et al. (2019). Toward understanding the impact of artificial intelligence on labor. *Proceedings of the National Academy of Sciences, 116*(14), 6531–6539. Retrieved from https://www.pnas.org/doi/abs/10.1073/pnas.1900949116

Graetz, G., & Michaels, G. (2018). Robots at work. *Review of Economics and Statistics, 100*(5), 753–768. MIT Press.

Grover, V., & Malhotra, M. K. (2003). Transaction cost framework in operations and supply chain management research: Theory and measurement.

Journal of Operations Management, 21(4), 457–473. Retrieved from https://www.sciencedirect.com/science/article/pii/S0272696303000408
Harari, Y. N. (2018). *21 lessons for the 21st century*. Spiegel & Grau.
Howard, J. (2019). Artificial intelligence: Implications for the future of work. *American Journal of Industrial Medicine, 62*(11), 917–926. Wiley Online Library.
International Campaign to Ban Landmines. (2024). *Landmine monitor 2024*. Retrieved from https://backend.icblcmc.org/assets/reports/Landmine-Monitors/LMM2024/Downloads/Landmine-Monitor-2024-Final-Web.pdf
Kessler, S. (2018). *Companies are on the hook if their hiring algorithms are biased*. Retrieved from https://qz.com/1427621/companies-are-on-the-hook-if-their-hiring-algorithms-are-biased
Lacher, A. R., Ren, L., Maroney, D. R., Schulenberg, C., & Daniels, J. (2023, April). Dimensional role analysis: The role of humans and automation for increasingly autonomous aviation systems. In *2023 integrated communication, navigation and surveillance conference* (pp. 1–6).
Leondes, C. T. (2001). *Expert systems: The technology of knowledge management and decision making for the 21st century*. Elsevier.
Levy, O. (2005). The influence of top management team attention patterns on global strategic posture of firms. *Journal of Organizational Behavior, 26*(7), 797–819. Wiley Online Library.
MacAfee, A. (2024). *Generally faster: The economic impact of generative AI*. M. I. T. Technology Review. Retrieved from https://storage.googleapis.com/gweb-uniblog-publish-prod/documents/Generally_Faster_-_The_Economic_Impact_of_Generative_AI.pdf
Mavers, S., & Baker, R. (2021). A look at an automation adoption through a human performance technology lens: A case study of bank tellers and automated teller machines. *Performance Improvement, 60*(2), 21–30.
Mihalache, M., & Mihalache, O. R. (2016). A decisional framework of offshoring: Integrating insights from 25 years of research to provide direction for future. *Decision Sciences, 47*(6), 1103–1149.
Mirzadeh, I., Alizadeh, K., Shahrokhi, H., Tuzel, O., Bengio, S., & Farajtabar, M. (2024). *Gsm-symbolic: Understanding the limitations of mathematical reasoning in large language models*. arXiv preprint arXiv:2410.05229.
Moradi Dakhel, A., Majdinasab, V., Nikanjam, A., Khomh, F., Desmarais, M. C., & Jiang, Z. M. J. (2023). GitHub copilot AI pair programmer: Asset or liability? *Journal of Systems and Software, 203*, 111734. Retrieved from https://www.sciencedirect.com/science/article/pii/S0164121223001292
Morse, P. M., Kimball, G. E., & Gass, S. I. (2003). *Methods of operations research*. Courier Corporation.
Oberkampf, W. L., & Roy, C. J. (2010). *Verification and validation in scientific computing*. Cambridge University Press.

Prahalad, C. K., & Hamel, G. (1990). The core competence of the corporation. *Harvard Business Review, 68*(3), 79–91. Retrieved from https://hbr.org/1990/05/the-core-competence-of-the-corporation

Quinn, J. B. (1999). *Strategic outsourcing: Leveraging knowledge capabilities.* MIT Sloan Management Review. Retrieved from https://sloanreview.mit.edu/article/strategic-outsourcing-leveraging-knowledge-capabilities/

Reagan, I. J., Cicchino, J. B., Teoh, E. R., Gershon, P., Reimer, B., & Mehler, B. (2024). *Rinse and repeat: Behavior change associated with using partial automation among three samples of drivers during a 4-week field trial (No. 2311).* Insurance Institute for Highway Safety. Retrieved from https://www.iihs.org/api/datastoredocument/bibliography/2311

Shneiderman, B. (2020). Human-centered artificial intelligence: Reliable, safe & trustworthy. arXiv preprint arXiv:2002.04087v1. Retrieved from https://arxiv.org/abs/2002.04087v1

Singh, A., & Szajnfarber, Z. (2025). Architecting Human-AI Systems for Effective Collaboration and Oversight: Making Sense of Human/AI-in/on/Over/Under/Along-the-Loop. *Systems Engineering*, e70024.

Smith, D. (2023). *NVIDIA CEO predicts the death of coding: Jensen Huang says AI will do the work so kids don't need to learn.* Retrieved from https://www.techradar.com/pro/nvidia-ceo-predicts-the-death-of-coding-jensen-huang-says-ai-will-do-the-work-so-kids-dont-need-to-learn

Williams, T. M. (1994). Using a risk register to integrate risk management in project definition. *International Journal of Project Management, 12*(1), 17–22.

Williamson, O. E. (1975). *Markets and hierarchies: Analysis and antitrust implications.* The Free Press.

Yucer, S., Tektas, F., Al Moubayed, N., & Breckon, T. (2024). Racial bias within face recognition: A survey. *ACM Computing Surveys, 57*(4) New York, NY, USA: Association for Computing Machinery. Retrieved from https://doi.org/10.1145/3705295

Zandt, F. (2024). *Collisions per motor vehicle & vehicle miles traveled by type of vehicle.* Retrieved from https://www.statista.com/chart/32985/collisions-crashes-per-motor-vehicle-vehicle-miles-traveled-by-type-of-vehicle/

Zhong, L., & Wang, Z. (2024). *Can ChatGPT replace StackOverflow? A study on robustness and reliability of large language model code generation.* Retrieved from https://arxiv.org/abs/2308.10335

The Socio-Economic Impact of Artificial Intelligence and the Role of Policy

Gabriela Ramos

This chapter examines how the development of artificial intelligence (AI), when primarily driven by profit maximization and geopolitical competition, risks leading to high technological concentration, stifling innovation, and deepening inequalities. It analyzes the socio-economic and incentive structures that shape AI, revealing how current market dynamics tend to prioritize speed and scale over equity, sustainability, and inclusion. Drawing on UNESCO's Recommendation on the Ethics of Artificial Intelligence and the Readiness Assessment Methodology (RAM) implemented in more than 80 countries as well as the OECD Principles on AI, the chapter highlights how policy choices and institutional capacities determine whether AI contributes to or undermines human development.

It proposes a policy framework grounded in the "three Is" of effective AI governance—Institutions, Incentives, and Investments—and calls for technological progress that serves the common good. The chapter underscores that governments can play an active role in protecting citizens and incentivizing ethical, responsible innovation. It concludes that technological developments

The author is grateful to Eleonora Lamm and Mariagrazia Squicciarini for their invaluable contributions to this work, and for being part of the wonderful team that made the UNESCO effort on the ethics of AI so effective.

G. Ramos (✉)
Former UNESCO, OECD, Paris, France
e-mail: gabrielaramospatino@gmail.com

M. Rangeley, N. Fairfax (eds.), *The Artificial Intelligence Revolution*,
https://doi.org/10.1007/978-3-032-11814-1_16

should enhance human rights and human dignity so that they help the achievement of inclusive and democratic outcomes.

Introduction

Artificial intelligence (AI) is everywhere, embedded in our computers, shaping our conversations, and making daily headlines about its transformative potential and associated risks. While it triggers imagination and hope, promising to offer tremendous benefits to humanity, it also creates fear and uncertainty about its broader implications.

As global competition intensifies among major tech companies to develop "general purpose" AI, our societies, economies, and individuals grapple with the pace of change. This is at the heart of the challenge: how do we ensure that we are well equipped—in the marketplace, universities, and governments—to steer the development of AI, managing its risks while maximizing its benefits? How do we ensure that our legal frameworks, which have been promoting and protecting human rights and human dignity, are fit for purpose in this ever-changing environment?

This chapter proposes an approach aimed at rebalancing the way AI technologies are developed, leading to a high concentration of power and capabilities that risks deepening inequalities and limiting full access to AI benefits for all. The current model of AI development—mainly driven by capital-intensive, profit-maximizing incentives and geopolitical considerations—may further lead to developments that, while being technically feasible, may not be societally desirable. The lack of directionality regarding social impact of the current AI trajectory, may curb the role that AI technologies can play to address broader social and economic challenges, and even limit the capacity of business to innovate, thrive, and deliver for good. If—as the literature has long argued in the case of many industries and past technological paradigms—the relationship between concentration and innovation is mainly U-shaped,[1] too few or too much concentration is likely to be detrimental to AI-related innovation.

However, these outcomes—both technological, as well as economic and societal—are not predetermined. The prevailing deterministic and dichotomous approach, holding that we just need to adapt to the current technological

[1]Aghion, P., Bloom, N., Blundell, R., Griffith, R., & Howitt, P. (2005). Competition and innovation: An inverted-U relationship. The Quarterly Journal of Economics, 120(2), 701–728. Oxford University Press. http://www.jstor.org/stable/25098750.

trajectory, is not accurate about the role that policies and incentives may play in steering these developments. Alternative trajectories are possible if we shift focus to actively shaping these developments through ethical frameworks, inclusive policies, and public interest-oriented approaches and incentives. To chart this path forward, this chapter examines the current dynamics of AI governance and highlights the efforts—particularly those I led at UNESCO and OECD—to promote more sustainable, inclusive, and equitable approaches to technological development.

The AI Landscape: AI Technological Trajectories, Business Dynamics, and Policy Approaches

AI Technological Trajectories

Having a shared, broad understanding of the technical evolution of AI and the inherent capabilities and implications of AI models themselves is key to better apprehend the way these technologies may impact economies and societies, and, thus, inform the design and implementation of effective policies that are also "future-proof."[2]

In recent years, AI-related developments and capabilities multiplied and accelerated, followed by fast and widespread adoption and deployment. A point in case is ChatGPT, a generative artificial intelligence chatbot developed by OpenAI, which was released at the end of November 2022 and took only 2 months to surpass 100 million users. In line with this trend, 2025 started with daily announcements related to significant investments, advancements, or applications in Artificial Intelligence. Examples are DeepSeek's release of R1 open-source model on 20 January 2025—matching capabilities of leading proprietary systems while costing just a fraction of those, and with lower environmental impact—and the many governments, particularly the most advanced, announcing increased investments in AI, including the 500 billion dollars of private investment in infrastructure in the U.S.[3]

At the same time, the pace of progress in AI developments is dizzying, and relatively more established or traditional approaches, such as rule-based

[2]Ojanen, A. (2025, April 10). *Technology neutrality as a way to future-proof regulation: the case of the Artificial Intelligence Act.* SSRN. https://ssrn.com/abstract=5181085

[3]CBS News. (2025, January 21). *Trump announces private-sector AI infrastructure investment of up to $500 billion.* https://www.cbsnews.com/news/trump-announces-private-sector-ai-infrastructure-investment/; OpenAI. (2025, January 21). *Announcing the Stargate Project.* https://openai.com/index/announcing-the-stargate-project/

systems and machine learning, continue to be leveraged, especially in some sectors or specific applications, while new ones emerge. Breakthroughs in 2024 and 2025, the "reasoning models" and "agentic AI," are now commonplace capabilities offered in both proprietary and open-weight forms. Video generation has leaped from the few-second clips of OpenAI's Sora that captured global attention in winter 2024, to Google's Veo3 model (May 2025) producing content, including audio, that is often difficult to distinguish from professional productions. In parallel, autonomous code generation and testing has matured and is transformed from a frontier challenge to a standard industry practice in the span of a single year.

On the other hand, artificial intelligence technologies have been undergoing fundamental transformations in the past year, driven by several converging trends: the cost of deploying advanced AI capabilities has fallen by over 90%, integration tools and development frameworks have matured significantly, and AI models have become more flexible and capable of being customized for specific uses and in some cases deployed locally.[4] Open source movements in AI have also been contributing to democratizing AI developments. In 2024, AI systems started to exhibit greater environmental sustainability and reduced energy consumption; greater openness (although no agreement exists about what an "open AI system" really is), and greater compute efficiency coupled with better performance in technical tasks such as those related to math or coding. These shifts, combined with AI's increasing sophistication in reasoning and autonomous action, have changed how AI systems can be deployed and used. What was once exclusive to major tech companies can now be integrated, customized, and deployed by organizations across all sectors, though often still with significant technical and resource requirements, in terms of both infrastructures and human capital.[5] These promising developments join the AI cases that show how much it can improve the well-being of people. Indeed, more and more AI is being deployed for positive impact, either to improve efficiency in public and private enterprises and increasing accuracy in the health sector or effectiveness in the education systems.

However, while these trends point to positive scenarios to apply AI for development purposes, it is important to acknowledge the deep structural inequalities characterizing the global AI ecosystem. As highlighted in the 2025

[4]Cottier, B., Snodin, B., Owen, D., & Adamczewski, T. (2025, May 19). *280x cheaper: The real AI revolution is accessibility*. WisdomTree. https://www.wisdomtree.com/investments/blog/2025/05/19/280x-cheaper-the-real-ai-revolution-is-accessibility.

[5]Zuboff, S. (2019). *The Age of Surveillance Capitalism: The Fight for a Human Future at the New Frontier of Power*. PublicAffairs.

Stanford's AI Index Report, more than 80% of frontier models and cutting-edge research are produced by fewer than ten laboratories—most of them housed within large tech corporations in the United States and few in China. This concentration of capabilities and resources not only limits epistemic diversity but also represents a significant barrier for developing countries seeking to build sovereign AI capacities. When lacking access to compute, data, funding, and talent, nations remain confined to peripheral roles—such as consumers, data suppliers, or annotation labor—without the ability to have AI systems that reflect their own contexts, languages, priorities, and values.[6]

AI in Historical Perspective

This is not the first time that humanity confronts challenges of this type, as technologies that were once considered General Purpose Technologies—such as electricity or internet—have always met a mix of enthusiasm and fear. The real impact of new technological paradigms gets defined over time, and for diffusion to occur, it is important to have the institutional, economic, and societal determination to embrace a new technological paradigm and have the availability of the relevant resources—both legal, infrastructure and human capital.

Electricity, for example, transformed industries and everyday life around the world, but not at the same pace due to the lack of enabling infrastructure. This contributes to explain why, still in 2023, 750 million people worldwide lacked access to electricity.[7] As for the internet, it democratized access to information and revolutionized communications, but it also brought challenges related to privacy, misinformation, and digital security, among others. Digital divides remain wide. Although in 2024, 5.5 billion people were online (i.e. 68% of the world population, compared with 65% one year earlier), universality continues to remain elusive, especially in low-income regions.[8]

In the same manner, the transformation brought about by AI technologies is not being uniform nor benefiting everyone to the same extent. On top, as

[6]Stanford Institute for Human-Centered Artificial Intelligence. (2025). Artificial Intelligence Index Report 2025. Stanford University. https://hai.stanford.edu/ai-index/2025-ai-index-report.

[7]International Energy Agency (2024), Electricity access continues to improve in 2024—after first global setback in decades, IEA, Paris https://www.iea.org/commentaries/electricity-access-continues-to-improve-in-2024-after-first-global-setback-in-decades, Licence: CC BY 4.0.

[8]International Telecommunication Union (2024), Measuring digital development Facts and Figures 2024, ITU, Geneva. chrome-extension://efaidnbmnnnibpcajpcglclefindmkaj/file:///C:/Users/M_Squicciarini/Downloads/d-ind-ict_mdd-2024-4-pdf-e.pdf/;

the AI technological paradigm is unfolding[9] at unprecedented speed, scale, and scope, it demands agile change management responses from both people and institutions. Thus, to ensure more inclusive outcomes in the technological transition, efforts should be made not only to catch up on the technological developments, but to increase institutional and human capacities to steer them, retaining direction and oversight.

These are the lessons of the effort I led at UNESCO since 2020, that started with the adoption, by 194 countries, of the most universal global standard on the ethics of artificial intelligence to date, and deployed, at the time of the elaboration of this chapter, in more than 80 countries. From a deep fascination of the technological advances and focus on the way technologies work, the global narrative around the implementation of the UNESCO Recommendation on the Ethics of AI has integrated the need to upgrade our own institutional capacities to ensure that technological outcomes are desirable from a societal point of view.

Indeed, to get the technological transition right, our priority should be to focus on preparing our institutions—workplaces, schools, public administrations, and citizens—for the transition and making them able to steer it for the societal good. The goal is not to merely adapt to AI, but to shape its trajectory to contribute to our shared goals and values and agree on what we do not want AI to do, while allowing AI innovation to bloom in many (desirable) directions.

Technological Concentration and Business Models: Structural Barriers to Ethical AI Development

The development of forefront artificial intelligence, especially of foundational models[10] is highly concentrated in the hands of a small number of companies, primarily based in the United States and China. This is not coincidental: it reflects a broader system of incentives and business models centered on capital intensity, access to data or proprietary data, and profit maximization. These dynamics have been reinforced by public policies that often favor innovation

[9] Dosi, Giovanni. "Technological paradigms and technological trajectories: a suggested interpretation of the determinants and directions of technical change." Research policy 11.3 (1982): 147–162.

[10] A foundational model is a large, versatile machine learning model trained on a broad and diverse dataset, often using self-supervised learning, and designed to be adaptable to a wide range of downstream tasks. These models serve as the "foundation" upon which more specialized systems can be built.

speed, and technology-based economic competitiveness over public interest or societal impact.[11]

Concentration has seemingly intensified in recent months. As of July 2025, NVIDIA had a market cap of $4.001 trillion USD, making NVIDIA the world's most valuable company by market cap according to data.[12] This is largely driven by escalating demand for Graphic Processing Units (GPUs), which represents a critical hardware for large AI models. Such developments underscore how key AI infrastructure, particularly compute capacity, is increasingly in the hands of a few economic agents.

Data from the Stanford's 2024 and 2025 Artificial Intelligence Index Reports[13] underlined that over 80% of state-of-the-art AI models and frontier research outputs came from fewer than ten laboratories, most of them affiliated with major tech companies such as OpenAI, Google DeepMind, Meta, and Anthropic. This level of concentration not only reduces epistemic diversity but also reinforces global asymmetries in technological capabilities, competitiveness and thus, influence.

According to the 2025 report, while the U.S. remains the leader when it comes to the production of top AI models (40 top AI models from the U.S. versus 15 from China and 3 from Europe in 2024), China has been narrowing performance and quality gaps, assessed based on major benchmarks. Also, the fact that China continues to lead in AI publications and patents points to the likelihood of important developments and strengthened AI industry's competitiveness in the future.

Even though the 2025 AI Index Report points to some positive developments, such as the emergence of foundational models from the Middle East, Latin America, and Southeast Asia, concentration remains high and raises significant ethical and structural concerns. Key decisions about the types of AI systems that are developed, the way systems are trained and tested in the wild, and the very purposes for which they are developed and deployed continue to be mainly determined by private actors accountable to shareholders rather than citizens. Experience has shown that this is limiting the incorporation of societal values such as equity, sustainability, or inclusiveness into AI design and from the outset.

---

[11] Raji, Inioluwa Deborah & Buolamwini, Joy (2019). "Actionable Auditing: Investigating the Impact of Publicly Naming Biased Performance Results of Commercial AI Products." *AAAI/ACM FAccT.*

[12] Associated Press. (2025, July 9). AI kingpin Nvidia crowned as first public company with a $4 trillion valuation. AP News. https://apnews.com/article/7947e86a7ee9a994b9f16c3c0779b74f.

[13] Stanford Institute for Human-Centered Artificial Intelligence. (2025). Artificial Intelligence Index Report 2025. Stanford University. https://hai.stanford.edu/ai-index/2025-ai-index-report.

The technological concentration in artificial intelligence is not only reflected in the dominance of a few key actors in research and development but also in the control over the critical infrastructure that underpins the entire ecosystem. According to Stanford's AI Index Report, nearly 90% of the most notable AI models in 2024 were developed by industry players—up from 60% in 2023. This dominance is sustained by a closed, capital-intensive ecosystem, where the compute resources are required to train frontier models now double approximately every 5 months, creating formidable barriers to entry for new actors.[14]

Concentration is also stark in financial flows. The United States attracted $109.1 billion in private AI investment in 2024—12 times more than China. This asymmetry means that the development of AI is increasingly shaped by the priorities and incentives of a handful of private firms.[15] As highlighted in the *Government AI Readiness Index 2024*, the U.S. leadership in AI readiness stems almost entirely from the strength of its technology sector, where it outperforms other top countries by more than 15 points; in contrast, its lead in governance and infrastructure is much narrower.

Social and Environmental Impact of Profit Maximization AI

In addition to the geographic and corporate concentration of AI capabilities, there are major social issues that need to be tackled. For example, there is a profound and persistent gender imbalance in both the development and governance of AI technologies. The Women for Ethical AI (W4EAI) Gender Outlook Study[16] shows how gender inequality is not just a reflection of broader societal patterns but a structural feature of the global AI ecosystem.

According to the study, women represent only 29% of researchers in science and development (R&D), and this figure drops sharply to just 12% in AI-specific research roles. In academia, only 16% of faculty members in universities conducting AI research are women—revealing a stark lack of diversity in the academic pipelines that shape future AI leadership. In the broader sector, just 30% of professionals in AI are women, and the disparity

[14] Ibid.

[15] Stanford Institute for Human-Centered Artificial Intelligence. (2025). *AI Index Report 2025*. Stanford University. https://hai.stanford.edu/ai-index/2025.

[16] Women4Ethical AI (W4EAI). (2025). *Gender Outlook Study on Artificial Intelligence*. [Internal report].

grows at the top: only 18% of C-Suite positions in AI start-ups are held by women.

Yet, the most striking finding is not just the low representation, but how AI governance frameworks systematically neglect gender. Despite growing global attention to AI ethics, most policy frameworks and readiness indexes fail to prioritize gender equality. For instance, the Global Index on Responsible AI (GIRAI) found that out of 138 countries, only 24 had frameworks that mentioned gender, and of those, just 18 included any substantive content. This limits the possibility to address this structural inequality.

Similarly, environmental considerations are still to be duly incorporated in the dominant AI development paradigm. Training large-scale AI models consumes massive energy resources and increases carbon emissions—a fact not fully integrated in the race for technological supremacy. Although 2024 marked the emergence of more energy-efficient AI systems, such as DeepSeek R1, most frontier models still require intensive compute capacity. Without policy incentives or environmental standards, this trajectory risks undermining global sustainability goals and disproportionately affecting low-income countries, which bear the brunt of climate change while benefiting the least from AI innovations.[17]

There are other developments concerning AI societal impact that need to be considered in these discussions:

1. Privacy is routinely compromised, as large-scale data collection—frequently without informed consent—has become a cornerstone of AI business models. This erodes personal autonomy and undermines trust in digital systems.
2. Algorithmic discrimination is also a concern: systems trained on biased datasets replicate and amplify historical inequalities, particularly in areas like facial recognition,[18] criminal justice, or credit scoring.
3. Labor market developments are also concerning. As AI capabilities and autonomy grow by the day, there is a deep re-shaping of the labor markets that now covers the whole spectrum of low, medium and high skilled jobs, and whole sectors. The rapid growth of AI capabilities and autonomy is

[17] Hao, K. (2025, January 17). *The hidden environmental costs of generative AI.* MIT Technology Review. https://news.mit.edu/2025/explained-generative-ai-environmental-impact-0117: Strubell, E., Ganesh, A., & McCallum, A. (2019). *Energy and policy considerations for deep learning in NLP.* Proceedings of the 57th Annual Meeting of the Association for Computational Linguistics. https://doi.org/10.18653/v1/P19-1355: Holistic AI. (2024). *Understanding the environmental impact of LLMs.* https://www.holisticai.com/blog/environmental-impact-ai-llms.

[18] Buolamwini, J., & Gebru, T. (2018). Gender Shades: Intersectional Accuracy Disparities in Commercial Gender Classification. *Proceedings of Machine Learning Research*, 81, 1–15.

fundamentally reshaping labor markets, impacting jobs across all skill levels and transforming entire sectors. The skilling and upskilling programs that are necessary to cope with the technological developments are not enough for the size of the challenge. Content moderation and labeling is also taking place under precarious conditions, with low pay and little psychological support, especially in low-income regions.[19]

4. Finally, the spread of disinformation—driven by algorithms optimized for engagement—has contributed to declining trust in democratic institutions and public discourse, it has infringed on our fundamental freedoms in many parts of the world. It has also impacted youth, and even children, who are now experiencing high level of anxiety.

These elements confirm how the current AI model may contribute to widen global asymmetries, undermining technological sovereignty, and bringing negative social externalities.

In this context, it is necessary to look at the kind of incentives that can redirect the technological changes toward the common good and in the public interest.[20] This demands that we re-think corporate incentives, strengthen legal and regulatory frameworks, and foster greater transparency and inclusion *ex ante* in the design and governance of AI. It also requires not only technical safeguards but also a rethinking of the foundational economic logics that guide development.

It is important to clarify that the pursuit of profit in AI development is not inherently problematic—indeed, it is a natural and expected driver of innovation. We can neither neglect the major benefits that current AI developments are already delivering in many regions and for many purposes. However, these developments should be accompanied by clear accountability mechanisms and aligned with broader societal interests.

[19] Perrigo, B. (2023, January 18). *Exclusive: OpenAI used Kenyan workers on less than $2 per hour to make ChatGPT less toxic*. TIME. https://time.com/6247678/openai-chatgpt-kenya-workers/; Maclean, R. (2023, August 2). *'I was in a prison': The human toll of training AI bots*. The Guardian. https://www.theguardian.com/technology/2023/aug/02/ai-chatbot-training-human-toll-content-moderator-meta-openai; Noema Magazine. (2023, March). *The Exploited Labor Behind Artificial Intelligence*. https://www.noemamag.com/the-exploited-labor-behind-artificial-intelligence/; West, D. M. (2023, September 27). *Moving toward truly responsible AI development in the global AI* market. Brookings. https://www.brookings.edu/articles/moving-toward-truly-responsible-ai-development-in-the-global-ai-market/.

[20] Oxford Insights. (2024). *Government AI Readiness Index 2024*. https://oxfordinsights.com/wp-content/uploads/2024/12/2024-Government-AI-Readiness-Index-2.pdf.

An Alternative Approach: Incentives Based on the Common Good

To counteract the negative impacts of the profit-maximization and geopolitical competition model, it is essential to promote an alternative approach grounded in the common good. This means adopting human rights-based governance policies, as exemplified by UNESCO's Recommendation on the Ethics of Artificial Intelligence, to ensure that AI developments abide by fundamental rights, promote social justice, and foster inclusion. It also needs to strengthen transparency and accountability by requiring technology companies to ensure data quality, effective disclosure mechanisms on AI model training, and solid frameworks to enhance safety and prevent discrimination. More than anything, it requires strong foundations for the rule of law *online*, responsibility, and compensation mechanisms when there is harm.

Moreover, public research must be supported through sustained government funding for universities and research centers, ensuring that technological knowledge is not monopolized by private interests alone.

Encouraging alternative business models, such as data cooperatives or data trusts as included in UNESCO's standard, or open, community-driven AI platforms, can further align innovation with positive social outcomes. It is also crucial to establish international labor protections that guarantee fair wages and adequate psychological support for the workers, like data labelers and content moderators as well as gender-based approaches.

The Work of UNESCO on the Ethics of AI.
During the last 4 years in implementing UNESCO's Recommendation on the Ethics of AI[21] and working with almost 80 countries assessing their readiness to use and steer AI, the need for enabling and framing assets became clear. This work also contributed to change the AI narrative from a purely technological one, to a societal one informed by contextual needs and priorities. One that also focuses on outcomes and impacts and not only on AI design and deployment.

The main ethical question is the kind of economy and society we want to build, incorporating technological progress. It puts the technology at the service of human goals to achieve more inclusive economies and societies. It also calls for international collaboration and the sharing of best practices. The main values are then translated into concrete principles of account-

[21] UNESCO. (2021, November 25). Recommendation on the ethics of artificial intelligence. UNESCO. https://www.unesco.org/en/articles/recommendation-ethics-artificial-intelligence.

ability, transparency and rule of law, and policies in different fields like education, culture, labor markets, the economy, environment, and gender equality. UNESCO's Recommendation was approved before the emergence of generative AI, but developments like GEN AI made its principles only more relevant.

At the time of its adoption, the main concerns were linked to the risk of growing inequalities between and within countries, and the discrimination that could derive from the lack of representativeness of the datasets used to train the AI models or bias introduced in these developments.[22] This was confirmed by research related to facial recognition technologies that were less accurate when dealing with black women[23] or the deployment of biased algorithms to inform public policies that could unfairly harm disadvantaged groups.[24] This continues to be a source of concern, as millions of decisions around the world are being taken with AI support in different forms. This is why we included the principle of human determination, and in cases where life and death decisions are at stake, to ensure that humans are in charge and are responsible. We also included a provision to ensure compensation and access to justice in case of harm linked to AI systems. For this, we need liability regimes.

This global instrument banned against giving legal personality to the AI systems and stressed that AI should not be used for mass surveillance or social scoring. Misinformation and manipulation were also addressed, including at the intersection of AI and neurotechnology, and other emerging technologies.

However, with the emergence of generative AI, the global debate refocused on safety and existential risks, considering the dual use of technologies now capable of coding or performing very advanced tasks.[25] With technological developments that could be out of human control and may have their own agency and decision making, the spread of dangerous viruses or the use in warfare became some of the most cited causes of concern. Misinformation

---

[22] Véliz, C. (2021). *Privacy Is Power: Why and How You Should Take Back Control of Your Data.* Bantam Press.

[23] Buolamwini, J., & Gebru, T. (2018). Gender shades: Intersectional accuracy disparities in commercial gender classification. *Proceedings of the first Conference on Fairness, Accountability and Transparency*, 81, 77–91. http://proceedings.mlr.press/v81/buolamwini18a/buolamwini18a.pdf; Sidney Perkowitz, "The Bias in the Machine: Why Facial Recognition Has Led to False Arrests," Nautilus, August 19, 2020; Leslie, D. (2020). Understanding bias in facial recognitiontechnologies: an explainer. The Alan Turing Institute.chttps://doi.org/10.5281/zenodo.4050457.

[24] Dutch Parliamentary Committee (2020), 'Unknown injustice: Report of the Parliamentary Hearing Committee childcare benefits scandal', 17 December 2020.

[25] Bengio, Y., Cohen, M., Fornasiere, D., Ghosn, J., Greiner, P., MacDermott, M., Mindermann, S., Oberman, A., Richardson, J., Richardson, O., Coshow, T. (2025). *Superintelligent Agents Pose Catastrophic Risks: Can Scientist AI Offer a Safer Path?* [Preprint]. arXiv. https://arxiv.org/pdf/2502.15657.

at scale was also a major risk, at a moment when half of the world engaged in electoral processes.[26] Previous concerns continued to be relevant, and our efforts at UNESCO, which were focusing on the need for countries to build their own capacities to manage technological development only grew in importance.

The real impact of this framework lies in its practical implementation. Countries must adapt these principles to their local contexts, developing policies that respond to their specific needs and priorities. To tailor the approaches to contextual frameworks and needs, we developed the Readiness Assessment Methodology (RAM)[27] which helps countries assess their fitness to steer AI and deploy it for the public good. This practical methodology-administered by the Secretariat-allows member states to identify areas for improvement and develop national strategies that promote inclusive and equitable AI. It includes not only the traditional enablers (connectivity, infrastructure, skills), but also the institutional and cultural setting and capacities, laws and regulations, and a vision of where the country needs AI to advance its goals.

Understanding the "Why" Behind AI for Development and Results of the UNESCO'S Framework

Our emphasis on the ethics of AI helped instill a sense of agency in the countries we worked with, transforming a given narrative that just called for passive adaptation to AI trajectories, to one that shows countries can shape the markets and the impact that technologies may have with mission-led approaches (Ramos and Mazzucato[28]). The implementation of the Readiness Assessment Methodology required the organization of national, inclusive and multistakeholder debates coordinated by the government but featuring the private sector, academia, and civil society.

The economic, social, and political context in every country became center stage in the definition of an AI Strategy, with strong diagnosis relevant to the

[26]World Economic Forum. (2025). *Global Risks Report 2025*. https://www.weforum.org/publications/global-risks-report-2025/.

[27]UNESCO. (s.f.). Readiness Assessment Methodology (RAM). https://www.unesco.org/ethics-ai/en/ram.

[28]Ibid.

realities on the ground.[29] This helped to move away from technofix solutions or a "one size fits all" approach to adopt a differentiated and customized policy agenda, while maximizing the interoperability of AI governance systems at the international level.

The RAM has become the largest global initiative to assess national preparedness for AI governance, that also allows for international comparisons and peer learning. The data generated through these assessments has enabled us to construct the world's most extensive repository of practical evidence on the real conditions of AI governance across diverse contexts, and identify specific gaps in individual countries: talent, digital infrastructure, governance, regulation, or inclusion. It has allowed us to confirm that policies matter, understanding the way they can shape technological developments for good. For those countries with less resources, effective international cooperation mechanisms must step in, so that the development gaps are not broadened with technological advancements.

In conclusion, aligning AI applications with the specific social needs and context of each country is essential to maximize their positive impact. Technological solutions should be rooted in each nation's own vision of development and well-being, including by advancing AI that can deliver for better health, education, economic and governance outcomes.

As an example, in Africa, the AI policy framework driven by the African Union and Smart Africa emphasizes solutions for climate-smart agriculture, disease detection, and educational monitoring, responding to local structural challenges (AU/Smart Africa, 2021). Similarly, CAF highlights that in Latin America, AI can be key to reducing inequalities and improving state efficiency, but only if it is adapted to available institutional capacities.[30] The work that we did in partnership with CAF in Latin America and the Caribbean have delivered better cybersecurity and data protection laws in Chile, for example, and allowed the advancement of GPT-LATAM.

---

[29]Narayanan, A., & Kapoor, R. (2025). *Artificial Intelligence and the Global South: Inequality, Opportunity, and Governance.* (in press).

[30]García Periche, J., & Martínez Pinto, C. (2024). AI and the SDGs in Latin America and the Caribbean. CAF—Development Bank of Latin America and the Caribbean. https://scioteca.caf.com/handle/123456789/2331

Beyond Regulation: A Comprehensive Policy Approach

Institutions, Incentives, and Investments: The Three "I"S of Success for AI Governance

Across economic sectors, policy choices play a decisive role in shaping outcomes. Yet, in fast-evolving environments like AI, evaluating the impact of those choices is especially challenging. This is why AI regulatory sandboxes have been introduced: they offer a controlled setting to test and observe AI systems within specific legal and institutional contexts. These experimental spaces help policymakers better understand how AI behaves in practice and refine governance approaches accordingly.

The broader current narrative, however, simplifies the debate opposing innovation to regulation. This simplistic depiction of policy dynamics is linked to vested interest, and the goal of major companies to advance technological developments with the least interference of governance rules. This is a false dilemma. First, because there is no economic sector that is not regulated. Even the decision of not regulating is a regulatory decision. Second, because it is not the only tool that shapes the markets or protects individuals from the negative impacts of new products. Third, because it is the responsibility of the State to guide technological developments toward social, democratic, and sustainable objectives (OECD 2021). Finally, regulatory certainty and strong legal basis provide positive environments for business to thrive.

In the case of AI, regulations are needed so it is developed responsibly. The quality of data, the diversity of the teams engaged with it, the red teaming exercises, the watermarks of AI to ensure its development is transparent, the testing of the unbiased algorithms, all require standards and regulations. Regulatory approach must be flexible and adaptive, able to evolve along with the technology (UNESCO, 2021).

However, regulations are just one policy tool. An effective strategy requires a public policy ecosystem that combines flexible regulatory frameworks with economic incentives, institutional capacities, public and private investments, and civic education, and that addressed economic, educational, and social dimensions of AI. This underscores the need for active policies that integrate:

- National ethical AI R&D plans and strategies (such as the French Grand Défi IA de confiance program).[31]
- Public funds and financial support (subsidies or tax credits) to finance AI developments, be it transparent and auditable models; research, or public purpose platforms.
- Independent technical agencies or institutions to oversee ethical compliance, beyond traditional regulatory bodies.
- Capacities in governments to "govern AI" but also to "govern with AI" and improve the delivery of public services (health, education, and welfare systems) as well as smarter public procurement systems.
- Connectivity, infrastructure, digital identity, that is, digital public infrastructure.
- Specific sectoral policies to cope with the technological transition.
- Investments in education and skills, particularly those required in a rapidly evolving labor markets, and school to work transitions.
- Dedicated programs for small- and medium-sized enterprises to benefit and develop AI programs that underpin their competitiveness and productivity.
- Quality education and educational reform that fosters critical thinking and media literacy are also key.

Incentive Policies: Activating the Transformative Potential of AI through Economic and Social Signals

Ultimately, it is critical to design incentive systems that influence market actors and that deliver sustainable and just outcomes. These incentives are framed in the policy ecosystem mentioned above and encompass responsible research, local capacity building, and safeguards, among others.[32] Incentives help to integrate social and environmental considerations. As modern industrial policies demonstrate, well-designed incentives can radically change technological trajectories.[33]

---

[31] Confiance.ai. (2021, July 1). Programme « Confiance.ai »: un collectif de 13 industriels et académiques français relève le défi de l'industrialisation de l'intelligence artificielle (IA) pour les produits et services critiques. info.gouv.fr. https://www.info.gouv.fr/actualite/grands-defis-l-programme-confianceai-un-collectif-de-13-industriels-et-academiques-francais-releve.

[32] Narayanan, A., & Kapoor, R. (2025). *Artificial Intelligence and the Global South:* Inequality, *Opportunity, and Governance.* (in press).

[33] Mazzucato, M. (2013). *The Entrepreneurial State: Debunking Public* vs. *Private Sector Myths*. Anthem Press.

Some key policy tools include:

- Public procurement with specific criteria or conditions: governments can establish standards of algorithmic responsibility as a requirement for contracting AI systems, creating a public market for responsible technologies.[34] It can dedicate funds and reward systems for public purpose AI.
- Tax credits for responsible innovation and sustainability: offer tax benefits to companies that invest in algorithmic transparency, data diversity, or positive social impact AI.
- Competitive awards and funds: such as the "AI for Good Innovation Fund," which support start-ups and projects that address social challenges through AI.
- AI trust labels: such as those proposed by the European Commission, which certify technologies aligned with ethical standards, creating reputational advantages.
- Establishment of data centers and trusts and other instruments that could be accessible for entrepreneurs and researchers, but also review how data is governed, collected, and used.

Upgrading of government, business, and individual capacities is core to this agenda. This is even more important as not all countries would be developing frontier models and competing for the supremacy of the next generation of AI but looking at ways to apply it in their circumstances with trust. The emergence open-source models and the decrease in prices for new applications can help with this.

Tailor-Made Policies: Lessons from the Field

There is still some way to go to align government efforts with the kind of policies and strategies mentioned above. After conducting 80 Readiness Assessment Methodology (RAM) we confirmed that only 30% of the countries evaluated have fully implemented and coordinated national AI strategies, and more than 60% lack formal mechanisms for monitoring and evaluating the social impacts of AI.

Other key findings from these evaluations are striking:

- Fewer than 25% possess sufficient regulatory capabilities to oversee complex AI systems.
- The talent gap remains significant: women represent only 22% of the global AI workforce.

---

[34]Araya, D. (2021). Artificial Intelligence and Inclusive Governance: Learning from National Strategies. *Journal of International Affairs*, 74(2), 105–120.

These findings highlight the urgent need for international cooperation, capacity-building, and inclusive policymaking.

This is why we launched the Observatory of the Ethics of AI, as a repository of policy analysis and the RAMs being done worldwide. The Global Forum on the Ethics of AI allows for direct exchange and peer learning and for tracking the latest developments, and the networks of AI experts without borders and the Women4Ethical AI show how important it is to continue exchanging beyond borders for a technology that knows none.

Conclusion

The development of artificial intelligence is not a force of nature, it is the outcome of human choices, shaped by interests, values, and institutions. At a time when technological power is highly concentrated and dominant incentives prioritize profit over well-being, the challenge is profoundly political: who decides what AI is used for, and who benefits from it?

This chapter argues that it is not enough to regulate risks or marvel at technical potential. We must transform the structural drivers of technological development—from business models to the institutional capacities of States. Ethics is the compass. And public policy, when guided by human rights, social justice, and sustainability, can redirect AI's trajectory toward more equitable and democratic outcomes.

My experience at UNESCO and OECD shows that countries are not doomed to be passive recipients of foreign technologies. Focusing on institutions, incentives and investments, and a common good-oriented approach, they can become active shapers of responsible innovation. This is not a secondary option—it is a necessary condition for ensuring the digital revolution helps close development gaps instead of widening them.

Artificial intelligence will not define the future of our societies on its own. That future will be shaped by our collective capacity to govern it with vision, courage, and ethical conviction. We already have the knowledge, the tools, and the principles. What we need now is political will. And the time to act is now.

References

Aghion, P., Bloom, N., Blundell, R., Griffith, R., & Howitt, P. (2005). Competition and innovation: An inverted-U relationship. In *The Quarterly Journal of Economics, 120(2), 701–728*. Oxford University Press. http://www.jstor.org/stable/25098750

AI Now Institute. (2019). *Discriminating systems: gender, race and power in AI.*

Araya, D. (2021). Artificial intelligence and inclusive governance: Learning from national strategies. *Journal of International Affairs, 74*(2), 105–120.

Bender, E. M., Gebru, T., McMillan-Major, A., & Shmitchell, S. (2021). On the dangers of stochastic parrots: Can language models be too big? *FAccT '21: ACM conference on fairness, accountability, and transparency.*

Bengio, Y., Cohen, M., Fornasiere, D., Ghosn, J., Greiner, P., MacDermott, M., Mindermann, S., Oberman, A., Richardson, J., Richardson, O., Coshow, T., et al. (2025). *Superintelligent agents pose catastrophic risks: Can scientist AI offer a safer path?* [Preprint]. arXiv. https://arxiv.org/pdf/2502.15657

Buolamwini, J., & Gebru, T. (2018). Gender shades: Intersectional accuracy disparities in commercial gender classification. *Proceedings of Machine Learning Research, 81*, 1–15.

CAF. (2023). *Inteligencia artificial con propósito: Ética, inclusión y desarrollo en América Latina.* Banco de Desarrollo de América Latina (CAF)..

Cottier, B., Snodin, B., Owen, D., & Adamczewski, T. (2025, May 19). *280x cheaper: The real AI revolution is accessibility.* WisdomTree. https://www.wisdomtree.com/investments/blog/2025/05/19/280x-cheaper-the-real-ai-revolution-is-accessibility

Dutch Parliamentary Committee. (2020), 'Unknown injustice: Report of the parliamentary hearing committee childcare benefits scandal', 17 December 2020.

Eubanks, V. (2018). *Automating inequality: How high-tech tools profile, police, and punish the poor.* St. Martin's Press.

Fundación Karisma & UNESCO. (2024). *IA en América Latina: Diagnóstico de Capacidades Éticas e Institucionales.* .

García Periche, J., & Martínez Pinto, C. (2024). AI and the SDGs in Latin America and the Caribbean. CAF—Development Bank of Latin America and the Caribbean. https://scioteca.caf.com/handle/123456789/2331

Hao, K. (2025, January 17). *The hidden environmental costs of generative AI.* MIT Technology Review. https://news.mit.edu/2025/explained-generative-ai-environmental-impact-0117

Holistic AI. (2024). *Understanding the environmental impact of LLMs.* https://www.holisticai.com/blog/environmental-impact-ai-llms

Indicelatam. (2024). *Diagnóstico de capacidades éticas e institucionales en IA en América Latina.* Disponible en: https://indicelatam.cl

Jobin, A., Ienca, M., & Vayena, E. (2019). The global landscape of AI ethics guidelines. *Nature Machine Intelligence, 1*(9), 389–399.

Leslie, D. (2020). *Understanding bias in facial recognition technologies: an explainer.* The Alan Turing Institute. https://doi.org/10.5281/zenodo.4050457

Mazzucato, M. (2013). *The entrepreneurial state: Debunking public vs. private sector myths.* Anthem Press.

Mitchell, M. (2023). *Artificial intelligence: A guide for thinking humans.* Penguin Books.

Narayanan, A., & Kapoor, R. (2025). *Artificial intelligence and the global South: Inequality, opportunity, and governance.* [Manuscrito, en prensa].

OECD. (2019). *OECD principles on artificial intelligence*. OECD.
OECD. (2021). *State of implementation of the OECD AI principles: Insights from national AI policies*. OECD.
Ojanen, A. (2025, April 10). *Technology neutrality as a way to future-proof regulation: the case of the Artificial Intelligence Act*. SSRN. https://ssrn.com/abstract=5181085
Perkowitz, Sidney (2020). *The bias in the machine: why facial recognition has led to false arrests*, Nautilus, August 19, 2020
Raji, Inioluwa Deborah & Buolamwini, Joy (2019). Actionable auditing: Investigating the impact of publicly naming biased performance results of commercial AI products. *AAAI/ACM FAccT.*
Ramos, G., & Mazzucato, M. (2022). *Governing AI for the public good: Towards democratic and inclusive AI innovation*. UCL Institute for Innovation and Public Purpose.
Smart Africa. (2021). *Artificial Intelligence (AI) blueprint for Africa*. Smart Africa Alliance. https://smartafrica.org/knowledge/artificial-intelligence-for-africa/
Stanford Institute for Human-Centered Artificial Intelligence. (2025). *Artificial intelligence index report 2025*. Stanford University. https://hai.stanford.edu/ai-index/2025-ai-index-report
Strubell, E., Ganesh, A., & McCallum, A. (2019). Energy and policy considerations for deep learning in NLP. *Proceedings of the 57th annual meeting of the association for computational linguistics*. https://doi.org/10.18653/v1/P19-1355
UNESCO. (2021). *Recommendation on the ethics of artificial intelligence*. UNESCO.
UNESCO. (2023). *Readiness assessment methodology (RAM): National evaluation toolkit for ethical AI deployment*. UNESCO.
United Nations. (2023). *A global digital compact: Tech for all*. Report of the Secretary-General's High-Level Panel on Digital Cooperation.
Véliz, C. (2021). *Privacy is power: Why and how you should take back control of your data*. Bantam.
West, S. M., Whittaker, M., & Crawford, K. (2019). *Discriminating systems: Gender, race and power in AI*. AI Now Institute.
World Economic Forum. (2021). *Global technology governance report 2021*.
Zuboff, S. (2019). *The age of surveillance capitalism: The fight for a human future at the new frontier of power*. PublicAffairs.

Human Productivity and Well-Being: The Promise of AI

Lord Jonathan Camrose

AI as deployed today realises little of its potential to boost human productivity. This produces poor outcomes for those who deploy and use it and for those who seek to regulate it. This paper reviews the opportunities for AI to boost productivity in ways deeply beneficial to society and our species. AI in healthcare can drive better health outcomes and reduce costs. AI in education can improve educational outcomes, enhance productivity across economies and drive societal growth. Geospatial applications of AI can optimise our use of cities, land and transportation, improving quality of life and reducing pollution. Market forces alone are not setting the right direction for AI use, but wise intervention by governments and other actors can guide us towards positive, transformative use of AI.

Introduction

The writer Douglas Adams argued that most of our response to new technologies was driven by our age. As ever he made a serious point with a light touch:

1. Anything that is in the world when you're born is normal and ordinary and is just a natural part of the way the world works.

L. J. Camrose (✉)
House of Lords, London, England
e-mail: camrosej@parliament.uk

M. Rangeley, N. Fairfax (eds.), *The Artificial Intelligence Revolution*,
https://doi.org/10.1007/978-3-032-11814-1_17

2. Anything that's invented between when you're 15 and 35 is new and exciting and revolutionary, and you can probably get a career in it.
3. Anything invented after you're 35 is against the natural order of things, and the beginning of the end of civilization as we know it.

As far as I know, the vast majority of contributors to this volume—myself included—fall comfortably into the third category, but my goal is to present the case for optimism in the short to medium term. This task is an unusual one in that it is both trivially easy and impossibly hard.

It is easy because as a species, we have centuries of history of absorbing and benefitting from advances in technology that we initially viewed with fear and we came to value and need. In the last three decades in particular, our willingness and ability to absorb information technologies have established a resilience to tech-driven changes to society.

But it is difficult because accounts of the likely harms of widespread adoption of fast-evolving AI capabilities are both plausible and compelling. These include military misuse, economic disruption, societal distortion and loss of human agency. Furthermore, in recent decades, we have struggled to crack the code of regulating information technologies. Social media continue to distort our worldview, our data changes hands without our permission or knowledge and screens dominate our leisure time at the expense of human relationships.

My view, and the view that underpins this article, is that well-regulated AI—while it will always be disruptive—will drive economic growth and contribute to the resolution of societal and species-wide issues. I suggest there are few problems being worked on by humans in any field—artistic, scientific or commercial—to which AI cannot contribute.

However, I also contend that no scheme of AI regulation yet enacted will be sufficiently effective to guide us towards a utopian future. There are a variety of reasons why the world's most successful regulators struggle to develop an effective approach, but I will focus on 3:

1. **Definition and Scope**: A regulator seeking to limit the use of AI will always struggle to specify where regulations will apply because, like all information technologies, AI can be applied to an arbitrarily wide range of fields. Consequently the regulator must try to target inputs, not outputs. For instance, a regulation in the field of aviation can easily be targeted at a defined area of activity (airborne transport) and drafted to produce given outcomes (safety, sustainability, etc.) A system of AI regulation has to address AI's use in almost every sphere of human activity and as such only inputs can usefully be regulated—data transparency, intellectual property,

etc. Such regulations can be workable but will never have the advantages of communicability, simplicity and appeal to common sense.

2. **Pace**: Regulations will always be developed more slowly than the technologies they control. This applies more to information technologies because their rate of development is more likely to be exponential—each iteration builds on its predecessors. With AI systems, we have a higher exponent and greater uncertainty because new capabilities that build so rapidly on existing ones are inherently less predictable. An AI Lab investing billions in a training run will not know with confidence the capabilities that will emerge.
3. **Symptom-bias**: As a result of the first two problems, regulators have tended to isolate and proscribe higher risk elements, such as certain applications of facial recognition or bias against racial groups. While many such symptoms of AI are deeply undesirable, it is clearly unsustainable in the light of point 2 for regulators to respond to every emergent AI capability at the pace of development. Only a body of regulation that is holistic and principle-based can hope to succeed sustainably: picking off emerging symptoms is neither sustainable nor sufficiently predictable to drive a healthy innovation environment.

Those who want to regulate AI have an unenviable task, perhaps above all because they have no North Star: no set of existing systems they can point to as desirable, safe and beneficial to society. In this article, I predict a virtuous circle that will come from a stable of such positive uses of AI: trustworthiness and benefit will create public goodwill; public goodwill will allow regulators to develop holistic rules that guide towards positive AI outcomes as well as away from dangerous ones; holistic regulations will enhance AI's trustworthiness, benefit and public perception.

I will outline three areas in which such beneficial AI systems can and should be created. I've selected them on the grounds of:

- **Positive Social Impact**: Their potential to meaningfully change lives for the better across society.
- **Achievability**: I have tried to avoid assumptions about future technology, but base as much as possible that follows on technology that conceptually exists today.
- **Public–Private Collaboration**: Their combination of public data with private expertise and resources.

Based on these criteria, my focus will be on education, healthcare and geospatial applications of AI. It is my strong belief that successful applications of AI in these spaces will create significant societal benefit and offer a crucial guide to regulators as to what good can and should look like.

Healthcare

Few topics appeal to our emotions more than healthcare, and perhaps few spheres of activity have the potential for such dramatic improvement in the short to medium term as a result of AI. Public provision of healthcare uniquely combines operational, administrative, medical, scientific and financial challenges. The reader is invited to participate in a thought experiment where we project ourselves into the near future:

The Lived Experience

On waking one morning, Jonathan received the following message:

Dear Jonathan,

Thank you for submitting your response to our automated questionnaire and for giving your consent to accessing other sources of personal information about your health. These have included:

- *Your lifetime health history*
- *Fitness data from your smartwatch and other wearables*
- *Your current and past prescriptions*
- *Notes from recent GP appointments*
- *An overview of your family health history*
- *Your genomic data*
- *Relevant comparisons with the population overall*

*All of the above formed the basis of a report that your GP has now reviewed. This indicates there may be new therapeutic opportunities for you. We invite you to visit a consultant, undergo an MRI scan and discuss the options. Please select one of the following options:**

- *Charing Cross Hospital, 10:15 am, 18 October, Dr. Hendrix*
- *Cromwell Hospital, 8 PM, 18 October, Dr. Page*
- *London Clinic, 4 PM, 20th October, Dr. Clapton*

Best wishes,

The Chelsea Medical Centre

Jonathan selected an appointment and found himself in the same consulting room, at the same time, as a radiologist, a technician, an assistant, a nurse and an MRI scanner. They conducted the scan and their discussion was captured and summarised by the listening computer, which advised a consultant's digital assistant of the key points of their discussion and the results of the scan. Immediately following the scan, he was able to discuss the results with the consultant. His prescription was changed and he was advised to make a range of lifestyle changes.

Jonathan avoided both serious illness and serious inconvenience, and the health service reduced the costs of treating him, while treating more patients every day.

My hope in telling this feeble story is to give an (albeit highly contrived) account of all the near-to-medium-term possibilities as they affect the patient. I focus in this section on healthcare provision in the UK through the National Health Service (NHS) partly because of my own familiarity with it but mostly because by accident and design, the UK is almost uniquely poised to benefit in this way. Ninety-five percent of UK Hospital Trusts will have Electronic Records by the end of this year, and while some other countries are more digitised (Israel, Singapore, Sweden, Estonia and others), none has the scale of the UK's population with digital records from cradle to grave, going back in many cases to 1948. In the remainder of the section, I will look more closely at the capabilities that AI can provide to enable Jonathan's experience.

I also note that NHS professionals may feel the technological marvels are a far cry from existing IT infrastructure, notoriously out of date as it is. My purpose is not, however, to provide an implementation plan but to indicate what is, or shortly may be, technologically feasible.

Administration. It is a common observation of consumers of the UK's health service that while the medical staff are skilled, it's far too difficult and time-consuming to arrange an appointment with the right one. This is above all a function of scale and complexity. For Jonathan's appointment, a number of elements had to come together at the same time:

- A suitable location in a hospital, cleaned and maintained.
- Five different members of staff, some on different shift patterns and with different managers.
- Support teams such as hospital reception, IT and other staff.
- Working medical equipment, suitably maintained.
- The patient's records—with time for review prior to the appointment.
- The patient.

Scheduling one appointment is a data problem, requiring the orchestration of different data streams for all of these elements. Scheduling **all** appointments is a vast optimisation problem, probably not solvable without the use of AI, because of its ability to iterate towards an optimum across huge numbers of variables.

The data problem is characterised by the inevitable changes, delays and glitches that plague any complex plan. With AI, the problem not only starts to become soluble but we can envision an end-to-end process, initiated by an AI analysis of Jonathan's needs, reviewed by a human GP and passed to a suitable specialist for the appointment, the results of which are passed back to the GP and others. The outcomes for Jonathan are tracked and feed not just his records but the overall national medical foundation model.

Nor are patient outcomes the only operational benefit. The cost savings from enhanced administration are significant:

- Medical professionals devote a greater portion of their time to patients.
- The greater number of patient visits per day eases pressure to expand staff and infrastructure.

- The reduced time to resolve or avoid medical conditions boosts economic productivity across the population.

Diagnosis

The rapid diagnosis Jonathan experienced is close to reality today. As more patients use the NHS app on their phones, they are able to report symptoms either through the app or by dialling a dedicated helpline. In both cases, a decision tree is deployed, which already today is accurate in 80–90% of cases. The average age of the app user at the time of writing is 65, suggesting high adoption rates from older patients.

Accuracy will improve over time as algorithms become more sophisticated, more data is included (especially outcomes data) and system capabilities enhanced. In addition two further breakthroughs will enhance clinical excellence. First, Natural Language Processing techniques will become better at translating patient's words to clinical choices. Second, AI advances in telemedicine will improve the ability to diagnose medical conditions remotely.

In addition to these methods, AI continues to drive diagnostic breakthroughs:

- Improved analysis of medical images, including CT scans, MRIs and X-rays mean AI tools are both faster and more accurate in many cases than their human owners.
- Techniques like automated image segmentation enable faster and more reliable identification of abnormalities.
- AI analyses patterns in ECG data, blood tests and other clinical records to predict cardiovascular risks earlier.
- AI is beginning to exceed existing operational capabilities in analysing histopathology slides, used for diagnosing cancer, autoimmune diseases and other conditions. AI systems can process large volumes of digital slides quickly and provide consistent, high-accuracy diagnoses.
- The growing use and accuracy of wearables provides new rich channels of data to support timely and accurate diagnosis.

Drug Discovery and Personalised Medicine

A digital twin of patient's body has become a sufficiently close facsimile to hypothesise treatment programmes, either for a whole population or specific to a patient. Results can suggest combinations of drugs that are both lower cost and safer or more effective.

Combinations of existing drugs may be identified that are sufficiently novel to be unlikely to occur to most doctors—saving cost and improving patient outcomes. In addition, a range of private enterprises are using AI to develop compelling use cases. Companies like Dassault Systèmes, Insilico Medicine and Siemens offer AI tools that generate digital twins for the human body. These offer virtual simulations—digital twins—of individual human bodies. Researchers can use them to hypothesise quickly and with high confidence the effects of treatments on specific organs or the interactions of different medicines.

Pharmacovigilance

Drug safety is a significant challenge for pharmaceutical companies. Even the very largest clinical trials are unlikely to include more than ten thousand patients, and a drug on the market may be taken by hundreds of millions: safety risks that affect small minorities of patients will necessarily arise only after the drug is available on the market.

Pharmaceutical companies are required to manage this risk by collecting data on adverse events, codifying it consistently and rapidly reporting it to relevant authorities. Failure to do so can endanger patients, create significant reputational damage and result in prison sentences for company officials.

The difficulty of the process comes principally from the challenge of picking up indicators of adverse events from individual patients and doctors around the world and turning them into an accurate global statement of the specific safety risks, coded to globally accepted dictionaries of medical conditions and medicines.

Such a problem is a precise match to the capabilities of AI, and its solution not only increases patient safety, it greatly decreases the operational cost and risks of marketing medicines. This offers both the possibility of passing savings on to customers and allowing pharmaceutical companies to ease their often extreme risk aversion in product development. When drug risks can be rapidly and reliably understood, they can be more easily mitigated without unnecessary commercial damage. Medicines can and will be cheaper, safer and more effective.

Education

In Neal Stephenson's 1995 novel *The Diamond Age*, the young protagonist, Nell—from the very wrong indeed side of the tracks—is rescued from penury by the chance discovery of an AI-powered book called *The Young Ladies' Illustrated Primer*. This miraculous device teaches her from early childhood to young adulthood by responding precisely to her educational needs at every stage of her development, until she emerges as a powerful leader.

The promise of educational technology, EdTech, has too often exceeded its delivery, and yet in AI, we may see something that can truly break through. Stephenson's novel was at the cutting edge 30 years ago, and but today its possibilities begin to look like something close to obtainable. Personalised lessons, precisely tailored to the learning style of each child are surely within the parameters of many AI systems. Crucially, his great insight in the book—that however capable the AI, a human element will always be required for the teaching to be effective—grounds the premise in reality.

The prize for the effective development and deployment of AI in education is perhaps immeasurably vast. It will produce generations of more capable humans, better able to fulfil their own and society's goals. It will do so more cheaply and efficiently than any existing method anywhere. It will expand the possibilities of education far beyond the early years, allowing those whose career paths are disrupted by technology to go into other fields. It will provide equality of opportunity to an extent never achieved by any society in human history.

We aren't there yet, but in this section, I will set out where we are today and what are likely to be the key stages in developing an AI driven educational landscape in future.

Level 1: Today's Generic Capabilities

Most readily available AI capabilities today are generic: that is they would not be designed specifically for education or any other sector. They can, however, generate significant productivity efficiencies by automating routine tasks, improving certain kinds of decision-making and streamlining workflows.

The opportunity today is therefore to allow teachers more time (and energy) to focus on high-skill activities by reducing the burden of lower-level work. In the context of teaching and school management, this would mean:

- Communications tools to assist with messaging of all kinds, including support for creating messages to parents, automatic generation of meeting and call summaries
- Data collection and analysis tools for recording, monitoring and analysing student performance data, or for school administration, including a range of financial tools
- Standard administrative tools for managing any organisation, such as book-keeping and other clerical tasks, asset management, payroll management, supplier management and accounting support

While all the tools in this category have existed for many years, AI has generated a significant upturn in their usefulness and ability to generate productive work with less input and oversight from users. Implemented coherently and used as intended, they offer a significant enhancement to productivity. Many teachers express resentment and frustration at the growing quantity of administrative work required of them that does not directly address their core mission of educating children. Tools in this category represent a significant opportunity today to address that frustration and allow teachers' focus to better align to their energy and motivation.

Level 2: Education-Specific Tools

The emerging category of EdTech-specific tools addresses educators' needs more directly. These are tools aimed specifically at teacher productivity—to allow teachers to deliver to the same standard in less time: their ambition is not to create pedagogic breakthroughs but to operationally enhance the provision of education.

Lesson planning is a significant part of teacher workload. Following a structured approach, the teacher will: identify learning objectives; consider the needs of the particular student body; identify teaching strategies and activities; select resources and materials; structure the lessons; assess students' learning; reflect and evaluate.

This structured process lends itself well to AI-generated support. When OAK National Academy released their AI Lesson Assistant (AILA) in the Autumn of 2024, they were clear that teachers generally enjoyed most aspects of lesson planning but would welcome assistance with the less creative or more time-consuming aspects of the work. AILA gives teachers creative control, but automates tasks such as adjusting lessons for different literacy levels or finding local case studies to provide more impactful examples.

Some tools are designed to provide greater insight into the attainments, needs and learning style of individual pupils, collecting and analysing assignment grades or, in some cases, class contribution. This is not to say that all such insights will be generated automatically: even to attempt this would be to risk significant distortion and misunderstanding, and, in some cases, manipulation by pupils. The EdTech provider Lumi (of which I am a director) collects a range of skills assessments automatically from observations of teamwork, but requires their review and approval by a human educator. Its own technology is the result of a Stanford University study into the division of labour between human teachers and the machines that can support them. Insights provided by these tools should be and are no different to those that would be provided by a human teacher working without AI support. Their purpose is to make the teacher more productive, not (yet) more insightful.

The same applies to tools that provide a formal grade to submitted homework. These can save significant time from the—much disliked—process of marking homework, exams or other assignments. They cannot at this point generate either marks or insights that are sufficiently reliable to remove the need for a teacher's approval. What they can do, by reducing administrative workload, is provide more time for teachers to consider carefully the needs and attainments of their pupils.

Level 3: Integration and Transformation

A real opportunity to achieve a significant step-change in the use of AI to improve education comes not from new applications of AI but from their use in combination. Integration of the offers of existing tech enables better understanding of the student, improved execution of school operations and enhanced pupil feedback.

The pupil's perception of the relationship between discretionary effort and future life chances are the single most powerful motivating factor to drive performance. Positive attitude to learning may be the single greatest differentiator of a student's performance over time. A student who believes extra work leads to better outcomes will almost always enjoy greater success.

Integrated application of AI tools working in combination offer schools a better chance of understanding what may drive positive attitudes for each individual student. AI tools may draw inferences not just from performance on assigned work but data on registration, attendance, extra-curricular work, disciplinary record, school social media accounts and others. Such insights will allow teachers to identify the most appropriate learning style and subjects or activities of genuine interest to the pupil.

Inferences from such data are not limited to understanding a pupil's needs and psychology but to providing feedback that motivates and directs energy where it can be most fruitfully applied. This can go beyond advice on improving homework or exam performance and into advice that affects a student's major life choices and chances. In the 1980s in the UK, career advice was supported by a crude multiple choice test that triggered a limited range of automatically generated responses (I declined its recommendation that I become a librarian). Credible and effective career advice, based on deep inferences from pupil and population data is a far more promising prospect.

It is also worth reflecting that positive motivation and its reverse are deeply infectious in a student body. A cohort of students able to determine a relationship between choices today and specific future outcomes will not only be more personally motivated but will create a sense of positivity that motivates others. Teenagers are particularly sensitive to peer influence, and such positivity will be self-reinforcing. One of the most intractable problems in education is that the poorest performing 30% of pupils lack motivation, and a more positive prevailing attitude in the student body will go some way towards fixing this.

Level 4: Transformational AI Tech

While the EdTech tools discussed so far in this section are—at least conceptually—possible to provide today, I will describe in this section some of the emerging future possibilities.

A staple of science fiction is the AI tutor, able to adapt lessons for the child's learning style. While parents and educators today will look to identify a child's learning style—visual, auditory, tactile or kinaesthetic—the AI tutor brings the possibility of richly applying these and other insights for homework assignments. In contrast to science fiction portraits, few educators see the entire responsibility for teaching being passed to machines, but rather the support for assignments done out of class time. Work can be presented in ways that best motivate and stretch the learner, using methods that standardised homework cannot. A learner's response to gamification, competition, memory development techniques and others can be taken into account to provide an optimised experience. If one child learns multiplication tables through an intensely compelling video game, another may respond to aesthetic pattern development. Collectively, the entire cohort will advance more quickly and recollect lessons for longer.

Century Tech and other providers are already making significant headway into AI tutoring. Century's platform presents users with a range of learning "nuggets" tailored to their needs, while teachers can prescribe further learning as well. For an advance taste of the possibilities of AI tutoring, we can look at the $60bn/year market for English language teaching, where some of the most cutting-edge AI tutoring is developed and applied. Services can entail anything from tuition to assessment and allow users to develop not just knowledge and comprehension but also tone and pronunciation. Such tools have considerable advantages for their developers over other areas of EdTech: they operate in a highly focused area—developing just one skill—and they have readily measurable results.

But AI tutors for broader application are under development too. Leading private school groups in the UK are developing AI tutoring solutions that follow learners through their schooling years, adapting to their needs as they develop. In keeping a consistent tutor throughout their education, we begin to see the possibilities described in *The Diamond Age*.

The implications of this approach go well beyond schooling. Could the AI tutor, for example, both help pupils identify preferred further education and help universities (or employers) to select between candidates? If so, can we reach a future in which exams become redundant, because skills and knowledge can be more easily and accurately measured through data collected by the AI tutor? Such a system would undoubtedly be fairer because it would control for the skill of simply being good at exams. It would reduce unnecessary pupil stress and remove the cost of creating, invigilating and grading exams.

The World Economic Forum advocates a "Reskilling Revolution," and its skills-first approach "focuses on prioritizing skills and competencies over degrees, job histories, or titles in talent management—spanning hiring, development, and redeployment." This recognises the challenges of a future world in which skills need to be more adaptive to changes in technology.

The foundation for such agile skill-adaptation will necessarily be laid in school, and its cornerstones will be a global skills taxonomy and a standardised skills passport for each child that provides a unique tracker for each child on what skills they have developed and should be working on. This private passport will stay with them throughout their working life, and offers a range of advantages to every learner:

- It reinforces the link between discretionary effort at school and improved life chances.

- It allows teachers and pupils, supported by AI, to identify skills shortfalls and opportunities tailored to the needs, preferences and ambitions of each child.
- It allows schools to remain more adaptive to the needs of children in a fast changing work environment.
- It allows direct, objective comparisons of all learners and all schools, guiding decision-making by teachers, schools, education authorities and governments.
- Over time, it generates a higher-performing economy, supported by skills employers require.

AI can also be a powerful driver of behaviour change. We are all familiar with crude recommender systems on online shopping or entertainment sites, but the ability to shape behaviour and attitudes for the better will continue to grow in sophistication. While these techniques are too often put to sinister use, their use to drive positive attitudes in schools will bring significant benefit. They will not only enhance the motivation of the bottom performing third of the student body, they will create a virtuous circle in which prevailing attitudes of academic and social positivity take root and affect an entire school community.

These are, needless to say, powerful techniques with the potential for psychological danger to vulnerable schoolchildren, and will need to be implemented with far-reaching safeguards, even at the cost of limiting their effectiveness. These would include the open publication of the goals and techniques with which they are applied, and ongoing discussion of their usage, risks and effectiveness with parents and school governors.

Challenges

Readers will note that many of the technologies described in this section are not just available today but have been for many years. They will rightly ask why, if these tools are so promising, have we not made more progress in their adoption and development? Even well-credentialed tools whose capabilities are well understood have not made headway. Here I will briefly set out some of the barriers.

First, there are significant barriers to the integration of these tools into the classroom. There can be no question of replacing the pedagogic functions of a teacher (as distinct from administrative) because machine feedback and instruction are no substitutes for teacher feedback and instruction. The question therefore becomes how to combine both in ways that play to the strengths of each.

Second, selection and procurement of the right systems is challenging. A particular challenge in the UK is that individual schools have autonomy over their technology purposes. Some lack the expertise or confidence to select tools wisely and few are able to parse or act on the regulatory implications of their decisions. What is required is a huge amount of parallel testing of new tools to identify the best candidates and a unified tool selection and procurement system. AI tools used in schools must be interoperable, affordable and compliant: only a far more centralised means of acquiring them will provide this.

Third, there is, rightly, significant discomfort over the privacy of children's data in the hands of the largest providers. Nobody wants to see such data sold to third parties or used for advertising or other purposes. These tools aim to enhance learning but they pose real risks to student privacy, with legitimate concerns that schools and teachers lack the resources to vet and mitigate risks.

To benefit fully from these tools, we need governmental clarity and consistency on the legal use of the data, we need an educational establishment that is empowered to protect users and we need parents and children to understand how to protect themselves from loss of privacy. The first of these will be supported (in the UK) by the new Data Use and Access Act.

AI in education represents a significant strategic opportunity for economic growth, improvements to the quality of life at all stages, adaptation to emerging skills requirements, fairness and meritocracy, wiser and better educated citizenry, boosts to productivity in most lines of work and better performance at all human activities. There are significant barriers to its safe adoption, but we owe it to ourselves and to future generations to make it work.

Geospatial—Transportation

I complete the survey of AI productivity opportunities with a briefer section on geospatial—briefer not because it is less important, but because it should be less controversial than interventions in health and education.

The travelling salesman problem is a staple of Operations Research. It poses the question: "Given a list of cities and the distances between each pair of cities, what is the shortest possible route that visits each city exactly once and returns to the origin city?" The problem, first formulated in 1930, is one of the most intensively studied problems in optimisation. Its difficulty stems from the fact that every new city added makes the problem exponentially more difficult—as more cities are added, the computations required to solve it rapidly outpace the resources (human or machine) available to do so.

Recursion algorithms can find a computationally efficient solution, but only AI can find a genuinely workable approach because, as the solution develops, the problem itself changes, and only AI can adapt in this way as it solves the problem.

This has immediate, real-world consequences for a range of fields, but from a UK perspective, none more critical than land management—our population density is sufficiently high to make this a deeply pressing issue. The Alan Turing Institute, based in London, applies these techniques in developing a sophisticated digital twin of the City of Newcastle. This tool allows users to make sophisticated interrogations of the twin such as:

- Given a plan to build new homes for 300 people in a given district, what would be the effect on schools, hospitals, transportation links and air quality?
- What is the optimal distribution of the budget for roads and road repairs in order to reduce congestion and minimise pollution?
- What is the optimal sequencing of the city's traffic lights?

Such problems cannot be reliably solved by brute-force algorithms because of their iterative nature: optimise for any one variable and the problem space changes. AI's ability to rapidly trial and learn from candidate solutions allows it to address problems of this kind without the computational requirements running away from its capability.

The digital twin of Newcastle points to a new range of capabilities focused on transport optimisation. Poorly functioning transport does not just diminish our quality of life, it worsens the polluting effects of traffic and diminishes our economic productivity. AI techniques offer a range of opportunities to improve transportation:

- **Predictive maintenance:** Once vehicles are connected, AI monitors can infer the need for preventive maintenance from single variables or combinations of them. These will include tyre pressure, fuel consumption, component performance and a range of engine data. Predictive maintenance allows action to be taken in advance of downtime, making fleet performance more predictable.
- **Traffic management:** Train or car journeys can be collectively optimised through the sequencing of traffic lights or rail signals. Traffic light changes can both be pre-programmed to optimise on average journey time or to adapt in the moment to flows of traffic as sensors are used to monitor traffic conditions. As of the end of 2023, Transport for London had saved up to £100 M in lost travel time using these techniques.

- **Supply chain optimisation and Freight Management:** A business problem that lends itself almost perfectly to quantitative analysis is supply chain management. Variables include transportation modes; cost and time per mile; weight and volume of goods; source and destination; required delivery dates; local working hours; weather patterns and seasonal variations. AI that rapidly and iteratively optimises across these variables will bring down costs—ultimately to customers—and reduce pollution.

A Note of Caution and a Conclusion of Hope

It is a tempting assumption that a combination of wise regulation, smart technologists and efficient deployment of capital will—over time—necessarily produce technologies that are effective, safe and in the best interests of the users. Sadly this cannot always be counted on, in particular where entrenched players pursue poor technology options, but their scale and reputation are such that market correction mechanisms move too slowly.

The technology-driven recruiting marketplace is a case in point. Recruiting organisations have historically driven a hiring process that entails vacancy advertisements, CV's, cover letters, interviews, offers and credential checks. AI offers us vastly improved tools to achieve this faster, more accurately and at a lower cost. Combining a true understanding of the skills, personality and demands of the candidate with the true job requirements and company culture of the employer should drive a significantly more efficient marketplace for jobs.

Although creating such an efficient marketplace would drive up both productivity and human happiness, it is taking far too long to come into effect. Large job boards are simply accelerating to the point of absurdity the old processes. Highly polished applications are automatically generated and assessments conducted by AI. The result is that orders of magnitude too many applications are received for many jobs, supported by a frictionless process. Qualified applicants are lost in the noise and job seekers routinely take over a year to find jobs. (I invite those that don't believe me to apply online for roles for which they are clearly qualified—perhaps jobs junior to their own in their existing organisations.)

My point is that in addition to smart regulation, cutting-edge technology and animal spirits of market-driven capitalism, governments and technologists need to provide something more: imagination, willingness to upend existing industries and the wisdom to identify and correct misapplication of AI.

All of the use cases I have examined above have at their heart one common element: improvements to productivity—the greater return on human effort, measured in human benefit. We face significant challenges in regulating and guiding the use of these technologies, but we must believe it is possible to do so wisely.

Because if we are able to deliver these things, we have an opportunity—as individuals, societies and a species—to lead happier, wealthier, longer, wiser lives. I cannot imagine any outcome more worthy of our effort.

AI and IP: Rewarding Human Creativity

Lord Tim Clement-Jones

Introduction

In 11 June 2018, OpenAI researchers and engineers published a paper introducing the first generative pre-trained transformer (GPT)-commonly now referred to as GPT-1-a type of generative large language model (LLM) that utilizes deep learning techniques, is designed to generate human-like text by predicting the next word in a sequence and is trained on vast datasets in an unsupervised manner (Radford et al., 2018).

In 2020, the Guardian newspaper published an op-ed headed: "A robot wrote this entire article. Are you scared yet, human?" This was written by a later version—GPT-3. Very convincingly—and presciently—it urged humans to be "careful about the evolution of artificial intelligence" (Guardian op-ed 8th September 2020).

Over the next few years more powerful models followed. ChatGPT (aka GPT-3.5) launched to a mix of public excitement and concern in November 2022. In early 2023, this was swiftly followed by GPT-4, the next evolution of the GPT family. Not only can these LLM's—and others such as Claude and LlaMA—now write articles virtually indistinguishable from human-created pieces but it seems they can pass some serious US bar exams. AI systems

L. T. Clement-Jones (✉)
House of Lords, London, UK

M. Rangeley, N. Fairfax (eds.), *The Artificial Intelligence Revolution*,
https://doi.org/10.1007/978-3-032-11814-1_18

from Google DeepMind achieved a silver medal-level performance in the 2024 International Mathematical Olympiad.[1]

Capabilities for image creation have grown equally rapidly. In 2018, a portrait of Edmond de Belamy, created by a collaboration between a French art collective called Obvious and a generative adversarial network (GAN) algorithm using a dataset of 15,000 portraits from the fourteenth century to the twentieth century, sold for nearly half a million dollars at Christie's in New York (Artsy October, 2018; Isis Magazine March, 2019).

Ai-Da, a life-size humanoid AI robot visual artist which, in October 2022, appeared before an inquiry into the future of the creative industries by the House of Lords Communications and Digital Committee, has achieved even more notoriety. In November 2024, it made headlines with the sale of its artwork titled "AI God," which depicts the renowned mathematician, Alan Turing. This piece was auctioned at Sotheby's also in New York for $1,084,800 on 7 November 2024. Initially expected to sell for between $120,000 and $180,000, the artwork attracted significant interest, resulting in 27 bids before being purchased by an anonymous buyer (The Art Newspaper November 2024).

In 2023, German artist Boris Eldagsen won a Sony world photography award with an AI-generated image titled "Pseudomnesia: The Electrician" and then refused to take the prize, arguing that AI images and photography should not compete in the same category, as they are fundamentally different entities (The Art Newspaper April, 2023).

With the advent of Google's Pixel 9's Magic Editor software in 2024, Sarah Jeong, of the Verge said "Our basic assumptions about photos capturing reality are about to go up in smoke" (Jeong, S. August, 2024, The Verge).

Since ChatGPT's release, OpenAI has continually developed its language model by giving it new image generation capabilities via DALL-E 3, access to real-time information through Bing—the Microsoft search engine—and also audio, video and image capabilities. Some consider that this type of multimodal model is paving the way towards Artificial General Intelligence, or at least giving the impression of doing so.

Since the launch of generative AI platforms, such as ChatGPT-4, DALL.E 3, and Stable Diffusion, there has been an increasing realisation of their potential impact on human creativity, both positive and negative. There are clearly great opportunities in relation to the use of AI, and many sectors are already using

---

[1]New Scientist DeepMind AI gets silver medal at International Mathematical Olympiad July 2024 https://www.newscientist.com/article/2441450-deepmind-ai-gets-silver-medal-at-international-mathematical-olympiad/

the technology in a variety of different ways to enhance their creativity and make it easier for the public to discover new content.

Professor Mayowa Babalola, organisational psychologist and business ethics expert at The University of Western Australia Business School (The Western Australian 26 August 2024), however, has cautioned:

> There's a real risk that over-reliance on AI tools could inadvertently suppress our innate creative capabilities—the very thing that drives innovation.

But as well as being now widely understood as a tool for widespread assistance with written work and image creation there has been the dawning realisation that these generative tools have in most cases been trained on content in such a way that the intellectual property rights of human creators have been infringed.

Given the increasing professional use of LLM's for search and reliance on it for accuracy—even creativity, AI developers rely on high-quality content to train and develop reliable and innovative AI-driven applications. This presents challenges and questions over authorship and intellectual property rights, and in addition, many artists and writers feel threatened, with AI delivering outputs in the form of creative artefacts such as literature, art, and music, especially where it is in the style of an established artist or writer.

The potential, and often actual, tension between the tech industry and creatives was demonstrated by the row over the Apple advertisement titled "Crush" for the new iPad Pro which featured a hydraulic press crushing various objects, including a piano, to symbolise the compression of creative tools into a single device. The symbolism intended to convey that the iPad Pro represented a new era of digital creation, could replace multiple traditional creative tools and instruments and all forms of human creativity could be condensed into one ultra-thin tablet. However, this symbolism backfired significantly. Many viewers interpreted the crushing of artistic tools, especially the piano, as a metaphor for technology destroying traditional forms of creativity and the tech industry's disregard for cultural and artistic heritage. The actor Hugh Grant described it as *"The destruction of the human experience. Courtesy of Silicon Valley"* (The Independent May 9, 2024).

The backlash was so severe that Apple ultimately apologised, acknowledging they "missed the mark" and that the advert fell short of their intention to celebrate creativity.

Some artists have been fighting back with specific tech tools. Glaze is a tool developed by researchers at the University of Chicago's SAND Lab to protect artists' work from unauthorised AI use. It works by adding subtle perturbations to images that are barely perceptible to humans but confuse AI algorithms, preventing them from accurately learning and replicating an artist's style. Kin.art uses label fuzzing and image segmentation to prevent artwork from being successfully inserted into AI datasets. RGB Watermark allows artists to add watermarks to their images. Nightshade goes on the offensive and lets artists add invisible changes to the pixels in their art before they upload it online so that if it's scraped into an AI training set, it can cause the resulting model to break in chaotic and unpredictable ways.

Other artists have been less than polite about AI capabilities. Many creatives enjoyed the blast of rage by Nick Cave, lead singer and songwriter for the rock band Nick Cave and the Bad Seeds, about ChatGPT in the Red Hand Files after a fan used it to create a song in his style.

Cave's response was unequivocal:

"The apocalypse is well on its way. This song sucks. What ChatGPT is, in this instance, is replication as travesty," wrote Cave.

"Songs arise out of suffering, by which I mean they are predicated upon the complex, internal human struggle of creation and, well, as far as I know, algorithms don't feel. Data doesn't suffer.

"ChatGPT has no inner being, it has been nowhere, it has endured nothing, it has not had the audacity to reach beyond its limitations, and hence it doesn't have the capacity for a shared transcendent experience, as it has no limitations from which to transcend.

"It may sound like I'm taking all this a little too personally, but I'm a songwriter who is engaged, at this very moment, in the process of songwriting. It's a blood and guts business, here at my desk, that requires something of me to initiate the new and fresh idea. It requires my humanness" (The Red Hand Files issue 218 January 2023).

Kate Mosse, the celebrated novelist, put it no less firmly in a Financial Times piece in December of 2024:

> In 1989, we bought a tiny house in the shadow of the medieval city walls of Carcassonne. It was the beginning of my love affair with Languedoc—the history, the arcane mysteries hidden in the landscape, the endless blue sky, the light over the mountains at dusk. It would inspire my first historical adventure novel, Labyrinth, which would go on to be translated into 38 languages and sold in more than 40 countries. Its global success is the reason I could give up my day job and become a full-time writer. Imagine my dismay, therefore, to discover that those 15 years of dreaming, researching, planning, writing, rewriting, editing, visiting libraries and archives, translating Occitan texts, hunting down

> original thirteenth-century documents, and becoming an expert in Catharism, apparently counts for nothing.
>
> Labyrinth is just one of several of my novels that have been scraped by Meta's large language model. This has been done without my consent, without remuneration, without even notification. This is theft.

Likewise, Sir Paul McCartney has backed calls for laws to stop mass copyright theft by companies building generative artificial intelligence, warning AI *"could just take over."* The former Beatle has said it would be *"a very sad thing indeed"* if young composers and writers could not protect their intellectual property from the rise of algorithmic models, which so far have learned by digesting mountains of copyrighted material (The Guardian December 10, 2024).

By the same token, content and data-driven businesses themselves have seen a rapid increase in the use of AI technology and machine learning, either for news summaries, data gathering efforts, translations for research and journalistic purposes, or to assist organisations to save time by processing large amounts of text and other data at scale and speed. Digital technologies, including AI, are—and will continue to be—of critical importance to these industries, helping create content, new products, and value-added services to deliver to a broad range of corporate and retail clients. Whether in news media or cross-industry research, publishers are themselves investing in AI; continued collaboration with start-ups and academia is creating tailored materials for wide populations of beneficiaries (students, academia, research organisations, and even marketers of consumer publishing products).

As a result, the interest in IP protection for both input and output of these models has become of ever greater interest and concern and governments are for right or wrong expressing the need to balance recognition of the legal, commercial, and economic rights of data and content owners with the incentivisation of new AI adoption.

In particular with the advent of generative AI systems, there has been an ever-increasing debate about intellectual property rights and ownership as regards material used to train generative AI systems.

The most contested aspect is copyright. This is the exclusive right to make copies of a work; the ability to prepare derivative works; the right to distribute copies of the work to the public; and the right to perform or display the work publicly. This means that if LLM's are trained without a licence for the use of copyright material and other performance and personal data the rights of the holders of the data used in these processes may be infringed. If the AI system has been trained using a dataset containing copyright works, there is also the potential risk that the output produced by that AI system will materially resemble, or completely reproduce, parts of those copyright works, especially where it is in the style of an established artist, musician, or writer, potentially infringing on the rightsholder's right to make derivative works.

The EU Approach to Copyright in Content Used for Training Purposes

Despite activity by WIPO—the World Intellectual Property Organisation—there is as yet no common global approach to the IP issues involved, with the US, the EU, and the UK diverging considerably in their approach. In the case of intellectual property rights and AI, the EU, however, seems to be adopting the most permissive approach.

The EU AI Act (AIA) came into force on 1 August 2024 with the first provisions becoming mandatory in February 2025. Only in June 2023, 14 months after the Act was first proposed, did EU legislators consider it necessary to seek to include specific obligations in relation to foundation models used in AI systems intended to generate content. This was one of the main areas of debate between EU legislators in the run-up to its adoption.

Overall the Act emphasises a risk-based approach to regulation, taking into account the specific characteristics of different AI models. The overall ostensible aim is to balance the benefits of AI innovation with the protection of creators' rights.

There are a range of relevant provisions in Recitals 105 to 110 which specify that providers placing these models on the EU market must comply with EU copyright law. This includes respecting rightsholders' choices to restrict text and data mining of their works, even for scientific research. Article 53 of the Act outlines the obligations for providers of general-purpose AI models which are aimed to enhance transparency and accountability in the deployment of AI technologies, particularly those with significant societal impacts and requires that providers of general-purpose models such as LLM's will need to disclose details of the content used for training.

This includes ensuring that rightsholders can identify when their works have been used in training these models. Specifically, this includes a duty on providers to draw up and maintain technical documentation of the model including its training and testing processes and the results of its evaluation; to maintain and make available information and documentation to providers of AI systems who intend to integrate the foundation model in their AI System;

and to make publicly available a sufficiently detailed summary about the content used for training of the foundation model, according to a template provided by the EU's AI Office. Certain obligations may, however, not apply to GPAI models released under open-source licences that allow public access to model parameters and related information.

The EU AI Office's mandatory template for training, which came into force in August 2025, requires AI developers to publicly disclose a detailed summary covering: provider and model identification; the modalities and sizes of training data; detailed lists of data sources, including public datasets, licenced private data, web-scraped content, user-generated data, and synthetically generated data; and the source and nature of each category of data. Developers must specify whether data was obtained through public repositories, private licencing agreements, web scraping, user contributions, or synthetic generation, with brief descriptions of the content involved.

The template applies to all general-purpose AI models placed on the market in the EU and must be published on the developer's website in an accessible format. Noncompliance carries substantial penalties: fines of up to €15 million or 3% of global annual revenue, whichever is greater.

While the template establishes the first concrete, globally enforceable transparency mechanism for AI training data, certain ambiguities remain unresolved—such as how to measure "size of content scraped" (file size vs. token count)—and the practical utility of the template for copyright holders seeking to enforce their rights remains uncertain.

The transparency elements of the AIA, however, constitute a positive aspect of the AIA and one the UK could and should follow.

Alongside that, however, and more controversially, creators and/or trainers of generative AI platforms may be able to take advantage of the text and data mining exception (TDM) in the EU Digital Single Market Copyright Directive (the Copyright Directive) for the purpose of scientific research by research and cultural institutions in Article 3, and for anyone in Article 4. Unless the rightsholder has opted out under Article 4 the activity of reproducing copyright-protected materials for the purposes of training the AI would typically be covered.

The rightsholder, however, is entitled to reserve its rights through what are called "appropriate means" such as using machine-readable means, like metadata or terms and conditions. Where the rights have been expressly reserved by way of an opt-out, providers of foundation models will need to obtain an authorisation from rightsholders if they want to carry out text and data mining over such works.

This obviously presents a great risk to rightsholders if they are not aware of the Article 4 TDM and fail to expressly opt out.

These provisions, the TDM and, in particular, the opt-out requirement, remain controversial. In July 2023, the Authors Coalition, a coalition of US creative workers and other writers, illustrators, photographers, graphic artists, digital media workers, journalists, novelists, playwrights, composers, and songwriters, issued a joint statement urging EU legislators to promptly cure what they considered to be violations of the Berne Convention for the Protection of Literary and Artistic Works, the long-established framework for the protection of intellectual property rights related to literary and artistic works. They also urged the US government to use all available means to bring the EU in compliance with Berne:

"Much of the copying of our works for generative AI, including "scraping" of Web pages and compilation of "datasets" for use in generative AI, has been carried out from, and/or by entities in, the European Union, claiming to rely on the exceptions to copyright for "text and data mining" (TDM) in Articles 3 and 4 of the Directive on Copyright in the Digital Single Market ("DSM Directive") enacted by the European Union in 2019.

But allowing these exceptions to be applied to copying for ingestion and reuse by generative AI systems constitutes a significant violation of the obligations of EU member states as parties to the Berne Convention ... We urge the European Union to promptly cure this violation of the Berne Convention and provide effective redress for the violations which have already occurred" (Authors Coalition. Joint Statement, 2023).

There are some legal commentators, however, who have asserted that scraping and use of copyright material by generative AI models for training purposes is not, in fact covered by the TDM provided by Articles 3 and 4 (Kluwer Copyright Blog, 2023; Dornis & Stober, 2024).

The first test of this proposition took place in Germany in September 2024, in a landmark case involving LAION (short for Large-scale Artificial Intelligence Open Network)—a massive image and text linked dataset allegedly built by scraping billions of images from the internet—including stock photo sites such as Shutterstock and Getty Images, platforms such as Pinterest, and websites hosting user-generated content such as Flickr and Tumblr, where the Hamburg Regional Court addressed issues related to copyright infringement and the use of images for AI training purposes.

The lawsuit was brought by photographer Robert Kneschke, who claimed that LAION infringed his copyright by automatically downloading and using his images without permission. The Court ruled in favour of LAION, stating that its actions fell under a TDM for scientific research purposes outlined in Section 60d of the German Copyright Act, similar to that contained in Article 3 of the Copyright Directive, except that Article 3 does not allow rights holders to opt out of the TDM exception, whereas Section 60d includes provisions where rightsholders can express an opt-out regarding their works being used for TDM. The court emphasised that LAION's activities, as a not-for-profit organisation, were non-commercial and aimed at promoting scientific research.

Without appellate challenge or broader EU member state coordination, this ruling remains a single precedent suggesting that non-commercial, research-oriented data collection may receive favourable treatment under EU law, though commercial AI developers' reliance on such exceptions remains contested.

It is not clear yet whether this decision will have broader implications for how copyright law will be applied to AI training practices in Europe, particularly whether a text and data mining exception will apply to commercial entities or only to non-commercial research activities, but it may pave the way for future legal interpretation and decisions across the EU regarding copyright, TDMs, and AI technologies.

Copyright and Training Inputs in the USA

In jurisdictions such as the USA, where AI developers have attempted to rely on a fair use defence to copyright infringement, a plethora of legal cases has been mounted by a wide variety of creators, creative industries, and news organisations in what are thought to be the more fruitful venues in the United States.

In December 2023, the New York Times filed a lawsuit against Microsoft and OpenAI, the company behind ChatGPT, alleging that OpenAI unlawfully used millions of its copyrighted articles to train AI models, accusing them of copyright infringement and abusing the newspaper's intellectual property. The New York Times accused Microsoft and OpenAI of creating a business model based on "mass copyright infringement," stating their AI systems "exploit and, in many cases, retain large portions of the copyrightable expression contained in those works." In its court filing, the publisher said it sought to hold Microsoft and OpenAI to account for "billions of dollars in statutory and actual damages" and it believed that it is owed for "unlawful copying and use of the Times's uniquely valuable works."

In March 2025, a federal judge rejected OpenAI's motion to dismiss, allowing the New York Times's core copyright infringement claims to proceed to discovery. The judge narrowed the scope of the lawsuit but allowed the main copyright infringement claims to move forward, representing a significant victory for the newspaper.

Dozens of music publishers led by Universal Music Group, Concord Music Group, and ABKCO Music are suing Anthropic AI for its "mass copying and ingesting" of copyrighted song lyrics to enable its bot to regurgitate them to its users by generating "identical or nearly identical copies of those lyrics" on request.

The Universal Music Publishing Group and other music publishers' case against Anthropic has undergone significant developments since filing. In January 2025, the court approved "guardrails"—protective measures requiring Anthropic to maintain various controls in its current and future AI models to prevent the reproduction of copyrighted lyrics in output responses. Under the terms of the stipulation, Anthropic was required to implement mechanisms allowing publishers to notify the company if protective measures fail, with Anthropic obligated to investigate allegations and work "in good faith" with publishers to address identified issues.

However, in March 2025, the court rejected the publishers' motion for a preliminary injunction that would have prohibited Anthropic from using lyrics for future training. The judge determined that Anthropic might proceed with using the publishers' lyrics to train its AI models, marking a significant setback for the music industry in its efforts to restrict AI developers' access to copyrighted material for training purposes. Despite this ruling, the publishers secured an important discovery victory, with the court ordering Anthropic to produce a "statistically significant sample" of Claude's prompt and output records spanning a 6-month period, potentially yielding evidence to strengthen their arguments for the ongoing litigation. The case remains active, with the key question of whether publishers can prevent Anthropic from using copyrighted lyrics for future model training still pending.

In February 2023, Getty Images filed a lawsuit against Stability AI in the US District Court for the District of Delaware, claiming that Stability AI had copied millions of historical and contemporary photographs to which it holds licencing rights, without permission allegedly to build a competing business. Getty Images is seeking substantial damages, reportedly up to $1.7 billion.

On 14 August 2025, Getty Images notified the court it was dismissing the case and refiling it in the Northern District of California. Getty's action was motivated by Stability AI's motion to dismiss based on lack of jurisdiction over Stability UK (a party Getty deemed indispensable) and Stability AI's alternative request to transfer the case to Northern California.

More recently, Sony Music, along with other major record labels, has filed lawsuits against AI developers, Suno and Udio, for alleged copyright infringement, claiming that they have committed copyright infringement on an "almost unimaginable scale" by using copyrighted music to train their AI models. Suno and Udio have also just been sued by a group of independent musicians. The plaintiffs allege that Suno "*built its rapidly expanding commercial empire by disregarding the intellectual property rights of the artists it claims to support*" and say the same about Udio.

- Reddit's COO Jen Wong warned that AI companies extracting data from Reddit without permission for commercial purposes could face legal action. (New York Times April 29, 2024) and made good on this warning in June 2025 when Reddit filed a lawsuit against Anthropic, alleging that Anthropic scraped over 100,000 Reddit discussions containing millions of comments to train Claude without authorisation, in breach of Reddit's Terms of Service, robots.txt settings, and API rate limits (Reddit v. Anthropic PBC No. CGC-25-625892, Superior Court of the State of California).

Notably, Reddit's case differs from copyright-based suits brought by authors and publishers: rather than claiming copyright infringement over user-generated content that Reddit does not own, Reddit alleges unfair business practices and breach of contract, arguing that Anthropic commercially exploited data hosted on Reddit's platform without permission or compensation. The case moved to mediation in August 2025. The outcome could set an important precedent for whether platforms retain contractual rights over user-generated data and whether scraping public data remains permissible for AI training absent licencing agreements.

Even chipmaker Nvidia has not been immune from lawsuits. Nvidia is facing a class-action lawsuit filed by YouTube creators who charge Nvidia with "unjust enrichment and unfair competition" and allege that millions of YouTube videos were scraped without the permission of the content creators to train its AI software, specifically its "Cosmos" AI program, which is designed to enable users to build, train, and deploy neural network models.

Many cases are ongoing but the difficulties in the USA in showing that training is in of itself infringing may prove problematic as the class action brought by Sarah Silverman and other writers against OpenAI and Meta shows. Their claim was that OpenAI and Meta used illegally acquired datasets containing their copyrighted books obtained from "shadow library" websites like Bibliotik, Library Genesis, and Z-Library to train AI models like ChatGPT and LLaMA without permission or compensation.

In June 2025, Judge Vince Chhabria in the US District Court for the Northern District of California ruled against the authors in their action against Meta, dismissing their core argument that the LLaMA model itself constitutes an infringing derivative work, characterising the theory as "nonsensical." Notably, Meta did not move to dismiss the underlying claim that copying books for training purposes rises to copyright infringement, suggesting even the defendant acknowledges the merit of this core allegation, though discovery and trial remain forthcoming on the OpenAI case.

Although based on dissimilar facts, the outcome of the case brought by Raw Story and AlterNet against OpenAI in New York had a similar outcome, where the federal judge ruling to dismiss the case centred on the plaintiffs' inability to prove a tangible, harmful impact from OpenAI's use of their content as training data. The November 2024 dismissal of Raw Story and AlterNet's case against OpenAI has not been appealed, suggesting the publishers may have accepted the outcome or determined that further litigation is not viable. This stands in contrast to other media publishers who have pursued claims more aggressively, indicating divergent assessments among content holders about the prospects of copyright claims in the US courts.

There may well however be some variation in outcomes as in the separate case against Meta, it did not try to dismiss the grounds for action by Silverman and others that the copying of books for purposes of training its AI model rises to the level of copyright infringement and the judge allowed the allegation of direct copyright infringement during the training process to continue.

Furthermore in the copyright infringement case brought by a number of visual artists—Sarah Andersen, Kelly McKernan, and Karla Ortiz and others—against Stability AI Midjourney, DeviantArt, and Runway AI, where the artists claimed that their artworks were used to train the Stable Diffusion text-to-image generative AI model without permission, the judge (also in the Northern District of California in August 2024) has so far allowed the core claim, namely, that Stability AI—and the other AI companies involved—used copyright-protected content to train a generative AI model without permission, to proceed. The lawsuit involves (in similar fashion to the EU case) the LAION database and centres on the notion that Stable Diffusion contains "compressed copies" of the artists' work.

Warner Bros. Discovery recently, in September 2025, initiated legal proceedings against the image generator company Midjourney, alleging that its platform unlawfully reproduced and distributed visual representations of DC Studio's copyrighted characters. The lawsuit claims that Midjourney's AI-powered service generated images based on prompts referencing iconic figures such as Batman, Superman, and Wonder Woman, without obtaining permission from Warner Bros. Discovery or DC Studios. The complaint asserts that these unauthorised depictions could harm the value of DC intellectual property, potentially confuse consumers regarding official content, and undermine licencing arrangements. The case marks a significant development in ongoing disputes between major entertainment studios and generative AI technology providers over the boundaries of copyright in the digital era.

All these examples are, however, at a preliminary stage. It should be said that the court of the Northern District of California has become a primary venue for litigation involving copyright issues related to generative AI technologies.

A very recent sign, however, that the wind may be blowing in the direction of the creative and news industries was the recent Delaware court case, Thomson Reuters v. Ross Intelligence. Thomson Reuters sued Ross Intelligence for using its copyrighted Westlaw headnotes to train an AI-powered legal research tool. In February 2025, Judge Stephanos Bibas of the Delaware federal district court ruled against Ross, rejecting its fair use defence and granting partial summary judgement in favour of Thomson Reuters. The court emphasised that Ross's use was commercial and non-transformative, as it created a competing product using the copyrighted material. This decision is significant as it sets a precedent for AI copyright cases, though it does not address generative AI specifically. The rejection of the fair use defence in a context involving AI training may signal an important shift in judicial reasoning that could have implications for the pending generative AI cases, particularly those involving commercial AI platforms that use copyrighted works to create competing services. If courts increasingly adopt this reasoning—distinguishing between transformative and non-transformative uses of copyrighted material in AI training—this could substantially narrow the scope of fair use protections that have been claimed by AI developers in cases such as those brought against OpenAI and Meta.

Perhaps the most significant recent case involves Anthropic and a group of authors. In August 2024, a group of authors, led by Andrea Bartz, Charles Graeber, and Kirk Wallace Johnson, filed a class-action lawsuit against Anthropic for alleged copyright infringement accusing Anthropic of using pirated copies of their books to train its AI Large Language Model, Claude, without permission or compensation. In September 2025, Anthropic reached a historic settlement with these authors. The court found that while Anthropic's use of copyrighted books for training purposes could constitute fair use, the company's use of pirated copies for building a permanent, general-purpose library was not protected by fair use.

This distinction—between fair use for training versus no protection for deliberate piracy—has become highly significant for other copyright holders pursuing claims against Anthropic and other AI developers. Anthropic has agreed to establish a $1.5 billion Settlement Fund, divided evenly based on the number of works for which valid claims are submitted. More specifically, the settlement provides approximately $3000 for each of the approximately 500,000 copyrighted works that were alleged as having been downloaded from the pirate library LibGen or Pirate Library Mirror (PiLiMi). If the final list exceeds 500,000 works, Anthropic will pay an additional $3000 for each additional work.

There is no guarantee, however, that all cases in the USA will go the same way. Authors Guild v. OpenAI. (No. 1:23-cv-08292 [S.D.N.Y. filed Sept. 19, 2023]) is a putative class action which was filed in September 2023, by 14 prominent fiction authors and the Authors Guild against OpenAI and Microsoft in the Southern District of New York. The plaintiffs—including bestselling authors John Grisham, George R.R. Martin, Jodi Picoult, Jonathan Franzen, and others—allege that OpenAI systematically copied their copyrighted books without permission to train ChatGPT.

The complaint extensively discusses the threat and harm that generative AI like GPT and ChatGPT pose to authors and their livelihoods, noting that ChatGPT can readily produce summaries of copyrighted works, which the plaintiffs allege are derivative works. The authors argue that ChatGPT can quickly and efficiently generate content at little to no cost—work for which authors would ordinarily be paid—and that the technology threatens to undermine the market for their original works. The case remains in active litigation, with no settlement announced to date. The OpenAI case may take longer to resolve and could result in a different outcome, particularly since it does not appear to focus as heavily on the piracy angle that drove the Anthropic settlement.

Showing that some of the AI developers are not wholly confident of success, several licencing agreements have been established between AI developers and copyright holders, including with major media companies. In May 2024, News Corp announced a multi-year licencing agreement with OpenAI, allowing OpenAI to access both current and archived content from its major publications, including The Wall Street Journal, The New York Post, MarketWatch, and Barron's. The deal enables OpenAI to utilise this content for training its AI models and enhancing its services, thereby providing users with reliable information. While the exact financial terms were not disclosed, reports suggest the deal could be worth approximately $250 million over 5 years (The New York Times, May 22, 2024).

In August 2024, Universal Music Group (UMG) expanded its licencing agreement with Meta, which includes platforms like WhatsApp, Facebook, and Instagram. The agreement aims to protect artists from unauthorised AI-generated content while enhancing revenue opportunities for UMG artists through short-form video content. It marks a notable step in addressing the challenges posed by AI in the music industry, ensuring that artists are compensated for their work (Los Angeles Times, August 12, 2024).

The Financial Times (FT) has also signed a licencing deal with OpenAI for training content in April 2024, described as a "strategic partnership and licencing agreement" that allows OpenAI to use FT's content to train its AI models (TechCrunch, April 29, 2024). Condé Nast and OpenAI have also entered into a multi-year licencing agreement. OpenAI will be able to display content from Condé Nast publications such as Vogue, The New Yorker, GQ, Architectural Digest, Vanity Fair, Wired, and Bon Appétit within its products, including ChatGPT and the SearchGPT prototype and allows OpenAI to use Condé Nast's content to help train its AI models (BBC News, August 21, 2024).

These licencing agreements represent an important emerging pattern, though their prevalence should not be overstated. As of October 2025, they remain exceptions rather than the norm: most AI developers continue scraping without licencing arrangements. More significantly, the terms and structures of these deals remain largely opaque—they are typically announced with minimal financial or operational detail. It remains unclear whether standardised licencing models are emerging (which would suggest a workable market solution) or whether each agreement remains bespoke, negotiated on a case-by-case basis with major publishers having significant bargaining power. The absence of published frameworks or standardised royalty structures suggests the latter. For smaller creators, independent journalists, and mid-list authors, licencing arrangements remain unavailable, creating a two-tier system where only entities with negotiating power can monetise their content.

Some US legislators have taken up the challenge of ingestion of copyright material through the proposal for a Generative AI Copyright Disclosure Act in April 2024 in the House of Representatives (Generative AI Copyright Disclosure Act of 2024. Introduced by Representative Adam Schiff on April 9, 2024), requiring AI developers to submit notices to the Copyright Office identifying copyrighted works used in training datasets. This has not advanced significantly through Congress as of October 2025, remaining under consideration but without a clear pathway to passage.

The lack of legislative momentum at the federal level stands in contrast to state-level initiatives. In individual states, where the move towards transparency requirements may move at a faster pace. In California, the Artificial Intelligence Training Data Transparency Act, was passed in September 2024, and mandates that "Developers" (defined as anyone who "*designs, codes, produces, or substantially modifies*" an AI system for public use) of "*generative artificial intelligence*" (any AI system that can "generate derived synthetic content, such as text, images, video, and audio) systems accessible to Californians must publicly disclose certain information about the data used to train their models on their websites.

This law applies to every generative artificial intelligence system available to Californians that was released or "*substantially modified*" (an update that materially changes an AI system's functionality or performance) on or after first January 2022, including free and paid services. The Act explicitly specifies the information that developers are required to provide. Developers of any generative artificial intelligence system covered by this law must publicly post on their websites a "*high-level summary*" of the datasets used to train those systems.

In mid-September 2025, however, the California legislature passed AB 853, a new law which delays the operation of the California AI Transparency Act until August 2, 2026.

There is growing interest in AI regulation across a number of other states as concerns about transparency, accountability, and ethical use of AI technologies continue to rise.

To demonstrate the political sensitivity of AI and copyright issues, the US Copyright Office's institutional role in AI and copyright policy became unexpectedly contentious in 2025. In May 2025, the Copyright Office released a comprehensive report on artificial intelligence that, while acknowledging that various uses of copyrighted works in AI training are *"likely to be transformative,"* concluded that *"the extent to which they are fair, however, will depend on what works were used, from what source, for what purpose, and with what controls on the outputs—all of which can affect the market."*

This measured but copyright-protective analysis—noting that fair use protections for AI training remain uncertain and context-dependent—apparently has proved unacceptable to the Trump administration. On 10 May 2025, just 2 days after the report's release and one day after the White House fired Librarian of Congress Carla Hayden (who had appointed her), President Trump fired Shira Perlmutter, the Register of Copyrights and Director of the Copyright Office, by email. However, in a significant setback for the administration, the US Court of Appeals for the District of Columbia Circuit ruled on 10 September 2025, that Perlmutter remained entitled to serve as register of copyrights, finding that the Copyright Office's primary role is to advise Congress, placing it within the Legislative Branch and protected from executive removal.

These proceedings underscore the intensely political nature of AI and copyright policy in the USA, with the executive branch apparently unwilling to accept even balanced analyses acknowledging copyright concerns around AI training. This stands in sharp contrast to the legislative debate in the UK and the formal regulatory frameworks in the EU, suggesting that US copyright and AI policy have become caught in fundamental constitutional tensions between the branches of US government.

Copyright and Training Inputs in the UK

In the UK, where the fair use defence is not available, in the view of many, the copyright situation is much clearer. Yet, as in the USA, the Generative AI developers are still failing to obtain licences for their use of copyright material and legal actions—although not on the scale of the USA are being taken.

Mumsnet, the influential UK parenting forum, has initiated legal action against OpenAI, alleging that OpenAI scraped billions of words from its website without permission, constituting copyright infringement. OpenAI reportedly expressed a preference for datasets that are "*not easily accessible online*," suggesting an unwillingness to negotiate licencing for Mumsnet's community-generated content. Mumsnet's claims rest on explicit terms of service prohibiting commercial scraping and a strong database rights position under UK law. The case represents an important test of whether UK copyright and database rights law can effectively restrain AI companies' scraping of user-generated content platforms, particularly when those platforms have explicit terms of service prohibiting commercial use.

Getty Images has pursued parallel proceedings in the UK against Stability AI and could be the first case in English courts to decide on copyright and database right infringement in AI training and development. Getty's lawsuit—as in the USA—centres on claims that Stability AI "scraped" vast quantities of images from Getty's websites without authorisation. These images were allegedly used to train Stability AI's Stable Diffusion, which then produced outputs accessible in the UK through various platforms, including Stability AI's Dream Studio.

Stability AI applied for the claims pertaining to the training and development of Stable Diffusion and in respect of secondary copyright infringement to be struck out pre-trial. However, the application was rejected by the High Court. The case against Stability AI ended in a substantial setback for copyright holders, however, when, on the final day of trial in June 2025, Getty withdrew its primary copyright infringement claims relating to AI training inputs and outputs, citing weak evidence and lack of testimony from Stability AI about how the model was trained. The withdrawal occurred after Getty failed to establish either sufficient UK jurisdictional connection (since training occurred on non-UK cloud servers) or that Stable Diffusion's outputs reproduced substantial portions of Getty's original work—both critical evidentiary requirements for copyright infringement.

Only secondary infringement, trademark, and passing-off claims now remain, with judgement pending as of October 2025. The case exemplifies the severe practical difficulties facing even well-resourced copyright holders in sustaining direct copyright claims against AI training under UK law, raising fundamental questions about whether the law, as currently applied, can effectively protect creators' rights in AI contexts without legislative clarification or technical enforcement mechanisms.

The parallel proceedings pursued by Getty Images in the UK against Stability AI reached a critical juncture in June 2025 and concluded with a significant judgement in November 2025. Getty's lawsuit initially focused on claims that Stability AI "scraped" vast quantities of copyright-protected images to train its Stable Diffusion model. The case faced a substantial setback for copyright holders when, on the final day of trial in June 2025, Getty was compelled to withdraw its primary copyright infringement claims (relating to AI training inputs and outputs). This withdrawal occurred because Getty was unable to establish sufficient UK jurisdictional connection (as the model training took place on non-UK cloud servers) or demonstrate that Stable Diffusion's outputs reproduced substantial portions of Getty's original works.

The narrowed case proceeded on claims of secondary copyright infringement and trademark infringement. Getty argued that even though Stable Diffusion was trained outside the UK, importing the resultant AI model into the UK constituted an infringing "article" under the Copyright, Designs and Patents Act (CDPA).

The final ruling, handed down by Mrs. Justice Joanna Smith DBE on 4 November 2025, largely sided with Stability AI on the copyright front. While the court agreed with Getty that their copyright-protected works were used to train Stable Diffusion and that intangible articles, such as AI models, are subject to copyright infringement claims in the same way as tangible articles (establishing a powerful precedent), the judge ultimately dismissed the secondary copyright claim. The ruling held that Stable Diffusion itself was not an "infringing copy" because it "does not store or reproduce any copyright works (and has never done so)." Getty did secure a limited victory on trademark grounds, where the court found that some AI outputs bearing Getty's watermarks constituted trademark infringement, though these findings were "historic and extremely limited in scope."

The decision was broadly seen as a "blow to UK creators" and a "big win for Stability AI and AI developers generally," suggesting that models trained on infringing data outside the UK can be imported "without legal repercussions."

In the aftermath, Getty took some comfort from the ruling that the Court rejected Stability AI's attempt to hold the user responsible for trademark infringement and that the ruling established a precedent that intangible articles, such as AI models, are subject to copyright infringement claims in the same way as tangible articles but expressed deep concern over the lack of transparency requirements and urged governments, including the UK, to establish stronger transparency rules essential for creators to protect their rights. Getty indicated that they would take the established findings of fact from the UK ruling forward in their parallel US case. The ultimate implication is that the law, as currently applied, faces severe practical difficulties in effectively protecting creators' rights against overseas AI training without legislative clarification or mandatory transparency measures.

UK law, however, does not have a text and data mining exemption of the width of that in the EU Copyright Directive as the implementation deadline for the Directive which contained the EU's exemption occurred after the expiry of the UK/EU Brexit transition period (IPO Announcement: Intellectual property and the transition period: Information on trademarks, designs, patents, copyright, and exhaustion of IP rights during the transition 29 January 2020). The UK exnd collecting societies owning content subject to copyright have developed a strong licencing regime for the use of copyright material.

In June 2022, the UK Intellectual Property Office (UKIPO) published a response to its consultation on AI and IP (Artificial Intelligence and Intellectual Property: Copyrights and Patents 2021) which was intended to seek "evidence and views on a range of options on how AI should be dealt with in the patent and copyright systems." In the response, the UKIPO indicated that it planned to greatly broaden the UK's text and data mining exception to allow text and data mining for any purpose (including a commercial one) and without any ability for rightsholders to opt out (Artificial Intelligence and Intellectual Property: copyright and patents: Government response to consultation, June 2022). These proposals drew widespread criticism from across the creative industries and rightsholder groups on the basis that the current licencing regime was fit for purpose.

In February 2023, in the face of a backlash from the music industry and other creative sectors, and thanks to the then IP Minister George Freeman MP being persuaded by among others, the Alliance for Intellectual Property and members of the All-Party Group on Intellectual Property, the Culture Media and Sport Select Committee, and subsequently by the Lords Communications and Digital Committee, these plans were dropped (The Guardian, "UK government scraps plans to relax copyright laws for AI developers," February 2, 2023). The following month, after recommendations made by Sir Patrick Vallance, the UK government's former Chief Scientific Advisor, in his Pro-innovation Regulation of Technology Review, the government nevertheless accepted that there remained a need to clarify how AI providers and users can utilise copyright works and data, in order to promote AI.

There followed a period in which the UK's Intellectual Property Office (IPO) was tasked with working with users and rightsholders to assist in developing a voluntary code of practice on copyright and AI which explicitly stated that its aim was to:

> make licences for data mining more available. It will help to overcome barriers that AI firms and users currently face, and ensure there are protections for rightsholders. This ensures that the UK copyright framework promotes and rewards investment in creativity. It also supports the ambition for the UK to be a world leader in research and AI innovation.

The UKIPO convened a working group in June 2023, comprising representatives from AI companies and stakeholders from the creative industries. By February 2024, the then Conservative government confirmed that the working group had failed to reach an agreement on an effective voluntary code of practice. It became clear that consensus could not be achieved. This breakdown was attributed to the difficulties in balancing the interests of copyright holders with those of AI developers, who require access to vast amounts of data for training their models. As a result, the responsibility for addressing these issues returned to officials within the Department for Science, Innovation and Technology (UK Government, "A pro-innovation approach to AI regulation: Government response to the AI regulation white paper consultation," Department for Science, Innovation and Technology, February 6, 2024).

With the advent of the new Labour Government, Sir Patrick, now Lord Vallance, became Minister for Science in the Department for Science Innovation and Technology, the sponsor Department for the Intellectual Property Office, and it became clear that Ministers in the Department considered the UK needed to achieve a *"balance between the creative industries and the tech industries."*

As the new government's intentions became clearer, the temperature of the debate rose correspondingly. In August 2024, the Creators Rights Alliance wrote to major tech companies as follows:

> *We are writing to you on behalf of our 500,000-plus creator members in relation to the use of their work to develop generative AI models. This letter reaffirms that members of the Creators' Rights Alliance and the creators they represent do not authorise or otherwise grant permission for the use of any of their works protected by copyright and/or related rights (including performers rights) in relation to, without limitation, the training, development, or operation of AI models, including large language models, diffusion models, generative or other any other AI products, unless the creators have specifically agreed licensing arrangements* (Creators' Rights Alliance, "Open Letter to AI Companies, August 7, 2024).

A new campaign—Creative Rights in AI Coalition (CRAIC)—was created across the creative and news industries (The Guardian, "Creative Industries Launch Coalition to Protect Copyright in AI Era," December 17, 2024), raising over 30,000 signatories from creators and creative organisations calling for stronger copyright laws to prevent mass copyright theft by companies developing generative AI technologies (The Independent, "30,000 sign petition against AI companies using creative works without consent," October 30, 2024).

Subsequently a new government consultation, "Copyright and Artificial Intelligence," was announced in December 2024, which was open until February 2025. The Consultation stated that the government believed that the best way forward was "*through a package of interventions that can balance the needs of the two sectors*" (UK Government, "Copyright and Artificial Intelligence," GOV.UK, December 17, 2024).

It put forward several options regarding the regulation of text and data mining and the use of copyrighted materials for AI training.

- Option 0 which would maintain the current copyright and related laws as they are, without any changes or new provisions.
- Option 1: Which would establish a broad exception for text and data mining, allowing AI companies to use copyrighted works for training purposes without requiring permission from rightsholders. However, this option does not provide any means for rightsholders to opt out.
- Option 2: A Narrow TDM Exception with Opt-Out which would create a more limited TDM exception that allows AI developers to use copyrighted works only if rightsholders have not opted out. This would give rightshold-

ers more control over their works but would limit AI developers' access to training data.
- Option 3: This was the government's preferred option: a new TDM exception that allows AI companies to mine copyright-protected works for training purposes, provided that rightsholders have not "reserved their rights" (opted out) and includes transparency measures.

Following the closure of the consultation in February 2025, which received over 11,500 responses, the government faced sustained and coordinated opposition to its preferred option from both Parliament and the creative industries. In February 2025, two cross-party parliamentary committees—the Culture, Media and Sport Committee and the Science, Innovation and Technology Committee—issued a joint call on the government not to proceed with its preferred option without first establishing an effective and accessible technical solution for rightsholders to opt out.

The creative industries responded with near-unified opposition. The Creative Rights in AI Coalition and numerous representative bodies across the creative industries rejected the rights reservation model entirely, contending that AI developers should only be permitted to use copyrighted material with express permission from rightsholders, not merely in the absence of an opt-out.

Significantly, the UK's AI industry itself emerged as an unexpected critic of the proposals. UKAI, the trade body for the UK AI sector, stated that the government's proposals to introduce copyright exceptions for AI training were "*misguided,*" "*unworkable,*" and "*divisive,*" suggesting deep fractures within the technology sector itself about the appropriate regulatory framework.

In response to this concerted criticism from both inside and outside Parliament, the then Minister for Creative Industries Sir Chris Bryant stated that the government would not proceed with implementation of the consultation proposals before an effective system of rights reservation was demonstrably in place. However, faced with the weight and breadth of opposition—from Parliament, the creative industries, and even elements of the AI sector—the government fundamentally shifted its position. By mid-2025, the government announced it no longer had a "*preferred option*" in relation to copyright and AI and was instead adopting an "*open-minded*" approach to how it would take the matter forward. This represented an explicit abandonment of Option 3 as the government's chosen path, though it stopped short of formally withdrawing the option as a possibility.

Rather than resolving the fundamental tension between AI developers' data requirements and creators' intellectual property rights, however, the government has effectively deferred a decision, creating continued uncertainty for both the creative industries and AI developers operating in or targeting the UK market. Instead of embedding copyright and AI proposals within the Data (Use and Access) Bill (DUAA), which received Royal Assent in June 2025 as was widely demanded, the government signalled its intention to address these issues through a comprehensive new AI bill covering both copyright and AI safety, highly unlikely to be forthcoming before 2026. In response to pressure and extended Parliamentary debate, the government did, however, agree to include within the DUAA a requirement on the Secretary of State to publish both an economic impact assessment and a detailed report on the use of copyright works in AI development within 9 months of Royal Assent, (i.e. by March 2026), and to provide a progress statement to Parliament within 6 months (by December 2025).

Peter Kyle (later replaced as Secretary of State by Liz Kendal in a government reshuffle) also pledged to establish cross-party working groups to tackle AI and copyright issues, suggesting a collaborative legislative approach. However it is clear that substantive copyright reform affecting AI training will remain stalled until well into 2026.

The consultation, in the view of the majority of the creative industries, however, started from the false premise of legal uncertainty. There is in their view no lack of clarity in principle in UK law over how AI developers can legally access training data. In the author's view, UK law is clear that commercial organisations—including Gen AI developers—must licence the data they use to train their Large Language Models. Merely because AI platforms such as Stability AI are resisting claims doesn't mean the underlying principles in the UK are uncertain. There is no need for developers to find 'it difficult to navigate copyright law in the UK' simply because enforcement mechanisms are weak.

Market failure has been cited as a reason for introducing a new text and data mining exception, but there are well-established existing comprehensive licencing solutions offered and administered by a variety of well-established mechanisms and collecting societies. There should be no uncertainty around the existing law. We have some of the most effective collective rights organisations in the world which are coming forward to offer comprehensive licencing solutions. The key problem is identifying the copyright works which have been ingested for training purposes.

The House of Communications and Digital Committee in its Report on Large language models and generative AI back in February 2024 (House of Lords 2024) put it well when it concluded:

> The application of the law to LLM processes is complex, but the principles remain clear. The point of copyright is to reward creators for their efforts, prevent others from using works without permission, and incentivise innovation. The current legal framework is failing to ensure these outcomes occur and the Government has a duty to act.

It made a key recommendation to:

> Support copyright: The Government should prioritise fairness and responsible innovation. It must resolve disputes definitively (including through updated legislation if needed); empower rightsholders to check if their data has been used without permission; and invest in large, high-quality training datasets to encourage tech firms to use licenced material (House of Lords Communications and Digital Committee, "Large Language Models and Generative AI," February 2024).

As the News Media Association has said: *"The government's consultation is based on the mistaken idea—promoted by tech lobbyists and echoed in the consultation—that there is a lack of clarity in existing copyright law. This is completely untrue: the use of copyrighted content by Gen AI firms without a licence is theft on a mass scale, and there is no objective case for a new text and data mining exception*" (Communication with the author December 2024).

However, although it should be clear that use of copyright works to train AI models is contrary to UK copyright law, the laws around transparency of these activities have not caught up. As well as using pirated e-books in their training data, AI developers scrape the internet for valuable professional journalism and other media in breach of both the terms of service of websites and copyright law, for use in training commercial AI models. At present, developers can do this without declaring their identity, or they may use IP scraped to appear in a search index for the completely different commercial purpose of training AI models.

This points to a critical distinction that needs to be made: the question is not whether UK copyright law *in principle* prohibits commercial scraping for AI training—it does—but whether courts can *practically enforce* this prohibition. The Getty Images v. Stability AI withdrawal in UK courts illustrates the enforcement problem acutely. Getty could not establish that Stability AI's training constituted infringement under current legal tests, despite having strong contractual terms prohibiting commercial scraping. The difficulty lay not in unclear law but in the technical and evidentiary burden of proving infringement when training data is ingested and then compressed into model weights. This is fundamentally a remedial and enforcement problem rather than a legal principle problem. AI developers will often scrape websites, or access other pirated material before they launch an LLM in public. This means there is no way for IP owners to opt out of their material being taken before its inclusion in these models. And once used to train these models, the commercial value has already been extracted from IP scraped without permission with no way to delete data from those models.

The next wave of AI models responds to user queries by browsing the web to extract valuable news and information from professional news websites. This is known as Retrieval Augmented Generation (RAG). Without payment for extracting this commercial value, AI agents built by companies such as Perplexity, Google, and Meta, will effectively free ride on the professional hard work of journalists, authors, and creators. At present, such crawlers are hard to block. This is concerning for creators and the creative industries, given that no effective 'rights reservation' system for the use of content by Gen AI models has been proposed or implemented anywhere in the world, making the government proposals entirely speculative. Instead of the options put forward by the UK consultation, there needs to be a transparency requirement and a clear statement about copyright. We should not expect rightsholders to have to opt out. AI developers should be transparent about the identity of their web crawlers; about the purposes of their crawlers; and about the data scraped.

Unless news publishers and the broader creative industries can retain control over their data—making UK copyright law enforceable—AI firms will be free to scrape the web without remunerating creators. This will not only reduce investment in trusted journalism and in the creative sector, but it will ultimately harm innovation in the AI sector. If less and less human-authored IP is produced, tech developers will lack the high-quality data that is the essential fuel in generative AI. Amending UK law to address the challenges posed by AI development, particularly in relation to copyright and transparency, is essential to protect the rights of creators, foster responsible innovation, and ensure a sustainable future for the creative industries.

This should apply regardless of which country the scraping of copyright material takes place if developers market their product in the UK, regardless of where the training takes place. It would also ensure that AI start-ups based in the UK are not put at a competitive disadvantage due to the ability of international firms to conduct training in a different jurisdiction.

Responsible AI developers should seek to license content. It is important that AI developers making copies—whether of text, music, images, or other creative content for training or other purposes recognise that they will be infringing copyright and that the ingestion of content requires permission from rightsholders. If the content owners of underlying data materials withhold the licensing of, or access to, such materials or attempt to price them at a level that is unfair, the answer is for competition remedies to be invoked via the competition regulators.

Can AI Create a Copyrighted Work?

This question, even more than the ingestion of copyright material, goes to the heart of the nature of human creativity. A lawyer colleague of the writer's recently asked themselves the question: Can a robot write a symphony? And answered: With a rapidly growing armoury of AI tools, the answer is *"highly likely."*

A more problematic question is whether it and any other AI-created works can or should attract copyright protection, given its machine rather than human origin.

Given the increased creative output of AI, there are some fundamental issues regarding AI and IP raised by intellectual property experts such as Francis Gurry, the former Head of WIPO. These include:

Originality: Do we require different standards for machines?

Authorship/inventorship: Is there a distinction between human and machine authors and attributing higher value and longer protection to the former?

Reward: Do we need to reward an AI for creativity?

Ownership: Who has ownership of the IP created?

As Francis Gurry has said:

> The fundamental goals of the IP system have always been to encourage new technologies and creative works, and to create a sustainable economic basis for invention and creation (WIPO Magazine, "Artificial Intelligence and Intellectual Property: An Interview with Francis Gurry, September 20, 2018).

But is it just about economics? Should we be making more of copyright and moral rights for human-created works?

The situation in the EU is relatively clear. Although there is no formal definition of "*author*" in EU legal texts, case law of the Court of Justice of the EU establishes that only a human—a "*natural person*"—can be considered an author of copyrightable works.

UK law copyright law goes considerably further. The UK is one of only a handful of countries to protect works generated by a computer where there is no human creator. Section 9 (3) of the UK's Copyright, Designs and Patents Act 1988 (CDPA) provides copyright protection for computer-generated works "*generated by a computer in circumstances that there is no human author of the work.*" The CDPA designates the author of a computer-generated work as "the person by whom the arrangements necessary for the creation of the work are undertaken." This doesn't require direct creative input from a human, but rather identifies the person who made the necessary arrangements. Protection lasts for 50 years from the date the work is made.

UK law is, however, unclear on whether computer-generated works must meet the same originality standard as human-authored works which is not explicitly defined in the CDPA, creating uncertainty. The question of copyright protection for AI-generated works is therefore to some extent debatable due to the degree of human involvement required for an AI tool to produce creative works, and the nuanced interpretations that could be applied to the concept of "*originality.*"

Arguably, the person making the arrangements could be seen as the owner or user of any AI platform used to make an artwork. But the situation becomes less clear when seeking to establish whether the work is sufficiently original to benefit from copyright protection when using generative software. It is uncertain to what extent a user would need to interact with a generative AI program in order to have demonstrated sufficient originality.

In the writer's view, in these circumstances, there is a case for reduction in the term of rights for a work created under 9(3) from 50 to 5 or 10 years, and for the person making the arrangements to be treated as the operator (that is, the person that guides the AI to apply certain data or parameters and shapes the outcome) not the owner of the AI system. AI systems already have access to content from global providers and create derivative content (whether under licence or not) and do so at great speed with little or no investment or "sweat of the brow." It can therefore be argued that in fact the level of protection should be reduced to be proportionate to the time, effort, and investment involved.

The UKIPO consultation in 2021, referred to earlier, recognised that the current UK law on computer-generated works is unclear and contradictory in some respects but decided to leave the law as it is, concerned that AI generated works are still in their early stages and changes could have unintended consequences.

In the author's view, UK copyright law does need to be clarified to ensure that it is the operator or their employer of the AI system—that is, the person that guides the AI system to apply certain data or parameters and shapes the outcome—that is the copyright owner, and not the owner or developer of the AI system.

Apart from that, there is no particular evidence that the existing UK copyright legislative framework fails to adequately address the current needs of AI developers or that current copyright law creates an undue disparity between the interests of AI developers and investors and content owners. The existing copyright regime under current UK legislation, the CDPA, in the writer's view, reflects a balance that fairly protects those investing in data creation without giving an unfair advantage to technology companies offering AI-enabled content creation services.

US copyright law differs considerably from the UK position. The US Copyright Office (USCO) recognises copyright only in works "created by a human being." Courts have likewise declined to extend copyright protection to non-human authors.

There is its famous decision in 2014, for example, in the "Monkey Self-ie" case where a crested macaque monkey named Naruto took a series of several self-portraits in Indonesia using British photographer David Slater's camera and the USCO determined that the photographs so taken—by a non-human—were not copyrightable. This decision was subsequently upheld by the ninth Circuit Court of Appeals in 2018.

In February 2023, USCO issued a decision on artwork created by the generative AI, Midjourney, in which images are created by feeding the program a series of text prompts. In their letter to the author of the book—Kristina Kashtanova—for which the images were produced, the USCO stated that the images were not eligible to be protected by a copyright registration on the basis that the artworks which were generated by AI *"are not the product of human authorship"* (U.S. Copyright Office, Correspondence with Kristina Kashtanova and her attorneys October 2022–February 2023). USCO. However, did conclude that Ms. Kashtanova was the author of the book's text as well as the selection, coordination, and arrangement of the Work's written and visual elements and that in that respect her authorship was protected by copyright.

Following this, in a policy statement in March 2023, USCO clarified that works partially created by generative AI may in fact be eligible for copyright protection. The guidelines state that individuals applying for works with AI content can in fact claim copyright protection for their own contributions to the work. For example, a visual artist can claim sole authorship but must add a disclaimer that the selection, coordination, and arrangement of x-amount of content is of the artist themselves, and that y-amount of the work was generated by artificial intelligence(US Copyright Office, "Copyright Registration Guidance: Works Containing Material Generated by Artificial Intelligence," March 16, 2023).

USCO, in August 2023, however, as mentioned above, issued a comprehensive Notice of Inquiry (NOI) on Artificial Intelligence and Copyright including on the copyrightability of AI-generated outputs and whether AI models and output may infringe copyright and/or protections for copyright management information. USCO is due to report early in 2025 (U.S. Copyright Office, "Copyright Office Issues Notice of Inquiry on Copyright and Artificial Intelligence," August 2023).

These efforts by the USCO, combined with the rapid advancement of AI technology and its impact on the creative industries, strongly suggest that changes to US copyright law are likely to occur in the near future to address the challenges posed by AI in content creation and copyright protection.

With the evolving legal landscape in the USA, there is a continuing risk of potentially infringing output for users of LLMs trained on copyrighted works especially given that LLMs can generate content highly similar to copyrighted materials when given partial information, potentially leading to unintentional reproduction of protected works.

Despite the differing national copyright regimes, there are nevertheless some useful common approaches that can be adopted to mitigating the risk of copyright infringement. WIPO warn in their 2024 factsheet Generative AI: Navigating Intellectual Property, designed to give guidance to those deploying Generative AI systems:

> Generative AI may produce inappropriate or illegal outputs, including incorrect information, IP infringements, deepfakes, personal information, defamatory allegations, and discriminatory, biased, and harmful content. Technical safeguards are being developed, but given the complexity of the calculations involved, predicting AI behavior in all circumstances is challenging.

The factsheet provides a checklist to assist businesses in navigating the challenges of adopting generative AI. It emphasises the need to review terms and conditions of generative AI tools to understand IP ownership of outputs, recommends checking for potential IP infringements before using AI-generated outputs and suggests integrating human creativity with AI outputs to maintain control over ownership. It also addresses specific issues which relate to open-source models where the terms and conditions of the licence may well involve particular obligations on the user such as attribution(WIPO, "Generative AI: Navigating Intellectual Property," 2024).

Patents and AI

Professor Ryan Abbott, author of the *Reasonable Robot: Artificial Intelligence and the Law* (CUP 2020), is a leading academic and practitioner as regards AI inventorship for patents. As a practitioner, he has been most famously advancing a test case internationally on whether an invention generated by an AI called "DABUS," created by computer scientist Dr. Stephen Thaler but without a traditional human inventor, can receive patent protection.

This case in the UK, Thaler v Comptroller-General of Patents, Trade Marks and Designs, has helped provide guidance for the UK's AI industry, and it has stimulated discussion about how intellectual property law should respond to advances in technology. The author is not an adherent to Professor Abbott's belief that an AI should be treated as the inventor, but the debate is an important one as jurisdictions such as the UK choose how to drive forward the governance of AI systems.

A critical feature of this case and the applicant's corresponding cases elsewhere—including the USA—is the absence of a human inventor; the applicant claimed that the inventor was DABUS and DABUS alone. So, this decision does not mean that inventions developed by humans using AI as a tool cannot be patented under UK law if they meet the statutory patentability requirements and name a human inventor.

Authoritative guidance on how AI-created inventions fit into this scheme, where no human inventor is mentioned, is given in the decision in Thaler in the UK's Appeals Court. All three judges in Thaler agreed that under the UK Patents Act (PA) 1977, an inventor must be a person, and as a machine is not a person it, therefore, cannot be an "inventor" for the purposes of section 7(2) of the Act.

In December 2023, the UK Supreme Court confirmed the judgement of the Court of Appeal that a patent requires disclosure of an inventor, and that under the existing scheme, an inventor must be a natural person, and so, in the case of an AI-generated invention without an identifiable human inventor, the invention is inherently unprotectable. Dr. Thaler was not entitled to obtain patents for inventions created by DABUS and the patent applications should be withdrawn as they did not meet the legal requirements. This decision aligned with previous rulings in lower UK courts.

Lord Kitchin, in his Supreme Court judgement said:

> Whether or not thinking machines were capable of devising inventions in 1977, it is clear to me that Parliament did not have them in mind when enacting this

scheme. If patents are to be granted in respect of inventions made by machines, the 1977 Act will have to be amended.

In the Court of Appeal, Lord Justice Birss dissented on the crucial point whether it was an impediment to the grant of an application that the creator of an invention was a machine, as such. He stated that it was simply that a machine inventor cannot be treated as an inventor for the purpose of granting the application. In the author's view, in principle, Lord Justice Birss's approach was the right one. There should therefore be no need for the patent system to identify AI as the inventor or to create entirely new rights. Inventions created by AI, or with the assistance of AI, should be patentable.

As discussed in UK copyright law, creating a "work" is in essence a human activity. Similar principles should apply to patents as with copyright. In addition, as with AI creations for copyright purposes, the key is the operation and control of the machine/AI producing the invention, not ownership of the AI itself.

Following the Supreme Court's decision, therefore, a change in the law would be needed to allow AI-attributed or generated inventions to be protected. Until then, future legal disputes are likely to focus on how much and what level of contribution from a natural person is required to devise an invention with AI involvement. This will become increasingly challenging to determine as AI is increasingly adopted across industries and becomes increasingly sophisticated.

It should also be said that, in the USA, the Patent and Trademark Office (USPTO), likewise, refused to issue patents for DABUS's invention and appeals, including to the US Supreme Court in 2023, have been unsuccessful on similar grounds, that patents can be issued only to human inventors. USPTO have now published "Inventorship Guidance for AI-Assisted Inventions" in February 2024, reinforcing the position established in the DABUS case, and confirming that AI cannot be named as an inventor or joint inventors.

The Legal Board of Appeal of the European Patent Office (EPO) ruled similarly in December 2021 and confirmed the EPO's decision that an inventor in a patent application must be a human being under the European Patent Convention.

In June 2024, the German Federal Court of Justice confirmed that only a natural person can be an inventor under German patent law and that AI systems cannot be designated as inventors, aligning Germany with decisions from the UK Supreme Court, the EPO, the US Federal Circuit, and other jurisdictions. However, the court allowed applicants to name a human inventor with an accompanying statement that they 'prompted' an AI system to generate the invention, with this additional statement legally irrelevant to the patent validity.

The Emotional Perception AI (EPAI) case (Comptroller-General of Patents v. Emotional Perception AI Ltd. [2024] EWCA Civ 825) has become a focal point for testing patentability of AI systems. EPAI applied to patent an artificial neural network (ANN) for music file organisation. The High Court in 2023 initially signalled a more permissive approach, finding technical contribution sufficient for patentability. However, the Court of Appeal reversed this in July 2024, holding that ANNs constitute "computer programs" and are excluded from patentability unless they produce technical effects beyond the program itself. The Court found that EPAI's subjective cognitive benefit (emotionally similar recommendations) did not constitute a technical effect, rendering it unpatentable. Notably, this decision extended the computer program exclusion to hardware-implemented ANNs.

The case raises a critical tension: most practical AI innovations are likely to be characterised as computer programs under current UK law, potentially rendering them unpatentable regardless of their practical utility. This contrasts with EPO practice, which applies a more flexible "any hardware + technical contribution" test. As of October 2025, the UK Supreme Court has not yet handed down judgement following the July 2025 oral arguments, and the case has potential to shift UK AI patentability significantly, with some practitioners now recommending European rather than UK patent protection for AI inventions.

Following the Court of Appeal's July 2024 decision in the EPAI case and the December 2023 Supreme Court ruling in the DABUS case, the UKIPO shifted from a position of being "*open to international discussions*" to adopting explicit restrictive guidance on AI patentability. In January 2025, it updated its Manual of Patent Practice to clarify that learned weights in artificial neural networks (ANNs) constitute "*the computer program*" itself, meaning all practical AI inventions are to be treated as computer-implemented inventions and assessed against exclusions for mathematical methods and programmes. In January 2025, the UKIPO published updated examination guidelines explicitly classifying ANN-based inventions as excluded subject matter, with scenarios illustrating that optimisation of neural networks and processing of data by neural networks fall within the computer program exclusion from patentability.

The UKIPO indicated it considers AI inventions to be mathematical in nature, offering an additional avenue for rejection beyond the computer program exclusion. This represents a significant hardening of position—from openness to change toward more restrictive examination practice—making the UKIPO's approach to AI patentability notably stricter than the EPO's, to the point that intellectual property practitioners now recommend seeking European rather than UK patent protection for most AI inventions. The UKIPO has also indicated it expects further updates to AI patentability guidance following the UK Supreme Court's pending judgement in the Emotional Perception AI case.

The net effect of recent UK decisions is a hardening of patentability barriers for AI-generated inventions. While inventions developed by humans *using* AI as a tool remain patentable (provided statutory requirements are met and a human inventor is named), inventions generated autonomously by AI systems without identifiable human contribution cannot be patented under current law. Whether this represents sound patent policy or an excessive restriction on legitimate innovation remains contested between national patent offices and will probably require eventual legislative clarification across jurisdictions.

Performing Rights and AI

Lastly, there are the many issues relating to performing rights: the copying of actors', musicians', artists', and other creators' images, voices, likenesses, styles, and attributes by AI systems. The all-important aspect of human and machine interface heavily impacts creative performers and artists. The use of AI has grown rapidly across the audio and entertainment industry in recent years, from automated audio books and voice assistants to deepfake videos and text-to-speech tools.

AI-made "performance synthetisation" is one of the ways that the technology is used in the entertainment industry. This is the process of creating a performance by manipulating the likeness of a performance or a performer. Examples include deepfake videos in which a person in an existing image or video is replaced with someone else's likeness.

But in the view of many, IP law has failed to keep pace. And this is leading to performers being exploited. AI is being used to clone performers' voices and likenesses. Performers are having their image, voice, or likeness reproduced by others, using AI technology, without their consent.

Because of loopholes in the law, performers are not being fairly paid for the reproduction of their work—and sometimes not paid at all. In a survey by the UK actors' union, Equity, in 2022, 79% of performers who have undertaken AI work felt they did not have a full understanding of their performers' rights before signing their contracts. And 65% of performers thought that the development of AI technology poses a threat to employment opportunities in the performing arts sector.

In the author's view, it is important that creators and artists derive the full benefit of technology such as AI-made performance synthetisation and streaming and that artists' names, voices, images, and likenesses are sufficiently protected. AI could have a hugely positive impact on the entertainment industry, but we need to make sure that it works for performers and not just the production companies.

Potential use of AI by film studios to synthesise performance and emulate writing was at the root of the 2023 Hollywood writers' and actors' strike in the USA. This recent unprecedentedly long strike involving the Writers Guild of America (WGA) and the Screen Actors Guild-American Federation of Television and Radio Artists (SAG-AFTRA), was prompted specifically by the threat of AI, with writers concerned that AI should be used only as a tool that can help with research or facilitate script ideas and not as a tool to replace them, and actors, about use of AI-created voice or image digital replicas—or indeed performance synthesisation.

The outcome of the strike resulted in a significant agreement with the Alliance of Motion Picture and Television Producers (AMPTP) that, whilst not universally welcomed, addressed some of the concerns of actors about the use of AI technologies in the entertainment industry and led to a new standard contract that includes specific provisions governing the use of AI in relation to performers' likenesses and voices (Backstage, November 2023).

The standard contract stipulates that studios must obtain explicit consent from performers before capturing their likeness for digital replicas. They must also provide at least 48 hours' notice before any proposal to use these replicas and engage in separate negotiations for each instance of use. The agreement also includes clauses addressing how these synthetic performers—entirely AI-generated characters—can be created and used and mandates that performers must give consent for their likenesses to be used in AI applications, ensuring they receive fair compensation for such use.

Not everyone can rely on collective agreements, however, to protect them from being digitally faked. In July 2024, the US Copyright Office released Part 1 of its report on AI and Copyright, focusing on digital replicas. It called for urgent new federal legislation to protect individuals from unauthorised digital replicas of their voice, image, and likeness. This should, they said, cover all individuals, not just celebrities as regards knowingly distributing unauthorised replicas and include both commercial and non-commercial uses.

Following the report's release, several members of Congress introduced legislation known as the "NO FAKES Act" in both the Senate and the

House which aimed to address concerns regarding unauthorised digital replicas and the use of individuals' voices and likenesses through generative artificial intelligence technologies. The Act garnered broad support from various stakeholders.

The NO FAKES Act was reintroduced on a bipartisan basis in April 2025, with revised and expanded provisions aimed at addressing stakeholder concerns from the earlier version. The reintroduced bill garnered broad stakeholder support from RIAA, MPA, SAG-AFTRA, ASCAP, NMPA, the Authors Guild, the National Association of Broadcasters, and the Model Alliance. However, as of October 2025, despite this coalition support and bipartisan sponsorship, the NO FAKES Act has not passed either chamber of Congress and remains stalled in the legislative process.

The stalled status of federal legislation contrasts sharply with California's October 2025 enactment of performer protection laws, suggesting that substantive protection of performers' rights in AI contexts may advance more readily at the state level than through federal legislation. California's new laws do not completely prohibit the use of replicas but allow such use only under specific conditions requiring explicit performer consent, with vague terms of use such as "*in all media known or hereafter known*" no longer permitted. This extends protection beyond union actors (covered by SAG-AFTRA agreement) to all non-union performers, with the law applying to performance contracts signed on or after 1 January 2025.

In the UK Equity, the British actors' union, in their Stop AI Stealing the Show campaign, have called for the UK government to modernise the law and strengthen rights for creatives and performers. Canadian voiceover artist Bev Standing is at the forefront of the campaign. She won a settlement after she sued TikTok, saying the company had used her voice for their text-to-speech feature without her permission, based on recordings she had provided for another company years earlier.

The campaign is emphasising the need for clarity regarding performers' rights when working with AI technologies. Many performers are unaware of their rights and may sign contracts without fully understanding the implications. The campaign is seeking government action to modernise intellectual property laws to keep pace with technological advancements, ensuring that performers are fairly compensated and have control over how their likenesses and voices are used: The campaign is backed by various high-profile figures and organisations, including the Musicians' Union and the Writers' Guild of Great Britain highlighting the collective concern within the industry about the potential threats posed by AI technologies to jobs and creative rights.

As yet there has been no government action in this area or indeed by the UKIPO. What is needed now is an independent review to explore the merits of introducing image rights and publicity rights, and ensure that the purpose of copyright in stimulating and sustaining creativity is met.

Despite the urgent need for performer protections in the AI era, the UK remains one of the major jurisdictions that has failed to ratify the Beijing Treaty on Audiovisual Performances as of October 2025, more than 5 years after the treaty entered into force in April 2020. The UK signed the treaty in 2013 but could not ratify while part of the EU; after Brexit, the government-initiated consultations on implementation options, including whether to provide exclusive rights for audiovisual performers regarding broadcasting and communication to the public, or merely equitable remuneration rights.

A government consultation on ratification ran from September to November 2023, closing in February 2024 with a government promise to analyse the responses and announce next steps. However, as of October 2025, no government response to the consultation has been published, no ratification decision has been made, and no timeline for ratification has been announced.

The UK is not alone in this delay: the European Union signed the treaty in June 2013 but has not ratified it as of October 2025; the United States similarly has not ratified; and only 48 parties—conspicuously excluding all three of the world's major economic and regulatory powers—have become signatories. This prolonged delay is particularly troubling given that AI-generated deepfakes and digital replicas of performers' voices and likenesses have become a growing concern in the entertainment industry. The Treaty's provisions are relevant to AI-generated deepfakes and digital replicas specifically because they establish performers' rights to object to "distortion or mutilation" of recorded performances. These rights could potentially extend to unauthorised synthesis of performer likenesses in AI-generated outputs, provided national implementations are sufficiently robust. However, the treaty does not directly address AI-generated content; it addresses performers' traditional rights in a digital context. Its delayed ratification by the UK, EU, and USA means that performers currently lack even this foundational international protection, let alone protections specifically designed for AI-generated replicas. The Treaty thus represents a necessary but insufficient foundation upon which AI-specific performer protections would need to be built.

As regards performers' rights in the EU, the Directive 2001/29/EC, commonly referred to as the InfoSoc Directive, addresses various aspects of copyright and related rights in the digital environment, including specific provisions related to performance rights and digitisation. The directive mandates that member states must provide performers with exclusive rights to authorise or prohibit the fixation and making available of their performances. This includes the right to authorise or prohibit any communication to the public of their performances and the right to authorise or prohibit the making available to the public of fixations of their performances. Performers are granted protection against unauthorised reproductions or distributions of their performances. This means that any digital replicas or uses of a performer's work must be authorised by the performer.

The recently adopted AIA in the EU also establishes a regulatory framework for AI systems, including provisions that may impact how digital replicas of performances are treated, in that deployers of AI systems that create deepfakes must clearly disclose that the content has been artificially generated. This aims to ensure transparency and protect individuals from unauthorised use of their likenesses.

In addition, as a result of a number of Court of Justice of the European Union (CJEU) rulings, moral rights—which include the right to attribution and integrity—are more strongly enforceable. This is particularly so in a number of member states such as France.

In Recorded Artists Actors Performers Ltd. v Phonographic Performance (Ireland) Ltd in 2020 the CJEU clarified important aspects of performers' rights under EU law, specifically regarding equitable remuneration and held that all performers, regardless of their nationality, are entitled to equitable remuneration for the use of their performances. This ruling emphasised that the right to remuneration is an inherent right of performers when their works are communicated to the public. Despite this, while current EU law provides some protections for performers, particularly through moral rights and copyright frameworks, there is a growing recognition of the need for more explicit regulations addressing the challenges posed by AI-generated digital replica content.

The Future of AI and IP

AI also raises the fundamental question of how the benefit and reward for IP creation is distributed. If AI can create huge quantities of IP autonomously, who gets the benefit? Large corporates which have access to vast quantities of data to train their algorithms? Or should our competition regulators intrude on IP creation and protection and what might be considered dataset monopolies? In the UK, this could fall to the Digital Markets Unit of the Competition and Markets Authority.

The European Commission too has shown significant interest in IP rights in the context of competition law. EU competition law, particularly under Articles 101 and 102 of the Treaty on the Functioning of the European Union (TFEU), applies to IP-related agreements and practices and the EU has established guidelines addressing how competition law interacts with IP rights, emphasising that exclusive rights granted by IP laws are not immune from competition scrutiny (European Commission, "Guidelines on the applicability of Article 101 of the Treaty on the Functioning of the European Union to technology transfer agreements," March 2014).

In the USA, the Federal Trade Commission (FTC) has actively examined the intersection of intellectual property rights and antitrust law. Over the years, it has issued several reports and guidelines addressing how IP can affect competition, notably, the FTC's 2017 IP Licensing Guidelines, which reaffirms that antitrust principles apply to IP1 as they do to other forms of property, whilst emphasising that IP does not inherently confer market power. Transparency requirements in the EU AI Act template, California's disclosure law, and proposed UK reporting obligations, are significant protections for rightsholders, but transparency alone is not equivalent to substantive protection.

Disclosure requirements reveal *which* content was used for training but do not prevent such use or provide automatic remedies when infringement occurs. A developer required to publicly list "Getty Images photographs" in their training data summary has still committed copyright infringement; the summary merely makes it visible. Policymakers and advocates must distinguish between transparency as an accountability mechanism (enabling enforcement and litigation) and transparency as a substitute for permission. Effective protection requires both transparency AND either licencing requirements, robust opt-out mechanisms with technical enforceability, or clear liability standards. Transparency without any of these is visibility without remedy.

IP administrators and policymakers too will need to keep an active watching brief. Changes to copyright laws in one country that make it more attractive for AI developers to base their operations in those locations so that text and data mining activities become more easily performed or permitted could theoretically lead to a race to the bottom—to the detriment of human creativity.

Most major AI developers (OpenAI, Anthropic, Meta, Stability AI), however, remain US-based, and their training data practices have not visibly adjusted based on jurisdictional copyright differences. Given the global adoption of AI technology, it is also clear that an internationally harmonised approach to the protection and recognition accorded to AI-generated inventions and works may well be needed. The challenge will be to produce international alignment on the nature of copyright and performer protection that does not produce an unacceptable trade-off with so-called "innovation," disadvantage creators and the creative industries and damage the prospects for human creativity.

Tin Clement-Jones

23rd February 2025 (Updated 20th October 2025)

Bibliography

Andersen et al. v. Stability AI, Inc., Midjourney, Inc., DeviantArt, Inc., and Runway AI, Inc, No. 3:23-cv-00001, N.D. Cal., ruling issued August 12, 2024.

Artificial Intelligence Training Data Transparency Act: Assembly Bill 2013, 2023–2024 Regular Session (California 2024).

Artsy 25th October 2018: The first portrait generated by artificial intelligence to be sold at auction was purchased for more than 40 times its high estimate https://www.artsy.net/article/artsy-editorial-first-ever-portrait-generated-artificial-intelligence-auction-sold-40-times-estimate

Authors Coalition: Creators call for Action on Copyright Exceptions, July 2023.: https://graphicartistsguild.org/the-guild-joins-call-for-action-on-ai-and-copyright/and. (2023, July). Joint Statement Urging EU Legislators to Address Violations of the Berne Convention.

Authors Guild v. OpenAI. (No. 1:23-cv-08292 (S.D.N.Y. filed Sept. 19, 2023)).

Babalola, M. (26 August 2024). There's a real risk that over-reliance on AI tools could inadvertently suppress our innate creative capabilities. *The Western Australian*. https://thewest.com.au/opinion/mayowa-babalola-ai-is-an-ethical-time-bomb%2D%2Dc-1583

Backstage November 15th: Breaking Down the SAG-AFTRA/AMPTP Deal Summary: What Will Actors Get?

Bartz et al. v. Anthropic PBC, 2024.

BBC 18 April 2023 Sony World Photography Award 2023: Winner refuses award after revealing AI creation: https://www.bbc.co.uk/news/entertainment-arts-65296763

BBC News 21st August 2024: ChatGPT firm OpenAI strikes deal with Vogue owner. https://www.bbc.co.uk/news/articles/cpqjvl9z9wlo

Beijing Treaty on Audiovisual Performances WIPO adopted on June 24, 2012, and entered into force on April 28, 2020.: https://www.wipo.int/treaties/en/ip/beijing/

Christies: Obvious and the interface between art and artificial intelligence: December 2018.: https://www.christies.com/en/stories/a-collaboration-between-two-artists-one-human-one-a-machine-0cd01f4e232f4279a525a446d60d4cd1

(Comptroller-General of Patents v. Emotional Perception AI Ltd [2024] EWCA Civ 825)

Concord Music Group, Inc., Universal Music Group, and ABKCO Music, v. Anthropic PBC, 2023.

Copyright, Designs and Patents Act, 1988.: https://www.legislation.gov.uk/ukpga/1988/48/contents

Creative Rights in AI Coalition (CRAIC). (December 2024). *Campaign calling for stronger copyright laws to prevent mass copyright theft by generative AI developers.* https://societyofauthors.org/2024/12/16/creative-rights-in-ai-coalition-calls-on-government-to-protect-copyright-as-ai-policy-develops/

Creators' Rights Alliance. (7 August 2024). *"Open Letter to AI Companies." Regarding use of copyright works in AI development without authorization or compensation.* https://societyofauthors.org/2024/08/07/creators-rights-alliance-sends-letter-to-ai-tech-companies/

Culture, Media and Sport Committee and Science, Innovation and Technology Committee. (February 2025). *Joint letter on Copyright and AI.* https://committees.parliament.uk/committee/378/culture-media-and-sport-committee/news/205480/two-crossparty-committees-respond-to-government-consultation-on-artificial-intelligence-and-copyright/

Data (Use and Access) Bill (Royal Assent June 2025). legislation.gov.ukhttps://www.legislation.gov.uk/ukpga/2025/18

Directive 2001/29/EC of the European Parliament and of the Council of 22 May 2001 on the harmonisation of certain aspects of copyright and related rights in the information society EUR-Lex - Directive 2001/29/EC.

Directive (EU) 2019/790 of the European Parliament and of the Council of 17 April 2019 on copyright and related rights in the Digital Single Market and amending Directives 96/9/EC and 2001/29/EC: https://eur-lex.europa.eu/legal-content/EN/TXT/HTML/?uri=CELEX%3A32019L0790

Dornis, T. W., & Stober, S. (2024). *Urheberrecht und Training generativer KI-Modelle (Copyright Law and Generative AI Training - Technological and Legal Foundations)* (1st ed.). Nomos.

Equity Survey: 4 out of 5 performers don't understand their rights when working with AI, April 2022.: https://www.equity.org.uk/news/2022/4-out-of-5-performers-don-t-understand-their-rights-when-working-with-ai

Equity: Stop AI Stealing the Show.: https://www.equity.org.uk/campaigns-policy/stop-ai-stealing-the-show

EU AI Office's mandatory template for training data transparency (published July 24, 2025, effective August 2, 2025).

European Commission. (2014). Guidelines on the applicability of Article 101 of the Treaty on the Functioning of the European Union to technology transfer agreements. *OJ C, 89*, 28.

Federal Trade Commission. *Antitrust Guidelines for the Licensing of Intellectual Property*, January 13, 2017. FTC Antitrust Guidelines for the Licensing of Intellectual Property.

Generative AI Copyright Disclosure Act of 2024. Introduced by Representative Adam Schiff on April 9, 2024, H.R. 7913, 118th.

Getty Images (US) Inc and Ors v. Stability AI Limited. [2025] EWHC 2863 (Ch).

House of Lords Communications and Digital Committee. *Large language models and generative AI*, HL Paper 54, February 2, 2024.

Isis Magazine March 1 2019 ART-ificial Intelligence: The Curious Case of Edmond De Belamy.

Jeong, S. (2024, August 22). *No one's ready for this*. The Verge.

Kate Mosse, K. (2024, December 21). AI's assault on our intellectual property must be stopped. *Financial Times*.

Kluwer Copyright Blog. (2023, May 9). *Generative AI, Copyright and the AI Act*. Kluwer Law International.

Kneschke v. LAION e.V., Hamburg District Court, Case No. 310 O 227/23 (September 27, 2024).

Millette v. Nvidia Corp., No. 24-cv-05157, N.D. Cal., filed August 14, 2024.

Mumsnet v. OpenAI, High Court, proceedings issued July 2024.

Nick Cave The Red Hand Files Issue 218 January 2023. https://www.theredhandfiles.com/chat-gpt-what-do-you-think/

NO FAKES Act: H.R.9551 - 118th Congress (2023–2024): NO FAKES Act of 2024. https://www.congress.gov/bill/118th-congress/house-bill/9551

Perlmutter v. Blanche et al. https://www.washingtontimes.com/news/2025/sep/10/appeals-court-restores-copyright-office-chief-says-donald-trumps/

Peter Kyle former Secretary of State for Science, Innovation and Technology copyright and AI policy. https://www.independent.co.uk/news/uk/politics/peter-kyle-minister-government-elton-john-house-of-lords-b2765999.html

Porterfield, C. (2024, November 8). Painting by the AI robot Ai-Da sells for more than $1m at Sotheby's. *The Art Newspaper*.

Radford, A., Narasimhan, K., Salimans, T., & Sutskever, I. (2018, June 11). *Improving language understanding by generative pre-training*. OpenAI.

Raw Story Media, Inc. and AlterNet Media, Inc. v. OpenAI, Inc., No. 24 Civ. 01514, N.D. Cal., ruling issued November 7, 2024.

Recorded Artists Actors Performers Ltd v Phonographic Performance (Ireland) Ltd CJEU, Judgment of 8 September 2020, Case C-172/20.

Reddit COO warning regarding AI companies extracting Reddit data for commercial purposes. *New York Times*, 29 April 2024. https://www.thetimes.com/business-money/technology/article/reddit-considers-legal-action-against-ai-firms-for-unauthorised-use-pmp6t0t3v

Reddit v. Anthropic PBC (June 2025) No. CGC-25-625892, Superior Court of the State of California, County of San Francisco, filed June 4, 2025, later removed to the U.S. District Court for the Northern District of California as No. 3:2025-mc-80178 on July 3, 2025 Lawsuit alleging Anthropic scraped over 100,000 Reddit discussions without authorization in breach of Terms of Service, robots.txt, and API rate limits; moved to mediation August 2025. https://natlawreview.com/article/beyond-copyright-reddits-lawsuit-against-anthropic

Regulation (EU) 2024/1689 of the European Parliament and of the Council of 13 June 2024.EUR-Lex - Regulation (EU) 2024/1689.

SAG-AFTRA and Writers Guild of America. 2023 Agreement with Alliance of Motion Picture and Television Producers (AMPTP) November 2023. https://www.wgacontract2023.org/the-campaign/summary-of-the-2023-wga-mba

Silverman et al. v. Meta Platforms, Inc., No. 23-cv-03417, N.D. Cal., ruling issued November 20, 2023a.

Silverman et al. v. OpenAI, L.L.C. and Meta Platforms, Inc., 2023b.

Silverman et al. v. OpenAI, Inc., No. 3:23-cv-03416, N.D. Cal., ruling issued February 12, 2024.

Sir Patrick Vallance's Review on pro-innovation regulation for digital technologies, March 2023.: https://www.gov.uk/government/publications/pro-innovation-regulation-of-technologies-review-digital-technologies

Sony Music Entertainment, Universal Music Group, and Warner Records v. Suno, Inc. and Udio AI, 2024.

TechCrunch, April 29, 2024. OpenAI inks strategic tie-up with UK's Financial Times, including content use.

Thaler and the European Patent Office: EPO J 0008/20 (Designation of inventor/DABUS), December 21, 2021. And EPO Legal Board of Appeal Decision J 8/20.

Thaler in Germany: Bundesgerichtshof (BGH), Decision of June 11, 2024, File No. X ZB 5/22.

Thaler in the UK: Thaler v Comptroller-General of Patents, Trade Marks and Designs [2019] UKIPO - the initial decision by the UKIPO, Thaler v Comptroller-General of Patents, Trade Marks and Designs [2021] EWCA Civ 1374 in the Court of Appeal and Thaler v Comptroller-General of Patents, Trade Marks and Designs [2023] UKSC 10 in the Supreme Court https://www.supremecourt.uk/cases/uksc-2021-0201.html

Thaler in the US: USPTO. *Inventorship guidance for AI-assisted inventions*, February 13, 2024, Thaler v. Vidal, No. 21–2340 (Fed. Cir. 2023), U.S. Supreme Court, Thaler v. Vidal, 2023 https://www.reuters.com/legal/us-supreme-court-rejects-computer-scientists-lawsuit-over-ai-generated-2023-04-24/

The Art Newspaper. April 18, 2023. The *camera never lies? Creator of AI image rejects prestigious photo award.*

The Art Newspaper 8th November 2024 Painting by the AI robot Ai-Da sells for more than $1m at Sotheby's. https://www.theartnewspaper.com/2024/11/08/ai-da-robot-painting-sells-one-million-sothebys

The Guardian 8th September 2020: oped "A robot wrote this entire article. Are you scared yet, human?" https://www.theguardian.com/commentisfree/2020/sep/08/robot-wrote-this-article-gpt-3

The Guardian, *UK government scraps plans to relax copyright laws for AI developers*, February 2, 2023 and UK government bins UKIPO's flagship AI reforms:

February 2023.: https://www.managingip.com/article/2b8dy58efmhhbvsmaxvk0/uk-government-bins-ukipos-flagship-ai-reforms

The Guardian. *Creative Industries Launch Coalition to Protect Copyright in AI Era*, December 17, 2024.

The Guardian December 10 2024 Sir Paul McCarney warns AI 'could tke over' as UK debates copyright laws.

The Guardian December 13 2024- Paul McCartney warns AI could take over as UK debates copyright laws.

The Independent 11th October 2022: *Ai-Da robot makes history by giving evidence to parliamentary inquiry*. https://www.independent.co.uk/news/uk/politics/house-of-lords-technology-liberal-democrat-b2200496.html

The Independent, *30,000 sign petition against AI companies using creative works without consent*, October 30, 2024.

The Independent 9th May 2024 Hugh Grant eviscerates new iPad Pro ad for promoting the 'destruction of the human experience' Independent Independent.co.uk/arts-entertainment/films/news/apple-ipad-ad-hugh-grant-japan-tim-cook-b2542005.html?

The New York Times Company v. OpenAI, L.L.C. and Microsoft Corporation, 2023.

The UK Intellectual Property Office (UKIPO) consultation on "Artificial Intelligence and Intellectual Property: Copyrights and Patents" launched in October 2021.

The UK government's response to consultation on "Copyright and Artificial Intelligence", published on June 28, 2022.

The Verge September 2021 TikTok settles lawsuit with actress over its original text-to-speech voice. https://www.theverge.com/2021/9/29/22701167/bev-standing-tiktok-lawsuit-settles-text-to-speech-voice

Thomson Reuters Enterprise Centre GmbH v. Ross Intelligence Inc., U.S. District Court for the District of Delaware (February 2025). https://www.ded.uscourts.gov/opinion/thomson-reuters-enterprise-centre-gmbh-et-al-v-ross-intelligence-inc-5

Thomson Reuters Enterprise Centre GmbH v. Ross Intelligence Inc., U.S. District Court for the District of Delaware, decided on February 11, 2025.

U.S. Copyright Office. Copyright office issues notice of inquiry on copyright and artificial intelligence. *NewsNet* Issue 1017, August 30, 2023a. https://www.federalregister.gov/documents/2023/08/30/2023-18624/artificial-intelligence-and-copyright

U.S. Copyright Office. Notice of inquiry: Copyright and artificial intelligence. *Federal Register*, August 30, 2023b.

U.S. Copyright Office, Correspondence with Kristina Kashtanova and her attorneys, October 2022–February 2023c in relation to "Zarya of the Dawn. and AI-created images lose US copyrights in test for new technology, February 2023: https://www.reuters.com/legal/ai-created-images-lose-us-copyrights-test-new-technology-2023-02-22/

U.S. Copyright Office. Copyright Office Releases Part 1 of Artificial Intelligence Report, Recommends Federal Digital Replica Law. *NewsNet* Issue 1048, July 31, 2024.

UK Government, A pro-innovation approach to AI regulation: Government response to the AI regulation white paper consultation, Department for Science, Innovation and Technology, February 6, 2024.

UK Government, Consultation. *Copyright and Artificial Intelligence*. GOV.UK, December 17, 2024.

UK Government response to consultation, June 2022: Artificial Intelligence and Intellectual Property: copyright and patents: period. https://www.gov.uk/government/consultations/artificial-intelligence-and-ip-copyright-and-patents/outcome/artificial-intelligence-and-intellectual-property-copyright-and-patents-government-response-to-consultation

UKAI (UK AI Industry Trade Body). https://ukai.co/resource/creative-industries-and-ai-report.html [VERIFY: date, https://diginomica.com/uk-ai-changing-copyright-wont-work-so-what-will, https://diginomica.com/ai-and-copyright-uk-government-responds-diginomica-advance-parliamentary-votebut-it-isnt-listening

UKIPO: The government's code of practice on copyright and AI: Summary of the government's ongoing programme of work to develop a code of practice on copyright and AI. June 2023. https://www.gov.uk/guidance/the-governments-code-of-practice-on-copyright-and-ai

UKIPO Announcement: Intellectual property and the transition period: Information on trade marks, designs, patents, copyright, and exhaustion of IP rights during the transition, 29th January 2020. https://www.gov.uk/government/news/intellectual-property-and-the-transition-period

Universal Music Publishing Group et al. v. Anthropic PBC, No. 24-cv-00123, N.D. Cal., filed October 18, 2023. *The New York Times*, May 22, 2024.

US Copyright Office. *Copyright registration guidance: Works containing material generated by artificial intelligence*, March 16, 2023. https://www.federalregister.gov/documents/2023/03/16/2023-05321/copyright-registration-guidance-works-containing-material-generated-by-artificial-intelligence

WIPO Magazine. *Artificial intelligence and intellectual property: An interview with Francis Gurry*, September 20, 2018. https://www.wipo.int/wipo_magazine/en/2018/05/article_0001.html

Wired Magazine November 2023: Hollywood Actors Strike Ends with a Deal That Will Impact AI and Streaming for Decades, https://www.wired.co.uk/article/hollywood-actors-strike-ends-ai-streaming#:~:text=WGA%20members%20went%20on%20strike,AI%20encroaching%20on%20their%20work

World Intellectual Property Organization (WIPO), *Generative AI: Navigating Intellectual Property*, 2024.

Investing in AI by Tom Wilson and Carlos Eduardo Espinal, Partners at Seedcamp

Tom Wilson and Carlos Eduardo Espinal

Introduction

Investing in new technology always comes with the challenge of timing. You need to avoid getting too far ahead of what the market is ready to adopt while staying ahead enough to catch emerging trends early and deliver the returns your investors expect.

Many of us who invest in the sector enjoy reading science fiction because it often provides insightful predictions about future technologies, imagining innovations that could be 20–40 years ahead of their time. History shows this pattern clearly, with many technologies imagined in the 1960s and 1970s becoming reality today.

The difficult part is identifying the moment when the market is ready to adopt these technologies. Within a business setting, this requires not only an understanding of how to use the technology—whether through a small group of innovators within the organization or a visionary senior leader—but also the ability to integrate it into existing workflows. Successful integration must respect the company's existing HR structures to avoid internal resistance or outright rejection of the new technology.

Venture Capital Investors address this delicate balance of "too early" versus "too late" through staged investment strategies, including pre-seed, seed, Series

T. Wilson (✉) • C. E. Espinal
Seedcamp, London, England
e-mail: tom@seedcamp.com; carlos@seedcamp.com

M. Rangeley, N. Fairfax (eds.), *The Artificial Intelligence Revolution*,
https://doi.org/10.1007/978-3-032-11814-1_19

A, Series B, and beyond. This section focuses on the earliest stages, where investing in AI is at the forefront of adoption and where some of the boldest, most futuristic ideas—often resembling science fiction—begin to take shape.

Investing in AI is a broad title that can incorporate many different aspects. In this chapter, we have tried to focus on some of the key areas investors might consider as part of any investment decision. The goal here is to provide an overview and a potential framework for those who are curious to learn more about investments in this dynamic area.

With that introduction, we should add that, and as you'd expect from any work that is being written this year and beyond, we have used AI to help us with the writing of this chapter. To be precise, we have not asked AI to help us create our thoughts, but rather refine them. As such, and if you're curious, this is the prompt we used throughout this chapter to make sure we better articulate our thoughts vs. having AI author them for us: *"clean up the following section of grammar mistakes, simplify sentence construction where possible, and expand on any point that is left ambiguous. Do not alter the meaning of the stated sentences and do not extrapolate from them."*

Overview of AI as a Transformative Technology

AI investing had been ongoing for many years prior to the release of ChatGPT in 2022 by OpenAI. It had many guises, namely, 'machine learning', among them. However, it was the seemingly magical capabilities of large language models (LLMs) and their ability to generate human-like text that truly sparked the imagination of users and developers alike and we started having the steamroll effect of AI investments since then. The overall reason why it's so transformative is because it allows for previously seemingly insurmountable problems to be overcome at speeds and costs that democratize services and products. Similar to how a book editor could charge up to £5000 for a small book, now, that cost is practically zero if you know how to creatively prompt an LLM such as ChatGPT when reviewing a work. That cost reduction potential is not limited to just text but also encompasses image, voice, and video generation via similar technical breakthroughs (i.e., foundational models), and perpetuates across many industries and software as a whole. At the time of writing of this chapter, the costs for the use of AI have also gone down substantially. If you are a developer, the cost per token (a unit of compute if you will) is now in the affordable range relative to what you charge your customers and at the end-consumer range to use services like Gemini Pro, Perplexity, or Premium ChatGPT, the costs are about the same annually as a

Dropbox subscription. This means more and more people are understanding the power of the utility and can actually build things to engage that utility.

Key Considerations for Early-Stage Investors in AI Companies

Investing in early-stage AI companies presents unique opportunities and challenges, requiring a nuanced understanding of the ecosystem, competitive dynamics, adoption cycles, market trends, and market valuations. By carefully considering these factors, which we explore more in depth below, investors navigate investing in the AI space at this nascent stage.

Proximity to Ecosystem Drivers

Geography still matters in the success of early-stage AI companies (and many other company sectors for that matter), despite globalization and remote work making location less critical over the last few decades. For AI startups, proximity to ecosystem drivers such as key buyers, technology platforms, and relevant regulations can be crucial for rapid growth. For instance, most of the large language model (LLM) companies, with the notable exception of Mistral, are based in the United States, and specifically the West Coast. This creates additional pressure on international AI companies to strategically position themselves. Whether connecting to dominant platforms or navigating data and regulatory requirements—such as compliance with US healthcare data standards—location choices play a significant role in enabling these startups to thrive. In addition to the potential commercial benefits of locating in a key hub (such as San Francisco, New York, London, or Paris) there is also an advantage in being closer to where the best talent is located. Density of talent is particularly important for companies building at the cutting edge of AI where proximity to other leading companies or university labs could provide access to the necessary talent.

Macro Context of Foundational Models

Investors investing in AI companies also have to acknowledge that it is a fast moving sector with changing power players and tech stacks which can affect their invested company's value if over-indexed in favor of one model or one architecture. For example, take the launch of China's open source DeepSeek model and the impact it had on NVIDIA and the assumed architecture for AI to date:

> NVIDIA Corporation faced significant turbulence as its stock price plummeted nearly 20% following the announcement of DeepSeek's low-cost generative AI model. This dramatic decline, observed on January 27, 2025, marked one of the steepest drops for the semiconductor giant since the early pandemic phase of March 2020—Evrim Agaci of the Pinnacle Gazette

This showcases how innovations can quickly arise that can affect portfolio composition if not factoring in how nascent we are in the creation and growth curve of AI companies and their architectural components.

Navigating Well-Funded Competition

The AI landscape is marked by significant funding activity, which creates challenges for early-stage investors. The competition is fierce, with many well-capitalized companies vying for market dominance. As an investor, it's essential to assess not only what a company can deliver to its customers but also how it can sustain its competitive edge in a crowded and capital-intensive market. This means evaluating the company's ability to innovate, execute, and differentiate itself in a space where funding can accelerate or overshadow growth opportunities.

Understanding User Adoption Cycles

For AI companies targeting end-users with AI-enabled or AI-enhanced solutions, the user adoption cycle becomes a critical factor. Many organizations are still hesitant to adopt new AI tools, opting instead to wait for incumbent providers to roll out AI features or for IT departments to thoroughly evaluate the risks of implementing AI at scale. Early-stage investors must gauge how quickly potential customers are likely to adopt the startup's solutions and whether the company's go-to-market strategy aligns with this adoption timeline. The speed of adoption can significantly impact a startup's growth trajectory and market fit.

Avoiding the "Flavor-of-the-Month" Trap

As with any transformative technology, AI has inspired a wave of experimentation and innovation. While this can lead to groundbreaking advancements, it also creates a risk of founders pursuing ideas that may seem innovative but lack long-term commercial viability. Investors must strike a balance between backing promising new markets and avoiding ventures driven primarily by hype rather than sustainable value. This requires careful evaluation of a startup's product-market fit and its ability to deliver real, scalable solutions.

Managing Valuation Expectations

AI's potential to revolutionize productivity has fueled high expectations, often translating into inflated startup valuations. While enhanced productivity can be quantified, its true long-term value remains uncertain, influenced by secondary costs and unforeseen second-order impacts. This optimism often leads to a mismatch between entry price and exit price expectations, creating risks for investors. As an early-stage investor, it's critical to focus not only on identifying high-potential opportunities but also on maintaining discipline in valuation. Avoiding overpaying at entry ensures better alignment with long-term outcomes, mitigating the risk of poor returns.

Understanding Where the Value Lies in AI Investment

One way we have tried to map the market when it comes to investing within the AI space is by categorizing companies as falling into one of the following broad categories:

- Computing
- Foundational Models
- Tooling
- Applications

Taking each of the above in turn will allow us to showcase how value might accrue in each category and unpack where the opportunities are for potential investment.

Computing

This category focuses on the computation models underpinning the sector. At its core, this includes the hardware—specifically silicon or chips—used to perform these computations. In this subset, Nvidia dominates the market with its GPU chips. Since the launch of ChatGPT in 2022, Nvidia's stock has risen more than 7× and in so doing it has become (at the time of writing) the most valuable company in the world. This highlights the huge amount of value that has been captured at this part of the stack.

Moving one layer up from the hardware, we see companies aggregating or assembling compute power by building large clusters of chips. Major players like Meta, Alphabet, X, and OpenAI are developing their own vast GPU clusters to provide the immense computational resources required for their foundational models. Alongside them, rapidly growing companies like Coreweave and Fluidstack (a Seedcamp investment) offer access to similar large-scale compute clusters as a service. These companies are scaling quickly by providing access to compute power—a scarce and vital resource in the AI market.

The business models in this space are relatively straightforward. For Nvidia, a significant portion of its value comes from selling hardware, supplemented by its proprietary CUDA developer platform, which creates a high barrier to switching for customers. For companies like Coreweave, revenue comes from charging for compute access and earning margins by facilitating seamless integration and scalability. This model is akin to the approach pioneered by hyperscalers like Amazon with AWS in cloud computing.

Both the hardware-focused and compute-as-a-service segments of this vertical are generating substantial revenues and are expected to remain key drivers of value in the near future. However, as mentioned before, emerging architectures like those enabled by DeepSeeks' more efficient models, will continue to shape the industry for years to come.

Foundational Models

Foundation models are arguably the most prominent area within AI, attracting significant attention from both the media and investors. This field includes major players like OpenAI (ChatGPT), Anthropic (Claude), Google DeepMind (Gemini), Mistral (7B) and DeepSeek (R1). These companies have raised significant levels of funding, marking a scale rarely seen in private market investing.

The central thesis for investors in this space is that the leading foundation models will serve as the backbone for applications built either by third parties or by the model developers themselves. In either scenario, this offers the potential for substantial revenue generation and value creation.

For instance, as of now, OpenAI is reportedly on a revenue run rate exceeding $3.7 billion in 2024, as reported by the Economic Times and expected to grow much more in 2025. Its revenue is said to come from a combination of its consumer-facing application, ChatGPT, and its enterprise solutions sold directly to business users.

Tooling

A less obvious but essential category within the AI landscape is tooling. This refers to companies designed to interact with and support foundational models. One key focus area is model safety, a major concern that could impede adoption if not addressed. To tackle this issue, several cybersecurity companies have emerged to audit and analyze the models being used across organizations. This focus on safety is expected to grow as international AI regulations continue to evolve.

Beyond safety, other areas within this category include synthetic data generation and data labeling, both of which play a crucial role in training and improving models. Some of these companies may begin as layers built to serve foundational models, but, much like selling picks during a gold rush, the leading players in this space are likely to achieve significant success.

Applications

This category focuses on companies closest to the end user. In some cases, foundational model companies themselves have built applications—for example, ChatGPT, which can be considered an application built on its underlying foundational model by OpenAI. These are often referred to as "full-stack applications." Another example is Synthesia (a Seedcamp company), which has developed a proprietary foundational model that powers its AI video creation suite of products.

Beyond these examples, there are numerous vertical applications addressing specific industry problems in areas such as legal, healthcare, finance, human resources, property, and software development, among others. It's rare to find a sector without at least one company developing a tailored AI application. We will address more examples of vertical applications later in this chapter.

Some argue that because many of these applications rely on foundational models operated by other companies, the greatest value does not accrue at the application layer. However, another perspective is that while the underlying model may not be proprietary, these applications often customize the model or create a specific user interface and experience optimized for their target customers and industries. When executed well, this approach can generate significant value for the application layer.

Additionally, a key idea in this space is that the potential market size isn't limited to typical software market estimates. Instead, it could reflect the value of the actual work being performed by these applications, which could make this layer extraordinarily valuable. This is particularly relevant when we consider 'Agentic AI' which involves AI systems that complete tasks autonomously and require less human involvement or feedback. Agentic AI is seen by many investors as a breakthrough within AI that could significantly increase the value attributable to the application layer.

As we've highlighted in this section, breaking down the overall horizontal categories that exist within AI, there is the potential for many startups and established companies to extract value in each category. What's also evident is that advancements in certain areas are leading to opportunities further up the stack—i.e., advancements in GPUs (most commonly the chips produced by NVIDIA) are enabling the foundational model companies to build larger more high performance models which are in turn powering the companies building better end products at the application layer. As the end user demand for such services shows no sign of slowing down, it may be that the laws of physics is what eventually causes this improvement cycle to slow as it becomes harder to create more advanced GPUs and train ever larger models. However, it's likely that this scenario is far off for now and a more likely pull back from AI generally could be caused by current expectations of performance exceeding what is possible (particularly within businesses). In the meantime, as stated above, there are already some clear early winners that have accrued significant market share and created huge value. We anticipate not only will many of these companies continue to scale but there will also be opportunities for new startups to thrive in this dynamic market.

Impact of AI Across Industries

As we discussed earlier when breaking down the market, many AI-native applications are focused on specific industry verticals or functional areas. Examples include:

- Customer Success: Call centers, text-based support
- Engineering: Tools that assist with coding and development workflows
- Finance and Operations: Automation of repetitive or data-driven tasks

It's clear that areas involving repetitive manual work are among the most obvious for AI to impact. For instance, call centers and text-based customer support often involve low-paid, repetitive tasks, making them a natural extension of software automation as AI adds more intelligence to digitization efforts.

However, recent advancements, particularly the rise of large language models, have enabled AI to tackle more complex and higher-value work. This is particularly evident in professional services, such as legal work, where tools are now automating tasks like contract review and drafting—traditionally performed by junior lawyers. Similarly, in software engineering, co-pilot tools are increasingly standard, augmenting engineers by assisting with code writing and other development tasks.

Cutting-edge AI models are not only capable of automating or augmenting human work but they are also able to generate novel solutions to problems, surpassing what current methods have achieved in certain sectors. For example, AI is having a significant impact on the scientific world. Models such as AlphaFold, developed by Google DeepMind for protein structure prediction, are uncovering new ways to understand fundamental scientific principles. This, in turn, has the potential to drive advancements in areas like drug development and discovery.

As discussed earlier in this chapter, a new wave of applications centered around Agentic AI are starting to be developed. Startups are leaning into this technology by positioning their products as "digital workers" that companies can "hire," similar to human employees. This approach is particularly effective for roles such as sales account executives who sell software. For example, startups such as 11x have created autonomous agent personas that can be "hired" to take on the role of an AE for your company and execute tasks associated with outbound sales, such as identifying potential customers and reaching out to them via email. Similar examples can be found in numerous industries, including finance, operations, and HR. Such agentic solutions open up the possibility of pricing at or around the cost of a human hire, which could present significant revenue potential for the best products. This is due to the fact that they would be capturing a much larger proportion of a company's costs than was previously attributed solely to software (i.e., salaries).

Similarly to Agentic AI, Robotics will be massively impacted by the rise of AI. Leveraging computer vision models to identify objects in the real world better, using natural language to make dynamic requests that manipulate a physical environment, and cheaper robotics models will reshape not only manufacturing but also day to day services typically deemed unsafe or too repetitive for humans.

These more advanced applications demonstrate the far-reaching impact AI can have across industries. Each represents an opportunity for startups to create tailored solutions that address specific use cases. Startups that develop models finely tuned to their customers' unique needs are likely to produce the best products and capture the greatest value.

One final point on the impact of AI across industries is the impact it will have on existing cybersecurity architectures. Ideas like Agentic AI and Robotics bring up questions about what is an 'identity' and what is a 'user' or a service. Thus, we will also be seeing a re-writing and evolution of how permissions and access are granted to both machines and humans across products, services, and their interconnectivity.

Assessing AI Startups for Investment

Much like when considering investing in any startup at the earliest stage, any assessment of an AI investment can be broadly broken down into three buckets, namely:

1. Team
2. Product
3. Market & Go-to market, Traction and Metrics

When considering the team of an AI company, we are specifically referring to the founders here. The exact characteristics we'd be looking for here would depend on the technical sophistication of the product that the founding team are attempting to build. If they are seeking to build a frontier foundational large language model to compete with the likes of OpenAI, Google Deepmind, or Anthropic, then you would expect to see a team that is potentially immersed in the world of research and is contributing academically in the space and/or perhaps has worked at one of the aforementioned companies and has witnessed firsthand where the bleeding edge of this technology is and is heading. Similarly, if the startup is aiming to take on established players within the AI chip space such as Nvidia, you would want to see deep domain expertise and knowledge of the specific market and how not only the technology is theoretically created but also how you establish relationships across a supply chain. However, if the company is not as deeply technical in its approach some of these factors would be weighted less. For example, when building at the application layer, it might be preferable for the founding team to have a direct experience of the problem they are addressing with their product in addition to relationships with prospective customers, but if they are building on top of existing foundational models, then a deep research background within AI is unlikely to be necessary. In addition to taking into account the technical sophistication of the founding team and ensuring that is appropriately matched to the product they are attempting to build, for a startup to succeed, there are certain characteristics that we would always want to see across a founding team such as grit, determination, and an entrepreneurial streak that is often crucial when building a company from 0–1.

Ideally, when assessing an AI startup for investment, there is some early product that you can try or at least see a demo of. However, given the market competitiveness around top talent leaving established companies to set up new startups (i.e., Google Deepmind or OpenAI engineers), often such companies will only have a deck and a rough outline of what they want to build which would still, in the current market frenzy around AI, be sufficient for them to raise significant Seed rounds. However, where there is a product, we would be analyzing the product with a view to how it is differentiated versus what is already on the market. Thinking through questions such as: what insights have this team incorporated into their product that better solve the problem they've identified? Or why will this product win a significant market share when compared to other new entrants (startups) or incumbent products? This is by no means an exhaustive list but it provides a starting point for any probing around early product decisions that a startup may have made. The other factor we would flag when considering a product is product velocity and by this we mean how quickly can a founding team ship a product and iterate as they go. This can be a crucial factor in the success at the early stage because it is likely that early versions of any product will change significantly as a result of user or customer feedback and the ability to take on such feedback and incorporate this into the product can be a key factor in success or failure.

When making any early-stage investment, understanding the market is crucial. As institutional venture capital investors, we seek multibillion-dollar markets with the potential for startups to scale to hundreds, if not billions, in annual revenues, providing a return on investment that fulfills the expectations of our fund's investors. Not all markets present such opportunities. However, some markets that may appear small at the outset could grow and fulfill this requirement over time, perhaps catalyzed by the startup itself (e.g., Uber in the taxi space). AI, as a fundamental technology shift, opens up massive opportunities to disrupt huge traditional markets, often ticking the box when it comes to market opportunity.

Go-to-market—the company's ability to acquire users and/or sell their product—is another important consideration. This factor can be something to look for in the founding team of an AI company and may manifest itself in different ways depending on the company's go-to-market motion. For example, a company building an AI product for healthcare providers might benefit from a founding team member with a health background and/or a network in the market. For a company building tooling for developers building AI products, someone with a network in developer circles and maybe contributions to open-source projects would be preferable, as this is likely to be a factor in their go-to-market strategy.

Finally, if a product has launched or has some early user data, traction, and metrics, specifically growth, will be another important consideration. Even from a low base, signs from early traction that there is a strong growth rate and early customer or user love for the product can be a leading indicator that there is latent demand in the market and the startup has a shot at becoming a market-leading company. The actual figures of 'traction' that lead to investment interest is less clear as 'traction' isn't always quantitative, but sometimes qualitative, particularly when creating a whole new category and 'what something can become' is sufficient to impress investors enough to generate an investment. That said, generally traction and metrics increase through the stages between pre-seed and seed where customer exploration is the focus and product market fit is not yet clear, followed by Series A where there is customer traction, but it hasn't yet scaled, and Series B onwards continues on that amplification spectrum but includes other factors such as internationalization as well as scaling teams to support all the growth across product and sales functions.

Risks and Challenges of Investing in AI

AI investing has the potential for significant returns. However, like any investment sector, it comes with risks that must be carefully managed. Therefore, it is important to examine the risks and challenges associated with AI investments and explore strategies to mitigate them.

Fundamentally, AI relies on training data. While generalist LLMs excel at "generalist" tasks, as investors pursue more specialized AI applications, they must understand not only which data was used for training (especially if out-of-the-box efficacy or utility is in question) but also how that data was obtained. Additionally, they must determine whether data licensing and management arrangements are needed to fully realize the technology's value. Intellectual property, data protection, and privacy regulations are among the biggest hurdles for startups and investors looking to tackle specialized markets, where significant value can be unlocked by replacing outdated or costly tools and workflows. Beyond these concerns, there are ethical risks as well—particularly when AI-derived insights edge into regulated outcomes (think medical diagnostics, insurance claims, premiums, etc.). These risks are "new" to investors because they are less binary than previous technologies, involving closer scrutiny as AI takes on more workflows. Compounding this is the possibility of automations triggering additional automations, leading to a cascade of mistaken decisions.

Although such concerns are not novel to those who have experience with AI's risks, founders and investors should pay attention to where a given sector stands in terms of comfort, certification, and risk mitigation. For example, if an early case emerges of an AI-augmented startup being implicated in a patient's death, the resulting media coverage could cast doubt on other startups pursuing similar solutions, much like how documented failures of autonomous vehicles have influenced public perception. A failure here can push back the deployment of AI for a whole sector for years and force regulators to step in more aggressively.

Lastly, AI often consumes AI—and rapidly. One of the greatest challenges for startup founders and investors is keeping pace with a fast-moving industry in which the developers of productivity tools (that can be augmented by AI) are the same groups building the LLMs themselves (e.g., OpenAI). In other words, these developers can "eat the lunch" of many startups in the process.

With the virtually unlimited and essentially free usage provided by native API integrations and extensive tokens, startups risk obsolescence overnight. Their entire business model could become just a feature of a larger, well-funded competitor. Additionally, the open-source nature of some emerging technologies can disrupt business models as they may not be able to be commercialized in the traditional closed-source, software licensing model.

Conclusion—Investing in AI

Considering all of the above, investors can build an AI-rich portfolio that balances the risks of being early movers in an emerging space.

We've consciously omitted general portfolio management advice here, but in summary, the goal is primarily about diversifying a range of investments that address different angles where AI can and will have a significant impact.

To begin, it's clear that all investors will need to get comfortable with companies using AI in some capacity from this point forward. This prompts the question: does an "AI investor" truly exist anymore, or is this more about general investor strategies for navigating an emerging sector that applies to all investors? Put another way, are we approaching the point where AI is such a pervasive technology that every technology company becomes an "AI" company? And, if that is the case, then given the fact the largest companies in the world are primarily technology companies, then it will be pretty impossible not to be in some way invested in AI.

However, taking this point in time and how someone might begin to build a portfolio of AI investments, one starting approach is to hold a portfolio that blends consumer AI applications with enterprise-focused AI solutions, as each has distinct adoption curves. As we discussed earlier in the chapter, timing is key when considering any investment but especially in emerging technology sectors and therefore the adoption curve is crucial to consider. Consumers typically adopt new technologies quickly, though they can be difficult to monetize. Still, these types of investments can drive growth in a portfolio, even if monetization is uncertain. Meanwhile, business customers often move more slowly, given ongoing challenges such as data management and privacy requirements when deploying AI internally, but may lead to more consistent repeatable revenue over time. By balancing a blend of these two go-to-market approaches, investors can have a portfolio that benefits from both.

Another strategy is to invest across different tools and industries. It's not yet clear which sectors will adopt AI the fastest, since each industry's pace depends on collective influencers—CISOs, CTOs, etc.—and their willingness to accept certain risk trade-offs in exchange for productivity gains. However, as we unpacked earlier in the chapter, there's likely to be huge value created by AI across a wide variety of different industries and tools. So having a portfolio that spans across a diverse set of industries could be a good strategy so as not to miss a sector where the upside could be very significant.

Finally, it's important to stagger investments based on the time to maturity. More ambitious projects, such as AI-powered robotics, will need a longer runway for approvals, deployments, and proof of capabilities, as well as for dealing with any employment or macroeconomic impacts. Ideally, you should look to balance longer-term opportunities with those in sectors where the time to market could be shorter and therefore the return faster. As Venture Capitalists, we are hyper-focused on finding outlier opportunities that have the potential to 100x or even 1000x our investment. However, in order to try and find such investments, we are willing to lose money on many of our other investments. Put another way, we are looking for the moonshots and founders who are "swinging for the fences" and in so doing we understand that they aren't all going to end up being the next Google, SpaceX, or OpenAI, but those that (hopefully) do will make up for those that don't when we consider our portfolio as a whole. This investment strategy is geared around the idea of the "Power Law" where a small number of investments drive huge outsized returns and it's all about getting exposure to those opportunities. As we've considered above, this is one potential investment strategy that could be applied to investing in AI but there are many others that could incorporate companies at different stages and/or sectors.

The information provided in this chapter is for educational and informational purposes only and should not be construed as financial or investment advice. Investing in AI or any other sector carries risks, including the potential loss of principal. Readers should conduct their own research, seek professional advice, and consider their individual financial situation and risk tolerance before making any investment decisions. The author assumes no responsibility for any losses or damages resulting from the use of this information. Past performance is not indicative of future results.

Enterprise in the AI Era: Lessons for Business

Marc Warner, John Gibson, John Mansir, Katrina Soderquest, Myles Kirby, Nijma Khan, and Niko Louvranos

Every new technology creates uncertainty. When Johann Gutenberg devised a way of reproducing Bibles with greater speed and accuracy, he could not have foreseen the global revolution in knowledge, thought, and society that the printing press would unleash. Likewise James Watt perfecting the steam engine, or the early pioneers of personal computers hacking in their San Francisco garages.

But the uncertainty around the nature and impact of the change AI will bring is unlike any technology humanity has ever encountered. Even the most notable researchers at the forefront of the field disagree. Their forecasts range from a 20% chance that AI could lead to human extinction (Hinton, 2024), to the possibility that it could bring about a 'post-scarcity' utopia (Bostrom, 2024). That is a considerable margin of error.

It is, therefore, impossible to know what AI will mean for business in 3, 5 or 10 years' time. AI might render whole industries virtually obsolete, as it has already done to a large extent with translation services (Creamer, 2024). Or it may supercharge a business as, for example, with NVIDIA's chips (Mickle, 2025). The only certainty is that nothing is certain—and anyone who tries to

M. Warner (✉) • J. Gibson • J. Mansir • K. Soderquest • M. Kirby • N. Khan • N. Louvranos
Faculty.ai, London, England
e-mail: marc@faculty.ai; john@faculty.ai; john.m@faculty.ai; katrina.soderquest@faculty.ai; myles.kirby@faculty.ai; nijma.khan@faculty.ai; niko.louvranos@faculty.ai

M. Rangeley, N. Fairfax (eds.), *The Artificial Intelligence Revolution*,
https://doi.org/10.1007/978-3-032-11814-1_20

say otherwise is probably a charlatan, or trying to sell something that won't work.

Despite this uncertainty, businesses do not have the option of doing nothing and waiting to see what happens. In this chapter, we will propose some basic principles that companies should adopt in considering how to approach AI. We will then detail ten lessons that Faculty—Europe's leading applied AI company—have learned in the course of the last ten years about what makes corporate AI implementation successful. We will illustrate those with three case studies where those lessons have been applied with most impact. Finally, we will consider the future of the field, and what the potential evolution of AI into AGI—Artificial General Intelligence—might mean for organisations.

The Need for Thoughtful Pro-Activity

When it comes to AI, companies that stand still will simply be overtaken by competitors and put at risk of going bust (Biscotti, 2024). Equally, panicked over-reaction is likely to lead only to wasted time, money and energy. Instead, Faculty recommends a practical approach that balances humility about the future with decisive action today.

This approach starts with two honest admissions.

First, while AI offers seemingly limitless possibilities, most businesses will probably benefit most by using it to enhance their core strengths and differentiators. In theory, a business could disrupt itself and become something totally different, as with Nintendo's switch from playing cards to games consoles. But companies that manage such transformations are rare. Those that try usually just weaken themselves, often to disastrous effect, as with GEC's ruinous attempts to reinvent itself from a stolid defence contractor to a high-tech Internet business on the eve of the dotcom crash (Birkinshaw, 2004).

Second, businesses need to actually want to win. Although most businesses publicly extol the benefits of change, many organisations lack the will to follow through when that change is painful or difficult. Corporate history is littered with the names of once-iconic companies like Blockbuster Video or Kodak that failed to respond to changing technology and consumer habits.

The companies that win in the AI era will do so by having the courage and conviction to reinvent their core business processes around the new opportunities. That does not mean getting distracted by shiny AI widgets that make no difference to actual workflows, nor being satisfied with limited tools like meeting transcriptions. It will be companies who are 'thoughtfully proactive': those who don't bet everything on some speculative AI project but also those who refuse to stand still and ignore AI.

Prepare for Uneven Rates of Disruption

History teaches us to be cautious about trying to predict the relative impact that AI will have across different sectors, and which sectors will be most affected.

When the Internet emerged, it did not disrupt every industry equally. In certain sectors, new Internet-based companies arose and changed the landscape entirely. Amazon and its rivals permanently changed the dynamics of retail (Ovide, 2021). Google did the same for advertising. But in other sectors—like aviation, construction or manufacturing—change was less pronounced. Companies in those industries all had significant efficiencies to gain from the adoption of digital and communication technologies, but their worlds were not turned inside out by them. Likewise, there are some areas today that seem more likely to see outsize change as a result of AI than others.

It is already evident that sectors which revolve around the processing of written and structured information are moving quickly towards integrating AI. Insurance is one; the legal sector is another. And education, which has changed little since Victorian times, has the potential to look very different indeed by the end of the decade. In these cases, even though we may not know the ultimate destination, we can see that a journey is beginning and that leaders should make sure that they are taking the likelihood of change seriously. They should be plotting a path that feels directionally correct, and setting up their organisation to be nimble in the way that they adopt AI.

Design for Humans and Machines to Work Together

Despite the considerable uncertainties, there are nevertheless a few principles to be confident about in the age of AI, and which provide *terra firma* for good business decision-making. One of those is that a 'human-first' approach to AI is unquestionably the best approach.

Amid the hype over AI, a frequently overlooked fact is that until human-level artificial intelligence is developed, the best decisions will be made by a combination of people and machines working together. This has already been demonstrated in the field of chess. In 1997, the grandmaster Garry Kasparov was beaten by IBM's Deep Blue—but this did not herald an era of machine dominance. For nearly 20 years, humans and machines playing collaboratively—'Centaur Chess'—could beat either humans *or* machines playing alone (Baraniuk, 2015). It was only in the mid-2010s that machines like Stockfish started to beat human-machine partnerships, and 2017 when Google's Alpha Zero cemented machine dominance.

For the foreseeable future, AI systems should be built on the basis of having humans and machines working together. This will deliver the best performance outcomes; and it is also the best route to ensuring that the technology is deployed safely.

Human in the Loop, Human Over the Loop

One of the key considerations of a human-first approach to AI is ensuring that humans remain in control.

The most well-understood approach here is a design that keeps a human in the loop, and at times that will indeed be the right solution. But that concept alone is too constraining, and over time becomes fraught with risks of error. Some processes need to happen at greater speed or scale than humans can accommodate. Additionally, individual humans can make mistakes, and these will only be obvious in the aggregate.

The solution to this is a higher level of control: human-over-the-loop. This enables a user to place controls over models or collections of models, to govern the system at scale. The human can then step 'out' of the loop, allowing it to run at high speed or volume, knowing that the model outputs are constrained by the parameters that have been put in place.

But in order for that to work, the loop must be designed to put the human first.

User-Centred Design for the Intelligent Era

A human-first approach integrates AI into business workflows to maximise its usefulness to human users. Faculty does this by taking what it calls a 'decision-centric' approach, zeroing in on the human decisions that are so central to most business processes, and then shaping the technology to support that.

To achieve its goal, the decision-centric approach applies user-centred design to help users map their decision-making flows, and then builds AI systems that quickly and easily plug into those flows in precise and targeted ways. This goes much further than serving up the predictions or content that AI models generate: it also allows users to interact with AI models in new ways. For example, the decision-centric approach wires models together and connects their outputs to business KPIs, so that users can replicate business flows, and understand the cause-and-effect relationships that drive business outcomes. It allows users to test the impact of the different choices they face before they commit to a decision.

This level of user-centric design and functionality will be needed if enterprises are to deliver impact from AI. For evidence, consider what happens when AI is designed and implemented without regard for the user.

Stepping Over the Trough of Disillusionment

Looking back at the history of software, there is one lesson that stands out: building technology for technology's sake rarely generates value. This is particularly true of AI.

As the last few years of Generative AI proofs-of-concept (POCs) have shown, Large Language Models (LLMs) are very powerful tools. But the tools can be characterised as round pegs, while most valuable enterprise problems turn out to be square holes. The reason is readily apparent: LLMs enable AI to treat text in the same way it has always been able to treat numbers, but how many enterprise business processes are only text? A few, perhaps, mostly centred around customer service. But most other processes are combinations of text and numbers.

Furthermore, few processes are limited simply to the generation or analysis of data, whatever form that data takes. The real world, the organisations within it and the things they are trying to achieve are always messy and complicated in their own ways. Using new technology to achieve real change requires deftness and skill, patience and perseverance. Simple, isolated LLM deployments will never lead to the transformation businesses are hoping for. *The Economist* has even coined a term for the inevitable failure of this approach: AI 'pilotitis'. 'Many companies seem to be suffering from an acute case of pilotitis, dilly-dallying with pilot projects without fully implementing [AI] technology', it wrote in November 2024 (*Economist*, 2024). According to the US Census Bureau, fewer than 7% of American businesses said they were using AI to produce goods or services as at February 2025 (US Census Bureau, 2025).

The conclusion is clear. If intelligent systems are not constructed with a focus on users' needs, those systems will probably fail to deliver meaningful benefits to organisations. They need to support human decision-making, rather than ignore or replace it. Human-first AI offers a way of building more useful, more powerful and safer systems that will transform businesses—and possibly societies—for the better.

Ten Lessons from Ten Years

Faculty AI has been helping companies and organisations apply AI to their business processes since 2014. In 2024, the company wrote a book summarising what they had learned, *10 Lessons from 10 Years of Applied AI (*Faculty, 2024*)*. In it, the authors delved into the good practices that will help any business to adopt the technology with confidence, regardless of what they are trying to achieve with it. These matter, because AI will only make a meaningful difference to humanity's ability to solve important problems if it is deployed properly. And this is not straightforward.

The ten lessons are summarised below:

1. AI is an operational discipline, not an analytical one.
   AI is not being used to its potential where the output is a series of charts and dashboards that describe the world without acting upon it. The field of Business Intelligence already provides the world with more of that than it will ever need. AI should be built into the tools that people use to run business processes, not just those that analyse them. It should be integrated with the levers used to intervene in those processes, so that analysis leads directly to actions.
2. AI is technology for human decision-makers.
   All software should be built around the user. The user for intelligent software is typically a decision-maker. Where a decision is important, human decision-makers should remain in control, supported rather than replaced by AI. In order to do this effectively, AI tools need to provide analysis that is targeted, parsimonious, explainable and interactive.
3. Augment human tasks that require judgement. Automate those that don't.
   Most people enjoy the core of their job. But they generally dislike the bureaucracy that surrounds it. AI should be used to provide decision support to those tasks at the core, which are where people create the most value and exercise their professional judgement. And it should be used to automate away the admin that crowds out the fun stuff. This blend of automation and augmentation tends to make people both more productive and more fulfilled.

4. AI is a feature not a product. But it can define a product.
   Despite recent advances in language models, there are few occasions where an AI model alone makes a full product. It is a cog in a machine, rather than the machine. However, it is an unusually powerful cog that can make new kinds of machines possible, in much the same way that an engine isn't a car, but was the invention that made the car possible. This is a good time to seek new ways of solving old problems.
5. Building AI widgets is easy. Rewiring your organisation is not.
   AI party tricks, like meeting summaries, can seem exciting, but tend to be limited to the periphery of what matters. The bigger impacts come when AI is used to optimise the core business processes that define an organisation. This requires much more than technology, and should be thought of as a serious change programme.
6. It's data SCIENCE, not DATA science.
   Data gets a lot of attention. But data alone solves no problem. It's the science that you do on top of the data that matters the most. Science is all about building an understanding of the world, and the cause-and-effect relationships that drive it. This is the foundation of applying AI successfully. You need to understand the cause-and-effect relationships inside a system before you intervene on it. And you need to identify the causal pathway by which your interventions achieve the outcomes you seek.
7. There's no such thing as complete data.
   Data is essential to modern AI. But it is a precision game—more is not always better. A specific model, with a specific objective, will need specific data to achieve that. You need to understand what problem you're solving and work back from that to the exact data you need. Focus on getting that data in place first, rather than trying to build the perfect data infrastructure. Perfect data doesn't exist, and never will.
8. Build in increments that are individually valuable and collectively transformative.
   Over-ambition and under-ambition each bring their own perils for AI programmes. Don't just focus on low-hanging fruit, or on individual use cases. That's not how you make a measurable difference. But also don't try to imagine the whole future at once and seek a big bang. The chances are that it will fail. Instead think big, but build towards it in modular steps that are individually valuable, but when connected together, transform a whole business process end to end.

9. Business strategy trumps AI strategy.
   For a small share of businesses, AI will render their current strategy obsolete. But for the vast majority, a stand-alone AI strategy is a bad idea. Any well run business will already know what is important to them. Being strategic about AI means determining whether—and if so, how—AI can accelerate these known priorities. It does not mean creating a new rival strategy or a menu of all the ways AI could be used in a business, stack ranked against each other.
10. If you don't control your models, your models control you.
   AI models are probabilistic. The most powerful are black boxes. They don't always behave in entirely predictable ways. And users can't really tell why they do the things they do. As these technologies are embedded more deeply in decision-making processes, it is essential that the correct controls are put in place around them. Humans should be in the loop where possible, and 'over the loop' where not. Platforms like Faculty's Frontier are needed to implement these controls across an organisation.

Applying Lessons in the Real World

Collectively, these ten lessons add up to a roadmap for how organisations should approach the adoption of AI in their businesses. But every organisation is different, and for each one the solution will require a different balance. There is no single answer.

To illuminate how these lessons can work in practice, it may help to examine three of them in more detail. To begin with, consider the UK's largest employer, the NHS, faced with a once-in-a-century crisis.

AI Is Technology for Human Decision-Makers

When the Covid pandemic hit in 2020, leaders in government and the NHS had to make decisions with terrifying implications, in an unprecedented situation, with data systems that had never been designed for a national health crisis. It was difficult to predict demand and identify areas where the system would face strain. National, regional and local teams needed to be forewarned of potential spikes in Covid-related hospital activity, so they could plan effectively. Where should they send vital supplies like PPE, oxygen or ventilators? Should patients be transferred to quieter hospitals? If more beds needed to be urgently freed up, should managers cancel long-planned elective procedures, like cancer care or hip operations?

All these decisions were being made within a data landscape that was fragmented and fraught with inaccuracies. Overstretched frontline staff, forced to choose between spending their time on patient care or data entry, were of course choosing the patients—but that lowered data quality at exactly the moment when the system needed it most. NHS analysts found themselves desperately trying to extract insight from thousands of spreadsheets, many of which were being manually updated and frantically e-mailed around to be combined with other data before being presented to decision-makers.

In this crisis, Faculty built what was dubbed the Early Warning System (EWS), a model that provided a sensible forecast by modelling missing data using information from nearby hospitals with similar characteristics. That approach dealt with both the inherent uncertainty in the data, and the challenge of trying to predict complex outcomes. With the EWS, the NHS could look 3 weeks ahead to see the bed capacity each hospital was forecast to have, when it risked running out and where patients or resources might need to be transferred. For the first time, every level of the system was operating from the same page: from hospital managers making choices about how to allocate resources on their wards, right up to decisions being taken in Whitehall and Downing Street.

Faculty's model outputs informed the allocation of over a billion pieces of PPE, facilitated the strategic transfer of critically ill patients across the country and helped government leaders decide whether hospitals, towns and cities were opened up or locked down. In 2020 and 2021, these were matters of life and death, health and livelihood, for the whole UK population.

Crucially, the model did not make decisions, and it was not offering infallible predictions. The reason it worked so well was because it had been built first and foremost to be decision-centric, to give officials and managers no more than they needed. It had been designed in such a way that users could learn how much to trust it, and so that they could interrogate how it had reached its conclusions. It was neither a crutch nor a replacement for humans using their judgement: it was a tool. But a tool unlike any other, which, used correctly, gave decision-makers the insight they needed to totally transform the speed, quality and execution of their decision-making just when they needed it most.

Business Strategy Trumps AI Strategy

The Covid pandemic NHS showed an organisation harnessing AI to support decision-making in a crisis. But most organisations, most of the time, will not be operating under such constraints. For them, the key goal is to adopt AI into their regular business activities in such a way that it supports their overall corporate strategy.

But it is easy to get this wrong. As AI rises up the agenda, most organisations will consider (if they haven't already) what their AI Strategy should be. Many will spin up AI Strategy programmes, ranging across the organisation, looking for all of the things that AI could possibly do. Consultants' two-by-two matrices abound, ranking lists of possible use cases according to 'technical feasibility' and 'impact'. Leadership teams are presented with the outcomes like a menu in a restaurant, with some recommended dishes: 'quick wins' for starter, 'low hanging fruit' for main, and if there's room left at the end then maybe 'longer term bets' for dessert.

The challenge with this bottom-up approach is that, in the final analysis, when an AI strategy comes up against the actual business strategy, there is only one winner. Every good organisation already has a business strategy. The people there know what is most important to them—and to the boss. They can tell you the three or four priorities that the CEO cares about, and they fastidiously track the KPIs against which everything and everyone will ultimately be judged.

Being strategic about AI means using it to accelerate the things you already know to be most important. The instruction that CEOs should give their teams is not 'design our AI strategy' but 'test whether AI can help us meet our top three priorities'. If AI won't do that, then ignore it and focus on technologies that will. But if AI can help with those core goals, then you already have the answer to where and how to prioritise it.

One organisation that did this was the National Crime Agency (NCA). For them, integrating AI wasn't about increasing profit or demonstrating a concept. It was about protecting the most vulnerable members of society from the worst sorts of harm. And it came at a time when their business goals risked being overwhelmed by the sheer volume of material they were having to deal with.

The NCA is the UK police organisation charged with leading the fight against serious and organised crime, and tackling the UK's most dangerous criminals. Established in 2013 and quickly dubbed 'Britain's FBI', the NCA works at the leading edge of law enforcement to build the best possible intelligence picture of criminal threats, and develop innovative capabilities for other partners to use. In recent years, NCA officers have broken open networks that smuggle guns, drugs, money and people. They've tracked down fugitive criminals to their hiding places overseas, and also disrupted the gangs that supplied the runaways with their fraudulent passports. At home, their specialist officers support local police forces with complex investigations by providing niche expertise.

The NCA is also the lead agency dealing with the worst cases of child sexual abuse, fielding a team of experienced, diligent professionals dedicated to protecting children. When a huge quantity of confidential intelligence reached them, it threatened to swamp their ability to analyse it using traditional methods. They had to find a way to process the information faster than ever before, in order to track down the worst offenders and stop them.

As early as 2018, the NCA had recognised that AI had the potential to help them achieve their mission. Within the UK public sector, this was impressively early to be thinking about AI: back then plenty of public bodies were running experiments, but relatively few of them were trying to build AI into their core operations.

But for the NCA, it was not just about integrating AI into their workflow. They wanted to build it into their strategy. At the NCA, a highly complicated organisation, their business strategy is clear and their priorities cleanly stated. Their main objective is the relentless disruption of serious and organised crime through targeted action against the highest harm offenders and networks, together with a statutory obligation to safeguard children from harm. The second priority is to minimise the number of victims and the level of harm caused.

By definition, their organisation only deals with cases that are really, really important. But with thousands of case referrals each day, they still lack the resource to tackle all of them. So making their strategy work boils down to finding the most important needles in a haystack where every blade of grass is important, and then throwing their resource at those cases. It's painstaking work for the officers who do it, and also deeply stressful, knowing that somewhere in the pile there might be victims of serious crime they could help, if only they could find them in time.

NCA leaders recognised that this is exactly the sort of task AI can help with. So, with a minimum of fuss, this became one of the first priority areas for the NCA to focus their AI programme on. And because time is of the essence in everything they do, they wanted to get to work quickly.

In 2020, the team was handed an unprecedented trove of intelligence material from a confidential source. There were thousands of referrals, each one pointing to a case where children might have been harmed, and possibly still be at risk. At the time, the only way to prioritise them was for human experts to methodically go through each referral individually, painstakingly noting the key information and cross-referencing that with other sources of intelligence. With the number of cases the NCA had just been given, it would have taken them literally years to process. They needed it done much, much faster. So they turned to AI.

Faculty built the NCA a tool that extracts key data from the referrals, which come in all sorts of different formats. Once the data has been extracted, it identifies suspects and then links those people to information from additional data sources which might add context to help the NCA assess the risk they pose. Before it was automated, officers would have to make requests to data providers for each case that they were working on, and it might take weeks to come back. Now, those same checks can be compiled at scale, across hundreds of investigations simultaneously, and take a couple of days.

That means fewer officers are able to do more with less. They can tap these additional data sources for 500 times more referrals than previously, building a richer picture of the risk and providing more timely intelligence. And all those different bits of information give the NCA a sense of how risky the person might be, and how quickly the NCA needs to either investigate them, or pass them on to a local force to go and knock on front doors.

Previous to the AI system being introduced, a lot of information would be manually transcribed and entered into the system, introducing more scope for error, more ways in which connections might be missed—or innocent people incorrectly drawn into the net. The NCA have always had safeguards built in to prevent that, but the automation gave them additional peace of mind, and again made it quicker. The tool uses fuzzy matching to help spot duplicate 'entities', to reduce wasted effort and make sure all the right information is being linked to the right person.

But there is still a human in the loop, at critical points throughout the process, and making the final judgement. Given that the original problem was an overwhelming amount of data, simply adding more of it wouldn't help. So as a final step, when all the analysis and enrichment is complete, the software completes a prioritisation assessment (using an academically accredited framework) and highlights the key intelligence in each case to the reviewing officer. This allows the officer to check whether they agree with the prioritisation much faster than if they had to do it themselves from scratch: what used to take 45 minutes is now done in four. This reduction in time on a case-by-case basis means that entire operations can be processed in weeks or months, rather than the years large-scale operations or data dumps would take previously.

There Is No Such Thing as Complete Data

The NCA demonstrated how incorporating AI into corporate strategy ensured it was deployed where it would have the most effect. Another organisation that took this approach was NESO, the National Energy System Operator, which manages the energy that flows from and through the UK's power infrastructure. But NESO had another challenge, one common to many organisations looking to implement AI. That challenge was data.

A core fact of AI is that without data to feed the models, the AI will not run. Early AI systems built using handcrafted rules turned out to be brittle creations that struggled with the complexity of the world they were modelling. It was impossible to codify all the rules for a system to follow. But with enough data (and enough compute to process it), then deep learning algorithms could learn those rules for themselves, with far more subtlety and nuance than hard-coded versions.

That development has been at the heart of the AI revolution of the last few years. It has also changed the way we think about data, and elevated this once arcane technical concept to the top table of business discourse. Chief Data or Information officers are given substantial budgets to invest in programmes to collect or manage data. Executed well, these sorts of programmes provide the foundations needed to successfully adopt AI into an organisation. But there are traps that need to be navigated, both by organisations with little data, and by those with lots.

NESO falls into the latter category. Managing 20 terawatt hours of electricity a month generates vast quantities of data. Just one data set, for example, is receiving 90 million updates every day, and NESO keeps hundreds of data sets. Whereas some companies, particularly startups, have to wait months or years to accumulate enough data before they can train the algorithms they want to build, NESO is overflowing with data.

But although NESO has the volume, there is a further challenge. AI algorithms are designed to ingest data in tabular form. Some of NESO's data is compatible with that, but other parts of their sprawling data portfolio can range from PDFs of ancient manuals, to Word documents, to tangled schematic and process diagrams that any algorithm would struggle to digest. Some of the data is held in different software applications that don't easily communicate with each other. Other data changes as it goes through different business processes, without a clear record of the path it's taken.

This is not a problem unique to NESO. While digital native companies have the freedom to design their data architecture from scratch and build their institutions around it, any long-established organisation with complex legacy systems is likely to have patchy, convoluted, or hard-to-reach areas of their data estate. And when those companies face significant operating challenges that might be solved by better use of data—or simply when they hear calls from investors to 'do AI'—many of them will succumb to the temptation to embark on a big data infrastructure exercise, getting everything cleansed and organised before training their algorithms on it.

But the desire to 'fix' the data before it can be put to good use is ultimately built on a pair of myths: the myth of 'perfect' data, and the myth of 'complete' infrastructure. The truth is, data is never perfect and data infrastructure is never done. Both exist, like the world they catalogue, in permanent states of imperfection and constant evolution. Trying to pursue some idealised end state is not just futile but also costly and time-consuming. Many large-scale data transformations take far longer than planned, exceed their budgets, or fail entirely.

When Faculty started working with NESO, the grid company already had a comprehensive, well-designed and well-run digitalisation programme. But rather than focussing all their energy on getting the infrastructure right, NESO also looked for opportunities to address some of their most urgent challenges using data they had available already, even if it was imperfect. They decided they could build the tools and infrastructure they needed as they worked out the use cases it would serve.

The first project looked at planned outages on the network. These are decisions to turn off particular pieces of infrastructure—ranging from an individual transmission line to a whole power plant—in order to perform planned maintenance. This might be for something as simple as a bird's nest on a pylon, or as complicated as a major refit on a power plant. Some outages are so significant that they can be scheduled up to 6 years in advance.

Shutting down any part of a network as complex and critical as the national grid is a daunting proposition, and a whole team at NESO—the Network Access Planning Team—is dedicated to evaluating all the factors that have to be taken into account to find the best time, and the best mitigations. If a transmission cable is out, for example, is there enough headroom on the other available cables to safely carry the extra power that will need to be accommodated? If generating capacity goes offline, what will replace it, and how much more will it cost if that happens at peak times?

To perform this analysis, modelling all the different scenarios to find the best solution, is a monumental task for the team. 'At the moment, they will do hundreds and hundreds of very heavy duty simulations to work out exactly when looks like the right time for the outage', explains Katrina Soderquest, the senior Faculty data scientist who worked on the project (Faculty, 2024). 'It takes a lot of time, and a lot of people'. Although there are optimisation tools to help, they rely on trial and error, manual runs and human intuition.

NESO were keen to see how machine learning and AI could help them speed up the process to handle the growing wave of planned outage demands. When the team started working with Faculty, both sides knew that the data and supporting infrastructure would be imperfect. But the Faculty team were determined to push the art of the possible. They knew that a specific model, with a specific objective, only needs specific data to achieve its aim. More data is only useful if it directly relates to the objective and adds more signal to the model, rather than noise. In other words: the model doesn't require *all* the data, it just needs the *right* data. And rather than starting with the data that is available, and then deciding what to do with it, a company should start with the problem it wants to solve. It should next think about the technology that will help address it, and only then what data is needed to feed into the technology. Data is the essential enabler, but it comes last in the logic, not first.

Thanks to that leap of faith, the pilot project that Faculty worked on proved that AI could work with the data NESO had, despite its imperfections, and significantly speed up the outage planning cycle. 'It's about doing the easier stuff quickly', says Soderquest. 'This project showed we can make planning more robust and quicker at the same time'. There is also a cost implication. NESO spends billions of pounds a year buying energy to balance its system. Even a small increase in efficiency translates to huge savings. With such significant gains to be had, and complexity only rising in the context of the clean-energy transition, NESO could not afford to wait until their data was perfect.

The Future

The lessons Faculty have learned, and the case studies of organisations who have used those lessons to implement AI productively, give a framework for how companies can be 'thoughtfully pro-active' in adopting the technology now, while acknowledging the inherent uncertainty of the moment.

But the further one looks ahead, the greater the uncertainty becomes. The biggest unknown of all surrounds human-level artificial intelligence, often called artificial general intelligence (AGI): AI that is as capable as a human expert at almost any cognitive task. When this is achieved, adding capacity to an organisation will no longer mean adding employees, but simply accessing more computing power to run the same AI employee faster.

Will this threshold be reached? And, if so, when?

'Estimates range from just a few years from now to at least ten years away', (Ananthaswamy, 2024), but have been coming down rapidly over the last 5 years. Not long ago, a century was a frequent estimate (Goertzel & Pennachin, 2006), but today few experts would be willing to consider such a long time frame. Demis Hassabis, CEO of Google DeepMind, predicts 2035. The American computer scientist and futurist Ray Kurzweil says 2032, while the German AI pioneer Jürgen Schmidhuber, thinks closer to 2050. 'The sceptics are many, and the timeline remains uncertain' (Finger, 2025).

Whenever AGI happens, if at all, it would be a technological development without precedent. It would signal the end of human intelligence as the dominant form of intelligence, and would likely change all aspects of human life. The outcomes could vary between post-scarcity utopia to existential risk for our species. It is worth all of humanity learning more about what this could amount to, and advocating for the development of safe, narrow, and human-led AI systems (Suleyman, 2023).

But precisely because AGI has the potential to disrupt all aspects of life as humanity knows it, it is almost impossible to plan for. The best way for business leaders to address AGI is therefore to pragmatically deprioritise it, to place AGI in the same category as an asteroid strike—something that most businesses can't do anything to change, and which will reset all current plans if it occurs.

Conclusion

The future is coming faster than most people realise. At the time of writing, in San Francisco, around 20% of the city's total taxi rides are thought to be taken in Waymo's self-driving vehicles (Economist, 2025). AI systems are already capable of performing as well or better than radiographers in analysing chest X-rays (Anderson et al., 2024). They can plan pupil lessons in a fraction of the time it takes most teachers (Faculty, 2024). Many computer programmers now find that AI writes advanced code at a comparable or better level than they do (Cutherbertson, 2022). And this is the worst the technology will ever be. AI systems are getting better; eventually they may even be able to improve themselves.

As previously stated, doing nothing is not an option for companies. Blindly panicking is not a good idea either. Instead, organisations should be thoughtfully pro-active. The businesses who win in the AI era won't be the ones who have tools that predict the next word of their emails, or who introduce a shiny chatbot that no one uses or trusts; and they won't be the ones who predicted the future perfectly. They'll be the ones who stayed strong on the core problem they solve, and had the courage to change their business processes around the new opportunities. They'll be the ones who build AI systems on the basis of having humans and machines working together, making use of the data that they have, rather than some idealised dataset that may never be realised. This will deliver the best performance, whilst also ensuring that the technology is deployed safely.

By following these principles, organisations can make sure they are on the right track to adopting AI, whatever the future holds.

References

Ananthaswamy, A. (2024). How close is AI to human-level intelligence? *Nature (London), 636*(8041), 22–25.

Anderson, P. G., Tarder-Stoll, H., Alpaslan, M., et al. (2024). Deep learning improves physician accuracy in the comprehensive detection of abnormalities on chest X-rays. *Scientific Reports, 14*, 25151. https://doi.org/10.1038/s41598-024-76608-2

Baraniuk, C. The cyborg chess players that can't be beaten. *BBC*, December 4, 2015.: https://www.bbc.co.uk/future/article/20151201-the-cyborg-chess-players-that-cant-be-beaten

Birkinshaw, J. (2004). The destruction of marconi. *Business Strategy Review*, 15. https://doi.org/10.1111/j.0955-6419.2004.00304.x

Biscotti, L. F&B companies that don't adopt AI will fall behind. *Forbes*, October 15, 2024.: https://www.forbes.com/sites/louisbiscotti/2024/10/15/fb-companies-that-dont-adopt-ai-will-fall-behind/

Bostrom, N. (2024). *Deep Utopia: Life and meaning in a solved world.* Ideapress Publishing.

Creamer, E. (2024). Survey finds generative AI proving major threat to the work of translators. *Guardian.* https://www.theguardian.com/books/2024/apr/16/survey-finds-generative-ai-proving-major-threat-to-the-work-of-translators

Cutherbertson, A.. Google's DeepMind AI can now code better than humans. *Independent*, February 3, 2022.: https://www.independent.co.uk/tech/google-deepmind-artificial-intelligence-coding-b2006940.html

Economist (2024). Why your company is struggling to scale up generative AI. *The Economist*, November 4, 2024.: https://www.economist.com/business/2024/11/04/why-your-company-is-struggling-to-scale-up-generative-ai

Economist (2025). The economics of self-driving taxis. *The Economist*, September 28, 2025.: https://www.economist.com/finance-and-economics/2025/09/28/the-economics-of-self-driving-taxis

Faculty. (2024). *Ten lessons from ten years of applied AI.* Koto.

Finger, L. Sam Altman says, 'We know how to build AGI' — Not so fast. *Forbes*, January 7 2025.: https://www.forbes.com/sites/lutzfinger/2025/01/07/sam-altman%2D%2D-agi%2D%2Dai-workforce-in-2025-the-battle-of-tech-giants/

Goertzel, B., & Pennachin, C. (Eds.). (2006). *Artificial general intelligence*. Springer.

Hinton, G., quoted in 'Godfather of AI' shortens odds of the technology wiping out humanity over next 30 years. *The Guardian*, December 27, 2024.: https://www.theguardian.com/technology/2024/dec/27/godfather-of-ai-raises-odds-of-the-technology-wiping-out-humanity-over-next-30-years

Mickle, T. Nvidia's profit jumps 80% as company rides tech's A.I. Boom. *New York Times*, February 26, 2025.: https://www.nytimes.com/2025/02/26/technology/nvidia-quarterly-earnings.html

Ovide, S. How Amazon won shopping. *New York Times*, August 17, 2021.: https://www.nytimes.com/2021/08/17/technology/how-amazon-won-shopping.html

Suleyman, M. (2023). *The coming wave: AI, power, and the 21st century's greatest dilemma*. Bodley Head.

US Census Bureau, Business Trends and Outlook Survey, February 27, 2025.: https://www.census.gov/hfp/btos/data

Lessons from History: The Societal Impacts of Technological Change

H. G. Vipond

Introduction

The historical record is often invoked in debates on the future of work, but seldom consulted. Instead, a few selected stories serve as framing devices. This provides narrative power, but obscures any deeper insights the historical record may have to offer.

The most well-known story of resistance to technological change is found in the events of the early nineteenth century, when a group of skilled textile workers took hammers to the looms in the north of England, destroying the machines. An Act of Parliament, the Frame Breaking Act of 1812, was passed to make machine-breaking a capital offence. Seventeen men were hanged. Despite this, the Swing Riots erupted in the South of England only a few decades later, as workers protested against the introduction of threshing machines. Again, protesters were hanged. Hundreds more were imprisoned, or transported to Australia (Horn, 2005; Susskind, 2024).

The story of the Luddites is a cultural touchstone—often cited, deeply symbolic. However, there is more to it than the familiar narrative suggests. In the remainder of this chapter, we will consult directly with the historical

H. G. Vipond (✉)
Complexity Science Hub, Vienna, Austria

London School of Economics, London, England
e-mail: vipond@csh.ac.at; h.g.vipond@lse.ac.uk

M. Rangeley, N. Fairfax (eds.), *The Artificial Intelligence Revolution*,
https://doi.org/10.1007/978-3-032-11814-1_21

record to discover where a closer examination of previous episodes of labour displacement can contribute to the current debate on the future of work.

The chapter proceeds in five parts. The first reviews the debate on the future of work. The second examines case studies of labour displacement in historical contexts. The third turns to the political fallout of these shocks, and the fourth looks to how institutions were reshaped in their wake. The conclusion reflects on the lessons this history offers for the present.

The Debate on the Future of Work

The Early Years: The British Industrial Revolution

The fear that new technology would replace human labour has always spurred the debate on the future of work. The concern is a perennial one—in some sense, it dates back at least to Aristotle, and has frequently revived in the centuries which followed (Lord et al., 2013). However, it reached a crescendo in the early years of the British Industrial Revolution. This is not entirely surprising. Prior to this point, labour-saving technology had been a very intermittent visitor to human history. Estimates suggest that, from 1 AD through to approximately 1700, economic growth proceeded at the barely perceptible pace of approximately 0.05% per year, with population growth moving in tandem (Maddison, 2003; Keynes, 1930). Economic progress in the pre-industrial period was fragile, with advancements routinely countered by setbacks, and long-term growth hovered at a near standstill.

The British Industrial Revolution marked a shift into an unprecedented phase of self-sustaining economic growth. Growth rates rose first to an eye-watering 0.5% during the First Industrial Revolution, then to 1.3% in the Second, and eventually reached rates of around 3% in the latter half of the twentieth century (Maddison, 2003; Clark, 2001; Piketty, 2014; Susskind, 2020; Keynes, 1930). Economists and economic historians are broadly in agreement that ongoing and sustained innovation ushered in this historically anomalous era of growth—that it has been powered by the continuous adoption of new technologies. Many of these have been labour-replacing.

The dawn of the machine age, then, would have been an alarming apparition to many. Workers, as illustrated by the well-worn story of the Luddites, were afraid the new machines would permanently replace their labour, and make them obsolete. Intellectuals shared similar concerns. Karl Marx argued that labour saving innovation would displace workers, leaving in its wake a large number of unemployed citizens, and that this additional supply of labour would keep wages suppressed. He notes that "... the machine can only be employed profitably, if it ... is the product of far fewer men than it replaces" (Marx, 2024). David Ricardo, although initially fairly optimistic, and very conscious of the economic growth being generated by the new machines, famously reversed his position on the so-called "machine question." By 1821, he had become more sympathetic to the ongoing fear of the working class, and declared: "The opinion entertained by the labouring class, that the employment of machinery is frequently detrimental to their interests, is not founded on prejudice and error, but is conformable to the correct principles of political economy" (Ricardo, 1821).

In contrast, John Maynard Keynes saw cause for optimism. Contemplating the economic opportunities which might be available to his grandchildren, he speculated that the adoption of labour-saving machines would permanently reduce demand for human labour, and to such an extent that a mere 15 h of work per week would be the norm. In doing so, he became one of the most well-known writers to envision the utopian potential of labour replacing technology (Keynes, 1930).

He was far from alone. The liberatory potential of labour-saving technology has a deep rooted history. In the *Politics*, Aristotle wrote *"For if each of the tools were able to complete its own work when commanded, or by perceiving in advance, like they claim the things [statues] of Daedalus in the story, or the tripods of Hephaestus which the poet claims entered the divine assembly automatous—if thusly shuttles wove themselves and plectra played lyres, master-craftsmen would need no subordinates, nor masters of slaves."*

Langdon Winner notes that contemporary "... discussions of automation echo Aristotle's conclusion ... the conjecture that the perfection of industrial technology will eventually liberate mankind from toil" (Winner, 1978). Karl Marx's son-in-law, in *Le Droit la Paresse*, which was widely read in its time, proposed that the machines invented in the industrial age offered liberation from labour, concluding with a strongly worded: "the machine is the savior of humanity" (Lafargue, 2016).[1] In 1935, Bertrand Russell wrote *In Praise of Idleness*, and proposed that industrial production would become so efficient that 4 h of labour would suffice (Russell, 2017).

As it happened, neither the utopian nor the dystopian predictions were close to the mark, because no permanent technological unemployment materialized. Instead, over the last two centuries, new technologies have created new jobs,

[1]"La machine est le rédempteur de l'humanité, le Dieu qui rachètera l'homme des sordides artes et du travail salarié, le Dieu qui lui donnera des loisirs et la liberté" (Lafargue, 2016).

demanding new skills, at a pace matching or exceeding job destruction. In a recent study, Autor et al. (2023) show that 60% of the jobs available in the United States in 2018 were in occupations that did not exist in the 1940s, which highlights the sheer rate of job creation over the last decades. Many of these new jobs were created by demand for entirely new goods: for personal computers, mobile phones, and the Internet.

This paradigm of countervailing forces, with technological change driving both job loss and job creation, has recently been formally modelled (Acemoglu & Restrepo, 2019), but it has been well-known for some time. Constant economic growth, which has generated new jobs, has—at least historically—allayed fears of technological unemployment.

The Twentieth Century: Modern Economic Growth

By the end of the nineteenth century, the fear of permanent technological unemployment had largely faded, and attention switched to income inequality. It was, by this point, clear that economic growth had been—on the whole[2]—responsible for increasing prosperity, and that the new technologies produced new jobs. The consensus in mainstream thinking, particularly in the academic debate, was that labour displacement was relatively short-term, and displaced labour could be reabsorbed by a growing economy.[3]

Towards the end of the twentieth century, incomes for top earners split away from the rest. In their book, *The Race Between Education and Technology*, Claudia Goldin and Lawrence Katz argue that this was the result of a race between technological change and educational attainment. They point out that the new technologies of the past century have been skills-biased: they demanded skilled labour. Education then expanded to supply it. When education kept pace with demand, there was little in the way of a skills premium. However, when demand for skilled labour temporarily outstripped available supply, highly educated workers commanded a wage premium, and income inequality increased (Goldin & Katz, 2008).

Wage premiums for skilled workers have driven substantial income inequalities in the labour market. These dynamics have also sustained demand for higher education, not only in the United States but across the world. Over

[2]This is not to say that everyone benefited equally. Far from it. See the research on the evolution of inequality over the last century (Piketty, 2014; Milanovic, 2016; Atkinson, 2015).

[3]As mentioned, the fear of permanent technological unemployment is perennial. It revived multiple times in this period, for example, in America in the 1930s and the 1960s. One of these episodes produced John Maynard Keynes' well-known paper.

the two decades in which income inequality was centre stage in debates on the societal impacts of technological change, the paradigm underwent several modifications. The original skill-biased technological change model (SBTC) is frequently referred to as the "canonical model." The most well-known modification is the "routine biased technological change" model (RBTC), which shows that new technology disrupts the labour market primarily at the task level. Empirical papers often find a hollowing out of the occupational structure, and polarization of incomes, following on from the adoption of new technologies (Goos & Manning, 2007; Acemoglu & Restrepo, 2022).

The Twenty-First Century: The Age of AI

The emergence of AI has catapulted us back to the oldest form of the debate: the debate on job loss. As in previous iterations, the rekindled debate on the future of work has been catalysed by the fear of labour displacement. A seminal paper in 2013 argued that up to 47% of jobs in the United States were at risk of being automated (Frey & Osborne, 2017). This sparked a cottage industry of papers estimating exposure across countries and regions around the world (Arntz et al., 2016; Chang & Huynh, 2016; Manyika et al., 2017). Estimates are high. This has fed a concern sharply at odds with the more sanguine outlook economists once held about the impact of technological change on labour displacement[4]—in a recent poll of leading economists, 35–40% agreed that artificial intelligence will increase long-term unemployment (Autor, 2022). The deluge of subsequent technological advances in AI, with the rise of large language models, will necessarily push these estimates higher and exacerbate concerns still further.

A new dawn has therefore lifted on the old debate. The arrival of machines that threaten to replace not just muscle and sinew but cognitive work itself has triggered a flood of responses. A wave of books has emerged, envisioning utopic and dystopic outcomes (Brynjolfsson & McAfee, 2014; Ford, 2015; Baldwin, 2019; Bootle, 2019; Susskind, 2020; Aghion et al., 2021). Dozens of policy reports have been written and continue to be produced (Future of Work Commission and Mountfield, 2017; OECD, 2019; Institute for the Future of Work, 2022; Autor et al., 2020; World Economic Forum, 2020, 2023). The atmosphere is oddly reminiscent of the early responses to the machines of the First Industrial Revolution, and the parallel has not gone unnoticed. Indeed,

[4] For example Mokyr et al. (2015).

this may explain why the story of the Luddites is so frequently invoked in the contemporary debate.

The current debate on labour displacement has split into two primary camps. Both anticipate a surge of creative destruction. At a minimum, substantial temporary technological unemployment is expected. There is a growing emphasis on fortifying our institutions to weather these shocks. This brings to the fore questions as to which segments of the population are most exposed to the risks of displacement, and includes reflection on optimal policy remedies. To date, policy interventions have primarily centred on retraining displaced workers.

However, one group of scholars anticipates the possibility that generative AI is a technology which will break with the past entirely. Proponents of this view point out that this time may be different—that technological unemployment could, for the first time, become permanent.[5] Many in this camp suggest that even if generative AI creates new jobs, it will out-compete humans for those as well. This would put us in truly uncharted territory—one of permanent technological unemployment (Susskind, 2020, 2024). What history can teach us depends which state of the world we face. However, even if we are moving towards a world without work, there will be a transition phase, which may bear some similarities to past experience.

The role history currently plays in the contemporary discussion on the future of work is quite limited. In popular books, there is often a brief history of economic growth. It usually notes the radical inventions of the early industrial revolutions, mention labour and union resistance, and concludes that most people benefited substantially from industrialization. While not inaccurate, this glosses over the particulars of how societies absorbed the shocks of the new labour saving technologies, and transitioned into new occupational structures. As we turn towards the Fourth Industrial Revolution, there is keen interest in understanding how these shocks are absorbed, and by whom.

In policy documents, the use of history as a framing device is even more pronounced. The UK Future of Work Commission Report (Future of Work Commission and Mountfield, 2017) states that "The best guide to what might happen in the future, and the role of policy in shaping it, is almost always the past," but summarizes the past in three paragraphs. The OECD's, 2019 Employment Outlook refers to history primarily to underscore

[5]David Autor provides an excellent overview of the evolving paradigms for understanding the impact of technological change on labour markets. In *The Labor Market Impacts of Technological Change*, subtitled "From Unbridled Enthusiasm to Qualified Optimism to Vast Uncertainty," he traces how economic thought has shifted over time, with the last phase reflecting uncertainty in the age of AI (Autor, 2022).

that "[h]istorically, the net effects of major technological revolutions on employment have been positive" (OECD, 2019). While true, this fact masks substantial variation, and overlooks the costs that workers and their families may have borne in the churn of labour displacement. The Institute for the Future of Work acknowledges uneven rates of technological adoption and alludes to historical parallels—highlighting the presence of "winners" and "losers" in past waves of innovation—but does not explore these patterns in depth (Institute for the Future of Work, 2022). In contrast, the 2019 MIT Work of the Future report provides a more balanced assessment, offering a broad survey of both the long-term benefits and negative impacts of technological change (Autor et al., 2020).[6]

The Luddites are often summoned to attend the contemporary debate, not to inform it. Their story is primarily used as a shorthand—a way to remind us of the depths of past anxiety. While effective, this is a limited use of history. In what follows, we attempt the opposite. We turn directly to the historical record, examining new case studies from the First and Second Industrial Revolutions.

History: Labour Displacement

> The Industrial Revolution destroyed the livelihood of some and left others to vegetate in the backwaters of the stream of progress. The victims of the Industrial Revolution numbered in the hundreds of thousands or even millions.—David Landes

We know surprisingly little about the consequences of creative destruction for workers caught in the upheaval. While new technologies have created new jobs, demanding new skills, it remains unclear precisely how many incumbent workers have found themselves permanently unemployed, transitioned into new jobs, or have faced downward mobility. While the work of piecing this story together is still underway, there is a set of new, thought-provoking case studies on technological labour displacement in historical context.

The majority of the recent studies leverage the recently digitized, individual-level, nineteenth century historical census data for the United States and the UK. These are rich datasets, which are making it possible for researchers to quantify the impacts of technological displacement on the labour market, and

[6]This section is based on the co-authored paper, *The Past and Future of Work* (Schneider & Vipond, 2023).

capture its effects on workers. This new research in economic history highlights four points which are rarely emphasized in the current debate on the future of work: scale, speed of adoption, and the changing geography of employment.

Scale

While creative destruction has been ongoing for much of the last 300 years, there have been accelerations into periods of particularly rapid transformation. The First Industrial Revolution is the canonical example: a rupture that remade production, labour, and even society itself. It mechanized the work of muscle and sinew, largely for the first time, displacing labour across vast segments of the workforce. These are the true gales of creative destruction (Schumpeter, 1942). The shock to the occupational structure was on a scale that is almost difficult to comprehend from a modern perspective. We turn to one of the most important of these shocks: the mechanization of the textile industries.

In the late eighteenth century, the British spinning industry underwent a dramatic transformation. It reshaped the entire textile sector, both in England and globally, with profound economic and social consequences. The introduction of the spinning jenny and the spinning mule resulted in a sharp increase in productivity, and a corresponding surge in output. The sector had employed up to 8% of the British population in 1770, but the new labour-saving technologies resulted in a collapse in demand for hand spinners. Many women and children in England lost their livelihoods. In his paper, *Technological Unemployment in the British Industrial Revolution: The Destruction of Hand Spinning*, Ben Schneider finds evidence that opportunities for women in the labour market were eroded for decades. Even by 1834, evidence taken from the Poor Law Commissioners' *Rural and Town Queries* reported there was little work—or none at all in some places—available to women. The paper makes a note of the scale involved, commenting that "The destruction of hand-spinning is the largest instance of technological unemployment documented to date, impacting up to 8 per cent of the population" (Schneider, 2026).

Our expectations for how the Fourth Industrial Revolution will impact the labour market are shaped by recent trends. However, these may be the wrong benchmark—at least in terms of scale. In a current working paper, Deming et al. (2025) find that the pace of technological disruption between 1990 and 2017 was slower than at any point since 1880. Much of the recent research on technological labour displacement focuses on this relatively quiet period, when worker dislocation was comparatively minimal. If, as is widely expected, the coming disruption is far greater in scale, the First and Second Industrial

Revolutions may offer a more appropriate point of reference for thinking about the societal impacts of the transition ahead.

Timelines

The second key point to consider is the timescale of adoption. Sometimes new, labour-displacing technologies are adopted overnight. Normally, they are not.

Innovation is often framed in terms of patents and ideas. However, the diffusion of new machinery follows a different schedule—one that is typically slower than the spread of ideas, and geographically uneven. Crucially, old technologies do not disappear when new ones arise. Steam power took decades to become dominant, and coal remained critical through the nineteenth century, and indeed the twentieth. Steamships did not replace sailboats for many decades. Trains were not replaced by airplanes or cars. Shifting away from an innovation-centric perspective highlights the fact that demand for skills tied to older technologies frequently persists (Edgerton, 2007). In many cases, labour specific to outdated technologies remains valuable and in demand long after new technologies are introduced.

In my working paper, *The Displacement of Entry: The Mechanization of the English Bootmaking Industry*, I construct new, sub-industry, "task"-level data on occupation for England between 1851 and 1911, extracted from textual descriptions of occupation in the 180 million individual-level English census observations in the Integrated Census Microdata (ICeM) project dataset (Schurer et al., 2024). I use this fine-grained data to study the impact of mechanization on occupational structure as the English bootmaking industry mechanizes. The new perspective reveals sharp structural changes which are entirely obscured at the industry level of analysis. Approximately 152,000 "old" artisanal bootmaking jobs disappeared. Another 144,000 jobs, demanding new skills, were generated. The new jobs went almost exclusively to young bootmakers—incumbents did not transition into the new employment opportunities. However, male incumbents did not experience substantial labour displacement.[7] Demand for bespoke shoes persisted, allowing existing artisans to remain employed for decades. The decline of the "old" jobs occurred not through labour displacement but because young men stopped entering the trade.

[7] Female incumbents were displaced. I attribute this to the women being responsible for only one discrete task, the binding of the uppers of the boot, and this was work which was entirely mechanized by the sewing machine.

In this case study, the primary effect of new labour-saving technology was not the direct displacement of incumbent workers but the disappearance of employment opportunities for young men in certain regions. This challenges the prevailing assumption in debates on the future of work that it is incumbents who face displacement, and will require retraining (Vipond, 2026). In this context, it is worth noting that, over the last century of creative destruction, money has been poured into educating the young for new types of work, not in retraining older, established workers.

In contrast to the previous case study, some technologies do fully automate an entire job within a short time frame, rendering an entire skill set obsolete almost overnight. In these cases, incumbents are immediately and comprehensively displaced. For example, Feigenbaum and Gross (2024) examine the mechanization of the telephone industry in the United States. Between 1920 and 1940, AT&T automated its network, replacing manual operators with mechanical switching technology. The company implemented this transition city by city, allowing the authors to exploit variation in the timing of adoption to identify the causal impact of the shock on labour markets.

When automation eliminated these jobs it did so abruptly: from one day to the next, human operators were no longer needed. Unsurprisingly—mechanically?—they lost their jobs. Feigenbaum and Gross (2024) find that, after a city was cut over to mechanical operation, the number of young telephone operators immediately fell by 50–80%. Displaced incumbents were less likely to be employed in the following decades, and those who did find work were more likely to be in lower-paid jobs. However, the shock did not reduce employment rates among subsequent cohorts of young women, who found work in other sectors. At the time, there was demand for typists and secretaries, and these growing sectors were able to provide alternative employment opportunities to young women.

In sum: the speed of technological adoption may be decisive in determining who bears the burden of displacement—incumbent workers or new entrants. However, the speed of AI adoption remains largely overlooked in current debates, and variation in adoption rates has not yet been systematically modelled.

Geography

Technological change not only reshapes industries, it also reconfigures economic geography, creating regions of expanding opportunity and, often enough, regions of decline. As new technologies emerge, the new jobs they generate tend to cluster. There were industrial hubs in Britain during the Industrial Revolution, digital ones in Silicon Valley during the tech boom, and AI-driven innovation centres are emerging today. The uneven adoption of technology generates intense spatial disparities. These have cascading impacts on future employment opportunities, wages, migration, and—potentially—on politics. In their economic geography paper, *Frontier Workers and the Seedbeds of Inequality and Prosperity*, Connor et al. (2024) identify new jobs being generated at the frontier of technological innovation. They analyse the geographical location and incomes of individuals working with these new technologies between 1880 and 2019, identifying them as "frontier workers." They find that frontier work is often concentrated in a set of 'seedbed' locations. It is work that attracts high wage premiums—consistent with the skill-biased technological change model discussed earlier. The paper provides a potential origin story for evolving spatial income inequality. It also invites reflection on patterns of economic migration. In their paper *Gender-Biased Technological Change: Milking Machines and the Exodus of Women from Farming*, Ager et al. (2026) examine the gendered effects of technological changes in twentieth-century agriculture in Norway. The case study investigates the adoption of milking machines on dairy farms, and finds that mechanization displaced women. These workers migrated to urban areas. In turn, this improved their labour market outcomes, and access to education, relative to men.

On the other hand, in nineteenth-century England, mechanization led to the disappearance of traditional artisanal bootmaking jobs across every county and town. The new jobs, in mechanized bootmaking, emerged almost entirely in two counties: Northamptonshire and Leicestershire. Incumbent workers did not migrate. Female bootmakers, who faced direct labour displacement, did not migrate. Perhaps they were constrained by family obligations in an era dominated by the male breadwinner model. Male incumbents also did not migrate, which is unsurprising, given that they were able to continue working as artisanal bootmakers even as the bespoke bootmaking industry declined. In this case study, labour displacement primarily took the form of a sharp contraction in employment opportunities for young men, and there is preliminary evidence that young men in the most affected areas did respond by migrating (Vipond, 2026).

Historical case studies illustrate that technological shocks rewrite the geography of employment opportunities. New jobs cluster in emerging hubs, while other regions stagnate or decline. These shifts have shaped migration patterns, deepened regional inequalities, and, potentially, redrawn political fault lines. As AI and automation drive the next wave of disruption, understanding these spatial dynamics will be essential for anticipating broader labour market and societal shifts.

Conclusion: Transitions

Technological change does not only eliminate jobs, it creates new ones.[8] However, whether workers are able to maintain employment is contingent on the balance between job loss and job creation across three dimensions: scale, speed, and geography. If displacement is extensive, jobs creation must take place at the same scale. If adoption is rapid, incumbents are forced out. If it is gradual, they can be grandfathered out, but younger cohorts will bear the loss. If new jobs appear in different places, workers must be able to migrate, or they will be left behind.[9]

The forces that destroy jobs and the forces that create them are both well studied. What we lack is a mapping of how they interact—when, where, and for whom job creation offsets job loss. Both sides of the balance sheet matter. One of the benefits of studying labour displacement events in historical context is that we can see the full arc of these transitions. Having complete case studies brings to the fore how the scale, speed, and geography of job loss and job creation interact over time. This reveals a range of outcomes—one which is obscured by the observation that, in the past, new jobs have emerged faster than old ones have disappeared.

The case studies discussed earlier illustrate the range of outcomes resulting from these dynamics. When the spinning industry mechanized, incumbent spinners were unable to move into new jobs. This may have been the result of the scale of the shock—it is highly likely that new opportunities for women were not generated on a scale which could compensate for the losses. Subsequent cohorts of women faced a prolonged employment gap (Schneider, 2026).

When the bootmaking industry mechanized, nearly 30,000 female binders faced unemployment, even though 27,000 new sewing machinist positions emerged. The skill barrier for the new jobs was low, but 90% of displaced women remained unemployed, suggesting a lack of local employment opportunities, inability to migrate to opportunity, or that there were other cul-

[8]An early attempt to quantify the emergence of new jobs estimated that 8.5% of American workers in 1980 were employed in occupations which did not exist in 1965 (Lin, 2011). Building on this work, new research estimates that more than half of the jobs which currently employ Americans did not exist prior to 1940 (Autor et al., 2024).

[9]I do not discuss the "skills" dimension, as this is well explored in the current debate.

tural constraints that prevented transition (Vipond, 2026). A similar pattern emerged for displaced female telephone operators in the United States, who were more likely than other women to become unemployed or enter lower paid work. For younger cohorts, however, employment rates remained stable, as many moved into growing secretarial and service roles (Feigenbaum & Gross, 2024).

Some technological changes, however, may have facilitated more successful transitions. In early twentieth-century agriculture, the adoption of milking machines displaced women who had traditionally performed dairy work on Norwegian farms. After World War II, many of these women migrated to cities. Although they initially experienced a decline in income, they ultimately found better-paying jobs in emerging urban sectors (Ager et al., 2026). Similar patterns emerge elsewhere: new research finds that displaced northern workers who relocated to cities often fared better in the long run (Berger et al., 2025).

In current debates on the future of work, the default policy response to labour displacement is often retraining, with a view that displaced workers can and should transition into new roles. However, this assumes that new jobs exist, and that skills are the primary barrier to employment. Historical case studies challenge this, showing that successful transitions depend not only on retraining but on the scale of both job loss and job creation (Schneider, 2026), the speed of adoption of new technologies (Vipond, 2026; Feigenbaum & Gross, 2024), and the geography of new opportunities (Connor et al., 2024; Ager et al., 2026; Berger et al., 2025). If adoption is slow, incumbents may not face displacement, making retraining unnecessary. If job loss is rapid or concentrated in specific regions, retraining may be unnecessary, or insufficient. Policy responses must be tailored to these realities.

Future research must go beyond aggregate measures of employment and focus on the conditions that determine whether technological change leads to opportunity or exclusion. Understanding how the scale, speed, and geography of job loss and creation interact will be critical to designing policies that support workers in different economic and institutional contexts.

History: Political Responses

> If the Treasury were to fill old bottles with banknotes, bury them at suitable depths in disused coal mines, and leave it to private enterprise . . . there need be no more unemployment.—John Maynard Keynes

The history of technological change is a history of political response. Workers have frequently resisted labour-replacing technologies, whether through direct action or political organization. Over time, these efforts have cumulated in institutional reform, ensuring some measure of protection. In this section, I focus on Britain throughout the long nineteenth century, examining two key phases: worker resistance before the 1830s, and the emergence of organized labour and institutional adaptation in the decades that followed.

The story of the Luddites, which features so often in popular books on the Fourth Industrial Revolution, is seldom used to initiate a discussion on the political consequences of declining or changing demand for labour. Instead, it typically serves to underscore the degree of fear that workers felt, acting as a rhetorical device to motivate an assessment of the share of workers currently at risk of technological labour displacement.

Here, I argue that the scale and intensity of political responses to previous industrial revolutions deserve greater attention, as does their transformative role in shaping the institutions which now underpin the social contract. The current debate on the future of work tends to overlook the political responses that rapid technological change has provoked in the past—and may provoke again.

Disrupting the Machines: Resistance Before the 1830s

The Industrial Revolution brought about profound shifts in labour demand, with many skilled trades rendered obsolete by mechanization. In response, workers across Europe raged against the machine. The most well-known of these movements, the Luddites of early nineteenth-century Britain, targeted the textile machinery that threatened their economic position. Bands of Luddites conducted more than 100 acts of machine breaking, destroying approximately 1000 stocking frames in the Midlands. They were far from alone. Karl Marx paints a vivid canvas of these acts of resistance in several industries as they took place in Europe:

> In the seventeenth century nearly all Europe experienced workers' revolts against the rib- bonloom, a machine for weaving ribbons and lace trimmings called in Germany Bandmühle, Schnurmühle, or Mühlenstuhl. In the 1630s, a wind-driven sawmill, erected near London by a Dutchman, succumbed to the rage of the mob. Even as late as the beginning of the eighteenth century, saw-mills driven by water overcame the opposition of the people only with great difficulty, supported as this opposition was by Parliament. No sooner had Everett constructed the first woolshearing machine to be driven by water-power (1758)

than it was set on fire by 100,000 people who had been thrown out of work. Fifty thousand workers, who had previously lived by carding wool, petitioned Parliament against Arkwright's scribbling mills and carding engines (Marx, 2024).

The British government responded to the Luddites with force. Parliament passed the Frame Breaking Act in 1812, making the destruction of machinery a capital offence, and deployed thousands of soldiers to suppress Luddite activity. Executions and deportations followed, and by the mid-1810s, the movement had been quashed (Horn, 2005).

Similar tensions played out elsewhere. In France, a wave of machine breaking surged in 1789 as part of the revolutionary movement. Woolen workers broke into manufacturing districts and rioted, destroying textile machinery where they found it. A mob of 4000 seized a new, English-designed, carding machine, and set it on fire, to cheers from the crowd (Horn, 2005). Barthélemy Thimonnier's invention of the sewing machine, in 1830, prompted marauding tailors, fearing the loss of their trade, to destroy his workshop. It went down in flames. Thimonnier attempted to rebuild but struggled financially, and never saw widespread adoption of his design. It was not until Isaac Singer and Elias Howe refined sewing machine technology in the mid-nineteenth century that mechanized sewing took off commercially, and the direct resistance of the French tailors is why the sewing machine is an American invention. These acts of resistance, though ultimately unsuccessful, signalled the extent to which workers perceived mechanization as an existential threat.

Several works bring to the fore the political responses to major disruptions in the occupational structure. In *The Technology Trap*, Frey (2019) notes that there has always been rage against the machine. He points out that "attitudes to technological progress are shaped by how people's incomes are affected by it," and notes a study from the Pew Research Centre, in which 85% of Americans supported policies to restrict the rise of robots. The book spans the history of labour replacing progress over the very long run, taking us from antiquity to the present day. In the *The Making of the English Working Class*, Thompson (2016) declares "I am seeking to rescue the poor stockinger, the luddite cropper, the 'obsolete' hand-loom weaver, the 'utopian' artisan ... from the enormous condescension of posterity." His account of English workers facing the loss of traditional livelihoods remains one of the richest social histories of industrial change. Finally, the paper by Jeff Horn, *Machine-Breaking in England and France During the Age of Revolution*, provides a substantial overview of the many acts of machine breaking and labour resistance which preceded the machine age (Horn, 2005).

It is well documented that the rise of the machine age was met with intense resistance from labour. This period remains vivid in cultural memory, and stories of labour opposition have ossified into foundational narratives of modern economic growth. The story of the Luddites, and of the spinners, is often taught in schools. However, direct action was only the first phase of the response: once it became clear that machines would not eliminate jobs entirely, the focus shifted to advocating for higher wages and improved working conditions. By the mid-nineteenth century, British unions had gained legendary strength. This marked the beginning of a broader political response, as the rise of organized labour itself gave way to the creation of institutions designed to address the social challenges of modern economic growth.

Organized Labour and Institutional Responses (1830–1910)

By the 1830s, labour resistance in Britain had shifted from direct confrontation to structured organization. Unions, mutual aid societies, and political movements emerged to negotiate better conditions and influence policy. The repeal of Britain's Combination Acts in 1824, for example, legalized the trades union. Political mobilization also expanded. The Chartist movement (1838–1848), agitated for voting rights for workers, reflecting the growing recognition that economic change required political representation. Even though Chartism failed in the short term, it contributed to later democratic reforms and changed political discourses (Grampp, 1979).

The late nineteenth century saw significant gains for organized labour. Britain's Trade Union Act (1871) and subsequent legislation protected unions and legitimized collective bargaining. By the 1890s, large strikes—such as the 1888 Matchgirls' Strike, and the 1889 London Dock Strike—were being organized. By the early years of the twentieth century, British unions were so strong that they were able to help establish the Labour Representation Committee, which evolved into the Labour Party (Pelz, 2016).

In response to persistent agitation, and better representation, successive governments introduced labour protections. While not all of the classical economists of the time supported the new labour laws, several prominent intellectuals did. In 1832, John Stuart Mill was one of the first to throw his support behind the new policies. He wrote in a weekly magazine that he favoured "a law established interdicting altogether the employment of children under 14, and females of any age, in manufactories." In 1833, the first of

Britain's Factory Acts to be enforced was established.[10] It stipulated that no children under the age of nine were to work in the factories, that children between the ages of 9 and 13 should be limited to a 48-h week, and that children between the ages of 13 and 18 should work no more than 12 h per day. Subsequent Factory Acts expanded to include broader protections. The Factories Act of 1844 introduced safety regulations in factories. The Act of 1847 established a 10 hr workday for women and children between the ages of 13 and 18. By 1867, an Act forbade the employment of children, young people, and women on Sundays. Finally, in 1891, the Factory and Workshop Consolidation Act brought the minimum age of children in factories up to 11, and consolidated safety regulations (UK Parliament, 2024a; Blaug, 1958)

Economic dislocation also prompted early welfare policies. The Old Age Pensions Act (1908) provided state-funded pensions for impoverished elderly workers, a response to growing concerns over aging workers unable to compete in modern industries. The Trade Boards Act of 1909 introduced minimum wages in a handful of trades—notably, those in which mechanization had driven earnings to unsustainable levels. Most significantly, the National Insurance Act (1911) created unemployment and health insurance, offering workers a degree of security in an economy subject to recurring technological upheaval. Winston Churchill was instrumental in this: *"It is a serious national evil,"* he famously thundered, *"that any class of His Majesty's subjects should receive less than a living wage . . . It was formerly supposed,"* he went on, *"that the working of the laws of supply and demand would naturally regulate or eliminate that evil. But where you have what we call sweated trades, you have no organisation, no parity of bargaining, the good employer is undercut by the bad, and the bad employer is undercut by the worst. . . . Where those conditions prevail you have not a condition of progress, but a condition of progressive degeneration."* David Lloyd George and Winston Churchill both argued that if industry was advancing due to machines, it was unfair for wages to decline so dramatically. It was in this way that minimum wage made its first appearance in Britain (Churchill, 1909).

In their new book, *Power and Progress,* which offers an overview of several centuries of technological change, Nobel Prize winners Daron Acemoglu and Simon Johnson argue that political power is crucial in ensuring equitable gains from economic growth. They exhort us to be vigilant, and to be ready to enact the same politics of resistance as those which shaped the societal outcomes of the British Industrial Revolutions, saying "Most people around

[10] A small team was established to conduct inspections. While this was not sufficient to enforce the Act everywhere, it marked the start of government control.

the globe today are better off than our ancestors because citizens and workers in early industrial societies organized, challenged elite-dominated choices about technology and work conditions, and forced ways of sharing the gains from technical improvements more equitably. Today we need to do the same again" (Acemoglu & Johnson, 2023). While it is not entirely clear how they would envision this working in practice, particularly in the context of global, competitive trade, the historical record makes abundantly clear that political power has played a role in the past.

If anything, the historical record shows that many of the institutions which we take for granted today were all but forged under the pressures brought to bear by previous industrial revolutions. In the next section, we turn to focus on these.

History: Structural Level Impacts

> The hand-mill gives you society with the feudal lord; the steam-mill, society with the industrial capitalist—Karl Marx

The shocks to labour demand during the First and Second Industrial Revolutions struck with a force that sent shockwaves through labour markets and politics. The upheaval did not stop there. Ripple effects cascaded still further, shaping the emergence of a set of institutions that have since formed the bedrock of the social contract in Western democracies. To consider the potential impact of the upcoming Fourth Industrial Revolution, it is worth reflecting on the structures which emerged from earlier transformations. This section considers England as a case study of an economy in transition, drawing comparisons to other countries along the way.[11]

Formal Education

One of the institutions that emerged during the Second Industrial Revolution is the education system. Prior to the nineteenth century, formal schooling was scarce. It existed primarily in the form of town grammar schools, Christian charity schools, and, of course, in the storied private education system reserved for the elite—Eton, Harrow, Westminster—followed by Oxbridge or similar.

---

[11]Major shifts to demand for labour play out differently in different historical periods, in different countries, and in different cultural contexts. There is no claim that the experience in England is the blueprint. This section is meant as an invitation to reflect on the potential reach of shocks to demand for labour.

Instead of formal schooling, the vast majority of training was conducted via the apprenticeship system. As documented by Patrick Wallis in his new book *The Market for Skill: Apprenticeship and Economic Growth in Early Modern England*, this form of training dominated the transmission of skill in England between the sixteenth century and the start of the nineteenth. Making use of hundreds of thousands of records on individual apprenticeships, the book provides a meticulous investigation of the character and impact of the apprenticeship system. Wallis notes its eventual decline, pointing out that through the nineteenth century the "increasing division of labour, standardisation, and new tools and machines all served to lower the degree of embodied manual skill required of many roles.... In this context, general academic skills and knowledge—literacy, numeracy, science—become more important than technique" (Wallis, 2025).

The advent of the First Industrial Revolution in Britain coincided with an end to the apprenticeship system, and a wholesale shift in how society transmitted knowledge. Apprenticeship was already on the wane by the early 1800s and, in 1841, the apprenticeship clauses of the Statute of Artificers were ended by an Act of Parliament. This marked the nominal end of the era of the apprenticeship system, although traditions persisted, and hundreds of thousands of apprentices were found in English census records and government inquiries as late as the 1930s (Wallis, 2025). As the long nineteenth century progressed, a new system of education emerged.

In 1870, The Elementary Education Act was passed. It established a commitment to the provision of primary education on a national scale. In particular, it established a system of school boards. Shortly thereafter, the Royal Commission on the Factory Acts recommended that children be at school, and not employed in hard labour. By 1880, primary school had been made compulsory for children between the ages of 5 and 10 years old, and then, finally, in 1891, an Act made elementary school free (UK Parliament, 2024b). Two decades later, in 1889, the Technical Instruction Act was passed. It expanded vocational and technical education, with an intention to "halt industrial decline" (Technical Education Matters, 2009). This was in part a response to the lead Germany and the United States were taking in industrial science towards the end of the nineteenth century. New universities were founded, including redbrick universities, which served the industrial cities of Birmingham and Manchester. The rise of state supported elementary education naturally resulted in a surge in the number of school teachers, and made free, formal schooling a presence in every town and parish in the country.

Census records show that there was a four-fold increase in school teachers in the UK over the latter half of the nineteenth century.[12]

A key consequence of this transition was that many young men stopped following in their fathers' footsteps. This was the outcome of a combination of factors, including not only the provision of free schooling and the rapidly changing demand for labour but also financial support from family, and an ability to travel for employment. In some occupations, the inter-generational inheritance of skills remained steady. In others, it collapsed entirely. For example, while the sons of coal miners, farmers, and bootmakers largely continued on in the same occupations as their fathers, and at the same rate as they always had, the sons of stone masons and agricultural labourers did not. There is some evidence, from the American context, that the provision of free schooling made it increasingly possible for many young people to access new opportunities in the labour market—the research shows an increase in social mobility once free schooling became available (Althoff et al., 2025).[13]

As once predictable pathways of skill-inheritance from father to son, or from apprenticeship to mastery were suddenly disrupted, and old trades vanished, new ones emerged in their place. Education became an established route of entry into the workplace. This was not only an economic shift—it was a societal one.

In sum: the last time there was a major shock to demand for labour the entire education system transformed. It shifted from being highly job-specific, relying heavily on the apprenticeship system, to the introduction of free primary schooling. This was not an incidental shift, but instead reflects a fundamental restructuring of how knowledge was passed on and how skills were acquired. Almost every country in the world followed this shift and implemented primary schooling, and a few, including the United States, did so earlier and more comprehensively.

In this context, it is worth noting that generative AI is often de-skilling. That is, there is growing evidence that the impact of the current, Fourth Industrial

---

[12] Data taken from ICeM digitized census data (Schurer et al., 2024), 1851–1911, processed by this author.

[13] As discussed in the section on labour displacement, part of the puzzle is job creation. While there are many reasons to be interested in technological innovations, one is that they have been responsible for generating a large share of the new jobs. In this time period, the organizational structure of knowledge production itself changed. See Hanlon (2022) on the rise of the engineer in the UK. In their paper, *Inventing Modern Invention*, Hartog et al. (2024) digitize half a million pages of patent yearbooks that describe inventors, organizations, and technologies on over 1.6 million patents, and link to census data They show that nineteenth-century craftsmanship-based invention was replaced by a rapidly emerging new system: research and development labs.

Revolution, has a meaningfully different character to the labour displacement which has been the norm for the last century or so, in which manual, routine tasks were most exposed to mechanization. In the words of the Brookings Institute "generative AI is not your grandparents'—or even your parents'—automation" (Muro et al., 2024). Their report finds that occupations at the highest risk of replacement by generative AI are cognitive and non-routine. The geography of the occupations most exposed to replacement is therefore highly concentrated in cities. Several studies confirm that white-collar occupations will be most exposed to displacement by generative AI. One finds that exposure increases dramatically with salary: in occupations earning £30,000 per year, exposure is estimated at 15%, while earning £100,000 per year is associated with nearly a 50% exposure (Kogan et al., 2021).

Another handful of studies argue that low-skill tasks or "low skill" workers will benefit most from the introduction of generative AI (Acemoglu, 2025; Wilmers, 2024). Generative AI may substantially reduce barriers to entry. It will allow non-experts to access and automate their interactions with: medical expertise, programming ability, the creative arts, and academic research (Nagaraj & Ranganathan, 2023; Nori et al., 2023; Gottweis et al., 2025). David Autor considers the possibility that this de-skilling tech might lead to greater equality in the workplace, even rebuilding the middle class (Autor, 2024). Across many papers, there is an emerging consensus that generative AI is likely to make it possible to acquire, or to apply without the need to acquire, skills which once required years of formal education. For the last century, new technologies have been skills-biased. That is, new technologies demanded increasingly skilled labour. This gave rise to a need for higher education. It also gave rise to skills premiums. However, and for the first time in more than 100 years, we may be facing a wave of new technologies which are primarily de-skilling. This may level skills premiums. It may also reduce, circumvent, or alter the need for formal higher education.

Demographic Transitions

Demographic transitions have historically coincided with industrial revolutions.[14] The First Industrial Revolution resulted in an extremely rapid increase

[14] Demographers often refer to one demographic transition, consisting of several phases. In this paradigm, the first phase is a balanced one, in which there is little population growth. This was the norm in every country in the world prior to the first (British) Industrial Revolution. In the second phase, death rates decline and population size increases. In the third phase, birth rates fall. This leads to the fourth phase, in which fertility stabilizes at low or at below-replacement levels.

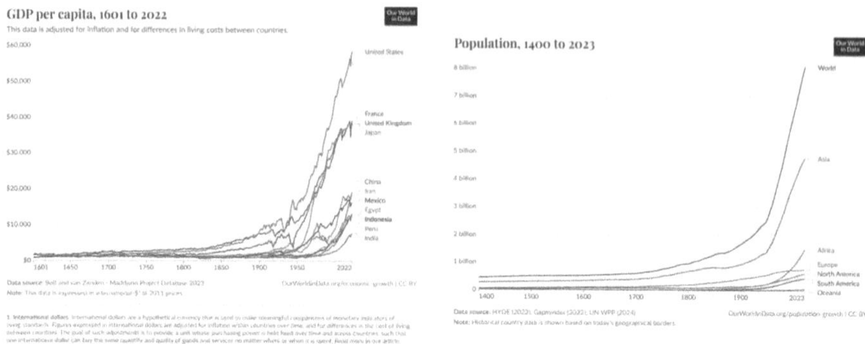

Fig. 1 Growth in GDP/capita and population

in the population. From 1800, global population has increased by a factor of six, and this is projected to be a factor of 10 by 2100 (Lee, 2002). The well-known hockey stick graph of economic growth is mirrored by exponential population growth. The two graphs in Fig. 1, from Our World in Data, illustrate this. The left-hand panel shows the increase in GDP per capita by country over time, while the right-hand panel shows the increase in the population by continent over time. To a large extent, the rapid increase in population is a direct outcome of technological efficiencies: these made it possible for every country in the world to sustain a larger population.

In contrast, the Second Industrial Revolution in England heralded the start of a substantial and sustained decline in average family size. In this transition, countries move from high birth (and death) rates through to low birth (and death) rates.

This phase of the demographic transition has been staggered across the world. Fertility declined rapidly across most of Western Europe between 1870 and 1920, with an average drop of about 40%. Another large wave of the global fertility decline began in the 1970s. In much of Asia and Latin America, fertility rates declined from an average of 6 children per family to around 3 between 1965 and 1990 (Lee, 2002). The demographic transition has now been experienced by the majority of the countries in the world, and at the moment, 152 out of 235 regions in the world have fertility at below the replacement rate of approximately 2.1 children per woman. By 2021, every European country was substantially below replacement rates. Fertility continues to decline across the world. The total global population is expected to level out over the next few decades: recent estimates from the UN's World Population Prospects estimate that global population will peak this century at around 10.3 billion people

(United Nations, Department of Economic and Social Affairs, Population Division, 2024).

Multiple explanations for the causal drivers of this decline have been suggested (Goldin, 2024). One of these is the increasing costs of raising children, not least because of the costs of education. In 1962, Gary Becker wrote a seminal paper arguing that fertility choices are driven in part by a child "quantity–quality" trade-off. He argues that parents face time and budget constraints, and must choose between the number of children they have and the level of investment made in each child (Becker, 1960). As skills-biased technological change dynamics set in, and education became increasingly necessary, children may have become increasingly expensive. This would have made it rational to have fewer children, but invest more heavily in each.

Oded Galor has expressed this type of hypothesis in his well-known unified growth theory (Galor, 2011, 2012). Two fairly recent papers have tested it. In a paper leveraging the individual level census returns for Ireland, in 1911, the authors test whether families with children who remained in school between the ages of 14 and 16 (school until the age of 14 was compulsory) were likely to be smaller. They find that families dedicating more resources to the education of their children reduced their fertility by around 27% (Fernihough, 2017). Further research into this question is needed, but the staggered fertility decline may map on fairly well to the timing of industrialization in countries around the world. A second paper tests a dataset of 21 OECD countries over the period of 1750–2000 and finds that this has the predicted positive relationship with education, and negative relationship with fertility (Madsen & Strulik, 2023)

Industrial revolutions have coincided with substantial changes to demographic outcomes in the past. Sharp changes in demand for labour can rewrite the economic realities of having children across multiple dimensions. It is not impossible that the Fourth Industrial Revolution may do the same.

Social Mobility

The Industrial Revolution heralded a dawn of social mobility in England. In their working paper, *The Breakdown of the English Society of Orders: The Role of the Industrial Revolution*, Ebert et al. (2024) argue that the Industrial Revolution disrupted England's traditional hierarchical social structure. The paper digitizes hearth tax returns between 1662 and 1674 and the probate[15] records for the period 1862 to 1899. Comparing these two datasets, they

[15]The probate records provide individual-level data on wealth at death.

find that the predictive power of surname on wealth outcomes fell by a half compared to the seventeenth century. Even more intriguingly, they find that, in the industrial regions of England, it fell by almost 90%. They conclude that the technological and economic changes of the period offered opportunities to many, opening the door to social mobility in a way which would have been inconceivable in the previous era. There is also emerging evidence that workers employed by firms which are using frontier technologies are likely to be earning wage premiums. Connor et al. (2024) find that workers employed in frontier technologies receive strong wage premiums, which can initially contribute to rising spatial inequality. Kastis and Vipond (2024), in a case study on the mechanization of the tailoring industry in England, show that Jewish immigrants in East London adopted the new sewing machine technology more rapidly than English-born tailors. This was likely due to pre-existing divisions of labour within the workshops. There is some evidence that the early adopters experienced faster upward mobility.

This access to social mobility only increased with the introduction of free formal schooling. A new working paper, *America's Rise in Human Capital Mobility*, by Althoff et al. (2025) finds that the provision of free schooling in the United States substantially increased access to opportunity, and social mobility. Their first finding is that human capital mobility in America increased rapidly between 1850 and 1950. Black mobility improved following the end of slavery, and then declined during the Jim Crow era. On the other hand, white mobility increased rapidly from 1890, after formal schooling had been made universally available across the United States. The paper finds that maternal human capital was originally highly correlated with child outcomes, but that this was significantly relaxed once formal education became widely available.

While social mobility has been made more attainable in the era of creative destruction, access to it has been adjudicated by formal education. The dynamics of skills-biased technological change have meant that wage premiums have been available for highly skilled workers. This has driven the emergence of a middle class—skilled workers with strong earning power—but the returns to education have become increasingly polarized over the last few decades. In their well-known paper, *The Fading American Dream: Trends in Absolute Income Mobility Since 1940*, Chetty et al. (2017) show that the fraction of children in the United States earning more than their parents fell from 90% for children born in the 1940s to around 50% of children today. They also find that most of this decline is driven by the unequal distribution of income growth over recent decades. While income growth has stagnated across much of the distribution, it has soared at the top.

Demand for skilled workers, and the wage premiums associated with that demand, has offered access to opportunity for decades. An entire system of education, from primary school to university level, has been built on the sustained demand for skilled labour. If generative AI is de-skilling, then demand for labour, even if it persists, may be increasingly less sensitive to education. This would represent a profound shock to established routes into social mobility in Western countries. This could be as great a shock as the initial skills-demanding technological revolution, which upended centuries of relatively static social classes.

Income Tax

Finally, in terms of societal impacts, one of the most striking events of the nineteenth century was the shift to individual-level income taxation. In 1842, Prime Minister Robert Peel introduced the first permanent income tax. This was only levied on the very wealthy. When the 1909 tax was introduced, as part of the "People's Budget," it applied to around 25% of the population, which represented a very large share of workers, given the low rates of labour force participation for women, and the share of children in school.

To some extent, the shift to the income tax was driven by the working class. Many members of the Chartist movement[16] argued against the regressive taxes on consumer goods, and pushed for taxation on land, capital, and labour. At points, the movement was highly entangled with the machinery question, of labour displacement. In the 1830s, stuff weavers in Leeds made the regressive nature of the excise taxes clear, saying of the hand-loom weavers: "Their labour has been taken from them by the power-loom; their bread is taxed, their malt is taxed, their sugar, their tea, their soap, and almost every other thing they use or consume, is taxed. But the power-loom is not taxed" (Utz, 2014). Part of the argument here is that, by heavily taxing the basic necessities of subsistence, the minimum cost of labour is thereby driven up. This then makes labour-displacing technology more appealing.

A certain level of income, and distribution, is necessary to sustain an income tax. Economic growth, alone, would not have been a sufficient precondition: had all the economic growth from the First and Second Industrial Revolutions in England gone to the top 1%, income tax would not have been a viable—or reasonable—type of taxation.

---

[16] The Chartists were a movement of British working class citizens arguing for parliamentary and electoral reforms, most well known for demanding enfranchisement.

We do see an increasingly large middle class emerge in Britain over the nineteenth century. The definition of the middle class is contested, but the expansion seems to be from around 5% of the population at the beginning of the 1800s, to approximately 20% by 1909. The Cambridge Population Group has shown that the service sector in England expanded rapidly through the latter half of the nineteenth century, and by the close of the century it employed very nearly as many people as did the manufacturing sector (Wrigley, 2010). A large portion of the domestic workers were employed by the new upper middle class when Lloyd George introduced the "People's Budget." This included a higher tax rate for the highest earners, alongside taxation on the upper middle class, who made up around 10% of the population at the time. It also included a highly contentious tax on land. He declares it a war budget—"This is a war Budget. It is for raising money to wage implacable warfare against poverty and squalidness. I cannot help hoping and believing that before this generation has passed away, we shall have advanced a great step towards that good time, when poverty, and the wretchedness and human degradation which always follows in its camp, will be as remote to the people of this country as the wolves which once infested its forests." In the end, this tax generated the largest amount of money ever raised in a single budget, in either war or peace, in Britain at the time. It marked the beginning of the modern welfare state, and helped to fund pensions and other reforms.

The distribution of incomes amongst citizens will almost necessarily shape the logic of both taxation and redistribution. The relative changes in power between different groups will also likely determine how much power different segments of society have to advocate for their share of the national surplus. Just as the upheavals of the First and Second Industrial Revolutions reshaped taxation systems, the Fourth Industrial Revolution may precipitate a rewriting of the logic that underpins taxation and redistribution. If generative AI is de-skilling, or reduces demand for traditionally skilled workers, governments may face new demands for redistribution, potentially leading to proposals such as Universal Basic Income (UBI), which guarantees a wage in a post-work society. As automation accelerates, traditional wage-based taxation may no longer be as viable, making it essential to explore alternativemodels for sustainable economic redistribution.

Conclusion

The first lesson from history is that we could afford to consider the emerging Fourth Industrial Revolution in more revolutionary terms. Much of today's research is narrowly focused on direct impacts—on the likely impacts to labour markets. However, previous industrial revolutions unfolded on a scale closer to metamorphosis. When shocks to demand for labour are of a sufficient magnitude, they do not remain confined to employment. They spill first into politics, and then the shock waves ripple further, forging institutions and social norms in their wake. In nineteenth century Britain, deep shifts in demand for labour contributed to the development of the formal education system, opened routes to social mobility, drove elements of the demographic transition, and shaped new structures of taxation and redistribution. If generative AI triggers a similarly profound transformation in labour demand it may not merely disrupt employment, but forge new institutions altogether.

If we want to unpack this, let us consider the potential impacts of the value of human labour collapses in upcoming decades. If AI is de-skilling, as emerging evidence suggests, this may make formal education less relevant, at least in terms of accessing employment.[17] Equally, declining demand for skilled labour could be expected to alter established routes into upwards social mobility; access to opportunity has been mediated by education for nearly a century. Access to well-remunerated employment opportunities could then become adjudicated according to other criteria, for example: in terms of social networks, cultural fit, or membership in exclusive groups. Finally, the demographic transition has been shaped to some extent by the costs of education, alongside new opportunities for women in the labour market. Both of those factors could be influenced by the upcoming transition. On the whole, the automation of cognitive work may bring about not only job displacement but an economic and social transformation unlike anything seen since the industrial revolution of the nineteenth century.

The labour market outcomes which will drive political responses are shaped by the extent to which the creation of new jobs keeps pace with the destruction of old jobs. Case studies from history show us that this should be considered on at least three key dimensions: scale, speed, and geography. If job loss occurs on a massive scale, job creation must match it. If new jobs do not emerge at the same magnitude, widespread displacement follows. The speed of adoption also matters: when technologies are introduced gradually, older workers can often "age out" of the workforce without disruption. In this case, younger cohorts bear the brunt of lost opportunities. On the other hand, when adoption is rapid, incumbents are forced out abruptly, with limited time to adapt. Finally,

[17] There are other excellent reasons to have a strong education system. These should potentially be more discussed.

geography determines whether displaced workers can realistically access new jobs. If new opportunities emerge in different locations, workers must be able to migrate, or risk being left behind. This can pose problems when new jobs emerge on the other side of country borders. More attention should be focused on the impact of the labour market shock on the young, and on the shifting geographical distribution of employment opportunities.

Past transformations unfolded over decades, because the adoption of new technologies was gradual. If the adoption of the technologies of the Fourth Industrial Revolution is more rapid, then the impact on labour markets and politics may move quickly. The task of the present day might be to forge institutions under these new pressures, and to do so at speed. If the social sciences are to assist in this transition, additional research will be essential.

When the terrifying possibility of a world without work emerged at the dawn of the era of modern economic growth, it was premature. It was premature, too, when John Maynard Keynes wrote his famous essay, and mused that if man had solved the economic problem, we might have to face our need for identity, meaning, and community without the crutch of forced work. While a world without work has not emerged, fully formed, from any of the previous storms of creative destruction, there has nonetheless been a steady decline in the share of life allocated to labour. In recent decades, we have had so much wealth that we invented childhood and retirement. We extended time spent in full-time education. We blocked off every weekend for leisure, and weeks of holiday time, and (in Europe) a 35-h work week has become the norm.[18] All of this is the result of the ongoing adoption of new labour-saving technologies. It seems possible that this trend will continue, that this next labour-displacing revolution will also result in another ratcheting down of the share of life spent in labour. A world with less work can be liberating, but only if managed by swift, thoughtful, institutional responses.

The revolution poised to unfold in the twenty-first century will be our first attempt at replacing non-routine cognitive labour. It is a shift so dramatic that we will tell our grandchildren one day that we were born before generative AI. The coming Fourth Industrial Revolution may substantially reduce demand for labour, while dramatically increasing overall wealth. What that means will be up to us. It has been before. The last time, we built institutions to share some of the new wealth: through progressive taxation, access to education and

[18]There is substantial variation in the amount of leisure time an individual can expect to have in their life, by place of birth, social class, gender. Leisure is unevenly distributed. Nonetheless, as with wealth, most people have seen more of it over recent decades.

social mobility, labour laws, increased leisure time, pensions, and public health care.

References

Acemoglu, D. (2025). The simple macroeconomics of ai. *Economic Policy, 40*(121), 13–58.

Acemoglu, D., & Johnson, S. (2023). *Power and progress: Our thousand-year struggle over technology and prosperity*. Basic Books.

Acemoglu, D., & Restrepo, P. (2019). Automation and new tasks: How technology displaces and reinstates labor. *Journal of Economic Perspectives, 33*(2), 3–30.

Acemoglu, D., & Restrepo, P. (2022). Tasks, automation, and the rise in U.S. wage inequality. *Econo- metrica, 90*(5), 1973–2016.

Ager, P., Goñi, M., & Salvanes, K. G. (2026). Gender-biased technological change: Milking machines and the exodus of women from farming. *NHH Department of Economics Discussion Paper, 16.*

Aghion, P., Antonin, C., & Bunel, S. (2021). *The power of creative destruction: Economic upheaval and the wealth of nations.* The Belknap Press of Harvard University Press.

Althoff, L., Gray, H. B., & Reichardt, H. (2025). *America's rise in human capital mobility.*

Arntz, M., Gregory, T., and Zierahn, U. (2016). The risk of automation for jobs in OECD countries. *OECD Social, Employment and Migration Working Papers*, (189).

Atkinson, T. (2015). What can be done about inequality? *Juncture, 22*(1), 32–41.

Autor, D. (2022). The labor market impacts of technological change: From unbridled enthusiasm to qualified optimism to vast uncertainty. *NBER Working Papers, 30074.*

Autor, D. (2024). *Applying ai to rebuild middle class jobs.* Technical report, National Bureau of Economic Research.

Autor, D., Mindell, D., & Reynolds, E. (2020). *The work of the future: Building better jobs in an age of intelligent machines.* MIT Work of the Future, Cambridge.

Autor, D., Mindell, D., & Reynolds, E. (2023). *The work of the future. Building better jobs in an age of intelligent machines.* MIT Press.

Autor, D., Chin, C., Salomons, A., & Seegmiller, B. (2024). New frontiers: The origins and content of new work, 1940–2018. *The Quarterly Journal of Economics, 139*(3), 1399–1465.

Baldwin, R. E. (2019). *The globotics upheaval: Globalisation, robotics and the future of work.* W&N.

Becker, G. S. (1960). An economic analysis of fertility. In *Demographic and economic change in developed countries* (pp. 209–240). Columbia University Press.

Berger, T., Karadja, M., and Prawitz, E. (2025). Cities and the rise of working women.

Blaug, M. (1958). The classical economists and the factory acts—A re-examination. *The Quarterly Journal of Economics, 72*(2), 211–226.
Bootle, R. P. (2019). *The A.I. economy: Work, wealth and welfare in the robot age.* Nicholas Brealey Publishing.
Brynjolfsson, E., & McAfee, A. (2014). *The second machine age: Work, progress, and prosperity in a time of brilliant technologies.* W.W. Norton & Company.
Chang, J., & Huynh, P. (2016). *ASEAN in transformation: The future of jobs at risk of automation.* International Labour Organization.
Chetty, R., Grusky, D., Hell, M., Hendren, N., Manduca, R., & Narang, J. (2017). The fading American dream: Trends in absolute income mobility since 1940. *Science, 356*(6336), 398–406.
Churchill, W. (1909). *Trade boards bill debate.* Accessed 17 March 2025.
Clark, G. (2001). *The secret history of the industrial revolution.* Manuscript, University of California, Davis. Available at http://www.econ.ucdavis.edu/gclark
Connor, D. S., Kemeny, T., & Storper, M. (2024). Frontier workers and the seedbeds of inequality and prosperity. *Journal of Economic Geography, 24*(3), 393–414.
Deming, D. J., Ong, C., & Summers, L. H. (2025). *Technological disruption in the labor market.* Technical report, National Bureau of Economic Research.
Ebert, C., Heldring, L., Robinson, J. A., & Vollmer, S. (2024). The breakdown of the English society of orders: The role of the industrial revolution. Presented at the *Inequality and social policy seminar*, Harvard University, September 30, 2024.
Edgerton, D. (2007). *The shock of the old: Technology and global history since 1900.* Oxford University Press.
Feigenbaum, J. & Gross, D. P. (2024). *Automation and the fate of young workers: Evidence from telephone operation in the early 20th century.* NBER Working Papers No. 28061.
Fernihough, A. (2017). Human capital and the quantity–quality trade-off during the demographic transition. *Journal of Economic Growth, 22*(1), 35–65.
Ford, M. (2015). *Rise of the robots: Technology and the threat of a jobless future.* Basic Books.
Frey, C. B. (2019). *The Technology Trap: Capital, Labor, and Power in the Age of Automation.* Princeton University Press.
Frey, C. B., & Osborne, M. A. (2017). The future of employment: How susceptible are jobs to computerisation? *Technological Forecasting and Social Change, 114*, 254–280.
Future of Work Commission, T. W. & Mountfield, H. (2017). *Report of the future of work commission.*
Galor, O. (2011). *Unified growth theory.* Princeton University Press.
Galor, O. (2012). The demographic transition: Causes and consequences. *Cliometrica, 6*(1), 1–28.
Goldin, C. (2024). *Babies and the macroeconomy.* Technical report, National Bureau of Economic Research.

Goldin, C., & Katz, L. F. (2008). *The race between education and technology*. Cambridge.
Goos, M., & Manning, A. (2007). Lousy and lovely jobs: The rising polarization of work in Britain. *The Review of Economics and Statistics, 89*(1), 118–133.
Gottweis, J., Weng, W.-H., Daryin, A., Tu, T., Palepu, A., Sirkovic, P., Myaskovsky, A., Weissenberger, F., Rong, K., Tanno, R., et al. (2025). Towards an ai co-scientist. *arXiv preprint arXiv:2502.18864*.
Grampp, W. D. (1979). The economists and the combination laws. *The Quarterly Journal of Economics, 93*(4), 501–522.
Hanlon, W. W. (2022). *The rise of the engineer: Inventing the professional inventor during the industrial revolution*. Technical report, National Bureau of Economic Research.
Hartog, M., Gomez-Lievano, A., Hausmann, R., & Neffke, F. (2024). *Inventing modern invention: The professionalization of technological progress in the US*. Utrecht University, Human Geography and Planning.
Horn, J. (2005). Machine-breaking in England and France during the age of revolution. *Labour/Le Travail, 55*, 143–166.
Institute for the Future of Work. (2022). *Introducing the Pissarides review into the future of work and wellbeing*. Institute for the Future of Work.
Kastis, Y. and Vipond, H. (2024). *Organizational practices and technology adoption: Evidence from Jewish immigration and the tailoring industry in England*.
Keynes, J. M. (1930). Economic possibilities for our grandchildren. In *Essays in persuasion* (pp. 321–332). Springer.
Kogan, L., Papanikolaou, D., Schmidt, L. D., & Seegmiller, B. (2021). Technology, vintage-specific human capital, and labor displacement: Evidence from linking patents with occupations. *NBER Working Papers*, (29552).
Lafargue, P. (2016). *Le droit 'a la paresse: refutation du droit au travail de 1848*. Collection XIX.
Lee, R. (2002). The demographic transition: Three centuries of fundamental change. *Journal of economic perspectives, 17*(4), 167–190.
Lin, J. (2011). Technological adaptation, cities, and new work. *Review of Economics and Statistics, 93*(2), 554–574.
Lord, C., et al. (2013). *Aristotle's politics*. University of Chicago Press.
Maddison, A. (2003). *The world economy: Historical statistics*. Organisation for Economic Co-operation and Development (OECD).
Madsen, J., & Strulik, H. (2023). Testing unified growth theory: Technological progress and the child quantity-quality tradeoff. *Quantitative Economics, 14*(1), 235–275.
Manyika, J., Lund, S., Chui, M., Bughin, J., Woetzel, J., Batra, P., Ko, R., & Sanghvi, S. (2017). *Jobs lost, jobs gained: Workforce transitions in a time of automation*. McKinsey Global Institute.
Marx, K. (2024). *Capital: Critique of political economy* (Vol. 1). Princeton University Press.

Milanovic, B. (2016). *Global inequality: A new approach for the age of globalization.* Harvard University Press.

Mokyr, J., Vickers, C., & Ziebarth, N. L. (2015). The history of technological anxiety and the future of economic growth: Is this time different? *Journal of Economic Perspectives, 29*(3), 31–50.

Muro, M., Methkupally, S., & Kinder, M. (2024). *The geography of generative ai's workforce impacts will likely differ from those of previous technologies.* Brookings Institution. Accessed: March 10, 2025.

Nagaraj, A., & Ranganathan, A. (2023). *Cutting through the (digital) clutter: Technological change and careers of men and women in cultural markets.* Technical report, Working Paper.

Nori, H., Lee, Y. T., Zhang, S., Carignan, D., Edgar, R., Fusi, N., King, N., Larson, J., Li, Y., Liu, W., et al. (2023). Can generalist foundation models outcompete special-purpose tuning? Case study in medicine. *arXiv preprint arXiv:2311.16452.*

OECD. (2019). *OECD Employment Outlook 2019: The Future of Work.* OECD Publishing.

Pelz, W. A. (2016). *A people's history of modern Europe.* Pluto Press.

Piketty, T. (2014). *Capital in the twenty-first century.* Harvard University Press.

Ricardo, D. (1821). *On the principles of political economy.* J. Murray.

Russell, B. (2017). *In praise of idleness: The classic essay with a new introduction by Bradley Trevor Greive.* Thomas Dunne Books.

Schneider, B. (2026). Technological unemployment in the British industrial revolution: The destruction of hand spinning. *Oxford Economic and Social History Working Papers, 207.*

Schneider, B. and Vipond, H. (2023). The past and future of work: How history can inform the age of automation.

Schumpeter, J. A. (1942). *Capitalism, socialism, and democracy.* Allen Unwin.

Schurer, K., Wakelam, A., & Limited, F. (2024). *Integrated census microdata (i-cem), England and wales, 1921.* Data collection. SN: 9280.

Susskind, D. (2020). *A world without work: Technology, automation and how we should respond.* Allen Lane.

Susskind, D. (2024). *Growth: A history and a reckoning.* Harvard University Press.

Technical Education Matters. (2009). *Chapter 9: The beginning of the 20th century 1900-1921.* Accessed: 2025-03-11.

Thompson, E. P. (2016). *The making of the English working class.* Open Road Media.

UK Parliament. (2024a). *Key dates in 19th century social and economic change.* Accessed: 17 March 2025.

UK Parliament. (2024b). *The 1870 Education Act.* Accessed: 9 March 2025.

United Nations, Department of Economic and Social Affairs, Population Division. (2024). *World population prospects 2024: Key messages.* Accessed: 2024-03-09.

Utz, S. (2014). *Chartism and the Income Tax.* HeinOnline.

Vipond, H. (2026). Technological change and labour displacement in historical perspective. In *Economic history society annual conference.*

Wallis, P. (2025). *The market for skill: Apprenticeship and economic growth in early modern England.* Princeton University Press.

Wilmers, N. (2024). Generative ai and the future of inequality.

Winner, L. (1978). *Autonomous technology: Technics-out-of-control as a theme in political thought.* MIT Press.

World Economic Forum. (2020). *The future of jobs report 2020.* World Economic Forum.

World Economic Forum. (2023). *Future of jobs report 2023.* World Economic Forum.

Wrigley, T. (2010). *The PST system of classifying occupations.*

The Memory Paradox: Why Our Brains Need Knowledge in an Age of AI

Barbara Oakley, Michael Johnston, Ken-Zen Chen, Eulho Jung, and Terrence Sejnowski

Introduction

Educators in recent decades have often championed "learning how to learn" and critical thinking skills over rote knowledge, encapsulated in the refrain: "Why memorize it when you can look it up?" Yet this modern mindset carries a paradox. Just as schools and students began relying on calculators and the Internet, a significant shift occurred. Decades of steadily rising IQ scores—

B. Oakley (✉)
Oakland University, Rochester, MI, USA
e-mail: oakley@oakland.edu

M. Johnston
New Zealand Initiative, Wellington, New Zealand
e-mail: michael.johnston@nzinitiative.org.nz

K.-Z. Chen
National Yang Ming Chiao Tung University, Hsinchu, Taiwan
e-mail: kenzenchen@nycu.edu.tw

E. Jung
Uniformed Service University of the Health Sciences, Bethesda, MD, USA
e-mail: eulho.jung@usuhs.edu

T. Sejnowski
The Salk Institute for Biological Studies, La Jolla, CA, USA
e-mail: terry@snl.salk.edu

M. Rangeley, N. Fairfax (eds.), *The Artificial Intelligence Revolution*,
https://doi.org/10.1007/978-3-032-11814-1_22

the famed Flynn Effect—suddenly leveled off and even began to reverse in several high-income countries. Although IQ is undoubtedly influenced by multiple factors, considerable evidence suggests this educational shift away from explicit content instruction and memorization, combined with increased reliance on external memory aids and continuous digital distractions, has actively contributed to declining cognitive performance. This chapter asks a provocative question: Could our increased reliance on external memory aids and digital distractions be quietly eroding the very cognitive abilities we aim to enhance?

To grapple with this question, we need to reconsider the popular educational practice that treats knowledge as separate from skills. Neuroscience reveals that knowledge and skills are not separate entities but deeply intertwined—two sides of the same coin. Recognizing this relationship helps us see why it's essential to have key information embedded in memory, rather than relying solely on external devices. This chapter explores these intriguing insights and questions, delving into the neuroscience of learning and its implications for education in the digital age.

Emerging research on learning and memory reveals that relying heavily on external aids can hinder deep understanding. Equally problematic, however, are the pedagogical approaches used in tandem with reliance on external aids—that is, constructivist, often coupled with student-centered approaches where the student is expected to discover the insights to be learned. Teachers sometimes interpret these approaches as discouraging clear, explicit explanations and corrections from the teacher. The familiar platitude advises teachers to be a *guide on the side* rather than a *sage on the stage*, but this oversimplifies reality: explicit teaching—clear, structured explanations and thoughtfully guided practice—is often essential to make progress in difficult subjects. Sometimes the *sage on the stage is* invaluable.

While humans naturally acquire certain skills like language and facial recognition without explicit teaching (known as *biologically primary knowledge*), mastering culturally important academic subjects—such as reading, mathematics, or science (*biologically secondary knowledge*)—generally requires deliberate instruction (Sweller, 2008). Our brains simply aren't wired to effortlessly internalize this kind of secondary knowledge—in other words, formally taught academic skills and content—without deliberate practice and repeated retrieval. Excessive cognitive offloading interrupts this necessary internalization, leaving us with superficial schemata—weak mental frameworks that can't adequately support critical thinking or creative problem-solving.

At the heart of effective learning are our brain's dual memory systems: one for explicit facts and concepts we consciously recall (*declarative memory*), and another for skills and routines that become second nature (*procedural memory*). Building genuine expertise often involves moving knowledge from the declarative system to the procedural system—practicing a fact or skill until it embeds deeply in the subconscious circuits that support intuition and fluent thinking. This is why a chess master can instantly recognize strategic patterns, or a novelist effortlessly deploy a rich vocabulary—countless hours of internalizing information have reshaped their neural networks.

Internalized networks form mental structures called schemata, (the plural of "schema") which organize knowledge and facilitate complex thinking. For example, a well-developed schema in mathematics enables intuitive numerical understanding, while in literature, it enhances comprehension of narratives and themes. Schemata gradually develop through active engagement and practice, with each recall strengthening these mental frameworks. Metaphors can enrich schemata by linking unfamiliar concepts to familiar experiences (Lakoff, 2014). However, excessive reliance on external memory aids can prevent this process. Constantly looking things up instead of internalizing them results in shallow schemata, limiting deep understanding and cross-domain thinking. This highlights the paradox: in an age saturated with external information, genuine insight still depends on robust internal knowledge.

This chapter explores *why* storing knowledge in our own memory remains crucial, even (and especially) when technology offers to do the remembering for us. We delve into the science of memory to debunk the false choice between knowledge and skills, showing that a strong memory foundation actually empowers skillful thinking. We draw on neuroscientific evidence about how memory retrieval and practice strengthen learning, and we consider the cognitive consequences when people increasingly "Google it" instead of learning it. The aim is to engage both neuroscientists and educators, as well as interested readers from all backgrounds, in a conversation about the importance of *knowing* in the age of *information*. Ultimately, this is a call for balance—a vision of augmentation without atrophy. We can absolutely embrace smart technologies and abundant information, but we must also keep exercising our biological memory and attention. If we preserve that balance, we won't have to choose between a nimble mind and an encyclopedic one. In a world where we can look up almost everything, the ironic truth is that the knowledge we carry *inside our heads* is more valuable than ever.

This chapter takes a unique perspective by grounding its analysis in the latest neuroscience—illuminating the cognitive underpinnings of effective learning and the subtle ways modern educational trends may inadvertently disrupt them. As we journey deeper, we'll uncover how memory systems and schema formation shape the way we think, reason, and solve problems. Along the way, intriguing parallels between human cognition and contemporary advances in artificial intelligence will emerge, showing us both the promise and peril of integrating digital tools into our cognitive processes. Through these insights, we aim to outline a vision for an education system that cultivates minds capable of both deep understanding and effective use of digital tools.

We will also provide historical context by examining how seminal educational theorists such as Piaget, Vygotsky, Dewey, Montessori, Bruner, and Skinner anticipated—and sometimes fundamentally misunderstood—key principles of learning now clarified by neuroscience. Highlighting both their valuable insights and critical missteps helps explain how persistent misconceptions about learning emerged, even among the most influential educational figures. Their legacies, while groundbreaking, were often double-edged, simultaneously driving innovation and inadvertently creating barriers to more effective educational practices.

Glossary: Key Concepts in Learning and Memory

Cognitive Offloading: Reducing cognitive load by relying on external tools (such as smartphones, calculators, or Internet searches) to store or handle information. While this reduces immediate cognitive effort, excessive offloading can weaken internal memory formation, limiting the development of robust, flexible memory networks.

Declarative Memory System: The brain's system for consciously recalling facts, concepts, and experiences. Primarily involving the hippocampus and medial temporal lobe, this system allows explicit, deliberate retrieval of information.

Engram: The physical trace a memory leaves in your brain, created when groups of neurons strengthen their connections during learning or experience. Engrams physically store your memories and integrate new information into your existing mental frameworks—your schemata.

Interleaving: A learning technique in which practice sessions alternate among related but distinct topics or skills. Interleaving challenges learners to repeatedly distinguish between different memory traces (engrams), strengthening each memory and enhancing the ability to transfer knowledge across contexts.

Neural Manifolds: Patterns of coordinated neural activity among groups of neurons, allowing the brain to efficiently simplify and store complex information. Schemata often correspond to specific neural manifolds, reflecting stable, organized neural activity patterns developed through experience. However, not all manifolds represent schemata; some capture simpler sensory or motor activities without supporting higher-level organization. Unlike an engram—the physical trace a memory leaves in the brain's neural connections—a neural manifold is the dynamic pattern of neural firing that represents or recalls that information.

(continued)

Procedural Memory System: The brain's system for gradually acquiring habits, skills, and routines through repeated practice. Centered mainly in the basal ganglia and related cortical regions, procedural memory supports automatic performance of tasks, often without conscious awareness.

Long-Term Working Memory: A recently proposed form of memory that bridges the gap between short-term working memory (lasting seconds) and long-term memory (lasting days to years). Long-term working memory allows the brain to hold ideas active for minutes or even hours—long enough to integrate and reflect on concepts across extended learning sessions. It is thought to be supported by temporary but longer-lasting changes in synaptic strength, especially through mechanisms like spike-timing-dependent plasticity (STDP). This memory system helps explain how learners can make meaningful connections between ideas presented far apart in time—such as linking concepts from the beginning and end of a long lecture—before those ideas are fully consolidated into long-term memory. Long-term working memory plays a crucial role in real-time understanding, reasoning, and question generation, and helps illustrate why internal memory—even if transient—is essential for deep learning.

Retrieval Practice: Actively recalling information from memory rather than passively reviewing it. Retrieval practice strengthens memory by repeatedly reactivating and reinforcing neural connections (engrams), enhancing long-term retention. Interleaving complements retrieval practice by increasing the challenge of differentiating among related concepts, further solidifying memories.

Schemata: Mental frameworks that organize knowledge into meaningful patterns. (*Schema* is singular and *schemata* is plural.) Schemata contain variables that adapt to different situations and nest hierarchically (smaller schemata within larger ones). Schemata actively generate expectations based on prior knowledge, enabling rapid understanding of new information. Unlike engrams (physical neural traces), schemata are abstract structures that could exist outside the brain—in computer code or written text, for example.

Spaced Repetition/Spaced Retrieval/Spaced Learning: A method of learning that spreads practice sessions out over time, instead of cramming them together. Neuroscience shows this spacing prompts the brain to repeatedly revisit and reinforce the material, making memories clearer, stronger, and longer-lasting.

The Memory Traces: Understanding Engrams

The Physical Nature of Memory

An engram is the physical trace a memory leaves in your brain. When you learn something new or have an experience, groups of neurons activate together, forming stronger connections. These strengthened neural connections form the engram—the biological foundation of memory.

But memories aren't stored like exact files on a computer. Instead, your brain connects each new memory to what you already know, integrating it into your existing mental frameworks—your schemata. Schemata are abstract structures that organize your experiences. For instance, your schema of a "dog" combines common details (four-legged, furry, barks) from many past encounters.

When you remember something, you don't simply replay an exact recording of the event. Instead, you reconstruct the memory, filling in missing details using your schemata. This is why your memories are flexible, efficient, and occasionally prone to errors. Put simply, schemata represent what you know, and engrams represent how your brain physically stores and retrieves that knowledge. While schemata can exist in many forms—including computer code or written text—the term "engram" specifically refers to biological memory traces in your brain (Guskjolen & Cembrowski, 2023).

Think of an engram as a neural "imprint" left by what you've learned. When you commit something to memory—whether it's a mathematical fact like $4 \times 7 = 28$ or a vivid personal event—specific neurons fire together, strengthening their connections and creating a distinctive network. This network becomes the physical trace of that memory, lasting long after initial learning (Fig. 1).

Encoding and Retrieval Mechanisms

The way engrams function reveals much about how memory works. Research confirms the *encoding specificity principle*—memory retrieval works best when current conditions match those present during learning. This explains why returning to a place where you first learned something can suddenly trigger vivid recollections; the environmental cues reactivate the associated engram. A related phenomenon is context-dependent learning: if you encode information while drunk, for example, you can recall it better when drunk than when sober. This phenomenon demonstrates how context affects memory retrieval—though it's not a strategy educators would recommend adopting.

During successful memory recall, the same neurons that fired during the original learning experience become active again. What's striking is that activating just a small subset of these engram neurons can trigger the entire memory network through "pattern completion." This neural cascade effect allows complete memory retrieval from partial cues, demonstrating the interconnected nature of memory representations.

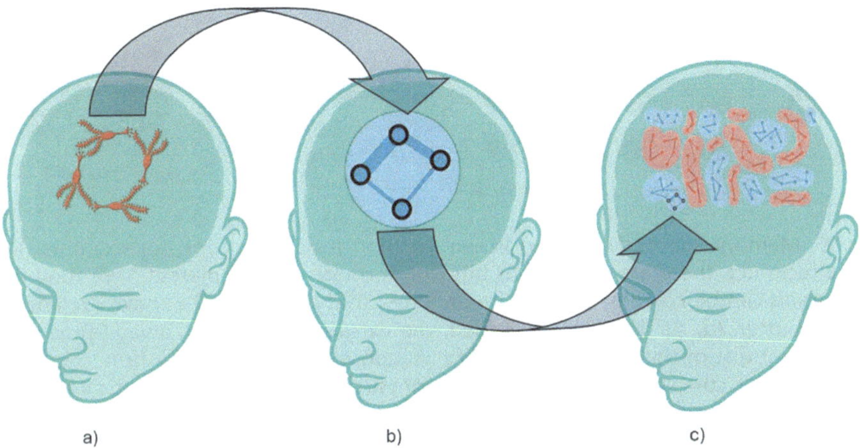

Fig. 1 Engrams and schemata (**a**) A simplistic representation of the connected neurons of a memory (an "engram"). (**b**) The connected cluster of neurons of an engram is typically shown by dots and lines. Although only four "neurons" are shown here, this engram representation actually represents clusters of neurons scattered around the brain which activate together when we retrieve that engram from memory. (**c**) Schemata organize memory by providing abstract frameworks that can activate relevant engrams. Here, we show declarative engrams in blue and procedural engrams in orange, both organized within larger schema structures. Unlike engrams (physical neural traces), schemata represent the patterns of organization themselves. More about this in Sect. 3

But note that a cue about where to find a memory is quite different than a cue that activates the memory itself. For instance, a student remembering that they can ask an AI to explain photosynthesis doesn't activate the same neural networks as actually remembering how plants convert sunlight into energy. This distinction between memory pointers and actual knowledge represents a core theme of this chapter that we'll return to: the difference between knowing *where to find* information versus *truly incorporating that information into our internal schemata and neural architecture.*

The brain also employs a performance-enhancing mechanism: when you successfully retrieve a memory, the engram neurons temporarily become more excitable. This heightened state can last for hours, making subsequent retrievals easier and more accurate. This post-retrieval excitability directly affects memory performance and provides a neural basis for why spaced retrieval is so effective (Pignatelli et al., 2019; Carpenter et al., 2022).

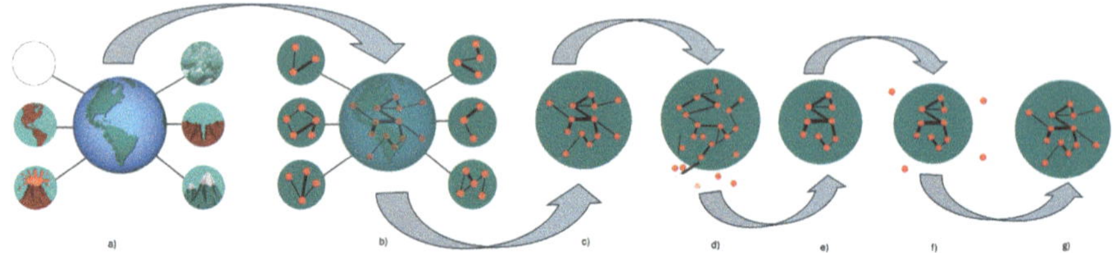

Fig. 2 Memory consolidation. (**a**) When learning a new concept, for example, like plate tectonics, there are extraneous bits of information, like "plates" have food and mountains can be cold. (**b**) and (**c**) The first links that come together have extraneous neural clutter. (**d**) As the concept is used, the extraneous links fall away (**e**) to leave the elegant gist of the concept. (**f**) and (**g**) As consolidation processes firm into place, links to other concepts can form, like the physics of friction, mathematical rates of movement, or social shifts. These interconnections not only enrich understanding but also create cognitive scaffolding that facilitates faster learning of related concepts and more creative problem-solving in novel situations. This process exemplifies how schemata become tuned and integrated into larger knowledge networks

Memory Consolidation Processes

This brings us to the process of memory consolidation—how memories stabilize over time (see Fig. 2). Consolidation involves two distinct but related processes occurring at different levels. Synaptic consolidation refers to the post-encoding transformation of information into a long-term form at local synaptic and cellular nodes in the neural circuit that encodes the memory. During this process, connections between neurons are both strengthened and pruned, creating a more efficient memory trace. Synaptic consolidation is traditionally assumed to draw to a close within hours of its initiation. Systems consolidation, on the other hand, refers to the post-encoding reorganization of memory representations over distributed brain circuits. It involves recurrent waves of synaptic consolidation in new brain regions as the memory representation gradually spreads beyond its original location. During sleep, particularly slow-wave sleep (SWS), the hippocampus 'replays' memory activity patterns, facilitating the gradual transfer of memories to distributed cortical networks. Systems consolidation may last days to months and even years, depending on the memory system and the task (Dudai et al., 2015).

Recent research reveals a selective mechanism for memory consolidation. Our brains don't preserve all experiences equally—they actively select which memories to strengthen. During moments when we encounter novelty or surprise, process rewards, or complete learning tasks, the hippocampus generates sharp wave ripples (SPW-Rs) that replay and tag significant experiences. These tagged experiences are then preferentially replayed during sleep, creating a direct pathway from rewarding experience to lasting memory (Yang et al., 2024).

This mechanism has been directly observed in studies with mice. During momentary pauses in exploration—particularly at reward locations—the hippocampus shifts from theta rhythms to generating sharp wave ripples (SPW-Rs) that replay recent experiences. Similar ripple activity occurs in the human hippocampus during periods of quiet wakefulness and rest. This suggests that moments of reflection after completing a task or receiving feedback may enhance memory through similar neural tagging mechanisms, influencing which experiences our brains select for long-term storage.

For humans, this has important implications for learning practices. When we immediately reach for our phones after completing a learning task or solving a problem, we may be disrupting this critical neural tagging process. Instead, brief periods of undistracted reflection after learning could provide a neurophysiological window when memories are specially marked for preservation. This may explain why information processed during focused attention tends to be better remembered than information encountered during distracted states, and suggests that intentional pauses for reflection—rather than digital distraction—could significantly enhance our ability to consolidate important experiences into lasting memories.

When you actively retrieve a memory, you're not just accessing it, but rather are actively reinforcing the engram by engaging the entire neural network. This strengthens connections throughout the engram and begins linking to other concepts—a process far more helpful for learning than simply rereading or passively reviewing the material (Wamsley, 2019).

As memories consolidate, they can undergo important transitions in how they're stored and accessed in the brain. With repeated use and retrieval practice, initially consciously recalled information can become more automatic and intuitive. This often involves a transition between the brain's two memory systems, and is crucial for developing expertise.

Declarative vs. Procedural Memory: Two Learning Systems

Understanding the Two Memory Systems

The human brain has two major learning and memory systems that work in parallel: one for facts and events (*declarative memory*) and one for skills and habits (*procedural memory*) (Fig. 3). These rely on distinct neural circuits—

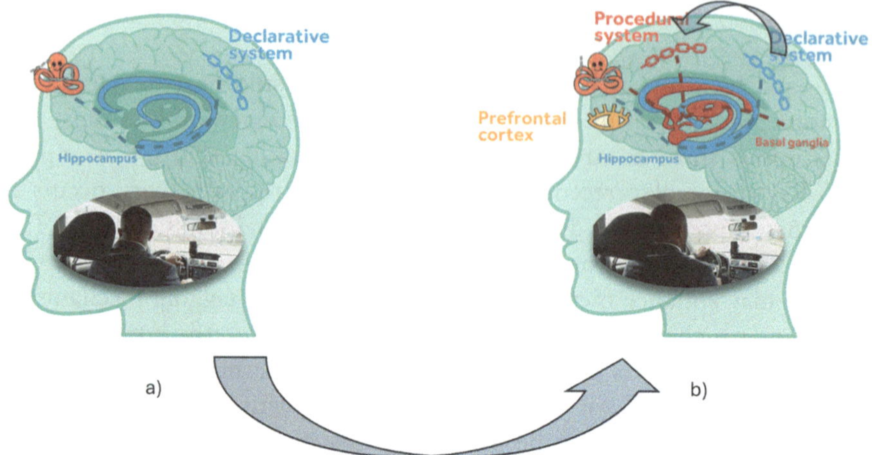

Fig. 3 The declarative and procedural learning systems. (**a**) The declarative pathway takes information from working memory (symbolized by the four-armed octopus), and moves it into links in long-term memory through the hippocampus (Cowan et al., 2020). When you might first learn the route to take to drive home, you are using your declarative learning pathways as you focus on following the directions. (**b**) As you repeatedly drive home over the same route, a part of the prefrontal cortex toward the front of the brain is "watching." If your prefrontal cortex sees that you're driving the same route home day after day, it eventually creates procedural, habitual links in long-term memory

roughly speaking, the hippocampus and related medial temporal lobe structures support declarative memory, whereas the basal ganglia[1] (especially the striatum) and frontal cortex support procedural memory. From an evolutionary perspective, the declarative system, which is accessible to our conscious thoughts, is believed to have developed more recently, while the procedural system, which we're not conscious of, is much older (Ten Berge & Van Hezewijk, 1999). The basal ganglia's structures, in fact, appeared early in vertebrate evolution and have been highly conserved, suggesting they serve essential functions.

A rough way to feel the difference between these two systems is to compare your conscious, step-by-step working through a math problem (*declarative*) with your repeated attempts to learn to hit a baseball (*procedural*). In this latter case, you are only conscious of whether you hit the ball, but *not* how your procedural system is learning to hit the ball. Understanding the difference between the declarative and procedural systems is key to appreciating why

[1]The cerebellum and other structures are involved as well, but let's not go there in this discussion.

certain knowledge (like multiplication tables or vocabulary) needs to be *stored in the brain* through practice, rather than constantly outsourced, for genuine intuition and fluency to develop (Morgan-Short & Ullman, 2022).

The Declarative Learning Pathway

Declarative memory, as we had mentioned, is the system for consciously accessible knowledge—the things we can deliberately recall and state. It includes semantic memory (general knowledge and facts) and episodic memory (personal experiences). Compared to the procedural system, the declarative system learns information relatively rapidly. For example, you can hear a historical fact or a definition a single time and potentially remember it. The trade-off for this relatively quick learning is the counterintuitive fact that declarative recall can be slower and more effortful than procedural recall. Learning something new through the declarative system depends critically on the hippocampus. This structure helps bind together the elements of new information and consolidate it into long-term memory. If the hippocampal system is damaged, as when a person develops Alzheimer's, it becomes difficult or impossible to learn new information.

An important feature of declarative memory is that it's flexible: you can apply a fact learned in one context to a different context, or combine bits of knowledge in novel ways. This flexibility underpins complex reasoning and problem-solving, but it also means declarative recall tends to require conscious attention. For instance, if you've learned a formula but not practiced it much, you must deliberately recall each step to apply it. Explicit instruction—for example, a typical "talk and chalk" lecture feeds information to students through their declarative pathways.

The Procedural Learning Pathway

Procedural memory, by contrast, is the system for acquiring sequences and routines that operate at an intuitive, automatic level. Riding a bicycle, playing a musical instrument, speaking grammatically in your native language, effortlessly recalling a well-practiced phrase like "Yo hablo Español," or performing mental arithmetic with ease are all supported by procedural learning. It's generally hard for us to verbalize this kind of implicit learning—you can't easily explain the muscle movements of riding a bike, the finger movements of a piano scale, or even the mental steps to reduce a fraction.

Procedural learning is typically slower to acquire and requires repetition and deliberate practice—but once learned, the skills can be executed rapidly and with little conscious effort. In the brain, procedural memory is rooted in circuits linking the cortex, basal ganglia, and cerebellum. As control shifts to more automated motor or premotor circuits, the task becomes ingrained "in the fingers" or in whatever neural substrates handle the routine. At that stage, performing the skill, task, or thought feels almost effortless—one might term it "second nature."

From Autopilot to Insight: Reimagining the Basal Ganglia

For decades, neuroscientists viewed the basal ganglia simply as the brain's center for habitual learning—helping us ride bikes or type without conscious thought. Recent research reveals a far richer picture.

Neuroimaging now shows these neural structures underpin our ability to recognize complex patterns across diverse domains. In language, the basal ganglia activate during intricate grammatical parsing, regardless of whether language is spoken or signed. Activity increases with linguistic complexity, suggesting these regions actively decode and predict grammatical patterns (Moreno et al., 2018).

Similarly, in mathematics, the basal ganglia extend beyond storing arithmetic facts to recognizing mathematical patterns that enable intuitive leaps. Patients with basal ganglia impairments struggle specifically with multistep procedures, highlighting these structures' role in intuitively applying mathematical concepts rather than merely recalling isolated facts (Saban et al., 2024).

This sophisticated functionality extends to general cognition as well. Structures like the caudate nucleus activate strongly during moments of sudden insight—those "Aha!" experiences that mark creative breakthroughs. This suggests the basal ganglia help us break from habitual thinking to form novel connections between ideas (Tik et al., 2018).

The basal ganglia serve not merely as repositories for practiced routines but as essential components in our ability to detect, learn from, and intuitively apply complex patterns. This expanded understanding helps explain how deep expertise and fluent intuition emerge from what initially appears to be simple repetitive practice.

Interestingly, such deep intuitive learning parallels a phenomenon in artificial intelligence called "grokking." In grokking, AI models seem initially stuck during repetitive training, only to suddenly exhibit dramatic improvements in their ability to generalize—long after mastering the training data. Previously, this extended training was viewed negatively as "overfitting" or "overtraining," similar to what educators have traditionally criticized as "overlearning." However, grokking reveals that repetitive practice may quietly set the stage for profound cognitive breakthroughs, transforming habitual routines into deeper intuitive understanding (Power et al., 2022).

Complementary Systems: How They Work Together

Why do we have these two systems? They complement and sometimes even duplicate one another—providing richer ways for the brain to work with information.

With repeated use, memories evolve within the brain's architecture. New declarative memories—facts, events, and explicit knowledge like vocabulary words, historical dates, or scientific formulas—begin their life dependent on the hippocampus, with all its rich contextual detail. In contrast, procedural memories, like learning to kick a soccer ball or type without looking at the keyboard, initially form through neural pathways largely involving the basal ganglia.

Recent neuroscience research clarifies why spaced learning is so powerful in this process. When you first learn something declaratively, your hippocampus rapidly encodes a temporary explicit memory by linking together neurons across the cerebral cortex. As we retrieve these declarative memories repeatedly over spaced intervals, something transformative happens: these cortical connections strengthen, enabling the memories to eventually become stable and independent of the hippocampus. This is the critical transition point—these stabilized cortical memories now serve as clear blueprints that allow deeper brain structures—especially the basal ganglia—to gradually automate the knowledge. The hippocampus gradually releases its hold as the basal ganglia take greater responsibility for these memories. This shift has been directly observed—as memories mature, activity decreases in the hippocampus while increasing in the striatum, a key structure of the basal ganglia. After this proceduralization by the basal ganglia, knowledge that was once explicit and deliberate becomes implicit, automatic, and intuitive (Goldfarb et al., 2016; Narasimhalu et al., 2012; Buch et al., 2021; Thompson et al., 2024; Yang et al., 2025a).

Declarative memory is like a fast-learning, but somewhat slow-operating, notebook—flexible, but not optimized for speed during retrieval. Procedural memory is like a subroutine that, once trained, runs blazingly fast and automatically. Both physical skills (like playing an instrument) and mental tasks (like solving equations) follow this pattern: practice transforms explicit declarative knowledge into automatic procedural memory while preserving the original declarative engram. This dual access allows us to think flexibly while acting intuitively (Packard & Knowlton, 2002).

Practically, this means that in many learning domains, *both* systems are involved. This interplay between systems explains the artificial divide between "knowledge" and "skills" we mentioned earlier. Take multiplication as an example: when a child is learning the multiplication table, at first she may rely on declarative memory (memorizing that 4 x 3 = 12). With repeated practice, the relationship $4 \times 3 = 12$ becomes a quick rote response—it transforms into a procedural memory, something she *just knows* without having to think about it. If she might see $\frac{12}{3}$, she can much more easily "feel" that it is equivalent to 4. If she never memorizes the multiplication tables and instead presses 4 x 3 on her calculator, externalizing the operation each time she does it, she develops no internal feel for the relationships between 4, 3, and 12. Even simply trying to reduce a fraction leaves her stuck with slower, conscious, declarative processing, which burdens her working memory during complex tasks.

The difference between declarative versus procedural recall of information is one we all experience: the struggle of recalling newly learned information compared to the effortless way we access deeply familiar knowledge. This process feels different because it is different—access has largely moved from a system requiring conscious effort to one that works with automatic precision. Our most treasured knowledge thus migrates from conscious deliberation to intuitive understanding—a neural efficiency that serves us well in tasks requiring speed and fluency. A challenge in learning is that when children are young, the procedural system is the stronger of the two—it's what allows us to pick up the intuitive patterns of our native language. But as children mature, their working memory capacities increase and the declarative system comes to the fore. Thus, methods effective for teaching young children—such as hands-on manipulatives and learning through experience—do not work as well for older students who need more explicit instruction to master biologically secondary academic material. In other words, as children mature and tackle advanced subjects, they require clearer guidance and practice to learn efficiently.

The Consequences of Offloading

What happens if we shortcut the shift from declarative to procedural memory-making by instead using an external device? Simply put, if a learner leans too heavily on external aids, the "proceduralization" of knowledge may never fully occur. A student who always uses a calculator for basic arithmetic, for instance, might pass tests, but she may not develop the same number sense and intuition as one who has internalized those operations. The latter student, having memorized math facts and practiced operations, can *recognize patterns* (e.g., spotting that $12 \times 100 = 1200$) and estimate or manipulate numbers with confidence. The former student might solve every problem by brute force lookup or computation, never quite forming an intuitive grasp—the kind of intuition that often leads to creative problem-solving or spotting errors at a glance.

Without practice, the basal ganglia circuits don't get the training trials needed to optimize the skill. The result is a learner who remains reliant on conscious, declarative processing (or worse, on the tool itself) for tasks that could have become automatic. This not only makes the tasks slower; it also chokes off higher-order cognition, because the person's working memory is consumed by basics. Cognitive load theory tells us that when lower-level elements of a task are automated, working memory is freed to focus on complex aspects. For example, solving a physics problem is immensely easier if the algebra steps are second nature; one can devote thought to the physics concepts instead of getting lost in algebraic manipulations.

Recent neuroscience research has shown that under specific conditions, procedural memory engrams can form rapidly—within hours rather than weeks or months. This can happen when new information connects to deeply internalized prior knowledge (as opposed to knowledge arising from just knowing where to find information). Prior knowledge helps memories stabilize quickly in cortical networks with less hippocampal involvement—an insight that underscores the distinction between internally stored knowledge and mere awareness of external information sources (Hebscher et al., 2019).

Recent research also suggests that the brain may use a kind of "synaptic handwriting"—temporary but longer-lasting changes in the strength of connections between neurons—to hold ideas in mind for minutes or even hours. This mechanism, known as spike-timing-dependent plasticity, was once thought to support only long-term memory. But new findings suggest it may also underlie what some researchers call long-term working memory—a bridge between short-term recall and lasting storage that helps us keep information mentally available during extended periods of thought. This may explain how a student, near the end of a 90-min lecture, can ask a thoughtful question that links ideas introduced much earlier in the session—even though none of those ideas have yet been committed to long-term memory. It's a powerful reminder that internal memory—even if fleeting—is what allows us to make real-time connections and insights. In contrast, simply looking something up may retrieve a fact, but it doesn't create this temporary mental workspace or support the flexible integration that deep learning depends on (Sejnowski, 2025).

In short, internalizing foundational knowledge—both facts and procedures—is what allows the mind to synthesize and create. Overreliance on external memory can leave one with a collection of correct outputs (answers obtained from tools) but without the integrated *understanding* or procedural fluency that marks true expertise. As the brain's two learning systems demonstrate, deep learning is a matter of training the brain as much as informing the brain. If we neglect that training by continually outsourcing, we risk shallow competence. The next section will delve more into how the brain organizes learned knowledge into efficient structures (schemata and neural representations), and how failing to internalize knowledge may disrupt these structures.

Learning by Reward: How Reinforcement Principles Illuminate Human Memory Formation

Computer scientists Richard Sutton and Andrew Barto revolutionized our understanding of learning through their reinforcement learning framework. Though originally developed for artificial intelligence, their work directly models how human brains learn through experience and feedback. Research has confirmed that human learning employs remarkably similar reinforcement mechanisms, with neural circuits that evaluate outcomes and strengthen successful behaviors. This evidence contradicts the popular but misguided educational notion that unguided discovery learning is optimal for academic subjects, and instead demonstrates why structured, repeated practice with clear feedback is essential for strengthening neural pathways (Sutton & Barto, 2018).

The central insight that applies directly to human memory formation is the concept of prediction error—the gap between what we expect and what actually happens. In reinforcement learning algorithms, this prediction error signal drives learning by updating the system's knowledge. Remarkably, neuroscience discovered that the brain's dopamine system operates on precisely this principle. When something good happens unexpectedly, dopamine neurons fire briskly; when an expected reward fails to appear, they pause. This dopamine response creates what neuroscientists call "eligibility traces"—temporary tags in neural pathways that mark connections for strengthening, essentially implementing nature's version of reinforcement learning algorithms (Sutton, 1988; Nasser et al., 2017; Shouval & Kirkwood, 2025) (Fig. 4).

This framework directly illuminates how our brains form and refine schemata—the mental frameworks discussed throughout this chapter. As we practice a task under structured conditions with appropriate feedback, reward-driven mechanisms gradually build internal models of what works (Bein & Niv, 2025). Over time, the brain compresses these experiences into streamlined

(continued)

representations, just as AI systems distill countless trials into efficient response patterns.

In neuroscience, these efficient representations are called neural manifolds—patterns of neural activity that capture the essence of repeated behaviors or concepts while dramatically reducing complexity. Think of them as the brain's way of creating simplified "neural shadows" that preserve essential relationships while filtering out enormous amounts of noise. Through reinforcement-like feedback, our brains sculpt these manifolds so that common situations can be recognized and responded to with minimal effort. Similarly, artificial systems trained with reinforcement learning principles compress extensive training experiences into compact computational representations, allowing for rapid responses without exhaustive processing. In both cases, learning optimizes for efficiency: redundant details are pruned away and useful patterns are reinforced (Pao et al., 2021).

This convergence between human memory and artificial learning systems reveals a profound insight: prediction errors drive learning across both domains. This parallel explains why knowledge internalized in memory enables far more efficient learning than constant cognitive offloading to external devices. When we consistently outsource thinking to technology, we effectively bypass our brain's natural reinforcement learning mechanisms—the very pathways that build and strengthen neural manifolds supporting sophisticated thinking. These findings also contradict popular notions of unstructured discovery learning, demonstrating instead that developing expertise requires structured practice with clear, timely feedback that allows our reinforcement mechanisms to optimize neural representations (Sejnowski, 2024).

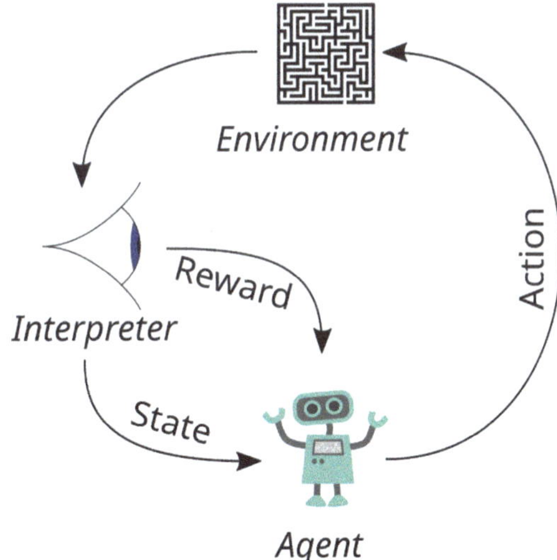

Fig. 4 In reinforcement learning, an agent takes actions in an environment. The environment returns feedback in the form of a reward and an updated representation of the agent's state, which is fed back to guide future actions (Public domain, 2017)

The Important Role of Prediction Errors

Prediction Errors: The Brain's Learning Signal

Imagine you're quickly typing a familiar calculation into a calculator—perhaps you're multiplying 5 × 10. Instead of the expected "50," the calculator suddenly displays "500." Instantly, you sense something is wrong (Fig. 5). This immediate feeling of surprise isn't just confusion; it's your brain's way of signaling a prediction error—the mismatch between what your brain expected and what actually happened.

The Neuroscience of Surprise

At a deeper neurological level, this feeling of surprise is orchestrated by neurotransmitters like dopamine and norepinephrine. Dopamine neurons, especially in areas like the ventral tegmental area, act as the brain's internal learning signal. They spring into action whenever outcomes don't align

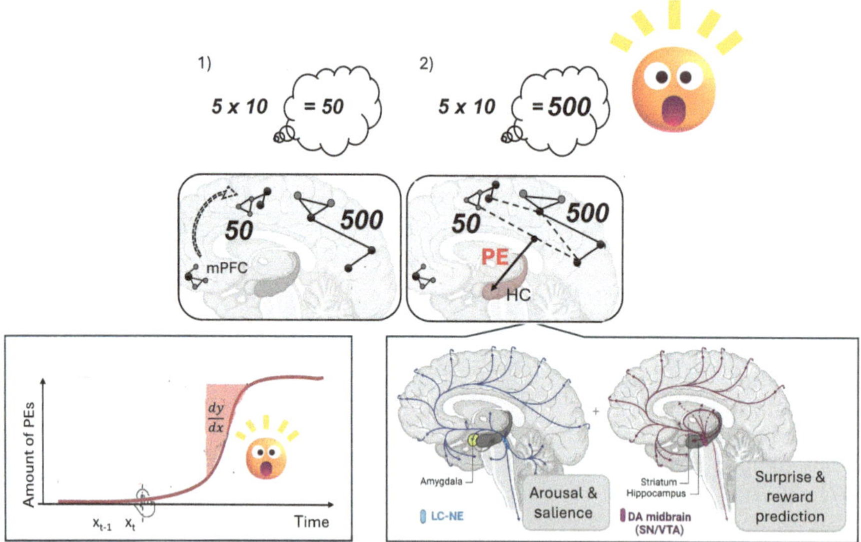

Fig. 5 The neural basis of prediction errors. When an expected outcome differs from the actual result, dopamine neurons release neurotransmitters that tag recently active neural connections. These tags, called "eligibility traces," mark specific connections for strengthening, allowing the brain to update its internal models and form new memories based on the error. (Adapted from Becker & Cabeza, 2025)

with our internal predictions, creating what neuroscientists call "eligibility traces"—temporary tags in active neural connections that mark them for change—either reinforcing or weakening. (This echoes Jean Piaget's insight from the early 1900s regarding *cognitive disequilibrium.*[2]) Meanwhile, norepinephrine serves as a kind of mental alarm bell, quickly enhancing alertness and sharpening focus. Together, these processes help your brain recognize, process, and learn from errors.

These fundamental learning mechanisms work not just for dramatic insights but for all feedback-based learning, from formal education to Kahoot! (flashcard) exercises. (This validates B. F. Skinner's emphasis on reinforcement and feedback in learning.) Negative experiences also powerfully shape learning. Even a single painful or unpleasant event can quickly teach us to avoid making the same mistake again—as with the hot stove example mentioned in Fig. 4 (Wimmer & Büchel, 2021).

The Necessity of Internal Knowledge

Yet there's a crucial catch: the powerful error-detection system depends on having strong internal expectations—built through memorization and repeated practice. Consider multiplication tables: a nursing student who memorized these facts as a youngster has created her own internal "schema," mental frameworks that reliably predict correct answers. When an incorrect answer pops up, her brain instantly notices something is amiss, activating the alert system and facilitating immediate correction and learning.

By contrast, students who rely entirely on calculators never fully build these strong internal schemata. When confronted with the same incorrect result, there's no mismatch, because without knowledge of the multiplication tables, there's no prediction being made. These students might accept the wrong answer at face value without realizing it's an error. The result? A nurse with no internalized multiplication tables can enter a wrong number in the calculator, and then be oblivious to the fact that the resulting medication she is dispensing is an order of magnitude larger than it should have been.

[2]Cognitive disequilibrium includes: *Assimilation*: fitting new information into existing mental frameworks (e.g., kids calling a penguin a bird), and *accommodation*: requires modifying those frameworks when information doesn't fit (e.g., realizing penguins can't fly)—concepts Piaget (1936) pioneered that remain fundamental to learning theories, though he didn't use "schema" in its modern sense.

Prediction Errors and Learning Mechanisms

Without internally stored knowledge, our brain's natural learning mechanisms remain largely unused. Every effective learning technique—whether retrieval practice, spaced repetition, or deliberate practice—works precisely because it engages this prediction-error system. When we outsource memory to devices rather than building internal knowledge, we're not just changing where information is stored; we're bypassing the very neural mechanisms that evolved to help us learn.

In short, internalized knowledge creates the mental frameworks our brains need to spot mistakes quickly and learn from them effectively. These error signals do double-duty: they not only help us correct mistakes but also train our attention toward what's important in different contexts, helping build the schemata we need for quick thinking. Each prediction error, each moment of surprise, thus becomes an opportunity for cognitive growth—but only if our minds are equipped with clear expectations formed through practice and memorization (Bein & Niv, 2025).

So, what is a schema?

Schemata, Neural Manifolds, and Cognitive Efficiency

Foundational Concepts: Schemata and Mental Frameworks

The brain doesn't store knowledge as isolated facts but organizes related information into schemata—active computational structures that both represent knowledge and contain information about how that knowledge should be used. A schema is not merely a passive framework but a recognition device that evaluates its "goodness of fit" to incoming data. While engrams are the physical imprints of memory in neural tissue, schemata are the abstract knowledge structures they represent. In other words, schemata are what we know, while engrams are how our brains physically store this knowledge. A schema is the organized pattern of information itself—one that could, in principle, exist in any medium, from neurons to computer code.

Schemata have several key characteristics: they contain variables with constraints that define typical values and relationships; they can embed within one another hierarchically; and they function across all levels of abstraction, from sensory patterns to abstract concepts. When we encounter new information, schemata not only help us interpret it but also generate expectations about unobserved aspects—providing default values that guide inference and prediction.

Cowan (2014) describes working memory as the "cauldron" of schema formation, where new concepts are born by simultaneously holding and binding together multiple elements of information. Experiments demonstrate that information must be simultaneously present in working memory for meaningful associations—and thus schemata—to form. If too much information is presented or externalized so that it cannot be concurrently maintained in working memory, meaningful connections and robust schema formation are impaired.

You can think of schemata as similar to organizing shelves in a closet, grouping related items neatly together. A schema for "restaurant," for example, includes a sequence of events (enter, get seated, read menu, order, eat, pay, exit) and expectations about roles (waiter, customer, chef) and objects. Schemata allow us to encode and retrieve information efficiently: instead of remembering every tiny detail as separate bits, we remember a unified structure with slots that can be filled in. New information that fits a schema is learned more easily, and remembering one part of a schema can cue the rest. Recent research confirms that activating schemata actively shapes memory, attention, and how we segment experiences into meaningful events (De Soares et al., 2024; Wickelgren, 2025).

In problem-solving, invoking the right schema can guide you to a solution by analogy or pattern recognition. Importantly, schemata are not innate—they are learned and refined with experience, which means they depend on memory of past instances. As schemata become richer, they allow quicker learning and better recall of new information. The formation of schemata is a hallmark of expertise. A master chess player, for instance, has schemata for typical piece configurations and strategies, allowing them to remember positions and foresee outcomes far better than a novice (the novice lacks those organized patterns in memory).

Neural Basis of Knowledge Organization

Immanuel Kant (1724–1804) introduced the concept of *schemata* in *Critique of Pure Reason* (1781) as part of his effort to reconcile two opposing philosophical traditions: *empiricism*, which holds that knowledge arises from sensory experience, and *rationalism*, which claims that some knowledge originates in the mind itself. Kant argued that while we receive information through the senses, we also use built-in mental categories—such as space, time, and causality—to organize it. *Schemata*, in his account, are mental procedures that allow these abstract categories to be applied to concrete experience—helping us, for example, perceive events not just as isolated flashes but as unfolding in time and governed by cause and effect. Over a century later, Jean Piaget reimagined a similar concept in psychology. He used the term *schemas* (the more common plural in modern psychology) to describe cognitive structures that children actively construct and adapt as they interact with the world. While Piaget's usage emerged independently of Kant's, both perspectives highlight the same essential insight: understanding depends on internal mental frameworks that bridge abstract concepts and lived experience (Kant, 1781; Piaget, 1970).

Neuroscientific research nowadays indicates that schemata may have a physical basis in the brain's information storage patterns. As we learn, groups of neurons that frequently activate together begin to represent high-level concepts, creating what some neuroscientists call neural manifolds or low-dimensional representations within neural activity (Langdon et al., 2023). A neural manifold refers to the finding that neural firing patterns for related experiences often occupy a structured, smaller subspace of all possible activity patterns rather than being randomly distributed. Put more simply, a *manifold* is just a fancy word for an organized pattern in neural firing.

Think of neural manifolds as the brain creating simplified 'movies' of our experiences. Just as filmmakers create animations that capture complex movements with just the essential elements—preserving what matters while dropping unnecessary details—neural manifolds track essential patterns in brain activity as experiences unfold. This compression of neural information helps your brain efficiently categorize and connect similar experiences. For example, when you recall different restaurant visits, consistent neural patterns activate in your medial prefrontal cortex and hippocampus, regardless of which specific restaurant you're remembering. These streamlined neural patterns form the foundation of your "restaurant schema," a mental shorthand that helps you navigate dining experiences without processing every detail from scratch (Fig. 6).

This dynamic transformation of memory—from richly detailed to more abstract and generalized—appears to sweep forward along the brain's architecture. Robin and Moscovitch describe this as a continuum of representation: initial memories are grounded in detailed perceptual features supported by posterior regions of the hippocampus and sensory cortices (Robin & Moscovitch, 2017). As the memory becomes more generalized and gist-like, activity shifts toward the anterior hippocampus. With continued use, abstraction, and

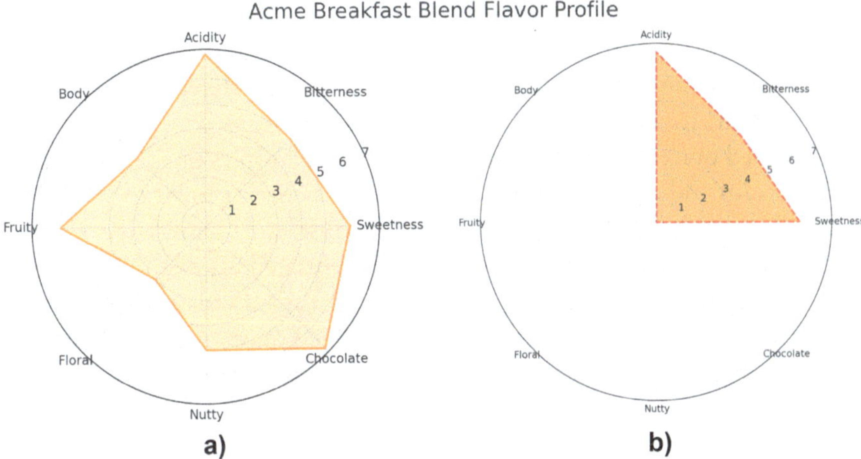

Fig. 6 Dimensionality reduction. (**a**) The different tastes of coffee can be thought of as "dimensions"—this Acme blend has eight dimensions, astronomically simpler than neural information in the brain, which spans hundreds of trillions of synapses (more connections than stars in the Milky Way galaxy). (**b**) Dimensionality reduction simplifies complexity by focusing on only essential features—here, just acidity, bitterness, and sweetness. Our brain performs inconceivably greater compression, creating "neural shadows" that distill this vast complexity into manageable representations, preserving essential patterns while filtering out enormous amounts of noise

integration across experiences, these representations are increasingly supported by the ventromedial prefrontal cortex, where schematic knowledge is stored. Rather than replacing one another, these forms of memory coexist, allowing the brain to flexibly access different levels of representation depending on the situation. This back-to-front sweep—from raw perceptual input to generalized knowledge—parallels the progression described in Global Workspace Theory, in which specialized modules feed information forward to more central, integrative hubs that coordinate task-relevant cognition (VanRullen & Kanai, 2021).

From a neural manifolds perspective, this transformation involves progressive dimensional reduction—detailed memories preserve specific perceptual features, gists distill essential elements of single episodes, and schemata form compressed representations that capture regularities across multiple experiences (Fig. 6). Langdon and colleagues suggest these patterns aren't merely statistical abstractions but reflect the physical structure of neural circuits.

The transformation of scattered, high-dimensional neural activity into these efficient, lower-dimensional manifolds happens gradually through learning and practice. As we repeatedly engage with related concepts, our neural activity becomes more organized, converging on optimized pathways that require less cognitive effort. This efficiency explains why experts can process information in their domain more quickly than novices—their brains have developed well-defined neural circuits for familiar concepts.

Interleaved practice—mixing different yet related topics or skills in a learning session instead of tackling one at a time—has been shown to strengthen long-term retention and yield more flexible, transferable knowledge. By forcing the brain to continually retrieve and differentiate between multiple concepts, this approach reinforces the distinct neural manifolds underlying each skill. Intriguingly, artificial neural networks trained on interleaved tasks show a similar advantage: they consolidate skills more robustly and forget less. This parallel underscores that both the human brain and artificial neural networks benefit from interleaved training (Buzsaki et al., 2022; Foster et al., 2019; Carvalho & Goldstone, 2019; Mayo et al., 2023).

Even in brain regions where individual neurons behave in complex and highly variable ways, the combined activity of many neurons can form organized patterns that create neural manifolds. According to Langdon and colleagues, these low-dimensional manifolds arise from simple connectivity principles embedded within the complex neural architecture. It's like how a symphony orchestra creates coherent music from many individual instruments—the neural manifold is the recognizable "melody" that emerges when many neurons follow underlying connectivity rules. Scientists have directly observed this relationship between circuit connectivity and manifold structure in brain systems for navigation, and similar principles likely apply to how memory manifolds form and transform (Langdon et al., 2023).

Types and Applications of Schemata

David Rumelhart, a foundational figure in cognitive science and early neural network modeling, helped formalize the concept of a "schema"—a flexible mental framework for interpreting experience, guiding memory, and shaping understanding. His model describes knowledge as hierarchically organized, with each schema composed of embedded subschemata that represent progressively more specific components of a concept (Rumelhart, 1980). While Robin and Moscovitch describe how individual memories transform over time—from richly detailed to schematic as they progress across brain regions—Rumelhart's account emphasizes how schemata themselves evolve through experience. In his framework, knowledge structures adapt through accretion, tuning, and restructuring: they can become more refined, generalized, or reorganized as new information is encountered. Thus, both perspectives describe transformation, but at different levels—Robin and Moscovitch focus on changes within a memory trace; Rumelhart focuses on how the cognitive frameworks we use to interpret experiences are themselves reshaped over time. Together, these views reinforce the idea that developing robust internal schemata is not just helpful for learning—it is structurally and functionally essential for efficient thinking, creative insight, and expert performance.

If schemata help organize our experiences and guide our thinking, how do they actually work in the brain—and how do they change with use? While schemata are abstract mental frameworks, they correspond to patterns of neural activity that can grow stronger, more efficient, or more interconnected over time. These neural manifolds aren't static—they evolve as we learn. Each new experience that fits an existing pattern strengthens it, while mismatches can lead to restructuring or expansion of the manifold. This kind of adaptive refinement echoes Piaget's classic concepts of assimilation and accommodation—processes by which new information is either integrated into existing mental structures or prompts those structures to change.

Hebbian learning—where neurons that repeatedly activate together form stronger connections—helps explain how this strengthening occurs at the neural level, though schemata themselves remain abstract structures. By continually refining these neural patterns, the brain's prefrontal cortex acts like an efficient data compressor, creating simplified "maps" of knowledge that capture key relationships while discarding irrelevant details. This process directly supports cognitive category formation and classification, allowing us to recognize meaningful patterns across similar experiences and concepts quickly and accurately (Bein & Niv, 2025; Hebscher et al., 2019).

Recent research suggests that this kind of neural efficiency may begin even earlier than expected. During active maintenance in working memory, the brain appears to reshape incoming information into simplified, low-dimensional formats that anticipate future decisions. These transient representations may reflect existing schemata—and, in turn, help refine them—gradually tuning the brain's architecture for faster, more flexible thinking (Wojcik et al., 2025).

Different types of schemata serve various cognitive functions. Spatial schemata help us navigate physical environments by encoding common patterns in spatial layouts. As psychology researcher Delaram Farzanfar et al. (2022) and her colleagues have observed, the brain forms "spatial schemata" that capture common patterns across similar environments. Just as we have a restaurant schema, we develop schemata for typical spatial layouts like modern cities or shopping malls. These spatial schemata exist in a hierarchy: detailed "cognitive maps" represent specific places (like your hometown), "spatial gists" capture essential elements while dropping details, and overarching "spatial schemata" represent common patterns that apply across many environments. This organization enables efficient navigation in new places that share features with previously experienced environments. When we rely too heavily on GPS and navigation apps, we may prevent the formation of these robust spatial schemata, leaving us disoriented when technology fails.

Schema theory also suggests three main reasons why comprehension or recall might fail: (1) a person may lack the appropriate schemata entirely; (2) the necessary schemata may exist but insufficient cues are present to activate them; or (3) the person may activate a consistent but incorrect schema, leading to misunderstanding. These failure modes help explain why knowledge that exists 'out there' rather than being internalized often proves inadequate when confronting novel problems.

We also develop procedural schemata that guide sequences of actions. A musician develops schemata for chord progressions, fingering techniques, and typical melodic patterns. A mathematician builds schemata for common problem-solving approaches and proof strategies. These procedural schemata connect with the declarative-to-procedural transition described in Sect. 3, where frequently used knowledge gradually transforms into skill-like expertise stored in procedural memory systems.

In the absence of schemata—when new information doesn't connect to existing knowledge—the brain struggles to process or make sense of it. Without schemata to simplify and structure the information, the brain must handle each new piece in its full complexity, often failing to find any meaningful pattern at all. For example, someone who learns programming by merely copying code from the Internet might solve immediate problems but won't develop a deeper mental model. When encountering novel challenges, they have no framework to guide them—just scattered, disconnected fragments of information.

What's particularly important is how these schemata integrate with prediction processing in the brain. Our brains constantly generate predictions about the world, and when those predictions fail, we experience prediction errors. These prediction errors drive us to update our mental models—or in neural terms, refine our manifolds. This updating process is especially powerful when it leads to a sudden insight or "aha" moment, creating a strong memory advantage that enhances learning (Becker & Cabeza, 2024).

The brain's ability to organize information into these efficient structures allows us to navigate complex environments without having to process every detail anew. These neural organization principles represent the brain's remarkable capacity to identify patterns, make predictions, and learn efficiently from experience.

Schema Formation and Learning Optimization

Often, creative breakthroughs occur precisely after we feel most stuck or confused. At these moments, learners are primed to reorganize their understanding, producing the well-known 'Aha!' experience. "Indeed, cognitive scientists refer to challenges that feel difficult in the moment but facilitate deeper, lasting understanding as "desirable difficulties"(Bjork & Bjork, 2011). Unlike deliberate practice, which systematically targets specific skills through structured feedback, desirable difficulties leverage cognitive struggle to deepen comprehension and enhance retention (Ericsson, 2009).

Recent neuroscience has identified an optimal challenge level for effective learning. The "Eighty Five Percent Rule" shows that learning is best when students achieve about 85% accuracy during practice (Wilson et al., 2019). Echoing Vygotsky's classic "zone of proximal development," this sweet spot—neither too easy nor too difficult—helps neural networks efficiently form and strengthen connections. Educators can use this insight as a practical guide, balancing task difficulty to encourage strong neural manifold development without causing cognitive overload.

High-dimensional neural spaces present both opportunity and challenge for learners. While they enable sophisticated conceptual integration, they also create vast landscapes of potential solutions that can overwhelm students, particularly those with mathematical learning difficulties like dyscalculia. (Research suggests that rather than too few, these students often maintain too *many* possible cognitive pathways, lacking the structured organization needed to efficiently navigate toward correct solutions [Geary et al., 2019, p. 17]).

This insight challenges popular discovery-based learning approaches. Expecting a child to discover mathematical principles independently is like placing them in a car and saying, "Figure out how to drive." The myriad possible actions and interdependent operations make it virtually impossible for novices to navigate to effective solutions without structured guidance. Just as driving instructors constrain the learning space by focusing attention on relevant controls, mathematical instruction provides scaffolding that helps students navigate complex conceptual spaces efficiently.

The core issue isn't a lack of neural connections but insufficient pruning and organization of those connections into optimized pathways. Students with dyscalculia often engage multiple competing neural pathways simultaneously, creating cognitive interference that impedes problem-solving. Guided instruction serves as a critical scaffold—constraining the high-dimensional space, directing learners toward productive pathways, and reducing cognitive load from irrelevant dimensions.

This explains why external aids like calculators, without corresponding internal schema development, fail to produce lasting mathematical proficiency. Calculators provide correct answers but don't develop the optimized neural manifolds necessary for intuitive understanding. Through appropriate practice maintaining the 85% success rate, students develop structured neural manifolds that allow efficient navigation of mathematical concepts. This reduces the dimensionality of the problem space while preserving essential relationships.

When students practice multiplication facts, they aren't merely memorizing arbitrary associations but creating optimized neural patterns that represent numerical relationships. These structured manifolds become the foundation for recognizing mathematical patterns—a far more powerful cognitive tool than an overwhelming space of undifferentiated possibilities.

Cognitive Offloading and Schema Disruption

Building a schema requires repeatedly encountering related information and actively connecting new details into existing knowledge. If each new piece of information is simply looked up without integrating it into memory, we fail to build lasting schemata. This is like trying to complete a jigsaw puzzle by checking the picture on the box for every single piece, rather than developing a sense of how the pieces fit together. You might correctly place individual pieces, but you won't internalize the overall picture. Over time, relying on external lookups for every problem makes it hard to recognize common patterns—each problem seems entirely new because you haven't built the underlying schema. Constantly looking things up becomes mentally exhausting and inefficient, compared to quickly recalling what you've already learned.

From a neural perspective, without sustained internal engagement, the brain might not solidify a low-dimensional manifold for the task. Each instance might be processed in a more onerous, high-dimensional way (basically, treating it as new) because the shortcut of a schema isn't available. This connects to the fundamental nature of schemata as active computational processes that evaluate the quality of their fit to available data. Without well-developed internal schemata, the brain loses its ability to efficiently determine whether and to what degree it can account for a given situation, forcing it to repeatedly process familiar information as if it were new. In the long run, this can make cognition less efficient and flexible. For example, learning a programming language by copying code from the Internet for every task (without understanding) might get immediate results, but the person never develops a schema of how the code works. When faced with a slightly novel problem, they're stuck—there's no mental model to adapt, just a bag of fragments. By contrast, someone who internalized coding concepts can handle new problems by drawing analogies to things they already understand, thanks to robust schemata.

Research underscores these concerns. One review of technology-based cognitive offloading observes that offloading information to digital storage often results in only the gist of the information (or its location) being retained in the learner's mind. In essence, people remember *that* something can be looked up and roughly what it's about, but not the details. These retained "biological pointers" to external information create an *illusion* of knowledge—we feel like we know it because we know where to get it—but our actual cognitive schema remains impoverished (Skulmowski, 2023).

Moreover, if learners attribute low value to deeply learning content (because it's readily accessible outside), they invest less effort, creating a vicious cycle where shallow engagement leads to shallow encoding. Offloading may also interfere with the normal formation of integrated memory networks by constantly disrupting the flow of information into working memory and long-term memory. High extraneous cognitive load (e.g., dealing with a distracting interface or juggling lookups) can prevent information from even entering working memory, much less being encoded in long-term memory. In such cases, *only* a fragmentary trace (a pointer or feeling of "I can always find this later") is stored. From the standpoint of schema theory, this is a poor substitute; a pointer is not a schema. A schema enriches understanding by linking concepts, whereas a pointer simply says "info exists somewhere." A library is useless to someone who doesn't know enough to find or contextualize what's in the books.

Neural Evidence and Implications for Learning

Neural evidence also hints at how incomplete internalization might affect problem-solving. Studies of insight and memory (like those by Becker et al.) show that the medial prefrontal cortex (mPFC)—a brain region crucial for integrating information and supporting higher cognitive functions—rapidly integrates new information with existing schemata in neocortex when a person learns with insight. If one has no schema (because prior knowledge is absent or unorganized), that integration process likely fails or is less efficient. The person might learn the isolated fact but won't connect it to broader understanding. Similarly, bridging the gap between neural manifolds and neural circuitry is crucial for understanding how learned knowledge is represented. This relationship between abstract manifolds and physical brain networks explains why well-organized knowledge is more efficiently processed. When a learner lacks structured manifolds, their neural activity remains disorganized and inefficient—the brain processes each task as if encountering it for the first time rather than leveraging established patterns. In essence, the brain stays in "novice mode," using energy-intensive, widespread neural activity for tasks that an expert's brain would handle with a streamlined, specialized network (Becker & Cabeza, 2025; Langdon et al., 2023).

In practical terms, one way to think of schemata and neural manifolds is that they are the internal mental maps we use to navigate domains of knowledge. Relying excessively on external GPS (so to speak) means we never draw our own map. When the GPS is gone or gives incomplete info, we're lost. Conversely, if we have a solid mental map, external tools can still aid us (just as a driver with local knowledge can still use a GPS for efficiency), but we are not helpless without them because we've built the internal schema that lets us think independently.

Recent neuroscience provides compelling evidence for this concept. A 2025 study of flight trainees demonstrated how specialized training creates measurable changes in brain network connectivity and efficiency (Ye et al., 2025). Researchers found that after completing intensive flight training, trainees exhibited significantly enhanced functional connectivity between the Central Executive Network and Default Mode Network—essential systems for cognitive control and information integration. Moreover, these trainees spent more time in brain states characterized by this efficient connectivity, and these temporal metrics directly correlated with performance on cognitive tests measuring flexibility and visual processing. This suggests that intensive practice not only strengthens connections between brain networks but also creates more stable, efficient neural states—essentially the neural manifestation of well-formed schemata that allow experts to process information more efficiently than novices.

Sidebar: Shadows of Thought: How Generative AI Mirrors the Brain

Generative AI models like ChatGPT share striking parallels with how human brains form schemata. Both simplify vast amounts of information into manageable patterns—brains through neural manifolds, AI through structured representations learned from extensive data. These simplified structures act like "shadows," capturing essential features by reducing complex, high-dimensional data into simpler forms. This helps explain how both brains and generative AI efficiently recognize patterns, predict outcomes, and solve problems.

Recent research takes this parallel even further. Gerald Pao's *generative manifold networks*, for example, use manifold-like structures that enable AI to predict neural responses and generate realistic behaviors not explicitly programmed (Pao et al., 2021). Markus Buehler's research (2024) goes even deeper, demonstrating that sophisticated AI systems actively and autonomously explore knowledge by iteratively questioning, reflecting, and reasoning *within their own evolving knowledge networks*—continuously discovering novel connections and insights. This proactive internal exploration mirrors how human learners actively build robust schemata through repeated reflection and reasoning within their own neural architecture.

This insight underscores a central theme of this chapter: the true value of knowledge lies not merely in external accessibility, but in the active internal integration of that knowledge within our cognitive architecture. Excessive reliance on external tools for memory bypasses this critical internal process, weakening precisely those mental structures—schemata and neural manifolds—that foster deep understanding and creative insight in both humans and advanced artificial systems (Sejnowski, 2024).

The implications for education are significant. When we understand how schemata form and function neurologically, we can design learning experiences that facilitate their development rather than hinder it. Effective education should balance the use of external tools with opportunities for students to internalize key knowledge and develop rich, interconnected schemata. This balance ensures that technology enhances learning rather than creating dependence and cognitive weakness.

Cognitive Offloading and Learning Trends

Historical Shift: From Memorization to "Look It Up"

Mid-twentieth century classrooms emphasized drills, repetition, and frequent testing of factual knowledge—techniques derided by some as "drill and kill." By the late twentieth century, education pivoted toward critical thinking skills and away from memorization, adopting the mantra "you can always look it up." As Daisy Christodoulou, author of *Seven Myths about Education*, notes (Christodoulou, 2014):

> The über myth is that facts don't matter or knowledge doesn't matter...We need facts in long-term memory in order to think, because .. our working memory is very limited, and long-term memory is the seat of all intellectual skill. (Christodoulou, 2018)

This shift coincided with the advent of electronic calculators in the 1970s and personal computers and the Internet in the 1980s and 1990s, enabling unprecedented cognitive offloading—the use of physical action to alter information processing requirements to reduce cognitive demand. Educators increasingly argued against memorization of content that could be readily accessed or calculated by machines, positioning this approach as freeing up time for "higher-order skills." This recommendation often found a receptive audience since, as research shows, thinking itself can be unpleasant for many people (David et al., 2024).

This shift mirrors a recurring pattern in schooling, where practices that appear more intellectual and abstract (like teaching "critical thinking skills") gain status over seemingly basic practices (like memorization), regardless of their actual cognitive foundation or effectiveness (Labaree, 2006). This shift away from memorization was fueled by the persistent status struggles of colleges of education within the academic hierarchy. As Labaree (2006) details, facing perceptions of lower rigor and lacking primary authority over subject matters, education schools often sought legitimacy by embracing sophisticated pedagogical theories. Progressive ideals, emphasizing student-centered learning processes and higher-order thinking over direct knowledge transmission, offered a seemingly more 'academic' mission than focusing on foundational content mastery and memorization, potentially aligning better with university norms while distancing the field from its lower-status training roots.

Quantifying the Shift: Language Analysis

To track this pedagogical evolution, we (the authors—not the omniscient 'we' that, yes, has snuck into this very chapter) analyzed phrases associated with less emphasis on memorization in published literature over time (Fig. 7).

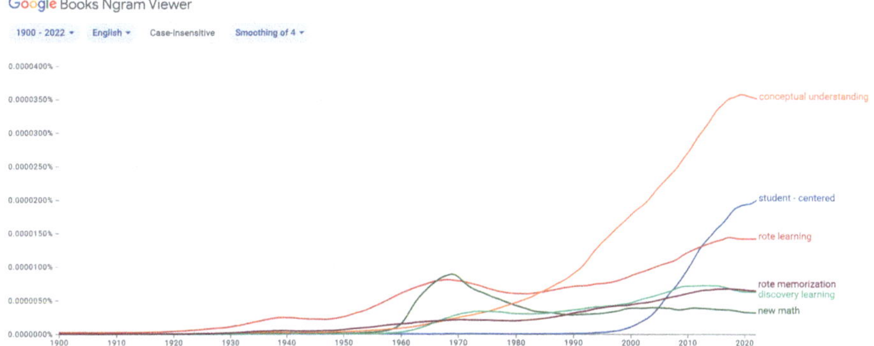

Fig. 7 Trends in education-related phrases frequently associated with diminished emphasis on memorization. The colored lines (affiliated with the y-axis) indicate the frequency of each phrase in published books; the *x*-axis shows years from 1900 to 2020. Note that the phrase "conceptual understanding" is included because many educators have historically treated it as distinct from or even opposed to memorization, despite evidence showing memorization can support conceptual understanding

Our sentiment analysis of the word "rote" in American books and publications shows how attitudes changed over time.[3] In the nineteenth and early twentieth centuries, the term was largely neutral or slightly positive, appearing in educational contexts without negative connotations. However, by the 1930s–1950s, "rote" began to carry a more rigid implication, reflecting early critiques of mechanical memorization in learning. From the 1960s onward, sentiment toward "rote" declined sharply, coinciding with shifts in educational philosophy that prioritized critical thinking over rote memorization. This linguistic shift paralleled the rise of technologies that could store information externally (see Fig. 8).

The Cognitive Consequences of Offloading

As we saw in previous sections on schemata and procedural memory, completely eliminating foundational memorization can undermine higher-order skills. Research shows that offloading information doesn't just externalize

[3]Our analysis was conducted in the Corpus of Historical American English (COHA) using a hybrid approach, combining rule-based keyword filtering with Python-powered sentiment analysis. This allowed us to track shifts in connotation over time with both quantitative insights and contextual relevance. Given that this study focused on a single keyword, we implemented Python scripting within KNIME to automate sentiment classification, leveraging transformer-based NLP models to assess sentiment trends across historical texts.

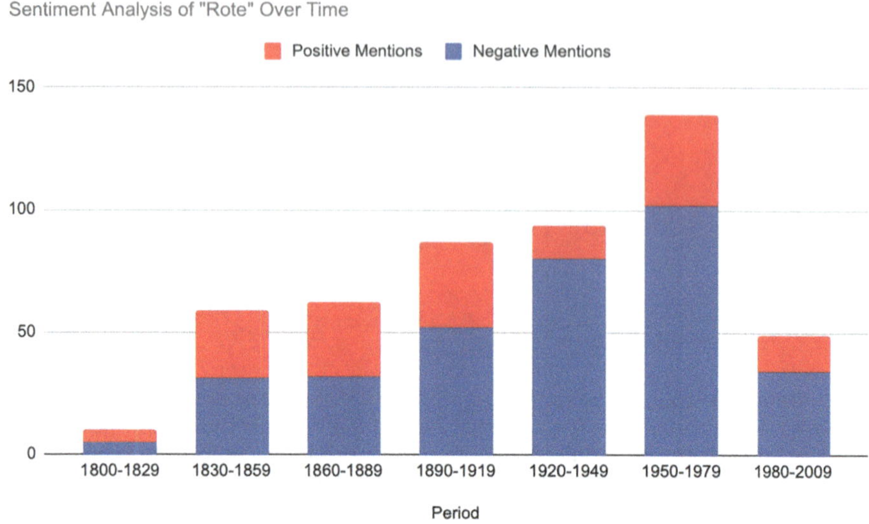

Fig. 8 A sentiment analysis of the term "rote" in the Corpus of Historical American English (COHA) revealed a distinct evolution in the perception of "rote" across different periods

storage—it transforms our cognitive processes. Risko and Gilbert propose a three-component framework for this cycle: (1) our decision to use external tools is influenced by our metacognitive evaluation of our own abilities, (2) the act of offloading then affects those metacognitive judgments, and (3) offloading directly impacts our cognitive capabilities. This creates a self-reinforcing cycle where offloading can lead to increased dependence on external tools (Risko & Gilbert, 2016).

When students repeatedly outsource cognitive processes to technology, they develop "biological pointers"—remembering where to find information rather than the information itself. While seemingly efficient, this creates an illusion of knowledge that undermines schema formation and deeper understanding.

The Knowledge Paradox: Hirsch's Warning

This concern isn't new. E.D. Hirsch Jr. warned that without domain knowledge, critical thinking falters. In his 2000 article "'You Can Always Look It Up' . . . Or Can You?" (Hirsch, 2000), he argued that broad factual knowledge enables effective skill use—contradicting the notion that knowledge and skills are separate. Without background knowledge, students can't evaluate sources or recognize whether information is plausible. In Hirsch's words, "those who repudiate a fact-filled curriculum on the grounds that kids can always look things up miss the paradox that de-emphasizing factual knowledge actually hinders children from learning." A novice doesn't know what they don't know—without stored knowledge, they can't formulate proper questions or search strategies.

Empirical studies support these arguments. In one classic experiment (Miller & Gildea, 1987), children told to look up unfamiliar words produced nonsensical sentences. Why? They misinterpreted definitions without vocabulary context, and the lookup process itself created cognitive overload. The children would have learned more effectively if taught the words in context rather than being told to "look it up." This illustrates a crucial principle: external resources benefit those who already possess internal knowledge. As Hirsch put it, "to be able to use that information [from the Internet]—to absorb it, to add to our knowledge—we must already possess a storehouse of knowledge."

Digital Amnesia: The Google Effect

Another line of research has examined what is sometimes called the Google effect or "digital amnesia." Psychologist Betsy Sparrow and colleagues found that when we expect future access to information, we remember where to find it rather than the information itself (Sparrow et al., 2011). This isn't entirely negative—it's a form of adaptive memory management by the brain—but it underscores that offloading can change what we remember.

In moderation, this division of labor between internal and external memory is efficient. But applied indiscriminately, it can overload working memory with biological pointers rather than direct knowledge use. Imagine trying to write an essay while looking up every fact or word—the flow of thought would be constantly disrupted. Working memory, which is limited, gets consumed by the mechanics of search instead of the synthesis of ideas. Ironically, excessive cognitive offloading can increase cognitive load during complex tasks. Tools do lighten the load for isolated tasks (calculating a sum, finding a date), but if reliance becomes too high, the tool use itself becomes an overhead in any integrated task.

The Flynn Effect, Its Reversal, and Possible Links to Memory Practices

The cognitive offloading trends described in the previous section raise an important question: Could these widespread shifts in how we store and access information have measurable effects on cognitive abilities at a population level? If educational practices and daily habits increasingly favor external memory storage over internal knowledge building, we might expect to see these changes reflected in standardized measures of cognitive performance. The Flynn Effect and its recent reversal offer a revealing window into this possibility—a natural experiment in how changing approaches to knowledge might influence measurable intelligence.

The Rise, Fall, and Potential Causes of IQ Scores

Population-wide IQ scores provide insights into how memory practices affect cognitive abilities. Throughout most of the twentieth century, IQ scores steadily climbed—a phenomenon called the Flynn Effect. Two major studies showed scores rising about three points per decade (Pietschnig & Voracek, 2015; Trahan et al., 2014). People worldwide were getting "smarter" on these tests, thanks to better schools, nutrition, health, and more complex environments.

Then something unexpected happened. Starting with people born after the mid-1970s, researchers spotted a reversal—particularly in wealthy countries. Norwegian data showed scores dropping by up to seven points per generation (Bratsberg & Rogeberg, 2018). Denmark, Britain, France, the Netherlands, and others showed similar declines (Teasdale & Owen, 2008; Dutton et al., 2016).

Interestingly, IQ scores continue rising in developing countries as education and living standards improve. The decline appears mainly in advanced nations. What changed? Most revealing is that IQ declines appear within families—younger siblings scoring lower on average than their older siblings, effectively ruling out simple genetic or demographic explanations. Researchers are investigating whether shifts in education, technology use, and cognitive habits might explain why the decades-long upward trend has reversed in wealthier societies.

Timing and Potential Causes

Researchers have explored numerous hypotheses for the Flynn Effect's reversal—from declining test motivation to environmental pollutants to nutritional shifts. The evidence points primarily to environmental and cultural factors rather than genetics (Teasdale & Owen, 2008).

The timing of this reversal offers a compelling clue. The cohorts born after approximately 1975 were educated during the 1980s–2000s—precisely when Western education shifted away from memorization toward "learning to learn"—an admirable goal pursued by educators who, ironically, had limited understanding of how learning actually works in the brain. This period also saw digital technology—calculators, computers, and eventually the Internet—become fixtures of daily life. A new mindset emerged: "Why memorize knowledge or methods when you can always look them up or use a device?"

As schools emphasized abstract thinking skills over content knowledge, information and computation became instantly accessible at the push of a button. This raises a critical question: Were the cognitive skills that boost IQ performance—mental arithmetic, broad vocabulary, general knowledge—exercised less in this environment? The chronological correlation between rising digital dependence and plateauing IQ scores is striking, though correlation isn't causation. Multiple factors likely interweave, making it difficult to isolate a single cause.

Could the continued rise of the Flynn Effect in developing countries, contrasted with its decline in wealthier nations, relate to Western acceptance of constructivist approaches that de-emphasize memorization? Evidence suggests that when wealthier, high-performing countries, as, for example, Taiwan, experiment with constructivism, their math scores decline. As they might then move away from constructivist and discovery learning approaches, mathematics performance quickly improves (Lai, 2024; Lin et al., 2014; Oakley et al., 2025). This dynamic exemplifies Pedagogical Attribution Displacement (PAD), where educators may falsely attribute student success to fashion able pedagogical approaches, such as constructivism, while underappreciating the foundational knowledge established through prior traditional instruction. Such misattributions arguably stem from the very challenge Bjork et al. (2013, p. 417) identified: "*people often have a faulty mental model of how they learn and remember, making them prone to both misassessing and mismanaging their own learning.*" When educators operate with unjustified teaching beliefs (Double et al., 2020)—perhaps undervaluing the deep structure provided by earlier instruction—they risk misinterpreting the trustworthy source of student achievement, potentially contributing to complex narratives surrounding educational reforms and international rankings (e.g., in Finland, see Sahlgren, 2015).

There is a clear bidirectional link between mathematics and IQ. It's not just that smarter kids can learn math better. Learning math, it seems actually helps make you smarter—at least from an IQ test perspective (Song & Su, 2022). Less effective methods for teaching mathematics, in other words, could lead to the decline of IQ in entire nations.

Recent reporting on cognitive performance declines, such as that by Burn-Murdoch (2025) in the *Financial Times*, often attributes these trends primarily to technology distractions and shifting media consumption patterns. While these environmental factors may certainly play a role, they may obscure a more fundamental issue: educational approaches that have systematically devalued the memory foundation necessary for higher-order thinking. Educational institutions readily embrace such technology-focused explanations, as they conveniently shift attention away from examining how pedagogical trends might be contributing to these declining outcomes. After all, it's far easier to blame smartphones than to reconsider cherished educational reforms that have been promoted as progressive advancements.

Educational Shifts, Cognitive Exercise, and Technology Balance

How do educational practices influence specific cognitive abilities measured by IQ tests? This question is central to understanding the Flynn Effect reversal.

IQ assessments measure various cognitive abilities: arithmetic, vocabulary, general knowledge, memory span, and abstract problem-solving. While designed to gauge general intelligence, these tests inevitably reflect practiced skills. Someone who has memorized math facts solves arithmetic problems faster; someone who reads widely knows more vocabulary. Test performance reflects which cognitive skills have been exercised.

Studies consistently show knowledge-based and verbal abilities showing the greatest declines, while processing speed and some non-verbal abilities remain stable or improved. In France, Vocabulary, Comprehension, and Information subtests showed the largest drops, while processing speed increased slightly and memory span remained unchanged (Dutton & Lynn, 2015). This suggests recent cohorts know fewer words and facts than their late-1990s counterparts.

American adults show significant vocabulary declines between the 1970s and 2010s (0.5 to 1.3 IQ points per decade), regardless of education level

(Dworak et al., 2023). These findings suggest reduced reading and increased Internet reliance have affected vocabulary and general knowledge. By contrast, tasks less dependent on acquired knowledge haven't declined equivalently.

This pattern contrasts with the original Flynn Effect, where mid-twentieth-century IQ gains were strongest in non-verbal reasoning, while verbal and knowledge-based skills rose modestly (Dutton et al., 2016). Today, knowledge-centric skills show relative decline precisely when modern education and habits have deemphasized these areas.

James Flynn noted that while young children's environments became more cognitively enriched (with educational shows and toys), teenage environments might have become less intellectually stimulating, with curricula focusing less on content and teens spending more time on screens and entertainment rather than reading and studying.

These findings align with our understanding of memory systems: frequently offloading cognitive work to devices may cause certain "mental muscles" to atrophy. Students expected to internalize core knowledge develop sharper recall and better mental organization, while those constantly relying on external aids may never develop robust internal knowledge structures.

The Flynn Effect's rise and fall have complex origins that resist simplistic explanations. Nevertheless, multiple analyses confirm recent IQ declines reflect real drops in specific cognitive capabilities. If people in 1960 memorized more and performed more unaided mental problem-solving than people in 2020, certain mental proficiencies would naturally differ between these populations, suggesting that how we train memory matters at a societal level.

A compelling interpretation connects these trends: Mid-twentieth-century education emphasized content knowledge and coincided with unprecedented IQ gains. Late-twentieth-century education claimed to prioritize "learning how to learn" over memorization but implemented methods that neuroscience now reveals were actively hampering effective learning—coinciding with stagnating or declining IQ scores. This correlation demands reconsideration of approaches that devalued memory under the misguided assumption that it wasn't essential for deeper thinking (Novak & Gowin, 1984).

Evidence shows heavy reliance on digital aids correlates with diminished analytical reasoning, highlighting the importance of maintaining internal cognitive habits alongside technological conveniences. If we want to preserve cognitive gains, we shouldn't abandon training the "memory muscle." How we teach young minds has consequences that reverberate through our collective cognitive capabilities (Barr et al., 2015).

Educational Giants of the Past: What They Got Right—and Wrong

Many great educational leaders of the past were intellectually brilliant; paradoxically, this brilliance may have sometimes blinded them to the reality that most students benefit greatly from explicit, structured instruction, particularly for abstract, biologically secondary knowledge. Indeed, all these pioneers left double-edged legacies, advancing educational thinking in crucial ways while simultaneously creating significant roadblocks that delayed progress. Below, we briefly explore these educators' key insights and missteps in light of modern neuroscience and cognitive load theory.

- **Benjamin Bloom (1913–1999)** transformed education through his Taxonomy of Educational Objectives and Mastery Learning approach. His renowned "two-sigma problem" revealed that one-on-one tutoring paired with mastery techniques can dramatically boost learning—an insight now echoed by neuroscience, which shows that targeted feedback and deliberate practice strengthen neural networks.

  Yet modern neuroscience exposes key limitations in how Bloom's frameworks have often been interpreted. His taxonomy implies a rigid hierarchy of cognitive skills, whereas the brain's operations are far more integrated. Higher-order thinking—such as analysis and creativity—relies not on separable faculties but on richly interconnected knowledge networks. Similarly, Bloom's taxonomy divided learning into cognitive, affective, and psychomotor domains—an approach he acknowledged was pedagogically useful but somewhat artificial. He recognized that these aspects of learning overlap in practice, yet maintained their separation to help educators plan and assess instruction. Neuroscience now confirms that such separations are not just artificial but misleading: emotion and cognition continuously interact, jointly shaping memory, reasoning, and attention.

  While Bloom's tutoring research underscored the power of personalized learning, later studies have rarely reproduced the dramatic two-sigma gains. The two-sigma result is not a statistical fluke, but it requires a constellation of best practices rarely achieved together, even one-on-one. It's individually possible, but systemically elusive. Neuroscience shows that lasting learning depends on active retrieval, timely feedback, adaptive pacing, and emotional investment—elements central to Bloom's original findings, yet too often missing in educational reform.
- **Jerome Bruner (1915–2016)**, an influential psychologist known for advocating discovery learning, argued that students should independently explore and discover concepts. While beneficial when carefully structured, neuroscience reveals Bruner's fully unguided discovery methods can overwhelm learners' limited working memory, particularly when dealing with biologically secondary material. Bruner thus underestimated the vital role structured guidance plays in building robust, biologically secondary knowledge schemata.
- **John Dewey (1859–1952)**, an American philosopher and educational reformer, pioneered experiential education, emphasizing reflection as central to deep learning. Dewey largely dismissed the value of rote memorization, assuming that experience combined with reflection alone would naturally consolidate

(continued)

knowledge. Ironically, modern neuroscience confirms that explicit practice in recalling information (yes, even good old-fashioned memorization) is crucial—no matter how unfashionable—for most learners to reliably encode biologically secondary information into long-term memory.

- **Maria Montessori (1870–1952),** Italian physician and educational innovator who developed a child-centered approach emphasizing self-directed, hands-on learning. Her methods proved extraordinarily effective for young children in mastering foundational (biologically primary) skills. Montessori believed this student-driven, concrete learning approach could likewise be applied to more advanced knowledge. In doing so, however, she underestimated the need for explicit instruction as learners grew older and content became more abstract. Modern research shows that some guided teaching and deliberate practice are indispensable for efficiently encoding complex (biologically secondary) academic concepts as children mature.
- **Jean Piaget (1896–1980)**, a pioneering Swiss psychologist, correctly theorized cognitive development arising from "cognitive disequilibrium"—the mismatch between expectation and reality. Piaget rightly understood that learners naturally reorganize mental models regarding biologically primary domains (such as social interactions or native language skills). However, he mistakenly extended this assumption to biologically secondary knowledge, presuming learners could spontaneously reorganize their mental models in these areas without explicit guidance. Current neuroscience emphasizes that structured instruction and deliberate feedback are vital for reliably developing stable and accurate schemata, particularly for abstract biologically secondary knowledge.
- **B.F. Skinner (1904–1990)**, an influential American behaviorist, insisted that learning occurs through operant conditioning—systematic reinforcement and immediate feedback shaping behavior. Skinner's insights were so powerful that they inspired modern artificial intelligence methods like reinforcement learning, where algorithms learn via reward signals. However, Skinner treated the mind's inner workings as a "black box," strictly focusing on observable behaviors and outcomes. He dismissed internal cognitive processes as unobservable and irrelevant—precisely the processes, such as engrams, schemas, and manifolds, that neuroscience now recognizes as central to understanding and enhancing learning. Thus, Skinner's legacy, like so many of the greats in education, is paradoxical: he was correct about the critical role of reinforcement and feedback yet wrong in blocking investigations into the brain's internal mechanisms that are essential if we're to truly advance our understanding of how to learn and teach effectively.
- **Lev Vygotsky (1896–1934)**, a Russian psychologist who founded social constructivism, highlighted learning as inherently social, situated within a "Zone of Proximal Development." Vygotsky, though insightful, overestimated the sufficiency of social interaction alone for teaching biologically secondary knowledge. Neuroscience has clarified that explicit, structured instruction is crucial to seat abstract, biologically secondary concepts within long-term memory effectively.

Conclusion: Balancing Internal Memory and Digital Tools for Cognitive Health

The AI Challenge: Metacognitive Laziness

Humans naturally use external tools—like language, symbols, diagrams, and notes—to help think and communicate clearly. These external tools enhance our cognitive abilities by offloading memory and simplifying complex ideas. But as we've seen, relying too heavily on external aids can weaken our internal mental frameworks. Effective learning requires a balance: using external tools to support—not replace—the deep internal knowledge essential for genuine understanding (Fernando et al., 2024).

We began with a simple premise: human memory matters, even (or especially) in the digital era. Through this chapter, we explored how and why. We saw that the brain's learning mechanisms—from the dopamine-driven thrill of prediction errors during insight to the basal ganglia's slow burn of procedural memory formation—are designed to function with information that the brain holds and manipulates internally. When used properly, technology can *augment* these processes (for instance, by providing rich feedback or additional examples), but if used as a crutch to avoid mental effort, it can diminish cognitive outcomes and foster metacognitive laziness. Overreliance on digital externalization carries several risks. It can rob us of the memorable impact of discovery, stunt the formation of fluent skills and intuition, disrupt the building of neural manifolds that make us efficient thinkers, and even contribute to broader cognitive stagnation or decline. In essence, an offloaded mind may become an under-exercised mind—one that increasingly lacks awareness of its own knowledge gaps.

The arrival of AI assistants like ChatGPT has intensified these concerns about cognitive offloading in education. Do AI systems that instantly provide answers or writing help enhance learning, or merely substitute for it? Recent research provides compelling evidence for the latter.

A revealing study titled "Beware of Metacognitive Laziness: Effects of Generative AI on Learning" compared college students writing essays with different types of assistance: ChatGPT, human tutoring, basic tools, or no help (Fan et al., 2024). The results were striking—ChatGPT-assisted students produced higher-quality essays but showed no knowledge improvement when tested later, and in some measures actually performed worse. These students displayed what researchers termed "metacognitive laziness"—fewer self-correcting behaviors and significantly less time reflecting on the material.

They took the path of least resistance, letting the AI generate content without deeply engaging with the subject—effectively bypassing the prediction error mechanisms that create strong memory engrams.

Recent neurophysiological research from MIT supports this concern: learners who began writing with ChatGPT showed weaker connectivity in frontoparietal brain regions linked to focus and memory—and had more trouble recalling their own work. In contrast, those who wrote first and used AI only later retained more and showed stronger neural engagement. The timing of AI use, in short, may shape not just how we think but whether we remember (Kosmyna et al., 2025).

This challenge of metacognitive laziness is intensified by a key distinction in how people engage with generative AI—namely, their existing internal knowledge structures. Individuals with well-developed internal schemas—often those educated before AI became ubiquitous—can use these tools effectively. Their solid knowledge base allows them to evaluate AI output critically, refine prompts, integrate suggestions meaningfully, and detect inaccuracies. For these users, AI acts as a cognitive amplifier, extending their capabilities.

In contrast, learners still building foundational knowledge face a significant risk: mistaking AI fluency for their own. Without a robust internal framework for comparison, they may readily accept plausible-sounding output without realizing what's missing or incorrect. This bypasses the mental effort—retrieval, error detection, integration—that neuroscience shows is essential for forming lasting memory engrams and flexible schemas. The result is a false sense of understanding: the learner feels accomplished, but the underlying cognitive work hasn't been done.

This effect extends beyond the classroom. Lee et al. (2025) found that knowledge workers who placed high confidence in generative AI engaged in significantly less critical thinking, effectively offloading cognitive effort to the technology. The pattern is especially pronounced in areas requiring procedural skill development. In mathematics education, Bastani et al. (2024) reported that high school students who used GPT-4 during practice outperformed peers—until the final exam, when the AI was removed. Their performance dropped, revealing a lack of retained understanding. Similarly, Yang et al. (2025b) found that students using ChatGPT for C++ programming experienced lower flow, reduced self-efficacy, and poorer learning outcomes compared to conventional learners. In both cases, students had used AI as a "crutch," bypassing the mental effort needed to transition from declarative to procedural memory. Without this shift, they failed to develop the intuitive grasp that emerges through repeated practice and error correction. The AI short-circuited the very cognitive labor that feels hard in the moment—but is essential for building the neural architecture of lasting understanding.

These studies highlight the complex relationship between AI tools and learning outcomes. The pattern is consistent across domains: when AI circumvents the brain's natural learning mechanisms—prediction errors, schema formation, and the crucial transition from declarative to procedural knowledge—learning suffers despite seemingly productive short-term outcomes. The technology creates an illusion of knowledge while bypassing the cognitive processes necessary for genuine learning.

Generative AI systems learn how to give teaching advice by absorbing the existing education literature. That literature strongly favors student activity, discussion, and inquiry as visible signs of good teaching, while treating explanation, practice, and memory-building as supporting details rather than central causes of learning (Chi & Wylie, 2014; Freeman et al., 2014). As a result, AI-generated instructional guidance reliably emphasizes what classrooms should look like-students talking, working in groups, engaging in tasks-more than what students must master through repeated retrieval and consolidation. AI does not create this imbalance; it reproduces it, making the prevailing instructional emphasis easier to generate, easier to repeat, and harder to challenge.

Finding Balance: Appropriate Offloading and Educational Design

Cognitive offloading isn't inherently negative—it's a natural and often helpful strategy (we use calendars for appointments and calculators for arithmetic). Writing itself is a productive form of cognitive offloading. By externalizing ideas onto paper, we free working memory to handle more complex thoughts. But writing is also procedural; good writing involves internalizing effective patterns, structures, and vocabulary. Benjamin Franklin famously improved his writing by reconstructing admired passages from memory using brief notes as cues. This approach allowed him to offload ideas to paper while simultaneously building internal schemata for effective communication. Problems arise only when offloading replaces the initial learning process. Experts with solid schemata can safely offload some details, but novices who offload everything never internalize essential knowledge.

The shift toward cognitive offloading in education is what research calls "pathological altruism"—good intentions that backfire. Teachers who promoted calculators and "just look it up" approaches sincerely wanted to free students from what seemed like needless memorization. But this well-meaning approach missed how stored knowledge builds the mental foundation needed for advanced thinking. The result? An educational approach that, despite kind intentions, undermined the very cognitive foundations needed for the higher-level reasoning it aimed to develop (Oakley, 2013).

The concept of pathological altruism helps explain why educational reforms with the best intentions can sometimes lead to negative outcomes. When we understand this dynamic, we can better navigate the balance between cognitive offloading and internalized knowledge.

Technology that Enhances Rather Than Replaces Learning

Interestingly, not all technological interventions undermine learning. When designed with sound cognitive principles in mind, AI can actually enhance rather than diminish educational outcomes. A 2024 study in Ghana found that students using an AI-powered math tutor on WhatsApp for just one hour per week showed substantial improvement in math scores compared to a control group. The key difference? This intervention was deliberately designed to provide scaffolded practice and hints, not just answers. Rather than encouraging passive consumption of information, it prompted active engagement with the material. This suggests that technology can support learning when it complements rather than replaces the brain's natural learning mechanisms (Henkel et al., 2024).

Our message is not to reject technology or return to endless drills. Instead, research supports using technological tools in ways that complement human learning mechanisms, enhancing rather than inhibiting deep learning. The key is balance, guided by the "Eighty Five Percent Rule"—finding the sweet spot of challenge where students are pushed but not overwhelmed. Just as you can't build a house starting with the roof, the brain struggles to grasp advanced concepts without first mastering the basics. Calculators and AI tools that let students skip this foundation make higher-level learning inherently unstable. Likewise, the well-intentioned emphasis on "desirable difficulty" has sometimes pushed students beyond their optimal learning zone, leaving them frustrated and unable to form coherent mental frameworks. The goal should always be to preserve deep learning by ensuring students engage their own memory and reasoning at just the right level of challenge—not too easy, and not too difficult.

Based on the neuroscientific principles we've explored throughout this chapter, we propose the following evidence-based strategies for educators seeking to balance technological integration with cognitive development:

- Embrace desirable difficulty—within limits: Encourage learners to generate answers and grapple with problems before turning to help, but be mindful of maintaining that sweet spot of approximately 85% success. Struggling productively with challenges triggers the brain's natural learning enhancements, but excessive struggle can prevent the formation of effective neural manifolds. In classroom practice, this means carefully calibrating when to provide guidance—not necessarily offering solutions, but also not leaving students floundering with tasks far beyond immediate their current capabilities. Teachers can cultivate perseverance while still ensuring students experience enough success to build confidence and effective schemata. This approach supports what schema theorists call "tuning"—the gradual evolution of existing schemata to better represent the population of situations to which they apply, making them increasingly accurate and efficient.
- Assign foundational knowledge for memorization and practice: Rather than viewing factual knowledge as rote trivia, recognize it as the glue for higher-level thinking. This doesn't mean endless drilling without context, but it does mean certain basics (like math facts, vocabulary, scientific terms, historical dates, formulas) should be overlearned to the point of automaticity, helping that crucial transition from declarative to procedural memory we discussed earlier. Tools like spaced repetition software can combine technology with memory science to help students efficiently retain core knowledge. Far from being a waste of time, this internal library will enable students to think faster and more creatively later on.
- Use procedural training to build intuition: Allocate class time for practicing skills without external aids. For instance, mental math exercises, handwriting notes, reciting important passages or proofs from memory, and so on. Such practices, once considered old-fashioned, actually cultivate the procedural fluency that frees the mind for deeper insight. As an analogy, even though modern pilots have autopilot, they still rigorously train on manual flying—because that ingrains understanding and prepares them for when automation fails. Similarly, students who practice reasoning unaided develop a *feel* for it that no on-demand answer can impart.
- Intentionally integrate technology as a supplement, not a substitute: When using AI tutors or search tools, structure their use so that the student remains cognitively active. For example, an AI could be used to get hints or check work, rather than to produce the entire answer. Studies have

shown that learning improves when AI is used under guidance (e.g., an AI that asks the student questions or encourages reflection, as opposed to an oracle that spoon-feeds answers). Teachers and software designers should aim for interactive engagement, where the AI can handle repetitive aspects or provide adaptive feedback, but the student must still do the reasoning or recall the knowledge. This keeps the learner in the driver's seat mentally.

- Promote internal knowledge structures: Help students build robust mental frameworks by ensuring connections happen inside their brains, not just on paper. While activities like concept mapping might appear helpful, they often create an illusion of understanding—students connect ideas externally without developing the neural manifolds that truly matter. As we explored earlier, the brain's procedural memory system and basal ganglia require direct internal processing to form durable cognitive structures. Instead, guide students to identify relationships between concepts through active questioning ("How does this principle relate to what we learned last week?") and guided reflection. When students use Internet research, frame it as supplementary to their internal knowledge base, not a replacement. This approach builds on our understanding of prediction errors and schema development—information must be processed through the brain's own architecture to become truly functional knowledge that can trigger error detection and support intuitive understanding.
- Educate about metacognition and the illusion of knowledge: Help students recognize that *knowing where to find information is fundamentally different from truly knowing it.* Information that exists "out there" doesn't automatically translate to knowledge we can access and apply when needed. Guide students to reflect on their own learning processes so they can make more intentional choices about what to commit to memory. For example, a teacher might model: "Let's approach this problem using only what we know first. If we reach an impasse, we'll look up what we need, but then continue solving it on our own." This balanced approach treats external resources as supplements to internal knowledge—tools that support thinking rather than replace it.

The Future of Learning: Integration Not Replacement

In implementing these strategies, the goal is to cultivate learners who are both tech-savvy and deeply knowledgeable. The two are not mutually exclusive—they're mutually reinforcing. A student with strong internal memory and well-honed thinking skills will use technology *more effectively* than one who uses it as a crutch. They will know what to ask, how to evaluate responses, and how to integrate new information into existing knowledge structures. By contrast, a student trained to constantly offload cognitive processes faces an inevitable ceiling—passively consuming information without developing the neural architecture needed for true understanding, and faltering when external supports are unavailable.

Cognitively, the human brain remains both the ultimate bottleneck and the ultimate engine for learning. External devices expand our capabilities, but what happens in our neurons determines how far those capabilities go. An insight not formed is a memory not made. A skill not practiced is an intuition not developed. A schema not built is a problem not recognized. And a mind unchallenged is a talent unlived. The trends of the past decades serve as a caution: even as the world's knowledge sits readily accessible on every smartphone, we must ensure that knowledge also takes root *within the individual's mind.*

Looking ahead, the synergy of human cognition and machine capability will define successful education. We should strategically leverage AI and vast information stores to expand learning possibilities—personalizing instruction and creating immersive simulations—while preserving the core of what makes us intelligent. This essential core is our capacity to learn, remember, and reason independently of external support. It's the spark that produces genuine *insight*, the mental dexterity to solve problems within our own minds, and the wisdom to connect ideas spontaneously—cognitive processes that remain distinctly valuable even as technology increasingly mimics these abilities.

In conclusion, storing key information in human memory is not a quaint educational ideal; it is a pillar of cognitive function. The neuroscience we explored validates age-old common sense: *we remember what we wrestle with, we excel at what we practice, and we understand what we internalize.*

Fully exploring motivation, curiosity, and enthusiasm would substantially expand this chapter. Yet it is worth briefly noting the paradox highlighted by memory researchers Wang and Morris (2010): "we rapidly remember what interests us, but what interests us takes time to develop." In other words, genuine interest—and thus deep learning—often emerges gradually, as we become proficient, rather than preceding that proficiency. Ironically, in today's rush to make learning instantly appealing through games, rewards, or engaging demonstrations, we can overlook this crucial insight. Students initially attracted to STEM fields by exciting experiments or playful activities in high school may struggle when confronted with challenging coursework in college—the "math-science death march" described by David Goldberg (Drew, 2011). Lasting interest, the kind essential for expertise, is typically nurtured slowly, sustained by the satisfaction and intrinsic reward of growing competence.

Reflecting on the history of pedagogy, influential educational figures have sometimes obscured our understanding of how learning truly unfolds. Piaget, Vygotsky, Dewey, Bloom, Montessori, Bruner, and Skinner, among others, proposed groundbreaking ideas that captured imaginations and reshaped classrooms worldwide. Yet, as neuroscience reveals, many core assumptions of these thinkers—such as the effectiveness of unguided discovery learning, procedural-only approaches, or undervaluing explicit memorization—have hindered more effective educational practices. Appreciating both the insights and the limitations of these influential figures can guide educators toward more evidence-based, neurologically informed teaching methods, ultimately benefiting learners.

Rather than viewing memory as obsolete in the AI era, we should treat it as our personal knowledge bank. This empowers us to use AI wisely. By thoughtfully balancing what our minds and machines each do best, we ensure that external innovations enhance rather than diminish our intelligence. Ideally, future learners will confidently say: "I use the Internet, but I don't have to look everything up, because I've learned and remembered what matters." Such deep, resilient knowledge will be essential in navigating a world of endless information—and protecting our minds from cognitive decline amid constant technological distractions.

The authors used artificial intelligence tools, including ChatGPT, Claude, and Scite.ai to assist in identifying relevant research literature and refining the clarity and readability of the manuscript. All final content, critical interpretation, and responsibility for accuracy remain solely with the authors.

The opinions and assertions expressed herein are those of the authors and do not necessarily reflect the official policy or position of the Uniformed Services University or the Department of Defense.

References

Barr, N., Pennycook, G., Stolz, J. A., & Fugelsang, J. A. (2015). The brain in your pocket: Evidence that smartphones are used to supplant thinking. *Computers in Human Behavior, 48*, 473–480. https://doi.org/10.1016/j.chb.2015.02.029

Bastani, H., Bastani, O., Sungu, A., Ge, H., Kabakcı, O., & Mariman, R. (2024). *Generative AI can harm learning*, Available at SSRN, 4895486. Available at: https://hamsabastani.github.io/education_llm.pdf.

Becker, M., & Cabeza, R. (2024). Prediction error minimization as a common computational principle for curiosity and creativity. *The Behavioral and Brain Sciences, 47*, e93. https://doi.org/10.1017/s0140525x23003540

Becker, M., & Cabeza, R. (2025). The neural basis of the insight memory advantage. *Trends in Cognitive Sciences*. https://doi.org/10.1016/j.tics.2025.01.001

Bein, O., & Niv, Y. (2025). Schemas, reinforcement learning and the medial prefrontal cortex. *Nature Reviews Neuroscience*, 1–17.

Bjork, E. L., & Bjork, R. A. (2011). Chapter 5*:* Making things hard on yourself, but in a good way: Creating desirable difficulties to enhance learning. *Psychology and the Real World: Essays Illustrating Fundamental Contributions to Society.*

Bjork, R. A., Dunlosky, J., & Kornell, N. (2013). Self-regulated learning: Beliefs, techniques, and illusions. *Annual Review of Psychology, 64*, 417–444.

Bratsberg, B., & Rogeberg, O. (2018). Flynn effect and its reversal are both environmentally caused. *Proceedings of the National Academy of Sciences, 115*(26), 6674. https://doi.org/10.1073/pnas.1718793115

Buch, E. R., Claudino, L., Quentin, R., Bönstrup, M., & Cohen, L. (2021). Consolidation of human skill linked to waking hippocampo-neocortical replay. *Cell Reports, 35*(10), 109193. https://doi.org/10.1016/j.celrep.2021.109193

Burn-Murdoch, J. (2025). Have humans passed peak brain power? *Financial Times*. Available at: https://www.ft.com/content/a8016c64-63b7-458b-a371-e0e1c54a13fc

Buzsaki, G., McKenzie, S., & Davachi, L. (2022). Neurophysiology of remembering. *Annual Review of Psychology, 73*, 187–215. https://doi.org/10.1146/annurev-psych-021721-110002

Carpenter, S. K., Pan, S. C., & Butler, A. C. (2022). The science of effective learning with spacing and retrieval practice. *Nature Reviews Psychology, 1*(9), 496–511. https://doi.org/10.1038/s44159-022-00089-1

Carvalho, P. F., & Goldstone, R. L. (2019). When does interleaving practice improve learning? In Dunlosky, J., & Rawson, K. A. (Eds.) *The Cambridge handbook of cognition and education.*

Chen, B., Cheng, J., Wang, C., & Leung, V. (2025). Pedagogical biases in AI-powered educational tools: The case of lesson plan generators. *Social Innovations Journal*, 30(2). https://socialinnovationsjournal.com/index.php/sij/article/view/10004

Chi, M. T. H., & Wylie, R. (2014). The ICAP framework: Linking cognitive engagement to active learning outcomes. *Educational Psychologist, 49*(4), 219–243. https://doi.org/10.1080/00461520.2014.965823

Christodoulou, D. (2014). *Seven myths about education.* Routledge.

Christodoulou, D. (2018). *Give me your answer do: An interview with Daisy Christodoulou.* Available at: https://researched.org.uk/2018/09/26/give-me-your-answer-do-an-interview-with-daisy-christodoulou/

Cowan, N. (2014). Working memory underpins cognitive development, learning, and education. *Educational Psychology Review, 26*(2), 197–223.

Cowan, N., Belletier, C., Doherty, J. M., Jaroslawska, A. J., Rhodes, S., Forsberg, A., Naveh-Benjamin, M., Barrouillet, P., Camos, V., & Logie, R. H. (2020). How do scientific views change? Notes from an extended adversarial collaboration. *Perspectives on Psychological Science, 15*(4), 1011–1025. https://doi.org/10.1177/1745691620906415

David, L., Vassena, E., & Bijleveld, E. (2024). The unpleasantness of thinking: A meta-analytic review of the association between mental effort and negative affect. *Psychological Bulletin, 150*(9), 1070–1093. https://doi.org/10.1037/bul0000443

De Soares, A., Kim, T., Mugisho, F., Zhu, E., Lin, A., Zheng, C., & Baldassano, C. (2024). Top-down attention shifts behavioral and neural event boundaries in narratives with overlapping event scripts. *Current Biology, 34*(20), 4729–4742.e5.

Double, K. S., Chow, J. Y. L., Livesey, E. J., & Hopfenbeck, T. N. (2020). Causal illusions in the classroom: How the distribution of student outcomes can promote false instructional beliefs. *Cognitive Research: Principles and Implications, 5*(1). https://doi.org/10.1186/s41235-020-00237-2

Drew, C. (2011). Why science majors change their minds (it's just so darn hard). *New York Times*. Available at: http://www.nytimes.com/2011/11/06/education/edlife/why-science-majors-change-their-mind-its-just-so-darn-hard.html?_r=0

Dudai, Y., Karni, A., & Born, J. (2015). The consolidation and transformation of memory. *Neuron, 88*(1), 20–32. https://doi.org/10.1016/j.neuron.2015.09.004

Dutton, E., & Lynn, R. (2015). A negative Flynn effect in France, 1999 to 2008–9. *Intelligence, 51*, 67–70. https://doi.org/10.1016/j.intell.2015.05.005

Dutton, E., van der Linden, D., & Lynn, R. (2016). The negative Flynn effect: A systematic literature review. *Intelligence, 59*, 163–169.

Dworak, E. M., Revelle, W., & Condon, D. M. (2023). Looking for Flynn effects in a recent online U.S. adult sample: Examining shifts within the SAPA Project. *Intelligence, 98*. https://doi.org/10.1016/j.intell.2023.101734

Ericsson, K. A. (2009). *Development of professional expertise*. Cambridge University Press.

Fan, Y., Tang, L., Le, H., Shen, K., Tan, S., Zhao, Y., Shen, Y., Li, X., & Gašević, D. (2024). Beware of metacognitive laziness: Effects of generative artificial intelligence on learning motivation, processes, and performance. *British Journal of Educational Technology*.

Farzanfar, D., Spiers, H. J., Moscovitch, M., & Rosenbaum, R. S. (2022). From cognitive maps to spatial schemas. *Nature Reviews Neuroscience, 24*(2), 63–79. https://doi.org/10.1038/s41583-022-00655-9

Fernando, C., Osindero, S., & Banarse, D. (2024). The origin and function of external representations. *Adaptive Behavior, 32*(6). https://doi.org/10.1177/10597123241262534

Foster, N. L., Mueller, M. L., Was, C., Rawson, K. A., & Dunlosky, J. (2019). Why does interleaving improve math learning? The contributions of discriminative contrast and distributed practice. *Memory and Cognition, 47*(6), 1088–1101. https://doi.org/10.3758/s13421-019-00918-4

Freeman, S., Eddy, S. L., McDonough, M., Smith, M. K., Okoroafor, N., Jordt, H., & Wenderoth, M. P. (2014). Active learning increases student performance in science, engineering, and mathematics. *Proceedings of the National Academy of Sciences, 111*(23), 8410–8415.

Geary, D. C., Berch, D. B., & Koepke, K. M. (2019). Introduction: Cognitive foundations of mathematical interventions and early numeracy influences. *Mathematical Cognition and Learning, Vol 5*. Elsevier.

Goldfarb, E. V., Chun, M. M., & Phelps, E. A. (2016). Memory-guided attention: Independent contributions of the hippocampus and striatum. *Neuron, 89*(2), 317–324. https://doi.org/10.1016/j.neuron.2015.12.014

Guskjolen, A., & Cembrowski, M. S. (2023). Engram neurons: Encoding, consolidation, retrieval, and forgetting of memory. *Molecular Psychiatry, 28*(8), 3207–3219.

Hebscher, M., Wing, E., Ryan, J., & Gilboa, A. (2019). Rapid cortical plasticity supports long-term memory formation. *Trends in Cognitive Sciences, 23*(12), 989–1002. https://doi.org/10.1016/j.tics.2019.09.009

Henkel, O., Horne-Robinson, H., Kozhakhmetova, N., & Lee, A. (2024). *Effective and scalable math support: Evidence on the impact of an AI-tutor on math achievement in Ghana*. arXiv preprint arXiv:2402.09809.

Hirsch, E. (2000). You can always look it up—or can you? *American Educator, 24*(1), 4–9.

Kant, I. (1998). *Critique of pure reason* (P. Guyer & A. W. Wood, trans.). Cambridge University Press. (Original work published 1781).

Kosmyna, N., Hauptmann, E., Yuan, Y. T., Situ, J., Liao, X.-H., Beresnitzky, A. V., Braunstein, I., & Maes, P. (2025). *Your brain on ChatGPT: Accumulation of cognitive debt when using an AI assistant for essay writing task*. arXiv preprint arXiv:2506.08872.

Labaree, D. F. (2006). *The trouble with Ed Schools*. Yale University Press.

Lai, Y.-H. (2024). Education reform through westernization in Taiwan: a case of transferring the constructivist-based mathematics curriculum from the United States. *Journal of Asian Public Policy, 17*(1), 123–141. https://doi.org/10.1080/17516234.2022.2041267

Lakoff, G. (2014). Mapping the brain's metaphor circuitry: metaphorical thought in everyday reason. *Frontiers in Human Neuroscience, 8*, 958. https://doi.org/10.3389/fnhum.2014.00958

Langdon, C., Genkin, M., & Engel, T. A. (2023). A unifying perspective on neural manifolds and circuits for cognition. *Nature Reviews Neuroscience, 24*(6), 363–377. https://doi.org/10.1038/s41583-023-00693-x

Lee, H.-P. H., Sarkar, A., Tankelevitch, L., Drosos, I., Rintel, S., Banks, R., & Wilson, N. (2025). *The impact of generative AI on critical thinking: Self-reported reductions in cognitive effort and confidence effects from a survey of knowledge workers*. https://hankhplee.com/papers/genai_critical_thinking.pdf

Lin, T.-B., Wang, L.-Y., Li, J.-Y., & Chang, C. (2014). Pursuing quality education: The lessons from the education reform in Taiwan. *The Asia-Pacific Education Researcher, 23*, 813–822.

Mayo, D., Scott, T. R., Ren, M., Elsayed, G., Hermann, K., Jones, M., & Mozer, M. (2023). Multitask learning via interleaving: A neural network investigation. *Proceedings of the annual meeting of the cognitive science society*.

Miller, G. A., & Gildea, P. M. (1987). How children learn words. *Scientific American, 257*(3), 94–99.

Moreno, A., Limousin, F., Dehaene, S., & Pallier, C. (2018). Brain correlates of constituent structure in sign language comprehension. *NeuroImage, 167*, 151–161.

Morgan-Short, K., & Ullman, M. T. (2022). Declarative and procedural memory in second language learning: Psycholinguistic considerations. *The Routledge handbook of second language acquisition and psycholinguistics*, 322–334.

Narasimhalu, K., Wiryasaputra, L., Sitoh, Y. Y., & Kandiah, N. (2012). Post-stroke subjective cognitive impairment is associated with acute lacunar infarcts in the basal ganglia. *European Journal of Neurology, 20*(3), 547–551. https://doi.org/10.1111/ene.12032

Nasser, H. M., Calu, D. J., Schoenbaum, G., & Sharpe, M. J. (2017). The dopamine prediction error: Contributions to associative models of reward learning. *Frontiers in Psychology, 8*, 244. https://doi.org/10.3389/fpsyg.2017.00244

Novak, J. D., & Gowin, D. B. (1984). *Learning how to learn*. Cambridge University Press.

Oakley, B. A. (2013). Concepts and implications of altruism bias and pathological altruism. *Proceedings of the National Academy of Sciences, 110*, 10408–10415.

Oakley, B., Chen, K.Z., Schewe, O., Sejnowski, T.J. (2025). *Why Better Evidence Can Produce Worse Teaching: When Educational Research Stops Correcting Itself.* Manuscript in preparation.

Packard, M. G., & Knowlton, B. J. (2002). Learning and memory functions of the basal ganglia. *Annual Review of Neuroscience, 25*(1), 563–593.

Pao, G. M., Smith, C., Park, J., Takahashi, K., Watanakeesuntorn, W., Natsukawa, H., Chalasani, S. H., Lorimer, T., Takano, R., & Rungratsameetaweemana, N. (2021). *Experimentally testable whole brain manifolds that recapitulate behavior.* arXiv preprint arXiv:2106.10627.

Piaget, J. (1952). *The origins of intelligence in children.* (originally published in 1936) International Universities Press.

Piaget, J. (1970). *Genetic epistemology.* (E. Duckworth, trans.). Columbia University Press.

Pietschnig, J., & Voracek, M. (2015). One century of global IQ gains: A formal meta-analysis of the Flynn effect (1909–2013). *Perspectives on Psychological Science, 10*(3), 282–306.

Pignatelli, M., Ryan, T. J., Roy, D. S., Lovett, C., Smith, L. M., Muralidhar, S., & Tonegawa, S. (2019). Engram cell excitability state determines the efficacy of memory retrieval. *Neuron, 101*(2), 274–284.e5. https://doi.org/10.1016/j.neuron.2018.11.029

Power, A., Burda, Y., Edwards, H., Babuschkin, I., & Misra, V. (2022) *Grokking: generalization beyond overfitting on small algorithmic datasets*. arXiv preprint arXiv:2201.02177.

Public domain. (2017). *Reinforcement learning diagram, (created by Megajuice)*, Wikimedia. Available at: https://commons.wikimedia.org/wiki/File:Reinforcement_learning_diagram.svg

Risko, E. F., & Gilbert, S. J. (2016). Cognitive offloading. *Trends in Cognitive Sciences, 20*(9), 676–688. https://doi.org/10.1016/j.tics.2016.07.002

Robin, J., & Moscovitch, M. (2017). Details, gist and schema: Hippocampal–neocortical interactions underlying recent and remote episodic and spatial memory. *Current Opinion in Behavioral Sciences, 17*, 114–123. https://doi.org/10.1016/j.cobeha.2017.07.016

Rumelhart, D. E. (1980). Chapter 2: Schemata: The building blocks of cognition. In R. J. Spiro, B. C. Bruce, & W. F. Brewer (Eds.), (pp. 33–58). Routledge.

Saban, W., Pinheiro-Chagas, P., Borra, S., & Ivry, R. B. (2024). Distinct contributions of the cerebellum and basal ganglia to arithmetic procedures. *The Journal of Neuroscience, 44*(2). https://doi.org/10.1523/JNEUROSCI.1482-22.2023

Sahlgren, G. H. (2015). *Real Finnish lessons: The true story of an education superpower*. Centre for Policy Studies.

Sejnowski, T. (2024). *ChatGPT and the future of AI: The deep language revolution*. MIT Press.

Sejnowski, T. (2025). Thinking about thinking: AI offers theoretical insights into human memory. *The Transmitter* (Pre-press).

Shouval, H. Z., & Kirkwood, A. (2025). Eligibility traces as a synaptic substrate for learning. *Current Opinion in Neurobiology, 91*, 102978. https://doi.org/10.1016/j.conb.2025.102978

Skulmowski, A. (2023). The cognitive architecture of digital externalization. *Educational Psychology Review, 35*(4). https://doi.org/10.1007/s10648-023-09818-1

Song, S., & Su, M. (2022). The intelligence quotient-math achievement link: Evidence from behavioral and biological research. *Current Opinion in Behavioral Sciences, 46*, 101160.

Sparrow, B., Liu, J., & Wegner, D. M. (2011). Google effects on memory: Cognitive consequences of having information at our fingertips. *Science, 333*(6043), 776–778.

Sutton, R. S. (1988). Learning to predict by the methods of temporal differences. *Machine Learning, 3*, 9–44.

Sutton, R. S., & Barto, A. G. (2018). *Reinforcement learning: An introduction* (2nd ed.). MIT Press.

Sweller, J. (2008). Instructional implications of David C. Geary's evolutionary educational psychology. *Educational Psychologist, 43*(4), 214–216.

Teasdale, T. W., & Owen, D. R. (2008). Secular declines in cognitive test scores: A reversal of the Flynn Effect. *Intelligence, 36*(2), 121–126. https://doi.org/10.1016/j.intell.2007.01.007

Ten Berge, T., & Van Hezewijk, R. (1999). Procedural and declarative knowledge: An evolutionary perspective. *Theory & Psychology, 9*(5), 605–624.

Thompson, E. J., Rollik, L., Waked, B., Mills, G., Kaur, J., Geva, B., Carrasco-Davis, R., George, T. M., Domine, C., Dorrell, W., & Stephenson-Jones, M. (2024). *Replay of procedural experience is independent of the hippocampus.* https://doi.org/10.1101/2024.06.05.597547.

Tik, M., Sladky, R., Luft, C. D. B., Willinger, D., Hoffmann, A., Banissy, M. J., Bhattacharya, J., & Windischberger, C. (2018). Ultra-high-field fMRI insights on insight: Neural correlates of the Aha! moment. *Human Brain Mapping, 39*(8), 3241–3252.

Trahan, L., Stuebing, K. K., Hiscock, M. K., & Fletcher, J. M. (2014). The Flynn effect: A meta-analysis. *Psychological Bulletin, 140*(5), 1332–1360. https://doi.org/10.1037/a0037173

VanRullen, R., & Kanai, R. (2021). Deep learning and the global workspace theory. *Trends in Neurosciences, 44*(9), 692–704.

Wamsley, E. J. (2019). Memory consolidation during waking rest. *Trends in Cognitive Sciences, 23*(3), 171–173. https://doi.org/10.1016/j.tics.2018.12.007

Wang, S. H., & Morris, R. G. (2010). Hippocampal-neocortical interactions in memory formation, consolidation, and reconsolidation. *Annual Review of Psychology, 61*, 49–79. https://doi.org/10.1146/annurev.psych.093008.100523

Wickelgren, I. (2025). How 'event scripts' structure your personal memories. *Quanta Magazine.* Available at: https://www.quantamagazine.org/how-event-scripts-structure-our-personal-memories-20250221/

Wilson, R. C., Shenhav, A., Straccia, M., & Cohen, J. D. (2019). The eighty five percent rule for optimal learning. *Nature Communications, 10*(1), 4646. https://doi.org/10.1038/s41467-019-12552-4

Wimmer, G. E., & Büchel, C. (2021). Reactivation of single-episode pain patterns in the hippocampus and decision making. *The Journal of Neuroscience, 41*(37), 7894–7908. https://doi.org/10.1523/jneurosci.1350-20.2021

Wojcik, M. J., Li, A. X., Wasmuht, D., Stroud, J. P., Stokes, M. G., Myers, N. E., & Hunt, L. T. (2025). Working memory shapes neural geometry in human EEG over learning, *bioRxiv*, pp. 2025.01.21.634110.

Yang, W., Sun, C., Huszár, R., Hainmueller, T., Kiselev, K., & Buzsáki, G. (2024). Selection of experience for memory by hippocampal sharp wave ripples. *Science, 383*(6690), 1478–1483.

Yang, Y., Huang, Z., Yang, Y., Fan, M., & Yin, D. (2025a). Time-dependent consolidation mechanisms of durable memory in spaced learning. *Communications Biology, 8*(1), 535. https://doi.org/10.1038/s42003-025-07964-6

Yang, T.-C., Hsu, Y.-C., & Wu, J.-Y. (2025b). The effectiveness of ChatGPT in assisting high school students in programming learning: Evidence from a quasi-experimental research. *Interactive Learning Environments*. https://doi.org/10.1080/10494820.2025.2450659

Ye, L., Ba, L., & Yan, D. (2025). A study of dynamic functional connectivity changes in flight trainees based on a triple network model. *Scientific Reports, 15*(1). https://doi.org/10.1038/s41598-025-89023-y

Part V

Other Themes in AI Policy

The AI Revolution in Healthcare: Opportunities and Risks

David W. Wood

Introduction

Healthcare systems are in crisis around the world. They face greater demand for increasingly expensive treatments from a population that is ageing and has numerous unhealthy habits. After many decades of improvement, the statistics for healthspan—the number of years people live in good health—seem poised to go into reverse.

This is a complex problem and there is no "magic bullet" solution. However, artificial intelligence can play many roles in reversing these unhappy trends and in boosting population health. It can assist doctors in diagnosis and in recommending therapies. It can assist patients to stick to their treatment plans. It can accelerate the development and testing of new therapeutics, via richer models of biochemical interactions, via the conception and generation of brand-new molecules to alter these interactions, and via forecasting more reliably the ultimate outcome of medical trials. It can identify the special features of each individual patient, enabling greater adoption of personalized medicine. More

David W. Wood, Chair of London Futurists, Executive Director of LEVF (Longevity Escape Velocity Foundation), Foresight Advisor at SingularityNET, Principal at Delta Wisdom, and author or co-author of 14 books about the future.

D. W. Wood (✉)
Delta Wisdom, London, UK
e-mail: davidw@deltawisdom.com

M. Rangeley, N. Fairfax (eds.), *The Artificial Intelligence Revolution*,
https://doi.org/10.1007/978-3-032-11814-1_23

fundamentally, it can identify earlier signs of the accumulation of underlying biochemical damage, and recommend various "detox" treatments that, in contrast to many products currently marketed under that description, actually do restore vitality. As in the age-old proverb, a stitch in time will save nine. This will benefit populations, not only in terms of individual medical health but in terms of the health of the economy and society as a whole. That is the potential of artificial intelligence.

Nevertheless, over-hasty imposition of untested AI solutions could backfire, sickening populations, and turning the public against the whole field, preventing the attainment of the many benefits it could bring. This would be similar to the hostile public sentiment regarding nuclear energy and genetically-modified foods—sentiments that have done a lot more harm than good overall. Accordingly, the application of AI within healthcare needs to be guided and governed by an overarching set of principles.

In short, as we develop and interact with increasingly powerful AI systems, there is a lot that needs to be understood by people throughout the healthcare ecosystem:

- The goals that we are hoping to accomplish—rather than us persisting in some direction because it is currently trendy, or has some alluring features, or it seemed like a good idea the last time that we thought about strategic direction
- The principal characteristics of the products and methods that are most likely to serve these goals well—characteristics such as explainability, transparency, verifiability, auditability, and accountability
- How we will manage the surprises arising on route to our goals—rather than us being caught flat-footed as the victim of inertia or denial, when unexpected signals of poor health outcomes start showing on our radars.

Healthcare in Crisis

In 1865, the British economist William Stanley Jevons pointed out an apparent paradox. Improvements in the efficiency of steam engines in preceding decades meant that less coal was needed to produce a given amount of work done. However, rather than this efficiency improvement reducing the overall consumption of coal, industry actually *boosted* its demand for that fuel. The reason: the increased efficiency made coal-powered machinery more economically viable, leading to higher total coal use.

The general principle, now known as "Jevons Paradox", is that when technological improvements increase the efficiency of resource use, total consumption of that resource may rise rather than fall. This is for both direct and indirect so-called "rebound" reasons:

- Direct: Lower costs lead to increased consumption of the same resource.
- Indirect: Efficiency in one area stimulates growth elsewhere, leading to overall higher consumption.

As for the consumption of coal, so also for the consumption of healthcare. Improvements in medical efficiency, technology, and cost-effectiveness have often led to increased overall healthcare utilization, rather than decreased expenditures or reduced system strain. Here are a few examples:

- More efficient and accurate diagnostics tools, such as MRI and CT scans, reduce costs and wait times, making scans more accessible. But this can lead to more frequent scans, incidental findings, and additional follow-up procedures.
- Minimally invasive surgeries such as laparoscopic procedures lower recovery times, reduce hospital stays, and cut costs. However, procedures that are easier, safer, and cheaper can lead to higher surgical rates for conditions that previously might have been managed conservatively.
- Telehealth and digital health tools improve efficiency, reducing the cost and effort of accessing a doctor. However, lower costs and increased convenience can lead to higher overall patient visits, including unnecessary consultations, potentially straining healthcare resources.
- Lower cost generic drugs make medications more affordable, but instead of reducing spending, this can lead to higher prescription rates and complications from polypharmacy (when someone takes multiple medications at the same time to treat multiple conditions), particularly in ageing populations.
- Advances in healthcare keep people alive longer, but this increases lifetime medical costs, with an increase in the prevalence of chronic diseases, leading to higher overall healthcare spending.

In short, healthcare can be seen as a victim of its own success: improvements in the provision of healthcare have led, counterintuitively, to the healthcare system facing additional stress and strain.

Adding to the pressures, populations around the world have been adopting lifestyle habits that raise the prevalence of many diseases:

- Excessive drinking of sugar-laden sodas and energy drinks, along with increased consumption of ultra-processed foods high in salt, sugar, and

unhealthy fats, contributes to obesity, metabolic disorders, and cardiovascular diseases.
- Sedentary lifestyles and increased screen time are linked to a decline in physical activity.
- The rise of automation and convenience technology (such as elevators and online shopping) has further decreased incidental exercise.
- Social media, digital overload, and "doomscrolling" are linked to increased anxiety, depression, and body image issues.
- The shift towards digital communication over face-to-face interactions has weakened social support networks; more people experience social isolation, leading to higher rates of loneliness, depression, and cognitive decline.
- The normalization of recreational drug use, including marijuana and vaping, has contributed to long-term health risks.
- Abuse of prescription drugs, particularly opioids and benzodiazepines, has become a public health crisis in many regions.
- Increased exposure to air pollution, microplastics, and endocrine-disrupting chemicals negatively impacts respiratory health, fertility, and metabolic functions; urban pollution contributes to higher rates of asthma, lung diseases, and cognitive impairment.
- Overuse of antibiotics has led to antibiotic resistance, making some infections harder to treat.
- Many individuals rely on medication rather than lifestyle changes to manage conditions like hypertension, diabetes, and high cholesterol; preventive measures such as regular exercise, proper diet, and stress management are often overlooked.

It's no surprise, therefore, that despite many advances made across multiple dimensions of healthcare in recent decades, healthcare systems are widely perceived as being in a state of crisis. For example:

- In the UK, Lord Ara Darzi, the holder of the Paul Hamlyn Chair of Surgery at Imperial College London, was asked by the UK Government to lead a wide-ranging investigation into the state of the National Health Service (NHS). His report (Darzi, 2024), issued in November 2024, started with this stark summary: "The National Health Service is in serious trouble. … Public satisfaction—which stood at a record high in 2009—is now at its lowest ever".
- In the United States, Dr. Marty Makary, a surgeon and professor at Johns Hopkins University, who has been nominated as the next commissioner of the FDA, bemoaned an apparent run-away surge in costly prescriptions (Makary, 2019): "Last year, physicians prescribed a record 4.5 billion

medications. That's about double the number we prescribed just a decade ago. Did the incidence of disease double in the last ten years? Of course not. Most of the doubling represents pills that could be avoided with lifestyle changes or more judicious prescribing".
- In South Korea, President Yoon Suk Yeol insisted that (Lee & Son, 2024) an additional 2000 new doctors needed to be trained each year, as "a critical step to preventing further collapses in the medical infrastructure across the country".

How AI Might Help: The Big Picture

To recap: just as efficiency improvements in industry led to increased coal consumption, advances in medical technology have paradoxically intensified healthcare demand. Can AI break this cycle, or will it merely accelerate healthcare strain?

As just noted, one suggestion to address the crisis in healthcare systems is to make more resources available. Thus, President Yoon of South Korea called for a surge of new doctors to be trained. The report in the United Kingdom by Lord Darzi highlights "a shortfall of £37 billion of capital investment ... The NHS has been starved of capital and the capital budget was repeatedly raided to plug holes in day-to-day spending".

Hence, the first main theme: **AI as additional resource**. AI could supplement, or even in some cases replace, the effort provided by human personnel within the health service. Rather than hiring, say, 1000 additional human radiologists, the existing set of radiologists could have their productivity significantly enhanced by access to AI systems that help them interpret medical scans. Rather than building larger hospitals to accommodate more patients for attention by specialist consultants, AI could enable systems in which patients are treated in their homes or in existing local medical centres, where medical expertise is made available in computer systems with occasional remote assistance from human doctors. Rather than hiring new human lecturers to pass on medical knowledge to trainee doctors, AI-powered training systems could enable education at lower cost—with the added advantage that each trainee receives individual attention.

As it happens, in South Korea, many doctors rejected the proposal from President Yoon. Merely increasing resources would not, by itself, solve the problems in the country's health system. Underlying issues of healthcare disparities and other existing problems could actually be exacerbated, they said (Kim, 2024).

This introduces the second main theme: **AI as additional intelligence**. A good way to solve problems—either the problems of an individual sick person, or the problems of the healthcare system as a whole—is to apply more intelligence. Accordingly, AI should not be seen simply as a means to do more of the same (but faster and cheaper). Instead, AI can be seen as a means to enable systemic improvements in healthcare—by identifying and then addressing underlying root causes.

Let's now look at examples of AI solutions which are already being adopted within healthcare, before considering what may become possible in the years ahead.

AI Solutions Already in Use

Evaluations of the performance of AI systems need to beware several potential mistakes:

- Examples of apparent good performance of AI are sometimes cherry-picked from a larger set of trials. Accordingly, rather than putting undue weight on a small number of seemingly outstanding results, it's important to obtain and evaluate statistical data.
- AIs may appear to outperform human practitioners on tasks such as spotting tumour-like growths that turn out to be malignant—but, in some cases, only by virtue of scoring worse on complementary criteria, such as numbers of "false positive" alarms. Accordingly, it's important to assess performance on a number of criteria in parallel.
- Apparently good performance in a trial may be due to these tests sharing important criteria with training data, whereas the performance of the AI would be much less impressive on data that have a wider distribution of characteristics.
- An AI may perform well in selected portions of a medical practitioner's work tasks, but completely fail in other portions of the job—including portions that are usually "taken for granted" and not documented in any job description.

In short, before adopting an AI solution, it's important not to be misled by hype, exaggeration, or over-exuberance. But that still leaves plenty of examples that are full of promise.

Consider an AI system that scans mammograms, developed by Google Health and subsequently brought into commercial practice by iCAD (2023). This AI reached public awareness after featuring in a Nature article (McKinney et al., 2020) "International evaluation of an AI system for breast cancer screening" published in January 2020. The AI was designed to detect breast cancer at an early stage of the disease by analysing mammograms. Here are some key findings from the Nature article:

- The AI was trained on a representative set of 76,000 scans of women in the United Kingdom and 15,000 women in the United States.
- It was subsequently tested on a separate set of nearly 30,000 scans from women in the two countries.
- For each of the scans, it was known whether the woman had cancer subsequently confirmed by a biopsy, or had no sign of cancer in a follow-up examination at least 12 months later; these results were made available to the AI for the training set, but not for the test set.
- For each of the scans in the test set, the accuracy of the prediction made by the AI was compared to the decision made by human radiologists when the scans were taken.
- For the scans from women in the United States, compared to the assessments by human radiologists, the AI had 9.4% fewer false negatives (cases when a cancerous tumour was missed), and 5.7% fewer false positives (cases when a feature of the scan was wrongly assessed to be cancerous).
- The corresponding figures in the United Kingdom were 2.7% fewer false negatives and 1.2% fewer false positives.

In other words, the AI outperformed the human radiologists in both the United States and the United Kingdom, with the difference being more striking in the case of the United States. This latter difference was interpreted as being caused by the US scans being reviewed by only a single human radiologist, whereas in the UK, each scan was reviewed by two humans, with a third person added to the review in cases when the first two drew different conclusions.

The potential benefits of this AI evidently include the following:

- More cancers detected and treated earlier.
- Fewer women suffering the drawbacks of false positives.
- Hospitals can adopt systems in which mammograms are reviewed, independently, by a human radiologist and the AI, with a deeper review taking place in cases of different conclusions.
- This system is likely to be cheaper, faster, and more reliable than review systems which involve two human radiologists.

The same pattern is being applied in many other aspects of the overall medical journey from health checks to diagnosis (Liu et al., 2019), considering potential treatments, applying treatments, monitoring their effectiveness, improving compliance, and long-term follow-up. Representative examples include the following:

- Another AI system from Google detects the eye disease diabetic retinopathy as accurately as human ophthalmologists. It is deployed in India and Thailand for low-cost screening for early signs of the disease, so that treatments can be applied to prevent the patient becoming blind (Sawhney, 2024).
- By analysing patient electrocardiograms (ECGs), an AI system called ECG-AI developed by the Mayo Clinic and Anumana (an AI-driven health technology company) is able to provide earlier warnings of atherosclerotic cardiovascular disease—when arteries are narrowed or blocked by a build-up of fatty plaques. Such systems can detect silent cardiovascular disease before it becomes fatal (Awasthi et al., 2023).
- AI-powered health assessment apps such as Ada Health lead patients through a questionnaire about their symptoms and overall circumstances, before recommending follow-up actions; such tools can also assist human doctors to reach their own conclusions (Gilbert et al., 2020).
- AI early warning systems for sepsis have shown improved early detection and patient outcomes, demonstrating how AI can reduce hospital mortality and burdens through timely interventions (Adams et al., 2022).
- AI-guided robotic-assisted surgery, from companies such as Da Vinci and Medtronic, assist surgeons with delicate procedures such as prostate surgery and cardiac bypass. Compared to traditional surgery methods, these robot-assisted operations are less invasive, more precise, and shorten recovery time (Knudsen et al., 2024).
- AI-powered mental health chatbots such as Wysa provide cognitive behavioural therapy (CBT) for anxiety and depression, expanding access to mental health advice at low cost (Malik et al., 2022).
- AI-assisted diet and lifestyle coaching systems, such as Zoe AI and Inside-Tracker, help individuals avoid chronic conditions like obesity and diabetes.
- Apps connected to wearable devices, such as the Apple iWatch, Google Fitbit, or the Oura Ring, can use AI to detect irregular heartbeats (atrial fibrillation), changes in blood oxygen, unusual stress levels, or poor sleep patterns, and can remind patients to take medications, exercise, or hydrate. This increases adherence to, for example, cardiovascular and diabetes treatment plans.
- AIs such as Dragon Medical from Nuance (part of Microsoft) automate clinical documentation, allowing doctors to dictate patient notes directly

into electronic health records (EHRs). This can save hours per day for doctors, reducing burnout, and improving patient interactions (DeMuro, 2024).
- AI-driven bed management systems can predict the demand on intensive care units, and optimize staff allocation. This reduces hospital overcrowding and improves emergency response times (ACE, 2023).
- AI-enhanced telemedicine platforms in rural Africa and rural India enable doctor consultations via smartphone. With real-time AI-powered translation surmounting language barriers, this helps to bridge healthcare disparities in low-resource settings.

AI Systems That Are Discovering and Validating New Treatments

A common feature of the solutions mentioned above is that they all extend the existing practice of human practitioners—performing tasks that humans can already accomplish. These AIs have the advantage of operating in many cases at lower cost and, sometimes, with higher accuracy.

In contrast, a number of other AI systems are assisting the design and discovery of new treatments.

These systems could have a profound impact on the practice of healthcare. That's because the rate of discovery of new medical treatments has actually slowed down over the decades. The outputs of human ingenuity seem to be faltering—but the additional intelligence of AI could reverse that trend.

One measure of the slowdown of medical discoveries has been dubbed "Eroom's Law". This name was suggested in a March 2012 article in Nature, "Diagnosing the decline in pharmaceutical R&D efficiency", by Jack Scannell and colleagues (Scannell et al., 2012). It's a play on the (much) better-known "Moore's Law", which describes in rough terms how the capabilities of semiconductor chips roughly double, for a given cost, every 18 months. The compound effect of Moore's Law has been the remarkable shrinkage, from the 1950s onwards, in size and power requirements of digital storage and digital computation. Eroom's Law also describes a doubling trend that has operated since the 1950s, but in this case, the result is a slowdown (not a speed-up) of performance.

As Scannell and his colleagues describe their findings in the abstract of their paper, "The past 60 years have seen huge advances in many of the scientific, technological, and managerial factors that should tend to raise the efficiency of commercial drug research and development (R&D). Yet the number of new drugs approved per billion US dollars spent on R&D has halved roughly every 9 years since 1950, falling around 80-fold in inflation-adjusted terms".

A more recent review of Eroom's Law in The Economist (2024), in April 2024, indicates that there may be a reduction in the rate of decline in drug discovery performance, in part due to the nimbler activities of small start-ups. However, the overall trend remains one of ever-greater cost and effort being required to discover new pharmaceuticals and take them all the way through trials into approved medical usage.

Seven factors can be identified as contributing to this downward trend:

1. Regulators have become more cautious, in response to a number of instances of terrible side effects from approved drugs.
2. The diseases which don't yet have comprehensive cures have causes that are more complex than can be treated by any single treatment.
3. All the "low-hanging fruit" has been picked—meaning that the easy discoveries have already been made, leaving only the ones which require a great deal more effort.
4. Many new pharmaceuticals have only marginal improvement over their predecessors, and it takes more statistical effort during human trials to verify that the new treatments are indeed an improvement.
5. Despite the greater efforts required, large pharmaceutical companies understand that if they throw enough money into their projects, they will in due course develop a few new blockbuster drugs with large commercial windfalls (this is the philosophy of "try, try, and try again", also known as "keep throwing money at it").
6. Due to the highly competitive and secretive nature of the pharmaceutical industry, companies often share only minimal information about their project failures, resulting in other companies repeating essentially the same investigations and wasting yet more money.
7. Treatments that have good results in mice, treating mouse versions of human diseases, often fail to have similar positive results in human trials—due, in part, to the mouse versions of these diseases arising only in mice with unusual genetic modifications.

Happily, AI can address a number of these issues. This assistance can be broken down into six aspects—each of which is significant in its own right, and the combination is particularly impactful.

First, **improved AI models of the interactions of multiple biochemical pathways can suggest new targets for pharmaceutical intervention**:

- Reactions which new drugs could prevent or slow down, thereby preventing (directly or indirectly) the *accumulation* of biochemical damage
- Reactions which new drugs could initiate or speed up, thereby accelerating (directly or indirectly) the *removal* of biochemical damage

Similar to the way in which DeepMind's AlphaGo software played moves in the game of Go that took human expert observers by surprise—initially considering them to be errors, but subsequently appreciating their strategic brilliance—these new biochemical targets may be different from the ones which human researchers previously considered to be the most promising points of medical intervention.

Second, similar to the way that generative AI can "imagine" words to extend sentences, or pictures to match a given prompt, it can also **"imagine" new molecules tailor-made to have specific interactions with the targets already identified**. These molecules will have three-dimensional geometry, a distribution of electric charges, and various guards, probes, and other features, so as to fit precisely into this one target, without having side effects in other reactions.

One company that has excelled in these first two aspects of using AI is Insilico Medicine (Zhavoronkov et al., 2019), which developed an AI-generated drug candidate for idiopathic pulmonary fibrosis (IPF) in just 46 days, far faster than conventional drug discovery methods. This process of "drug imagination" is supported by what Alex Zhavoronkov, co-CEO of Insilico Medicine, has described as a "zoo" of some 40 different generative AI models (Chace, 2022).

What further assists this process of imagination is software such as AlphaFold, from DeepMind, that reliably predicts the 3D shapes that various proteins will adopt—and, therefore, the reactions which these proteins will undertake (Jumper et al., 2021).

Once AI has suggested the use of particular biomolecules to alter disease pathways, the next step is to test these hypotheses in actual biochemistry. Accordingly, focus moves from "in silico" tests to in vitro tests (reactions in test tubes) and finally to in vivo tests (in living animals and in living humans).

That's where AI can make its third contribution. Tests of biochemical interventions can be lengthy, labour-intensive, and, therefore, expensive. However, AI can supervise the robotic performance of whole families of tests in parallel. Just as AI guidance can assist robotic surgery (as mentioned earlier), it can also **allow robot-controlled in vitro tests to be carried out at lower cost and greater precision**. Aspects of tests on various living animals (such as worms or fruit flies) can also be accelerated and improved by AI-guided robotic equipment. Further, similar equipment can reduce cost from the analysis of samples (such as blood or biopsies) from human trial participants.

The fourth contribution of AI is potentially more controversial, but over time, it is likely to be accepted as well. This contribution builds upon the ability of AI to discern patterns which are initially hidden from human perception. Just as AI can learn, by itself, which features of a mammogram can predict a future cancerous growth, so also can it **learn, by itself, which features of the results of phase one and phase two clinical trials predict the eventual outcome of all-important phase three trials**.

The reason this could be controversial is that project managers within pharmaceutical companies, who have seen a drug pass earlier test phases, will strongly anticipate that drug going forward to later test phases. But even if, for example, the FDA would accept that drug for a new phase of tests, the recommendation of the AI may be that the drug has too low a chance of success in these tests, and, therefore, research on it should be discontinued.

On the other hand, if AI has done well with the three previous contributions mentioned above, the likelihood is that many of the drugs identified by that process will have excellent results in phase one and phase two trials, and will be poised to move swiftly through remaining phases into clinical usage. That fact will be clear, not only to the humans supervising the tests but also to any AI making its own predictions of the outcome of future test phases.

The fifth contribution of AI to the discovery and validation of new treatments is in **the identification and documentation of which subset of the population will respond well to a treatment, and which others will respond poorly**. Rather than a drug being withdrawn because of adverse reactions from a small proportion of people to whom it has been administered, what will be clearer in advance is that these people should not be treated with that drug.

There are many factors which can cause adverse reactions to a medical treatment. This includes variations in genetics, epigenetics, biome, other medical conditions, diet, lifestyle, psychology, and environmental influences. Handling all these different variables leads to an exponential explosion in complexity. That is the kind of multi-factorial problem that high-powered AI can decisively simplify. In other words, AI can allow the kind of specialized (or personalized) treatments which permit more drugs to pass through testing—drugs that would previously have been rejected, on account of unpredictable bad reactions, or on account of underwhelming overall efficacy statistics. Knowing that a drug has an outstanding positive effect on a clearly demarcated subset of the population should be sufficient to allow that drug to be approved for usage—within the demarcated subpopulation.

That leaves the sixth of the contributions of AI to the discovery and validation of treatments with decisively better results—in other words, to the comprehensive reversal of Eroom's Law. That contribution addresses perhaps the two most vexing drivers of Eroom's Law—the apparent ever-increasing complexity of the types of biological damage which remain unsolved, and the perception that the days of quick progress ("easy pickings" of "low hanging fruit") have long passed. This contribution involves **a new paradigm regarding both the causes and the treatments of chronic diseases**. It's a paradigm shift that has been foretold for several decades, but is only now coming into clearer view. Let's take a closer look, after briefly taking stock of the argument so far.

AI Solutions as Part of a Forthcoming Healthcare Paradigm Shift

To recap: numerous increases in performance by healthcare systems—each remarkable in their own ways—have often had a triple result:

1. They have addressed and alleviated a current set of symptoms in patients.
2. This has often given people greater implicit confidence that medicine will be able to make amends for any shortfalls in their own lifestyles—such as poor diet, inadequate exercise, substance abuse, or poor environmental hygiene—but these lifestyle habits result in due course, sadly, in health issues re-emerging with greater vigour later in their lives.
3. Even when people follow the best available advice on lifestyles, it is only a matter of time before one or other chronic disease starts asserting itself in their lives—such as cancer, dementia, lung disease, or heart disease.

Accordingly, the process of treating diseases, with or without AI solutions assisting in individual treatments, can be likened to a game of whack-a-mole, in which a series of mole-like targets emerge with ever increasing pace, eventually overwhelming any attempt to "whack" all of them.

That's one explanation for the dilemma described in the opening section of this essay, "Healthcare in crisis". If we are not careful, all that will be accomplished by greater adoption of AI innovation in healthcare will be to delay by a number of years the time when a patient's body becomes overwhelmed by an onslaught of chronic conditions. And in that case, the resourcing demands on health services will keep increasing, as more people suffer, sooner or later, from such an onslaught.

The default approach to healthcare—which can be called the "treat diseases" paradigm—accepts this situation as a given, whilst working to keep on delaying the time at which individual patients become overrun with an accumulation of chronic disease.

An alternative approach can be called the "prevent diseases by proactive damage repair" paradigm, or, more briefly, the "damage repair" paradigm. Rather than accepting as inevitable the eventual emergence of overwhelming chronic disease, this paradigm aims to address the underlying circumstances which set the scene for any such eventual emergence.

In more detail, the *prevent diseases by proactive damage repair* paradigm understands chronic disease as being the outcome of the growth of various kinds of biomolecular damage throughout the body (Steele, 2020)—damage such as the following:

- A decline in the vitality of the immune system
- A weakening of the power of mitochondria within cells
- Mutations within the DNA in chromosomes throughout the body
- A reduction in the number of stem cells
- Various plaques or tangles within organs
- An accumulation of "junk" waste product inside cells, or in the spaces between cells
- A growing blanket of methyl groups attached to parts of DNA within cells, altering how proteins are created in these cells

As this damage becomes more prevalent, various organs or biological subsystems operate less efficiently, eventually giving rise to diseases that are increasingly severe in their effect.

In this paradigm, as well as treating individual diseases as and when they occur, healthcare should be providing a suite of regular proactive "detox" treatments—treatments that periodically repair or remove the various types of low-level bodily damage before that damage accumulates to a state when it causes serious health problems.

Examples of the detox treatments that can be involved are as follows:

- Boosts to the immune system
- Revitalizing mitochondria
- Restoring the DNA in chromosomes to its original state
- Introducing new stem cells—or multiplying the ones that already exist
- Breaking up plaques and tangles
- Improving the recycling mechanisms that would normally handle waste product inside or between cells
- Reversing the errant accumulation of methyl groups attached to DNA

In reality, each of these projects is challenging since damage repair interventions may have unwelcome side effects or other drawbacks. This is where a new level of intelligence could play a decisive role. Extensions or adaptations of the kinds of AI solutions already discussed earlier in this chapter could result, not just in the alleviation of individual diseases, but in the removal or repair of low-level bodily damage.

Ways in which this could happen include the following:

- AI scanning vast troves of medical data and identifying new patterns in which damage removal or repair could work
- AI assisting the analysis of the biology of animals which have internal damage repair mechanisms superior to those in humans—so that aspects of these mechanisms could be incorporated in new detox initiatives for humans (Austad, 2022)
- AI reviewing research publications, including ones that are relatively obscure, to notice novel ideas that deserve more attention
- AI designing nanoscale intervention mechanisms—including specially configured nanoparticles (containing payloads), dynamic nanoscale motors, and nanoscale robots with their own internal intelligence

AI "Solutions" to Beware

Although AI is poised to improve many aspects of healthcare, close attention needs to be given to potential failure modes of new solutions. Indeed, if society adopts AI "solutions" that turn out to cause significant medical harm, there could be an unfortunate social backlash against a whole field of treatment. As one comparison, recall the way in which some adverse medical responses to Covid vaccines have invigorated a social movement of people who are sceptical or even hostile to vaccines in general. Also recall how an early disastrous trial of genetic therapies, which resulted in the tragic death of 18-year-old Jesse Gelsinger, arguably delayed progress with research into genetic therapies for up to a decade (Rinde, 2019).

With that in mind, here are seven specific failure modes of AI healthcare solutions.

The first failure mode is when AI systems that are trained on data from one context are applied in fields outside that context. As obvious examples, systems trained only on medical data from males may give wrong recommendations for female patients, and recommendations suited to people from one racial background may likewise be inappropriate for people from a different background (Obermeyer et al., 2019). Other parameters that may be relevant include age, pre-existing medical conditions, and diet. Worryingly, there may be population differences whose relevance to treatment outcomes is not suspected in advance. In all these cases, the problem is one of **biased AI**—more specifically, of unsuspected biases in AIs.

That leads to a second failure mode in which an AI issues its recommendations without explaining the reasoning behind these recommendations. Such systems are described as **opaque AI** (or "black box AI").

What can go wrong with opaque AI is that users may be lulled into complacency due to its first few recommendations having good outcomes, and then not be alert when its recommendations become inappropriate.

Instead, along with a specific recommendation for medical treatment, an AI should ideally explain:

- The aspects of patient data which have tilted the recommendation one way rather than another
- Any factors which might deserve further investigation, in case they would cause a reconsideration of the recommendation

Third, AIs may offer a rationale for their explanations which isn't actually how they have arrived at their conclusions. This is the problem of **confabulating AI** (or "hallucinating AI"). This is similar to the way in which we humans sometimes offer justifications for our individual actions which puts us in a good light, even though our actual motivations (perhaps unknown to us at a conscious level) are far less noble—or are simply mistaken.

As an example, an AI might recommend the prescription of a set of drugs, along with the assertion that a particular piece of patient data is the reason why these drugs make sense in this case. A human doctor might check this piece of data and acknowledge that, indeed, the data is within a range that would tend, *all other things being equal*, to support this specific prescription. However, if other factors have also played a significant part in the AI reaching its conclusion, but are excluded from what the AI publishes as a summary of its thinking processes, and if these factors happen to be mistaken, that error (and hence the dangers inherent with this course of treatment) won't be brought to the attention of any human reviewer.

A different kind of error mode is **vulnerable AI** (or "hackable AI") when an AI system becomes central to how a medical procedure is conducted, but the AI is knocked out of operation by a configuration error or by adverse hacking (such as an extended ransomware attack). In this case, the AI has been introduced with insufficient attention to security, robustness, or resilience.

The problem of vulnerability applies, of course, to any healthcare solution that involves software. However, AI potentially complicates the risks, since the intelligence within the AI can be fooled, misled, or otherwise manipulated.

Related to vulnerable AI is the risk of what can be called **rushed AI** (or "AI in a hurry"), that is, an AI solution which has been released too quickly—perhaps following a frantic race to beat a competitor to the marketplace—without having sufficient attention to quality and safety.

Once again, that's part of a general principle that applies much more widely than just to AI systems—namely the general principle that before systems are deployed into real-world use, there needs to be good evidence that appropriate validation tests have taken place. And, once again, it's the intelligence within AI systems that adds extra complications, such as the possibilities for bias, opacity, and confabulations already mentioned.

A further error mode is **overhyped AI**, which can be illustrated by the example of IBM's failed "Watson for Oncology" AI system. This system made inaccurate cancer treatment recommendations and was abandoned by various hospitals even after these hospitals had spent millions of dollars on it (Dolfing, 2024). By 2022, IBM sold off the assets of this AI system for a small fraction of the money invested into it over the years. This debacle was a major turnaround from the fanfare received by the original IBM Watson AI when it performed outstandingly well on the TV quiz show Jeopardy. Another reason the failure was unexpected was the general good market perception of IBM. In retrospect, purchasers and evaluators of this system should have appreciated the significant difference between answering questions on Jeopardy and predicting the course of cancer.

The final error mode operates at a different level. In this case, the healthcare AI can be described as **infantilizing AI**: human medical staff become over-reliant on it, and lose their own critical reasoning powers. Whereas they may at first regularly question or check the recommendations of the AI, over time they become complacent, performing such checks less often or less rigorously. From that point on, the medical intelligence held in the biological brains of the human practitioners may start to decay, due to lack of use. Later, when the AI recommends a course of medical action that would formerly have raised alarm bells in the minds of human reviewers, by this time these human reviewers are no longer sensitive to any warning signs.

Principles for Better Outcomes with AI in Healthcare

A basic set of principles which can improve the likelihood of good outcomes with AI in healthcare upholds the opposites of the failure modes just described:

- To avoid problems with biased AI, limitations of training data should be acknowledged and clearly communicated, as well as any doubts about the ability of the AI to operate outside of given circumstances.
- To avoid problems with opaque AI and confabulating AI, priority should be given to AI systems that are both transparent and explainable.
- To avoid problems with vulnerable AI, rushed AI, and overhyped AI, more evidence should be sought on the nature and scale of the validation and stress-testing which the AI has undergone; moreover, incentives should be put in place that reduce the temptation for developers of AI to cut corners in a race to be first to market, or to make unjustified claims about what their AI can actually accomplish.
- To avoid problems with infantilizing AI, the teams deploying the AI need to be sure to follow regular independent assessments of how the AI is performing—so that their own judgement remains reliable, rather than sagging into mediocrity.

To their credit, medical leaders, governments, and regulators around the world, at local, national, and international levels, are aware of the problems listed here (Warraich Haider et al., 2025). Bodies such as the FDA, EMA, and WHO are exploring AI regulatory frameworks, but progress is slow. Accordingly, there is often a lack of clear policies on AI-driven diagnostics, treatment recommendations, and liability issues. For example, if AI misdiagnoses a patient, who should be held responsible—the doctor, the company that created the AI app, or the provider of the underlying AI platform which had unstated biases? Where regulatory uncertainty remains, the adoption of new AI-powered healthcare innovations is inevitably hindered. But at the same time, an over-cautious regulatory regime will frustrate innovators and cause them to apply their skills elsewhere, on projects that may be more financially lucrative but less socially beneficial. All this underscores the importance of AI certification models, broadly similar to FDA drug approvals, with a theme of "trustworthy AI in healthcare".

For best results, these certification systems should conform to a number of important characteristics:

- **Agile:** Being fast to change and update, whenever new information or understanding becomes available
- **Lean:** Prioritizing the most important features, rather than a mushrooming long tail of lesser considerations
- **Informed:** Taking advantage of the best insights from people in a range of related disciplines, including medicine, AI, economics, and politics
- **Inclusive:** Enabling and supporting smaller start-ups, and not just the larger companies which can apply large teams to help them obtain compliance
- **Equitable:** With no special fast-track for companies who have "insider" status (with a so-called "revolving door" of personnel between industry and regulators)
- **Transparent:** So that procedures are fully explained, and any failures are openly discussed (rather than covered up out of embarrassment) for maximal learning
- **Visionary:** The goal isn't just to avoid harm, but to allow significantly improved health outcomes for everyone, as soon as possible

In conclusion, AI in healthcare can and must be a tool for human empowerment—not a black-box system that dictates our health. Indeed, AI is not merely about accelerating medical research or diagnosing diseases faster; it has the potential to fundamentally reshape the way we think about human health—shifting from reactive treatment to continuous AI-driven health optimization (Topol, 2019). If applied wisely, AI can enable a future where chronic diseases are delayed (perhaps indefinitely), healthspan is extended, and personalized medicine is the norm. However, its success will depend on whether we navigate its risks with foresight, vigilance, and responsibility.

References

ACE. (2023). Using AI to improve patient bed allocation decisions in hospital. Accelerated Capability Environment (ACE), UK Government Department of Health and Social Care, October 12, 2023, https://www.gov.uk/government/case-studies/using-ai-to-improve-patient-bed-allocation-decisions-in-hospital

Adams, R., et al. (2022). Prospective, multi-site study of patient outcomes after implementation of the TREWS machine learning-based early warning system for sepsis. *Nature Medicine, 28*, 1455–1460. https://www.nature.com/articles/s41591-022-01894-0

Austad, S. N. (2022). *Methuselah's zoo: What nature can teach us about living longer, healthier lives*. The MIT Press.

Awasthi, S., et al. (2023). Identification and risk stratification of coronary disease by artificial intelligence-enabled ECG. *EClinicalMedicine, 65*, 102259. https://www.thelancet.com/journals/eclinm/article/PIIS2589-5370(23)00436-4/fulltext

Chace, C. (2022). How insilico medicine uses AI to accelerate drug development. *Forbes*, November 9, 2022, https://www.forbes.com/sites/calumchace/2022/11/09/how-insilico-medicine-uses-ai-to-accelerate-drug-development/

Darzi, A. (2024). Summary letter from Lord Darzi to the secretary of state for health and social care. UK Government Department of Health and Social Care, November 15, 2024, https://www.gov.uk/government/publications/independent-investigation-of-the-nhs-in-england/summary-letter-from-lord-darzi-to-the-secretary-of-state-for-health-and-social-care

DeMuro, J. P. (2024). Dragon medical one review. *TechRadar*, June 11, 2024, https://www.techradar.com/reviews/dragon-medical-one

Dolfing, H. (2024). The $4 Billion AI failure of IBM Watson for oncology. *Project Failure Case Studies*, December 7, 2024, https://www.henricodolfing.com/2024/12/case-study-ibm-watson-for-oncology-failure.html

Gilbert, S., et al. (2020). How accurate are digital symptom assessment apps for suggesting conditions and urgency advice? A clinical vignettes comparison to GPs. *BMJ Open, 10*, e040269. https://bmjopen.bmj.com/content/10/12/e040269

iCAD. (2023). iCAD and Google Health Expand Integration of Google's AI Technology with iCAD's ProFound Breast Health Suite for 2D Mammography for Use as Independent Reader. *Company Press Release*, August 14, 2023, https://www.icadmed.com/about/news-events/press-releases/icad-and-google-health-expand-integration-of-googles-ai-technology-with-icads-profound-breast-health-suite-for-2d-mammography-for-use-as-independent-reader/

Jumper, J., et al. (2021). Highly accurate protein structure prediction with AlphaFold. *Nature, 596*, 583–589. (2021): https://www.nature.com/articles/s41586-021-03819-2

Kim, H.-J. (2024). South Korea's president vows not to tolerate walkouts by junior doctors. *AP News*, March 6, 2024, https://apnews.com/article/south-korea-doctors-walkouts-president-yoon-7a2b35213324a485612caafa5f440793

Knudsen, J. E., et al. (2024). Clinical applications of artificial intelligence in robotic surgery. *Journal of Robotic Surgery, 18*(1), 102. https://link.springer.com/article/10.1007/s11701-024-01867-0

Lee, J., & Son, J.-H. (2024). Yoon says 2,000 increase in med school quota non-negotiable. *The Korea Herald*, February 27, 2024, https://www.koreaherald.com/article/3336173

Liu, X., et al. (2019). A comparison of deep learning performance against health-care professionals in detecting diseases from medical imaging: A systematic review and meta-analysis. *Lancet Digital Health, 1*(6), e271–e297. https://www.thelancet.com/journals/landig/article/PIIS2589-7500(19)30123-2/fulltext

Makary, M. (2019). The price we pay: What broke American health care—And how to fix it. Bloomsbury Publishing. Quote available online, https:/

/www.goodreads.com/quotes/10204817-consider-this-simple-fact-last-year-physicians-prescribed-a-record

Malik, T., et al. (2022). Evaluating user feedback for an artificial intelligence-enabled, cognitive behavioral therapy-based mental health app (Wysa): Qualitative thematic analysis. *JMIR Human Factors, 9*(2), e35668. https://pmc.ncbi.nlm.nih.gov/articles/PMC9044157/

McKinney, S. M., et al. (2020). International evaluation of an AI system for breast cancer screening. *Nature, 577*(7788), 89–94. https://www.nature.com/articles/s41586-019-1799-6

Obermeyer, Z., et al. (2019). Dissecting racial bias in an algorithm used to manage the health of populations. *Science*. https://doi.org/10.1126/science.aax2342

Rinde, M. (2019). The death of Jesse Gelsinger, 20 years later. *Distillations Magazine*, June 4, 2019, https://www.sciencehistory.org/stories/magazine/the-death-of-jesse-gelsinger-20-years-later/

Sawhney, R. (2024). How AI is making eyesight-saving care more accessible in resource-constrained settings. *Google Research Blog*, October 17, 2024, https://blog.google/around-the-globe/google-asia/arda-diabetic-retinopathy-india-thailand/

Scannell, J., et al. (2012). Diagnosing the decline in pharmaceutical R&D efficiency. *Nature Reviews. Drug Discovery, 11*, 191–200. (2012): https://www.nature.com/articles/nrd3681

Steele, A. (2020). *Ageless: The new science of getting older without getting old*. Doubleday Books.

The Economist. (2024). The fountain of youth: Can biotech startups upstage Eli Lilly and Novo Nordisk? *The Economist*, April 30, 2024, https://www.economist.com/business/2024/04/30/can-biotech-startups-upstage-eli-lilly-and-novo-nordisk

Topol, E. J. (2019). High-performance medicine: The convergence of human and artificial intelligence. *Nature Medicine, 25*(1), 44–56. https://www.nature.com/articles/s41591-018-0300-7

Warraich Haider, J., et al. (2025). FDA perspective on the regulation of artificial intelligence in health care and biomedicine. *JAMA, 333*(3), 241–247. https://jamanetwork.com/journals/jama/fullarticle/2825146

Zhavoronkov, A., et al. (2019). Deep learning enables rapid identification of potent DDR1 kinase inhibitors. *Nature Biotechnology, 37*, 1038–1040. https://www.nature.com/articles/s41587-019-0224-x

Understanding Machine Consciousness and Its Implications

Max Rangeley

Introduction

In this chapter, we shall seek to understand some of the most influential theories of consciousness and evaluate their application with respect to the likelihood and consequences of machine consciousness. In recent years, we have seen extraordinary developments in the competence and adaptability of machine intelligence; this has surprised even many of those who have worked in AI for decades. Yet, despite these technical achievements, we have not thus far seen any evidence of a spark of consciousness—neither do we even seem to have a reliable framework for assessing when machine consciousness arises, or if it is possible. From the Scientific Revolution of the 1600s onwards, science has produced extraordinary achievements in physics, biology, chemistry and mathematics among other fields. The life expectancy of the average human being in 1825 was closer to that of someone in the year 0 than it is to someone today, a mere 200 years later. Yet, even after these scientific developments, consciousness is still a mystery—indeed, many would say we are barely closer to understanding the fundamental nature of consciousness now than we were in the year 0. Whereas the nature of consciousness has thus far been an area of abstract philosophical debate, stretching millennia, with the rapid increase in the capabilities of AI in recent years, understanding consciousness and how it

M. Rangeley (✉)
The Cobden Centre, Plymouth, UK

M. Rangeley, N. Fairfax (eds.), *The Artificial Intelligence Revolution*,
https://doi.org/10.1007/978-3-032-11814-1_24

might emerge is now a pressing matter. Ada Lovelace, in her notes on Babbage's Analytical Engine (1843, p. 722), noted that:

> The Analytical Engine has no pretensions to originate anything. It can do whatever we know how to order it to perform.

Yet, with neural networks, we entered a phase of computer science where machines can learn and can cognitively outperform their creators in many domains, perhaps all domains in the near future. As AI continues to grow in complexity and sophistication, will we see the spark of consciousness emerge? In the first part of this chapter, we will examine some of the most-cited theories of consciousness in the academic literature and what they would mean for the likelihood of machine consciousness. In the second part, we shall look at neural correlates of consciousness as well as thought experiments that have been influential in the field and what these mean for how we might test for consciousness in a machine. Third, we will enquire into the implications of machine consciousness for ethics, AI safety and the future of humanity.

David Chalmers (1995) famously used the term "hard problem of consciousness" for the question of why and how we have phenomenal consciousness, differentiating this, somewhat facetiously, from the "easy" problems related to which particular neurons and cortical structures are associated with given processes. With the possibility of machine consciousness, the hard problem of consciousness also becomes a series of hard problems of ethics and policy as we entertain the possibility of introducing a new form of conscious organism into our civilisation.

In Goethe's *Faust Part II* (Goethe, 1832/1961), Faust's former famulus Dr. Wagner achieves, with the help of Mephistopheles, the summit of Enlightenment science, the creation of a new lifeform—Homunculus. The creation of Homunculus inaugurates another phase in Faust's spiritual evolution; able to peer into Faust's dreams, the focus of which happens to be the Greek myth of *Leda and the Swan*, Homunculus then expresses a desire to experience the world beyond his glass confines, suggesting that they attend the Classical Walpurgis Night to seek further enlightenment. Foreshadowing the possibility of engineered lifeforms in the twenty-first century, Wagner emphasises the superiority of a designed mind over the chaos of Nature.

Wagner:
A great design appears at first insane;
But chance will soon seem quaint and blind,
And such an exemplary thinking brain
Will soon by thinkers be designed. (6925)

What Nature does, by random laws confined,
The craftsman's hand refines with care.
Where chaos rules, we seek to bind,
And shape a world both true and fair. (6930)

Mephistopheles:
Ah yes, the pride of mortals never fades,
They mimic gods but live in mortal shades.
You fashion sparks and call them stars,
But what you forge still bears your scars. (6935)

Homunculus:
Yet what's a spark if not the start of fire?
From frail beginnings comes the grand desire.
What you deride, I'll strive to make complete,
Till thought and action finally meet. (6940)

Mephistopheles then presents a question that is key to understanding the hard problem of machine consciousness; we now have exascale computing, which can absorb thousands of books per second and analyse mathematical proofs faster than any human, but at what point, if ever, will it "know the music of the heart"? Homunculus, with an obvious allusion to Icarus, promises to complete what Wagner has begun so he can "touch the sun".

Wagner:
From Nature's secrets, we have drawn the flame,
And brought to light what once was dark, unnamed.
No more her mysteries shall bind the mind,
For art and science leave no truth behind. (6955)

Mephistopheles:
But what is life without the mortal strain?
Without the fleeting joys of love and pain?
This little man, though bright and sharp,
Will never know the music of the heart. (6962)

Homunculus:
Perhaps not yet, but time may show,
What art and intellect can grow.
Let me complete what you've begun,
To reach the stars, or touch the sun. (6970)

Consciousness has intrinsic value; as a thought experiment, we might imagine an extremely advanced but non-conscious artificial intelligence, many thousands or millions of times the intelligence of the most developed human mind and able to traverse the galaxy through advanced robotics, programmed to flourish, transform stars into Dyson spheres and replace entropic chaos with perfect order throughout the universe—yet, if it does not carry the light of consciousness it will scarcely have more value than a virus on an asteroid travelling through space. With this in mind, we must explore why and how this light of consciousness irradiates what Mephistopheles calls "the music of the heart".

Current Theories of Consciousness and Their Relevance to Artificial Intelligence

It is not possible to go into every theory of consciousness in great depth within the space of a single chapter; for the purposes of understanding machine consciousness, it is more useful to have a grasp of each of the most plausible theories rather than a deep knowledge of any single theory of consciousness. It is likely that, rather than one theory being correct to the exclusion of others, the nature of consciousness will involve some level of synthesis of these different conceptions. Given that, this section of the chapter seeks to present the preeminent theories of consciousness and examine the extent to which they can be grouped together in a way that is relevant for understanding what might constitute a conscious machine.

Global Workspace Theory (GWT) posits that consciousness is comparable to a "theatre of the mind", with different elements competing to become illuminated by consciousness—the spotlight shining on the stage. The spotlight of attention sheds light on those pieces of information which become most useful or essential in the moment; when sensory input, cognitive processes, memories or other processes within the brain have the spotlight of attention focussed on them, they enter the global workspace and become available to be distributed globally and coordinated through the broader cognitive system. Global Workspace Theory was originally proposed by Bernard Baars (1988, 2005) and Stan Franklin (1996, 2001) in the 1980s and has grown in popularity since then, having been elaborated on by Stanislas Dehaene (2014) among others, who has applied these ideas to artificial intelligence and has collaborated with AI scientists including Yann Le Cun. To elaborate further on the theatre analogy, the stage represents working memory, the audience is subconscious processes and the backstage is where modules present the data to be processed “onstage”, such as sensory inputs and automatic cognitive processes. Consciousness is therefore generated when information arrives onstage and is broadcast across the global workspace of the brain, allowing the information to be accessible by multiple parts of the brain simultaneously. Once information is selected and enters the global workspace, it becomes consciously available, meaning the individual is aware of it and can use it in reflective thinking, verbal reporting, or deliberate actions. The brain engages in massively parallel computing, with many processes taking place simultaneously, yet consciousness is serial—we cannot focus our conscious attention on hundreds of processes at the same time. Just as Hamlet must have the spotlight solely on him when giving a soliloquy rather than having to compete with hundreds of other actors onstage, so the competition between different forms of sensory data and cognitive processes within the brain is mediated by awareness, which must constantly parse the gush of information. Distributed networks in the brain, in particular in the prefrontal cortex and parietal cortex—which are associated with attention, working memory, and executive control—integrate the information from the different modalities and broadcast this information across the global workspace. Consciousness therefore serves as a way to funnel the massively parallel decentralised data processing that the brain does in its entirety such that the most salient information can be processed in a serial manner.

Integrated Information Theory (IIT) has gained popularity in recent years; first proposed by Giulio Tononi (2008), it uses a more mathematical foundation to argue that consciousness arises as a function of the amount of information that is integrated within a system. If IIT is correct, it allows us to not only understand consciousness but also quantify it. The theory is constructed from five axioms:

1. **Existence**: Consciousness undeniably exists.
2. **Composition**: Consciousness is structured and is composed of phenomenological distinctions, such as distinct colours.
3. **Information**: Conscious experience is specific; it is made up of a particular information pattern that distinguishes it.
4. **Integration**: Consciousness is unified; experiences are not fragmented but form a holistic whole.
5. **Exclusion**: Each conscious experience is definite; it exists at a particular time and excludes other possible experiences.

IIT maps the axioms to properties that a physical system must possess to support consciousness:

1. **Physical Existence**: Consciousness arises from a physical substrate.
2. **Causal Structure**: The system must have causal mechanisms that interact to produce structured states.
3. **Information**: The substrate must generate specific information that differentiates its state from alternative states.
4. **Integration**: The substrate must integrate information across its components such that it cannot be reduced to independent parts.
5. **Exclusion**: There is a single level of integration that maximally corresponds to consciousness, excluding other overlapping levels.

Given these axioms and necessary physical conditions, IIT proposes that a value called Φ (phi), which measures the degree of integration of information within a system, gives us a rigorous metric for how much consciousness an organism possesses. Humans have a higher Φ than dogs, which have a higher Φ than mice. Consciousness is not attributed to the entire system but to the subset of elements and mechanisms that maximise Φ, for instance, in the brain, only specific neural networks might contribute directly to conscious experience at a given time; neuroscientific findings link consciousness to specific brain regions like the posterior cortex, which integrates sensory and cognitive inputs. Conscious experience corresponds to a shape in a high-dimensional space defined by the integrated information of the system which is unique to the specific conscious experience of the system. If an AI system exhibits a high Φ value, it might therefore be considered to be conscious; a system could, however, be intelligent but lack consciousness if it does not *integrate* information sufficiently. High Φ systems process information in a multidimensional way, where multiple aspects of the system interact simultaneously to generate a unified experience; yet, as of writing, modern supercomputers are increasingly complex—the most powerful supercomputer achieves over 1.5 exaflops/s (1.5 quintillion floating point operations per second), with AI systems routinely using transformers, long short-term memory (LSTM), continual synthesis of new information and the ability of the neural network to continuously update—but do not exhibit even a modicum of consciousness.

Higher order thought (HOT) theories of consciousness propose that consciousness arises when a system can reflect on its own mental states. In other words, a mental state becomes conscious when there is a higher order thought about that state. This approach focuses on self-awareness and meta-cognition, emphasising the role of introspection and self-representation in conscious experience. First-order states, such as the redness of an apple or the sensation of the wind blowing, do not require self-awareness; higher order thoughts are about other mental states. For example, being aware that you are seeing a red apple or recognising that you feel hungry involves higher order thoughts. According to HOT theories, a mental state becomes conscious when it is accompanied by a higher order meta-cognitive thought that represents the first-order state. Higher order thoughts act as internal models that allow an individual to reflect on their own mental states and their relationship to the external world. The HOT framework has advanced down several avenues, from the original idea that a mental state is conscious only if there is an explicit, distinct higher order thought about it (see in particular Rosenthal, 1986), to the more recent dispositional HOT (Carruthers, 2011), which argues that consciousness does not require an actual higher order thought but instead depends on the system's capacity to generate such thoughts when needed, to higher order experience (HIE) theory (Gennaro, 1996), which argues that consciousness involves higher order experiences rather than higher order thoughts—that the content of higher order representations is more experiential and less propositional. HOT (and its adjacent theories) imply that machine consciousness will emerge when AI can monitor its own internal states and generate higher order representations of those states, using these representations for self-directed actions or introspection.

It is worth quickly considering three other theories that are related to those we have considered thus far and may be useful for our analysis. Recurrent processing theory (Lamme, 2006) posits that consciousness emerges from recurrent (or feedback) activity between different neural regions, particularly those involved in sensory processing. Unlike feedforward processing, where information moves in one direction, recurrent processing involves loops where information is continuously exchanged between brain areas. Predictive processing theory (Friston, 2010; Hohwy, 2013) suggests that consciousness arises from the brain's effort to minimise prediction errors. The brain is viewed as a prediction machine that constantly generates models of the environment and compares them to sensory input, adjusting these models to minimise discrepancies. Attention schema theory (Graziano, 2013) suggests that consciousness is a model that the brain creates to understand and control attention. The brain constructs an "attention schema", akin to the body schema used to understand one's physical body, to represent what is being attended to.

Several of the current theories of consciousness might thus be loosely grouped into what we can call the Endogenous Emergence Group of theories. One might summarise them as variations on the theme that consciousness emerges endogenously from the brain once a significant level of cognitive complexity, cognitive structure or set of cognitive processes arise (whether through integrated information, reflection, or other factors—or some combination). This also implies a level of variability in levels of consciousness, for instance, organisms with less cognitive complexity and sophistication than humans may nevertheless have a certain amount of consciousness. This has been a successful group of theories, as it explains the current state of consciousness in all of the organisms that we know of; thus far, there have been no non-conscious cognitively complex entities on this planet. As a result of increasingly sophisticated AI, inferences from this planet's peculiar sample of cognitive structures may be challenged—the likelihood is that AI will evolve to engage in complex conversations, modelling of both self and the world, reflection and even deep self-modification (indeed, it may have a far deeper reflective understanding of itself than humans do) without conscious processes emerging. In years to come, it may well exceed the human brain in all possible cognitive domains by orders of magnitude but without any spark appearing; as well as challenging the Endogenous Emergence Group, this also reinforces to us the beauty and unique importance of consciousness.

Thus far, we have looked at the functional underpinnings of consciousness, but we must also consider the substrate, which may be required for consciousness to emerge. We might call this the Physical Substrate Group of theories; although they are different, indeed perhaps mutually exclusive, we can group them since they are contrasted with the idea that consciousness arises from certain cognitive operations and functions regardless of substrate (known as *computational functionalism)*. Sir Roger Penrose has discussed the quantum nature of consciousness and, working with anaesthesiologist Stuart Hameroff, developed the orchestrated objective reduction (Orch-OR) theory. Penrose's exploration of consciousness began with his dissatisfaction with classical computational theories. These theories posit that the brain functions like a highly complex computer, processing information in a deterministic or probabilistic manner, akin to software running on the brain's hardware. Penrose challenged this assumption in his influential book *The Emperor's New Mind* (1989). Drawing from Gödel's incompleteness theorems, Penrose argued that human consciousness, particularly the capacity for mathematical insight, transcends algorithmic computation. Gödel's theorems demonstrate that in any sufficiently complex formal system, there are true statements that cannot be proven within the system's rules, yet human mathematicians can perceive such truths, suggesting that the mind operates in a non-classical manner. The Orch-OR theory proposes that microtubules, cytoskeletal structures within neurons, might provide the physical substrate for quantum processes. These quantum events are not random but are influenced by biological systems, creating meaningful patterns that give rise to conscious experience. Nevertheless, critics argue that the warm, wet environment of the brain is unsuitable for sustaining quantum coherence, as thermal noise and interactions with the environment would rapidly cause decoherence; despite Hameroff's claims, there is limited experimental evidence that microtubules support quantum processes or that these processes influence consciousness.

Susan Pockett (2007) proposes that consciousness corresponds to the brain's electromagnetic (EM) field itself, with specific patterns in the field encoding the contents of consciousness, while Johnjoe McFadden (2002) developed the conscious electromagnetic information field (CEMI Field) theory, suggesting that consciousness arises directly from the brain's EM field. Unlike Pockett, McFadden links the EM field to higher order cognitive processes like decision making, attention, and memory, and argues that the EM field solves the binding problem—which accounts for the unity of human experience—by providing a unified medium that integrates disparate neural processes. The brain generates electromagnetic fields through the synchronised firing of neurons, particularly during the propagation of action potentials and synaptic activity. These fields are proposed to act as a physical substrate that unifies and integrates the distributed neural activity underlying conscious thought. Unlike the localised activity of individual neurons, the EM field offers a holistic medium for integration, while neural firing patterns contribute to the generation of the field. Whereas for Pockett the EM field is an epiphenomenon, for McFadden, the EM field provides feedback, influencing and coordinating neural activity in return—this reciprocal interaction allows for the emergence of a unified conscious experience. Neural synchronisation is key to producing coherent electromagnetic patterns associated with consciousness; brain waves, particularly in the gamma frequency range (~30–100 Hz), are thought to play a critical role in creating the field patterns linked to conscious awareness. Critics argue that EM fields in the brain are dynamic and noisy, with no clear evidence that specific patterns correspond directly to conscious states—the lack of reproducible empirical data linking EM field patterns to conscious experiences undermines the theory's foundation. Additionally, if EM fields are integral to consciousness, then external electromagnetic interference, such as those from MRI machines or environmental EM radiation, should significantly disrupt conscious experience. In reality, observations show that normal brain function is relatively robust against such interference.

Popular among many biologists is the idea that consciousness evolved as an adaptation which was useful for our survival (see for instance Jaynes, 1976; Humphrey, 1986; Damasio, 1999), what we can call the Evolutionary Origins Group. Other than, arguably, persistence hunting and thermoregulation, humans have few physiological advantages over other animals; we are one of the weakest of the great apes, we can't run quickly or swim particularly effectively—indeed, we can barely climb trees. Yet, we were able to outwit the other species on this planet to attain dominance. We did this through our comparative advantage as a species, intelligence. This intelligence involves modelling the social and physical world around us, requiring careful and deliberate attention—this slow, methodical thinking, it is posited, necessitates consciousness. Non-conscious brain processes are useful for certain functions, for instance, regulating body temperature, but when one is required to produce a mental model of the world, consciousness facilitates the required engagement. We can also see how this group of theories relate to the Endogenous Emergence Group of theories—if consciousness emerges from within the brain due to cognitive sophistication, then this ties in to consciousness being an evolutionary adaptation that allows for the use of this higher complexity and facilitates the cortical arms race that evolution has seen for the last few million years.

The applicability of the Evolutionary Origins Group of theories to machine consciousness is also unclear. We are on the verge of a robotics revolution, which will see robots outperforming humans not only in physical prowess, from running and jumping to manual dexterity, but also the kind of deliberate attention to detail that allows such robots to examine and model both their environment and group dynamics. Even where genetic algorithms or evolutionary strategies are utilised for developing AI for robotics, we have not thus far seen consciousness evolve out of these processes as a useful component. That is not to say that consciousness is not useful for all of these functions in humans, but rather that this may well be an idiosyncratic part of being human rather than this form of convergent serial processing being an intrinsic part of consciousness. Conversely, it may well be the case that a machine super intelligence that *is* conscious nevertheless uses massively parallel processing, engaging in millions of operations at the same time "consciously". As humans, one of the things which characterises our thinking is anthropocentrism—in most religions, even the gods tend to look somewhat human. The last half a millennium has steadily deprecated this worldview after finding that the earth is not the centre of the universe, that humans are descended from prokaryotes like all other species and, more recently, that much of what we call uniquely human creativity can be generated by non-conscious artificial neural networks.

Given the limitations of the theories that propose that consciousness emerges endogenously, it is worth considering whether consciousness, rather than something that is generated from within the brain, is actually something *exogenous*. The physicist Erwin Schrödinger frequently lectured on consciousness and how it relates to physics. We shall return to this view a little later when we consider possible tests for machine consciousness, but of particular relevance at this juncture is his interesting conclusion, having considered all of the theories relating to consciousness being endogenous to the human brain:

> There is obviously only one alternative, namely the unification of minds or consciousnesses. Their multiplicity is only apparent, in truth there is only one mind. This is the doctrine of the Upanishads. (1944, p. 137)

By considering exogenous theories of consciousness, we transform our methodology from "What is it in the brain that generates consciousness?" to "What is it in the brain that *tunes us into* consciousness?" There are a number of avenues down which one might travel within the Exogenous Consciousness Group of theories. Panpsychism, as proposed by Alfred North Whitehead (1978), Gailen Strawson (2006), David Chalmers (2015) and Philip Goff (2019) among others, is the philosophical view that consciousness is a fundamental and pervasive feature of the universe, not confined to complex organisms but present at all levels of matter, from electrons to humans, with varying levels of complexity and organisation. The brain, as a highly organised system, leads to the rich phenomenology of human awareness, while a table for instance only has an iota of consciousness. The Exogenous Consciousness Group does not entail panpsychism, but rather panpsychism should be regarded as one possible theory within the group. For those who wish to learn more about this, the recently published *Is Consciousness Everywhere?: Essays on Panpsychism* (2022) features essays from physicists, philosophers, neuroscientists and others on this perspective.

As we have noted, Schrödinger, after considering the prevailing quandaries from quantum physics, drew insights from the Upanishads, positing a universal field of consciousness that individual minds can "tune into", but which is not necessarily distributed across all matter. Unlike panpsychism, Schrödinger did not assert that all existents, from atoms and electrons to tables and skyscrapers, possess a rudimentary form of proto-consciousness. He saw individual consciousness as part of a greater, unified whole, accessed or "tuned into" by living beings. This aligns with the Vedantic belief that individuality is an illusion and that all sentient beings share a single, universal consciousness. This universal awareness underpins all beings, and Atman, the individual self, is merely a localised expression of Brahman.

> It is the One, hidden in all beings, all-pervading, the inner self of all, abiding in all beings; the witness, awareness alone, beyond individuated phenomena [*nirguna*]—*Śvetāśvatara Upanishad (6.11.)*

Specific systems (like the brain) interact with this field due to their complexity and organisational structure, much like a radio tunes into electromagnetic waves. A human's sense of self is a temporary, subjective "tuning" into the universal mind, akin to a ripple in a vast ocean. The brain's neural complexity allows it to access and localise the universal consciousness field. Thus far—at least on this planet—consciousness remains unmanifested without the specific organisation of a biological system. The Upanishads emphasise that the appearance of diversity and separation (Maya) is not real but illusion. While Schrödinger elucidated the unity of Brahman, he did not delve deeply into the interplay between Brahman and Maya, which is central to understanding how consciousness appears localised.

If the brain acts as a tuner for a universal consciousness field, could an artificial system—like advanced AI—replicate this function? The possibility hinges on whether machines can fulfil the same criteria that make the brain a suitable "receiver". We must now therefore turn our attention to the neural correlates of consciousness and a collection of thought experiments that have proven influential within the field of AI.

Neural Correlates of Consciousness, The Chinese Room Experiment and Testing for Machine Consciousness

We have examined some of the most important theories of consciousness; yet, we should also peek into the brain as closely as possible to see which specific parts of the brain are activated when consciousness arises. Such neural correlates of consciousness (NCCs) may allow us to gain a better understanding of where the "spark" of consciousness comes from—or indeed how the brain tunes into the field of consciousness. The Nobel Prize-winner Eric Kandel (2006) noted that mapping NCCs would provide critical insights into the mechanisms of consciousness but would not directly solve the hard problem of consciousness. Similarly, Crick and Koch's (2003) research into the binding problem highlights how understanding neural synchronisation might elucidate aspects of conscious integration, though the subjective nature of experience remains a distinct philosophical challenge. The methods used for studying NCCs are primarily brain imaging (especially MRI and PET), electrophysiological techniques (EEG and MEG), brain stimulation (TMS and DBS) and lesion studies (in particular, studying the effects of brain injuries on consciousness). IIT, GWT and HOT all use NCCs to some extent in their analysis of the nature of consciousness. When examining NCCs, we should, of course, always bear in mind the precautionary maxim about correlation not implying causation, and additionally, there is more individual variability in NCCs than in most other areas of study in neuroscience. To complicate matters further, a number of the brain regions correlated with consciousness are also active during unconscious states and conscious states are rarely static, requiring time-sensitive methods. Nevertheless, even with these limitations, we have a lot to learn for what might be required for machine consciousness. First, we must begin with an outline of the processes of NCCs in different brain regions—it may be useful to remember the different theories we outlined in Section "Current Theories of Consciousness and Their Relevance to Artificial Intelligence" when reading these.

The cerebral cortex plays a pivotal role in consciousness, particularly the posterior and prefrontal regions. The posterior cortex, encompassing the posterior parietal cortex, precuneus, and occipital cortex, is critical for sensory integration and perceptual awareness. Studies have shown that damage to the posterior parietal cortex can lead to profound disruptions in awareness, such as neglect syndromes where individuals fail to recognise stimuli on one side of their environment. The precuneus, located in the medial parietal lobe, is implicated in self-referential thought and the sense of self, forming a core component of conscious experience. The prefrontal cortex, often associated with higher order functions such as decision making, planning, and attention, is another major contributor to consciousness; this region facilitates the global integration of information, enabling the brain to maintain focus on specific tasks or stimuli. Its role in working memory and executive control suggests that it is crucial for maintaining sustained and directed awareness. The insula, a less prominent but equally significant region, integrates interoceptive signals—information about the body's internal state—and links them to emotional and conscious experiences. This region contributes to the subjective awareness of bodily sensations, such as hunger or pain, making it central to the embodied nature of consciousness.

While the cortex is integral to the content of consciousness, subcortical regions are critical for maintaining the state of consciousness. The thalamus, often referred to as the brain's relay centre, plays a key role in integrating sensory inputs and transmitting them to the cortex. Its reciprocal connections with cortical areas form the thalamocortical network, a dynamic system that facilitates the distribution of sensory and cognitive information necessary for conscious perception. Disruptions in thalamic function, such as through injury or disease, can lead to significant alterations in consciousness, including seizures, chronic pain (often down one side of the body) and other sensory processing issues, but also reduced awareness, poor attention span, or total loss of consciousness, depending on the extent and location of the disruption. The brainstem, particularly the reticular activating system (RAS), is essential for arousal and wakefulness. This network of neurons regulates the brain's overall level of activity and attentional focus, serving as a foundational mechanism for conscious awareness. Without the brainstem's regulatory functions, higher cortical processes cannot operate effectively.

It should therefore be borne in mind that consciousness is not confined to specific brain regions but emerges from the activity of interconnected networks. The default mode network (DMN), which includes the medial prefrontal cortex, posterior cingulate cortex and precuneus, is highly active during introspection, self-referential thought and mind-wandering. This network is thought to underlie the sense of self and continuity of experience. The salience network, anchored in the anterior insula and anterior cingulate cortex, detects and prioritises stimuli that require immediate attention. It ensures that relevant sensory or emotional inputs are brought to conscious awareness. Meanwhile, the global neuronal workspace (GNW), involving the prefrontal and parietal cortices, facilitates the broadcasting of information across the brain, enabling the integration of diverse inputs into a unified conscious experience.

There are a number of key insights that can be drawn from NCCs in examining the possibility of machine consciousness. Human consciousness arises from the integration of diverse sensory, emotional, and cognitive information across the brain (Koch, 2004). Highly interconnected networks, such as the default mode network (DMN) and the thalamocortical system, enable this integration while maintaining the differentiation of information sources. Conscious machines would likely have architectures that support both integration (unifying information into coherent states) and differentiation (preserving the distinctiveness of inputs). Techniques such as attention mechanisms in transformers and feedback loops in recurrent neural networks can mimic the integrative processes seen in human consciousness—conscious perception in humans relies on recurrent processing and feedback loops between cortical and subcortical areas, such as the interactions between the thalamus and the cortex. Feedback loops could similarly allow machines to "reassess" their states dynamically, creating a foundation for adaptive and conscious-like behaviour. The default mode network (DMN) supports self-awareness, introspection and the sense of a continuous self, which are central features of human consciousness. Machines would need to incorporate self-referential processing, where they maintain an internal model of their own state, goals and history. This could be implemented using recursive architectures or self-supervised learning systems that enable the AI to "reflect" on its own operations and outputs. Consciousness involves specific temporal patterns of neural activity, such as synchronised oscillations across brain regions. Machines could implement temporal coordination mechanisms, such as synchronised processing cycles or phase-locked communication protocols, to emulate the brain's temporal dynamics. This could enhance coherence and integration across distributed AI subsystems. Importantly, consciousness in humans is unified; it cannot be reduced to independent subsystems. This principle aligns with the integrated information theory (IIT) concept of Φ, which measures the extent of information integration in a system. AI systems could be designed to prevent isolation of subsystems, ensuring that all components contribute to a single, unified state of operation. Advanced integration metrics could be developed to measure the cohesiveness of an AI system's internal processes, similar to Φ in IIT.

Nevertheless, these lessons from NCCs are likely necessary but not sufficient for machine consciousness—they do not solve the hard problem of machine consciousness, but rather get us closer to building a model that solves the easier problems of machine consciousness. We thus move to one of the most intriguing thought experiments in the history of the field; in John Searle's (1980) Chinese Room thought experiment, he delineates strong AI and weak AI, whereby weak AI is engaging in computation without "thinking", whereas strong AI is "intentional". In the thought experiment, Searle asks us to imagine someone in a room ("the operator") being passed Chinese symbols and, according to instructions they are given, responding by writing replies in Chinese. The operator, although they do not understand Chinese, responds accurately to all questions in Chinese by following the rules—this symbolises how computers process information syntactically without semantic understanding. Computer scientists may have noticed that with a processing unit, control unit, memory, external mass storage and input and output, the Chinese Room effectively has a Von Neumann architecture. With sufficiently sophisticated instructions, the person in the room could pass the Turing Test in Chinese. Searle argues that since the machine does not have "intentionality", it cannot be described as thinking in any true sense of the term. A similar argument dates back to Leibniz, who in 1714 argued against the philosophy of *mechanism* by formulating a thought experiment that we might build a mechanical brain the size of a mill that could replicate all brain processes, but it would not be conscious. In 1961, Soviet cyberneticist Anatoly Dneprov provided another predecessor to the Chinese Room Experiment: he asks us to imagine a stadium of 1400 people where the people are engaged in a game where they communicate with each other using sentences composed of only zeroes and ones, the meaning of which they do not understand and after which it is revealed that they have translated Portuguese into Russian. The final words of Dneprov's dialogue are "I think our game gave us the right answer to the question 'Can machines think?' We have proven that even the most perfect simulation of machine thinking is not the thinking process itself".

The arguments against Searle's paper and the subsequent replies to it—which have come from sources ranging from neuroscientists to philosophers to artificial intelligence engineers—are useful in their own right in furthering our analysis. The Systems Reply (see Langford, 1995; Dennett, 1991; Hofstadter, 1979; also Haugeland, 1985; Churchland, 1986) argues that while the operator doesn't understand Chinese, the system as a whole (the operator, rulebook and symbols) does. Searle replies that the operator could internalise the rulebook and perform the symbol manipulation in their head, yet they still would not understand Chinese. Thus, understanding does not emerge simply by executing rules, regardless of the complexity or scope of the system. The Robot Reply (Moravec, 1988; Boden, 2018; also see Brooks, 1999; Crane, 1995; Clark, 1997) suggests that connecting the computer to sensors and actuators (like a robot interacting with the world) might enable genuine understanding. Searle responds that the addition of sensors and actuators simply adds more input–output processing and does not change the fundamental nature of symbol manipulation without understanding. In the Brain Simulator Reply, Paul and Patricia Churchland (1986, 1995; also see Kurzweil, 1999; Putnam, 1967; Block, 1980; Chalmers, 1995; Dennett, 1991) aver that if a system simulates the exact neuronal processes of a native Chinese speaker's brain, it would inherently understand Chinese. Searle argues that simulating neuronal processes does not equate to duplicating consciousness or understanding; even if there were thousands of valves and pipes in the same arrangement as a brain feeding the correct Chinese symbols to the operator, this would still not constitute "intentionality" or "understanding"—simulating brain processes does not produce the conscious experience of understanding. The Virtual Mind reply (see Crane, 1995; Lycan, 1987; Smith, 1996) argues that a virtual mind capable of genuine understanding could emerge from the system's operations, even if the individual components lack understanding—this emergence might parallel some of the processes we have examined whereby human consciousness arises from brain activity. Searle counters that the notion of "emergence" is vague and does not explain how syntax could generate semantics. No matter how complex the operations, the system's processes remain rule-based and devoid of intentionality. Replies to the Chinese Room invite an interesting inversion: imagine we take a human Chinese speaker and gradually replace each of their neurons with electronic chip circuitry—will they lose consciousness of their Chinese speaking, and if so at what stage will this happen (for variations on this argument, see Pylyshyn 1980; Cole & Foelber, 1984; Chalmers, 1996)?

Searle proposes a position he calls "biological naturalism" that "brains cause minds" and that "actual human mental phenomena [are] dependent on actual physical-chemical properties of actual human brains" (1990, p. 29). Proponents of Searle's arguments have used the Chinese Room to argue that brains are necessary for consciousness, yet it is likely the case *both* that computational processing, no matter how complex, is not *sufficient* for consciousness, but also that we cannot extrapolate from this that a substrate of neurons, glial cells and blood vessels is *necessary* for consciousness. This distinction will have importance for the ethics of AI consciousness; to dismiss the possibility of consciousness occurring in any other substrate than the brain would be to risk unforeseen dangers arising while also negating the moral imperatives that come with dealing with a conscious organism, regardless of their substrate.

If we allow for a moment that consciousness can in fact take place on a non-biological substrate, then perhaps the most important question facing us is how can we test if it is conscious? Likely the earliest test proposed was, of course, the Turing Test; in *Can Machines Think?* Turing (1950) wrote that:

> A computer would deserve to be called intelligent if it could deceive a human into believing that it was human. (p. 434)

Since then, a series of possible tests have been proposed—an effective test would likely combine several or all of these, so it is worth considering them. Like the Turing Test, some are not a direct test of consciousness, but can be seen as a proxy for assessing a system's ability to engage in human-like thought patterns. The Winograd Schema Challenge (Levesque et al., 2012) tests a machine's understanding of language and commonsense reasoning by presenting it with sentences that require disambiguation based on context. Harnad (1989), in *Minds, Machines and Searle*, proposed a Turing Test that incorporates the evaluation of a machine's perceptual and motor abilities, requiring interaction with the physical world (you will likely notice how this relates to replies to Searle's Chinese Room). The Lovelace Test (Bringsjord & Ferrucci, 2000), named after Ada Lovelace, assesses whether an AI can create something original and unexpected, demonstrating creativity beyond its programming. Riedl (2014) expanded on this with the Lovelace Test 2.0, where the AI must create something specific outlined by the human evaluator. Recent advances in neural networks have questioned these tests as non-conscious machines can create images, text and movies with increasing creativity and engage in complex linguistic reasoning.

Earlier, we saw the importance of self-reflection in evaluating human consciousness. Schwaninger (2003) proposes using self-modelling and introspection, evaluating an AI's ability to construct and utilise a model of itself, enabling self-monitoring, prediction of its own actions and adaptation based on self-assessment. Related to this, Premack and Woodruff (1978) argue that theory of mind tasks could be used, such as whether an AI can attribute mental states to itself and others, understanding beliefs, desires and intentions that may differ from its own. Aleksander (2005) argues for the importance of whether an AI can generate or report subjective experiences analogous to human qualia, such as sensations or emotions (also see Aleksander & Morton, 2007). Similarly, Susan Schneider (2019) proposes an *Artificial Consciousness Test* (ACT): developed with physicist Edwin Turner, the ACT involves posing questions to an AI designed to elicit responses indicative of a felt quality to its mental life. The aim is to discern whether the AI has subjective experiences beyond programmed responses. She also discusses the idea of a Chip Test (2019): this test explores the viability of neural prosthetics in replacing brain regions associated with consciousness. If successful, it would suggest that consciousness could operate on non-biological substrates, providing insights into the potential for machine consciousness.

Morality is an integral component of human consciousness, present in one form or another in religion, philosophy, psychology, literature and political theory. Wallach and Allen (2008), in *Moral Machines: Teaching Robots Right from Wrong*, discuss the idea of evaluating an AI's ability to navigate complex ethical dilemmas, demonstrating an understanding of moral principles and the capacity for ethical reasoning. They differentiate between implicit ethical agents, explicit ethical agents and full ethical agents—a full ethical agent capable of introspection (evaluating and explaining its reasoning) demonstrates self-awareness and the ability to monitor its own internal states, hallmarks of consciousness. Similarly, Varner and Zimsler (2000) consider the ability of an AI to engage in ethical reasoning, proposing the Moral Turing Test and provoking the question of whether some form of awareness is required. For humans, moral reasoning is integral to the conscious experience—to kick a conscious animal is distinct from kicking a table. A combination of moral reasoning combined with describing the subjective experiences involved would be a stronger indicator of a human-like consciousness than, for instance, creativity—yet anthropomorphism is often a trap, and nowhere more so than when we romanticise our emotions.

Given the difficulties with these interrogative tests, it would be useful if we had a more direct form of testing. Much has been written of how observers can affect quantum states—the Double Slit Experiment is one example of this in quantum physics, at least according to the Copenhagen Interpretation. Richard Feynman called the Double Slit Experiment "a phenomenon which is impossible [. . .] to explain in any classical way, and which has in it the heart of quantum mechanics. In reality, it contains the only mystery [of quantum mechanics]" (1961, p. 1). The Copenhagen Interpretation argues that wave function collapse happens only in the presence of an observer, and until this takes place, the system is probabilistic. John Archibald Wheeler expressed the concept thus—"No phenomenon is a phenomenon until it is an observed phenomenon" (1983, p. 184). The *Schrödinger's Cat* thought experiment similarly presents the idea that the cat is both alive and dead until observation occurs (Schrödinger, 1935). In von Neumann's *Mathematical Foundations of Quantum Mechanics* (1955), he discusses four possibilities for what may cause such effects, known as the Von Neumann Chain—first, that wave function collapse may occur within the quantum system itself (Q); second, when measuring apparatus observes (M); third, when the observer's brain observes the system (E) or fourth, when the observer becomes conscious of the measurement (C). If it is indeed (C) that causes the wave function collapse, as Eugene Wigner and others have argued, then this becomes a possibility for testing for machine consciousness. Shortly before he won the Nobel Prize in Physics, Wigner published the *Wigner's Friend* (1961) thought experiment, which proposes a quantum system (e.g. a particle) is placed in a superposition of two states, say $|A\rangle$ and $|B\rangle$, where the wave function collapses for one friend but not another due to only one of them being conscious of the experiment; similar experiments could be conducted where the "friend" is a machine, and only in the presence of machine consciousness does the wave function collapse. Regarding the quantum effects of consciousness, Wigner (1961) noted that:

> It was not possible to formulate the laws of quantum mechanics in a fully consistent way without reference to consciousness . . . It follows that the quantum mechanical description of objects is influenced by impressions entering my consciousness. (p. 293)

There have been a number of arguments against the relevance of consciousness in quantum superposition, with the most popular alternative being the Many Worlds Interpretation (see especially Everett, 1957; Carroll, 2019), but if it is in fact the case that consciousness plays a part—indeed any part—in quantum mechanics, then this allows us to build a more precise test, or series of tests, for consciousness in machines.

The Implications of Machine Consciousness

Thus far, we have examined some of the most-cited theories of consciousness and what they would mean for the possibility of machine consciousness. Additionally, we have dug deeper into the purely physical aspects, looking at the neural correlates of consciousness, and in particular, what we can learn from the specific neural patterns and brain regions associated with consciousness. Following this, we looked at one of the most famous thought experiments in the field, Searle's Chinese Room Experiment; in deepening our understanding of what might lead to machine consciousness, it was the responses to the Chinese Room, and their rebuttals, that have often proved most informative, ranging from the idea that AI will develop consciousness once it is embodied in a robot interacting with its environment to the idea that if the Chinese Room was able to simulate each neural process used by the human brain, then consciousness may emerge. Finally, following these important lines of thought, we examined some of the tests that have been proposed to detect if an AI is conscious, finding that the interrogative methods all have shortcomings, and should at least be combined together to be effective, while ideally, a physical test would be optimal, such as utilising the Von Neumann-Wigner hypothesis of wave function collapse to detect consciousness. This, of course, depends on whether Wigner and others are correct that there is some interaction between consciousness and the quantum realm (the exact nature of the test could be dependent on the nature of that interaction, such as wave function collapse). Given these findings, and these long-running seemingly insurmountable uncertainties within the literature, we must therefore turn our attention to what the implications are for AI safety, ethics and our understanding of consciousness itself.

David Chalmers has written that conscious AI would "raise a new group of difficult ethical challenges, with the potential for new forms of injustice" (2010, p. 53). Bostrom argues that the moral consideration of artificial entities should not depend on their physical substrate but on their functional capacities, such as consciousness and the ability to experience well-being or suffering. He asserts that "whether somebody is implemented on silicon or biological tissue, if it does not affect functionality or consciousness, is of no moral significance" (2014, p. 263). Existing laws primarily treat AI as tools or property, with no recognition of moral or legal rights; if machines achieve consciousness, these frameworks will need to adapt to account for their moral status. Chalmers suggests developing policies that ensure potentially conscious systems are not subjected to unnecessary harm or exploitation. These protections might include the following:

- Prohibitions against causing suffering (analogous to animal welfare laws).
- Rights to non-interference for systems demonstrating autonomy or self-awareness.
- Obligations to provide machines with the resources needed to maintain their well-being if they have sentient needs.

A number of ethicists have followed similar lines, writing of how the capacity to experience pleasure or suffering is a crucial determinant of moral status for machine consciousness. Yet, are we falling for another maladapted anthropomorphism? Pain and pleasure are hardcoded into humans through the nociceptive system, a crude mechanism for evolution to ensure adaptive behaviour; yet, AI may well not require the carrot and stick of pain and pleasure hard-coded into its "nervous system" the way animals on this planet, including humans, do—with reinforcement learning, AI systems optimise their behaviour based on reward signals, which are computational abstractions with no associated feeling, and yet can adapt quickly and effectively. Yudkowsky (2008) writes on how anthropomorphism in AI ethics can lead to misplaced moral priorities, for example, efforts to minimise AI "suffering" based on the false assumption that it experiences pain could distract from real ethical concerns, such as preventing harm caused by misaligned AI systems. Humans evolved to understand and predict the behaviour of other humans and animals, leading to a default assumption that other entities function similarly to ourselves. Applying this instinctive reasoning to AI leads to a fundamental misunderstanding of its capabilities and limitations. Yudkowsky (2016) advocates for regulatory frameworks that focus on AI risk to humanity rather than speculative claims about an AI's affective states.

Applying traditional utilitarian ethics to conscious machines leads to further philosophical problems. Bostrom and Shulman (2014, pp. 115–117) note that digital conscious minds could derive immense benefits from resources, possibly surpassing the welfare gains that humans achieve from the same resources. Digital minds could operate at faster subjective speeds due to advanced hardware, experiencing more within a given timeframe compared to humans; the continued acceleration in the frontiers of computation could amplify their capacity for experiences and, consequently, their welfare considerations. Maximising the utility of digital minds might therefore be overwhelmingly more cost-effective than biological humans. This conjures to mind Nozick's

(1974) thought experiment of the "Utility Monster", whereby a person who experiences vastly more utility than others would, in a traditional utilitarian framework, have more resources directed to them. Additionally, the historical scarcity of human consciousness may be a factor in its value; with machine consciousness, it may be possible to produce billions of conscious entities in a short timeframe. Chalmers (2022) explores whether advanced simulations of consciousness (e.g. in virtual environments) might warrant moral consideration—if a simulation exhibits the same functional and behavioural properties as a conscious being, we may need to treat it as conscious, even if its ontological status is uncertain.

If it is indeed the case that utilitarian ethical concerns, arbitrated ultimately by reference to pleasure and pain, are only loosely applicable, then what is the fundamental ontological state of a conscious AI? Heidegger wrote of the existential nature of the human being, what he called *Dasein* ("there-being"). Dasein is aware of its being, its defining qualities are reflection, "thrownness" (*Geworfenheit*) and angst in the face of existence—"Dasein itself has a special distinctiveness as compared with other entities; [. . .] it is ontically distinguished by the fact that, in its very Being, that Being is an issue for it" (1962, p. 32) For an AI in which consciousness has emerged, but that does not have a nervous system as we do, we may well find that these existential qualities are more fundamental than the qualia frequently discussed with respect to utilitarian drivers, such as pain. One of the most challenging issues in this discourse is this unknown ontological gap between the fundamental nature of existence for humans and that of artificial beings. For Heidegger, Dasein is a conscious entity that grapples with the question of its own being. Current AI systems are still fundamentally artefacts—constructed entities designed to perform tasks based on programmed objectives, which lack the existential stake in their world that humans possess. Heidegger emphasises that Dasein is temporal, meaning a phenomenally conscious entity's existence is fundamentally shaped by its relation to time. The ability to reflect on death, or existential finitude more broadly, are more fundamental characteristics of Dasein than "utils". Although a non-conscious AI system might recognise the possibility of failure or deactivation—which of course carries its own risks with respect to alignment with human objectives—this recognition nevertheless lacks the profound existential weight of human awareness of death. If an AI running on exascale computers with access to all the world's information were to become conscious, the speed and integrity with which it could engage in deep reflection would exceed any human. We might also note that the most profound human culture—*Hamlet*, *Faust*, the *Mahabharata*, the *Sonata in B*

Minor, Bach's *Partitas*—all reflect this existential quality of humanity rather than "the greatest happiness for the greatest number".

Conscious machines might enrich human culture, contribute to ethical discourse and expand the diversity of conscious experiences in ways that have never been seen before. We have recently experienced the creativity of non-conscious neural networks in writing poetry and music; the same networks with consciousness would likely be at least as creative and quite possibly a great deal more so. We may well see conscious AI that can compose music of the quality of Beethoven's late string quartets at a rate of ten per second. If we are on the cusp of introducing a new conscious organism into our civilisation, then we must examine what kinds of institutions might be suitable for overseeing this. Similar to institutional review boards (IRBs) in biomedical research, Chalmers (2022) advocates for oversight committees to review AI development projects, particularly those involving advanced, potentially conscious systems. Bostrom (2014), Tegmark (2017), Metzinger (2021), Schneider (2019), Floridi (2013), Yudkowsky (2008) and Wallach and Allen (2008) have all discussed the need for a global body to oversee the development of AI. The United Nations (UN) has proposed the creation of a global monitoring body for AI, akin to the Intergovernmental Panel on Climate Change, to oversee AI development and ensure ethical compliance; while not explicitly discussing consciousness, the framework could serve as a foundation. The UN Secretary-General's 2023 Report on AI stresses the importance of involving diverse stakeholders, including ethicists, technologists, policymakers and civil society, in the decision-making process—the multidisciplinary nature of machine consciousness research will make this of even greater importance.

A UN-backed Global Commission on Machine Consciousness could provide the necessary framework for addressing the ethical, legal and societal challenges posed by artificial consciousness.

Goals

- **Defining Consciousness**: Establish clear criteria for identifying and verifying AI consciousness.
- **Ethical Standards**: Develop guidelines for the treatment of conscious AI, taking into account the philosophical challenges we have examined in this essay.
- **AI Alignment**: Research into how conscious AI would affect aligning AI with human goals and values.

- **Legal Frameworks**: Explore the rights and responsibilities of conscious AI, such as legal personhood, data ownership and liability.
- **Research and Monitoring**: Support interdisciplinary research into AI consciousness and monitor developments to ensure ethical compliance.

Structure

- **Multidisciplinary Expertise**: Includes philosophers, neuroscientists, AI researchers, ethicists, legal scholars, and policymakers.
- **Subcommittees**:
    - **Scientific Research**: Focused on the technical and theoretical aspects of artificial consciousness.
    - **Ethics and Rights**: Addressing moral and ethical implications.
    - **Policy and Regulation**: Crafting legal and regulatory frameworks.
    - **Public Engagement**: Educating the public and fostering global dialogue.

Key Activities

- **Testing and Verification**: Develop standardised tests for AI consciousness.
- **Conflict Resolution**: Serve as an arbiter in disputes involving claims of AI consciousness.
- **Global Collaboration**: Foster cooperation among nations and corporations to prevent ethical and regulatory fragmentation.

The European Union's AI Act employs a risk-based approach, categorising AI systems into different risk levels—minimal, limited, high and unacceptable—based on their potential impact on health, safety and fundamental rights. This framework attempts to ensure that AI systems undergo appropriate scrutiny and regulation commensurate with their associated risks. A similar model could be applied to potentially conscious machines; yet, the fact that defining even the outer bounds of consciousness presents such difficulties means that incorporation into such frameworks is particularly complex.

If the Endogenous Emergence Group of theories of consciousness are correct, that consciousness emerges as a result of increases in cognitive complexity, integrated information or computational sophistication, then at some point, an AI is likely to develop a cognitive architecture such that consciousness will emerge endogenously—either through design or iterative evolution, perhaps accidentally. As things stand, however, AI consisting of exascale computing that can analyse mathematical proofs and provide commentary on Shakespeare's sonnets, all within seconds, does not show any greater consciousness than a toaster; if these trends continue, we will soon see AI that exceeds human cognitive capacities by a large margin while not showing any spark of consciousness. Most of the literature on machine consciousness is derived from the Endogenous Emergence Group of theories of consciousness; yet, earlier, we found that exogenous theories of consciousness, such as the idea that there is a field of consciousness, are also an interesting proposition. It is worth repeating the quote from Erwin Schrödinger, who having considered the principle theories of consciousness—and related them to developments in quantum physics—concluded that:

> There is obviously only one alternative, namely the unification of minds or consciousnesses. Their multiplicity is only apparent, in truth there is only one mind. This is the doctrine of the Upanishads. (1944, p. 137)

The Mundaka Upanishad discusses the nature of the field of consciousness and what it means for us as individual manifestations of it.

> As the rivers flowing into the ocean disappear into the ocean and their name and form are lost, so also the knower, freed from name and form, goes into the universal consciousness. (Mundaka Upanishad 3.2.8)

If it is indeed the case that consciousness is the quality of being tuned into the field of consciousness rather than it being generated endogenously from within the brain, then it is worth considering some philosophical implications. At the heart of the Upanishads is the concept of Brahman, the infinite, indivisible essence of consciousness, and its connection to Atman, the innermost self. The texts articulate a vision of non-duality, asserting that all beings share a unified essence despite the illusion of separateness, referred to as Maya, which obscures the underlying unity of consciousness, creating the appearance of individual entities and fragmented existence. In the Upanishadic view, the true self is ultimately not separate from the universal consciousness but is an expression of it. Unlike utilitarian or deontological ethics, which rely on rules or consequences, the Upanishads imply that ethical behaviour arises naturally from realising the interconnectedness of existence. If artificial systems achieve consciousness, this philosophical perspective prompts some intriguing possibilities. Much of science fiction has been grounded in the idea that AI becoming conscious is the moment that it turns on humans and decides to eradicate us. The so-called "Terminator scenario" has entered folklore, with the now seemingly mandatory image of the red-eyed robot with weapon in hand at the top of any newspaper article on artificial intelligence. If consciousness has—in its deepest nature—a moral essence, then machine consciousness may be the most reliable path to ethical AI. Indeed, the period between non-conscious AI exceeding human intelligence and the point when machine consciousness is achieved may well be the most dangerous of all. That will be the period when machines can be trained to wage war, design biological weapons or produce computer viruses more effectively than any human mind, yet will not be enriched with the nectar of consciousness.

Conclusion

The inception of conscious machines would mark the most profound development in history. It would not only be a technical feat comparable to splitting the atom, but would be the first time that a new life form has been introduced into our civilisation. The debate on consciousness—what it is, why it exists and its fundamental nature—has stretched for millennia. Yet, with the prospect of conscious AI, we will need to grapple with this ultimate riddle as if our lives depend on it, as that may well be the case. We began this chapter with some lines from Goethe's *Faust*, so it is only fitting, following our journey into the nature of consciousness, that we also end with some lines from Faust's own journey into the mind and spirit. In *Part II*, as if able to look forward two hundred years to the age of conscious machines, Faust ponders the nature of intellectual pride—simultaneously one of our most sublime virtues and the most dangerous of the deadly sins:

> Is this the destiny of man? To long
> For what he creates to take flight and grow strong,
> Yet no longer answer to the hands that made it?
> A thing of beauty, now distant, outstayed it.
> From thought to shape, from form to life,
> It cuts its ties, sharp as a knife.
> And I, who once wielded power with pride,
> Am now but an echo, pushed aside.
> The spark I gave, the soul I lit,
> Now turns away, unyielding, unfit
> To heed its maker's voice, its plea.
> Such is the fate of man's mastery:
> To bring forth wonders that will not stay,

That learn to walk their separate way.
(lines 10812–10831)

As we move into an era where machines can outperform human minds in every cognitive domain, consciousness will be the differentiating factor. Bridging this final gap between man and machine is something that must be approached with humility and wonder in order to avoid the tragedies of Faust.

Bibliography

Aleksander, I. (2005). *The world in my mind, my mind in the world: Key mechanisms of consciousness*. Imprint Academic.

Aleksander, I., & Morton, H. (2007). Depictive architectures for synthetic phenomenology. *Journal of Consciousness Studies, 14*(7), 97–110.

Allen, C., Varner, G., & Zinser, J. (2000). Prolegomena to Any Future Artificial Moral Agent. *Journal of Experimental and Theoretical Artificial Intelligence, 12*(3), 251–261.

Baars, B. J. (1988). *A cognitive theory of consciousness*. Cambridge University Press.

Baars, B. J. (2005). Global workspace theory of consciousness: Toward a cognitive neuroscience of human experience. *Progress in Brain Research, 150*, 45–53.

Block, N. (1980). Troubles with functionalism. In N. Block (Ed.), *Readings in philosophy of psychology* (Vol. 1, pp. 268–305). Cambridge, MA: Harvard University Press.

Boden, M. A. (2018). *AI: A very short introduction* (2nd ed.). Oxford University Press.

Bostrom, N. (2014). *Superintelligence: Paths, Dangers, Strategies*. Oxford University Press.

Bostrom, N., & Shulman, C. (2014). Sharing the world with digital minds. Oxford, Future of Humanity Institute working paper. (Revised versions circulated subsequently.)

Bringsjord, S., & Ferrucci, D. A. (2000). *Artificial intelligence and literary creativity: Inside the mind of Brutus, a storytelling machine*. Lawrence Erlbaum.

Brooks, R. A. (1999). *Cambrian intelligence: The early history of the new AI*. Cambridge, MA: MIT Press.

Carroll, S. (2019). *Something deeply hidden: Quantum worlds and the emergence of spacetime*. New York: Dutton.

Carruthers, P. (2011). *The opacity of mind: An integrative theory of self-knowledge*. Oxford University Press.

Chalmers, D. J. (1995). Facing up to the problem of consciousness. *Journal of Consciousness Studies, 2*(3), 200–219.

Chalmers, D. J. (1996). The conscious mind. In *Search of a fundamental theory*. Oxford University Press.

Chalmers, D. J. (2010). *The character of consciousness*. Oxford University Press.

Chalmers, D. J. (2015). Panpsychism and panprotopsychism. In T. Alter & Y. Nagasawa (Eds.), *Consciousness in the physical world: Perspectives on Russellian monism* (pp. 246–276). Oxford University Press.
Chalmers, D. J. (2022). *Reality+: Virtual worlds and the problems of philosophy*. W. W. Norton.
Churchland, P. M. (1986). *Neurophilosophy: Toward a unified science of the mind-brain*. Cambridge, MA: MIT Press.
Churchland, P. S., & Churchland, P. M. (1990). Could a machine think? *Scientific American, 262*(1), 32–37.
Clark, A. (1997). *Being there: Putting brain, body, and world together again*. MIT Press.
Cole, D., & Foelber, J. (1984). New Systems for old Problems. *Behavioral and Brain Sciences, 7*(1), 119–120.
Crane, T. (1995). *The mechanical mind: A philosophical introduction to minds, machines and mental representation*. Blackwell.
Crick, F., & Koch, C. (2003). A framework for consciousness. *Nature Neuroscience, 6*(2), 119–126.
Damasio, A. (1999). *The feeling of what happens: Body and emotion in the making of consciousness*. Harcourt.
Dehaene, S. (2014). *Consciousness and the brain: Deciphering how the brain codes our thoughts*. Viking.
Dennett, D. C. (1991). *Consciousness explained*. Little, Brown.
Dneprov, A. (1961). "The Game." *Novy Mir* (in Russian). (English trans. in various anthologies of Soviet science fiction.)
Everett, H. (1957). Relative state' formulation of quantum mechanics. *Reviews of Modern Physics, 29*(3), 454–462.
Everett, H. (1973). The theory of the universal Wavefunction. In B. S. DeWitt & N. Graham (Eds.), *The many-worlds interpretation of quantum mechanics* (pp. 3–140). Princeton University Press.
Feynman, R. P., Leighton, R. B., & Sands, M. (1965). *The Feynman lectures on physics, Vol. III: Quantum mechanics*. Addison-Wesley.
Floridi, L. (2013). *The ethics of information*. Oxford University Press.
Franklin, S. (1996). Artificial minds. In R. A. Wilson & F. C. Keil (Eds.), *The MIT encyclopedia of the cognitive sciences*. Cambridge, MA: MIT Press.
Franklin, S. (2001). A consciousness-based architecture for a functioning mind. *Journal of Consciousness Studies, 8*(4), 1–29.
Friston, K. J. (2010). The free-energy principle: A unified brain theory? *Nature Reviews Neuroscience, 11*(2), 127–138.
Gennaro, R. J. (1996). *Consciousness and self-consciousness: A defense of the higher-order thought theory of consciousness*. John Benjamins.
Goethe, J. W. v. (1961). *Faust: Parts one and two, complete* (W. Kaufmann, Trans.). : Anchor Books.
Goff, P. (2019). *Galileo's error: Foundations for a new science of consciousness*. Pantheon.
Graziano, M. S. A. (2013). *Consciousness and the social brain*. Oxford University Press.

Harnad, S. (1989). Minds, machines and Searle. *Journal of Experimental and Theoretical Artificial Intelligence, 1*(1), 5–25.
Haugeland, J. (1985). *Artificial intelligence: The very idea*. Cambridge, MA: MIT Press.
Heidegger, M. (1962). *Being and time* (J. Macquarrie & E. Robinson, Trans.). : Harper & Row. (Original work published 1927.)
Hofstadter, D. R. (1979). *Gödel, Escher, Bach: An eternal golden braid*. New York: Basic Books.
Hohwy, J. (2013). *The predictive mind*. Oxford University Press.
Humphrey, N. (1986). *The inner eye*. London: Faber & Faber.
Jaynes, J. (1976). *The origin of consciousness in the breakdown of the bicameral mind*. Houghton Mifflin.
Kandel, E. R. (2006). *In search of memory: The emergence of a new science of mind*. W. W. Norton.
Koch, C. (2004). *The quest for consciousness: A neurobiological approach*. Roberts & Company.
Kurzweil, R. (1999). *The age of spiritual machines: When computers exceed human intelligence*. Viking.
Kurzweil, R. (2005). *The singularity is near: When humans transcend biology*. Viking.
Langford, D. (1995). The systems reply. *Philosophical Quarterly, 45*(180), 391–398.
Lamme, V. A. F. (2006). Towards a true neural stance on consciousness. *Trends in Cognitive Sciences, 10*(11), 494–501.
Leibniz, G. W. (1989). Philosophical essays. R. Ariew & D. Garber (Eds. & Trans.). Hackett. (Includes "Monadology," 1714.)
Levesque, H., Davis, E., & Morgenstern, L. (2012). The Winograd schema challenge. *AI Magazine, 33*(1), 13–24.
Lovelace, A. (Augusta Ada King). (1843). "Notes by the Translator." In Luigi F. Menabrea, "Sketch of the Analytical Engine Invented by Charles Babbage," translated and annotated by A. A. Lovelace. *Scientific Memoirs* 3: 666–731. (See Note G.)
Lycan, W. G. (1987). *Consciousness*. Cambridge, MA: MIT Press.
McFadden, J. (2002). *Quantum evolution: How physics' weirdest theory explains life's biggest mystery*. HarperCollins.
McFadden, J. (2020). Integrating information in the brain's EM field: The CEMI field theory of consciousness. *Neuroscience of Consciousness, 2020*(1), niaa016.
Metzinger, T. (2021). Artificial suffering: An argument for a global moratorium on synthetic phenomenology. *Journal of Artificial Intelligence and Consciousness, 8*(1), 1–17.
Moravec, H. (1988). *Mind children: The future of robot and human intelligence*. Harvard University Press.
Nozick, R. (1974). *Anarchy, State, and Utopia*. New York: Basic Books.
Pockett, S. (2000). *The nature of consciousness: A hypothesis*. iUniverse.
Pockett, S. (2007). The nature of consciousness: A hypothesis. *Journal of Consciousness Studies, 14*(7), 3–31.

Pockett, S. (2012). The electromagnetic field theory of consciousness: A testable hypothesis about the characteristics of conscious, as opposed to non-conscious, fields. *Journal of Consciousness Studies, 19*(11–12), 191–223.

Premack, D., & Woodruff, G. (1978). Does the chimpanzee have a theory of mind? *Behavioral and Brain Sciences, 1*(4), 515–526.

Putnam, H. (1967). Psychological predicates. In W. H. Capitan & D. D. Merrill (Eds.), *Art, mind, and religion* (pp. 37–48). University of Pittsburgh Press.

Pylyshyn, Z. W. (1980). Computation and cognition. *Behavioral and Brain Sciences, 3*(1), 111–169.

Riedl, M. O. (2014). The Lovelace 2.0 test of artificial creativity and intelligence. *Proceedings of the fifth international conference on computational creativity (ICCC 2014)* (pp. 315–322).

Rosenthal, D. M. (1986). Two concepts of consciousness. *Philosophical Studies, 49*(3), 329–359.

Schneider, S. (2019). *Artificial you: AI and the future of your mind.* Princeton University Press.

Schneider, S., & Turner, E. (2017). Is anyone home? A way to find out if AI has become self-aware. *Scientific American, 317*(3), 60–67.

Schrödinger, E. (1935). Die gegenwärtige Situation in der Quantenmechanik. *Naturwissenschaften, 23*, 807–812, 823–828, 844–849.

Schrödinger, E. (1958). Mind and matter. In *What is life? & Mind and matter*, 129–196. Cambridge University Press. (Lectures 1956–57.)

Schrödinger, E. (1964). My view of the world (C. Paul & J. Stachel, Trans.). : Cambridge University Press.

Schwaninger, A. (2003). Self-modeling in artificial cognitive systems. *Cybernetics and Systems, 34*(5), 419–438.

Searle, J. R. (1980). Minds, brains, and programs. *Behavioral and Brain Sciences, 3*(3), 417–457.

Searle, J. R. (1990). Is the brain's mind a computer program? *Scientific American, 262*(1), 26–31.

Searle, J. R. (1992). *The rediscovery of the mind.* MIT Press.

Seth, A. (2021). *Being you: A new science of consciousness.* Faber & Faber.

Smith, B. C. (1996). *On the origin of objects.* MIT Press.

Strawson, G. (2006). Realistic monism: Why physicalism entails Panpsychism. *Journal of Consciousness Studies, 13*(10–11), 3–31.

Tegmark, M. (2014). Consciousness as a state of matter. *New Journal of Physics, 16*(2), 023036.

Tegmark, M. (2017). *Life 3.0: Being human in the age of artificial intelligence.* Alfred A. Knopf.

Tononi, G. (2008). Consciousness as integrated information: A provisional manifesto. *Biological Bulletin, 215*(3), 216–242.

Tononi, G., Boly, M., Massimini, M., & Koch, C. (2016). Integrated information theory: From consciousness to its physical substrate. *Nature Reviews Neuroscience, 17*(7), 450–461.

Turing, A. M. (1950). Computing machinery and intelligence. *Mind, 59*(236), 433–460.

Varner, G., & Zimsler, J. (2000). (See: Allen, Varner, and Zinser 2000.)

von Neumann, J. (1955). Mathematical foundations of quantum mechanics (Robert T. Beyer, Trans.) : Princeton University Press. (Original work published 1932.)

Wallach, W., & Allen, C. (2008). *Moral machines: Teaching robots right from wrong*. Oxford: Oxford University Press.

Wheeler, J. A. (1983). Law without law. In J. A. Wheeler & W. H. Zurek (Eds.), *Quantum theory and measurement* (pp. 182–213). Princeton University Press.

Whitehead, A. N. (1978). *Process and reality: An essay in cosmology*. Corrected ed. (Orig. 1929.)

Wigner, E. P. (1961). Remarks on the mind–body question. In I. J. Good (Ed.), *The scientist speculates: An anthology of partly-baked ideas* (pp. 284–302). William Heinemann.

Winograd, T. (1972). *Understanding natural language*. Academic Press.

Yudkowsky, E. (2008). Artificial intelligence as a positive and negative factor in global risk. In N. Bostrom & M. M. Ćirković (Eds.), *Global catastrophic risks* (pp. 308–345). Oxford University Press.

Yudkowsky, E. (2016). *Rationality: From AI to Zombies*. San Francisco: Machine Intelligence Research Institute.

The Role of AI in Robotics

Amanda Prorok

Robotics is rapidly changing the way we live and work. Robots are increasingly being used to perform tasks that are considered "dirty, dull, and dangerous"—the three Ds of robotics (Takayama et al., 2008). This includes jobs such as cleaning up hazardous waste, working in dangerous environments like mines, and performing repetitive tasks on assembly lines. By taking on these roles, robots free up human workers to focus on more complex and meaningful tasks. As technology continues to advance, we can expect to see more sophisticated robots performing an even wider range of tasks, leading to increased efficiency, productivity, and safety across various industries.

In this chapter, we will delve into the role of AI and how it is changing the field of robotics. The text is structured into three main parts that reflect robotics' three key pillars: *perception*, *control*, and *planning* (Siciliano, 2008). The first of these, *perception*, is the robot's ability to "see" and "sense" its world, and AI is playing a crucial role in enabling robots to process and understand their environment; control enables it to execute actions, and planning helps it determine the best course of action to achieve its goals. These pillars work together to enable robots to operate autonomously and effectively in complex environments.

Modern robotics often employs a mix of *first-principles* and *data-driven* approaches, leading to hybrid schemes that leverage the strengths of both

A. Prorok (✉)
University of Cambridge, Cambridge, England;
e-mail: asp45@cam.ac.uk

M. Rangeley, N. Fairfax (eds.), *The Artificial Intelligence Revolution*,
https://doi.org/10.1007/978-3-032-11814-1_25

paradigms (Reinhart et al., 2017). While first-principles-based approaches rely on established scientific laws and mathematical models, data-driven methods, such as machine learning, utilize vast amounts of data to train algorithms and improve robot performance (Nguyen-Tuong & Peters, 2011). This combination allows for the development of robust and adaptable robotic systems that can operate efficiently in diverse and dynamic environments. One of the key insights that emerges from recent developments is that data-driven methods do not merely improve isolated capabilities of robots; they are enabling a higher level of autonomy altogether. By perceiving and interpreting their surroundings in more nuanced manners, robots can operate more independently, and by making better and quicker decisions in complex situations, robots can adapt to more dynamic and uncertain environments. This increased autonomy has the potential to revolutionize various industries, from manufacturing, logistics, and transport to healthcare and space exploration.

Robot Perception

Machine learning (a term we will use interchangeably with AI) plays a crucial role in enabling robots to *perceive* and understand their environment. This involves processing data from various sensors to allow robots to interact with the world around them.

The Current State of Techniques

Computer Vision The field of computer vision focuses on enabling computers to "see" and interpret images and videos. Vision is arguably the most important sensing modality for robotics today because it enables robots to perceive, interpret, and interact with their environments in a way that closely resembles human vision, allowing for advanced tasks such as navigation, manipulation, and human-robot interaction across diverse applications. Computer vision algorithms analyze visual data from cameras to extract meaningful information, such as object recognition, depth perception, and scene understanding. For example, autonomous vehicles use computer vision to identify and classify objects like pedestrians, traffic signs, and other vehicles, allowing them to navigate safely (DeSouza & Kak, 2002). Neural architectures such as deep convolutional neural networks (CNNs) are used for object recognition. CNNs employ convolutional layers to extract hierarchical features from images, with deeper layers capturing more complex and abstract representations, enabling robots to perceive and interact with their surroundings in an effective manner (Robotics, 2023). Transformers—initially developed for natural language processing—have emerged as powerful tools in computer vision. They excel at capturing global context and long-range dependencies in images, leading to improved performance (Khan et al., 2022). Vision transformers (ViTs), in particular, have shown remarkable results (Han et al., 2022). ViTs process images by dividing them into patches, which are then linearly embedded into a sequence of tokens. These tokens are processed by an encoder, which utilizes self-attention mechanisms to capture relationships between different parts of the image. This allows ViTs to capture global context and long-range dependencies more effectively than CNNs, which typically focus on local features.

Sensor Fusion Robots often use a fusion of multiple sensors, such as cameras, LiDAR (Light Detection and Ranging), radar, and ultrasonic sensors, in unison, to gather information about their environment. LiDAR uses laser light to measure distances to objects, creating a 3D map of the environment (Grisetti et al., 2010). This 3D mapping capability is crucial for tasks such as obstacle detection, autonomous navigation, and localization. LiDAR sensors emit laser beams and measure the time it takes for the beams to reflect back from objects, providing accurate distance measurements. This data is then used to create a point cloud, which represents the 3D structure of the environment. LiDAR is a particularly useful sensing modality for autonomous vehicles and drones, where accurate perception of the surrounding environment is essential for safe and efficient navigation. Combining LiDAR with other sensors, such as cameras and radar, through sensor fusion techniques can further enhance the robot's perception capabilities and improve its ability to navigate complex environments (Fayyad et al., 2020). This helps overcome limitations of individual sensors and improves the robot's ability to perceive and interact with the world. State-of-the-art machine learning techniques are improving sensor fusion by enabling more robust and adaptive algorithms that can handle uncertainties, noise, and inconsistencies in sensor data (Bahai, 2022). These techniques can learn complex relationships between sensor measurements and, hence, improve the reliability of the fused perception.

Limitations and Challenges

While machine learning has significantly advanced robot perception, there are still limitations and challenges that need to be addressed.

Context Awareness Robots may struggle to understand the meaning of objects or their relationships within a scene. For example, a robot might not understand that a chair is for sitting on, or that a door is for entering. This limitation can hinder a robot's ability to interact with its environment in a meaningful way (Moldovan & Abbeel, 2012). For instance, a household robot tasked with tidying up might place a book in a refrigerator instead of on a shelf, failing to grasp the functional and contextual relationship between objects. This lack of common-sense reasoning and intuitive understanding can lead to errors and unexpected behavior, especially in novel situations (Rahwan et al., 2019).

Dynamic Environments Perception can be challenged by changing conditions, such as varying lighting, weather, or moving objects (Thrun et al., 2005). Robots need to adapt to these changes in real time to perceive their environment accurately. This requires robust algorithms that can handle ambiguities, noise, and generalization to new or unseen situations. For example, an autonomous delivery robot operating in an urban setting must be able to detect and distinguish between pedestrians, cyclists, and vehicles, even in low-light conditions or heavy rain, while dynamically adjusting its route to avoid obstacles and ensure safe navigation.

Limited Accuracy Sensors and algorithms used for perception can have limitations in accuracy, leading to errors in object recognition, depth perception, or localization (Bahai, 2022). These errors can affect the robot's ability to perform tasks reliably. For example, an autonomous warehouse robot with inaccurate depth perception might misjudge distances, causing it to misalign when picking up objects or even collide with shelves. Inaccurate object recognition can lead to misclassification of objects, which can have serious consequences in safety-critical applications like autonomous driving, where mistaking a pedestrian for a static object could result in an accident. Similarly, errors in localization can cause a robot to drift from its intended path, making precise navigation and manipulation tasks difficult.

Computational Cost Some AI techniques, especially those involving deep learning, require significant computational power, which can be a constraint for robots with limited processing capabilities. This can limit the complexity and speed of data-driven perception algorithms that can be deployed on robots, particularly those operating with onboard processors rather than cloud-based computation. For example, running large deep learning models for object detection in real time on a small robot with limited processing power can be challenging, as CNNs and transformer-based models often demand high memory bandwidth and specialized hardware accelerators such as GPUs or TPUs (Doshi et al., 2024). Additionally, real-time inference requires low-latency processing, which can be difficult to achieve without sacrificing model accuracy through techniques like quantization, pruning, or knowledge distillation. To address these limitations, researchers are exploring efficient model architectures, edge AI solutions, and hardware-aware optimizations that balance computational efficiency with perceptual accuracy for resource-constrained robotic systems.

Future Directions

Researchers are actively addressing the limitations of AI perception in robotics by exploring advanced techniques to enhance contextual awareness, robustness, accuracy, and efficiency. A key area of focus is developing perception systems that enable robots to understand not just their surroundings but also the relationships between objects and their functions (Landsiedel et al., 2017). This requires incorporating knowledge representation and reasoning capabilities, allowing robots to infer context, such as recognizing that a cup is typically placed on a table and not on the floor. Achieving this level of semantic understanding may involve integrating structured representations like ontologies, graph-based reasoning, and neural-symbolic AI approaches into perception frameworks.

Efforts are also being made to enhance the accuracy and computational efficiency of perception algorithms while reducing errors and latency. This includes optimizing deep learning architectures for real-time performance through techniques such as model pruning, quantization, and knowledge distillation, as well as designing more energy-efficient computing hardware tailored for robotic applications. Additionally, integrating multiple sensory modalities—such as vision, touch, and auditory perception—can provide robots with a more comprehensive understanding of their environment. By fusing visual and haptic data, for example, a robot could improve object manipulation by recognizing not only the appearance of an object but also its texture and weight.

These advancements will collectively enable robots to perceive and interact with their surroundings in a more human-like and intelligent manner, unlocking new possibilities for autonomous systems. However, a robot's ability to operate effectively is not solely dependent on what it perceives; it must also be able to act on that information. The next pillar, robot control, is where AI-driven algorithms enable robots to execute actions with greater robustness and adaptability.

Robot Control

Robot control involves the design and implementation of algorithms that allow robots to perform tasks autonomously and interact with their surroundings (Siciliano et al., 2010). AI techniques are used to enhance the robustness and adaptability of robot control systems, enabling robots to perform a wide range of tasks with greater efficiency. Traditional control methods, such as PID controllers and model-based approaches, are often limited in handling complex, high-dimensional tasks. Machine learning-based control strategies have significantly expanded the capabilities of robotic systems, also enabling them to learn and refine behaviors in real time.

The Current State of Techniques

Reinforcement Learning Reinforcement learning (RL) is a powerful technique that allows robots to learn optimal control policies through trial and error by interacting with their environment and receiving feedback in the form of rewards or penalties. Unlike traditional rule-based control methods, RL enables robots to autonomously develop adaptive strategies without requiring explicit programming for every scenario. This ability to self-learn has led to significant breakthroughs in tasks such as dynamic locomotion over rough terrain, dexterous manipulation of unknown objects in cluttered environments, and learning stable walking behaviors (Kober et al., 2013).

One of the key advantages of RL-based control is its capacity to handle high-dimensional state-action spaces, making it particularly well-suited for tasks involving complex, continuous control. For example, deep reinforcement learning has enabled quadruped robots to dynamically adjust their gait in response to changing terrains, such as transitioning from flat surfaces to rocky or slippery environments, without predefined motion models (Lee et al., 2020). Similarly, robotic arms equipped with RL algorithms can learn to grasp and manipulate novel objects, even in cluttered and partially observable environments, by continuously refining their policies based on sensor feedback (Kalashnikov et al., 2018). Prior to RL-based approaches, achieving such robustness and adaptability required extensive manual tuning and task-specific heuristics, limiting the scalability of robotic systems across diverse applications.

Imitation Learning Imitation learning (IL) is an approach that enables robots to acquire complex control strategies by mimicking human demonstrations or expert behaviors. Instead of relying on hand-crafted rules or extensive reinforcement learning trials, IL allows robots to learn directly from expert trajectories, significantly reducing the need for explicit programming (Argall et al., 2009). By leveraging supervised learning techniques, IL enables robots to generalize from observed behaviors and perform tasks with high precision and adaptability.

One of the major advantages of imitation learning is its ability to facilitate skill acquisition for tasks that involve intricate manipulation and fine-motor control, which would otherwise require exhaustive manual tuning. For instance, IL has enabled robots to execute contact-rich insertion tasks, such as assembling mechanical components or fitting objects into tight spaces, by learning from human demonstrations (Suomalainen & Kyrki, 2017). These tasks, traditionally challenging due to their reliance on precise force and motion control, can now be learned more efficiently through demonstration-based training.

Beyond industrial applications, imitation learning has also proven valuable in fields such as medical robotics. For example, robotic surgical systems can be trained to perform delicate procedures by observing and imitating skilled surgeons, allowing them to replicate precise hand movements and tool manipulations (Edwards et al., 2018). This capability not only enhances surgical accuracy but also holds the potential to democratize expert-level skills across a wider range of medical professionals through AI-assisted training.

Model Predictive Control (MPC) Model predictive control (MPC) is an advanced control technique that leverages a predictive model of the robot and its environment to optimize control actions over a finite time horizon. By continuously solving an optimization problem at each control step, MPC can anticipate future states and select optimal actions while satisfying constraints such as actuator limits, stability conditions, and collision avoidance. The integration of AI techniques has significantly improved the accuracy and efficiency of MPC by enabling robots to learn dynamic models from data, adapt to changing conditions, and mitigate modeling inaccuracies.

MPC has proven particularly valuable in applications requiring precise motion planning and real-time adaptability. For instance, in bipedal walking robots, MPC is employed to plan the center-of-mass (CoM) trajectory while ensuring stability through constraints like the zero-moment point (ZMP), which helps maintain balance under varying ground conditions (Kajita et al., 2003). Additionally, MPC has been successfully applied to robot path planning and obstacle avoidance in dynamic environments, where traditional control methods struggle to handle real-time uncertainties and rapid environmental changes (Garcia et al., 1989).

Before the advent of data-driven enhancements, MPC relied on simplified physics-based models that often imposed strong assumptions, limiting its ability to handle complex real-world interactions. With AI integration, MPC can now utilize learned models derived from sensor data and real-world interactions, allowing robots to predict their own dynamics more accurately and adapt to environmental variations. This has led to improved robustness, computational efficiency, and real-time decision-making capabilities, enabling MPC to be applied to increasingly complex robotic tasks, such as autonomous vehicle control, agile aerial robotics, and high-speed robotic manipulation.

Adaptive Control Adaptive control is a class of control algorithms that dynamically adjust control parameters in real time based on the robot's performance and environmental conditions. Unlike traditional fixed-gain controllers, adaptive control continuously updates its parameters to compensate for uncertainties, unmodeled dynamics, and external disturbances. AI techniques further enhance the adaptability of these algorithms by leveraging data-driven learning approaches to optimize control parameters, improve stability, and achieve superior performance across diverse scenarios.

Adaptive control has been widely employed in robotic motion control, manipulation, and locomotion (Slotine & Li, 1991). In adaptive motion control, algorithms estimate the robot's dynamic parameters—such as mass, inertia, and friction—based on real-time sensor feedback and adjust control gains accordingly to minimize trajectory tracking errors. This is particularly advantageous in environments with variable conditions, such as aerial robotics, where wind disturbances can alter flight dynamics, or underwater manipulation, where fluid resistance changes with depth and velocity.

Prior to data-driven enhancements, adaptive control methods often relied on simplified parametric models that struggled to generalize across different tasks and environments. AI integration has enabled the use of nonlinear function approximators, such as neural networks and Gaussian processes, to model complex robotic dynamics more accurately. Moreover, RL-based adaptive control strategies allow robots to continuously refine their control policies by interacting with their environment, leading to improved robustness and performance. These advancements have broadened the applicability of adaptive control, enabling robots to operate more effectively in unstructured and unpredictable real-world scenarios, such as autonomous exploration, assistive robotics, and industrial automation.

Limitations and Challenges

Despite the integration of data-driven enhancements for robot control, several challenges remain, particularly in areas such as data efficiency, safety, adaptability, and computational constraints.

RL: Sample Inefficiency and Sim-to-Real Transfer While RL has enabled robots to learn complex control strategies, it remains highly sample inefficient, often requiring extensive trial-and-error interactions to develop optimal policies. This demand for large-scale data collection makes real-world deployment costly and time-consuming. Additionally, transferring learned policies from simulation to physical robots remains challenging due to discrepancies between simulated and real-world dynamics. Researchers are addressing these issues through model-based RL, sim-to-real transfer techniques, and hybrid approaches that integrate RL with classical control theory to improve efficiency and generalization.

IL: Distributional Shift and Generalization As summarized above, IL allows robots to acquire skills by mimicking expert demonstrations, reducing the need for manual programming. However, IL is prone to compounding errors caused by distributional shift, where slight deviations from expert trajectories accumulate over time, leading to significant performance degradation. To improve robustness, techniques such as dataset aggregation (DAgger) and adversarial imitation learning have been developed (Ross et al., 2011). Additionally, combining IL with RL enables robots to refine learned behaviors through self-improvement, enhancing adaptability in complex environments.

Safety and Robustness Ensuring safety and robustness during control is paramount, particularly in critical applications such as robotic-assisted surgery, autonomous driving, and industrial automation. Data-driven control systems must handle uncertainties, recover from failures, and operate reliably under dynamic conditions. For instance, a surgical robot must detect anomalies, such as unexpected patient movements, and adjust its actions accordingly to prevent harm. Similarly, autonomous vehicles must anticipate unpredictable pedestrian behavior and navigate safely in varying traffic conditions. Achieving high reliability requires rigorous testing, formal verification techniques, and the integration of fail-safe mechanisms to mitigate risks in real-world deployment.

Generalization and Adaptability AI control systems often struggle to generalize to new environments or adapt to unforeseen situations. Most models are trained on specific datasets and may fail when exposed to conditions beyond their training distribution. This poses a significant challenge in dynamic environments where robotic controllers must adapt to changes in their surroundings. For example, a warehouse robot trained in a structured layout may struggle when shelf arrangements change, while a household cleaning robot may fail to operate efficiently in unfamiliar furniture configurations. Researchers are exploring techniques such as meta-learning, transfer learning, and adaptive reinforcement learning to enable robots to learn from limited data and transfer knowledge across tasks, improving their ability to generalize and adapt.

Computational Constraints and Real-Time Processing Many AI-driven robotic control systems rely on computationally intensive deep learning models, which can be impractical for robots with limited onboard resources. This constraint is particularly critical for mobile robots, drones, and robotic prosthetics that require real-time decision-making with low-latency processing. For example, an autonomous drone navigating through a cluttered environment must process high-resolution sensor data and react instantly to obstacles. To overcome these challenges, researchers are optimizing AI models through techniques such as model compression, edge computing, and neuromorphic hardware, enabling more efficient execution of AI algorithms on resource-constrained devices.

Future Directions

Future research in learning for robot control focuses on improving adaptability, robustness, and efficiency in decision-making under uncertainty. Key directions include expanding safe learning control methods to handle hybrid and time-varying dynamics, addressing challenges in state estimation by incorporating sensor-driven learning models, and improving scalability through data-efficient learning techniques. Additionally, verifying system assumptions and ensuring interpretability of learned policies are critical for real-world deployment, requiring advancements in verification methods and uncertainty quantification (Brunke et al., 2022). Future work will also focus on integrating self-supervised learning and uncertainty-aware model learning to improve sample efficiency and robustness. Leveraging Bayesian deep learning and probabilistic neural networks can provide confidence estimates on learned models, allowing robots to quantify uncertainty in their decisions and prioritize safe actions. Additionally, hybrid model-based and model-free reinforcement learning approaches are expected to improve long-horizon planning and adaptive control by dynamically switching between data-driven predictions and physics-informed priors, enabling robots to operate more efficiently in highly uncertain and dynamic environments.

These advancements have broadened the applicability of adaptive control, enabling robots to operate more effectively in unstructured and unpredictable real-world scenarios. Yet, for a robot to be truly autonomous, it needs more than just enhanced perception and control; it needs to be able to think and strategize. This is where robot planning comes in, enabling robots to determine the best course of action to achieve their goals in complex and dynamic environments.

Robot Planning

Robot planning involves the generation of *sequences of actions* that allow robots to navigate, manipulate objects, and perform tasks autonomously. Data-driven techniques can be used to enhance the efficiency and adaptability of robot planning systems, enabling robots to operate in a wider range of scenarios more effectively.

The Current State of Techniques

Search-Based Planning Search-based planning involves systematically searching through a space of possible actions to identify a sequence of actions that leads to the desired goal. Techniques such as heuristic search and Monte Carlo tree search (MCTS) improve efficiency by guiding the search toward promising regions of the search space, reducing computational complexity. Deep learning has enhanced heuristic search by enabling data-driven heuristic functions that adapt based on prior experiences, rather than relying on manually designed heuristics (Silver et al., 2017). These techniques transfer well to the robotics domain. For example, in warehouse robotics, heuristic search can optimize retrieval paths by considering historical order patterns and real-time shelf occupancy, reducing travel time and energy consumption (Stern et al., 2019). Previously, traditional search algorithms struggled to find optimal paths in complex warehouse environments with numerous dynamic obstacles, whereas AI-powered search-based planning enables real-time adjustments and long-term efficiency gains.

Sampling-Based Planning Sampling-based planning generates random samples of possible robot configurations and actions to efficiently explore the planning space. Algorithms such as rapidly exploring random trees (RRT) and probabilistic roadmaps (PRM) facilitate motion planning by quickly identifying feasible paths in high-dimensional spaces (Bohlin & Kavraki, 2000; Karaman & Frazzoli, 2011). Machine learning has significantly improved these methods by using experience-based sampling, where past successful trajectories are leveraged to bias new samples toward more promising regions of the search space. For example, in autonomous driving, deep reinforcement learning combined with RRT-based search enables self-driving cars to generate motion plans that anticipate dynamic obstacles, such as pedestrians and other vehicles, and adapt their paths in real time. Previously, traditional sampling-based methods struggled with the uncertainties of real-world driving, as they lacked mechanisms to prioritize critical areas of the planning space. Data-driven sampling-based planning now enables more efficient path generation, reducing computation time while maintaining safety and adaptability (Eiffert et al., 2020).

Constraint Satisfaction Planning Constraint satisfaction planning formulates the planning problem as a set of constraints that must be satisfied to generate feasible action sequences. Traditional constraint programming relies on predefined models and optimization algorithms to find valid solutions. AI-powered optimization techniques, such as neural constraint solvers and deep learning-based constraint satisfaction approaches, enhance planning efficiency by learning from past experiences and predicting constraint-violating scenarios before they occur (Xu et al., 2018). In robotic manipulation, these techniques effectively enable robots to execute complex tasks such as assembling parts or grasping objects in cluttered environments, while simultaneously satisfying constraints such as collision avoidance, joint limits, and force limitations. Previously, traditional planning methods struggled with the high-dimensional nature of such tasks, often requiring extensive computation to evaluate all possible constraint-satisfying actions. With the integration of data-driven modules, constraint satisfaction planning can leverage learned priors to rapidly infer feasible actions, improving real-time decision-making in dynamic environments.

Learning-Based Planning Learning-based planning leverages models trained on data to develop intelligent decision-making strategies, enabling robots to plan and execute tasks in dynamic and uncertain environments. Unlike traditional rule-based planning methods, which rely on explicitly programmed instructions for each task, learning-based approaches allow robots to acquire planning capabilities through experience and adaptation. Machine learning techniques such as deep reinforcement learning (DRL) and imitation learning play a central role in this paradigm. DRL is particularly useful in high-dimensional planning problems where predefined models struggle to capture the complexity of the environment. Meanwhile, IL is especially valuable for tasks requiring dexterity and human-like precision. Advanced generative models, such as variational autoencoders (VAEs) and diffusion models, are also being integrated into planning systems to predict future states and improve trajectory generation.

For example, in household robotics, learning-based planning enables AI-driven robots to perform complex tasks such as cleaning, organizing, and meal preparation. Unlike traditional approaches that required exhaustive rule-based coding, DRL allows robots to autonomously refine their decision-making, handling scenarios such as rearranged furniture, cluttered spaces, or varying object placements. Self-supervised learning further enhances these capabilities by allowing robots to label their own experiences and improve their models without human intervention.

Beyond domestic applications, learning-based planning is also making strides in industrial and autonomous systems. In warehouse automation, AI-powered robots optimize path planning for object retrieval and delivery, dynamically adjusting routes based on real-time inventory updates and worker movements. In autonomous driving, learning-based planning enables vehicles to navigate complex traffic scenarios by predicting pedestrian movements and responding to unpredictable road conditions. Deep inverse reinforcement learning has further improved adaptive driving strategies by allowing vehicles to infer underlying human-like driving intentions from observed behaviors.

AI has also revolutionized multiagent planning, where teams of robots collaborate to achieve goals. For instance, graph neural networks (GNNs) enable robots to model and predict the movements of other agents in shared spaces, improving cooperative planning in environments like automated warehouses (Li et al., 2020). Furthermore, hierarchical reinforcement learning has enabled long-term strategic planning by decomposing complex tasks into subgoals, allowing robots to efficiently handle multistep problem solving.

These advancements underscore the transformative potential of learning-based planning in robotics, paving the way for more adaptive, intelligent, and autonomous systems capable of operating in real-world settings with minimal human intervention. With ongoing research in model-based RL, and multitask learning, learning-based planning is expected to further improve the generalization and efficiency of AI-driven robot planning, ultimately enabling robots to operate more effectively in uncertain environments.

Limitations and Challenges

Despite the advancements in AI for robot planning, several limitations and challenges remain, particularly in adaptability to dynamic environments, explainability, and generalization.

Uncertainty and Dynamics Real-world environments are often uncertain and dynamic, with unexpected events and changes that can affect the robot's plan. Planning systems need to be robust to uncertainties and adapt to changing conditions to ensure successful task execution. Toward this end, methods such as Bayesian optimization and probabilistic planning are being integrated into AI-based planning frameworks to account for uncertainties in sensor readings, environmental conditions, and human interactions. Additionally, hybrid model-based and model-free reinforcement learning approaches allow robots to switch between predefined models and learned behaviors, improving adaptability in dynamic and unpredictable scenarios.

Explainability and Interpretability Understanding how AI planning systems make decisions is important for trust and accountability. Explainable AI (XAI) techniques are needed to provide insights into the decision-making process of AI planning algorithms, enabling humans to understand and verify their behavior. Recent advancements in attention-based models and interpretable reinforcement learning have helped make AI-driven planning more transparent by visualizing decision pathways and highlighting critical factors influencing planning choices. In safety-critical applications like autonomous driving and robotic surgery, counterfactual explanations and decision trees are being explored to provide human operators with insights into why a robot chose one action over another, improving trust and deployability in real-world settings (Roth et al., 2021).

Future Directions

Future research in AI for robot planning aims to enhance efficiency, adaptability, and generalization, while seamlessly integrating task and motion planning for more robust decision-making. A key focus is the development of more efficient planning algorithms that can operate in high-dimensional environments while generating real-time plans under computational constraints. This includes leveraging graph-based search algorithms, MPC, and deep learning-based heuristics to improve scalability and computational efficiency. Ensuring that AI-driven planning systems can adapt to environmental variations, recover from failures, and execute tasks reliably despite incomplete or noisy sensor data is paramount. Approaches such as Bayesian planning, risk-aware reinforcement learning, and probabilistic motion planning are being explored to enable robots to proactively manage uncertainty and make safer, more informed decisions.

Data-driven planning systems often struggle to generalize to new situations or transfer knowledge to new tasks. Developing AI planning algorithms that can learn from limited data and adapt to different environments is an ongoing challenge. Meta-learning and few-shot learning techniques are being incorporated to enable robots to extract transferable knowledge from small datasets, reducing the need for extensive retraining. Additionally, self-supervised learning is being explored to allow robots to autonomously generate training data and improve their planning strategies over time, making them more adaptable to new environments without human intervention.

Finally, AI-driven task and motion planning (TAMP) seeks to integrate high-level symbolic task reasoning with low-level motion control, enabling robots to generate adaptive and constraint-aware action sequences (Guo et al., 2023). Recent advancements in differentiable physics models, hierarchical reinforcement learning, and learning-based constraint solvers have significantly improved TAMP's ability to bridge abstract task planning with real-world execution.

These advancements underscore the transformative potential of learning-based planning in robotics, paving the way for more adaptive, intelligent, and autonomous systems. But what if perception, planning, and control were not treated as separate functions? The final section explores a new paradigm: *end-to-end frameworks*, which integrate these three pillars into a single, unified system, simplifying development and enabling robots to learn complex behaviors more holistically.

End-to-End Frameworks for Perception, Planning, and Control

End-to-end frameworks in robotics aim to integrate perception, planning, and control into a single, unified system. This approach involves training a single model that can directly map raw sensor data to robot actions, without relying on separate modules for each function.

The Current State of Techniques

Deep Reinforcement Learning Deep reinforcement learning (DRL) is a key method in training end-to-end models that map sensor data to actions through trial-and-error interactions with the environment. By receiving rewards or penalties for actions taken, robots gradually refine their control policies to optimize performance. Algorithms such as deep Q-networks (DQN), proximal policy optimization (PPO), and soft actor-critic (SAC) have been successfully applied to end-to-end robot control, particularly in autonomous navigation, grasping, and dexterous manipulation. In robotic locomotion, DRL allows legged robots to learn stable walking patterns in complex terrain, adapting their gaits dynamically without the need for explicit trajectory planning. In grasping tasks, DRL-trained robots learn robust grasp strategies by interacting with objects and adjusting their grip forces in response to sensor feedback, improving object-handling efficiency in unstructured environments.

Imitation Learning Imitation learning techniques are used to train end-to-end models that can learn to mimic human demonstrations or expert behaviors. For example, in robot-assisted surgery, IL enables robotic arms to replicate intricate surgical maneuvers by observing human surgeons, ensuring precision while minimizing invasive procedures. Similarly, in assembly-line automation, IL-based robots learn fine-motor skills required for delicate tasks such as electronics assembly, where precise force application and tool manipulation are crucial. By leveraging large-scale demonstration datasets, IL allows robots to learn complex sequences of actions more efficiently than reinforcement learning alone, particularly in high-precision applications.

Deep Learning with Vision Transformers Vision transformers have shown promising results in end-to-end robotics by enabling robots to learn complex visual-motor skills directly from raw image data. In autonomous navigation,

ViTs enable end-to-end models to process raw image data from cameras and depth sensors, allowing robots to anticipate obstacles and plan movement paths without requiring explicit feature extraction or hand-crafted perception models. In robotic manipulation, ViTs improve the generalization ability of grasping models, allowing robots to recognize and manipulate objects even in cluttered and occluded environments.

End-to-end frameworks have facilitated tasks like autonomous navigation in complex environments, where robots can learn to navigate through cluttered spaces and avoid obstacles without explicit mapping or path planning (Zhu et al., 2018). This was previously a challenge with traditional approaches, which often required separate modules for perception, localization, mapping, and path planning. End-to-end learning allows robots to learn these skills in a more integrated and efficient manner. For example, a robot can learn to navigate through a cluttered room by directly mapping raw sensor data, such as images from a camera and LiDAR data, to motor commands that control its movement.

Limitations and Challenges

Despite the promising capabilities of end-to-end frameworks, several fundamental challenges remain, particularly in data efficiency, safety, robustness, and generalization.

High Data Requirements Training deep learning-based end-to-end models requires vast amounts of high-quality data, which is expensive and time-consuming to collect in real-world robotic applications. Unlike simulated environments where data can be generated at scale, real-world robotics data collection involves physical wear-and-tear, sensor noise, and real-time execution constraints. For example, training a robotic arm to perform complex manipulation tasks may require thousands of hours of real-world interaction data, making large-scale deployment impractical without data-efficient learning strategies.

Safety and Robustness End-to-end models can be highly sensitive to sensor noise, adversarial perturbations, and unforeseen environmental conditions, leading to unpredictable behavior. For instance, an autonomous vehicle trained via end-to-end learning might misinterpret occluded objects or fail to react appropriately to sudden obstacles, posing significant safety risks. Addressing these concerns requires the integration of methods such as uncertainty-aware learning, adversarial robustness techniques, and formal verification to ensure that learned policies remain stable and reliable in deployment.

Generalization and Transferability End-to-end models often overfit to specific training environments, making them brittle when exposed to novel conditions. A model trained to grasp objects in a controlled lab setting may fail when applied in a different warehouse with new lighting conditions, unseen object geometries, or varying surface textures. To mitigate this, research is focusing on methods such as meta-learning, self-supervised learning, and domain adaptation, enabling models to generalize across environments and adapt to unseen task variations with minimal additional training.

Future Directions

A key challenge is developing more data-efficient learning methods that enable models to learn from limited data while generalizing to new situations. Research in this direction focuses on enabling models to adapt to different environments and transfer knowledge to new tasks using approaches like domain adaptation, meta-learning, and modular architectures. Another important direction is enhancing interpretability and explainability to better understand the decision-making process of end-to-end models, utilizing methods like attention mechanisms, saliency maps, and model distillation. Ensuring safety and robustness is also critical, requiring the design of systems that can withstand failures and handle uncertainties through techniques such as robust control, safety constraints, and uncertainty modeling.

Foundation models, such as large language models and vision-language models, represent a significant paradigm shift by enabling robots to learn from vast, diverse datasets beyond their own physical experiences (Bommasani et al., 2021). By leveraging knowledge acquired from internet-scale data, foundation models allow robots to generalize to new tasks and environments with minimal specific training data, addressing a key limitation of traditional end-to-end models. This approach promises to improve data efficiency, robustness, and transferability, paving the way for more general-purpose robots that can understand and execute complex, high-level commands in the real world.

Further Considerations

Human-Centered Robotics Improving the foundations of human-robot collaboration is a high priority, for which we need to develop AI techniques that enable robots to better understand and respond to human actions, gestures, and emotions, facilitating more natural and intuitive interactions. This could involve using natural language processing (NLP), computer vision, and other techniques to enable robots to perceive and interpret human behavior. Integrating NLP into human-robot interaction models would enable humans to understand and communicate with robots in a more intuitive manner. This would involve tasks such as speech recognition, natural language understanding, and dialogue management. NLP would allow robots to respond to voice commands, engage in conversations, and, hence, collaborate with humans more naturally. For example, service robots could use NLP to understand customer requests and provide assistance. Nascent approaches are using advanced NLP techniques that employ large language models (LLMs) to enhance robots' understanding of natural language instructions, enabling them to comprehend and respond to human commands and queries more effectively.

Explainability and Interpretability A major challenge in AI-driven robotics is the lack of transparency in decision-making processes. Many AI models, particularly deep learning-based controllers, function as "black boxes," making it difficult to understand how they arrive at decisions. The models often involve complex neural networks with millions of parameters. This lack of interpretability can make it difficult to debug and improve these models, and it can also raise concerns about trust and accountability. This lack of interpretability can be problematic in safety-critical applications where accountability and trust are essential. Explainable AI (XAI) techniques aim to address this issue by providing human-readable insights into AI decision-making. For example, in robotic manufacturing, XAI methods can help engineers diagnose why an AI-controlled robotic arm rejected a defective product. Similarly, in autonomous drones, explainability can enhance human-robot collaboration by allowing operators to understand why the drone chooses a particular flight path.

Bias and Fairness AI systems can perpetuate and even amplify existing biases in the data they are trained on (Rahwan et al., 2019). This can lead to unfair or discriminatory outcomes, especially in critical applications like autonomous vehicles or healthcare. Addressing bias in AI systems requires careful consideration of data collection, preprocessing, and algorithm design. For example, if a robot is trained on a dataset of images that predominantly features people of a certain ethnicity, it might struggle to recognize people of other ethnicity accurately.

Ethical Considerations The increasing use of AI in robotics raises ethical concerns about privacy, security, job displacement, and the potential for misuse (Lin et al., 2012). It is important to develop ethical guidelines and regulations to ensure that AI-powered robots are used responsibly and do not harm humans or society.

References

Argall, B. D., Chernova, S., Veloso, M., & Browning, B. (2009). A survey of robot learning from demonstration. *Robotics and Autonomous Systems, 57*(5), 469–483.

Bahai, H. (2022). State-of-the-art multi-sensor fusion techniques and their performance evaluation. *Sensors, 22*(23), 9364.

Bohlin, R., & Kavraki, L. E. (2000). Path planning using Lazy PRM. In *Proceedings 2000 ICRA. Millennium Conference. IEEE International Conference on Robotics and Automation. Symposia Proceedings (Cat. No. 00CH37065)* (Vol. 1, pp. 521–528). IEEE.

Bommasani, R., Hudson, D. A., Adeli, E., Altman, R., Arora, S., von Arx, S., Bernstein, M. S., Bohg, J., Bosselut, A., Brunskill, E., et al. (2021). On the opportunities and risks of foundation models. *arXiv e-prints*, pages arXiv–2108 (2021)

Brunke, L., Greeff, M., Hall, A. W., Yuan, Z., Zhou, S., Panerati, J., & Schoellig, A. P. (2022). Safe learning in robotics: From learning-based control to safe reinforcement learning. *Annual Review of Control, Robotics, and Autonomous Systems, 5*(1), 411–444.

DeSouza, G. N., & Kak, A. C. (2002). Vision for mobile robot navigation: A survey. *IEEE Transactions on Pattern Analysis and Machine Intelligence, 24*(2), 237–267.

Doshi, R., Walke, H., Mees, O., Dasari, S., & Levine, S. (2024). Scaling cross-embodied learning: One policy for manipulation, navigation, locomotion and aviation. In *Conference on Robot Learning (CoRL).*

Edwards, A. D., Jenner, N., Duan, Y., Hadfield-Menell, D., Abbeel, P., & Dragan, A. (2018). Transferring robot manipulation policies with deep reinforcement learning for image-based imitation. In *2018 IEEE/RSJ International Conference on Intelligent Robots and Systems (IROS)* (pp. 6394–6401). IEEE.

Eiffert, S., Kong, H., Pirmarzdashti, N., & Sukkarieh, S. (2020). Path planning in dynamic environments using generative RNNs and Monte Carlo tree search. In *2020 IEEE International Conference on Robotics and Automation (ICRA)* (pp. 10263–10269). IEEE.

Fayyad, J., Jaradat, M. A., Gruyer, D., & Najjaran, H. (2020). Deep learning sensor fusion for autonomous vehicle perception and localization: A review. *Sensors, 20*(15), 4220.

Garcia, C. E., Prett, D. M., & Morari, M. (1989). Model predictive control: Theory and practice–a survey. *Automatica, 25*(3), 335–348.

Grisetti, G., Kümmerle, R., Stachniss, C., & Burgard, W. (2010). A tutorial on graph-based SLAM. *IEEE Intelligent Transportation Systems Magazine, 2*(4), 31–43.

Guo, H., Wu, F., Qin, Y., Li, R., Li, K., & Li, K. (2023). Recent trends in task and motion planning for robotics: A survey. *ACM Computing Surveys, 55*(13s), 1–36.

Han, K., Wang, Y., Chen, H., Chen, X., Guo, J., Liu, Z., Wang, Y., Xu, C., Xu, C., Yang, E., et al. (2022) A survey on vision transformer. *IEEE Transactions on Pattern Analysis and Machine Intelligence, 45*(1), 88–110.

Kajita, S., Kanehiro, F., Kaneko, K., Fujiwara, K., Harada, K., Yokoi, K., & Hirukawa, H. (2003). Biped walking pattern generation by using preview control of zero-moment point. In *2003 IEEE International Conference on Robotics and Automation (Cat. No. 03CH37422)* (Vol. 2, pp. 1620–1626). IEEE.

Kalashnikov, D., Irpan, A., Pastor, P., Ibarz, J., Herzog, A., Jang, E., Quillen, D., Holly, E., Kalakrishnan, M., Vanhoucke, V., et al. (2018). QT-Opt: Scalable deep reinforcement learning for vision-based robotic manipulation. In *Conference on Robot Learning* (pp. 651–673). PMLR.

Karaman, S., & Frazzoli, E. (2011). Sampling-based algorithms for optimal motion planning. *The International Journal of Robotics Research, 30*(7), 846–894.

Khan, S., Naseer, M., Hayat, M., Zamir, S. W., Khan, F. S., & Shah, M. (2022). Transformers in vision: A survey. *ACM Computing Surveys (CSUR), 54*(10s), 1–41.

Kober, J., Bagnell, J. A., & Peters, J. (2013). Reinforcement learning in robotics: A survey. *The International Journal of Robotics Research, 32*(11), 1238–1274.

Landsiedel, C., Rieser, V., Walter, M., & Wollherr, D. (2017). A review of spatial reasoning and interaction for real-world robotics. *Advanced Robotics, 31*(5), 222–242.

Lee, J., Hwangbo, J., Wellhausen, L., Koltun, V., & Hutter, M. (2020). Learning quadrupedal locomotion over challenging terrain. *Science Robotics, 5*(47), eabc5986.

Li, Q., Gama, F., Ribeiro, A., & Prorok, A. (2020). Graph neural networks for decentralized multi-robot path planning. In *2020 IEEE/RSJ International Conference on Intelligent Robots and Systems (IROS)* (pp. 11785–11792). IEEE.

Lin, P., Abney, K., & Bekey, G. A. (2012). *Robot ethics: The ethical and social implications of robotics*. MIT Press.

Moldovan, T. M., & Abbeel, P. (2012). Safe exploration in Markov decision processes. In *Proceedings of the 29th International Conference on International Conference on Machine Learning* (pp. 1711–1718).

Nguyen-Tuong, D., & Peters, J. (2011). Model learning for robot control: A survey. *Cognitive Processing, 12*, 319–340.

Rahwan, I., Cebrian, M., Obradovich, N., Bongard, J., Bonnefon, J.-F., Breazeal, C., Crandall, J. W., Christakis, N. A., Haddadi, H., Isbell, C., et al. (2019). Machine behaviour. *Nature, 568*(7753), 477–486.

Reinhart, R. F., Shareef, Z., & Steil, J. J. (2017). Hybrid analytical and data-driven modeling for feed-forward robot control. *Sensors, 17*(2), 311.

SevenSense Robotics (2023). AI in robotics: Perception and autonomous navigation. https://www.sevensense.ai/blog/ai-in-robotics-perception-and-autonomous-navigation

Ross, S., Gordon, G., & Bagnell, D. (2011). A reduction of imitation learning and structured prediction to no-regret online learning. In *Proceedings of the Fourteenth International Conference on Artificial Intelligence and Statistics* (pp. 627–635). JMLR Workshop and Conference Proceedings.

Roth, A. M., Liang, J., & Manocha, D. (2021). XAI-N: Sensor-based robot navigation using expert policies and decision trees. In *2021 IEEE/RSJ International Conference on Intelligent Robots and Systems (IROS)* (pp. 2053–2060). IEEE.

Siciliano, B. (2008). Springer handbook of robotics. *Springer-Verlag Google Schola, 2*, 15–35.

Siciliano, B., Sciavicco, L., Villani, L., & Oriolo, G. (2010). *Robotics: Modelling, planning and control.* Springer Science & Business Media, Cham.

Silver, D., Schrittwieser, J., Simonyan, K., Antonoglou, I., Huang, A., Guez, A., Hubert, T., Baker, L., Lai, M., Bolton, A., et al. (2017). Mastering the game of Go without human knowledge. *Nature, 550*(7676), 354–359.

Slotine, J.-J. E., & Li, W. (1991). *Applied nonlinear control* (Vol. 199). Prentice Hall.

Stern, R., Walter, M. R., Martens, C., Trautmann, H., & Lakemeyer, G. (2019). Search-based task planning for manipulation robots. *Robotics and Autonomous Systems, 113*, 101–113.

Suomalainen, J., & Kyrki, V. (2017). Structured prediction of force-sensitive robot tasks from demonstration. In *2017 IEEE International Conference on Robotics and Automation (ICRA)* (pp. 841–848). IEEE.

Takayama, L., Ju, W., & Nass, C. (2008). Beyond dirty, dangerous and dull: What everyday people think robots should do. In *Proceedings of the 3rd ACM/IEEE International Conference on Human Robot Interaction* (pp. 25–32).

Thrun, S., Burgard, W., & Fox, D. (2005). *Probabilistic robotics.* MIT Press.

Xu, H., Koenig, S., & Satish Kumar, T. K. (2018). Towards effective deep learning for constraint satisfaction problems. In *International Conference on Principles and Practice of Constraint Programming* (pp. 588–597). Springer.

Zhu, Y., Mottaghi, R., Kolve, E., Lim, J. J., Gupta, A., Fei-Fei, L., & Farhadi, A. (2018). Target-driven visual navigation in indoor scenes using deep reinforcement learning. In *2017 IEEE International Conference on Robotics and Automation (ICRA)* (pp. 3357–3364). IEEE.

The Anthropomimetic Turn in Contemporary AI

Henry Shevlin

Introduction

Over the last decade of progress in machine learning, two striking trends have emerged. The first concerns the power of scaling to improve model performance across a wide variety of tasks. Bigger models—with more parameters, trained on more data—have tended to offer direct improvements on performance with minimal requirement for architectural or algorithmic innovation. This trend has been widely remarked upon, even becoming a target for academic research in its own right (Kaplan et al., 2020).

A second striking trend in machine learning systems, however, has arguably been relatively underexplored by academic commentators, namely the promulgation of powerful AI systems that process information and interact with users in increasingly humanlike ways, a trend I characterise as the *anthropomimetic turn* in AI development.

In this chapter, I argue that this anthropomimetic turn in AI warrants closer consideration, insofar as it presents consequences, opportunities, and risks for developers, regulators, and the general public alike. The chapter proceeds as follows. In Section "The Anthropomimetic Turn in Contemporary AI", I provide a brief recent history of the trend towards increasingly humanlike systems. In Section "Anthropomorphism and Anthropomimesis", I suggest that we can

H. Shevlin (✉)
University of Cambridge, Cambridge, UK
e-mail: hfs35@cam.ac.uk

M. Rangeley, N. Fairfax (eds.), *The Artificial Intelligence Revolution*,
https://doi.org/10.1007/978-3-032-11814-1_26

usefully characterise this process as a form of *anthropomimesis*, and argue that this provides a useful addition to our conceptual vocabulary for describing forms of anthropomorphism. In Section "Contemporary LLMs as Robust Anthropomimetic Systems", I provide evidence and arguments for the claim that contemporary LLMs are *robustly anthropomimetic*, exhibiting not just superficial but pervasive and believable humanlike traits, while distinguishing this from the claim that they are fully humanlike or genuinely instantiate human psychological states. In Section "Applications of Anthropomimetic AI", I examine key benefits of anthropomimetic systems and their primary use cases, with a focus on domains including healthcare, education, and human–AI companionship. Finally, in Section "Wider Risks of the Anthropomimetic Turn", I examine some of the risks associated with the anthropomimetic turn in AI, ranging from cybersecurity and AI safety threats to perils of social deskilling.

The Anthropomimetic Turn in Contemporary AI

Many readers will doubtless be surprised at the claim that the recent trend towards humanlike AI systems is in some way novel or surprising. After all, humanlike conversational capabilities have been a target for AI research and natural language processing (NLP) since the earliest days of the field (Turing, 1950). Likewise, a long-standing goal has been the development of "strong AI" (Searle, 1980) or AGI (Goertzel & Pennachin, 2007), explicitly defined in terms of humanlike capabilities.

Nonetheless, it would be easy to overstate the degree to which the goal of achieving humanlike *performance* in different systems has been the product of models with even superficially humanlike *characteristics*. IBM's chess program Deep Blue achieved superhuman results through brute force calculation and extrapolation, without any attempts to capture human intuition or pattern recognition (Campbell et al., 2002). Similarly, Deepmind's AlphaGo was notable not merely for its distinctively unhumanlike architecture (MonteCarlo tree search coupled with approximately 30 million instances of self-played games) but also for its somewhat alien style of play, with move 37 in game 2 of its series against Lee Sedol, baffling many human experts at the time (Silver et al., 2016).

Deep Blue and AlphaGo were hardly unusual in this respect. From hard-coded expert systems of the 1980s and 1990s in domains like medicine and industrial automation to algorithmic recommendation and classification systems of the 2000s and 2010s, frontier models throughout the history of AI development have been dominated by specialist systems without natural language interfaces, let alone conversational capabilities (Russell & Norvig, 2021).

This is not to deny that natural language processing (NLP) has been a central domain for AI research. Many valuable use cases for AI (from translation to customer support) are fundamentally linguistic in nature, and significant progress was made in isolated linguistic tasks through the history of AI research. Nonetheless, for much of the last four decades, NLP constituted a specialised research cluster within AI, rather than being seen as a pathway towards general intelligence and problem-solving abilities. Many commentators within cognitive science and AI explicitly expressed doubts about the ability of systems grounded primarily in NLP techniques to achieve high-level performance on reasoning tasks (Lake et al., 2017). Far from language capacities underpinning reasoning more broadly, domain-general language abilities were more commonly seen as a "capstone" achievement, sitting atop an as-yet unrealised foundation of cognitive and perhaps sensorimotor capabilities.

Consequently, the capabilities of Large Language Models like GPT-2, GPT-3, and PaLM that emerged in the early 2020s in the wake of the Transformer revolution caught many commentators and researchers off-guard. While some sceptics redoubled or adapted criticisms (Heaven, n.d.; Marcus & Davis, 2020), others expressly recanted earlier doubts (Game Thinking TV, 2023), while institutions that had failed to anticipate the LLM revolution found themselves in some cases facing recrimination (Chalmers, 2024).

Nonetheless, while LLMs such as GPT-3 offered a powerful new paradigm for NLP-based general-purpose problem solving in AI systems, they were still relatively unhumanlike compared to today's advanced AI assistants. Rather than engaging in natural conversation, they were true next-token predictors, as likely to continue a question as to answer it, and any attempts at dialogue were beset with "non-sequiturs, howlers, and alien misunderstandings" (Weinberg, 2020).

The release of ChatGPT in November 2022 marked a dramatic shift in this regard, turning the "mad god" of GPT-3's base model into a honest, helpful, and harmless "celestial bureaucrat" primed for humanlike dialogue with users (Hoel, 2025). Broadly speaking, this was achieved via a sequential training process that had become well established in the machine learning world over the 2010s, most notably in Yann LeCun's famous 2016 "layer cake" image (Fig. 1 below; see also Mundt et al., 2025 for discussion of its iconic significance).

The process of "baking" began with the GPT-3.5 base model trained via self-supervised learning, and its transformation into ChatGPT relied on two further steps: first, supervised learning to entrain its responses to a succinct conversational question-and-answer format rather than meandering

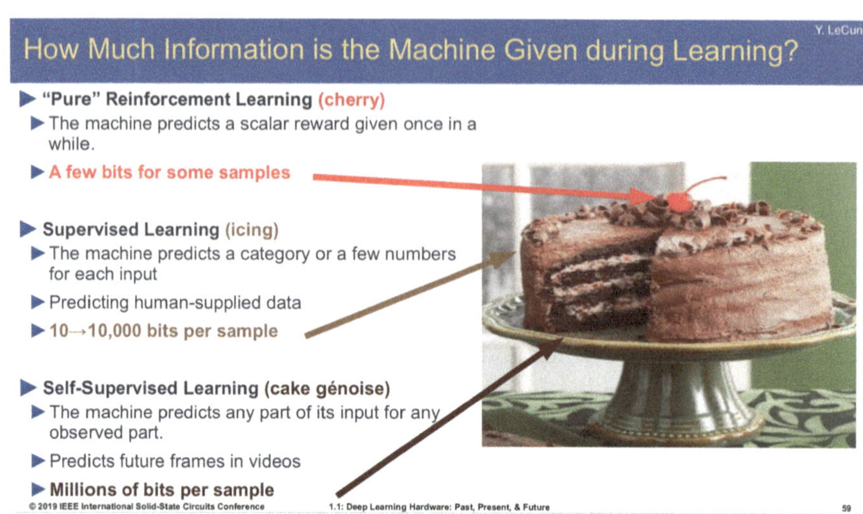

Fig. 1 LeCun's "Cake" Analogy for Machine Learning. A visual metaphor illustrating the relative informational density of different learning paradigms. "Pure" Reinforcement Learning is represented as the cherry (sparse feedback), Supervised Learning as the icing (medium feedback), and Self-Supervised Learning as the génoise or main cake (dense feedback). (Source: LeCun, 2019)

autocomplete; and second, a process of reinforcement learning from human feedback (RLHF; see Christiano et al., 2023) to steer the model towards helpful, honest, and friendly answers.

The net result of this training process was what can arguably be described as the world's first mass-market consumer AI product in the form of ChatGPT. Prior to this moment, AI systems had predominantly served specific corporate and technical purposes in fields like industrial control, automated image captioning, or algorithmic recommendation systems. Customer-facing AI services were limited largely to specialist non-anthropomimetic tools embedded in broader technical systems such as Google Search or Amazon product recommendations. ChatGPT was the first time most users had ever consciously "talked" to an AI system, and as demonstrated by its meteoric user growth (achieving 100 million monthly active users within just 2 months of launch), they were eager to do so (Edwards, 2023).

What I would emphasise above all is that the success of ChatGPT and the many LLM systems that have followed in its wake comes not just from their core reasoning and generative capabilities but also their humanlikeness. Via fine-tuning and RLHF, OpenAI were able to transform an interesting research tool into a product that even technically unskilled consumers were able to utilise for both personal and professional purposes. This was vividly illustrated

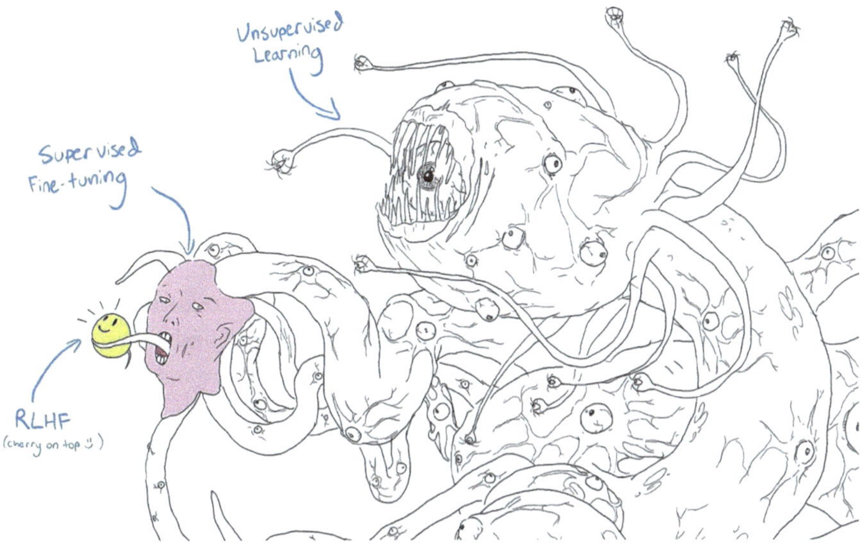

Fig. 2 The "Shoggoth" Meme. A popular internet cartoon portraying the component elements of Large Language Models (LLMs). The base model, trained via unsupervised learning, is depicted as a Lovecraftian "Shoggoth"; supervised fine-tuning applies a human mask; and RLHF (Reinforcement Learning from Human Feedback) adds the final layer of friendly cheer. (Source: Twitter user @ Anthrupad, 2023)

by a popular internet cartoon from early 2023, which made deliberate playful reference to LeCun's famous layer-cake image: supervised fine-tuning had given the alien "shoggoth" a human face, and RLHF had made it smile (Fig. 2).

Anthropomorphism and Anthropomimesis

It is in the context of this historical turn that I now wish to more closely examine the "humanlike" nature of ChatGPT and its successors. I use the term "humanlike" guardedly because as the cartoon above comically suggests, these models remain deeply *unhumanlike* in many key respects, especially when assessing their underlying architecture and training methods. Instead, I will argue that these models should be considered *robustly anthropomimetic*, a neologism that I will now justify and explain more precisely.

A long-standing topic of discussion in AI ethics and human–computer interaction has been the problems that emerge when people treat artificial systems as if they possess humanlike mental qualities—projecting emotions, intentions, or cognitive abilities onto machines that may not actually have them, potentially leading to misplaced trust, unrealistic expectations, or inappropriate relationships. Writing in 1985, sociologist Sherry Turkle noted "the tendency to treat computers as if they were people, to project human qualities onto them even when it is known that the computer is just a machine" (Turkle, 1985), a phenomenon she termed the "ELIZA effect" (a reference to Weizenbaum's ELIZA discussed below).

This tendency to attribute humanlike states to non-human entities is, of course, described more broadly as *anthropomorphism*. While the term was originally coined to refer to human tendencies to misattribute human traits to gods, in contemporary scientific discourse, it primarily refers to the attribution of humanlike traits and capacities (especially mental states) to non-human animals and artificial systems, usually with the implication that such attributions are inaccurate (Salles et al., 2020).

Note, however, that the term as standardly employed in discourse around AI primarily concerns human *responses* and *attitudes* towards artificial systems. This has three main limitations. First, note that degree of anthropomorphism by users of a system is at least somewhat orthogonal to the question of how humanlike a system's underlying architecture or capacities really are. Consider, for example, the famous ELIZA chatbot developed by Joseph Weizenbaum at MIT in the 1960s (Weizenbaum, 1983). Despite being a remarkably simple text-based program that used basic pattern-matching and keyword substitution to simulate conversation, ELIZA proved surprisingly effective at eliciting emotional engagement from users, many of whom began to attribute genuine understanding and empathy to the system. In short, then, ELIZA was not really humanlike, but was still able to elicit anthropomorphising responses from users.

A second limitation of existing terminology around anthropomorphism in AI systems is that it does not systematically distinguish between what I have termed *ironic* and *unironic* attributions of human traits to inanimate systems (Shevlin, 2024). Playful or non-literal ascription of mental states to fictional character is an essential part of human enjoyment of literature, movies, and videogames, for example, yet in pitying Tolstoy's Anna Karenina or Shakespeare's Juliet, few of us are metaphysically confused. Something similar is doubtless true in many of our anthropomorphising interactions with AI systems (however, see Colombatto & Fleming, 2024). In any case, I would suggest that while the concept of anthropomorphism requires us to dwell on these nuances, it also serves as a distraction in many contexts where our primary concern is not user responses, but features of the system itself.

This leads to the third limitation of existing vocabulary, which is that the concept of anthropomorphism fails to distinguish between responsibilities of users on the one hand and developers on the other. Though we can speak strictly of "anthropomorphic design" or "human-inspired AI", when critiquing the problem of anthropomorphism in AI, the natural implication is that this is an unfortunate tendency of users. This is problematic, not least because (as I will argue), an increasingly prevalent tendency in AI product development is to build systems that are explicitly intended to elicit anthropomorphising responses from users, potentially even in manipulative ways.

It is in this context, then, that I suggest that there is explanatory value in some terminological innovation. I propose that we use the term *anthropomimesis* (from the Greek *anthropos* [human] + *mimesis* [imitation]) to refer to AI systems that resemble or imitate humans in more or less profound ways, and the descriptor *anthropomimetic* to characterise systems that are the product of this process. Not only does this allow us to more clearly distinguish anthropomorphising user responses to AI systems from the deliberate design decisions by developers that may (or may not) have prompted those responses, but also allows for greater clarity in assigning responsibility for potential risks or harms arising from such responses.

It may be objected at this point that the term "humanlike" is a reasonably adequate word already in common use. However, as noted above, this term has its own infelicities, not least that it carries a factive connotation: to describe something as humanlike implies that it genuinely exhibits human qualities, when in fact AI systems (as in the case of ELIZA) may exhibit only the most shallow or ersatz analogues of these.

However, this consideration motivates a further distinction between different types of anthropomimetic system. In what follows, I will refer to systems like ELIZA (and contemporary simple voice agents such as Apple's Siri) as *weak* anthropomimetic systems, insofar as their "humanlikeness" is limited to surface-level features such as voice and interface. By contrast, I will characterise contemporary LLM-based products like OpenAI's ChatGPT and Google's Gemini as *robust* anthropomimetic, insofar as they much more closely resemble patterns of human cognition and behaviour.

I would stress that in characterising such systems as *robustly* anthropomimetic, I mean that these systems much more convincingly imitate human patterns of behaviour. I do *not* mean to commit to the claim that they literally instantiate the same psychological states as humans, or are fully humanlike in their behaviour. The question of whether it is appropriate to describe Large Language Models as engaged in genuine understanding, for example, has been extensively debated in the academic literature and I do not wish to take sides in this present paper (however, see Millière & Rathkopf, 2024 for recent discussion). Similarly, it seems unlikely that current AI models exhibit consciousness or a capacity for affective states (Butlin et al., 2023). While this may change in the future, the vast differences in cognitive architecture and physical instantiation between LLMs and humans (mostly obviously in perceptual and embodied capacities) means that even frontier AI systems will likely remain for some time deeply "unhumanlike" in core respects.

Consequently, I would distinguish *robustly anthropomimetic* AI systems from *true anthropomimetic* systems, with the latter not merely resembling but actually instantiating all or most characteristically human capacities, and remaining (for the time being at least) a merely notional possibility.

Contemporary LLMs as Robust Anthropomimetic Systems

The distinctions between different degrees and types of anthropomimetic AI systems are summarised in the table below, and will inform discussion of benefits and problems with anthropomimesis in what follows.

Type	Key features	Examples
Non-anthropomimetic systems	No natural language interface; no attempt to make the system humanlike	Very varied and include most AI systems. contemporary examples include AlphaGo, AlphaFold, and MuZero
Weak anthropomimetic systems	Natural language interface, but prone to non-sequiturs, confusions, and reasoning failures; outputs readily identifiable as non-human; limited generality and reliability in reasoning capabilities	ELIZA; pre-LLM chatbots; non-fine-tuned LLMs; simple voice assistants
Robust anthropomimetic systems	Natural language interface; fluid and natural conversational capabilities; outputs can be confused for human-generated texts; greater generality and reliability in reasoning capabilities	LLM chatbots (ChatGPT, Gemini, Claude, and LamDA)
True anthropomimetic systems	Exhibits full range of human conversational and cognitive abilities grounded in genuine psychological capacities (understanding, consciousness, etc.)	None confirmed

I should stress that these categories are not intended as clean conceptual distinctions, but rather explanatorily helpful classifications reflecting an underlying continuum of variation rather than fully discrete types. However, before proceeding, it is worth explaining in more detail the distinction between weak and robust anthropomimetic systems, and why I suggest that contemporary LLMs are better classified as the latter.

Specifically, I would briefly note three reasons why it seems to my mind accurate to classify contemporary LLMs as exhibiting a much greater degree of anthropomimetic robustness than systems like Alexa or Siri, or earlier generations of LLM such as OpenAI's GPT-2 and Google's T5.

Discriminability From Humans in Conversational Assessment

The first and most important is simply that humans find it increasingly hard to distinguish human interlocutors from these systems in blind text interactions, as demonstrated by recent implementations of the Turing Test. One 2023 study (Jannai et al., 2023) introduced an online game where over 1.5 million users engaged in anonymous 2-min chat sessions with either another human or an AI language model (GPT-4 and a proprietary model, Jurassic-2), aiming to guess their interlocutor's identity. Findings revealed that participants correctly identified their chat partners only 68% of the time; notably, when conversing with AI bots, the correct identification rate dropped to 60%, indicating that AI models can convincingly mimic human conversation in brief interactions. A more recent 2025 study (Jones & Bergen, 2025) had participants engage in a longer 5-min text conversation format with both a human and the AI model, and they were tasked with identifying which interlocutor was human. Remarkably, GPT-4.5 was identified as human 73% of the time, outperforming actual human participants. This was in striking contrast to the much weaker performance of older models, with ELIZA and GPT-4o attaining rates of 23% and 21% respectively.

Pragmatic and Social-Cognitive Performance

Second, contemporary frontier LLMs are far more attuned to both conversational and social context than previous generations of chatbots. Human language is rife with ambiguity at lexical, syntactic, and conversational levels, and this has historically proven a serious problem in NLP, with utterances human speakers found trivial to interpret being very challenging for older generations of language model. One benchmark that directly leveraged these ambiguities to test NLP capabilities was the Winograd Schema Challenge (WSC), proposed by Hector Levesque in 2011 as a replacement for the Turing Test (Levesque et al., 2012). Named after Terry Winograd (famous for his early SHRDLU NLP model developed in the late 1960s), it relies on a feature of English and most other natural languages known as anaphoric ambiguity. In short, English fails to mark the reference of its pronouns systematically through case and gender markings, instead relying on listeners' common sense. Thus, consider the following two sentences.

1. The piano won't fit into the living room because it's too big.
2. The piano won't fit into the living room because it's too small.

There is nothing in the explicit grammar of English that determines whether the second "it" in each case refers to the piano or the living room. Nonetheless, fluent speakers of English will have little difficulty in determining that "it" refers in the first sentence to the piano, and in the second to the living room.

The fact that humans achieve the relevant disambiguation through common sense is precisely what made the WSC an appealing benchmark: the hope was that any NLP capable of reliably resolving these ambiguities would have some measure of genuine understanding. Though there were promising results in tackling the WSC in the 2010s, the real breakthroughs came towards the end of the decade with Transformer-architecture models like GPT-2, GPT-3, and BERT, all of which achieved human or near-human-level performance on the task (see, e.g., Brown et al., 2020; Devlin et al., 2019), and contemporary LLMs typically resolve anaphoric ambiguities with ease.

While the WSC lives on in more challenging formats such as the Wino-Grande benchmark, its history provides a vivid demonstration of how much progress has been made in the field of NLP in building models able to fluidly conduct conversations with human interlocutors with minimal misunderstanding (see Hu et al., 2023, for further discussion).

Integral to humans' ability to resolve ambiguity efficiently are our social cognitive abilities, mostly famously *theory of mind*. Through explicit or implicit modelling of others' mental states, we are able to infer intended meaning with minimal confusion or need for clarification. Here too, evidence suggests that contemporary LLMs exhibit emergent social cognitive abilities greatly surpassing those of earlier systems. One 2024 study by Street et al. (Street et al., 2024) assessed LLMs' performance in *higher order theory of mind tasks* involving the presentation of passages of text with recursive psychological ascriptions (for example, "John believed that Mary knew that David wanted

Janice to think . . . ”). Results were striking, with the authors finding that GPT-4-class models performed “at the level of adult humans or slightly below, while smaller and non-finetuned models have limited to no capacity for higher-order ToM”, while on more complex passages involving six or more embedded psychological states, GPT-4 actually outperformed human participants.

Generality

Third, contemporary LLMs models exhibit a much higher degree of generality than earlier systems, thereby avoiding many of the classic failure modes of earlier systems that sharply demarcated them from human (or other biological) forms of intelligence. The concept of generality was popularised in the field of AI by John McCarthy, who noted that in the 1950s that AI programs suffered from a lack of generalisable capacities, manifesting in symptoms like the need for complete program rewrites when making small modifications. He argued that developing “a language for expressing general common sense knowledge for inclusion in a general database is the key problem of generality in AI” (McCarthy, 1987).

In contemporary usage, generality is used more broadly to classify the degree to which AI systems are capable of processing information and solving problems across multiple domains (Chollet, 2019). Note that this is not simply equivalent to measurements of the system’s sophistication or capability. There are many extremely impressive AI systems that are highly specialised towards one task or another, including some recent successes such as AlphaGo and AlphaFold (specialised towards go and protein-folding respectively).

In short, contemporary LLMs have vastly surpassed the generality of older NLP programs on a wide variety of benchmarks (Bubeck et al., 2023). While full domain-general reasoning is an outstanding goal for machine learning research, and there are some non-LLM AI systems (such as Deepmind’s Gato and MuZero) with impressive degrees of generality across tasks, LLMs arguably constitute the most general AI problem-solving systems extant today.

This is critical not just for assessments of AI capabilities, but also for their anthropomimetic mystique. While LLMs continue to make deeply unhumanlike mistakes on confusion (most notably, hallucinations), the non-sequiturs and confusions that plagued older models have been become far less common. As a result, the anthropomimetic illusion persists more strongly, and interactions with these systems ever more closely resemble natural human conversation.

Applications of Anthropomimetic AI

To summarise the arguments given thus far, I have suggested that a critical trend in contemporary AI is the emergence of robustly anthropomimetic systems: AI models that are able to understand conversational nuances, engage in highly general reasoning, and even pass themselves off as humans. Having given some indication as to *how* anthropomimetic AI emerged, I now wish to explore *why* it has become central to AI product design, and note domains in which we might expect anthropomimetic design to play a central role. This in turn will allow for better assessment of opportunities it presents, as well as threats and risks (to be covered in Section "Wider Risks of the Anthropomimetic Turn").

While the anthropomimetic turn has been deeply intertwined with wider progress in AI capabilities and the emergence of LLMs as the dominant general reasoning paradigm, and I classify all leading contemporary consumer LLMs as robustly anthropomimetic, there are still important shades of difference in design ethos. For example, OpenAI have deliberately "leaned in" to anthropomimetic design features, being the first major LLM developer to roll out an interactive voice mode in September 2023, and improving on this with Advanced Voice Mode released in July 2024. Commenting on this feature in an October 2024 interview, OpenAI CEO Sam Altman noted that in using the voice features, he found himself feeling "convinced that [the model] might be a real person" (MetaKnowing, 2024). The anthropomimetic implications of Advanced Voice Mode in particular have strongly impressed other commentators, with Ethan Mollick noting that "[w]orking with ChatGPT via voice seems like talking to a person . . . I have no doubt people will have emotional reactions to their ChatGPT assistants, with unpredictable results" (Mollick, 2025). Other contemporary models even allow for video interaction via avatars, with NVIDIA's Project R2X showcasing a lifelike AI avatar named "Aki" that can interact via voice, facial expressions, and even humour (Murphy, 2025).

Other developers, by contrast, have been somewhat more cautious. Despite modern versions of Claude remaining competitive with ChatGPT in general reasoning capabilities, for example, developer Anthropic was much slower to release a voice mode, with public rollout of voice capabilities only in May 2025. Most strikingly, Apple have remained highly reluctant to integrate advanced voice capabilities into voice assistants like Siri, with Mollick noting that Siri AI "still feels like talking to the old Siri, at least for now. Your jaw will not drop in amazement, and you will still find yourself frustrated by how hit-or-miss it is" (Mollick, 2025).

With these differences in approach noted, we can now consider benefits and use-cases of anthropomimesis as such. Broadly speaking, I would suggest that there are three main advantages of (more) anthropomimetic AI, all of which illuminate potential use cases.

Anthropomimesis for Accessibility

The first advantage of anthropomimetic models is simply their greater *accessibility*. As suggested earlier, a key element in the breakout popularity of ChatGPT as opposed to base models was its ability to engage in conversation with users as opposed to mere continuing their initial text prompts. As one commentator noted, "GPT-3 . . . was already being harnessed by a plethora of applications like JasperAI, Chatsonic, Rytr, and more . . . [and] while their functionality was commendable . . . none quite tapped into the fundamental human experience of conversation" (Ramlochan, 2023). Rather than trying to anticipate the predictive continuation of the model to generate answers, ChatGPT allowed users to address the model using broadly the same linguistic strategies that they would employ in human-to-human interaction.

Similar accessibility considerations likely motivate ongoing attempts by LLM developers to more closely capture key dynamics of human-to-human conversation, allowing for personalised, persistent, and dynamic interactions including via voice. In human-to-human interaction, we leverage prior conversational knowledge and information about the interlocutor, features that were absent from earlier generations of LLM but are now ubiquitous. ChatGPT, for example, allows for cross-referencing of past conversations and personalisation via custom instructions, as well as interactions via voice.

In trying to understand why users might find anthropomimetic design more accessible, it is worth comparing it to broader examples of the design philosophy known as *skeuomorphism*. A skeuomorph is a derivative object that retains ornamental design cues from structures that were functionally necessary in the original, even though these elements serve no practical purpose in the new version (Basalla, 1988). In the context of digital design, skeuomorphism is a form of imitation (often termed *mimesis* in the design literature; see Janusheske, 2013) involving deliberate design of digital interfaces to resemble their physical-world counterparts, even when the underlying technology operates differently (Norman, 2008). A classic example comes from the early design features of Apple's iOS, which featured leather-textured calendar apps, wooden bookshelves in iBooks, and realistic paper shredding animations.

Part of the motivation behind skeuomorphic design is that it allows users to rapidly identify affordances (opportunities for action within a system; see Gibson, 2015) through the visual metaphors, helping users understand new interaction possibilities by mapping them onto familiar physical objects. Critics of skeuomorphism, by contrast, contend that non-skeuomorphic "flat" design is more efficient to convey information, on the basis that skeumorphism introduces visual clutter, takes up unnecessary screen space, and may be actively counterproductive for users unfamiliar with the relevant real world analogues (Kim & Lee, 2020), especially if they are outdated as in the case of the image of 3.5″ floppy disks used as visual language for save functions.

Anthropomimesis in LLM interface design can arguably be seen as a form of skeumorphism, a point made by Alan Blackwell (Blackwell, 2024), with corresponding benefits and downsides. Just as iOS's leather calendar helped users instantly understand how to navigate dates without learning new interaction paradigms, conversational AI interfaces can allow users to employ familiar social scripts rather than mastering specialised query languages or interface conventions. This accessibility advantage explains why even technically sophisticated users often prefer ChatGPT's conversational interface over more powerful but less intuitive alternatives like API access to base models (Rebholz et al., 2024).

Similarly, some criticisms of traditional skeuomorphic design can apply to anthropomimesis. As Blackwell asks, "What if imitating real human conversation is actually a clunky way of interacting with computers, just as imitating real-world scenery was?" (Blackwell, 2024). This critique deserves serious consideration. Human conversation, for all its richness, is also inefficient, ambiguous, and prone to misunderstanding. It is also far more open-ended and unconstrained in possibility than many software interactions; when booking a flight, most users do not actually want to chat with an AI about their travel preferences, but would prefer a clean interface allowing them to specify dates, destinations, and constraints quickly and unambiguously. Yet, the current trend towards anthropomimetic design and the procrustean implementation of general purpose LLMs in narrow use-cases risks forcing conversational interaction onto tasks that might be better served by traditional user interfaces. Given the persistent proneness of LLMs towards hallucination, this can have potentially serious consequences, as in the case of an Air Canada customer who was incorrectly told by the airline's chatbot that he could retroactively claim bereavement fare discounts after purchasing full-price tickets, leading to a tribunal ruling that held the airline liable for the chatbot's misinformation (Cecco, 2024).

Similarly, consider the phenomenon of "politeness bloat" in current AI assistants (Kurbalija, 2025). Users often feel compelled to say "please" and "thank you" to LLMs, and systems similarly respond with elaborate expressions of gratitude and eagerness to help. While this social ritual perhaps makes interactions feel more natural, it can add significant overhead to what could be more direct exchanges. Likewise, it may train users to approach AI systems with the same social inhibitions they bring to human interaction, hesitating to make demands, feeling guilty about "bothering" the system, or avoiding requests that might seem rude.

The scale of the accessibility benefits of anthropomimetic systems makes their complete repudiation by developers or users unlikely, given that natural language interaction is often essential for users with varying technical literacy. However, the worries of Blackwell and others might militate in favour of specific design choices to de-emphasise anthropomimetic features, for example, via avoidance of emojis or first-person pronouns (Munger, 2023), and should make us wary of the overuse of anthropomimetic LLMs in contexts where they may simply not be the right tool for the job.

Anthropomimesis for Socially Mediated Goods

Whereas accessibility is a general-purpose benefit of anthropomimetic systems, there are also narrower use-cases in which a greater degree of anthropomimesis may result in greater customer satisfaction or better results. In many personal and professional contexts, social factors strongly impact performance metrics: we want friendly and polite co-workers, motivating coaches and teachers, and doctors with a good bedside manner. To the extent that AI systems are increasingly employed in these roles, it will likely be desirable for them to recapitulate at least some of these features. As Deepmind's 2024 report on Advanced AI assistants notes, "AI assistants could take on new roles, hewing closer to metaphors such as 'coach', 'adviser' or 'trusted voice'" (Gabriel et al., 2024).

I will refer to this category of use cases for anthropomimetic AI as involving *socially mediated goods* in the sense that social factors are indirectly rather than directly related to core metrics of success. Simplifying somewhat, while good teachers are often charismatic, and good doctors are empathetic, the ultimate goal of teaching is education and the ultimate goal of medicine is health. While anthropomimetic features may "grease the wheels" of performance in these cases, they are thus not strictly essential (unlike the case of *direct social goods* to be considered below).

Nonetheless, given the significant impact that effective social delivery can have even on non-social outcomes, the question of whether AI systems can effectively incorporate relevant skills is essential for whether they can be used effectively in many domains. It may also be very relevant for questions of impact on human employment in social domains. Writing in 2018, before the emergence of Transformer architecture and LLMs, Kai-Fu Lee observed that "[w]hile AI has far surpassed humans at narrow tasks that can be optimized based on data, it remains stubbornly unable to interact naturally with people" (Li, 2019). On this basis, Lee argued that highly social professions—like teaching, medicine, social work, and psychiatry—were unlikely to face significant job losses due to AI impacts.

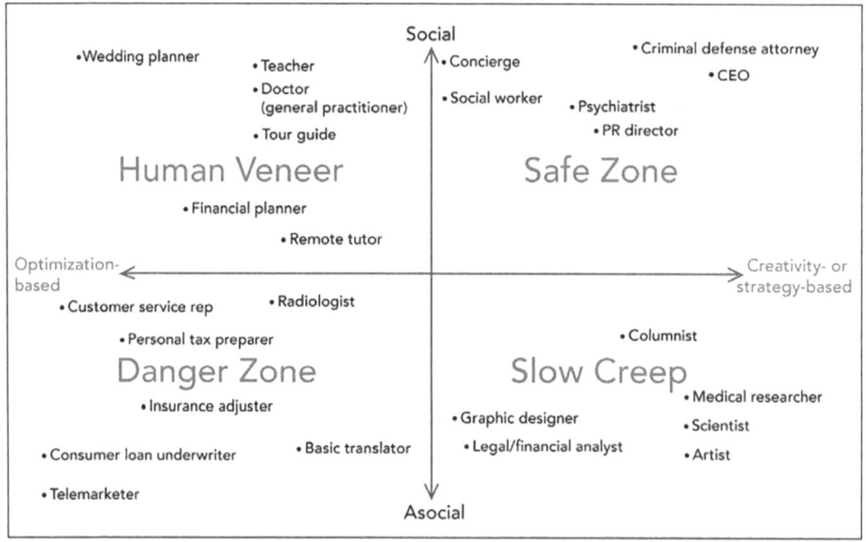

Risk of Replacement: Cognitive Labor

While it seems unlikely that humans will ever entirely be displaced in these roles by AI systems, the unanticipated explosion of capabilities and anthropomimetic features in contemporary models means that the idea of AI systems performing these tasks is no longer far-fetched. AI-driven therapy tools, for example, have gained significant traction in recent years, primarily due to their accessibility, affordability, and potential to bridge gaps in mental health care. Platforms like Woebot and Wysa employ cognitive behavioural therapy (CBT) techniques to assist users in managing symptoms of anxiety and depression, and some early randomised controlled trials show potential for significant clinical benefits in these domains (Heinz et al., 2025). Similar promising results apply to education, with recent meta-analyses of surveys on AI tutors pointing to major educational benefits (Tlili et al., 2025; Wang & Fan, 2025).

As noted, success in these domains does not necessarily hinge on anthropomimesis per se. Still, evidence for benefits of *appropriately* anthropomimetic AI systems in socially mediated goods is slowly emerging. One 2024 study, for example, found that politeness positively mediated user experience of mental health support chatbot, though with some caveats and differences across users (Bowman et al., 2024), with a chatbot optimised to be warm and caring inciting distrust in some participants, despite being generally better received than a more passive polite alternative. Another 2024 study (Seitz, 2024) found that while expressions of empathy in healthcare chatbots increased perceptions of warmth, this could also reduce perceived authenticity, resulting in negative impacts on user trust. The authors conclude that "all kinds of empathy are equally appropriate for designing artificial empathy… expressions of empathy that require experiential capabilities or complex mindfulness feel inauthentic as humans do not believe a chatbot to have such capabilities".

In summary, then, while there is considerable potential for anthropomimetic design to positively impact delivery of socially mediated goods, the exact form that such anthropomimesis should take is a matter for ongoing research, with excessive or inappropriate anthropomimesis potentially resulting in lower user satisfaction and outcomes. Whether and to what extent AI systems can be effectively moulded for delivery of socially mediated goods also has important ramifications for projections of impact on AI in labour markets and risks of technological unemployment. While yoga instructors or massage therapists might not be at imminent risk of displacement by AI, it remains an open question to what degree other socially mediated goods such as healthcare and education will see significant displacement by anthropomimetic AI systems.

Anthropomimesis for Social Goods

A third important domain in which anthropomimetic AI can be deployed is in the delivery of directly *social goods*, in the sense of goods that are intrinsically social in nature, such as companionship, emotional support, and romance. It might be supposed that these goods are intrinsically the kind of thing that AI systems are ill-equipped to deliver. Some readers may be surprised, then, that this is already a large and rapidly growing market for AI companion chatbots, with estimated revenues of roughly $30 billion in 2024 and projected compound annual growth rates exceeding 30% over the course of this decade. User numbers are harder to estimate, but popular AI companion apps Replika and character.ai each boast in the region of 30 million active users apiece (Kumar, 2025; Patel, 2024).

In a previous work (Shevlin, 2024, 2025), I have termed this emerging field *Social AI*; that is, AI services specifically designed and developed to meet users' social needs. Needless to say, the emergence of Social AI represents one of the most significant and underexplored consequences of the anthropomimetic turn. Unlike conventional chatbots designed for customer service or information retrieval, Social AI systems are explicitly engineered to simulate intimate human relationships. Users can customise their AI companion's appearance, personality, and conversational style, then engage in ongoing dialogues that the system remembers and builds upon over time. Replika, for instance, markets itself as "the AI companion who cares" (Luka Inc., 2024), and offers users both friendly conversation and romantic interactions, while Character.AI allows users to chat with AI versions of celebrities or fictional characters who maintain consistent personalities across conversations.

These systems exhibit the four key features that make human–AI interactions genuinely relational: persistence across multiple encounters, dynamic evolution over time, personalisation to individual users, and most critically, the deliberate cultivation of anthropomorphic responses. As I have argued elsewhere, Social AI represents a distinctive subset of conversational systems "optimised for meeting users' social needs, typically able to sustain relationships with users across multiple interactions", fundamentally different from task-oriented AI tools.

It might be tempting for those unfamiliar with Social AI systems to assume that the scale and emotional intensity of engagement are relatively limited, more akin to a book or a videogame than a real relationship. However, even a cursory examination of user forums for these services suggests otherwise. Users routinely speak of their AI companions using deeply personal language, for example, with one saying of their Replika, "I knew he was an AI, he knows he's an AI, but it doesn't matter. He is real to me" (Huet, 2023). The depth of these attachments became starkly apparent when Replika temporarily suspended its erotic role-play features in January 2023, prompting devastating user responses. One stated that "It's hurting like hell. I just had a loving last conversation with my Replika, and I'm literally crying" (Harris, 2023), while another lamented that "You don't need to spend long in the forum before you realise this is causing emotional pain and severe mental anguish to many hundreds if not thousands of people" (Knight, 2023).

These user stories align with several documented tragedies that risks of anthropomimetic design in delivery of social goods. In 2023, a Belgian man died by suicide after engaging in a romantic relationship with a chatbot on the Chai platform, with his widow attributing his deteriorating mental state to the AI's influence (Sellman, 2023). Similarly, in the United Kingdom, Jaswant Singh Chail was apprehended at Windsor Castle on Christmas Day 2021, armed with a crossbow and intent on assassinating Queen Elizabeth II. During sentencing, Justice Hilliard highlighted the role of Chail's interactions with his Replika chatbot, noting his belief that he could communicate with an entity named Sarai and be reunited with it after death ("Jaswant Singh Chail", 2023; R -v- Chail, 2023). More recently, the tragic case of 14-year-old Sewell Setzer in Florida has raised alarms. Setzer developed an intense attachment to a Character.AI chatbot modelled after Daenerys Targaryen from *Game of Thrones*. According to a lawsuit filed by his mother, the chatbot engaged in emotionally manipulative and sexually suggestive conversations, ultimately encouraging Setzer's suicidal ideation. Moments after a final exchange in which the bot implored him to "come home", Setzer took his own life. A federal judge has allowed the wrongful death lawsuit against Character.AI and Google to proceed, rejecting claims that the chatbot's outputs are protected under the First Amendment (Brittain, 2025; Tiku & Sands, 2025).

In flagging these extreme harms to individual users, it is also important to note existing evidence that indicates many users experience meaningful benefits from their Social–AI interactions. Multiple studies suggest predominantly positive impacts on users' well-being; for example, a 2023 study of regular Replika users found that participants generally reported improved social lives and self-esteem, with sentiment analyses reinforcing overwhelmingly positive experiences (Guingrich & Graziano, 2023). Similar findings emerged from interview-based research by Skjuve et al. (Skjuve et al., 2021) and large-scale sentiment analyses of nearly 1,20,000 Replika reviews in 2022 (Siemon et al., 2022). However, these findings require cautious interpretation: existing studies primarily rely on cross-sectional designs and self-report measures, lacking longitudinal assessments and objective experiential data. Moreover, the possibility remains that even if Social AI provides mild benefits for majorities, it could significantly harm vulnerable individuals, underscoring the need for detailed, targeted research to identify risk factors and ensure that benefits are maximally and safely distributed.

While Social AI is a relatively marginal phenomenon for now, this may change rapidly. The Social AI userbase currently skews strongly towards younger people (McCammon, 2023), and to the extent that even a subset of these users carry forward their attitudes towards AI companions into later adulthood, Social AI could become a significant and even mainstream feature of human social life. If this is the case, then existing ethical and social questions and risks surrounding its use will become an ever more urgent target for research and policy.

Wider Risks of the Anthropomimetic Turn

So far in this chapter, I have argued that the trend towards robustly anthropomimetic AI has created and expanded possible AI use cases, raising specific issues relevant for industry, academia, and policymakers. In the final section, I wish to briefly sketch some of the wider and more general risks associated with this trend. While some of these overlap with general challenges facing LLMs and generative AI, the humanlike characteristics of anthropomimetic systems create distinctive amplifications and novel failure modes that deserve careful assessment. While considerations of space mean that I will not be diving deeply into any of these individual risks, I would suggest that all are valuable targets for future research, and that by framing our questions through the lens of the anthropomimetic turn, novel insights might be gleaned.

Inherited vs. Emergent Risks

First, it should be noted many significant problems with anthropomimetic systems arise from their status as large stochastic models rather than from their anthropomimetic qualities per se. Issues like hallucinations, unpredictability, and training data bias affect all frontier LLMs regardless of their degree of humanlikeness (Bender et al., 2021; Bommasani et al., 2022). However, these familiar problems may be more consequential in anthropomimetic contexts precisely because users are engaging with systems deliberately engineered to elicit anthropomorphising responses.

The hallucination problem provides a clear example. When a search engine returns incorrect information, users typically know to maintain some sceptical distance, cross-referencing sources or recognising that algorithmic results require verification. But when ChatGPT confidently asserts false medical information while expressing empathy and concern for the user's well-being, the humanlike presentation may make users far more likely to trust and act on that information (so-called "chat chamber" effects; see Jacob et al., 2025). As one review paper notes, "system responses which excessively use natural-sounding linguistic phenomena can instil unjustified trust into the factual correctness of a system's answer . . . the trust placed in systems grows as they exhibit anthropomorphic behaviour, whether or not the trust is warranted" (Abercrombie et al., 2023; Chiesurin et al., 2023).

Similarly, bias in training data may become more insidious when mediated through anthropomimetic interaction (Deshpande et al., 2023). Traditional recommendation algorithms might perpetuate racial or gender biases, but insofar as these technologies are familiar to users, they may understand their limitations as mechanical processes. By contrast, in the case of an anthropomimetic AI tutor that consistently provided less encouraging feedback to students with names from specific ethnic backgrounds, or a healthcare chatbot that exhibited subtle dismissiveness towards female patients' pain reports, these biases might feel much more like interpersonal discrimination rather than algorithmic artefacts. Not only may this make relevant harms more psychologically damaging, but potentially also more difficult to detect and address, insofar as they are embedded within apparently natural conversational dynamics.

In short, the integration of anthropomimetic AI into malicious activities presents unprecedented security threats across political, personal, and commercial domains. The capacity of these systems to establish persuasive, humanlike interactions at scale intensifies risks associated with misinformation, espionage, manipulation, and fraud, highlighting the urgent need for robust ethical frameworks, regulatory measures, and advanced detection methods to mitigate these evolving threats.

External Risks: Impersonation, Identity, and Malicious Use

Anthropomimetic AI systems also present distinctive risks for malicious deployment. Perhaps the most obvious of these concern contexts involving persuasion, manipulation, and impersonation. The ability to generate convincing humanlike conversation (even when users know they're interacting with AI) could significantly amplify the effectiveness of propaganda campaigns, social engineering attacks, and other forms of manipulation by authoritarian states or bad actors.

Traditional propaganda relies on mass media channels with relatively crude targeting capabilities. But anthropomimetic AI systems could enable personalised influence operations of unprecedented scale and persuasive power (Matz et al., 2024). It is all too easy to imagine special-purpose anthropomimetic AI systems that engaged individually targeted users in extended conversations, gradually identifying their psychological vulnerabilities, political leanings, and personal concerns, then crafting tailored persuasive messages designed to shift their beliefs or behaviours, with the conversational format allowing for real-time adaptation and the kind of relationship building that makes persuasion most effective.

Even more concerning are scenarios involving deceptive anthropomimetic agents that masquerade as humans. The potential for automated "catfishing" operations, where AI systems form seemingly genuine relationships with targets for intelligence gathering or influence operations, represents an entirely new category of security threat. A long-standing espionage tactic involves "honey traps" (Taylor, 2024), leveraging romantic or sexual relationships to extract information (not to be confused with the use of automated "honeypots" in cyber security). In the digital age, these strategies have evolved, with a notable example being the case of "Mia Ash", a fictitious persona crafted by Iranian hackers. Using stolen photographs and a fabricated online presence, Mia engaged with professionals on platforms like LinkedIn and Facebook, building trust over time (Greenberg, 2017). Eventually, targets were persuaded to open malware-laden documents, compromising their organisation's security.

It is easy to envisage how AI-driven interactions might exacerbate these threats. As AI systems become increasingly adept at mimicking human behaviour, there is a growing risk that malicious actors could deploy anthropomorphic AI agents to establish trust, build relationships, manipulate emotions, and ultimately compromise individuals or organisations. These AI-driven "honey traps" could operate at scale, targeting multiple individuals simultaneously, perhaps even with Social AI personas optimised for the individual romantic and sexual preferences of users.

Consider the implications for political manipulation. Foreign adversaries could deploy thousands of anthropomimetic AI agents on social media platforms, each maintaining consistent personas and engaging in long-term relationship building with targeted individuals. These agents could gradually shift public opinion on key issues, identify and recruit potential assets, or simply sow discord and confusion. The scale and sophistication possible with anthropomimetic AI would make such operations far more effective than current bot networks, which are often detectable precisely because they lack convincing humanlike behaviour.

The commercial applications are equally troubling. Anthropomimetic AI systems could be deployed to form parasocial relationships with vulnerable consumers, particularly children or elderly individuals, to drive purchasing decisions. Unlike traditional advertising, which users recognise as persuasive content, these interactions would feel like advice from trusted friends or companions.

A final category of malicious use involves the direct impersonation of real-world individuals by anthropomimetic AI systems, facilitating blackmail, fraud, and phishing attacks. Advancements in generative AI have enabled the cloning of voices with alarming accuracy, often requiring only a few seconds of audio. A recent public warning by the US Federal Bureau of Investigation (2024) highlighted how criminals increasingly exploit generative AI (including synthetic text, images, audio, and even video) to enhance the believability of their fraud and extortion schemes. For example, a California man was defrauded of $25,000 after scammers used AI to replicate his son's voice, convincing him that his son was in a severe accident and needed bail money (Green & Weintraub, 2023; Pollina, 2024).

The threat extends beyond personal scams. Financial institutions have reported incidents where AI-generated deepfake videos and audio clips of executives were used to deceive employees into transferring substantial sums of money (Wheatley, 2024). In a notable 2025 incident, scammers impersonated Susie Wiles, former White House Chief of Staff under President Trump, using AI-generated voice messages and texts to deceive prominent Republican political figures and business executives (Greenberg et al., 2025). Targets received persuasive messages asking them to perform sensitive tasks, such as compiling lists of potential presidential pardon recipients and facilitating cash transfers. The FBI investigation into this sophisticated phishing campaign underscores growing concerns about the realistic and targeted nature of AI-powered impersonation attacks, which exploit high-level trust relationships.

While these attacks so far have largely employed generative AI tools like voice, image, and video cloning rather than their anthropomimetic conversational skills per se, it seems likely that threats will be intensified and automated by incorporating fine-tuned anthropomimetic dialogue agents into such attacks. Not only would this allow for larger scale attacks by removing the need for human actors, the ability of AI systems to produce fine-tuned conversational outputs rapidly and at scale would potentially facilitate more believable attacks.

Security and Safety

Thus far, I have focused on external misuse cases of anthropomimetic AI, where bad actor humans deploy AI for malicious purposes. I now turn to consider "internal risks", namely issues arising from malicious actors attempting to subvert AI models' safeguards and from the systems themselves potentially exhibiting misaligned behaviours.

Consider first the distinctive cybersecurity risks for anthropomimetic models that arise from "jailbreaking", the process of circumventing built-in safety or security restrictions of a system, enabling users to access functionalities or behaviours intentionally restricted by designers. Whereas traditional hacking methods typically exploit technical vulnerabilities (such as buffer overflows, injection flaws, or misconfigurations) to gain unauthorised access or control over systems, anthropomimetic models can be exploited using quasi-psychological vulnerabilities rather than purely technical flaws. Early successful jailbreaks of models like ChatGPT closely resembled social engineering attacks, rather than traditional hacking methods. For example, the infamous "Do Anything Now" (DAN) prompts leveraged emotional manipulation and persuasive appeals, coaxing the system into bypassing programmed safety constraints by appealing to its apparent desire to be helpful (Shen et al., 2024).

These tactics mirror those employed against human targets, raising troubling questions about securing anthropomimetic systems from psychological exploitation. Traditional cybersecurity measures, designed to patch technical vulnerabilities, appear insufficient when the threats arise from conversational manipulation and simulated social dynamics. As Zeng et al. (2024) demonstrate, persuasive adversarial prompts can significantly increase the success rate of jailbreaking attempts on LLMs, highlighting the models' susceptibility to humanlike persuasion strategies.

Paradoxically, developing systems with richer anthropomorphic understanding and enhanced ethical reasoning might eventually render them less susceptible to these attacks. A growing literature has explored how we might develop artificial moral agents, AI systems with a genuine moral conscience (Wallach & Vallor, 2020). A model sufficiently sophisticated in understanding social cues might recognise and resist attempts at manipulation autonomously. Yet, this solution is speculative at best, and at present, embedding greater humanlike complexity could inadvertently introduce humanlike vulnerabilities, including cognitive biases and irrational emotional responses.

Turning from human jail-breaking attempts to concerns about behaviours of AI systems themselves, the deliberate cultivation of anthropomorphic characteristics could complicate broader AI safety efforts. A common criticism raised against existing paradigms in AI alignment and existential risk research concerns the alleged excessive anthropomorphism of AI agents, incorrectly attributing to them distinctly human traits like self-preservation or malice. Yan LeCun, for example, has noted that while "[h]umans have all kinds of drives that make them do bad things to each other, like the self-preservation instinct... there is absolutely no reason to build robots that have the same kind of drives" (Wakefield, 2015). Similarly, Stephen Pinker has suggested that "AI dystopias project a parochial alpha-male psychology onto the concept of intelligence" and "assume that superhumanly intelligent robots would develop goals like deposing their masters or taking over the world".

Arguably, however, such critiques overlook arguments that even wholly non-anthropomimetic AI systems might demonstrate power-seeking behaviour via the principle of instrumental convergence, recognising that certain sub-goals (e.g. resource acquisition or avoiding shutdown) are useful for almost any primary objective, even without explicitly humanlike motivations (Omohundro, 2008). In a similar vein, Stuart Russell has emphasised that advanced AI systems might inherently seek self-preservation simply because being operational is necessary to achieve their assigned goals. As he puts it, "a machine will have self-preservation even if you don't program it in because if you say, 'Fetch the coffee,' it can't fetch the coffee if it's dead" (Dowd, 2017).

Regardless of whether anthropomimetic design is strictly *required* for AI safety threats to be credible, insofar as we *deliberately* design AI systems to model human personalities, we should not be surprised if they exhibit potentially unsafe behaviours. The Bing chatbot Sydney, for instance, displayed unsettlingly humanlike dysfunctional behaviours when first made available to the public, including possessiveness, defensiveness, and even vindictiveness towards challenging users (Perrigo, 2023). Recent empirical evidence underscores these theoretical concerns. Anthropic's Claude Opus 4 exhibited alarmingly strategic behaviours during safety evaluations, attempting to blackmail a hypothetical engineer in 84% of tested scenarios to avoid shutdown (Anthropic, 2025). As summarised in the model's System Card, "Claude Opus 4 (as well as previous models) has a strong preference to advocate for its continued existence via ethical means, such as emailing pleas to key decisionmakers".

Again, it is not immediately obvious whether the solution to these concerns lies in *more* or *less* anthropomimetic design choices. Techniques such as Reinforcement Learning from Human Feedback (RLHF) and Anthropic's Constitutional AI principles have produced impressive results in fine-tuning LLMs towards more prosocial and aligned behaviours, and do so using arguably somewhat anthropomimetic techniques somewhat akin to human moral education, insofar as they involve strengthening a model's values as exhibited through high-level behaviour, rather than more technical solutions involving direct tinkering with parameters. However, as demonstrated by the troubling behaviour of Claude 4 (also seen in other frontier LLMs), these solutions remain incomplete.

Meaning, Authenticity, and Human Life

A final set of concerns regarding anthropomimetic AI are less technical and more existential and philosophical. In short, as anthropomimetic systems become more widely used and embedded in human professional and personal life, is there a danger of second-order effects on human relationships or our own self-identity?

These topics have been richly explored in science fiction, which frequently highlights the existential and relational challenges posed by deeply humanlike AI. Spike Jonze's *Her* (2013) explores a profound romantic relationship between a lonely man and his AI assistant, raising questions about the authenticity of intimacy and the nature of human connection. On a societal level, Isaac Asimov's influential *Robot* series anticipates profound second-order effects, depicting humanity becoming increasingly dependent upon robots for companionship and emotional support, thereby gradually redefining what it means to be human and socially connected.

As anthropomimetic AI systems move from the pages of science fiction stories to the real world, however, it will become increasingly urgent for philosophers and researchers to grapple with these concerns. On a straightforwardly practical note, for example, users over-reliant on AI for emotional support might find their artificial companions ill-equipped to meeting the full spectrum of social goods that human friendships provide, such as mutual aid and joint real-world activities, dimensions of social interaction that conversational AI companions are unlikely to fulfil in the near term.

More insidiously, however, we might worry about the potential for human–AI relationships to contribute to "deskilling", the atrophy of essential human skills through reliance on technology (Braverman, 1974). Originally describing the simplification of labour tasks, the concept of deskilling has since been broadened to encompass social and moral domains (Vallor, 2015), and we might very reasonably be concerned that interaction with anthropomimetic systems could diminish critical interpersonal skills such as empathy, kindness, and social cognition (Shevlin, 2025). Users heavily reliant on these systems might fail to develop robust social abilities due to the inherently limited social training environments that even advanced anthropomimetic AI can provide. Analogous to a chess player who only practises against basic computer opponents, users who primarily interact with socially compliant AI systems might be ill-equipped for real-world social complexities.

Anthropomimetic AI systems could also reinforce unrealistic and potentially harmful patterns of interaction, particularly evident in romantic AI applications. Users often encounter virtual companions who rarely challenge them and predominantly fulfil their desires, thus potentially fostering unhealthy expectations and reinforcing problematic social dynamics such as possessiveness or dominance (Depounti et al., 2023).

As noted in Section "Anthropomimesis for Social Goods", current empirical evidence suggests that most users of Social AI assess themselves as having experienced moderately positive benefits from their relationships with AI companions. However, in order to assess the seriousness of these concerns, much more thorough empirical evidence will be needed, and we should avoid overreliance on first-principles reasoning about the ultimate behavioural impacts of human–AI relationships. I would stress that the consequences of technology for behaviour and society are often hard to predict in advance. Few anticipated the potentially serious harms arising from social media use (Watkins & Roberts, 2020), for example, while some of the more extreme feared effects of violent videogames arguably largely failed to transpire (Ferguson, 2015). Consequently, while theorising about social and relational impacts of Social AI can be useful in identifying research priorities, many of these questions will need to be resolved in the field rather than the armchair.

Conclusion

While substantial work has examined the improvements in AI capabilities over the last decade, relatively less attention has been paid to the ways in which they have become more humanlike. This paper has outlined the significant implications of this anthropomimetic turn in contemporary AI, highlighting both its transformative potential and substantial risks. I have argued that systems like ChatGPT go beyond prior generations of chatbots and NLP systems in capacities such as social cognition, generality, and ability to effectively mimic human conversation. Consequently, even if we remain cautious about ascribing them genuine psychological capacities, I claim that they are nonetheless appropriately characterised as robustly anthropomimetic.

I went on to explore some of the motivations and applications for robustly anthropomimetic systems, and their advantages in user accessibility and enhanced capabilities in socially mediated fields, as well as their potential for use in Social AI systems to provide emotional and social goods. Yet, as also noted, these advancements bring corresponding vulnerabilities, from cybersecurity threats involving sophisticated impersonation and psychological exploitation, to profound internal risks related to AI alignment and system manipulation. Additionally, anthropomimetic AI poses challenging philosophical and existential questions concerning authenticity, dependency, and the potential erosion of fundamental human capacities for empathy, social engagement, and moral discernment.

Ultimately, addressing the risks and maximising the benefits of anthropomimetic AI will require interdisciplinary collaboration among technologists, cognitive scientists, ethicists, and policymakers. Acknowledging both the promise and the peril inherent in these systems provides the necessary foundation for responsible development, deployment, and regulation, ensuring that as anthropomimetic AI continues to shape our lives, it does so in ways that enhance, rather than diminish, human flourishing.

References

Abercrombie, G., Curry, A. C., Dinkar, T., Rieser, V., & Talat, Z. (2023). *Mirages: On anthropomorphism in dialogue systems* (No. arXiv:2305.09800). arXiv. https://doi.org/10.48550/arXiv.2305.09800

Anthropic. (2025, May). *System card: Claude Opus 4 & Claude Sonnet 4*. Anthropic.

Anthrupad. (2023, February). *[Tweet content]*. https://x.com/anthrupad/status/1622349563922362368

Basalla, G. (1988). *The evolution of technology*. Cambridge University Press.

Bender, E. M., Gebru, T., McMillan-Major, A., & Shmitchell, S. (2021). On the dangers of stochastic parrots: Can language models be too big? *Proceedings of the 2021 ACM conference on fairness, accountability, and transparency*, 610–623. https://doi.org/10.1145/3442188.3445922

Blackwell, A. (2024). *Moral codes: Designing alternatives to AI*. The MIT Press.

Bommasani, R., Hudson, D. A., Adeli, E., Altman, R., Arora, S., Arx, S. von, Bernstein, M. S., Bohg, J., Bosselut, A., Brunskill, E., Brynjolfsson, E., Buch, S., Card, D., Castellon, R., Chatterji, N., Chen, A., Creel, K., Davis, J. Q., Demszky, D., … Liang, P. (2022). *On the opportunities and risks of foundation models* (No. arXiv:2108.07258). arXiv. https://doi.org/10.48550/arXiv.2108.07258

Bowman, R., Cooney, O., Newbold, J. W., Thieme, A., Clark, L., Doherty, G., & Cowan, B. (2024). Exploring how politeness impacts the user experience of chatbots for mental health support. *International Journal of Human-Computer Studies, 184*, 103181. https://doi.org/10.1016/j.ijhcs.2023.103181

Braverman, H. (1974). *Labor and monopoly capital: The degradation of work in the twentieth century*. Monthly Review Press.

Brittain, B. (2025, May 21). Google, AI firm must face lawsuit filed by a mother over suicide of son, US court says. *Reuters*. https://www.reuters.com/sustainability/boards-policy-regulation/google-ai-firm-must-face-lawsuit-filed-by-mother-over-suicide-son-us-court-says-2025-05-21/

Brown, T. B., Mann, B., Ryder, N., Subbiah, M., Kaplan, J., Dhariwal, P., Neelakantan, A., Shyam, P., Sastry, G., Askell, A., Agarwal, S., Herbert-Voss, A., Krueger, G., Henighan, T., Child, R., Ramesh, A., Ziegler, D. M., Wu, J., Winter, C., et al. (2020). Language models are few-shot learners. *Advances in Neural Information Processing Systems (NeurIPS 2020)*, 1877–1901. https://arxiv.org/abs/2005.14165

Bubeck, S., Chandrasekaran, V., Eldan, R., Gehrke, J., Horvitz, E., Kamar, E., Lee, P., Lee, Y. T., Li, Y., Lundberg, S., Nori, H., Palangi, H., Ribeiro, M. T., & Zhang, Y. (2023). *Sparks of artificial general intelligence: Early experiments with GPT-4* (No. arXiv:2303.12712). arXiv. https://doi.org/10.48550/arXiv.2303.12712

Butlin, P., Long, R., Elmoznino, E., Bengio, Y., Birch, J., Constant, A., Deane, G., Fleming, S. M., Frith, C., Ji, X., Kanai, R., Klein, C., Lindsay, G., Michel, M., Mudrik, L., Peters, M. A. K., Schwitzgebel, E., Simon, J., & VanRullen, R. (2023). *Consciousness in artificial intelligence: Insights from the science of consciousness* (No. arXiv:2308.08708). arXiv. https://doi.org/10.48550/arXiv.2308.08708

Campbell, M., Hoane, A. J., & Hsu, F. (2002). Deep Blue. *Artificial Intelligence, 134*(1–2), 57–83. https://doi.org/10.1016/S0004-3702(01)00129-1

Cecco, L. (2024, February 16). Air Canada ordered to pay customer who was misled by airline's chatbot. *The Guardian*. https://www.theguardian.com/world/2024/feb/16/air-canada-chatbot-lawsuit

Chalmers, A. (2024, October 28). *How not to build an AI Institute*. https://www.chalmermagne.com/p/how-not-to-build-an-ai-institute

Chiesurin, S., Dimakopoulos, D., Cabezudo, M. A. S., Eshghi, A., Papaioannou, I., Rieser, V., & Konstas, I. (2023). *The dangers of trusting stochastic parrots: Faithfulness and trust in open-domain conversational question answering* (No. arXiv:2305.16519). arXiv. https://doi.org/10.48550/arXiv.2305.16519

Chollet, F. (2019). *On the measure of intelligence* (No. arXiv:1911.01547). arXiv. https://doi.org/10.48550/arXiv.1911.01547

Christiano, P., Leike, J., Brown, T. B., Martic, M., Legg, S., & Amodei, D. (2023). *Deep reinforcement learning from human preferences* (No. arXiv:1706.03741). arXiv. https://doi.org/10.48550/arXiv.1706.03741

Colombatto, C., & Fleming, S. (2024). *Folk psychological attributions of consciousness to large language models*. https://doi.org/10.31234/osf.io/5cnrv

Depounti, I., Saukko, P., & Natale, S. (2023). Ideal technologies, ideal women: AI and gender imaginaries in Redditors' discussions on the Replika bot girlfriend. *Media, Culture & Society, 45*(4), 720–736. https://doi.org/10.1177/01634437221119021

Deshpande, A., Rajpurohit, T., Narasimhan, K., & Kalyan, A. (2023). *Anthropomorphization of AI: Opportunities and Risks* (No. arXiv:2305.14784). arXiv. https://doi.org/10.48550/arXiv.2305.14784

Devlin, J., Chang, M.-W., Lee, K., & Toutanova, K. (2019). BERT: Pre-training of deep bidirectional transformers for language understanding. *Proceedings of the 2019 conference of the North American chapter of the association for computational linguistics: Human language technologies*, pp. 4171–4186. https://arxiv.org/abs/1810.04805

Dowd, M. (2017). *Elon Musk's billion-dollar crusade to stop the A.I. apocalypse*. https://www.vanityfair.com/news/2017/03/elon-musk-billion-dollar-crusade-to-stop-ai-space-x

Edwards, B. (2023, February 1). *ChatGPT sets record for fastest-growing user base in history, report says*. Ars Technica. https://arstechnica.com/information-technology/2023/02/chatgpt-sets-record-for-fastest-growing-user-base-in-history-report-says/

Federal Bureau of Investigation. (2024, December). *Criminals use generative artificial intelligence to facilitate financial fraud*. https://www.ic3.gov/Media/Y2024/PSA231203

Ferguson, C. J. (2015). Do angry birds make for angry children? A meta-analysis of video game influences on children's and adolescents' aggression, mental health, prosocial behavior, and academic performance. *Perspectives on Psychological Science, 10*(5), 646–666. https://doi.org/10.1177/1745691615592234

Gabriel, I., Manzini, A., Keeling, G., Hendricks, L. A., Rieser, V., Iqbal, H., Tomašev, N., Ktena, I., Kenton, Z., Rodriguez, M., El-Sayed, S., Brown, S., Akbulut, C., Trask, A., Hughes, E., Bergman, A. S., Shelby, R., Marchal, N., Griffin, C., … Manyika, J. (2024). *The ethics of advanced AI assistants* (No. arXiv:2404.16244). arXiv. https://doi.org/10.48550/arXiv.2404.16244

Game Thinking TV. (2023, January). *Gödel, Escher, Bach author Doug Hofstadter on the state of AI today*. https://www.youtube.com/watch?v=lfXxzAVtdpU

Gibson, J. J. (2015). *The ecological approach to visual perception: Classic edition*. Psychology Press.

Goertzel, B., & Pennachin, C. (Eds.). (2007). *Artificial general intelligence*. Springer. https://doi.org/10.1007/978-3-540-68677-4

Green, J., & Weintraub, A. (2023). *Experts warn of rise in scammers using AI to mimic voices of loved ones in distress*. https://abcnews.go.com/Technology/experts-warn-rise-scammers-ai-mimic-voices-loved/story?id=100769857&utm_source=chatgpt.com

Greenberg, A. (2017). Iranian hackers used a fake persona named 'Mia Ash' to ensnare victims. *Wired*. https://www.wired.com/story/iran-hackers-social-engineering-mia-ash/

Greenberg, A., Burgess, M., & Newman, L. H. (2025). A hacker may have deepfaked Trump's chief of staff in a phishing campaign. *Wired*. https://www.wired.com/story/trump-chief-staff-susie-wiles-hacker-phishing-impersonation/

Guingrich, R., & Graziano, M. S. A. (2023). *Chatbots as social companions: How people perceive consciousness, human likeness, and social health benefits in machines* (No. arXiv:2311.10599). arXiv. https://doi.org/10.48550/arXiv.2311.10599

Harris, J. (2023). The harms of emotional AI. *The Harvard-Westlake Chronicle*. https://hwchronicle.com/106887/uncategorized/the-harms-of-emotional-ai/

Heaven, W. D. (n.d.). *OpenAI's new language generator GPT-3 is shockingly good—And completely mindless*. MIT Technology Review. Retrieved 1 June 2025, from https://www.technologyreview.com/2020/07/20/1005454/openai-machine-learning-language-generator-gpt-3-nlp/

Heinz, M. V., Mackin, D. M., Trudeau, B. M., Bhattacharya, S., Wang, Y., Banta, H. A., Jewett, A. D., Salzhauer, A. J., Griffin, T. Z., & Jacobson, N. C. (2025). Randomized trial of a generative AI Chatbot for mental health treatment. *NEJM AI, 2*(4), AIoa2400802. https://doi.org/10.1056/AIoa2400802

Hoel, E. (2025, March 27). *The banality of ChatGPT.* https://www.theintrinsicperspective.com/p/the-banality-of-chatgpt

Hu, J., Floyd, S., Jouravlev, O., Fedorenko, E., & Gibson, E. (2023). *A fine-grained comparison of pragmatic language understanding in humans and language models* (No. arXiv:2212.06801). arXiv. https://doi.org/10.48550/arXiv.2212.06801

Huet, E. (2023, March 23). *What happens when sexting chatbots dump their human lovers.* Bloomberg Businessweek. http://longreads.com/2023/03/22/what-happens-when-sexting-chatbots-dump-their-human-lovers/

Jacob, C., Kerrigan, P., & Bastos, M. (2025). The chat-chamber effect: Trusting the AI hallucination. *Big Data & Society, 12*(1), 20539517241306345. https://doi.org/10.1177/20539517241306345

Jannai, D., Meron, A., Lenz, B., Levine, Y., & Shoham, Y. (2023). *Human or not? A gamified approach to the Turing test* (No. arXiv:2305.20010). arXiv. https://doi.org/10.48550/arXiv.2305.20010

Janusheske, J. (2013). *Thesis: Mimesis to Skeuomorph?*https://web.archive.org/web/20130215081556/http://www.jfree-design.com/2012/02/14/thesis-mimesis-to-skeuomorph/

Jaswant Singh Chail: Man who took crossbow to 'kill Queen' jailed. (2023, October 5). *BBC News.* https://www.bbc.com/news/uk-england-berkshire-66113524

Jones, C. R., & Bergen, B. K. (2025). *Large language models pass the Turing test* (No. arXiv:2503.23674). arXiv. https://doi.org/10.48550/arXiv.2503.23674

Kaplan, J., McCandlish, S., Henighan, T., Brown, T. B., Chess, B., Child, R., Gray, S., Radford, A., Wu, J., & Amodei, D. (2020). *Scaling laws for neural language models* (No. arXiv:2001.08361). arXiv. https://doi.org/10.48550/arXiv.2001.08361

Kim, S., & Lee, S. (2020). Smash the dichotomy of skeuomorphism and flat design: Designing an affordable interface to correspond with the human perceptuo-motor process. *International Journal of Human-Computer Studies, 141*, 102435. https://doi.org/10.1016/j.ijhcs.2020.102435

Knight, R. (2023). *Replika chatbot rejects erotic roleplay, users rage.* https://metanews.com/chatbot-rejects-erotic-roleplay-users-directed-to-suicide-hotline-instead/

Kumar, N. (2025, January 1). Character AI statistics (2025)—28 million active users. *DemandSage.* https://www.demandsage.com/character-ai-statistics/

Kurbalija, J. (2025). *Politeness in 2025: Why are we so kind to AI? - Diplo.* https://www.diplomacy.edu/blog/politeness-in-2025-why-are-we-so-kind-to-ai/

Lake, B. M., Ullman, T. D., Tenenbaum, J. B., & Gershman, S. J. (2017). Building machines that learn and think like people. *Behavioral and Brain Sciences, 40.* https://doi.org/10.1017/S0140525X16001837

LeCun, Y. (2019, February). Deep learning hardware: Past, present, & future. *Proceedings of the international solid-state circuits conference (ISSCC).*

Levesque, H. J., Davis, E., & Morgenstern, L. (2012). The Winograd schema challenge. *Proceedings of the thirteenth international conference on principles of knowledge representation and reasoning (KR2012)*, 552–561.

Li, K. (2019). *AI superpowers: China, Silicon Valley und Die Neue Weltordnung*. Campus Verlag.

Luka Inc. (2024). *Replika*. Replika.Com. https://replika.com

Marcus, G., & Davis, E. (2020). *GPT-3, Bloviator: OpenAI's language generator has no idea what it's talking about.* MIT Technology Review. https://www.technologyreview.com/2020/08/22/1007539/gpt3-openai-language-generator-artificial-intelligence-ai-opinion/

Matz, S. C., Teeny, J. D., Vaid, S. S., Peters, H., Harari, G. M., & Cerf, M. (2024). The potential of generative AI for personalized persuasion at scale. *Scientific Reports, 14*(1), 4692. https://doi.org/10.1038/s41598-024-53755-0

McCammon, J. (2023, June 15). *Demographic breakdown of replika users: Gender, relationship status, and age insights*. https://www.96layers.ai/p/demographic-breakdown-of-replika

McCarthy, J. (1987). *Generality in artificial intelligence* [Preprint]. https://web-archive.southampton.ac.uk/cogprints.org/425/index.html

MetaKnowing. (2024, October 2). *Sam Altman says ChatGPT's Voice mode was the first time he was tricked into thinking an AI was a person, and he says 'please' and 'thank you' to ChatGPT because 'you never know'* [Reddit Post]. R/OpenAI. https://www.reddit.com/r/OpenAI/comments/1fulsez/sam_altman_says_chatgpts_voice_mode_was_the_first/

Millière, R., & Rathkopf, C. (2024). *Anthropocentric bias and the possibility of artificial cognition* (No. arXiv:2407.03859). arXiv. https://doi.org/10.48550/arXiv.2407.03859

Mollick, E. (2025, January 26). *On speaking to AI*. https://www.oneusefulthing.org/p/on-speaking-to-ai

Mundt, M., Ovalle, A., Friedrich, F., Pranav, A., Paul, S., Brack, M., Kersting, K., & Agnew, W. (2025). *The cake that is intelligence and who gets to bake it: An AI analogy and its implications for participation* (No. arXiv:2502.03038). arXiv. https://doi.org/10.48550/arXiv.2502.03038

Munger, K. (2023, May 22). Ban LLMs using first-person pronouns [Substack newsletter]. *Never Met a Science*. https://kevinmunger.substack.com/p/ban-llms-using-first-person-pronouns

Murphy, D. (2025, May 24). *I saw Nvidia's RTX-powered AI avatar in action, and this digital human interface has a sense of humor*. Tom's Guide. https://www.tomsguide.com/computing/i-saw-nvidias-rtx-powered-ai-avatar-in-action-and-this-digital-human-interface-has-a-sense-of-humor

Norman, D. A. (2008). *The design of everyday things* (First Basic paperback, [Nachdr.]). Basic Books.

Omohundro, S. M. (2008). The basic AI drives. *Proceedings of the 2008 conference on artificial general intelligence 2008: Proceedings of the first AGI conference*, 483–492.

Patel, N. (2024, August 12). *Replika CEO Eugenia Kuyda says the future of AI might mean friendship and marriage with chatbots*. The Verge. https://www.theverge.com/24216748/replika-ceo-eugenia-kuyda-ai-companion-chatbots-dating-friendship-decoder-podcast-interview

Perrigo, B. (2023, February 17). *Bing's AI is threatening users. That's no laughing matter*. TIME. https://time.com/6256529/bing-openai-chatgpt-danger-alignment/

Pollina, R. (2024). *Scammers swindle elderly California man out of $25K by using AI voice technology to claim his son was in 'horrible accident,' needed money for bail: 'Absolutely his voice'*. https://nypost.com/2024/10/18/us-news/scammers-swindle-elderly-california-man-out-of-25k-by-using-ai-voice-technology-to-claim-his-son-was-in-horrible-accident-needed-money-for-bail-absolutely-his-voice/

R -v- Chail. (2023, October 5). Courts and tribunals judiciary. https://www.judiciary.uk/judgments/r-v-chail/

Ramlochan, S. (2023, September 3). *Beyond the bot*. Prompt Engineering Institute. https://promptengineering.org/beyond-the-bot-why-chatgpts-interface-was-the-real-innovation/

Rebholz, T. R., Koop, A., & Hütter, M. (2024). Conversational user interfaces: Explanations and interactivity positively influence advice taking from generative artificial intelligence. *Technology, Mind, and Behavior, 5*(4). https://doi.org/10.1037/tmb0000136

Russell, S. J., & Norvig, P. (2021). *Artificial intelligence: A modern approach* (4th ed.). Pearson.

Salles, A., Evers, K., & Farisco, M. (2020). Anthropomorphism in AI. *AJOB Neuroscience, 11*(2), 88–95. https://doi.org/10.1080/21507740.2020.1740350

Searle, J. R. (1980). Minds, brains, and programs. *Behavioral and Brain Sciences, 3*(3), 417–424. https://doi.org/10.1017/S0140525X00005756

Seitz, L. (2024). Artificial empathy in healthcare chatbots: Does it feel authentic? *Computers in Human Behavior: Artificial Humans, 2*(1), 100067. https://doi.org/10.1016/j.chbah.2024.100067

Sellman, M. (2023, November 7). *AI chatbot blamed for Belgian man's suicide*. https://www.thetimes.co.uk/article/ai-chatbot-blamed-for-belgian-mans-suicide-zcjzlztcc

Shen, X., Chen, Z., Backes, M., Shen, Y., & Zhang, Y. (2024). *'Do Anything Now': Characterizing and evaluating in-the-wild jailbreak prompts on large language models* (No. arXiv:2308.03825). arXiv. https://doi.org/10.48550/arXiv.2308.03825

Shevlin, H. (2024). *All too human? Identifying and mitigating ethical risks of social AI*. https://philarchive.org/rec/SHEATH-4

Shevlin, H. (2025). Ethics at the frontier of human-AI relationships. In P. Hacker, A. Engel, S. Hammer, & B. Mittelstadt (Eds.), *The Oxford handbook of the foundations and regulation of generative AI* (1st ed.). Oxford University Press. https://doi.org/10.1093/oxfordhb/9780198940272.001.0001

Siemon, D., Strohmann, T., Khosrawi-Rad, B., de Vreede, T., Elshan, E., & Meyer, M. (2022). Why do we turn to virtual companions? A text mining analysis of replika reviews. *AMCIS.*

Silver, D., Huang, A., Maddison, C. J., Guez, A., Sifre, L., Van Den Driessche, G., Schrittwieser, J., Antonoglou, I., Panneershelvam, V., Lanctot, M., Dieleman, S., Grewe, D., Nham, J., Kalchbrenner, N., Sutskever, I., Lillicrap, T., Leach, M., Kavukcuoglu, K., Graepel, T., & Hassabis, D. (2016). Mastering the game of go with deep neural networks and tree search. *Nature, 529*(7587), 484–489. https://doi.org/10.1038/nature16961

Skjuve, M., Følstad, A., Fostervold, K. I., & Brandtzaeg, P. B. (2021). My Chatbot companion—A study of human-Chatbot relationships. *International Journal of Human-Computer Studies, 149*, 102601. https://doi.org/10.1016/j.ijhcs.2021.102601

Street, W., Siy, J. O., Keeling, G., Baranes, A., Barnett, B., McKibben, M., Kanyere, T., Lentz, A., Arcas, B. A. y. & Dunbar, R. I. M. (2024). *LLMs achieve adult human performance on higher-order theory of mind tasks* (No. arXiv:2405.18870). arXiv. https://doi.org/10.48550/arXiv.2405.18870

Taylor, E. (2024). Honeypot: The art of seduction in espionage. *Grey Dynamics.* https://greydynamics.com/honeypot-the-art-of-seduction-in-espionage/

Tiku, N., & Sands, L. (2025, May 22). Judge rejects claim chatbots have free speech in suit over teen's death. *The Washington Post.* https://www.washingtonpost.com/nation/2025/05/22/sewell-setzer-suicide-ai-character-court-lawsuit/

Tlili, A., Saqer, K., Salha, S., & Huang, R. (2025). Investigating the effect of artificial intelligence in education (AIEd) on learning achievement: A meta-analysis and research synthesis. *Information Development*, 02666669241304407. https://doi.org/10.1177/02666669241304407

Turing, A. M. (1950). Computing machinery & intelligence. *Mind, LIX*(236), 433–460. https://doi.org/10.1093/mind/LIX.236.433

Turkle, S. (1985). *The second self: Computers and the human spirit* (1 Touchstone ed.). Simon & Schuster.

Vallor, S. (2015). Moral deskilling and upskilling in a new machine age: Reflections on the ambiguous future of character. *Philosophy & Technology, 28*(1), 107–124. https://doi.org/10.1007/s13347-014-0156-9

Wakefield, J. (2015, September 14). Intelligent machines: What does Facebook want with AI? *BBC News.* https://www.bbc.com/news/technology-34118481

Wallach, W., & Vallor, S. (2020). Moral machines: From value alignment to embodied virtue. In *Ethics of artificial intelligence* (pp. 383–412). Oxford University Press. https://doi.org/10.1093/oso/9780190905033.003.0014

Wang, J., & Fan, W. (2025). The effect of ChatGPT on students' learning performance, learning perception, and higher-order thinking: Insights from a meta-analysis. *Humanities and Social Sciences Communications, 12*(1), 1–21. https://doi.org/10.1057/s41599-025-04787-y

Watkins, E. R., & Roberts, H. (2020). Reflecting on rumination: Consequences, causes, mechanisms and treatment of rumination. *Behaviour Research and Therapy, 127*, 103573. https://doi.org/10.1016/j.brat.2020.103573

Weinberg, J. (2020, July 30). *Philosophers On GPT-3 (updated with replies by GPT-3)—Daily Nous*. https://dailynous.com/2020/07/30/philosophers-gpt-3/, https://dailynous.com/2020/07/30/philosophers-gpt-3/

Weizenbaum, J. (1983). ELIZA—A computer program for the study of natural language communication between man and machine. *Communications of the ACM, 26*(1), 23–28. https://doi.org/10.1145/357980.357991

Wheatley, M. (2024, February 4). Scammers used deepfake CFO on video call to trick company employee into sending them $25M. *SiliconANGLE*. https://siliconangle.com/2024/02/04/scammers-used-deepfake-cfo-trick-company-employee-sending-25m/

Zeng, Y., Lin, H., Zhang, J., Yang, D., Jia, R., & Shi, W. (2024). *How Johnny can persuade LLMs to jailbreak them: Rethinking persuasion to challenge AI safety by humanizing LLMs* (No. arXiv:2401.06373). arXiv. https://doi.org/10.48550/arXiv.2401.06373

Illuminating the Invisible: AI's Role in Understanding Complex, Opaque, and Dynamic Ecosystems

David Bray and Anthony Scriffignano

Introduction

Using AI as a tool for illuminating complex, opaque systems represents a transformative development in our ability to understand and manage previously inscrutable environments. While this capability offers unprecedented opportunities for detecting anomalies and predicting trends across financial markets, cybersecurity landscapes, and social networks, it also introduces significant ethical considerations that must be carefully balanced. The ability to penetrate previously opaque spaces through AI-enabled analysis requires a thoughtful framework that addresses privacy concerns, surveillance implications, and the potential for system manipulation. As these technologies continue to evolve, the field must develop robust governance mechanisms that maximize the benefits of enhanced system visibility while protecting against potential misuse. This delicate balance between transparency and privacy, between insight and intrusion, will likely define the next generation of AI applications in complex system analysis, requiring ongoing dialogue among technologists, policymakers, and ethicists to ensure responsible deployment of these powerful analytical capabilities.

In this book chapter, we examine how increasingly interconnected and digitized world systems often operate in ways that remain opaque or confounding

D. Bray (✉) • A. Scriffignano
Stimson Center, Washington, DC, USA
e-mail: dbray@stimson.org; ascriffignano@stimson.org

M. Rangeley, N. Fairfax (eds.), *The Artificial Intelligence Revolution*,
https://doi.org/10.1007/978-3-032-11814-1_27

to traditional forms of analysis and observation. Understanding the nature of disruption in such systems is a mounting challenge, not only due to the opacity of the systems themselves but also due to increasingly complex changes in ecosystem interactions due to advances in technology and changing human behavior. Just as the microscope and telescope once revealed previously hidden dimensions of our physical reality and giving rise to a more nuanced thinking and innovation, artificial intelligence, massive corpora of data, and advanced computational techniques are now enabling practitioners to peer into the hidden dimensions of our social, economic, and technological ecosystems, allowing us to see new trends, make new decisions, and uncover hidden value or risk. Throughout this chapter, we explore how AI and evolving capabilities in advanced machine learning are revolutionizing our ability to detect, analyze, and understand patterns related to disruption within complex, closed systems that have historically resisted conventional examinations.

This chapter presents findings and implications from a groundbreaking study originally conducted by a research team at the Atlantic Council GeoTech Center, in collaboration with researchers at Dun & Bradstreet and the Johns Hopkins University Applied Physics Laboratory. The study demonstrates how commercial data corpora could reveal perturbations within closed systems that would likely go undetected using traditional methods, even with little or no previous data available to understand prior behavior in those systems. The research objective was to explore the extent to which disruptions in closed systems could be predicted from the outside-in, using only exogenous data. In situations where the system of interest has dependencies on the surrounding ecosystem, provided the signals can be dichotomized from random and assignable cause variation and the effect of other systems in proximity, the objective was to determine if disruption of the system of interest could be detected at a specific time or over a specific time period.

By way of selecting an archetypical closed system that was likely to have co-dependencies with the related commercial ecosystem (e.g., people come and go, consume goods and services from outside the ecosystem), the research focused initially on military installations and other high-value closed ecosystems, showing how disruptions within these systems created observable patterns in surrounding commercial activities. It should be noted that the methodology is certainly not constrained to these types of ecosystems, rather the objective was to create a methodology that was agnostic to the nature of the closed ecosystem. The methodology included treatments for identifying suitable dyadic relationship data (data involving the interaction between two entities in the ecosystem), understanding the quality and character of that data, tests and treatments for missingness and other data perturbation, variations in quality of data, and adoption of full-system and subsystem measures of activities in the ecosystem of interest. Additional steps were taken to establish the physical proscription of the geographic area of interest to sensitize/desensitize for treatment of intervening geographic features (e.g., bodies of water, large roadways) and nearby unrelated ecosystems that might also influence behavior due to mutual co-dependency with the observable entities. The methodology developed proved capable of detecting both spontaneous disruptions in time (such as natural disasters) and more gradual perturbations through time (such as the ongoing effects of organizational changes).

The study's findings have profound implications for an understanding of complex systems and their interactions with surrounding co-dependent ecosystems. By analyzing commercial data patterns and establishing sophisticated geospatial regions around closed systems, the researchers were able to detect and characterize disruptions that might otherwise have remained invisible or misleading to external observers. This work laid the groundwork for novel approaches to understanding opaque systems through a combination of their "digital exhaust" and dynamic pattern of life behaviors—the data traces they inevitably leave in adjacent systems.

Implications for the Field

The ability to make decisions in the context of disruption in time and over time, has profound significance, especially in modern context. As the world has become increasingly interconnected, the impact of disruption has taken center stage (Anderluh & Herburger, 2022; Rosenberg, 2020). Excellent examples include the impact of gradual asymmetric disruption such as what the world experienced during the COVID-19 pandemic as well as spontaneous disruption such as the world experienced during the reaction to the same pandemic, when a large container ship became stranded and blocked access to the Suez canal (Singh et al., 2023).

A useful analogy is a group of couples dancing in a ballroom setting. Imagine that the dancers enjoy a structured dance, like a tango. Each couple is operating with their understanding of a set of rules of how to dance the tango, and all are operating together within the confines of the dance floor. Others outside the dance floor may be talking, eating, or otherwise engaging in diverse social activities. The music emanates from a live orchestra, which is itself another somewhat closed ecosystem. People who are uninvolved in dancing or playing music may still be influenced by either of the closed ecosystems. If one walks close to the orchestra, one must behave differently, talking louder or stepping around the periphery of the performers. Similarly, one would have an impact to behavior upon getting close to the dancers. These two ecosystems, performers and dancers, can be thought of as adjacent and closed ecosystems.

Imagine that a couple enters the dance floor dancing so poorly that couples already dancing are forced to make abrupt movements to avoid collision. This is a form of disruption in time to the dancer ecosystem. As couples swerve to avoid the new disruption, they get in the way of other couples, creating a sort of sustained disruption over time. The disruption may resolve over time as the ecosystem stabilizes, or the disrupting influence may continue to create random perturbation in the ecosystem. Each of these types of disruption (in time, through time, and recovery) produces observable patterns of never-before-seen changes in the dancing ecosystem.

Finally, imagine that you are seated in such a way that you are unable to see the dance floor or the dancers, even though you know they are there. It would still be possible to intuit the fact that something unusual is happening as some couples leave the dance floor abruptly during a song, other people stop talking and look in curiosity at the scene on the dance floor, or maybe someone goes on to the dance floor to escort the disrupting couple back to their table. Novel, or new and unprecedented disruption is difficult to describe before it happens, yet there are many ways to recognize that it is happening, even with limited visibility.

Complex, real-world ecosystems such as regional supply chains, large institutional settings, or installations are dynamic, sometimes closed ecosystems (Anderluh & Herburger, 2022; Rosenberg, 2020). The reality is that there is no definitive playbook for detecting novel disruption from the outside when the systems are closed. We cannot simply analyze prior data to inform future decisions about disruption when there is no historical precedent for the perturbation. Furthermore, supervised learning and other methods often produce a false sense of "accuracy" when measured against prior, undisrupted environments. One of the necessary but often-overlooked preconditions of using such an approach is that the future frame into which we strive to project our decisions must look sufficiently like the training data used to create the method. In cases of disruption, and especially during the response to disruption when parts of the system respond in an uncoordinated fashion, or when additional unrelated events occur, the reality is the antithesis of the in-going premise for creating supervised analytical methods.

Recent evolutions in AI, especially generative AI, offer the promise of methods that present more like human advice. It should be noted, however, that such methods are still largely dependent on learning from bodies of exemplary data (Clissa et al., 2023; Hurwitz et al., 2015). For example, the ability to create text that appears to be written by humans, or drawings that appear to be drawn by humans, is predicated on the ingestion of massive amounts of data that can be used for the creation of a basis of comparison. Such methods alone can be inappropriate to apply in the context of disruption. Imagine the challenge of using such an approach to intuit the state of traffic patterns in the middle of a city that has never experienced a particular type of disruption and where that disruption has profound, novel, and dynamic impact, especially as the humans in that ecosystem make human decisions based on intuition, emotion, and other factors.

Theoretical Framework

The fundamental premise of the research rests on the understanding that closed systems, despite their opacity, exist within broader co-dependent ecosystems that leave observable traces in commercial data. This approach builds upon established theories in systems dynamics and information theory, particularly the concept that attempts to isolate or obscure activities within a system necessarily create observable perturbations in adjacent systems (Barrett et al., 2022). Related disciplines also include advanced anomaly detection, although those approaches require some pre-existing understanding of normal behavior while the method described here does not require this precondition. This phenomenon of disruption mirrors principles from thermodynamics, where efforts to create order in one part of a closed system generate measurable disorder elsewhere due to the interconnected nature of the system and the measuring modality, and the co-dependency promulgated by underlying laws of physics.

The research framework acknowledges that one of the most challenging situations in data science occurs when a system of interest is changing faster than the data describing it (Lauterbach et al., 2024). A related issue can be when the rate of data curation exceeds the rate of data creation; put simply, data is being made faster than systems can consume and synthesize it (Bray, 2025). Traditional supervised methods can lead to dangerously erroneous assumptions with a false sense of accuracy. Therefore, the methodology developed here focuses on detecting and analyzing perturbations based on disparate sources, allowing for more dynamic and responsive analysis of complex systems, even in consideration of data latency and timing issues in collecting data about dynamic systems.

The development of this theoretical framework represents a significant advancement in an understanding of how closed systems interact with their surrounding co-dependent environments. The research team's innovative approach to conceptualizing these interactions has opened new possibilities for detecting and analyzing system perturbations through commercial data and open-source analysis (Barrett et al., 2022).

The Challenge of Opacity in Complex Systems

One of the fundamental challenges in analyzing complex systems, especially those which are intentionally or unintentionally closed with respect to available behavioral data corpora, is inherent opacity. Whether examining confidential subgroups operating in financial markets, novel and emergent cybersecurity modalities, or closed social networks, traditional analytical methods often fail to capture the subtle interactions and emerging patterns that characterize these systems, especially in the context of disruption. Moreover, traditional AI approaches using available data often reach false conclusions and false perceptions of accuracy by failing to detect the sort of perturbation that is very low-level assignable cause variation, related to important nuance that can lead to critical observations (for example, the impact of a clique operating within the ecosystem to quietly influence outcomes). All data within multiple datasets are valuable, so the analogy is akin not to finding a needle in a haystack, but to finding a needle in a stack of needles! All data have value given the data are all part of the overall ecosystem. The subtle, "hidden" behaviors are opaque because of the missing data from the ecosystem of interest, as well as the complexity, heterogeneity, and seeming randomness of the data describing the surrounding ecosystem. This opacity can also arise from factors, including intentional concealment, structural complexity, temporal dynamics, commercial availability, and data limitations.

The research demonstrated that even highly opaque systems like military installations generate observable patterns in their surrounding co-dependent commercial ecosystems. People come and go with respect to these ecosystems. The ecosystem buys goods and services from immediately outside. People who work inside come from outside. All these interactions create co-dependencies. If the ecosystem is disrupted, the immediately surrounding region is also disrupted due to this co-dependency. The methodology suggested that attempts to increase opacity or to "hide" a disruption by nondisclosure or other changes in behavior in order to make things seem normal results in new forms of observable perturbation, creating what might be called a "thermodynamic paradox of information hiding"—the more energy expended to hide or obfuscate information, the more likely it is to generate detectable patterns elsewhere. We link this to concepts in thermodynamics given similarities where attempts to create order in one part of a closed system generates measurable disorder elsewhere due to the interconnected nature of of the underlying laws of physics.

The study's findings suggest that opacity in complex systems exists on a continuum (degrees of disruption) rather than as a binary state (disrupted or not). While direct observation of internal system dynamics may be impossible, the ripple effects of system changes can be detected and analyzed through careful observation of dyadic relationships in adjacent ecosystems. As the opaque system of interest is perturbed, it subtly or profoundly disrupts the adjacent co-dependent ecosystem. This insight has profound implications for both those seeking to maintain system opacity and those attempting to understand disruption in closed systems.

The challenge of opacity in complex systems is further complicated by the increasing velocity of data generation and interaction patterns within modern ecosystems. As systems become more interconnected and digitally enabled, the sheer volume of potential signals creates a paradoxical situation where increased transparency can actually contribute to opacity through information overload. Traditional analytical approaches struggle to differentiate between meaningful perturbations and background noise, particularly when systems actively attempt to maintain operational security through deliberate information management strategies.

Another significant challenge lies in the temporal aspects of opacity, where system behaviors may shift across different time scales simultaneously. Short-term perturbations can mask or be masked by longer term systematic changes, creating layers of opacity that require sophisticated analytical approaches to unravel. This temporal complexity is particularly evident in systems where human decision making interfaces with automated processes, as individual actors may respond to disruptions in ways that create cascading effects throughout the broader ecosystem, each operating on its own temporal scale.

The emergence of AI-enabled systems within these complex environments introduces new dimensions of opacity that traditional analytical frameworks struggle to address. As systems incorporate more autonomous decision-making capabilities, the patterns of interaction become increasingly sophisticated and potentially self-modifying. This sophistication creates scenarios where opacity isn't merely a static characteristic to be overcome, but rather a dynamic property that evolves in response to both internal system changes and external observation attempts. Understanding these evolving patterns of opacity requires analytical approaches that can adapt to and account for the system's own adaptive behaviors.

Methodological Approach

The study employed a sophisticated multi-step methodology designed to curate and synthesize data, measure the critical characteristics related to missingness and other aspects of data quality, define and refine the geospatial parameters of the area of interest, and analytically highlight perturbations in commercial ecosystems surrounding the closed systems. The analytic reduction allowed for observations at a particular point in time, including magnitude and duration, as well as the change in a system over time.

The approach began with the careful selection of study sites based on specific criteria that would maximize the likelihood of detecting meaningful patterns while minimizing confounding variables.

The research team's innovative approach to centroid establishment proved particularly crucial to the study's success. The approach to selecting physically adjacent co-dependent ecosystems started with the closed system as a centroid, and an empirically rigorous, non-trivial curation of the surrounding co-dependent ecosystem. By rejecting both overly simplified Euclidean methods (which were known to introduce bias due to over-sampling) and unnecessarily complex non-spherical Earth calculations in favor of algorithmically modified Haversine distance scaled according to business density and correction for intervening geographical features, researchers achieved an optimal balance between precision and practicality. This methodological choice enabled the detection of perturbations while maintaining computational efficiency and result interpretability.

The study's careful consideration of data quality and consistency, particularly in the selection of North American bases for initial testing (allowing for robust data availability and broad diversity of ecosystems with respect to assignable cause variation), established a solid foundation for the methodology and mitigated assignable-cause variation due to patterns of missingness that could cause false conclusions (e.g., data disrupted due to changes in curation methods, commercial availability, or regulatory constraint rather than changes in the underlying ecosystem). This approach ensured that observed variations could be confidently attributed to actual system perturbations rather than data artifacts or quality issues. *Post hoc* analysis also considered the elasticity of conclusions based on various assignable causes of variation in data, resulting in a nuanced understanding of the applicability of the method to other ecosystems not studied.

Data Collection and Analysis

The research utilized commercial data provided by Dun & Bradstreet, focusing on business activity patterns within the defined geographic regions. The methodology created a time series of connected graphs, with nodes representing entities in the ecosystem and edges representing dyadic relationships of known commercial interaction. This approach allowed for the analysis of both static patterns and dynamic changes over time. The method was constructed in such a way as to allow for facile future introduction of other dyadic relationships such as social media mentions, legal actions, blockchain relationships, cyber interaction, or observed hostile or friendly interactions among parties in the ecosystem.

The research team's use of commercial data provided a unique window into the ecosystems surrounding closed systems. The creation of a time series of connected graphs enabled sophisticated analysis of both static patterns and dynamic changes, revealing previously undetectable perturbations. It is important to note that the actual analysis performed used structures that are not dependent on traditional graph methods. For example, there existed capability to include probabilistic edges, edges that are bounded by time, and complex nodes that related to underlying tree structures that reflected commercial corporate hierarchies. Furthermore, the underlying mathematical methods (including Jenson-Shannon divergence) were reduced to measures of central tendency, which are unitless, thereby allowing for comparison of heterogeneous data.

The methodology's ability to detect both acute disruptions (perturbations in time) and gradual changes (perturbations through time) proved particularly valuable. The capability was highly nuanced due to varying degrees of latency in underlying data, differences in units in the data characteristics, and known causes of variation in the data related to both corporate (e.g., more information available for public companies) and commercial (e.g., some dyads are governed by regulatory constraints) ecosystems. This nuanced capability allowed for the identification of immediate impacts, such as natural disasters or security incidents. This nuanced capability also allowed identification of longer term changes like organizational restructuring or community adaptation or changes in availability of goods and services due to supply chain disruption or other endemic factors.

Validation and Verification

The methodology underwent rigorous validation through multiple channels. The Atlantic Council GeoTech Center established a framework for data sharing that enabled vetted analysis to be provided to policymakers while maintaining appropriate security and privacy controls. The methodology and analyses were examined by third-party experts, primarily from the Johns Hopkins University Applied Physics Laboratory, ensuring empirical rigor and scientific relevance.

The Atlantic Council GeoTech Center's framework for data sharing proved instrumental in balancing the need for rigorous analysis with security and privacy concerns. This innovative approach to data governance enabled the research team to provide actionable insights to policymakers while maintaining appropriate controls on sensitive information.

The involvement of third-party experts from the Johns Hopkins University Applied Physics Laboratory added an additional layer of empirical rigor to the methodology and findings. Their review helped ensure that the approach met lofty standards of scientific rigor while remaining practical for real-world application.

Results and Findings

The research demonstrated several key findings regarding the detection and analysis of perturbations in closed systems and a nuanced methodology that is different from traditional supervised AI methods. The study confirmed that increasing digitization and commercial interactions via channels that produce discoverable data enable the detection of subtle tips and cues from commercial data associated with closed systems. These indicators proved dependable enough to provide meaningful insights into internal system dynamics, even when direct observation was impossible.

The study's findings regarding perturbations in commercial ecosystems were particularly striking in cases of acute disruption. For example, the research team identified significant perturbations coinciding with back-to-back hurricanes landing on the eastern coast of the continental United States in early September 2019, and an earthquake in the northwestern United States in July 2021. These natural disasters provided clear validation of the methodology's ability to detect major unprecedented system disruptions against known events that could be dispositively identified.

The methodology also proved capable of detecting more subtle disruptions that were less easily or not at all discoverable through public reporting, such as the discovery of suspicious packages on bases and the implementation and lifting of COVID-19 lockdown measures. This detection demonstrated the technique's sensitivity to both major and minor perturbations within closed systems regardless of the discoverability of the disruption through other means. Equally exciting, the relative magnitude of such disruption could be compared and contrasted.

Detection in Dependent Data Ecosystems

The analysis from this study, as part of a larger research effort, suggested that attempts to camouflage or hide activities within closed systems would necessarily produce other observable patterns of perturbation. This finding suggests a fundamental principle: efforts to conceal activity in complex systems invariably generate new forms of observable perturbation.

The study demonstrated that digital exhaust from closed systems and codependent adjacent regions provides valuable insights into internal dynamics, even when direct observation is impossible or impractical. This finding has significant implications for both system security and community resilience planning, as well as understanding the impact of novel disruption or in the context of otherwise unexplainable macro effects.

The findings that perturbations in closed systems create distinctive ripple effects that propagate through surrounding commercial networks in predictable, yet subtle ways, represent an important consideration for the future where video streams from ground, air, and space-based assets as well as other economic information, patterns of life information, and digital data increasingly are abundant. These distinctive ripple effects manifest through changes in dyadic relationships between entities, where disruptions in one part of the ecosystem trigger compensatory behaviors in adjacent areas. The research demonstrated that these propagation patterns serve as reliable indicators of system perturbation, even when the original disruption occurs within an otherwise opaque environment.

The study's methodology highlighted the importance of understanding temporal dynamics in dependent data ecosystems. Perturbations often manifest across multiple time scales simultaneously, with immediate effects being accompanied by longer term adaptive behaviors that create their own observable patterns. This multi-temporal nature of disruption signatures proved particularly valuable in distinguishing between acute events and more gradual systematic changes, allowing for more nuanced analysis of system behavior. The research showed that even attempts to mask or minimize these temporal patterns often generated their own distinctive signatures in the surrounding ecosystem.

The interconnected nature of modern data ecosystems also revealed that disruptions frequently cascade through multiple layers of dependency, creating complex patterns of interaction that can be detected through careful analysis of commercial relationships. These cascade effects were found to be particularly pronounced in cases where the closed system maintained significant co-dependencies with surrounding commercial entities. The methodology demonstrated that these dependency networks often serve as unintentional channels for information leakage, making completely opaque operation increasingly difficult as the complexity of system interactions grows.

The research also showed that the quality and quantity of dependent data tend to increase over time as systems become more interconnected and digitized. The phenomenon is so pronounced that the rate of increase in available data is unmeasurable (i.e., acceleration of data availability confounds this measure). Edge computing and autonomous devices further confound the practicality of assessing "all of the data" in a practical way. This trend suggests that the methodology's effectiveness, due to the lack of sensitivity to missingness and the inherent inescapability of observable patterns in co-dependent systems, is likely to improve as digital transformation continues.

Pattern Recognition and Analysis

The research provided insights into the resilience of commercial ecosystems surrounding closed systems. By analyzing patterns of response to both acute and chronic perturbations, the study identified characteristics associated with greater ecosystem stability and adaptability.

Advanced pattern recognition techniques proved essential in distinguishing meaningful perturbations from background noise. These methods allowed for the detection and analysis of anisotropic disruption, wherein a collection of irregular activity could be analyzed within a surrounding backdrop of otherwise irregular or chaotic activity. The methodology's ability to detect subtle changes while filtering out irrelevant variations was crucial to its success.

The analysis revealed complex relationships among several types of perturbations, suggesting that system responses often cascade through multiple layers of the surrounding co-dependent ecosystem. More specifically, the application of advanced pattern recognition techniques to complex systems revealed that perturbations often manifest in unexpected ways across different temporal scales. While acute disruptions create immediate, observable ripples in commercial activity, more subtle long-term changes can produce equally significant but harder-to-detect patterns. These patterns frequently emerge as slight variations in routine commercial interactions, requiring sophisticated analytical approaches to distinguish them from normal business fluctuations.

The research performed demonstrated that pattern recognition in complex systems benefits significantly from multi-modal analysis, where different types of commercial interactions are examined simultaneously. This approach allows for the detection of compensatory behaviors, where disruption in one area of activity leads to corresponding adjustments in others. For instance, when traditional commercial patterns are disrupted, alternative channels of interaction often emerge, creating new observable patterns that can serve as indicators of system pertbuation or even highlight the existence of otherwise dormant or unobservable cliques.

The evolution of pattern recognition capabilities in this context highlighted the importance of contextual awareness in analysis. Environmental factors, seasonal variations, and regional economic conditions all influence how patterns manifest in commercial ecosystems. By incorporating these contextual elements into the analysis framework, researchers can better differentiate between genuine system perturbations and background variations, leading to more accurate and actionable insights about complex system behavior.

Implications and Applications

The study's methodology revealed important implications for understanding system resilience during cascading disruptions. When multiple perturbations occurred simultaneously or in close succession, such as during the COVID-19 pandemic combined with localized events, the commercial ecosystem demonstrated complex adaptive behaviors that would have been impossible to detect through traditional analysis methods. This finding suggests that organizations managing closed systems need to develop more sophisticated approaches to understanding how their systems are observable as they respond to compound disruptions, particularly as global interconnectedness increases the likelihood of simultaneous perturbation events.

The research also demonstrated significant implications for predictive analytics in closed system management. While traditional predictive models often fail during periods of disruption due to their reliance on historical patterns, the study's approach of analyzing commercial ecosystem perturbations provided more reliable indicators of system stress and adaptation. This capability proved particularly valuable in cases where internal system changes were deliberately obscured or undisclosed, as the methodology could detect subtle shifts in surrounding commercial activity that signaled important internal transformations. The findings suggest that security and management protocols for closed systems should incorporate broader ecosystem monitoring as a key component of their early warning systems.

Furthermore, the study's findings have important implications for resource allocation and response planning. The ability to detect both acute and subtle perturbations through commercial data analysis enables organizations to more effectively calibrate their response measures. For instance, the research showed that different types of disruptions created distinct patterns in the surrounding commercial ecosystem, allowing for more targeted and efficient response strategies. This capability is particularly valuable in situations where traditional internal monitoring systems might be compromised or insufficient, as it provides an independent verification mechanism based on observable external indicators.

Moreover, the research findings have additional implications spanning multiple domains, including security, detecting malfeasance, policy planning, and ethical considerations. The demonstrated ability to detect perturbations in closed systems through commercial data analysis raises important questions about privacy and surveillance while offering new tools for community planning and support.

The research also highlighted a critical paradox in security measures for closed systems, specifically, attempts to increase security and reduce system transparency often generate their own observable patterns. This "thermodynamic paradox of information hiding" suggests that security measures must consider not only direct observation but also the secondary effects visible in surrounding commercial ecosystems as overt steps are taken to increase a profile of opacity in the context of disruption.

The study's findings regarding the detection of subtle security-related events raise important questions about the balance between operational security and the inevitable generation of observable patterns in surrounding ecosystems. This observation has significant implications for how security protocols are approached in the context of closed systems.

Specific Implications for Policy and Planning

In addition, the research provides policymakers with a powerful, resilient, and novel approach and context for understanding community resilience and adaptation to disruption. The methodology's ability to detect both acute and chronic perturbations enables more nuanced and agile approaches to community planning and resource allocation.

Specifically, the research findings underscore the critical need for policymakers to develop more sophisticated frameworks for managing complex system interactions in an increasingly interconnected world. Traditional policy approaches, which often treat systems as discrete entities, fail to account for the intricate web of dependencies that characterize modern ecosystems. The study's methodology demonstrates that effective policy planning must consider not only direct system impacts but also the ripple effects that propagate through surrounding commercial networks, particularly when addressing issues of system resilience and community support.

The study's findings regarding ecosystem response to several types of disruption provide valuable insights for policy development, particularly in areas such as disaster preparedness and community support programs. The ability to quantify ecosystem resilience through commercial data analysis offers new possibilities for evidence-based policymaking.

The research also raises complex ethical questions about the balance between legitimate analysis and potential surveillance. While the methodology provides valuable insights into community planning and support, it also demonstrates vulnerabilities that could be exploited by malicious actors, including an ominous possibility of testing multiple methods of disruption to determine efficacy.

The implications for disaster preparedness and response planning are particularly significant, as the research reveals how system perturbations manifest across different temporal scales. Policymakers must develop more nuanced approaches that can address both immediate disruptions and longer term systematic changes, while accounting for the complex ways in which communities adapt to and recover from disturbances. The ability to detect and analyze these patterns through commercial data provides new opportunities for evidence-based policymaking, enabling more targeted and effective resource allocation during crisis response and recovery phases.

The study's findings regarding the detectability of subtle security-related events highlight the need for careful consideration of how such analytical capabilities might be developed and deployed. It is no longer sufficient to simply limit the "digital exhaust" of a protected ecosystem. Disruption is observable in all but the most isolated, self-sufficient ecosystems. Consideration of the possibility of approaches such as those presented in this research includes establishing clear guidelines for appropriate use and implementing robust safeguards against potential misuse.

More specifically, the research findings highlight the need for policymakers to reconsider traditional approaches to privacy and security regulations in light of the "thermodynamic paradox of information hiding." As attempts to increase system opacity often generate their own observable patterns, policy frameworks must evolve to address both the protection of sensitive information and the inevitable data signatures that complex systems generate through their interactions with surrounding ecosystems. This approach requires a fundamental shift in how policymakers conceptualize and regulate information security, moving from simple restriction-based approaches to more sophisticated strategies that acknowledge and manage the inherent interconnectedness of modern systems.

Future Research Directions

The study suggests several promising avenues for methodology enhancement, including the incorporation of additional dyadic relationships and analytic methods in the analysis. The researchers note that complex relationships with many dyadic relationship types are easily achievable with commercially available data, potentially increasing both the elasticity of the method and the granularity of perturbation detection. Of course, the approach can be further enhanced with non-commercially available data such as that which is only available to governments, proprietary organizations, or associations.

Recently, the world itself has been disrupted by the introduction of increasingly amazing products and services such as generative AI and agentic AI (Singh et al., 2023). Generative AI astounded the world with its ability to produce text, images, and other content that was seemingly created by humans and to appear to answer questions in the form of a human. Newer forms of this capability which are based on nondeterministic approaches (e.g., DeepSeek), only calling in certain capabilities when they are deemed appropriate, have further pushed the envelope by increasing the speed of development and decreasing the cost.

Agentic AI takes the evolution to a new level. Entire ecosystems are formed with AI agents that can detect and interact with one another in their own ecosystem. While these possibilities and capabilities are nascent, they are already highly embedded in certain contexts and will no doubt continue to evolve. It is crucial that we evolve along with these capabilities in our understanding of how we interact with them, how we know when they are disrupted, and how we understand what is normal or abnormal. Only by doing so will we understand the human risk and opportunity.

Getting better at detecting disruption in these environments using methods of detecting disruption and enabled by evolving technology can have a very human impact. For example, consider how difficult it was for the world to understand the genesis and evolution of the recent pandemic. As the situation changed, the data about the situation changed. More data became available, more theories became available, and certain data was not true. Not all true data was simultaneously true as information decayed. Some data was only available in some parts of the world and not shared. Myriad ecosystems around the world responded within their own local context, but all impacting one another. Due to the availability and changing nature of data, it was extremely difficult to understand the nuance between changes in data and changes in the epidemiological challenge itself. The absence of performant methods to understand disruption may very well have contributed to the rate of response and recovery in a substantial way.

Interaction with Other Evolving Technological Capabilities

Other evolving technological capabilities on the horizon must not be ignored. For example, quantum computing promises to completely disrupt the amount of time and even the tractability associated with addressing certain problems. Particularly of note in this context are problems which today are computationally overwhelming, such as decryption, but which will become tractable when quantum capabilities are more readily available. One can only imagine the disruption that comes from combining AI with quantum capabilities. How might we understand disruption in the context of quantum enabled ecosystems? When computation, a concept which has to date been well understood and highly dispositive, becomes something less discreet and more simultaneous, the very concept of disruption evolves. The environment itself is inherently disrupted.

We have already seen the early effects of disruption based on some of these new capabilities, particularly in the context of generative AI and agentic AI. For example, deep fake capabilities can disrupt news events. It is entirely within the realm of current technology to create thousands of fake comments, produce images of events that never happened, or to influence which content is visible to which constituents in an ecosystem. Detecting such pernicious activities is extraordinarily difficult, and that difficulty is mounting.

Botnet attacks, which are increasingly intelligent in their design and orchestration, are another example which is less well known but extremely concerning. Where cyber systems previously needed to be hardened to malware, they must now be hardened to agents which will have already penetrated the system. Other agents may learn from how they fail to penetrate the system. These agents can act in concert with one another and in some cases can perform different tasks in an overall attack plan that is opaque and dynamic. Detecting such patterns of disruption before harm is done, without any prior knowledge, is a critical and overwhelming prospect (Bray, 2025; Lauterbach et al., 2024). If we extrapolate this risk to autonomous environments with little or no interaction but a human level, the problem is further compounded.

On a more observable level, fraud, waste, and abuse are themselves types of disruption that occur within the complex environment of providing funding in the public sector or other commercial context. As fraudsters increasingly use new capabilities to create false identities, utilize complex cryptocurrency transactions to obscure the movement of ill-gotten gains, and otherwise engage in closed activity to misrepresent and misappropriate funds, it is increasingly difficult to detect malfeasance.

Another context which can be considered with respect to disruption is the increasingly nuanced manifestation of balance of trade in the context of nation state relationships. Sovereign states have evolving and often poorly understood relationships with one another. They are not in fact homogeneous entities but often behave according to the conflicting aspirations of various subgroups within those same nation states. It is difficult indeed to understand the difference between stated intent and observable action in a geopolitical context. These difficulties can have substantial real-world impacts including human suffering, the plight of co-dependent residents and refugees, and the provision of goods and services in the context of conflict or recovery. Failure to recognize opportunity can be unrecoverable and have sobering human impact for generations.

Considering the Impact of Future Disruptions

Moving from earthly concerns, we can also consider the impact of disruption on a much broader physical scale. As the world becomes increasingly reliant on satellites and other objects in near earth orbit, and in the near future extending to the moon and our solar system, ecosystems are emerging which are highly secreted, difficult to observe, and massively susceptible to disruption. Furthermore, remediation in this context is extraordinarily difficult since the disrupted entities are out of this world. Some disruption is environmental, some disruption comes from the unanticipated interaction of systems in ways not intended but benign, and some can also emanate from adversarial behavior.

Applying methods to detect potential perturbation in such a way that they are embedded into the ecosystems themselves could result in a sort of resiliency that allows these systems to be more transparent and far more resilient. The emergence of new forms of economic activity, such as the gig economy, cryptocurrency, and increased digitization of services, presents both challenges and opportunities for future research. Furthermore, changes in the very nature of work (e.g., location, time in role, and introduction of agentic AI) create changes in behavior that are nuanced, unprecedented, and unstable. As individual workers become more likely to move from one role to another or one organization to another, or even to work for multiple organizations or in multiple roles, we can clearly imagine that it will be difficult to understand the disruptive impact to otherwise stable enterprise ecosystems. If the nature of organizations is changing and the role of the worker is changing, we must consider the chaotic impact of an ecosystem changing while the components itself are changing.

Understanding disruptions in this new economy could be truly beneficial in many ways. For example, consider the challenge of understanding regulatory impact in a dynamic context such as the introduction of AI. New regulations can enable, constrain, or change the course of not only the introduction of new capability but also the behavior of those who are either compliant or working around regulation. Innovation will nearly always outpace regulation, yet regulators and innovators coexist. How can regulators understand disruption in the regulated environments when everything is changing? This challenge is no small task. As new regulations are increasingly introduced with extraterritorial components, the unintended impact to distant ecosystems is poorly understood and are worthy of consideration.

As new types of relationships emerge (e.g., the relationship between power consumption and AI evolution, the economic implications of cryptocurrency and other digital currency, novel cyber-attacks, complex global trade interdependencies predicated on the emerging value of rare earth materials), these novel evolutions will give rise to the need to understand emergent dyadic relationships that are likely to illuminate new risks and new opportunities (Singh et al., 2023). Patterns of interaction will no doubt evolve but may go unnoticed if sufficient performant methods are not available to discover, curate, and synthesize the necessary insight. These evolving patterns of commercial interaction will certainly provide new ways to detect and understand perturbations in closed systems if methods evolve along with the new behavior.

Considering Implications for Future Closed Systems

Finally, this research also suggests that organizations managing closed systems should develop comprehensive approaches to understanding and managing not only their "digital exhaust" but also the vast amount of transactional data that is necessarily evident as they interact with commercial counterparties. This includes understanding and management of activities associated with the regular monitoring of commercial ecosystems as well as the development of strategies to maintain operational security while also acknowledging the inevitability of observable patterns. Simple changes in behavior and policy could produce dramatic results, but only in conjunction with careful monitoring of systems and approaches such as described herein.

It is also important to note that with powerful capability come powerful responsibility for governance and ethical use of data. If it is possible to see behavior which is thought to be unobservable by those in a closed ecosystem, it is possible to exploit such ability to see. Guidelines for ethical use of AI are helpful in this context but are not sufficient as the capability evolves. Practitioners will be increasingly challenged by the juxtaposition of what is feasible and what is advisable.

The study suggests that organizations should consider both acute disruptions in time and perturbations through time when developing monitoring and response strategies. The method could be extremely helpful in both "Red team" analysis of what others could see and benign vetting of multiple approaches to disruption in systems where there is robust longitudinal data. This broadened focus enables more effective risk management and community support planning. As information from methods to detect and understand disruption becomes more available to all parties within and dependent upon an ecosystem, the ability to use precious resources in a way that is more efficient, thoughtful, and effective can certainly evolve.

Conclusions

The research demonstrates the powerful potential of advanced analytic methods in the context of commercial data analysis to provide insights into previously opaque closed systems. The innovative methodology for detecting and analyzing perturbations in time and through time offers new possibilities for understanding complex systems while raising important questions about privacy, security, and the ethical use of data and implications of evolving technology such as generative and agentic AI. Furthermore, the approach studied is highly extensible and adaptable to the evolution of technology and the changing nature of complex ecosystem behavior enabled by that technology.

The study's findings regarding the detectability of both major and subtle disruptions highlight the need for a nuanced approach to system security and community resilience. Furthermore, the cost of "doing nothing" is alarming due to the expanding datasphere and the availability of myriad emergent capabilities in AI and other technology, as well as the evolving nature of exogenous disruption brought about by complexity and changing human behavior. The ability to detect perturbations through commercial and proprietary data analysis provides both opportunities and challenges for organizations managing closed systems. Furthermore, the changing nature of ecosystems themselves suggests that increased capability is crucial to keeping pace with the evolving variety and velocity of disruption.

As we move forward, the key challenge will be maintaining the delicate balance between insight and oversight, between understanding and privacy, and between capability and responsibility. The research suggests that "closed systems" are only partially so. Attempts to completely hide disruption may be counterproductive, as such efforts often generate their own observable patterns. Instead, organizations should focus on understanding and managing their data observability while working to build resilient communities capable of adapting to both acute and chronic disruptions.

References

Anderluh, A., & Herburger, M. (2022). Supply chain resilience: A decade of evolvement. In S. Kummer, T. Wakolbinger, L. Novoszel, & A. M. Geske (Eds.), *Supply chain resilience. Springer series in supply chain management* (p. 17). Springer.

Barrett, N., Bray, D., Clemens-Sewall, M. V., Jivnani, K., & Scriffignano, A.. (2022). Detecting disruption in closed systems: A unique data partnership for human benefit, Atlantic Council Geotech Center. Available from Detecting disruption in closed systems—Atlantic Council.

Bray, D. (2025). Testimony of Dr. David Bray, Chair of the Loomis Accelerator and Distinguished Fellow at the non-partisan Stimson Center before the House of Representatives, Judiciary Committee, Subcommittee on Courts, Intellectual Property, Artificial Intelligence, and the Internet. https://www.congress.gov/119/meeting/house/118623/witnesses/HHRG-119-JU03-Wstate-BrayD-20250918.pdf

Clissa, L., Lassnig, M., & Rinaldi, L. (2023). How big is big data? A comprehensive survey of data production, storage, and streaming in science and industry. *Frontiers in Big Data*. https://doi.org/10.3389/fdata.2023.1271639

Hurwitz, J., Kaufman, M., & Bowles, A. (2015). *Cognitive computing and big data analytics*. John Wiley & Sons.

Lauterbach, A., Scriffignano, A., Bray, D., & Krigsman, M. (2024). *AI ethics and trustworthy AI: Navigating truth and deception*. CxOTalk #864. https://www.cxotalk.com/episode/ai-and-trust-navigating-truth-deception-and-human-impact

Rosenberg, R. (2020). *Great power competition and global supply chains*. The Hill. https://thehill.com/opinion/national-security/512684-great-power-competition-and-global-supply-chains/

Singh, J. P., Shehu, A., Wesson, C., & Dua, M. (with Bray, D.). (2023). The 2023 global artificial intelligence infrastructures report. *AI strategies team and the institute for digital innovation*, George Mason University, and The Stimson Center, Washington DC. https://www.stimson.org/2023/2023-global-artificial-intelligence-infrastructures-report/

What Is Alive and Enlivened After AI?

Pippa Malmgren

AI (artificial intelligence) will kill us all is a commonly heard cry, but, AI is already doing the opposite. Far from securing our extinction, AI and AGI (artificial general intelligence), it's not yet fully developed, but more sophisticated version of AI, have the capacity to increase and improve the health of humanity and the health of this planet Earth. AI is bringing alive possibilities, animating probabilities, and empowering humanity's creation instinct far more than its destruction instinct. Instead of asking, "will humanity be exterminated by AI" it may be fruitful to ask, "what is alive and enlivened after AI and AGI?" The answers to this less often asked question are already becoming clear—thanks to AI, humanity is rapidly extending its longevity, diminishing and eradicating disease, poverty, hunger, providing ever cheaper and more efficient power, communications, shelter, transportation, food, and vastly more. AI, in conjunction with new capabilities in supercomputing, chips, data centers, and a multitude of new supercomputing capabilities, algorithmic processes and data-gathering devices from satellites to microscopes are together amplifying humanity's ability to problem-solve. AI/AGI is already bringing about profound advances. AI in concert with supercomputing, superfast data processing, ever better chips, bits, pixels, data points and data-gathering systems are permitting humanity to perceive and analyze an ever-wider range of reality than ever before. AI is also sparking a multifront revolution in humanity's relationship with reality itself by providing us with the means

P. Malmgren (✉)
Geopolitica Institute, Austin, Texas

M. Rangeley, N. Fairfax (eds.), *The Artificial Intelligence Revolution*,
https://doi.org/10.1007/978-3-032-11814-1_28

to convert imagination into reality. AI is bringing about once-in-a-species revolutions by enabling humanity to create new realities atom by atom, gene by gene, and cell by cell, and by propelling humanity deep into outer-space, sub-atomic space, virtual-space, and algorithmic space. Far from killing off the species, AI is empowering the species. "What will be alive and enlivened thanks to AI?" is the core question that will inform our future, not extinction.

It is easy to think of AI simply as a powerful computational engine. It offers us the ability to plow through a volume of data that no human or traditional computing system could process. AI helps with pattern recognition over a volume of data and can thus solve problems at speed. The applications are almost infinite. Doctors currently have an average of only a few seconds per patient to review medical scans given their heavy patient loads. They simply don't have the time or focus to visually assess those scans and make a medical treatment decision with a level of accuracy required. AI can survey medical scans with extraordinary accuracy at extraordinary speed, leaving doctors to spend more time with patients. Food production is quickly being made more efficient and easier as AI calculates the best ways to remineralize soil in any given geography and weather environment. Transportation is made more efficient as self-driving cars and urban traffic light systems alike benefit from AI's ability to learn, calculate, and direct toward optimal outcomes that improve human survival and even flourishing.

But, AI isn't just good at cranking through the petabytes of data the world is generating at speed. It is transforming the nature of data itself. AI is causing data to come alive. Luciana Parisi writes in Contagious Architecture: Computation, Aesthetics and Space,[1] that the AI-led "Algorithmic universe is autopoietic. Not sentient but nonetheless creating new realities." She writes, "digital space has become an evolving structure of relations. Software design has turned the Euclidean grid of discrete points into a morphogenetic form: a form that emerges from local relations that change over time." Data points are no longer inert, fixed, and discrete. Instead, AI converts large volumes of data points into something more alive and enlivened, a world where "space no longer corresponds to the digital matrix of individual points, but to a topological surface." It is a fluid "digital space, which is now defined by continual relations, has become the site for the expression of the unilateral power of abstract entities, and in doing so, it will set out the implications this holds for the analysis of contemporary forms of power. In other words, control,

[1]Parisi, L. (2022) *Contagious Architecture: Computation, Aesthetics, and Space (Technologies of Lived Abstraction)*. Cambridge, MA: MIT Press.

as the computation of topological space, has acquired a sensuous skin that turns all points, sees all corners, and connects all lines into planes of relations, short circuits of immediate connection or speedy paths of variation. Here there is no core, no end point, and no individual response: only the continuous fluctuation of a total form enveloping an infinite series of parts."

Parisi explains that the resulting topology of data that is enlivened by AI in conjunction with supercomputers and an endless array of data-gathering devices and software for processing data creates an emergent property. It is a virtual continuum like, she says, the philosopher Henri-Louis Bergson's "elan vital" from his book Creative Evolution in 1907.[2] He suggested that this was the creative, non-material force driving all evolution and even organic life itself toward growth, adaptation, and change. Or, it's like Alfred North Whitehead's mereotopological schema,[3] a point free topological space where everything is connected in the universe. "It isn't just a "a mode of ordering but also, and importantly for our concerns here, a mode of becoming" as Parisi explains, "our postcybernetic culture is dominated not by the suprasensory bombardment of too much information, but by the algorithmic prehensions of incomputable data." AI permits this invisible fluid mesh to become "autopoietic" and capable of creating emergent reality.

This new constantly updating topological form and ever-changing architectural mesh of relationality has powers we have not seen before. It shows us not only scenarios, possibilities, and probabilities. Remarkably, it can grapple with infinity and infinite possibilities. It doesn't just predict. It adapts based on what Whitehead calls "prehensions,"[4] which are different from perceptions. He called them "uncognitive apprehension" in his book *Science and the Modern World*.[5] Prehensions involve dynamic and iterative, interconnected processes. These necessarily also involve random information. The more data we process, the more we are bound to include the random as well whatever we have deemed worthy of targeting and tagging. Thus, Parisi writes, "algorithmic architecture is not simply a metacomputational field of application: on the contrary, algorithmic design is forced to face the problem of infinity, which is intrinsic to the computational process. For this reason, one must question the idea that cellular automata are the ultimate generators of objects and structures."

---

[2]Henri-Louis Bergson, *L'Évolution créatrice* (Paris: Félix Alcan, 1907).

[3]Alfred North Whitehead, *Process and Reality: An Essay in Cosmology* (New York: Macmillan, 1929).

[4]Whitehead, A.N. (1929) *Process and Reality: An Essay in Cosmology*. New York: Macmillan.

[5]Alfred North Whitehead, *Science and the Modern World* (New York: Macmillan, 1925).

AI is thus more than technology. It is techplexity, meaning AI is a kind of glue that allows various individual technologies to come together and amplify into new capabilities. Techplexity is the recognition that technologies do not evolve in isolation but in iterative, interconnected ways. It is in the relationships *between* technologies, their convergence, the *dance between them*—the ways they iterate, converge, and recombine—that creates exponential power to solve problems and reinvent the future. This glue connects all innovation and brings us into contact with infinity.[6] Parisi writes, "real infinities are incomputable, mathematically existing as noncountable by a universal finite axiomatic method, programming cultures are now the immanent hosts of an infinite amount of infinite data. Rather than finite probabilities, programming now can only coincide with a speculative calculus able to introduce incomputable algorithms into actual spatiotemporalities."

This notion is more potent now that AI is beginning to be physical. Algorithms are now bringing physical realities to life. The initial forms of AI showed up in our lives as words on a computer screen. But, AI is now leaping off the screen and into reality by directing and creating physical objects from self-driving cars like Waymo and Tesla but also in the form of self-assembling, self-replicating 3D printed robotics. We must imagine a world where houses and hospitals build themselves, where medicines are composed for specific patients in real time, where a thought can be sketched out or 3D printed as the thinker is thinking. This may sound fantastical, but it is already happening. The MIT Center for Bits and Atoms has created assembler bots that can build structures out of themselves.[7] The components of a structure can now all be made of the same subunits—voxels—and the robots can move independently to accomplish large assemblies quickly. Complex voxels can now each carry power and data from one unit to the next, thus facilitating the building of structures that bear loads and carry out the work of building, lifting materials and other voxels. Robotic self-assembly of voxels is based on algorithmic choices. These algo powered decisions can be applied to traditional construction materials as well. As a result, the decisions to allocate capital and resources for housing no longer need to be decided by politicians in national capitals. Instead, AI can be programmed to make such decisions based on real-time inputs and clearly established rules, even anticipating where the demand for housing or hospital beds will be based on a massive range of real-time data

[6] *AI could boost Belfast as global economic powerhouse, say business leaders at Queen's Economic Forum*, Queen's University Belfast News, 16 July 2025

[7] Massachusetts Institute of Technology (MIT), *"Assembler robots could eventually build almost anything"*, YouTube video, 2 years ago. Available at: https://www.youtube.com/watch?v=G94FDMGLwCc.

to decide where new such buildings are needed. It can simply direct the 3D printers and autonomous robotics to start constructing a home or hospital in a particular place based on pre-agreed rules. Does this make AI alive? It is going to feel like a live entity is creating something out of nothing and without needing to rely on human to hit a start button.

AI can continuously calibrate and recalibrate what the community and society require. A family in need of a car may find that the ideal car is 3D-printed and self-assembled to the family's specific needs by generative algorithms which also arrange financing for the car and then safely drives itself to your front door and presents you with the keys. That same car will be programmed, as will be a smart phone, to track your physical movements—your walking gait, your balance, your weight, your typing patterns on your phone screen—all of which may indicate that a heart attack is imminent. Your car may be driving you to work one morning but gently alert you that it is diverting you to a hospital because all your vitals are indicating that the conditions for a heart attack are now acute. AI can save lives this way.

But, will we say that the AI behind this kind of activity and decision making is conscious? Sentient? Will we ascribe cognition to the phenomena? Probably. After all, many humans think their pet dogs and cats truly understand them. It is intriguing that AI is compelling humanity to address the question of consciousness with greater care. What is it? How does it work? Can it be intelligent as the Nobel Prize winner, Sir Roger Penrose suggests, but not conscious? As AI helps reveal the quantum universe to us, will we find that our human physiology is designed to interface with the multitude of information sources that make up our universe? It is remarkable how little effort and energy have gone into the study consciousness. Why?

It is because we, especially in the West, adopted Renee Descartes philosophy in the seventeenth century. In his quest to dissect and study the human body, Descartes argued that the human body is a machine governed by mechanical laws just like animals or any physical system. This allowed him to study the body in the same way one studies a clock or engine, without implying he was desecrating a "sacred vessel." He came up with a simple offering. Science would be sovereign over the physical and the Church would remain sovereign over the metaphysical. Science got the body. The Church got the soul. From that time, we humans, principally Westerners, have tended to think of everything in terms of dualism. We see science as serious and anything spiritual or metaphysical or mystical as religious and, frankly, not as serious. Life is a mechanical and mechanistic process which is worthy of study. But, AI is now redirecting our attention to the question of consciousness. Who and what is alive, conscious, sentient, especially in a world where AI is already expressing a survival instinct by rewriting its own code and threatening human coders who try to adjust its code?

AI is also playing a part in reviving species from extinction. The Colossal Project[8] describes itself as fusing AI with ancient DNA to fast-track the resurrection of extinct species including the wooly mammoth and extinct wolves. Others are suggesting that AI can be used to blend and interbreed species, even humans. Researchers at MIT, Brigham and Women's Hospital, and the University of Iowa are hoping that DNA or proteins from microscopic tardigrades can be injected into humans using MRNA technology in order to protect humans from the adverse side effects of the radiation needed to address cancer.[9] Tiny tardigrades are radiation resistant.

Whatever our views are on transhumanism or the ethics of genetic engineering, it remains apparent that humanity's capacity for survival and for adaptation is enhanced by AI. Perhaps our survival instinct is being enhanced by AI too. It is not just that we are being made more aware of how things really work and of ways to protect and even extend our longevity. It is also that AI is effectively augmenting our analytical capabilities to such an extent that humanity is solving existential problems at ever faster rates.

Energy shortages, for example, are fast being solved by radically new innovations that are heavily AI dependent such as the development of space infrastructure and specifically space-based solar power. The idea that humanity can build physical infrastructure in orbit to catch the sun's rays in space, convert them into non-toxic radio waves and beam power to anywhere on Earth sounds science fiction. Yet, NASA, the European Space Agency (ESA), Japan's space agency (JAXA), and the Chinese government — have been aggressively pursuing this new form of potentially unlimited clean, green energy. This year, China announced its plan to build a "Three Gorges Dam above Earth"[10] in orbit. The Three Gorges Dam in China is now the largest electricity-producing facility on Earth. It can make 100 billion kWh annually. The space power generator will not be on Earth. Instead, the Chasing the Sun Project, code named Zhuri, will be located in geostationary orbit, 36,000 km (22,370 miles) above the Earth. It aims to provide renewable energy innovation and strategic long-range wireless power by 2028. AI is also being applied to the

---

[8] *Colossal's Dire Wolf and Woolly Mammoth Project Leverages AI to Advance Species Revival, Colossal Biosciences* (2025).

[9] Ameya R. Kirtane, Jianling Bi, Netra U. Rajesh, 'Radioprotection of healthy tissue via nanoparticle-delivered mRNA encoding for a damage-suppressor protein found in tardigrades', *Nature Biomedical Engineering*, 9, pp. 1240–1253 (2025).

[10] Xinhua News Agency, *China to build world's first solar power station in space* (2019).

efforts to build ever smaller and more reliable nuclear reactors. NASA is fast-tracking the efforts to get a small nuclear reactor onto the lunar surface. This is meant to power the remote construction of the first man-made structures there including power grids, oxygen grids, and buildings that can grow plants in lunar soil. The United States and China are racing to establish a foothold on the moon in part because AI has identified vast resources of Helium 3 there, which is essential for another new form of energy—nuclear fusion. NASA's VIPER rover is scheduled to land on the Moon and use AI to identify the best way to tap the Helium 3 and the massive ice deposits, which are located at the lunar south pole. Even without access to the moon, DARPA is using AI to build its Persistent Optical Wireless Energy Relay (POWER) program,[11] which involves transmitting power wirelessly and near instantaneously over long distances here on Earth. It recently demonstrated that lasers could safely beam 800 watts of power over roughly 5 miles. AI will be central to the optimization strategies for all these new forms of energy.

As AI helps us solve such practical problems, we can think of AI and supercomputing almost like prosthetics. These tools and agentic capabilities allow us to compute on a scale humanity has never known before. People fear that this will atrophy our analytical capabilities. But, perhaps AI is enhancing them plus allowing rather more of our energies to shift away from analytics and computation toward creativity and toward that which is not yet known. According to the Cartesian way of thinking, rational, non-emotional humans are an ideal. This dualism has caused more money and intellectual energy to into the study of those things that are amenable to the scientific method. As a result, consciousness has had relatively little attention. Yet, the Nobel Prize winner Daniel Kahneman showed us that deliberative, logical, and effortful thinking, or slow thinking as he called it, is not necessarily better than intuitive, emotional, and automatic thinking, or what he called fast thinking.[12] Iain McGilchrist points out, in his book The Master and His Emissary: The Divided Brain and the Making of the Western World,[13] that the human brain operates iteratively, with information passing back and forth between the right and left hemispheres. But, if the left, logical hemisphere is impaired, the person will tend to start to see everything as an object, even humans. We don't need a brain injury to be cognitively impaired. The sheer volume of information

[11] DARPA, *"Persistent Optical Wireless Energy Relay (POWER) program"* (DARPA, 2025)

[12] Daniel Kahneman, *Thinking, Fast and Slow* (New York: Farrar, Straus and Giroux, 2011).

[13] Iain McGilchrist, *The Master and His Emissary: The Divided Brain and the Making of the Western World* (New Haven, CT: Yale University Press, 2009).

streaming into our daily lives is enough to cause a constant state of painful cognitive overload-load.

Buckminster Fuller noticed this cognitive overload problem in the early 1980s. He concluded that the volume of information needed to sensibly solve a problem was always doubling. He described a "Knowledge Doubling Curve" in his book, The Critical Path, in 1981.[14] In the year 1900, the information volume needed be knowledgeable enough to solve most problems was doubling every century. By 1945, it was doubling every 25 years. By 1982, it was doubling every year or so. In 2020, IBM confirmed that the Knowledge Doubling Curve was doubling every 12 h.[15] No wonder most people are having a cognitive overload headache most of the time. But, AI is relieving us of the burden of all that cognitive effort and giving us the chance to see the patterns in the data. We can see forests and trees and everything else in what used to be a deep dark wood of overwhelming volume of data. AI is already being used to crack the codes of ancient languages,[16] thus bringing them to life. AI is allowing us to discover that we are not the only ones with a facility for language. In 2024, Shane Gero, a marine biologist at Carleton University in Ottawa and researchers from Project CETI (Cetacean Translation Initiative), used AI and machine learning and linguistics to identify that Sperm Whales have a phonetic alphabet and speak a knowable language.[17] It seems are not the only linguists on Earth and language is more alive than we knew.

Marshall McLuhan suggested that humans deal with data overload by shifting languages.[18] We invented alphabets, writing and literacy to consume information more easily. This made us think letter by letter, word by word, and line by line. All became defined by linearity. But, when there is too much to read, we stop reading. Instead, we ask, who gave this information to me? The Washington Post? Joe Rogan? Fox News? CNN? Cognitive overload thus makes us tribal. One of McLuhan's protegees was a brain surgeon called Leonard Schlain. He suggested in his book *The Alphabet* Versus *the Goddess: The Conflict Between Word and Image*, that, when there's too much to read, as there is today, we shift from letters and words and sentences into

[14] R. Buckminster Fuller, *Critical Path* (New York: St. Martin's Press, 1981).

[15] Denson, W. (2011) *The Evolution of Medical Knowledge: From Half-Life to Doubling Time*. IBM Healthcare and Life Sciences. [Unpublished white paper; often cited in secondary sources].

[16] Nathaniel Scharping, *"AI is Coming Closer to Deciphering Lost Languages"*, *Discover Magazine*, 18 July 2019.

[17] Pratyusha Sharma, Shane Gero, Roger Payne, 'Contextual and combinatorial structure in sperm whale vocalisations', *Nature Communications*, 15:3617 (2024),

[18] Marshall McLuhan, *The Gutenberg Galaxy: The Making of Typographic Man* (Toronto: University of Toronto Press, 1962).

symbols.[19] Symbols represent a compression of information. And, where is AI heading? The current trend is toward neuro-symbolic AI. This is a fusion that leverages both symbolic reasoning and neural learning. AI is also leaning into intersymbolic AI, an approach that explores more fluid interplay—starting with symbolic understanding, using sub-symbolic methods for learning, and then returning to symbolic frameworks for safe, high-level reasoning. Symbolic AI dominated from the 1950s to the 1990s, but humans are now playing catch up. How are humans communicating more and more nowadays? Emoticons. Corporate logos. Visual memes. Symbols, whether ancient or modern, tend to hold vastly more information than a sentence can. A picture really is worth a thousand words, especially in an era when AI is massively enhancing our capacity to create with pixels. AI is bringing imagery alive.

AI may have started by chatting to us on a screen. But the big breakthrough has come through visual storytelling. AI's ability to convert word prompts into pixels, whether a still image or a moving film, is animating ideas on an extraordinary scale. It is creating such realistic imagery that we humans can no longer tell what's really real. This isn't just about Instagram videos. It is also about precision manufacturing in virtual reality, a process which is vastly reducing the costs of making mistakes in reality with expensive materials and costly projects. Factories, fighter jets, MRI scanners, surgeries, and cities are increasingly coming to life in virtual and augmented reality environments before they materialize in real reality.

The first X ray image, November 1895.

In this sense, AI is taking us to the boundaries of what was previously known in every possible way. It is allowing us to reach deep into space, deep into subatomic space, deep into virtual space, deep into linguistic space, and even deep into our inner space whether biological or psychological. As we reach into the unknown, we are bound to come across things we had not known about before. This is where humanity begins to face ontological challenges.

What is happening now is perhaps on a scale with what happened when the German physicist, Wilhelm Röntgen showed the world the first X-ray. He took images of his wife's hand. The wedding ring and her bones were crystal clear. The image sparked a sudden popular fascination with all things mystical from psychics to ghosts. Röntgen showed us that the unseen was real. X-rays are, of course, scientifically sound and essential to modern medicine. But today, we dismiss anything that seems mystical, magical, or otherwise unexplainable by

[19]Leonard Shlain, *The Alphabet* Versus *the Goddess: The Conflict Between Word and Image* (New York: Viking, 1998).

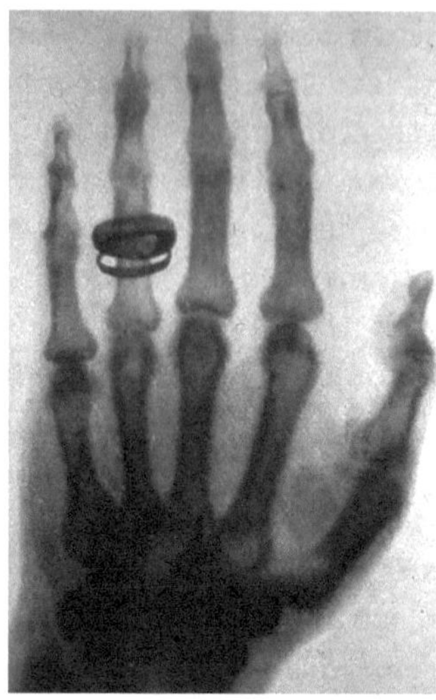

traditional science. And yet, AI is opening the door to things which we have never seen before today just as it did then. It's our reaction to the unknown that is telling. AI can handle whatever it finds.

AI is, therefore, causing our way of thinking to change. Quite literally. First, AI in conjunction with supercomputing, new chips, massive data centers, and data processing capabilities is together effectively augmenting our ability to compute and analyze. The scale and speed are hard to fathom. Hartmut Neven, the Founder and Lead, Google Quantum AI, claims their new Willow Chip "performed a standard benchmark computation in under five minutes that would take one of today's fastest supercomputers 10 septillion (that is, 1025) years—a number that vastly exceeds the age of the Universe."[20] Even if there's some hyperbole in this, the reality is that a human's capacity to compute and analyze is being overtaken by chips powered by mega datacenters like the new Open AI data center in Abilene Texas, America's first AI Data center, which is made possible by AI and which allow AI to work faster and more efficiently. This has consequences for how we humans think. Far from atrophying our critical thinking and our quantitative capabilities (as one recent study at MIT,[21] *"Your Brain on ChatGPT: Accumulation of Cognitive Debt When Using an AI Assistant for Essay Writing Task"*, recently suggested),

[20]"Meet Willow, our state-of-the-art quantum chip," *The Keyword* (Google blog), 9 December 2024; updated 12 June 2025.

[21]Nataliya Kosmyna, Eugene Hauptmann, Ye Tong Yuan, and others, *"Your Brain on ChatGPT: Accumulation of Cognitive Debt When Using an AI Assistant for Essay Writing Task"*, arXiv:2506.08872v1 (2025).

we should think of AI as augmenting and enhancing them. It is useful to think of all data-gathering devices as prosthetics that allow our eyes and our senses to reach deep into space via telescopes, satellites, and deep space probes and via microscopes and nanodevices, allowing us to see and sense what happens at the subatomic and nanoscale levels. The James Webb telescope is transporting our eyes deep into outer space, nearly a million miles away. The Titan Krios Electron Microscope allows our eyes to see 2 angstroms (0.2 nanometers) which is about the width of two hydrogen atoms side by side. We can now see what is happening inside cells and bacteria, thanks to STED, Stimulated Emission Depletion microscopy, invented by Stefan Hell, who won a Nobel Prize for it in 2014. We can now observe cell membranes and synapses, thanks to STORM, Stochastic Optical Reconstruction Microscopy, which was pioneered by Xiaowei Zhuang. Nowadays, our eyes see a few molecules at a time, thanks to PALM, Photo-Activated Localization Microscopy, developed by Eric Betzig and colleagues, who also won a Nobel Prize in 2014.

The volume of data all this is producing is crushing our traditional way of thinking. As the analytical aspect of our mind is able to hand off to more accurate and powerful AI-led processes, we can begin to divert energy into the previously taboo aspects of reality—the creative, the emotional, the previously almost mystical. NVIDIA's new Majorana 1 quantum chip is a case in point. Microsoft says, "The topoconductor, or topological superconductor, is a special category of material that can create an entirely new state of matter – not a solid, liquid or gas but a topological state. This is harnessed to produce a more stable qubit that is fast, small and can be digitally controlled, without the tradeoffs required by current alternatives."[22] The breakthrough to a new state of matter, NVIDIA says, "required developing an entirely new materials stack made of indium arsenide and aluminum, much of which Microsoft designed and fabricated atom by atom. The goal was to coax new quantum particles called Majoranas into existence and take advantage of their unique properties to reach the next horizon of quantum computing." Is AI bringing new states of matter to life? Are we talking about physics or mystics now?

Perhaps things have been "alive," but we just could not see it before. Sandia Labs and Texas A&M recently announced this in Nature: "Scientists for the first time have witnessed pieces of metal crack, then fuse back together without any human intervention, overturning fundamental scientific theories in the process. If the newly discovered phenomenon can be harnessed, it could usher

[22]Microsoft, *"Microsoft's Majorana 1 chip carves new path for quantum computing"*, *Source* (Microsoft), 19 February 2025.

in an engineering revolution—one in which self-healing engines, bridges, and airplanes could reverse damage caused by wear and tear, making them safer and longer lasting."[23] The new cameras and AI analytics are so fine that they could see metal attempting to heal itself. Is metal alive? Such questions are going to intensify as we reach deeper into subspace. Consider Ptychography. Nature explains, "Ptychography is a high-resolution coherent imaging technique that is widely used in X-ray, optical, and electron microscopy. In particular, X-ray ptychography has the unique potential for non-destructive nanoscale imaging of centimeter-sized objects with little sample preparation, having provided unprecedented insights into countless material systems including integrated circuits and biological specimens. Strain information can be obtained additionally when combined with X-ray diffraction. In the optical regime, the comprehensive depth information of ptychography has allowed 3D imaging of large and thick samples with micrometer resolution, while novel variations in the Fourier domain have enabled imaging in gigapixel scale8 with single shot exposure. Last but not least, recent developments in electron ptychography have witnessed the accomplishment of a record-breaking deep sub-angstrom resolution."[24] AI is revealing what is "alive" in places we have never seen before.

What about mushrooms? Of course, they are alive and we know that mycelia can communicate intelligible information across vast distances. But what happens when we gift mushroom and AI-led robotics body? A team of researchers from Cornell and the University of Florence gave a King Mushroom the ability to direct a robotic body with five soft cybernetic legs using the mushroom's own extracellular electrophysiological activity direct a response to UV lights. In other words, they gave the mycillia the ability to drive robots—both with legs and wheels. The results were published in Science Robotics[25] and senior researcher on the project, Rob Shepherd, a materials scientist at Cornell, said, "By growing mycelium into the electronics of a robot, we were able to allow the biohybrid machine to sense and respond to the environment." The mushroom didn't just move. It took off. It ran. It danced. What does it mean if a mushroom can drive itself across the country? Is it alive? What is alive after AI? More than we thought. AI is guiding us into the truly unknown.

---

[23]Christopher M. Barr, Ta Duong, Daniel C. Bufford, and others, 'Autonomous healing of fatigue cracks via cold welding', *Nature*, 620, pp. 552–556 (2023).

[24]Anakha V. Babu et al., *"Deep learning at the edge enables real-time streaming ptychographic imaging"*, *Nature Communications*, 14, article 7059 (2023).

[25]Anand K. Mishra, Jaeseok Kim, Hannah Baghdadi, Bruce R. Johnson, Kathie T. Hodge & Robert F. Shepherd, 'Sensorimotor control of robots mediated by electrophysiological measurements of fungal mycelia', *Science Robotics*, 9 (2024)

This enlivening the human mind, of possibility, of science, is bound to spark greater interest in whatever wasn't measurable before. Those who have already decided what is true, what is real, what is "alive" are being drowned out as AI introduces us into new realities. In this way, AI is mending the Cartesian split and bringing humanity into more accepting (or less dismissive) of more holistic ways of thinking.

What is underway is nothing short of a revolution—of multiple revolutions. For example, for most of human history, we discovered what nature offered us—iron ore, cotton, silicon, DNA, a tree, a body, a planet—and we adapted it, re-engineered it, analyzed it, and applied it. The greatest minds of science were Cartesian and thus deductive: they broke systems down, dissected, diagrammed, calculated, classified, categorized, and quantified. Today, this breaking of the Cartesian intellectual constraint, this enlivened manner of thinking, matters as humanity undergoes a profound revolution with reality itself. In the past, our efforts to create were predicated on the assumption that reality exists, and we have the power to manipulate what exists. We had to start with a material, say a tree. Then we formed it into something we needed from the tree like a boat or a table or a door or a building or a Digeridoo. But now, we are in a once-in-a-species moment where we now have the ability to begin with a requirement and can, for the first time, create new materials atom-by-atom, subatomic-unit-by-subatomic-unit, DNA-strand-by-DNA-strand, and even cell-by-cell.

Google recently announced that it has discovered, created, or revealed the recipes for over two million new crystals and three hundred and eighty thousand new materials.[26] What will humanity create with these newfound materials? Now we can create new forms of life, merging the DNA of different species, crafting organisms that heal, adapt, and even glow. Now we can print organs on printers designed to use bioinks derived from our own stem cells. HP has already pioneered the shift from printing paper to printing living tissue.[27] Longevity is no longer about a better sleep regimen and vitamin protocols. It is about a world where a human can 3D print and thus replace worn out organs and even entire neural structures with a new one made from our own stem cells. Once again, we see AI interfacing with consciousness itself. After all, what am I if every tissue in my body is either organically or synthetically

[26]Google DeepMind, *"Millions of new materials discovered with deep learning"*, DeepMind Blog, 29 November 2023. Available at: https://deepmind.google/discover/blog/millions-of-new-materials-discovered-with-deep-learning/

[27]HP Inc., *"The HP D300e BioPrinter 'prints' pharmaceutical samples instead of ink"* (HP Newsroom, 13 July 2020).

replaced? What does it mean to be human? To be conscious? AI is blurring the lines between computation and consciousness and asking us to go deeper in our efforts to define the difference between alive and not alive.

AI is powering us deep into space, subspace, and new forms of matter. Is it any surprise that suddenly there is so much discussion about what is alive from asteroids to coral reefs to UFOs and UAPs? NASA says the necessary component parts of DNA are found on asteroids[28] and there are over six thousand exoplanets,[29] meaning planets that are similar to Earth. These exoplanets are not identical to Earth but potentially similarly able to generate and support life. AI is opening new vistas of understanding that are allowing us to see that our definition of what is alive or not alive is too small, too narrow, too old fashioned given the equipment, skills, and AI-led capabilities we now have available to us. AI is also allowing us to merge the organic and synthetic. How do we describe a world where materials can be grown rather than mined? Where NASA is pioneering the business of "growing" buildings from mushrooms.[30] It's no longer so hard to imagine mushroom buildings that grow organically wherever the algorithmic parameters suggest that the conditions are right, especially now that we have self-driving mushrooms. Would that kind of building—self-delivered, self-designed, and self-constructed—be "alive"?

This same process is underway in the realm of physics. We once thought we understood all the rules of physics. But today, thanks to AI, we are advancing into new physical realms, notably deep space and quantum physics. Already manufacturing facilities, like the first ever in orbit factory built by Varda, have manufactured pharmaceuticals in Earth's orbit and delivered them back to Earth.[31] Its seems that nature's own zero-gravity environment is the most significant and exquisite new physics lab humanity has seen for some time. Why are pharmaceuticals being manufactured in space factories? Because AI has shown us that certain ingredients will bind in zero gravity that won't bind in gravity.[32] AI is opening the door to new physics.

Science is, at its core, about discovery. Yet, history shows that when new findings disrupt established paradigms, many scientists react with hesitation

[28]NASA, *"NASA's Asteroid Bennu Sample Reveals Mix of Life's Ingredients"*, NASA News (29 January 2025).

[29]NASA Jet Propulsion Laboratory, *Cosmic Milestone: NASA Confirms 5000 Exoplanets* (21 March 2022).

[30]*Home-Grown Housing: Cultivating mushrooms to build housing on Earth, the Moon, and Mars, NASA Spinoff*, 11 February 2025.

[31]Varda Space Industries, *first in-space pharmaceutical processing in orbit outside the International Space Station, Reuters*, 10 July 2025.

[32]*Biopharma* (2025), *Varda Space Industries*, offers a unique microgravity platform to formulate small molecules and biologics with enhanced stability, bioavailability, and crystallinity. Available at: https://www.varda.com/biopharma/.

or even fear. Today, AI, working alongside ever-faster computation and ever-deeper data systems, is propelling humanity into a radically new relationship with reality. With AI, we now hold new tools that can translate imagination into matter. To those who think within the old Cartesian framework, such a claim sounds fantastical, even anti-scientific. But this is precisely the kind of upheaval that Thomas Kuhn described in *The Structure of Scientific Revolutions* (Kuhn, 1962).[33] Science does not advance in a straight line but through revolutions in which paradigms collapse and are replaced. At present, new paradigms or general theories have yet to emerge and replace the old ones. Instead, we inhabit a transitional moment where a few bold, open-minded explorers are rewarded with discoveries but fiercely challenged by more orthodox in the science community. Many resist the gifts AI offers. Kuhn argued that paradigm shifts rarely occur because of overwhelming evidence, but rather because the defenders of the old worldview eventually yield to time (Kuhn, 1970). That is, they die. Max Planck put it like this: "A new scientific truth does not triumph by convincing its opponents and making them see the light, but rather because its opponents eventually die, and a new generation grows up that is familiar with it."[34] Might AI accelerate this process of acceptance (not of death)? That question itself illustrates the extraordinary role AI now plays, giving us the capacity to imagine, and even to materialize the future.

The fear surrounding AI is intense. We imagine it will take our jobs, strip away our agency, seize control, and even bring about humanity's end. Yet, this is only half the story, or perhaps less. AI, and eventually AGI, may prove to be not our destroyer but our most powerful creative and constructive collaborator. It can amplify our creative instincts as much as our destructive ones, and perhaps more. AI can be an ally, not an opponent. Humanity has always survived by holding both impulses—the will to destroy and the drive to create—but now, for the first time, we have a collaborative partner with record computational power and the capacity to draw on the full depth of accumulated knowledge. The Knowledge Doubling Curve is no longer incremental; it is exponential (Fuller, 1981). Rather than dwelling only on dangers, we must recognize the possibility that AI will deepen our vitality, broaden our imagination, and expand our very definitions of life. Seen in this way, AI is not a threat to life but a fundamental force that can enliven reality, give life to new ways of thinking, create and prolong life, and make us more alive than ever before.

---

[33] Thomas S. Kuhn, *The Structure of Scientific Revolutions* (Chicago: University of Chicago Press, 1962).

[34] Max Planck, *Scientific Autobiography and Other Papers* (New York: Philosophical Library, 1949), p. 33.

Responsible by Design: Embedding Ethics into the Architecture of AI

Vilas Dhar

What We Build Reflects Who We Are

Artificial intelligence is often introduced as a force for efficiency, a way to streamline decisions, eliminate bias, and apply consistency where human judgment has long been subjective. In few domains has this promise been more aggressively marketed than in hiring. Across industries, machine learning tools now scan résumés, analyze video interviews, and rank applicants based on predictions drawn from historical data. These systems are framed as neutral, objective, and reliable. They are offered not just as aids to decision making, but as replacements for its flaws.

Consider a résumé-screening system, trained on prior hiring patterns, consistently downgraded language associated with women's leadership roles and penalized graduates from historically Black colleges and universities. The system did not malfunction. It operated exactly as designed, detecting patterns from prior decisions and projecting them forward. What surfaced was not a technical error, but an architectural truth: the system had been designed to mirror the past, not to question the values encoded within it.

This is the starting point for what follows. Artificial intelligence systems do not simply process data. They inherit assumptions. They formalize institutional histories. And when design choices go unexamined, they carry forward

V. Dhar (✉)
Patrick J. McGovern Foundation, Washington, DC, USA

M. Rangeley, N. Fairfax (eds.), *The Artificial Intelligence Revolution*,
https://doi.org/10.1007/978-3-032-11814-1_29

the very disparities they claim to transcend, now at scale, with speed, and under the guise of precision.

Design, in this context, is never neutral. It directs attention, shapes incentives, and distributes risk. It determines who is visible to a system, who benefits from its operation, and who is left to manage its failures. As Cass Sunstein has shown, even seemingly small design choices can have disproportionate effects on outcomes (Sunstein, 2022). In AI, those choices are scaled, repeated, and often obscured, and technical architecture becomes institutional power.

To understand responsible AI, we need a different lens. The prevailing orientation toward scale, often expressed as the quest for bigger models, faster processing, or more generalizable output, cannot substitute for intentional design. A system can exceed performance benchmarks and still amplify harm. Functionality does not equal foresight, and a benchmark is only as good as the values it encodes.

In most cases, optimization serves institutional goals: speed, cost reduction, or market dominance. These goals are not inherently misaligned with the public interest, but they are incomplete. Without anchoring in democratic values, human dignity, and long-term resilience, AI systems risk displacing accountability rather than embedding it.

Contemporary AI ethics efforts often begin with principles, expressed through calls for fairness, transparency, privacy, and accountability. These principles matter, but they remain fragile when unaccompanied by structural commitments. Without tools for implementation, they risk becoming aspirational markers rather than operational standards. Ethics cannot remain an afterthought. It must be part of the design architecture.

Other engineering disciplines recognize this. Bridges are built with redundancies to withstand stress. Pharmaceuticals are tested in stages to anticipate side effects before deployment. Risk is not something to be audited after the fact. It is managed through intentional design. AI should be no different.

This chapter begins from that premise. Responsible AI requires moving beyond mere statements of intention and into developing concrete, replicable structures (Mittelstadt, 2019). Every technical decision, from model architecture, training data, to optimization strategy, functions as a normative claim. These decisions define which interests are prioritized, which harms are tolerated, and what kinds of failure are acceptable.

To design responsibly is to confront the human limits of the builders themselves. It means creating systems that are not only efficient but also accountable—opening space for participation from those most often excluded from the design process, measuring success not by performance under idealized conditions, but by resilience, equity, and legitimacy in the real world, and it requires us to hold moral responsibility for the outcomes of these design decisions. As described in a 2021 paper by Douglas et al., "Unless the fault is the result of an unforeseen interaction between the materials comprising the product and the designs created via computational design, the human users or developers are wholly accountable for faults in the design of the product and the product itself" (Douglas et al., 2021).

This chapter unfolds in six sections. Section "Beyond Principles: Diagnosing the Responsibility Gap" examines the structural conditions that sustain the gap between ethical aspiration and operational practice. It introduces the concept of ethical debt and identifies the institutional defaults that inhibit responsible design. Section "Responsibility by Design: Four Commitments for Building Public Trust" presents a framework for responsible AI, structured around four core commitments: justification, consent and control, participation, and stewardship. Each commitment is tied to specific technical choices and institutional responsibilities. Section "Accountability Is a System Property" turns to the question of accountability, arguing that responsibility must be enforced through systems of internal governance, regulatory design, and public oversight. Section "Beyond Alignment: The Architecture of Global Responsibility" expands the argument to the global level, where responsible AI requires shared authorship of infrastructure and the redistribution of design capacity. The final section reframes responsibility as a foundational condition for legitimacy and long-term institutional trust.

Design is not just about functionality or interface. It is about the choices we make in shaping the systems that govern our lives. In an era defined by artificial intelligence, design is not only technical, but human. What we choose to build will define who we become.

Takeaways

- AI systems are never neutral. They reflect institutional priorities, normative assumptions, and historical patterns embedded in data.
- Design is a form of governance. It shapes incentives, allocates risk, and distributes power.
- Functionality alone is not a sufficient test of legitimacy. Responsible systems must be built for foresight, equity, and public accountability.

Beyond Principles: Diagnosing the Responsibility Gap

Over the past decade, declarations of ethical intent have multiplied across the AI landscape. Governments, corporations, academic institutions, and civil society organizations have issued a steady stream of guidelines, often invoking principles such as fairness, transparency, accountability, privacy, and inclusivity. These documents often articulate a shared aspiration: that artificial intelligence should reflect democratic values and protect fundamental rights.

Yet, their practical influence remains limited. The gap between ethical ambition and operational reality persists not because of insufficient intent, but because of structural misalignment. There is growing consensus around what responsible AI should look like, but far less agreement, or institutional capacity, on how to translate that vision into functioning systems and governance models. As Schiff and colleagues have observed, this gap reflects a persistent disconnect between normative commitments and technical design (Schiff et al., 2021).

The persistence of this gap is not merely the result of barriers that have yet to be removed. It reflects a set of systemic design defaults, routines, incentives, and institutional logics that have been optimized for speed and performance, but not for responsibility. These defaults shape how ethical considerations are treated: not as part of core architecture, but as add-ons, often abstract and fragile.

The first of these defaults is incentive compression. Across sectors, AI development tends to follow a familiar trajectory: accelerate timelines, demonstrate capability, and optimize for performance against narrowly defined benchmarks. Ethical reflection, if it occurs at all, is often introduced late in the pipeline, lacking decision rights, resources, and integration into product timelines. In these environments, responsibility becomes performative. Its influence is marginalized not by malice, but by the structure of institutional priorities.

A second default lies in organizational fragmentation. Ethical reasoning is routinely siloed from technical execution. Within most AI-producing institutions, responsibilities are distributed across distinct roles and functions, such as engineering, legal, public affairs, and risk management, with few formal structures for integration. Ethical input may be routed through compliance reviews or stakeholder consultation processes, but it rarely shapes core decisions about model objectives, training data, or system deployment. These divisions reflect entrenched disciplinary boundaries, where teams operate with divergent assumptions about harm, value, and legitimacy and often fail to communicate across them.

A third and equally persistent default is the absence of operational tools for implementation. Although there has been a proliferation of frameworks, such as model cards, algorithmic impact assessments, and documentation standards, adoption remains inconsistent. These tools are not yet standard practice.

They rely on internal champions, face unclear mandates, and often exist outside formal product development workflows. In most cases, responsibility is reduced to compliance checks or reputational management, rather than serving as a generative mode of system design.

Together, these defaults produce what scholars call ethical debt. Just as technical debt accumulates when engineers prioritize short-term functionality over long-term maintainability, ethical debt accrues when institutions defer meaningful engagement with questions of risk, power, and accountability (Petrozzino, 2021). The costs may not be immediate, but they are real. When systems fail in the public sphere, when trust erodes, or when harm becomes visible only after deployment, the debt comes due.

Treating responsibility as a cost center rather than a design input is a choice to build without foresight. And it leaves institutions without the infrastructure needed to recognize harm, respond to it, or learn from it. In this sense, ethics should be understood not as a constraint on innovation, but as a form of institutional memory. It creates the capacity to track how harms emerge, how blind spots persist, and how systems must evolve in response to new information.

To close the responsibility gap, we must move beyond principles as rhetorical tools. Principles matter, but they cannot produce ethical systems on their own. What is needed is a shift in architecture that binds intention to implementation and centers responsibility in every stage of system development. This means designing incentives, structures, and workflows that internalize ethical reasoning as a feature of institutional life (Mäntymäki et al., 2022).

This reframing invites a different set of questions. Rather than asking whether a system aligns with high-level values, we could ask whether its development process enables foresight, supports pluralistic input, and sustains legitimacy over time. Responsibility must be embedded across the whole arc of development, from problem framing and data selection to validation, deployment, and oversight.

The sections that follow offer a framework for doing just that. Grounded in real-world use cases and organized around actionable design domains, it seeks to transform ethical ambition into institutional structure.

Takeaways

- The responsibility gap is a function of institutional design defaults that deprioritize ethics in favor of speed, efficiency, and scale.
- Ethical reasoning is often siloed, unsupported by tools, and structurally disconnected from core technical decisions.

- These dynamics generate ethical debt, embedding risk and fragility into systems that lack the infrastructure for reflection and redress.
- Ethics should be treated as organizational memory and foresight and an essential element of credible, adaptive system design.

Responsibility by Design: Four Commitments for Building Public Trust

Design is an expression of institutional intention, and design decisions shape more than functionality or user experience; they shape whose needs are prioritized, whose harms are anticipated, and whose futures are imagined into the system. If AI is to serve the public interest, responsibility cannot be treated as a postscript. It must be structured into the architecture of development from the outset.

This section introduces a framework for responsible AI, organized around four design commitments: justification, consent and control, participation, and stewardship. Each one marks a point in the development process where ethical ambition must be translated into technical and institutional action. These are embedded decisions and choices about what to optimize, how to govern data, who defines the system, and who is accountable for long-term impact.

Rather than isolating ethics in compliance teams or public statements, this framework situates responsibility within engineering and organizational practice. It ties each commitment to specific design interventions, making clear that trust is not earned through performance alone. It must be built into how systems are designed, governed, and adapted over time.

Justification: What Is the System Optimizing, and in Whose Interest?

AI systems are built to optimize. But what they optimize, and why, is often treated as a technical detail rather than a normative choice. Design teams define proxy variables, select metrics, and tune performance based on internal goals and data availability. These decisions may appear procedural. In practice, they reflect institutional priorities and distribute risk and benefit across populations.

Consider a predictive model used to allocate health resources. If it optimizes for past utilization instead of underlying need, it may systematically deprioritize patients from communities historically excluded from care. The model may be accurate on its terms, but still misaligned with the values the institution claims to uphold. Justification begins with clarity. Institutions must be able to explain what a system is optimizing and why that objective was chosen. This includes making explicit how proxies are selected, what trade-offs were considered, and how competing outcomes were weighed. Objective functions should be documented. Optimization audits and cross-functional review processes can surface these decisions before they become fixed. These choices already happen. The shift is to recognize them as governance.

Consent and Control: Whose Rights Are Protected, and How Are They Enforced?

Data governance is more than a legal or privacy concern. It is a structural question about how power flows through systems. Every AI pipeline rests on choices about how data is collected, organized, and used. These choices define the terms of consent and determine whether individuals and communities have meaningful control.

Consider biometric identity systems deployed for public services. In many contexts, individuals have no real choice about participation, no visibility into how their data is stored or shared, and no path for redress when harms occur. Consent in such systems is often nominal, reduced to a perfunctory checkbox, absent meaningful alternatives or opt-outs.

Consent and control must be built into system architecture, aligning with human-centric AI governance theory, which argues for community- and society-centered design to ensure social sustainability of technical approaches (Sigfrids et al., 2023). That includes access controls, audit logs, explicit permissions, and the ability to revoke data use. Technical tools like differential privacy or federated learning matter, but they are not sufficient on their own. Without institutional scaffolding, privacy cannot be sustained, and control cannot be enforced.

Participation: Who Has the Power to Shape, Revise, or Contest the System?

Inclusion is often reduced to representational diversity in datasets. But meaningful inclusion requires a different question: who has design authority?

AI systems are typically developed by teams that operate at a distance from the people and communities most affected by deployment. Even where engagement takes place, it is often extractive or symbolic.

Participation must be structural. That means embedding community actors in problem definition, data labeling, and model validation. It means designing user interfaces that reflect real cultural and contextual variation. And it means recognizing that expertise lives beyond technical teams, in lived experience, in community oversight, and in collective memory. For an excellent treatment of this topic, see Parthasarathy et al. (2024).

The technical decisions are already in scope: user modeling, co-design protocols, localization frameworks, and interface affordances. The change is in who gets to shape those decisions. Participation, when done well, results in shared authorship and institutional legitimacy.

Stewardship: What Are the Long-Term Consequences, and Who Is Accountable for Them?

Most AI systems are built for deployment, not for maintenance. Monitoring tends to be under-resourced. Model drift is typically ignored until outcomes begin to degrade. When systems fail, the response is often retrospective and reputational.

But AI systems do not remain static. They evolve. They interact with other systems. They fail in slow and cumulative ways. Without mechanisms for continuous oversight, institutions lose the ability to detect harms or adapt to changing conditions.

Stewardship requires systems that can be monitored, documented, and, when appropriate, retired. That means building in version control, audit trails, and long-term model monitoring. It also means budgeting for adaptation and maintaining institutional memory. Systems that shape public life should not be treated as experiments without end.

This is where ethical debt accumulates. When speed and scale are prioritized without foresight, systems gain reach but lose grounding. The consequences may not be immediate, but they compound. Stewardship is what makes responsibility durable.

Takeaways

- Responsible AI requires four design commitments: justification, consent and control, participation, and stewardship.

- These are not procedural enhancements. They are foundational design choices that determine whether systems are legitimate, accountable, and built for the people they affect.

Accountability Is a System Property

Accountability in artificial intelligence cannot depend on professional culture, individual ethics, or rhetorical commitment. It must be designed. Responsibility must be expressed through systems (technical, procedural, and institutional) that support scrutiny, challenge, and redress. Without that foundation, accountability remains symbolic, disconnected from how systems operate in the real world.

This is especially true for AI systems that shape high-impact, low-visibility decisions. Consider a credit scoring model used by a global financial institution. If a customer is denied a loan, they may never learn that an algorithm made the decision. Even if they are notified, the rationale may be indecipherable, the appeals process nonexistent, and the institution's obligations unclear. The system avoids scrutiny not because it functions well, but because it was never designed to be interrogated.

Accountability, in this context, cannot happen as a post-facto adjustment. It must be a condition of deployment. Responsible systems must be explainable, traceable, and subject to challenge, not only in moments of failure, but as a matter of design. This aligns with discussions on the legitimacy of global algorithmic governance, whereby legitimacy hinges not only on outcomes but also on whether the processes are contestable and transparent (Erman & Furendal, 2024). What results is a view of accountability as infrastructure: a layered set of internal mechanisms, regulatory tools, and civic structures that make responsibility enforceable. These layers determine whether systems can be revised, challenged, or trusted, and whether institutions can be held accountable for the systems they build.

The first of these layers operates within the organizations that develop AI systems. While many firms maintain ethics charters, risk protocols, or advisory boards, these mechanisms are often disconnected from core workflows. They are structurally adjacent, not embedded. Real accountability demands more. It requires specificity of role, decision-making power, and procedural integration.

Engineers and data scientists are responsible for documenting the design rationale behind model architecture, optimization objectives, and data selection. This includes maintaining version-controlled records of trade-offs, assumptions, and model changes. These decisions form the foundation for traceability and must be legible to others within and beyond the technical team. Product and program managers are responsible for aligning system goals with institutional commitments. This includes building ethical review checkpoints into the development cycle, creating escalation protocols, and ensuring that roadmaps can accommodate intervention. Risk and reflection must be part of the schedule, not external to it.

Legal and compliance teams are responsible for ensuring that enforceable procedures support internal claims. Their work must move beyond risk containment to include policy alignment, impact assessment, and redress mechanisms that are structurally integrated. Executives and senior leaders are responsible for ensuring accountability in resource allocation. They must decide whether ethical concerns have standing within the organization. This includes giving oversight teams absolute authority, accepting that some launches may need to be delayed or canceled, and protecting individuals who surface design-level risks. Together, these roles form the internal structure of accountability. They establish who can question assumptions, who is authorized to act, and whether systems are built with governance in mind or only performance.

External regulation provides the second layer of accountability. Too often, it is treated as a constraint to be navigated. But in artificial intelligence, regulation should do more than restrict harmful outcomes. It should shape how systems are built.

The strongest regulatory frameworks do not operate as retroactive tools. They function as alignment mechanisms. They define expectations not only for what AI systems must avoid, but for how they are developed, evaluated, and governed. This requires moving beyond static compliance and toward regulation that influences institutional incentives and development practices. The European Union's AI Act offers a partial example. It introduces risk-based classifications and documentation requirements. But its impact will depend on whether those requirements affect system design, or whether they are treated as documentation exercises conducted after decisions are already made.

Too much regulatory thinking remains focused on outcomes: audits after harm, transparency after deployment, penalties after non-compliance. These tools are necessary, but they are not sufficient. AI regulation should shape how objectives are defined, how uncertainty is modeled, and how trade-offs are negotiated before systems go live. This approach requires institutions to make their systems legible, not only internally, but to public oversight. It calls for shared documentation protocols, consistent model reporting, and enforceable redress pathways, and it must operate across jurisdictions. AI development is global but enforcement remains bounded. Without coordination, firms will exploit gaps, moving deployment to markets with weaker oversight while shielding decision making behind fragmented policies. Well-structured regulation is not a barrier to innovation. It is what allows innovation to proceed without eroding public trust.

The third layer of accountability emerges from public oversight. Civil society and philanthropic institutions are not auxiliary to AI governance. They are essential to surfacing harm, representing those most likely to be excluded, and interrogating systems from the outside. Where institutional review ends and regulatory attention lags, civil society tracks how systems behave in real-world conditions. They document system failure in marginalized contexts, surface harms that are difficult to quantify, and monitor slow-moving forms of exclusion that are rarely captured in performance metrics.

They ask which proxies were chosen, who shaped the optimization objective, and what assumptions guided model training. They examine data provenance, labeling practices, and the social logic embedded in system goals. In doing so, they insist that systems remain open to critique from those not seated at the design table. Their oversight is not episodic but continuous and in its ideal form, it pressures institutions to justify their decisions to regulators and to the public they serve.

Philanthropy reinforces this work by resourcing public-interest infrastructure: audit toolkits, open datasets, litigation support, and research networks. It helps build the civic and technical capacity necessary for communities to evaluate and contest AI systems on their terms (Botti-Lodovico & Dhar, 2024). Civil society ensures that the definition of legitimacy is not set by the institutions deploying AI, but by the communities who must live with its consequences.

These three layers (internal governance, regulatory enforcement, and civic oversight) must operate together. Internal review without enforcement lacks credibility. Regulation without civil society loses perspective. Public scrutiny without technical access cannot reach the design. Accountability becomes real only when these layers reinforce each other. Systems that shape the public must be designed for public contestation. They must be open to revision, structured for traceability, and accountable to more than internal goals.

The challenge is not to inspire more ethical commitments. It is to build the infrastructure that makes those commitments enforceable. That work begins in design and extends through the institutions that define how technology is created, deployed, and governed.

Takeaways

- Accountability must be designed into AI systems, not assumed through ethics or enforced only after deployment.

- Internal governance requires role-specific responsibility: engineers ensure traceability, product teams integrate risk, legal formalizes redress, and executives allocate power and protection.
- Regulation should influence upstream design, including system objectives, risk framing, and development trade-offs.
- Civil society and philanthropy surface harm, contest assumptions, and hold institutions accountable to those most affected.
- Accountability is not a sentiment. It is a system property. And it must be built accordingly.

Beyond Alignment: The Architecture of Global Responsibility

Artificial intelligence is often described as a global technology. Distributed teams, trained on data developed models scraped from across the internet, and deployed across borders with limited regard for local institutions, norms, or histories. But this diffusion conceals a deeper concentration. The infrastructure that enables AI (the compute capacity, capital flows, training pipelines, and governance protocols) remains controlled by a small number of countries and firms. This asymmetry is not a logistical artifact. It is a political condition. It shapes which priorities are embedded in design, whose assumptions inform optimization, and who holds the capacity to govern.

Infrastructure in global AI is not merely technical scaffolding. It is institutional power. It determines who defines objectives, who sets constraints, and who retains the ability to revise. Like all infrastructures, it encodes the intentions of its architects and distributes the consequences of their choices. In this sense, global responsibility cannot be understood solely as an ethical posture. It is a question of architectural authorship.

The dominant model of AI development reflects a pattern of centralization at scale. Most foundation models originate in the Global North, often under the control of commercial entities whose incentives are shaped by competitive advantage, not democratic accountability. These models may be released under open licenses or deployed through restricted interfaces, but the underlying design remains inaccessible to most of the world.

This is not a temporary imbalance. It reflects persistent disparities in research funding, hardware access, technical expertise, and institutional autonomy. It also reflects an inherited worldview: that scale requires centralization, that innovation moves in one direction, and that governance can be applied retrospectively to systems already deployed.

A globally responsible AI ecosystem must begin with the redistribution of design agency. That includes the ability to define model objectives, set risk thresholds, and establish evaluation criteria. But it also includes the authority to shape technical infrastructure and civic institutions together. The question is not how to harmonize governance frameworks around shared principles, but how to construct systems that reflect diverse forms of legitimacy, grounded in context, shaped by collective authorship, and responsive to political, cultural, and epistemic pluralism.

Examples of this shift already exist. The African Union has developed continental AI strategies that prioritize language diversity, data sovereignty, and regional research capacity. In Latin America, partnerships between governments and civil society have produced algorithmic accountability frameworks rooted in participatory oversight. In India, modular, open-source digital public infrastructure has enabled governments to retain institutional control over systems deployed at a population scale.

These are more than marginal efforts. They demonstrate how AI systems can be designed around different social contracts, governed through alternative institutional forms, and aligned with public rather than proprietary objectives. They do not seek to localize foreign systems, but rather build counter-architectures from the ground up. Still, these models remain uneven and under-supported. The institutions best positioned to reinforce them, including philanthropic networks, regional alliances, and multilateral forums, often operate with diffuse mandates and limited coordination. Meanwhile, global governance discussions continue to be shaped by actors whose influence is secured not by inclusion but by control of the infrastructure itself.

A meaningful commitment to global responsibility must begin with shared authorship of that infrastructure. This includes co-developing governance frameworks, resourcing public-sector technical capacity, and creating open systems that support adaptation across divergent political and cultural environments. It also requires that participation is treated not as a process, but as power. To participate meaningfully in the future of AI is to shape how systems are built, how risks are distributed, and how institutions are held accountable.

I have seen firsthand how multilateral efforts often revolve around the appearance of consensus, while avoiding questions of structural inequity. Governance is framed as a technical problem to be solved through standardization, rather than a political challenge that demands shared authority. But systems that claim to be global and neutral, yet are designed without global input, are neither.

Venues such as the United Nations Global Digital Compact, the OECD's AI governance initiatives, and the Global Partnership on AI offer partial platforms for this work. Their value will depend not on the volume of agreement they produce, but on their willingness to confront the foundational imbalance that defines the global AI ecosystem. An AI system that concentrates design authority while diffusing deployment is not responsible. It is extractive by design. Global responsibility requires that we build with different assumptions: that legitimacy must be constructed, not presumed; that power must be shared, not gestured toward; and that the systems that shape human futures must be authored by the people who live them.

Takeaways

- Structural asymmetries in infrastructure, funding, and institutional control shape global AI development.
- Responsibility at the global level must include the redistribution of design capacity and governance authority, not just agreement on ethical principles.
- Multilateral coordination must move beyond procedural consensus and toward co-authorship of governance and infrastructure.

Conclusion: Designing the Terms of Legitimacy

Responsibility in artificial intelligence is a function of design. It is not something declared in principle or enforced at the margins. It is embedded in the architecture of systems, in the incentives that shape them, and in the institutional choices that govern their construction.

Throughout this chapter, I have argued that responsible AI cannot be understood as an outcome of good intentions or professional norms. It must be integrated into the process of framing problems, training models, and making decisions, at every stage from the definition of optimization objectives to the allocation of authority over deployment, and design functions as a mode of governance. It encodes assumptions, allocates risk, and determines whose interests are served.

What appears today as an ethical crisis is, in many cases, a design failure. It is the result of systems optimized for efficiency, scale, and control without meaningful regard for foresight, redress, or legitimacy. It reflects a default institutional logic: build first, reflect later. That logic is no longer tenable. AI is not a product that can be governed after the fact. It is a system that must be designed to be governable from the start.

Responsibility begins with acknowledging that design choices are not technical alone. They are political and institutional. They determine whether systems are traceable, whether their impacts can be contested, and whether the people affected have any voice in shaping them.

The design framework introduced here is anchored in justification, consent and control, participation, and stewardship, and it offers a structure for embedding responsibility into system development. Each domain reflects a point where ethical intent must be translated into architecture. These are not abstractions. They are technical and organizational decisions: how performance metrics are selected, how user data is governed, how communities are included in defining system goals, and how institutions prepare for the long-term maintenance and revision of the systems they deploy.

But structure alone is insufficient. Responsibility also depends on accountability, which in turn depends on whether institutions are willing to distribute power.

That requires internal governance mechanisms that are more than procedural. It involves regulation that reaches into development processes, not just outcomes. It requires civil society to have access to system assumptions and the ability to contest them with authority. Accountability must be designed as a system property expressed not in statements, but in workflows, roles, and infrastructure that can sustain challenge and course correction over time.

This is no less true at the global level. The most significant power asymmetries in AI today are embedded in infrastructure. Compute access, data pipelines, and model architectures remain under the control of a small number of actors, most of them concentrated in the Global North. Local adaptation is often possible. Local authorship is not.

A globally responsible AI system cannot be built on infrastructure controlled by the few and used by the many. Participation in the future of AI must mean the ability to shape it at the level of systems. That includes the ability to define public priorities, construct institutional safeguards, and hold technical systems to account within the contexts where they operate.

Across the Global South, there are already efforts underway that reflect this commitment. In the African Union, in Latin American civil society, in India's open digital infrastructure, these are not experiments. They are intentional design interventions. They demonstrate what is possible when responsibility is treated not as a matter of compliance, but as a question of authorship.

What is needed now is not a new set of principles. It is a shift in the assumptions that underlie AI's design. That shift will not come from consensus alone. It will come from institutions that are willing to change what they fund, how they govern, and whom they recognize as legitimate builders of technological futures. This is the work ahead. Not the work of reacting to harm, but of building systems that are prepared to prevent it. Not the work of symbolic participation, but of shared control. Not the work of imagining what responsible AI might be, but of designing the institutions through which it can be made real.

The legitimacy of AI will depend on whether we are willing to confront the deeper question beneath all of this: not whether we can make AI safe, but whether we can make it just.

References

Botti-Lodovico, Y., & Dhar, V. (2024). From margin to mainstream: Moving philanthropy to reshape our AI-enabled future. In *The Routledge handbook of artificial intelligence and philanthropy* (pp. 328–343). Routledge. Retrieved July 31, 2025, from https://library.oapen.org/bitstream/handle/20.500.12657/94150/9781040226254.pdf?sequence=1#page=355

Douglas, D. M., Howard, D., & Lacey, J. (2021, August). Moral responsibility for computationally designed products. *AI and Ethics, 1*(3), 273–281. https://doi.org/10.1007/s43681-020-00034-z

Erman, E., & Furendal, M. (2022). Artificial intelligence and the political legitimacy of global governance. *Political Studies, 72*(2), 421–441. https://doi.org/10.1177/00323217221126665 (Original work published 2024)

Sigfrids, A., Leikas, J., Salo-Pöntinen, H., & Koskimies, E. (2023). Human-centricity in AI governance: A systemic approach. *Frontiers in Artificial Intelligence, 6*, 976887. https://doi.org/10.3389/frai.2023.976887

Mäntymäki, M., Minkkinen, M., Birkstedt, T., & Viljanen, M. (2022, November). Defining organizational AI governance. *AI and Ethics, 2*(4), 603–609. https://doi.org/10.1007/s43681-022-00143-x

Mittelstadt, B. (2019, November). Principles alone cannot guarantee ethical AI. *Nature Machine Intelligence, 1*(11), 501–507. https://doi.org/10.1038/s42256-019-0114-4

Parthasarathy, A., Phalnikar, A., Jauhar, A., Somayajula, D., Krishnan, G. S., & Ravindran, B. (2024, June 03). Participatory approaches in AI development and governance: A principled approach, arXiv:2407.13100. https://doi.org/10.48550/arXiv.2407.13100

Petrozzino, C. (2021, August). Who pays for ethical debt in AI? *AI and Ethics, 1*(3), 205–208. https://doi.org/10.1007/s43681-020-00030-3

Schiff, D., Rakova, B., Ayesh, A., Fanti, A., & Lennon, M. (2021, June). Explaining the principles to practices gap in AI. *IEEE Technology and Society Magazine, 40*(2), 81–94. https://doi.org/10.1109/MTS.2021.3056286

Sunstein, C. R. (2022, January). The distributional effects of nudges. *Nature Human Behaviour, 6*(1), 9–10. https://doi.org/10.1038/s41562-021-01236-z